AD
ULTIMO

AD ULTIMO

A Memoir of international relations in war and peace

Volume 2

John Deverill

G

Ad Ultimo

Published by Gilgamesh Publishing in 2015
Email: info@gilgamesh-publishing.co.uk
www.gilgamesh-publishing.co.uk

ISBN 978-1-908531-51-3

CIP Data: A catalogue for this book is
available from the British Library

CONTENTS

Interlude

L. INTER(*ludium f. ludus* play). I could not put it better myself. A break in play, not half-time, but a period of R and R (rest and recuperation). After arriving home on 25 October 1950 at Lyneham in Wilts, the RAF Transport Command base, by Halifax bomber converted to carry stretcher casualties, I was taken by ambulance to RAF Hospital Wroughton not far away, and then allowed to go home to Alton by train, with strict instructions to return on the Monday. From there, on 30 October, I was given a railway warrant to Aylesbury, whence I was collected by car and taken to RAF Hospital Halton, to commence treatment for amoebic dysentery again. This time I was to have the complete Morton course, named after Air Vice Marshal Morton, a specialist in tropical diseases, who had devised his course of treatment for amoebic dysentery by using himself instead of the usual guinea-pig(s).

I had felt very cold at home, partly because I was painfully thin, weighing under 11 stone, which for a height of over 6'1" is not heavy. The winter was cold and wet and windy and I was quite glad to get into a warm hospital bed at Halton. There were about thirty patients, mostly medical cases, in my ward. The beds nearest the entrance door of the ward were kept, it was said, for those about to die, so that the staff would not have so far to wheel them out, presumably to the mortuary. This certainly seemed to be so, and we saw several patients disposed of in this way. The humour in the ward was always a bit black, a "Here's to the next man to die" attitude. My course of treatment was much the same as at Ismailia: a week of emetine injections, followed by ten days of Emetine bismuth iodide tablets. The emetine seemed to have a more pronounced effect than before; and I found I could not stand up steadily even on those few occasions when I managed to evade the predatory nurses. I was not even allowed to go for a bath without an escort.

The nurses were a mixed bunch, all Queen Alexandra's Nursing Service, some pretty, but most not, and some tyrannical, both to us, and to their colleagues. It was now my turn to get sugar from home. Very little was served in the hospital and I hungered for it. Dad drove up at least once a week, quite a long journey, and brought me pounds of the sugar I had sent him from the Middle East. I discouraged other visitors, such as Babs, because I thought I looked very poorly and better kept under covers. However, Mary Warren and other British Red Cross nurses who had worked with me at Shunni came to visit me, which I enjoyed a lot. Mary Warren and Ella Jordan were off to Korea to serve our troops there, work for which Ella later got an O.B.E. I put off my sister Mary because I thought she would be rude to the nurses.

After three weeks at Halton, I was allowed home for eight days from 18 November to recover from the treatment before returning to Halton for a course of Yatrin enemata. Yatrin was a thickish black tarry compound, related to iodine, which smelt somewhat like creosote. As a result of its thickness it was not easy to administer (if that is the word for applying an enema). First thing each morning the bottom of my bed was raised about a foot and a nurse inserted a tube into my bowels to which she attached a large container of Yatrin, which gradually filled up my colon and anything attached to it. This had to be retained for several hours, in which period I could not move of course. On one occasion the nurse, a nice young thing, got her tubes mixed up and my bed was deluged with the tarry compound. The senior sister came hurrying to condemn the nurse in the roundest terms, and the enema session was suspended while I was cleaned up and moved to a new bed. It was not a nice two weeks. After I had been deemed as OK to get up and move about, I was again sent home for another week off.

An adjacent bed was occupied for a week or more by a Flight Lieutenant Wickham-Barnes, recently returned from flying Sabre fighters with the USAF in Korea. Some of us were bemused when he left the ward for several days and then returned as a Wing Commander. He rose rapidly to Air rank (Air Commodore and above) and then retired or resigned, and was seen no more. A meteoric career!

My father came to take me home from Halton Hospital on 9 December and I then started several months of accumulated leave. In fact, apart from three weeks back at Halton for tests and ameliorative treatment from 15 February, I did not return to RAF service until 10 April. The treatment at Halton was penicillin injections daily, 24 sulfasalazine tablets daily and a protein rich diet including proteolised liver. The antibiotics were to combat ulcerative colitis and the food to put some of my weight back.

On Sunday 11 February I was at home and so were Mary and Titus in addition to my father and Jessie, the housekeeper. At about two o'clock in the morning I was woken by Mary's voice calling from the large bedroom, where she was sleeping with Titus, to ask if I had heard a noise from downstairs. I said No, but shortly afterwards heard scraping noises, followed by a crash of broken glass from the kitchen. I jumped out of bed and grabbed a Gurkha kukri I had obtained in Singapore. Bounding downstairs, stark naked, and entering the kitchen I saw the dog cowering under the northern kitchen window in which most of the panes were broken. I raced to the door, opened it and ran round the back brandishing my weapon. I saw a shape pounding across the garden towards the hedge 70 yards away. I chased it as fast as I could run, but the intruder escaped over the fence and I returned frustrated to the house. Titus had dialled 999 and reported the break-in to the police, but to the Aldershot police who took Alton calls over the weekend. Consequently they sent a patrol car to Kings Road, Aldershot, found nothing abnormal and phoned us later to make further inquiries, not turning up at Valverde until next day. By then we had worked it out that the would-be burglar had stuck surgical tape over the centre pane of the leaded light, and then hit it, with the probable intention of removing the taped pane and opening the catch inside. What happened was that every pane other than the taped pane broke into fragments, making the noise which had finally attracted our attention. The dog, whose basket was in the kitchen, close to the window, peed in fright and kept doggo.

While I was at home in February I saw Leslie Kerridge several times about the car I wanted – a Hillman Minx. Production of these had started just after the war and the price new was about £250. However delivery of a new car could take up to two years from order. So I inquired about second-hand. These fetched four times the price new, but I wanted a car now and had the money, so asked Les to look out for a good one for me. After a short time he came up with a 1949 Minx, in mint condition, low mileage, grey/fawn colour – £995. I took the car out for a run down the A32, enthused about it and collected it from Kerridge's garage in Alton on 2 March. My RAF salary at the time as a Flight Lieutenant was £49.7s.4d per month, net. A Flight Lieutenant now gets 40 times more, say £2,500 p.m. A new car now for £15K would not be unreasonable for an officer of that rank. But would today's Flight Lieutenant pay £40K for immediate delivery of the same car second-hand?

How times have changed. Even so, I was not skint, having sold £594 worth of National Savings Certificates. Not long afterwards I paid a large bill of £77.9s to my tailor, Mr Wilkinson, in St George's Square, this at a time when for a three-piece suit he charged 20 guineas + tax, say £25. I also paid my first annual subscription of £7 to the London Library in St James's Square, to which I had been introduced by Titus. This was a kindness from Titus, for which I have always been grateful. Until my 65th birthday I remained a member of this admirable institution, started by Disraeli for poor students, but now used more by authors researching books, of which the London Library has an incomparable collection. The annual subscription in 2003 was £170, an increase of 24.5 times, not unreasonable when compared with other prices, especially houses in the south-east – 100+ times.

After further checks of my guts at Halton I drove down to Chippenham to see Babs and her parents. Her father was now stationed at RAF Rudloe Manor as Unit Commander of a very hush-hush unit concerned with Sigint (Signals Intelligence). The old manor on the surface was connected by lifts and stairs with an underground complex of tunnels. I did not stay with the Taylors for long. Babs had joined the WRAF as an officer and was off to start her training at RAF Biggin Hill, which had been a famous Fighter Command station during the war. She occasionally came home to Alton with me.

On 10 April I drove up to RAF Moreton-in-Marsh to start No.6 CFS Refresher Course on Harvard aircraft. The purpose of this course was to update pilots destined to go to the RAF Central Flying School to train to be flying instructors. The Harvard was an American ab initio flying trainer, a single-engined monoplane with tandem seating for instructor and pupil. The standard aircraft ended up with a Pratt and Whitney Wasp radial 600hp engine. Its prominent characteristic was the deafening roar made by its two-bladed airscrew. More than 17000 Harvards were built which made it the premier basic flying trainer of the war. The RAF ordered a number in 1938 and gave it the name Harvard. I did not like it much. It was easy to fly, but more of a motorbike than an aircraft. In April and May I completed about 50 hours flying on the Harvard, and regained my Master Green Instrument Rating Card.

All the pilots on the course were "refreshing" their flying after months or years on the ground and we suffered a number of accidents, including four fatalities, when one aircraft landed on top of another. The visibility from the cockpit when landing was restricted by the radial engine, and as with many such single-engined aircraft, it was standard practice to land off a steeply descending curve. In some circumstances when two aircraft were landing at roughly the same time, if one were above the other, only the lower aircraft could see the upper and not even that if the speeds of approach differed widely. In such circumstances it would have been the responsibility of the Duty Pilot or the Controller in the Tower to warn the pilots of the danger by radio or by pooping off a red Verey light.

Whatever happened in this case, the upper aircraft landed on the lower, and all four pilots were killed. This was another case where we fellow students formed a Guard of Honour at the subsequent funeral of the one pilot buried in the cemetery at Moreton-in-Marsh. (The relatives of the others took them home). The funeral was marred by the presence of two women both claiming to be the wife of the deceased. On a dreadfully cold and rainy day, the funeral cortege was held up under the lych-gate while the officiating padre tried to make peace between the two women and their families. Not a nice re-introduction to flying.

At the end of my refresher course I had several days back at home before leaving in my car for Italy. On Sunday 27 May I drove to Dover and boarded the ferry. At that time there were no drive-on car ferries. One drove the car on to a railway flat truck and this was joined to the train ferry for transport across the Channel. At Dunkirk the French had no locomotive immediately available to pull the trucks off the ferry, so it was already evening by the time I got onto the road south (a regional road; there were as yet no motorways). By 21.00 I had got as far as Ham, and being tired and hungry stopped at the only hotel in the town – one star. Although the kitchen was shut, a very nice girl immediately said she would make me a meal – a cheese omelette with petits pois and chips, with two glasses of wine and a gateau for sweet. Very nice indeed, with a comfortable bed overnight.

The next day I drove via Soissons, Troyes, Chaumont, Langres, Gray, Besançon and Pontarlier to Lausanne, arriving there at 2000. I put up at a luxurious hotel. I see that I had paid Thomas Cook £101.10s.11d for travel expenses. This probably included the return ferry fare and the balance in Travellers' Cheques. The following year travel abroad became much more difficult with Exchange Control limiting sterling exports to £25 per person. It was just as well I had some spare cash because driving east from Lausanne the next morning of 29 May the carburettor packed up near Montreux. The first garage I encountered employed a mechanic who spoke good English and was a good engineer to boot. He took the carb. to pieces, cleaned and reassembled it and within two hours I was on the road again.

At Brigue I was told that the next train with flat trucks to carry cars through the Simplon tunnel would not leave until 1630, but that the pass over the top was open. So after a splendid meal of spaghetti cooked with walnuts (a speciality of the area I was told) I set off up the steep incline. Towards the top, the road ran between 10' walls of frozen snow but the weather was beautiful and the scenery magnificent. The weather had in fact been lovely since Langres where the clouds, which had been thinning since I left England, finally broke. On the Italian side

I passed Domodossola, which I knew from my mother's travels was where Italy really started, but did not stop until I reached Stresa, where I had tea. Then on via Arona, Borgomanero, Novara and the autostrada to Turin. Before the war under Mussolini autostrade had been built to link the more important Italian cities and construction continued after the war. In the 50s the autostrade had vast advertisements alongside or straddling the roads, ruining the views of the countryside. These were demolished in the 60s (but soon factories took their place). Arriving in Turin on 30 May 1950 I did not go straight to Zia Albina's flat in Via del Carmine, but put up at the Hotel Venezia, in preference to the Piemonte, which was too expensive at £5 for bed and breakfast.

I spent the following day with Albina and Pola. The former was better from what I had discovered was heart trouble, or even a heart attack, and not TB, as they had feared when I visited them in early 1949, but she had put on a lot of weight. Pola was her usual self, elegant, pretty and sad. She was still teaching disegno (what might in England be called art) in primary schools south of Turin. She wanted me to stay with them in Turin, but I was keen to see more of Italy, and after a couple of days drove off via Asti, Novara and Genova to Portofino, which I found to be no more beautiful than the average Arab fishing village.

I got back to the UK via the Dunkirk ferry on 10 June 1951 and two days later reported to RAF South Cerney to start the RAF Central Flying School Course in flying instruction. Almost immediately the gut problems resurfaced, and back I went to the RAF Hospital at Halton where I was by now practically accepted as a permanent resident. I left on sick leave on 17 July, medically boarded AT GT (T for temporary) i.e. suitable for no service anywhere in any capacity, until a further Medical Board on 17 August when I received A2 G7, meaning restricted flying (below 10000') and ground duties in the UK only. The height limitation was because gas in the intestines expands painfully with altitude.

While on one sick leave I accompanied Babs to the Festival of Britain. She took the train to London and we met at Waterloo. She was dressed up to the nines and had a stretch of tulle or some such material threaded through her picture hat. I confiscated both and stuffed them in my briefcase. The Festival of Britain was supposed to be a formal end to the austerity of the war. Modernistic (for those days) structures had been built as semi-permanent features on the South Bank of the Thames, some of which have survived to this day; for instance – the Festival Hall. Others were demolished later, including a mini-Dome and the Skylon (an alloy flêche mounted vertically on cables) and a radar dish mounted atop the old shot tower from which one could send a radar pulse to the moon and receive the reflection back a few moments later. Great stuff! The Festival lasted from May to September 1951 and was a great success.

Then for a short while I went back to South Cerney, but only to collect my things. I was then posted to RAF Moreton-in-Marsh on 6 September 1951, which now held No 1 Advanced Flying School equipped with Oxford aircraft. However, I was not going to fly them. I was Adjutant to the unit, and responsible to the Wing Commander (Administration) – Wing Commander Lewis, Black Lewis by nickname.

Black Lewis was a much-decorated wartime bomber pilot, a Welshman, with black beetling eyebrows, which gave him his sobriquet. I moved into a wooden hut close to the Officers' Mess. All the accommodation blocks were large wooden huts with pitched roofs. Only the Mess was brick. I quickly located a horse for hire from a local farmer several hundred yards down the road towards Chipping Norton. Riding round the airfield in the evening, sometimes only the horse's head, and my body from the waist up, were above the thick layer of mist which often collected over the airfield. The airmen in the Guardroom told me that this looked extremely ghostly. I greatly liked working for Black Lewis, who was quite an eccentric. He started a pig farm to consume the very large quantities of swill made from the food rejected by the airmen, Corporals and Sergeants, who obviously did not like the food served up and probably went out to eat in local pubs.

In the Officers' Mess the food was bad too. Black Lewis did not mind this because it all meant more swill for his pigs. As he was nominally responsible for the various messes on the station, he invested large sums of money in automatic dish-washers, floor cleaners and other devices and was later called to account for this, with threats from higher command about formal inquiries. Eventually the pigs developed swine fever and all of them, about sixty, had to be put down, again with considerable financial loss, for which he was held to blame. Not that he took this very seriously. Sometimes I drove in with him to Broadway, the beautiful Cotswold village west of Stow-on-the-Wold, to have lunch with contractors with whom he had business. At other times he invited me home to eat with him and his wife, a woman equally eccentric and very good-looking. They had a baby of about eight months. Black Lewis was insistent that their son should not grow up a weakling and put him out naked in his pram even in the frost. He turned pink but did not seem to suffer greatly.

Speaking of babies Mary was heavily pregnant and at the end of September 1951 was nearing her time, as they say. On 3 October I walked with Mary and Titus in Regent's Park, where large sculptures by Henry Moore were installed among the trees. Later that night, provoked by the walking or by Henry Moore's "Mother and Child", Mary went into labour and was transferred to St Mary's Hospital, where their son, John, was born on 4 October. I photographed Mary and John in the hospital bed next day. Shortly afterwards I went to Nottingham University to take a course in communism which lasted a week, possibly to prepare me for my next job at Wellesbourne Mountford where I was to be Chief Ground Instructor with responsibilities including Current Affairs, in which communism featured. About the same time I was regraded medically to A2 G4 – OK for most things but not quite everything.

At Moreton I was Mess Secretary for my sins, and was responsible for organising Mess functions including dances. As we had more than a hundred trainee pilots on the station, all away from home and all keen on finding partners to dance with, etc. (especially the etc.), I got to know the Matrons of local hospitals and through them invited their nurses to attend dances. They came from as far away as Oxford (27 miles) where the Radcliffe Infirmary always contributed a coach-load. Invariably we had more than a hundred nice young (well fairly nice and fairly young) girls at our dances, which took place about once a fortnight. The Matron of the Radcliffe Infirmary was very definite that she wanted her girls back, sober, and not pregnant, by midnight. She minced no words; her nurses were on duty the next day and there would be hell to pay if they were not sent home in good order. Unfortunately, on one occasion several nurses were the worse for wear when inspected on arrival at 1 a.m. and I was summoned to the Infirmary to receive the Matron's dressing down, although she did relent and let them come back for the next dance.

We were to have an even larger than normal dance at Christmas 1951, and a week or so before then I was summoned by Black Lewis, who first swore me to secrecy and then asked for my help in a rather painful matter involving a girl working at the Manor House Hotel in Moreton-in-Marsh. The Manor House had once been just that, but had been bought by a Miss Gray, a well-moneyed lady, who had turned it into a very good hotel, providing for the hunters, shooters and equally well-moneyed local squires and squiresses as well as those from as far afield as America, who came to tour the Cotswolds or hunt foxes or wager money at the nearby race courses.

To staff the Manor House, and the Bay Tree Hotel at Burford, which she also owned, Miss Gray recruited personable young girls to "learn hotel management". For this, they or their parents had to pay quite substantially, but the staff were therefore more the sort of girls one might find attending a Swiss finishing school. They were a pretty undisciplined lot. On one occasion, when I was having lunch, the door from the kitchen swung open and ejected a flushed laughing girl in an apron, followed by a cream loaded whisk which hit her in the back of the neck, scattering cream among the diners. Gals will be gals! The RAF Station was only several hundred yards distant and therefore the officers especially patronised the Manor House and the bar was never without a quota of pilots. Indeed the atmosphere was such, that in the hotel I still sense the ghostly presence of aircrew officers, chatting and laughing.

The girls lived on the premises. They cooked, cleaned, manned the bar and kept the books, usually under the eye of a more experienced female manager, always of the same class – upper middle. One of these girls was Josephine Butler, aged 20. She came from Torquay, where her father and mother ran a private primary school with about 60 boys, a third boarding and the rest local. The whole of the Butler family had to play their part and both Jo and her elder sister cooked, cleaned and served meals under their parents' supervision. So the Manor House Hotel experience was not unlike what she had been doing at home. Jo's favourite activity when she was not attending her parents' school, working or being taught, was riding horses. At this she was brilliant; she jumped at the White City, won prizes galore and for one or more seasons was whipper-in to the Vale of the White Horse hunt. Jo said she had come to the Manor House to get away from home, where she did not relish her school duties.

Black Lewis explained that a Flight Lieutenant Kuhlenkampf, a flying instructor at Moreton-in-Marsh, had formed an attachment to Jo which Black Lewis wanted to nip in the bud, because he knew from Kuhlenkampf's documents that he was married with a wife and children living not far away. He also knew from the Station Medical Officer that Kuhlenkampf had only a short time to live. He had leukaemia of a type that was then untreatable. Black Lewis was adamant that a nice girl like Jo should not be disappointed by an unfaithful married man with a limited life. He had therefore ordered Kuhlenkampf not to attend the dance nor associate further with Jo. But Jo had been invited to the dance and Black Lewis ordered me to look after her. Never having met her, I had my reservations. Also I had doubts about Black Lewis's authority to interfere in the personal lives of officers under his command. But as Babs, now in the WRAF and serving at RAF Benson, had told me that it was her duty to attend her own station's Christmas dance, thus depriving me of a partner, I decided to do my "duty" to Black Lewis.

Jo appealed to me enormously. She was of medium height, splendid figure of the sort to which a lot of physical exercise had contributed, black wavy hair worn fairly short, healthy complexion with glowing cheeks and a confident rather cheeky expression often on her face. She was a tom-boy, an extrovert, even eccentric. Nothing too conventional appealed to her. I had not met anyone like her before. We hit it off at once and had a good time at the dance, not exclusive to each other, anything but. Jo had lots of admirers and I had duties to perform in that as Mess Secretary I was responsible for order, food, drinks, senior officers and civilian dignitaries, and, most importantly, the behaviour of the nurses and their escorts. The dance was a great success but it was my last as Black Lewis's adjutant, because on 27 December I was posted as Chief Ground Instructor (CGI) to 9 Advanced Flying Training School at RAF Wellesbourne Mountford near Stratford on Avon.

For this post I was promoted to Acting Squadron Leader with appropriate salary, which was welcome. Wellesbourne was only a 20 minute drive from Moreton, so I saw Jo quite often. Her sister, Anne, two years older than Jo, was married to a Flight Lieutenant Wakeford, a flying instructor at Little Rissington and we went there once or twice. Dick was a month younger than I and we shared some career postings in the RAF – Coastal and Training Commands and intelligence posts later. They remained in the RAF much longer than I, and ended up as Air Marshal Sir Richard and Lady Wakeford. Jo and I often visited Oxford to see films and plays at the Playhouse. I loved Oxford and the academic atmosphere. We also often visited the Memorial Theatre at Stratford and in my 10 months at Wellesbourne Mountford, spanning two theatrical seasons I saw every Stratford production. Taking Jo "home" to the hotel sometimes presented problems because the doors were locked at midnight. On several occasions we had to break in, usually through a window left unfastened. I remember one occasion when the whole of a heavy pelmet and the rails and curtains attached to it came down on my neck as I negotiated a sofa left against the window. We usually brewed mugs of cocoa before parting and in the early hours the kitchen floor was alive with cockroaches.

As CGI, I was in charge of all the ground training of the hundred or more student pilots we had at 9 AFTS and I myself lectured on meteorology, pilot navigation, and aspects of current affairs. I had a small staff of other full-time lecturers, and about 30 non-commissioned officers and airmen, some of them National Servicemen, led by a Sergeant Marlborough, a splendid man who would have been a credit to Blenheim Palace, not far away. Our Ground School was a large aircraft hangar with the two ends bricked up. Such a vast amount of space was very useful. We adapted a part as an instructional cinema, which we also used for showing films as entertainment, and I was able to borrow some splendid productions from various sources, both service and civilian. Our projector was a professional one and made a great deal of noise because we had no projection room, but had to project from a stand at the back of the audience. I was determined to get a projection room by hook or crook. One evening I saw lengths of angle iron lying outside the Station Equipment Section. It was there for several days unattended.

Putting my architectural experience to good use, I designed the sort of projection booth that could be constructed using strawboard as in-fill. Some derelict huts on the airfield perimeter track were clad with 8' x 4' sheets of 4" strawboard. One night Sgt Marlborough and his merry men moved the angle iron into our hangar. The next night we had one of our staff who knew about these things cut up the angle iron to sizes I had worked out and then weld them into a strong box-like structure. The next night our volunteers stripped out enough strawboard, leaving the huts even more derelict than before, and within a week the projection booth was in use, painted and spick and span. It was at least a fortnight before the senior equipment officer discovered that his stock of angle iron for new shelving had disappeared. There was quite a row when it was discovered that it was welded irrecoverably into a projection kiosk used for the instruction of pilots under training as well as for entertainment for the troops. The matter was dropped when the Station Commander intervened on our side.

The station commander was Group Captain N. de W. Boult, DFC, AFC. He was married with a wife and family whom I met occasionally when I was invited round to his married quarter. He was a very thoughtful and even religious person, but troubled by some sort of doubt as many thinking people are. I never learned the detail but one day, in the officers' mess bar I think, our conversation led me to tell him of my view that all human beings, animals too, indeed all living organisms, and inanimate things, that are, were, or will be, were a unity and that death, as a final outcome, did not exist any more than life. Some years later he approached me in some foreign place, through which we were both by chance passing, and said that my opinions had helped to keep him sane and saved his life. I was gratified but mystified. What had I done?

As CGI my duties included arranging decompression experience for the courses of pilots at Wellesbourne. This involved driving with half a dozen u/t pilots to a nearby Bomber Command station with a decompression chamber. I think this was Gaydon, about 20 minutes away in a RAF pick-up. The decompression chamber resembled a ship's boiler about 20' long and 6' in diameter, entered through a porthole at one end, which was sealed up once the "crew" to be decompressed were in their rather cramped seats. Oxygen masks were donned and inspected for fit, and when all were ready the air was pumped out of the chamber and an altimeter inside showed the equivalent height. At 20,000' it was my task, as the senior officer present, to remove my oxygen mask so that the students might see how long it would take me to lose consciousness. After a short period of anoxia when the "demonstrator" (me) behaved rather as in the first stages of drunkenness, stupid jokes, decreasing responsibility, you pass out. A second instructor in the chamber then instructs students to remove something from the unconscious demonstrator, (his watch or belt for instance) and then his mask is put back over his nose and mouth. Recovery is instantaneous and you frequently carry on saying what you had started before losing consciousness. It is important to demonstrate to student pilots the stages of anoxia because an anoxic rarely knows what has happened until it is too late.

The chamber was then further evacuated to a height of 35,000' where we stayed for a longer period to check if any students were particularly predisposed to the bends (caisson disease). Gaining a lot of height quickly from ground level has a similar effect to returning to the surface from deep in the sea. Do it more quickly than your body can adapt, and nitrogen in the blood starts forming bubbles, which can be painful. The first stage is not too bad and feels like breadcrumbs in the joints, but in worse cases it can be extremely painful, even life threatening. In the worse case of all one may lose consciousness. One day at 35,000' I was with half a dozen students and an instructor, Flight Lieutenant Williams. He suddenly passed out. I suspected altitude sickness, related to the bends and anoxia in that it results from a change in altitude to which the body cannot adapt sufficiently quickly. I immediately asked the Medical Officer, always present outside the chamber and keeping an eye on the occupants through a porthole, to bring us down to ground level as soon as possible. However, after about 10,000' a student started to complain about his ears. He had a bad cold and should not have been with us. We could not carry on down without damaging his ear drums so I managed to seal him in a small one-man subsidiary chamber at the end of ours. We left him there at 20,000'and came on down with Williams to ground level. By then he had recovered consciousness but the MO insisted he be taken to Sick Quarters for examination. He was allowed to drive home with us with instructions that if he were to be taken ill that night he should phone the MO at once, or his wife should, and I was asked to phone Mrs Williams to warn her, which must have worried her no end. There are several types of altitude sickness and they can be life threatening. In this case Flight Lieutenant Williams was OK.

Another project I developed was an initiative and endurance exercise for syndicates of students. We drove in RAF transports through Hereford to the Black

Mountains in Wales. Syndicates, minimally equipped, with barely adequate rations, were dropped off on tracks in the hills and given routes to follow and grid references showing where they should aim to be at set times. They had the best part of 100 miles to cover in three days and nights. DS (directing staff) monitored arrivals and departures from the key points and marks were awarded for the best performance. I established myself at a central point (a reservoir) and used a horse hired from a local farmer to make random visits to syndicates to check on progress and on health. Quite a few u/t pilots developed massive blisters on their feet as well as different types of exhaustion necessitating their evacuation for treatment. But on the whole we all enjoyed the fun. These exercises were mounted about once a month. Less frequently we had "escape" exercises where students were put in the position of escapees from a Stalag Luft, chased by the local police and army units. The students had to live off the land and these exercises were discontinued because farmers and others cut up rough at having things stolen from their farms and kitchens.

Come spring, and I wanted to visit Italy again, and asked Jo to accompany me. I was naïve enough to think that no eyebrows would be raised, because who could possibly raise objections to a person like me, somewhat in love, but with no carnal intentions, taking a girl like Jo, similarly minded I thought, to see a country I loved and of which I was a part in many respects. However, Jo's parents, whom she had never been keen for me to meet, objected mightily to our intentions and wrote me a letter, which I considered rude and inconsiderate. I replied with a card inscribed "*Honi soit qui mal y pense*", which was rash I suppose, if I expected to meet and get on with them later.

Undeterred Jo and I set off in the Hillman Minx from the Manor House in Moreton-in-Marsh on 7 June 1952, crossed the Channel by ferry from Dover to Calais later that day and drove south through France and Switzerland towards Venice. The weather was poor initially so we decided to press on to the south until it cleared. Venice we found far too expensive to think of a hotel. The foreign exchange allowance had been reduced to £25 each, annotated at the back of our passports and £50 did not go far even in those days. Looking for somewhere else to stay I decided to try Grado, a seaside town over which I had nearly been shot down in July 1944 when unbeknown to our Intelligence, a German HQ had been moved there, with heavy and light flak defences. The first I knew about it was when we were illuminated by cones of searchlights and then saw and felt heavy AckAck exploding around us. I corkscrewed the aircraft and turned south out to sea on the instant.

By now Grado was a seaside resort. We found a very nice and cheap hotel on the front there and made it our base for the next week. Grado was a spa, and on the beach, apart from sun-bathers, were many bodies covered in mud, which was supposed to help their rheumatism. The hotel management were delightful. Knowing that we had no more than a pittance on which to live, they gave us free food, fruit and wine, and I think thought well of these two "love birds" having a holiday together on their uppers. From Grado we made two excursions to Trieste, not far to the east, where my uncle Mario had been Senior Naval Officer at the end of the war, and where he was captured by the Yugoslav partisans and taken away to be shot. From Trieste we drove down the coast of Istria to Pirano, where I had dropped a stick of bombs on the night of 28 July 1944. I always felt guilty about this but despite having air photos of the bomb bursts, there was no trace of any damage. Jo and I did not like Yugoslavia. It had a mean look and so did the people. There were many scruffy uniformed soldiers about and it seemed a thoroughly down-at-heel and unfriendly place. We were glad to get back to Grado. As our money was giving out we left for England. The hotel gave us food for the journey, wine and even flowers. Driving via the Brenner Pass, Austria, Germany and France we crossed the Channel on 21 June after exactly two weeks abroad. This was the first time Jo had been abroad to Europe and she had been most impressed. Loved it and me too.

In early August I drove Jo home to Torquay nominally for me to meet her parents, possibly as a peace offering. The meeting was no more than a very brief introduction. Jo had been nervous about their reaction to me, and rightly. They made it clear that they did not like me to be associated with their daughter. To compensate, Jo took me to meet her grandmother, whom Jo called Nana Buts. She was a dear, and Jo loved her above her own father and mother. She was of French origin and lived in her own little house in Torquay. Jo also had a younger brother, whom I did not meet at the time.

Jo had a predilection for histrionics. She could mimic people accurately and cruelly and loved doing so. With a couple of drinks under her belt she would play to the gallery until the cows came home getting progressively more flushed and excited, evincing roars of laughter from her audience and less enthusiasm from any friends of those she was imitating. I was sometimes slightly embarrassed by this trait, which seemed at odds with Jo's character as I saw it. She had many admirers and on one occasion when I drove up to the Manor House to collect her, she was trying to disengage herself from a Flight Lieutenant Ellison, who had taken over from me as adjutant to Black Lewis. He was very upset to see me and swung a fist, which I parried. He went off weeping, which was very embarrassing for both of us.

On Friday 5 September a course was passing out from Wellesbourne with a parade attended by parents and relatives of the graduates. I invited Dad up and he enjoyed the occasion, with the opportunity to inspect the Station after tea in the Officers' Mess and finally cocktails also in the Officers' Mess. These days I expect driving after cocktails would be frowned on. Dad drove home in his car and Jo and I followed in my Minx. It is 90 miles so we were tired on arrival. The next day, Saturday 6 September, Jo and I drove to the SBAC (Society of British Aircraft Constructors) Farnborough Air Show. This turned out to be a truly tragic event. We drove in and parked in the morning to have a look at the ground display and in order to be there in good time for the flying display starting at 2 p.m. At this time aircraft capable of supersonic flight were being developed and test pilots demonstrating such aircraft at Farnborough used to dive on the audience to subject them to the double boom produced when the shock wave generated by exceeding Mach 1 reached the ground. I think the first aircraft to do this on 6 September was the prototype Hawker Hunter. Later it was the turn of the De Havilland 110 to show its paces. It was a swept wing double hull aircraft showing a family resemblance to the Vampire and Venom, but bigger and heavier and with two engines instead of one. Also, unlike the earlier aircraft, it carried an observer in addition to the pilot. John Derry was the test pilot and Tony Richards his observer.

The DH 110 had done similar displays on the previous four days of the SBAC week. After take-off from Hatfield, the De Havilland factory airfield, John Derry climbed the aircraft to about 40,000' and then dived back towards Farnborough from the northeast, generating a very satisfactory double boom as it accelerated through Mach 1. Decelerating, it went into a wide turn and came in from the south in a high speed run at between 50' and 100'. Over the Black Sheds, as they were called, the aircraft gained height in a wide turn through north-west and pulled back fairly hard as if to start a slow roll towards us watching from the ground. It then appeared that the outboard portion of the starboard wing flipped up and broke away, following which in seconds the rest of the aircraft disintegrated. The nose portion was coming directly towards Jo and me in part of the crowd of many thousands clustered on slightly rising ground, which we had chosen for a good view. The commentary over the loudspeakers stopped as the commentator saw what had happened and surmised what was about to happen. I pushed Jo down to the ground and lay above her while still watching the nose cone and cockpit enclosure, which hit the ground several hundred yards ahead of us but bounced on, finally coming to rest no more than 20 yards away, killing, we later discovered, someone in the front row of spectators and injuring more.

The two engines of the DH 110, visibly red hot, wailing like banshees, passed over us at low level, one crashing into a hangar and the other into the crown of the hill from which we were watching, killing another 19 spectators and injuring many more, of whom some died later. The total death role was eventually 30 including John Derry and his observer. In an inquest on the following Monday, the Coroner held no one to blame. The deaths were accidental, and he noted that spectators at such displays must realise that accidents do happen. Following this serious accident, the SBAC ruled that aircraft engaged in displays should as far as possible avoid heading towards the crowd and should perform aerobatics and fly-pasts no closer to spectators than the runway and parallel to it.

For Jo and me the accident was a chastening experience. We returned to the car and drove home to Alton, thoughtful but thankful that we had not been killed too. But not downhearted. Being of the opinion that it would be nice for our future life together if Jo knew more about flying, I had earlier suggested that she might try to enter BOAC (the British Overseas Airways Corporation) as an air hostess. Jo was nearing the end of her contracted period working at the Manor House Hotel and the Bay Tree Hotel in Burford, did not want to return home to the school, and was thinking what else she might do. She liked the idea of becoming a hostess, a glamorous and prestigious job in those days. So I got her the application forms and she sent them off.

I had also been thinking about my own future. I did not relish the idea of remaining a penguin, a grounded pilot, but had to think of some way of escaping Training Command. The Station Commander, Group Captain Boult, wanted me to stay at Wellesbourne for at least the normal tour of two years. Any application I made for a posting would have to go through him, and it would be his prerogative to turn it down, or to send it up to Training Command with a recommendation that it be refused. I therefore hit on the idea of applying for posts that could not be turned down at intermediate levels but had to be sent directly to Air Ministry. Three options emerged from a study of Air Ministry Orders (AMOs): the RAF desperately needed parachute jumping instructors; the Embassy in Iraq wanted an Assistant Air Attache; and officers were wanted for a course in Russian language. I applied for all three, doubting whether my guts would be OK for the Baghdad position.

A few days later we were back at work, Jo at the Manor House and me at Wellesbourne. The Station Commander had deputed me to play the leading part in organising Battle of Britain Week 1952. At that time many RAF stations were open to the public in September to celebrate the Battle of Britain, usually over the week spanning 15 September on which day in 1940 the RAF had shot down so many German raiding aircraft that Hitler, and more specifically Goring, abandoned the planned invasion of Britain as being unachievable, and turned to Operation Barbarossa against the Soviet Union. The Battle of Britain anniversaries were still taken very seriously in 1952. Battle of Britain Weeks were celebrated at many RAF stations. One major objective was to raise money for the RAF Benevolent Fund, the charity responsible for helping ex-members of the RAF and their dependants. Collections, rather similar to those on Armistice Day, were held in towns and streets on most days and on one, usually the Saturday, each RAF station was open to the public from 1000 to dusk. The aim was to give the public the chance to see the RAF at work, the workplaces, training schemes, equipment etc., anything to impress visitors with the Service, its aims and achievements. A major part of the open day was a good flying display, usually starting early in the afternoon.

We had plenty of RAF squadrons and plenty of aircraft in those days, and it was fairly easy to line up an air show, with individual aircraft or flights, even squadrons, covering several air displays at different stations one after the other. Coordinating the events was more difficult because with a fairly precise programme for each station it would not do for aircraft to turn up unexpectedly. I left gaps in the displays by visiting aircraft which we filled locally, as it were. One set-piece was entirely my idea. It simulated the capture of a pilot who had force-landed in the desert (let us say the Iraqi desert). He was flying a Tiger Moth, standing in for the Wapiti or whatever other biplane might have been used in the 20s in Iraq. He simulated engine trouble by blipping the ignition switches when overhead and then landed bumpily close to a bedu encampment. The locals, suitably dressed in bedu gear, winkled him out of the cockpit and tied him up on the ground outside their tents. Fortunately his plight had been spotted by colleagues who turned up in three other Tiger Moths to effect a rescue, first bombing the bedu to terrorise them into submission.

The bombing was an art I set out to learn. I had the idea of having a passenger in the rear seat of each Tiger Moth throw bags of flour at the bedu, but I soon discovered that 1lb bags of MacDougalls self-raising were too heavy and the paper bags did not split readily, constituting a danger for the bedu on the ground – me, because we tested all this out for days beforehand, with me as a target. Being hit on the head by a bag of MacDougalls could be damaging, if not fatal. Also the flour did not spread very satisfactorily for an audience watching in safety from several hundred yards away. I then had the idea of using talcum powder, which was obtainable in quantity from a firm in Birmingham. Their contribution to the RAF Benevolent Fund was 2cwt of talcum powder, which we loaded into 1lb paper bags from a stationer, also provided in exchange for a couple of invitations to our Open Day. The talcum powder, which had to be kept completely dry until used, was very successful and we had several target practices on the airfield with me in my overalls as the target.

Most other items needed for the Open Day were wheedled out of factories and shop-keepers in the area and all were acknowledged in the programme, which was also very well printed free for us by Parkes and Mainwarings Ltd., of Birmingham. Full page advertisements in the programme were sold to local firms, and Hercules, the well-known bicycle manufacturer in Birmingham, also gave a bicycle as a prize in our raffle. Altogether I must have raised several thousand pounds in cash or kind from local firms and individuals. The RAF At Home, as it was then called, within Battle of Britain Week 1952, was on Saturday 20 September. The flying display went off splendidly, with me doing the commentary from the Control Tower. Up there I could hear the W/T traffic between the Controller and the participating aircraft and was able to introduce each event from notes made earlier.

The display opened at 1345 with a demonstration of a Meteor NF 11, a new night fighter just introduced into service. This was followed by Tiger Moth aerobatics and a formation of Oxfords from our local resources, flown by our instructors. Then came a Hastings, a Canberra (jet medium bomber) and a variety of new and not so new aircraft, each occupying the stage for from five to ten minutes, the shorter period for a simple fly-past and the longer for aerobatics. Sometimes I had to fill in gaps between the arrival of aircraft with commentary on performance, potential or pilots, but generally everything went according to plan, with a Vampire formation roaring over to complete the show at 1715. Jo was not with me in the Control Tower, which was small and crowded with people like me doing a job, but I had found her a chair in a good position close by.

Afterwards there was tea and I showed Jo round the Ground School hangar, which was my pride and joy. To show the populace the weapons that the RAF could drop I had successfully applied for a complete set of bombs, from the 14lb practice bomb, through 250lbers and 500lbers, and incendiaries of various types and weights, to the larger bombs dropped by the RAF during the war, including the mighty 20,000lber invented by Barnes Wallis. This was so large that we had to knock a hole in the hangar wall to get it in, which I then immediately had cemented up. Some weeks later. when the unit providing the bombs wanted them back, I was able to retain them permanently because it would have been too costly to demolish and rebuild the hangar wall.

For the Official Programme printed for us by Parkes and Mainwaring I selected a photograph of Spitfires over Kent for the title page and below it printed Churchill's:

"*Never in the field of human conflict was so much owed by so many to so few*"

and beneath it the words of General de Larminat:

"*The sacrifice of the elite is a cruel thing, yet without this willingness to sacrifice they would not be the elite, and a nation is built on its elite. Thank God, those to whom Great Britain gave birth did not fail her or civilisation. Let us bow low and ponder this lesson, both as soldiers and citizens.*"

Where I got this latter passage from I have forgotten, but I thought it was very apposite. The following week I learned that I would be going to London University to study Russian for nine months from 3 October.

Russian

I needed somewhere to live in London within reach of Russell Square, where the School of Slavonic and East European Studies of London University was located partly in Senate House and partly in an Annex at 28 Russell Square, a house on four floors of a Victorian terrace in the north-west corner of the square. I asked Sue Ridley, my sister Mary's friend, who had played a part in introducing me to fencing, for advice. She and her partner ran a Salle near Victoria and recommended possible places in the Earl's Court area. After a couple of visits I found accommodation at 2 Templeton Place which was comparatively quiet for London and from where I could easily reach Russell Square by underground – eight stations east along the Piccadilly Line. An important factor was that, if I were using my Hillman Minx, it was easy for me to reach Hammersmith Bridge and the Kingston Bypass (A3) to Guildford, and thence by the A31 to Alton. Parking was usually available in Templeton Place. No 2 had a dozen or more rooms on three floors, and I was able to rent a large attic room at the top, with an exit onto the roof, of which more later. The other tenants were mostly young women, often secretaries, who frequently blew up the bathroom on each floor because they could not control the gas geysers. There would be a dull explosion and after a few seconds the door would open and in a cloud of smoke a distraught naked girl with singed hair would run out, very like the appearance of the demon king in pantomimes.

I was a member of No 7 Russian Course under a scheme aiming to give selected officers a sound knowledge of the Russian language up to Civil Service Interpretership standard. It was inter-service but each service administered its own students. As far as the RAF was represented, we had 22 officers, including me, and as an Acting Squadron Leader I was appointed senior RAF student, responsible for certain admin. functions, and acting as the conduit for orders to all and any of us. Most of the officers were Flight Lieutenants and nine of us were aircrew. This course at SSEES paralleled a much larger course or series of courses for National Servicemen, who spent half of their two years' service learning Russian, and then the remainder using it in intelligence posts including the Signals Intelligence centre at Cheltenham. They were all volunteers but screened to make sure only those with a penchant for languages were selected. However, we did not share all of our instructors. We had several specifically for ourselves, of whom Peter Norman was the senior tutor, assisted by Mrs Cholerton, a formidable Russian émigré.

The pace of the course was hot. As had been the case with Arabic, we were given the Russian alphabet (32 letters) on the first day and were attempting to read and write it the next. The course assembled on Monday 6 October 1952 and was scheduled to disperse on 11 July 1953 after three terms of 11, 12, and 13 weeks respectively. Some, but not all, of those who completed this part of the course would then live with Russian émigré families in Ireland or Paris until needed to take up their RAF posts. Our course was similar to the National Service course in one respect; there were examinations at the end of each term and failure meant RTU (Return to Unit, to normal Service duties). And it seemed that the last two or three students in each exam marks list were scrubbed anyway. In this sense it was competitive. By the end of the third term we had lost six students. There was a lot of homework to be done and studies set one evening would be examined first thing next day. Courses in other east European languages for Service officers, but mainly the Army, were continuing in parallel with ours. Bulgarian, Czech, Serbo-Croat, Hungarian and Polish all had smaller groups of students, split between Senate House and 28 Russell Square. But we had so much to do with Russian that we saw little of these other would-be linguists although we sometimes met them at lunch in the dining hall in Senate House. I sometimes had lunch there with Tom Sheasby, an Army officer studying Bulgarian, who became quite a close friend.

For us students of Russian, work usually started with a plenary lecture in Masaryk Hall in Senate House from 0930 to 1030, on some general grammatical or syntactical aspect of Russian (Russian numerals, stress, aspects of the verb, etc.) preceded by announcements common to all students. After that we walked round to No. 28 for our coffee break followed by Syndicate work until 1245. Then lunch in the Senate House canteen, followed by more classroom work until 1500, when we went home with our very considerable homework. This always included thirty or more new words to memorise, as well as a page or two of specialist aviation terms, for which we had a technical instructor, translations from English to Russian and vice versa, and essays.

There were also "jingles" to memorise to help us with Russian pronunciation. One was:

Piripilá i tittirivá ni litayut v'nibisakh
Quail and ptarmigan do not fly in the skies.

This illustrated that unstressed "e" and "i" are undifferentiated and pronounced in the same way as a neutral "eh". There were many similar aids to pronunciation, mostly devised by Ronald Hingley, who was one of our senior lecturers, more concerned with National Servicemen. Later he became a professor at Oxford University and wrote an important biography of Chekhov among other books.

Another of Ronald Hingley's innovations was for us students to memorise a list he compiled of interjections, by which I mean both words and groups of words meaning very little in themselves but serving to string out an answer or a conversation – a form of temporising. These exist in all languages and in Russian the most common is probably "ну", pronounced "noo", in English "well" or even just "er", but there are many others. In oral examinations, these interjections enabled us gain time to think of what we were going to say next – a very useful adjunct.

The large amount of homework made any sort of social life difficult. I continued to see as much as I could of Jo. After finishing her contract at the Manor House Hotel, she got a job initially at the Soup Kitchen, started by Terence Conran in Knightsbridge, his first restaurant. Then she moved to manage a small hotel, the Majestic, in the Cromwell Road, where she was obliged to live in. We were still very close to each other, and she usually came home with me at weekends, and, having left the Manor House, she kept all her personal belongings at Valverde in cupboards and drawers in various rooms. She very seldom visited her parents in Torquay and Dad was worried about this and encouraged her to go down occasionally. But she was distressed that her mother and father took such a poor view of me, and of her for consorting with me. She wrote to my father that she wished that her parents treated me as he treated her. We managed to go to the occasional play at the Royal Court Theatre and concerts at the Festival Hall, but most nights I was working on Russian until after midnight.

One of the great differences between studying Russian and Arabic is that there is relatively little Arabic literature, whereas Russian literature is vast and as western in character as Russian music. Consequently I was much more interested in Russian than Arabic. The first book we were given to read by our Russian teachers was Dni I Nochi (Days and Nights) by Konstantin Simonov. It is a novel based on the siege of Stalingrad (and was therefore probably seen as particularly suitable for a course of Service officers). Simonov was a poet as well as a novelist. As a War Correspondent he covered the Stalingrad battle and knew his facts. Later I came to know and love his poetry, fairly unconvoluted, very emotional and nationalistic. But splendid! "Zhdi Minya" (Wait for Me) still brings a tear to my eye.

From day one we had to read passages from Dni I Nochi out loud, usually with Mrs Cholerton to correct our pronunciation. She was a tyrant and sadist as far as I was concerned, always getting at me to repeat passages where she thought I was at fault, as I was, and asking me for explanations (in Russian) of things I had not entirely understood, usually because I had not prepared in sufficient depth the night before. Later when I came to know her better, I appreciated that she had a particularly soft spot for me and thought it very important that I should attain complete fluency in Russian, and come to love it as she did. She had one daughter who became an architect and married a diplomat in the Foreign Office, later to be an Ambassador.

A problem in London was Russian conversation. At SSEES we spoke Russian in classes, corrected and supervised by our teachers, usually Peter Norman and Mrs Cholerton, and we read aloud to them and used Russian as much as possible, but this was not the sort of everyday Russian spoken in an office or family. I therefore located a home for elderly Russians in Nevern Square, a stone's throw from Templeton Place, and went there for evening meals under an arrangement made with the management. The management were a stern lot, presided over by a female scion of the Tolstoy family. The old people, who in many cases spoke no English other than a heavily accented Yes and No, were not well treated in my opinion. The food they were served for supper was execrable, badly cooked, never hot, quite awful. I put up with it for the conversation, which was fascinating. Occasionally the female Tolstoy appeared, often dressed in breeches and riding boots, with a riding crop, with which I imagined her striking any Russian veteran who asked for a second helping of kartoshki (spuds). Nobody ever did because they knew their place and in any case the kartoshki were close to inedible. Every few days, to recover from this diet, I returned to supper at 2 Templeton Place.

In December 1952 there occurred the Great Smog of London. From 5 to 10 December, we experienced the worst ever smog, fog mixed with smoke, fog caused largely by smoke particles in visible water vapour condensing in the weather conditions of the time – an inversion, no wind, cold temperature. At times I could not see across my attic at 2 Templeton Place. I could not drive; nobody could drive. Very few buses braved the smog. The underground still operated so I was able to get to work. In the streets after dark the visibility was up to ten feet. At the Earls Court Exhibition nearby there was a cattle show, with prize animals from all over the UK being exhibited for sale. Many of them died. Owners and accompanying drovers tried to save their animals by hanging whisky soaked sacks over their muzzles, but to no effect. They died. So did many elderly Londoners. The smog aggravated their bronchitis and other respiratory troubles and they died in their hundreds. The smog made the government realise that here was an emergency to be confronted. The 1952 smog resulted in the Clean Air Act of 1956, as a consequence of which it became illegal to burn anything other than smokeless fuel in the millions of domestic grates and heating boilers of London. This took some time to take effect and even after the Great Smog I remember difficulties driving back to London from Alton, times when I had to ask Jo to get out of the car and find the nearside kerb.

Christmas 1952 we spent at home in Alton. I had two weeks off; Jo less. After the Christmas holiday I returned to SSEES to find two officers already returned to their units because they had done badly in the December examinations. Not long afterwards we lost another officer – Flying Officer A.W.H. Frenzel, previously a staff pilot flying trainee navigators at RAF Hullavington near Malmesbury. He had seemed to me an odd choice for a course in Russian, in which language he seemed completely disinterested. One day he came to me as senior RAF officer on the course and asked for a private word. It emerged that he was to appear at Bow Street Police Station charged with indecency from the stage of the Palladium Theatre. He confessed that he and his wife were a double comedian act and that they had succeeded in getting a booking at the Palladium, and their act had led to complaints and prosecution. What should he do, he asked? I consulted "higher authority" and Flying Officer Frenzel was removed from the course forthwith. I always wondered what he and his wife got up to on the stage. As to using a language course in order to fulfil a stage engagement: that surely was unique. But people came on the course for all sorts of reasons, not always linguistic. Some were sent by their Commanding Officers because it was a good way of getting rid of them.

From my attic I could climb out of the window, scramble perilously along behind the parapet wall and access a large chimney block, from which most of the pots had been removed and the flues bricked in. There were about two square yards of flat space between the remaining pots and when signs of spring became apparent, I used to climb up there with a chair and my books and study, watching with envy aircraft approaching and climbing away from Heathrow. City life did not suit me one bit and I pined for the freedom of fields and sky and the opportunity to climb above them. Early in 1953 Jo left the Majestic and moved temporarily to The Old Mill Hotel and Restaurant near Salisbury. There she managed the hotel side. We discovered this beautiful old place after visiting the cathedral. The Old Mill was in the water meadows just south of the cathedral, a vantage point for many painters of the still quite mediaeval scene.

From 28 March to 12 April 1953 we had a break for the Easter holiday and I flew to Amman as described at the end of the chapter "The Arab Legion Air Force", spending ten days there and in Beirut. It had been the original intention to meet Jo there for a holiday together but the arrangements were impossible to coordinate and although we both went out, I was there first, and she followed, with addresses of friends of mine in the Lebanon and Amman who would look after her. She managed very well, even getting into Israel through the agency of a Christian Lebanese, a prominent personality and a friend of Israel, who was able to get her over the frontier and back. In Jordan she was helped by Bob Young, who took photographs of her, which arrived back home only months later.

On her return to London to be near me, Jo moved to a room at 3 Trebovir Road which I arranged. Working again at the Majestic as a receptionist she was by no means happy and looked for other temporary employment until she would hear from BOAC. She was offered a post, intended to be permanent, managing Bendick's chocolate shop and café in Mayfair. Bendicks had been started by Mr Benson and Colonel Dickson in Kensington 30 years earlier to make quality chocolates. After the Second World War they had a second shop in Mayfair and chocolate manufacture was moved to Winchester (where it still is, but on an industrial site outside the town). The Bendicks job would have been well paid but Jo turned it down when in May she had a letter from BOAC inviting her for interview on 9 July. She was accepted immediately and within days was training on the job, flying as a hostess to the USA in Stratocruisers and to Australia in Constellations. Formal training had been minimal – a few days in a dummy fuselage at Heathrow learning exit techniques for crash landings and ditchings in the sea. Between flights the aircrews were accommodated at Dormy House near Virginia Water and I sometimes drove Jo there or to Heathrow, where we ate in the terminal buildings – in those days huts on the north side of the airfield with access to the Great West Road (A4).

On 11 July 1953 the first part of the Russian course at SSEES ended, and I was posted to learn to fly Meteor aircraft at Tarrant Rushton, south of Salisbury. This was a lovely airfield in the middle of open country. The only other users of Tarrant Rushton were Flight Refuelling Limited, a firm started by Sir Alan

Cobham to develop aerial refuelling techniques. As far as I know this preceded American work on this aspect of aviation, designed to extend the range of fighter and bomber aircraft. The dozen or so Meteor VIIs and IIIs of No.210 Advanced Flying School were serviced by Sir Alan Cobham's set-up. I usually practised aerobatics over the Old Mill which Jo still treated as a home from home.

For me flying a Meteor was a completely new experience. I exulted in the great surge of power when one opened the throttles for take-off. I was troubled by the speed with which one needed to carry out landing checks. Instead of the unhurried survey of the cockpit, checking dial readings, warning lights, etc., against mnemonics, and confirming completed checks to Ground Control at leisure, there was a frantic gallop to get this done in a tenth of the time available in a piston-engined aircraft. To take-off and make a circuit of the airfield before landing again took about four minutes instead of 15. Turning on to the final approach to the runway about three miles from the threshold there was barely time to call "Turning Final. Three Greens" (preceded by the Control Tower call-sign and your own), confirming that you were on the final approach and that all three lights were showing green on the undercarriage indicator on the control panel. By then one was within seconds of touch-down, and usually prepared to roll the wheels on the ground and go straight off to do another circuit, and then another, each taking several minutes.

Stalling, spinning and aerobatics were more physically demanding than in a piston-engined aircraft because one could exert quite a few g on one's body. g expresses gravity; 1g is the gravity one experiences in normal life. In a turn in an aircraft one is pressed down in one's seat, giving the body twice or more times g. A person sitting in an aircraft cockpit pulling back on the control column, as in a steep turn, can exert 4g or more on the body. Blood, being a liquid, drains into the lower limbs and away from the brain. This is noticeable, because it is not only physically uncomfortable, but, as the blood leaves the eyes and brain, sight dims, called a "grey-out", and increased g brings "black-out" and unconsciousness, which immediately returns if g is relaxed by easing the control column forward. It is possible to regulate one's pressure on the control column to achieve an acceptable state between clarity of sight and grey-out. Moving one's head, clenching one's leg muscles, can delay the onset of grey-out. A g-suit, the legs of which automatically inflate in conditions of heightened g can make high g quite tolerable.

High speed runs in a Meteor were also very interesting. Because of its wing design a Meteor could not exceed the speed of sound, Mach 1 at ground level, but approaching it, the shock wave generated in front of the wings would eventually cause loss of lift from one wing or the other, resulting in a stall, and unless speed were immediately reduced the aircraft would become uncontrollable, unable to respond to controls and diving to even greater speeds until at a lower altitude the air became thick enough to reduce speed and restore controllability. Mach .82 was achievable in a Meteor and it was one of our exercises to climb to height, increase speed in a gentle dive to the limiting Mach Number where one could feel the aircraft start to shake as the shock wave disturbed airflow. The cure – throttle back and air brakes out. In seconds the aircraft was back under control.

A maximum rate descent was also an eye-opener. To get down from height as soon as possible, which might be necessary for a variety of reasons, for instance oxygen supply failure, one rolled the aircraft onto its back, pulled back on the control column to achieve a steep angle of descent, extended air brakes and adjusted the throttle to give an optimum rate of descent. I think we aimed at 6,000' a minute. The altimeter needle circled the dial like a mad thing and one had to be observant and start to decrease the angle of descent well before you hit the ground. One normally practised this exercise under control from the ground because as often as not it meant descending through other aircraft doing their own thing at normal heights and speeds. For someone brought up on Wellingtons and Dakotas, jets were an exciting and sometimes frightening experience. By the end of July I had completed 15 hours' flying Meteors, which does not sound much but which involved 22 flights in two weeks, less the weekends of course, when I was at home in Alton with Jo.

The other students on the Russian course had had a more restful time. They had received a list of addresses for the second phase of the course, involving residence with a Russian émigré family in Ireland, or for those most favoured, in Paris. Sixteen of us had been chosen to go to Paris and there was a list of sixteen addresses to which students could write to make arrangements with their hosts. This meant a certain amount of competition, on the first come, first serve principle. As I had been away flying and only arrived back in London three days after the lots were drawn, I drew the last straw – a Madame Vorontsova-Velyaminova, living at 1 Rue Claude Matrat, Issy-les-Moulineaux, close to the Porte de Versailles. There were no other addresses so I wrote out to see what the score might be. I was answered by Flying Officer Christine Hickling, a WRAF officer, who had spent her language consolidation period with the family. I learned that Mme Vorontsova-Velyaminova was dying of cancer and would not last more than a few months at most.

She was living with her son by her second marriage, Aleksei Burnashov, a taxi-driver, and his daughter, Alyonushka (short for Lena from Helena), aged 11. In fact Christine, who had got to know the family very well, had taken Alyonushka to live with her in her flat in Pinner until the grandmother died. So I would be arriving in tragic circumstances. However, the family needed the money the RAF was paying for accommodation, etc. and there was no option really but to go ahead. I say etc. because the family had the responsibility of helping their guest in mastering fluent Russian conversation. They were paid for this and of course for providing meals.

On 10 August 1953 I drove to Paris in my Hillman Minx via the Dover-Bologne car ferry, arriving at my host's that evening. I arranged to park my car in the garage of an adjacent block of flats for a quite pricey monthly payment. Mme Vorontsova-Velyaminova occupied a flat on the third floor of a cement block of similar flats. It was not impressive from outside, nor inside. I had my own small room with bed and cupboard, lit by a window overlooking the next identical cement block. The small kitchen was the only venue for eating, talking and writing, and of course cooking, which was usually done by one of the Russian medsestri (nurses) attending Mme VV. She had her own room and Aleksei had a bed in the single reception/sitting/dining room. One or other medsestra slept on a camp bed in the corridor for the last week or so of the old lady's life. They kept her clean, (fairly), fed her, and administered pain killers. Occasionally she tottered out of her room in her tattered dressing gown, long grey hair in disorder over her face and shoulders, for all the world like a character from one of Ibsen's more depressing plays.

Keeping clean was also a problem for me. I had not had a hot bath since I left England. There was no hot water. I managed a cold bath most days but the weather was getting cool and the water colder. A kettle of warm water from the kitchen took the chill off for shaving. I had to do most of my own washing, except towels and handkerchiefs, which had to be taken to a communal laundry in the basement from where I collected the wet washing and dried and ironed it as best I could. I kept my own room clean but the bathroom and loo were beyond my jurisdiction. Only I used the bath, but as often as not it was full of dirty sheets awaiting laundering. I did not dare ask Jo round for fear she might have doubts about my own standards (that I might be prepared to live in such conditions). At the flat I spent most of my time in the kitchen, fairly clean, but very small, cluttered with old pots and pans, rather like the view one sometimes glimpsed of the poky kitchen of a small restaurant in Soho.

The food was OK – very Russian, with lots of nourishing soups (borshch, shchi, respectively beetroot and cabbage soup, but always with a slab of meat in the bottom of the plate) and pirozhki (cabbage pie in puff-pastry). And grechnevaya kasha (buckwheat roasted and then steamed to make a satisfying brown earthy-tasting alternative to potatoes or rice). Slightly salted, with a knob of butter on top – delicious! "Grechnevaya kasha – Mat' nasha!" (Grechnevaya kasha – Our mother!), the Russian swaddy used to say. Sometimes Aleksei cooked if both nurses were away. For breakfast I usually had a Monsieur cheese, a splendid soft but not pongy cheese in a 2" diameter wooden box. With a freshly baked baton and coffee (with hot milk) who could want more.

Aleksei plied an ancient Peugeot taxi, which he had used at the end of the war to ferry urban partisans about their business. With a cloth over the taximeter the car also served as family transport. There were plenty of family – two or three of Mme VV's other sons by her first husband and their families, as well as Aleksei's married daughter and her family. They were all very supportive of each other and concerned about their mother. She died at the end of August and from then on the flat was full of funeral preparations, arrival of the coffin, laying out, women in black crêpe, representatives of the Russian Orthodox Church. I did not attend the funeral service in one of the dozen or more Russian churches in Paris.

The early lives of Aleksei's two daughters had been unorthodox. Natasha was the older, possibly 28, married to an artist, Yves Penau, and living in Paris XVII. Her mother was very devout and within weeks of Natasha's birth had left Aleksei and her child to enter a convent, where she stayed for some 10 years, leaving Aleksei to bring up his daughter as best he could. She then decided to make peace with her husband and leave the convent (obviously she had not taken vows) to live again as a wife. However, after the birth of her second daughter, Alyonushka, back the mother went to her nunnery. And there she remained. She had made more overtures to Aleksei about returning to the bosom of the family, but this time Aleksei was not having it.

He himself had an interesting history. He had been a praporshchik (cadet) in the Czarist army, graduating just after the Revolution. A monarchist, he had joined Denikin's army advancing against the Bolsheviks from the south. He was the gunnery officer in a British made tank, which the British "interventionists" had given to the forces opposing Bolshevism. During an advance from the Don, Aleksei's tank was cut off from the main column when the fuel pump broke down. The pump repaired, the tank commander decided to try to rejoin the column, but the Bolsheviks sought to prevent this by setting fire to a bridge over a river, which had to be crossed. The commander decided to risk a crossing, but when the tank was well onto the wooden structure it collapsed into the bottom of the ravine. The tank caught fire, but because Aleksei was in the turret of the tank he managed to get out, the only survivor. He suffered severe burns: much of his face and his nose were burnt as well as his ears. After some months in hospital he was discharged with a badly scarred face and was made a Colonel (Artillery) in the Bolshevik army. Some time later it became known that there would be a "purge" to get rid of anyone in the Army who had supported the Czarist regime. Aleksei decided to escape to the West. He took a train skirting and occasionally crossing the Finnish frontier, and jumped out when he thought he was in Finland. This was a mistake because he was still in Russia.

On the journey under escort back to Leningrad, he again jumped off the train from a toilet window, and this time was successful. Making his way to Berlin he settled there and his case came to the notice of the Grand Duchess Xenia (who later occupied a grace and favour apartment at Hampton Court). She paid for plastic surgery on Aleksei's face, which improved his appearance, although when I met him he still looked a bit like a clown, which suited his well-developed sense of humour. This helped him in dealing with his wife and family, and with me for that matter. These Russian hosts of ours were often poorly off and certainly Aleksei's household depended almost entirely on the money paid by the RAF. The taxi brought in some income, but very little. The terms of the agreement with the RAF included housing and feeding me as well as helping me with my colloquial Russian. In this Aleksei was good value because he had an excellent library of Russian books and was well informed about Russian literature as well as Russian cultural events in Paris of which there were many. At the time there were many thousands of families of Russian extraction in Paris, possibly hundreds of thousands. Apart from a Cathedral and at least a dozen Russian churches, they had Russian trades' unions, Russian restaurants and cafes (Bistro is a Russian word meaning "Be quick about it!"), a Russian opera and ballet. The Russian ballet was more than just a performing company; they had a world famous Russian school, including Serge Lifar and many other famous names. One could live Russian in Paris and I spoke very little French because there were always Russians to provide the services I needed.

Not the postal services though. That August the French postal service was on strike and I had to fix up an alternative service for us students via the Air Attaché in the British Embassy. Peter Norman came over from SSEES quite often to teach, examine and advise. Lectures and tutorials were often in a mosaic artist's studio in Vanves. Once a week we all gathered for a glass of wine in a café on the Boulevard de Montparnasse towards Les Invalides. The main aim was to discuss admin and common (and uncommon) problems some of which I might need to bring to the notice of Air Ministry. I myself used to take my books to work on in the Café Select at the other end of Montparnasse. As the autumn came and the temperature decreased, the Select was a very fine place to read and study because it had glass panelled screens erected out on to the pavement and hot water radiators coupled to pipes under the paving stones. I would settle down in a chair beside a radiator and several cups of coffee would see me through the morning. I was surrounded by tables of others with quite similar intentions – some reading for hours on end, others chatting or heatedly discussing politics or the latest articles in Le Monde and Figaro. The next table to mine was often occupied by Kokoshka (the well-known artist) and several of his cronies.

Our man at the Air Ministry was Squadron Leader Michael Forter, the oldest squadron leader in the RAF it was said. He was pushing 60 but was retained beyond his retirement date because he was Russian, spoke several languages in addition to Russian, had served in the Czarist Army, and knew the Russians in exile better than anyone else. He was a charming man with diplomatic skills which would have done the Foreign Office proud. (His son became a British Ambassador). He served in a Department of Air Ministry known as DDAFL (Deputy Directorate of Air Forces Liaison). Shortly after we reached Paris he came over to organise examinations and to visit students and their hosts. He appreciated that my host, now just Aleksei (and his daughter Alyenushka, who had returned from London) were not ideal from some points of view. As the living conditions were difficult for me he sought to arrange a transfer to a Mme Maslova. But I turned down this idea because I felt that Aleksei depended on me for financial support. There was also another factor. When Squadron Leader Forter arrived from London he told me that I was first choice to replace the Assistant Air Attaché in the British Embassy in Moscow. What did I think of that prospect? With the greatest pleasure was my answer.

Squadron Leader Forter then said that to assist my Russian he would introduce me to a tutor who was one of his greatest friends (in fact she had been a pre-revolutionary girlfriend). We visited her for supper. Mme Starova was a very distinguished Russian lady. Starova had been her maiden name. She had married a Russian Jew, Loury, who had given his name to their son Georges, with whom she said she had escaped on foot over the snow into Germany, with the baby boy in her arms. She told me later that her husband had been a good for nothing and she had parted from him for ever. Now Yekaterina Nikolaevna lived on her own in a small but comfortable flat at 20 bis Rue de Jouvenet in Auteil, a modish suburb of Paris, within a long walk of my abode with Aleksei. On my first visit to her she agreed that I might use her bathroom any time I wanted a bath, and to leave laundry for her maid to do. With these facilities, I decided I could put up with the domestic conditions in Issy-les-Moulineaux. Later still Yekaterina

Nikolaevna admitted that she was unable to teach me much about the Russian language, and in any case she found that boring (as did I) but volunteered instead to introduce me to all the interesting Russians in Paris, and she knew many of them. Her son, Georges Loury, had a delightful little nine year old daughter, Katyusha, who was adored by her grandmother, and sometimes put on traditional Russian dress to entertain me with Russian dances.

Jo came over to Paris in late August directly she got back from a flight to Australia. She had been looking forward to this since the end of July, when she had spent a weekend at home with me and Dad, writing to him from Calcutta on 6 August:

> *At the moment I am sitting at the swimming pool and finding it very sticky weather. Every 10 to 15 minutes I have to take a dip in the pool to recover. I did so enjoy staying with you at "Valverde"- thank you for being so kind and understanding. I do so wish my parents would do for John all you have done for me – it would make things so much easier, and everyone would be much happier. At the moment I know John never wants to meet my parents again because on the two short occasions that they have met him they have not been kind to him and now they try to judge him and say things about us. They just don't know him and this hurts and worries me a lot. Let's hope that in the next few months this will all clear up – I do hope so. We're happy and we want everyone else to be happy too. The trouble is that I find it much easier to talk to you about my worries and troubles than I do to talk to my parents.*

We had a splendid week together. Of course I was unable to have her accommodated with Aleksei; there was no room, so we stayed in various B & B's, both in Paris and down the Seine to the west. I introduced Jo to some of my more select Russian friends and to Russian Course colleagues, and apart from visits in Paris itself (Eiffel Tower, etc.) we used the Hillman Minx for visits outside to Chartres Cathedral, which was beautiful, and to Versailles to see what may have been the first Son et Lumiere. I had explained all this to Dad in a letter dated 6 September:

> *Mme VV died on Tuesday. You can probably realise the state of affairs: women in black crêpe, arrival of the coffin, flowers, mourners, family, all very miserable, and you can imagine how inconvenient my presence*

could have been. Therefore Jo's arrival was a blessing. I have been able, as far as possible, to keep out of the family circle, preoccupied with the funeral and associated functions – meals after the religious services, of which there have been many, etc, always very harrowing. Both Jo and I have had "tum trouble", rather unpleasant. Jo is still uncomfortable. Now lets look at the bright side.

The Palace of Versailles has been having twice-weekly illuminations, when the whole enormous and beautiful structure is floodlit section by section, while the audience in the wonderful formal gardens are treated to a dramatised historical commentary given by a world-famous cast of actors – more or less a theatrical production, with beautiful music by the National Broadcasting Company's orchestra. E.g. the commentary has reached the Revolution. The Great Hall of Mirrors is slowly illuminated from within by soft red lights. You hear the roar of the revolutionaries breaking in – shots, cries, Marie Antoinette's voice beseeching mercy for her children. The lights and noises surge up and down from one end of the Palace to the other, controlled by the operators of the many loudspeakers concealed about the building. The lights and voices die until only one faint light can be seen high in a room of the central block. The noise and commentary take over again, moving forward another step in history. We went on Tuesday. It was very, very beautiful. I shall remember it all my life.

After the Palace, the gardens were illuminated and dealt with similarly, with the great fountains turned on at appropriate moments until one might imagine oneself in some fantastic Valhalla. Thereby hangs a tale. On arrival both Jo and I wanted to spend pennies. I asked an official where the toilets might be. He replied "Pas de toilettes!" Remembering the large formal gardens with pruned yews and the like, on each side of the main terrace at the rear of the Palace, Jo and I descended the marble steps and each of us in turn disappeared along the lawns among the lines of bushes, while the other kept cave. Then, as the music was starting, we walked back up the staircase. It was a dark night, stars only. We stood on the gravel near several other people watching the building. I thought it was very quiet. There were thousands of cars in front of the Palace, but only five of us here. Then I noticed that the men were turning large "keys" in the ground, and that the noise of the fountains was becoming louder. I realised that we were standing next to workmen turning on the waterworks. I muttered to Jo that we seemed to be in the wrong place, looked around and saw a faint white line of hurdles about 50 yards away. We walked over. An agitated gendarme ran out and shooed us inside the enclosure with all the missing thousands. Seconds later the music rose to a crescendo and the whole fairylike Palace was flooded with light, and our formal yew garden in glaring green. We had missed being floodlit by about two minutes. Just think of the roar of laughter that would have gone up had we been caught with our trousers down.

Jo and I did many other things too – went to Chartres Cathedral and lit a candle to our future happiness. It is a wonderful old cathedral – great glowing stained glass windows, and practically no light inside except that from dozens, maybe hundreds, of candles round a side chapel. We took Nonie (UNESCO) and her partner Paul to dinner in a Russian restaurant. Nonie was enamoured of the Russian language and hoped to learn it, but never did. Paul worked for a record cutting firm, but was poorly off.

During this week together in Paris, Jo and I met Squadron Leader Forter who talked to us about Moscow and what we would need to take there. Jo and I drafted an announcement of our engagement which I sent to Dad, asking him to put it in the Telegraph and the local paper (The Herald) as soon as possible, our intention being to marry the following spring. Squadron Leader Forter had confirmed that I would be going to Moscow, directly my predecessor (Peter Knapton) returned. He had applied for a six month extension, so might not be leaving Moscow until September 1954. The post was for an accompanied Squadron Leader so there would be no difficulty about Jo accompanying me.

At home (at 1 Rue Claude Matrat) we were having housekeeper problems. One of the nurses who had been looking after Mme VV had stayed on to keep house for Aleksei and me and Alyonushka. But very soon Aleksei discovered she had been taking increasing doses of Mme VV's painkillers, notably morphine, which, as a nurse, she could get without much difficulty. Aleksei concluded that this was intolerable, especially with a young girl in the house. He then found another woman, who had a heart attack on the kitchen floor and was hauled off to hospital. He then found Valentina Honig, a well-born Russian Polish lady with some money and three children – an engineer, a married daughter and a younger daughter all in the USA. She hoped to join them, but meanwhile was happy to work for Aleksei, who paid her generously from his RAF money. Valentina had worked for 20 years for the American Foreign Service in Latvia, Poland and

Germany. I never discovered in what capacity, but she had extraordinary tales to tell of the war in Germany, where she had been cut off, living in Munich. She was a very good cook, spoke English, French, German and Russian well, was spotlessly clean and brought some sort of order into Aleksei's somewhat Bohemiam ménage. Not hot water though; that was impossible. After a few weeks Valentina decided that before she obtained her visa to go to the USA to stay with her children, she would move with a friend, a Dr Maria Ploetz, to Sigmaringendorf in Hohenzollern, Germany, where Dr Ploetz had a house. We were therefore back to Square One.

Aleksei then heard of a Mrs Nina Balcomb, whose father had been a Scot in the service of a Russian family before the Revolution. Nina had been Nanny to Russian children (many aristocratic Russians had Scottish or English nannies before the Revolution). Nina (maiden name unknown to me) had married a British consular official about 1910 and they had one son, Eric Oswold, born in St Petersburg on 26 October 1913. At the height of the Revolution, Eric's father, posted to be the British Consul General in Vladivostock, decided to send his wife and child back to Britain for safety, but he regarded it as his duty to remain in Vladivostock until ordered to return home or move elsewhere. For some reason or other, Nina left the ship in Japan, and settled down to make her living there. Eric, aged about six, travelled on to the UK in the care of friends and was met by Balcomb relatives and put into the boarding school where a place had been reserved for him. Later he was joined in London by his father.

Of Nina there was no news, but by 1939 she had made her way back towards the UK as far as Paris. Unable to get back to the UK because of the war, Nina had acted from then on as housekeeper for an elderly Czarist general. This is how she came to be known to Aleksei, who, hearing of the General's death, thought Nina might welcome looking after us. We put a cloth over the taximeter and drove off in Aleksei's taxi to find Nina. We found her on an upper floor of a poor tenement in a distant suburb of Paris. She came to the door dressed in a green knitted garment that hung from her bony frame like seaweed. Her face was sadly twisted as a result of an operation on her jaw some years earlier. When I spoke to her in English she replied in fluent Scots and broke down in floods of tears. We had no option but to take her on, although initially Alyonushka was frightened of her face. It turned out that after the war Nina had approached the British Embassy to find out if her husband and son were still alive, but had been so scared by the attitude of the officials and the forms they wished her to complete that she never dared go there again. However, I decided to do what I could to help and visited the Embassy myself, providing them with all necessary information. It was discovered that Nina's husband died in an air raid on London during the Blitz, but her son was alive and well, with a wife and children, working for the Post Office in Liverpool.

The Foreign Office put mother and son in touch and later Nina moved to live with him and his family. Later still I received a "I am directed by Secretary Sir Anthony Eden" letter from the FO conveying general thanks for my part in the reunion. Later still I had a letter from Eric to say that the advent of his mother had upset the children and broken up his marriage. There must be a moral there. Whatever her virtues and faults, Nina, short for Antonina, was a good cook of what might be called plain Russian food, and kept the household in reasonable order.

In any case, I was obtaining my share of the luxuries of life from Mme Starova and her friends. These included Prince (Kniaz) Felix Youssoupoff and his wife Princess (Kniagina) Irina; Grand Prince (Veliki Knias) Andrei Vladimirovich; Countess (Grafinia) Grabbé, Count (Graf) Alexander Schmemann and his wife; Mme Bibbikova; Mme Sofia Mikhaelovna Zernova, and a dozen or more others, many of them aristocrats, academics and professionals, or all three. Members of this circle were always entertaining each other. And Yekaterina Nikolaevna made sure I was always involved. The Youssoupoffs were a very interesting couple. They lived at 38 bis rue Pierre Guerin, in a beautifully converted Mews house, expensively decorated and furnished, with splendid paintings and portraits. They were fabulously well-off.

The Youssoupoffs had lived in Russia in a Versailles look-alike at Arkangelskoye between Moscow and St Petersburg. I visited it later when I was in Moscow; part of it was then a home for retired theatrical personalities. They also had large houses (mansions) in Moscow and Leningrad, Prince Youssoupoff had managed to get a great deal of his wealth out to the west. He also made a great deal of money from law suits against Hollywood picture makers depicting him inaccurately. When I knew him he was just editing the English language version of his book *Lost Splendour*[1] and I helped him. The book is a good introduction to his rather depraved life, the key element being his part in murdering Rasputin. He frequently retold this story, differently each time. For relaxation he sang gypsy songs, accompanying himself on the guitar. His wife, Princess Irina, was a self-opinionated woman, as she had to be with a husband like that.

La Contesse Grabbé was a rather heavily made-up elderly blonde (by elderly I probably mean in her fifties). She had been a mannequin for the fashion house of Captain Molyneux in Paris. She was a bosom pal of Princess Irina and of

Yekaterina Nikolaevna Starova, whom I think she had met when both of them had just arrived from Russia and had set up a business sewing luxury underclothes to go with the garments made by Parisian fashion houses. Later Mme Starova also became involved in a business making exquisite artificial flowers, also for the fashion market. This workshop still existed when I was in Paris and I visited it on one occasion and was amazed to see the quality of these flowers, mostly made of silks, stiffened in various ways. Even heather was indistinguishable from real heather, with each tiny flower exactly replicated. Grafinia Grabbé always had a lot to say about everything, as they all did, on every subject under the sun.

The Schmemanns, Sofia Mikhaelovna Zernova and Sofia Mikhaelovna Bibbikova were more serious. Alexander Schmemann was deeply religious, Russian Orthodox of course. He seemed to be a pillar of the Church and was very friendly with Sofia Mikhaelovna Zernova. Sofia Mikhaelovna lived at 395 Rue de Vaugirard, the very long road starting at the Place de Versailles and running right through Paris from west to east. She was at the heart of Russian charitable concerns, including the Centre d'Aide aux Refugiés Russes en France and others. In September 1953, she and Mme Starova and the Schmemanns were working on a project to provide a new Russian Dyetski Dom (orphanage). The earlier orphanage, for about 80 Russian children, had been sold by the owner, without a by your leave, and there was an urgent need to find another building to accommodate children and staff. Mme Bibbikova was also involved in this. She was a soft-spoken lady who had been a school teacher. No husband or children as far as I knew, but a very nice kind person to know.

Suppers/dinners with all or any of these friends were usually in the flat of one or other, and they were always delightful meals. I do not think they ever cooked, although all of them had part-time staff. In Paris, if one knew one's way around, one could always purchase delicious entrees – delicacies in aspic; beluga caviar accompanied by vodka; the wherewithal for Boeuf Stroganoff or other specialities; little tartlets of alpine strawberries. Main dishes were often delivered from restaurants and kept hot in the oven. The wine was always superb. When I went to Paris I had some knowledge of wine from the bottles my father usually kept on the sideboard, but in Paris I learned a great deal more. Mme Starova had a good way of serving vodka. Both the bottle and the glasses were put in the deep-freeze compartment of the refrigerator. Consequently both bottle and glasses were cold enough to exhibit drops of condensation when brought to the table. Essential in Yekaterina Nikolaevna's opinion.

The contrast between life with Aleksei and his family and friends, and life in the rarified circumstances of Mme Starova and her friends was striking. They never met and only knew of each other through me. I happily used both environments. I had keys both to Aleksei's flat and to Yekaterina Nikolaevna's flat and had free access to both, although I was more careful about entering the latter, usually giving warning of when I wanted a bath! On 28 October Yekaterina Nikolaevna invited me out to meet her son, Georges Loury, at his very fine house in Garches, more or less in the countryside, not far from the Pasteur Institute. He was a successful architect, the apple of his mother's eye, divorced from his first wife and living with another woman and Katyusha (Katyushka, Katyenka – any number of diminutives) and her younger sister. The house was beautifully furnished with antique furniture and splendid paintings, and had a large garden of half an acre or more, with a gardener in attendance. Katya, dressed in her Russian "maiden's" clothes sang and danced for us. Georges was very French, with no sign of his Russian provenance. An elderly Russian General lunched with us, after which we all went for a walk in the Parc de St Cloud to see the Lafayette memorial. The General must have been cavalry rather than infantry and brought up the rear, dragging his feet.

Two days later Aleksei took me, one of his brothers and his wife, and our housekeeper, Nina, to the opening performance of the Russian theatre – a play called *The Last Victim*. Nobody had ever heard of it, but these first nights were key social events. At least half the audience turned up to take their seats half an hour after the first act should have started, but, knowing their audience, the curtain did not rise until an hour later. For the next afternoon Aleksei and I had received invitations from the President of the Republic (French) to the opening of the autumn Salon (Art and Sculpture) in a gallery off the Champs Elysées. It had been explained to me that to get invitations it would be best to be titled, so I was invited as Lord Deverill and Aleksei as "Le Comte".

On 31 October Dad received another card of the many Jo sent him from stops on her flights. This was dated 29 October and from Geneva where her flight to Australia had been delayed for 24 hours. It was in her usual style, saying she was well and promising a further letter when she had time. On 10 November 1953 I had a very short letter from Jo in Karachi, calling off our engagement and saying she would not be seeing me again. I was astonished and distraught. I telephoned my father about it and he was outraged and concluded that Jo had been using both of us, using Valverde as a convenient home from home. I sent him off the keys to various boxes in which Jo had stored her more precious possessions, including the linen and silver we had bought for our married life together. Before he could send this off to Torquay she arrived at home by car.

Letter from home, 26 November 1953:

> *When I went home to tea today, Jessie told me that Jo had turned up in a car with a type she called "Ron", had gone upstairs with her keys, emptied the plate chest of all the things, except a bed cover and some sheets and towels, and her hat, and packed them all in your Officer's Trunk and off they went. Jessie said she would telephone to inform me at the office, but Jo would not let her do so — said it didn't matter. I thought perhaps she would have written to me but have heard nothing since so I presume she has gone off to Australia again as she told Jessie she was on stand-by at London Airport.*
>
> *Well John I am not sorry for you any more. I am glad this break had occurred, the reasons for which I do not understand, but I can only say that a girl who can treat one who has befriended her, and given her the greatest hospitality over a period of two years, in such a manner, is worse than worthless. I do not want to hear any more about her. I have told Mary and Michael, and others who have asked after you and Jo. Les, for instance, was greatly shocked. He wondered if it was because you were hoping to go to Russia and she could not stand the idea.*

I never discovered why Jo had behaved like this. She knew about my forthcoming posting to our Embassy in Moscow, and the duties and privileges of an Assistant Air Attaché and his wife. Michael Forter had described them. She did not seem to be much good at languages and at that time of the Cold War, Russians were in the doghouse and portrayed by the media as so many devils. There was also the point that nominally I was a Catholic, whereas Jo's parents, if not Jo herself, were very Protestant. On the other hand it may just have been that during our periods of separation she had fallen in love with Ron Carter (I only discovered his surname much later), and thought that he offered more the sort of life that appealed to her. Ron was a Flight Engineer on Constellations and must often have been on flights to Australia with Jo. He also had a "corner shop" in a Dorset village. A thought that occurred to me much later, in 2004, when Herta and I visited our youngest son in Queensland and we visited a rodeo, was that Jo, who was very much the outdoor girl, loved horses and excelled in horsemanship, had on at least one occasion to my knowledge, stopped over in Australia for several weeks between flights and helped herd cattle in Queensland or Northern Territory. This must have attracted her greatly and Ron may have agreed that they might move to Australia later. There could be no greater contrast with the life I was to lead in Moscow.

Several days after the end of the affair I was surprised to get a letter from Jo's mother in the vein of Oh-well-we'll-have-to-put-up-with-it-now, proposing that the wedding should be "like Anne's", Anne being Jo's sister married to Dick Wakeford. It was clear that the parents had not yet heard of Jo's decision. Of course Jo did have a very high opinion of herself, very like Marilyn Monroe some people were supposed to have told her. Her figure was similar, and she could mimic Marilyn Monroe. But her face was completely her own: she had a wide gap between her two front teeth and with the help of two fingers could stop a taxi in Trafalgar Square with a whistle from Buckingham Palace.

Life must go on. My Russian friends responded magnificently. Aleksei produced a bottle of gin in which to drown our sorrows and then put a sock over the taximeter and took me and his two daughters and half-brother, an engineer recently returned from the Cameroons, to a famous Italian marionette show, I Piccoli di Monreco, playing in the Champs Elyseés Theatre, an unprecedented event as it did not start until 9 p.m. and Alyonushka was not in bed until long after midnight. Apart from everything else I was depressed because I thought I might lose the Moscow appointment where a married man was preferred. Yekaterina Nikolaevna and her friends were equally helpful, inviting me to the Russian Naval Ball on 27 November. This was held in the ballroom of the French Military Club. As a partner I took one of the WRAF officers on the Russian course, but more and more Russian friends kept joining us until we numbered about a dozen. At 5 a.m. we took a bus to Les Halles, the French equivalent of Covent Garden, and ate onion soup at the renowned "Le Chien qui Fume". The soup was splendid hot stuff, dripping tendrils of molten cheese. Bed at 7 a.m. but up at 11 a.m. for work. I had done well in the latest Russian exams, being 6th out of the 15 of us, with an overall percentage of 70 (the highest was 78%).

I had numerous sessions over tea, lunch or supper with Mme Starova and the Grand Prince Andrei Vladimirovich, who were keen to use me (and my car) to collect various things to sell at the forthcoming fête/bazaar to raise money for the new orphanage. Apart from picking up artificial flowers from Mme Starova's former workshop, baskets of fruit and bottles of spirits, I visited Mme Rimsky-Korsakov's jewellery in the Rue de Rivoli and was given some quite expensive pieces of schmuck. I was asked to visit the apartment of Marc Chagall to collect a promised picture. When I rang the flat intercom, a woman opened the door and took my message, asked me to wait, closed the door and returned after a few minutes to say that M. Chagall would send the picture down in a short time. Ten minutes later she reappeared with a still damp unframed Chagall with all the usual features – diaphanous female floating above, moon, a devil or goat or two, fairly lurid undergrowth etc. I handed it over to Mme Starova and never saw it again, but trust it was sold to inflate the orphanage fund.

A final Council of War was held over dinner with Yekaterina Nikolaevna on 4 December, attended by Dodik, ex-General, former ADC to Grand Prince Andrei Vladimirovich; a Princess (name forgotten), Sofia Mikhaelovna Zernova, Graf Schmemann and his wife, and me. A great deal of vodka was drunk to the success of the fête and those involved in its organisation, followed by the usual excellent meal and champagne. The combination of drink and food and interesting conversation was exhilarating, and instead of sinking deeper into the gloom of introspection that had been my lot since the break-up with Jo, I drove down the newly built autoroute to Versailles reaching speeds fantastic for a Hillman Minx.

The fête was on Sunday 5 December in the Shell building on the Champs Elysées. A large sum of money was raised throughout the day and the organisers were well pleased. I had visited the building destined to become the new orphanage several times. It was about 20 miles south of Paris in the village of Montgeron on a tributary of the Seine. The story goes that Anna Yaroslavna, born in Kiev in 1024, daughter of Yaroslav the Wise, married Henry I of France in Rheims in 1049. The marriage was political, to achieve an alliance against the Holy Roman Empire. She bore Henry a large number of children, among whom was Philip I of France. Henry died in 1060 and Anna then reigned as Regent until her son was of age. Anna founded an order of monks and nuns based in Senlis, north of Paris. After a while the monks decided they needed a flour mill to provide their houses with bread, and built the Moulin de Senlis at Montgeron. Anna's signature has been preserved and there is a sculpture of her in the portal of the church of Saint Vincent at Senlis.

It is said that Anna brought to France the technique of tapestry making and that the Bayeux Tapestry is an example of the work of Kievan tapestry workers or those they taught. At a later stage, when the orphanage was running, pieces of the tapestry were sold in the orphanage shop. I visited the Mill and associated Chateau du Moulin de Senlis with Yekaterina Nikolaevna. It badly needed restoration and was completely surrounded by water, a very dangerous place for children I thought. Gothic, with flying buttresses, the basic structure was superb. Inside there were immense oak beams of great age. The Mill mechanisms, water wheel, gears, and cogs, seemed to be all intact. Three tributaries of the Seine met at the Mill, in a walled garden, with Bougainvillaea and creepers cascading from the walls, and willow, birch and fruit trees everywhere around. The scene was of a "magical" lost garden, as in a setting for

The Sleeping Beauty.

Letter home, 11 December 1953:

The bazaar to raise money for the Russian orphanage was a great success. Most of the RAF officers turned up with their hosts, friends and girlfriends to swell the crowd and contributed substantially. I met a great many people there. All displaced communities have in common webs of relationships, based on faith, hope and charity. To get to know a community one has to get involved in the web, and then simply follow the threads.

On Tuesday there was film show and soirée in aid of a Russian ecclesiastical school. I transported the buffet and bar and established them in the hall, somewhere in Avenue d'Iena. There was only one bottle of vodka and a limited amount of caviar, so Mme Starova and Graf Schmemann (32, bearded, Russian art broker), kept it under the counter and we finished it off ourselves. I like caviar; it goes perfectly with vodka. The film was awful – an old Shirley Temple, but of course ecclesiastical schools have to play safe – no latter-day American indecencies like Salome *or* Quo Vadis *would be tolerated. A quartet sang some very fine Russian folk songs.*

On Thursday there was a most engaging evening. A long time ago Mme Starova had asked me to accompany her to hear the famous Russian Kedroff Quartet, who have given four concerts to packed houses here over the last few months. It turned out that this time the concert would be in the church of St Severin, down near the river in the Latin Quarter. Something fairly serious was expected, so I put on a dark blue suit and sober tie (and shaved). Another quite ancient Russian lady came with us and I drove there to arrive at about 9 p.m. The quartet sang very well, but it was rather dull, more a lecture with examples of the development of Russian plain-chant from AD *1100 to* AD *1900.*

The lecture was in French and the singing in Russian, the singers being in full evening dress (frack). My Russians were a bit put out when the whole affair ended with a complete Catholic Benediction service. Russian Orthodox are anything but keen on Roman Catholic ceremonies. At the end I was introduced to the quartet and to the mother of their leader, Mme Kedrova, who is over 80 and a Professor at the French Conservatoire de Musique. Extraordinary old lady –

shrivelled up like a skinless chestnut.

Also met a beautiful and heart-breaking Russian lady, whose 21-year-old daughter, a veritable angel, they say, is dying of cancer in a hospital here. She is the only daughter – lung cancer, with secondaries after an operation on a tumour in her leg a year ago. She has about a week left of life. We are not so very unlucky, are we?

When we finally got away from the church in a dark brown mood, Mme Starova, who is the sort of aunt I would like to have, suggested we should have a look at Les Oubliettes, the dungeons where, in pre-Bastille days, prisoners were tortured and then disposed of in the Seine, through chutes in the dungeon walls. They now house a variant of night-club. Seated in semi-darkness in oak pews (it is small and intimate as dungeons go) surrounded by the old instruments of torture, one drinks, watches, listens, and joins in the songs and choruses (if one knows the words) of a pretty riotous and, by anyone's standards, indecent floor-show. No nudity – nothing so crude – but the subtle indecencies which nearly offend taste, but not quite. The French are so good at it! Taste is like a knife-edge or tight-rope on which the French love to turn somersaults, pretend to fall off and so on, but on which they balance superbly. Mme Starova had not expected quite such "breadth" or whatever you would like to call it, and was a bit worried about the reactions of her elderly companion. But she kept repeating that it was indecent really, but all the same… that was life, and after a sticky strong drink of cherries in eau de vie, put on a resigned smile (and went on to orangeade). We stayed until 1 a.m.

As part of the final exams we have to read and interpret Russian script, handwriting, that sort of thing. Any number of people have lent me handwritten manuscripts to read – the Grand Prince Andrei Vladimirovich; a Russian Admiral who was with the communists; Princes and Princesses. I have memoirs not to be published for 50 years, confidential drafts about the organisation of the Russian armed services, texts of books, private letters, all on condition that I return the papers to their owners and disclose nothing to others.

Yesterday I arranged to take Natasha, the taxi-driver's elder daughter, to see a new Russian film, with Aleksei, and Alyonushka and Natasha's husband. This because Natasha expects a baby any minute now and might otherwise have no chance of seeing the film, a very beautiful Soviet production of the legend Sadko. As it happened the performance yesterday was private. So we are going today, in a few minutes.

As to coming home for Christmas, I should arrive at London Airport or at Northolt on Monday 21 December at about 9 p.m. A complete aircraft will carry all of us. We have no choice over the flight because it is an RAF aircraft and it has to arrive off peak. I will write again next week to confirm details. Can you meet me? Please make me an appointment for a hair cut with Eburnes (Mayfair 4600) on 22 December after lunch, and ask the Robinsons if they have a hunter for me for Boxing Day.

I was home a week for the warmest Christmas for years. Dad had arranged for my haircut, but there was no horse available from the Robinsons for hunting on Boxing Day. They had ceased hiring out horses and now did livery only. The house was quite crowded – with my sister, Titus her husband and their son, John, in the large bedroom; Dad and Michael (as yet unmarried) in the front room; me in the north-facing room; and Jessie the housekeeper in her usual bedroom. The weather was so warm on Boxing Day that we drank our pre-lunch sherry in the garden, and watched the Hampshire Hunt stream down the hills to the north – first the fox several hundred yards in front of the first hounds, and the huntsmen not appearing for another ten minutes. I was back in Paris on 30 December. As usual there was a postal strike in progress and mail in the two directions could only be via the Air Attaché in Paris.

Letter home, 8 January 1954:

I have been, and am, very busy, or it would be truer to say "occupied" – for I do not do specific study, i.e. I do not sit down behind a desk and swot words. At the moment at midday I am sitting in an old armchair in my room occasionally exchanging words with the rest of the family through the open door, quenching an unusual thirst with cups of sweet hot milkless tea. This is after a party last night at Mme Starova's, for yesterday was Russian Christmas Day.

The party was dinner-type and quiet. Present were Yekaterina Nikolaevna of course, Prince Youssoupoff and Princess Irina, Mme Zernova, Grafinia Grabbé, and self. In fact – same as last time. Once again it was a most interesting evening. The more I see of people the more I realise that children never grow up. They grow up but not old. In so far as logic and commonsense are concerned, children grow "down".

I have described Princess Irina before – she is about 60, society-faced, a bit blasé in a faded fed-up way, grey, tight-lipped, sharp-tongued. Prince Y – very tall, dressed in a dark grey suit with a red bow-tie, about 66. He has a long face with soft grey aristocratic eyes and lashes and there is something womanish about the way his lips tend to purse. He has a lot of devil in him, and will, for instance, bring out some embarrassing anecdote specifically to embarrass anyone he considers to be narrow. Above all he is immensely conceited; it comes out in his book, his conversation and his behaviour. And he knows it and even takes definite pride in being so perverse as to think so much of himself. But it is very easy to pierce his mask of superiority, for he is not over-intelligent. All you get is laughter though, for he has a sparkling sense of humour, even when the joke is on him.

Grafinia Grabbé had an awful cold. She is an elderly blonde, separated from her husband many years ago – once a leading model. She was beautiful once, but now in her sixties, has faded a bit, although still as lively as a filly and with a figure even Mick's girlfriend would envy. Princess Irina fished an ivory ball on the end of a thread out of her handbag and holding it over the Countess's outstretched hand, diagnosed the state of her liver and lights from the movements of the ball. She went on to confirm whether the wines and foods we were eating were good or bad for herself and for the rest of us. There was a furious argument about this, Sofia Mikhaelovna Zernova and myself proclaiming and demonstrating that it was tomfoolery.

We also argued long about faith healing. The Prince's butler and general handyman, Grisha, has cancer of the throat, which the doctors say is incurable, but controllable for a time using X-ray treatment, which he is receiving from the hands of the best French specialist in such things. But, in addition, the Prince, influenced by his wife and Mme Starova, has called in a faith-healer, who, after praying for a while, looked up with a sweet smile (she is a girl) and said: "He is quite cured!" The Prince asked if she was absolutely certain and if he should now leave off the X-ray treatments. She replied (after more prayers); "He is quite cured!" The Prince now intends to keep on with the X-rays until Grisha's red blood cell count becomes too low for further treatment, and then to wait and see. After all, what more could be done. (In fact Grisha died three months later).

We also discussed God more or less heatedly, depending on the beliefs and doubts of those present. I am restricted here to some extent because although I understand everything in Russian, I cannot yet speak with sufficient confidence and speed in a free-for-all, especially on such a subject. One thing I remember that I said was: "Do you think it would be a good idea to save with modern medicine and science the lives of all those in India who would otherwise die in the next year?" "Yes" said Mme Zernova with conviction. And then" I continued "what about the famine which will result next year?" Said Mme Zernova: "That is God's natural way of controlling the population". We got back onto the problem of how one is to decide if one's immediate actions are good or bad. "By one's conscience" was the general opinion. What informs "conscience" was then discussed. This sort of discussion is not unusual whenever one or more Russians are gathered together. Love, death, life, evil, any of the great imponderables are pondered.

I am going over to the Youssoupoffs for lunch on Wednesday. He wants some help in sending off replies to many English letters he has received following the publication in English of his book Lost Splendour. *A second book of his is to be published in April, and he is going to give me the proofs to peruse to see if they read well in English. Princess Irina is visiting England in February and has asked me to visit her, and her mother, who is living in a Grace and Favour apartment in Hampton Court.*

Yesterday we lit the Yolka (Christmas Tree) here at home, and exchanged presents. I gave Alyonushka the dress from Phil Chesterfield, which fits, a little brown knitted hat (very cute) and a pair of skiing trousers to keep her legs warm at school. She gave me a book. She was wildly excited with everything yesterday. As a result, back at school today has been an anticlimax. Nina, our old Scottish lady, has no idea how to control children and weakens her position by trying to persuade or shame Alyona into doing things. As Alyona is as sharp as a sparrow, she notices discrepancies between the behaviour expected of her and the example set by the grown-ups and she invariably gets the better of any verbal arguments with the old lady.

Day before yesterday I went to the Russian Church for the Christmas Eve service with the whole family – taxidriver, both his brothers, their wives and five children. Mishka, for whom I got those Dinky Toys (bus and Jeep) served at the service and looked incredibly innocent and good, until he got outside afterwards and two hours of stillness had to be worked off. He is four and his sister nine and they are demons, like bear cubs, as their father is like a bear. Life for them is one long roughhouse. We went back to their house for dinner after church and lit the Christmas Tree and the children sang Russian carols. Going back a week to our own New Year's Eve, we spent that at 1 Rue Claude Matrat, again with all the family. First at 10 p.m. we listened by radio to the Kremlin bells and the Soviet National Anthem broadcast from Moscow at their midnight; then, at French midnight, to the Marseillaise; and then at London midnight to Big Ben and the National Anthem. I was astonished and most moved when they all rose at the first notes of "God Save the Queen" and stood stiffly to attention throughout, heads high in the air, without the ghost of a smile. Tomorrow I am off to the Russian children's orphanage (still the old one) for their Christmas party. I am driving Mme Starova and Mme Zernova.

Yekaterina Nikolaevna suggested we should pay a visit to Mathilde-Maria Kschessinskaya, aged 82, once prima ballerina assoluta of the Imperial Russian Ballet. After the Revolution she left Russia for Paris in 1920 and taught there ever afterwards. I bought her a large box of the most expensive chocolates I could find and we drove in the Hillman Minx and parked close to her residence and ballet school. We found her in a wheelchair to which she had been confined for some years. She was instructing a class of young would-be ballerinas, using her voice and hands to show them how to express themselves in this very athletic and artistic medium. She was very small and old but beautiful. After an introduction from Yekaterina Nikolaevna, and my explanation (in Russian) that I was soon going to Moscow, Mme K (as we might call her) advised me to visit the Bolshoi in Moscow and the Kirov in Leningrad (as it was then) to see the ballet there, and observe their different styles. When I presented her with the chocolates she burst into tears, which moved me greatly. She had known Nicholas II of Russia, and, according to the Youssoupoffs, had been "served up to him" at a banquet in a large pirozhok (pie), from inside which she broke the crust and emerged naked, no doubt to execute the 32 consecutive pirouettes which she was the first Russian ballerina to achieve. But maybe this was just another of Felix Youssoupoff's slightly scandalous stories.

January had turned very cold, so cold that the pissoirs (a la Clochemerle) were filled with columns of ice like stalagmites, formed from the dripping flush hole. In one case I was unable to enter a pissoir because of this obstruction. The pavements were very treacherous and the Hillman Minx hard to start.

Letter home, 19 January 1954:

> *Saw in the Russian New Year with a party at Tania's tiny flat. She invited all of us RAF officers learning Russian in Paris and there must have been 40 present. The flat consisted of one room with a minute loo/bathroom opening from it and a cooking facility on the landing outside. Flt Lt Gill, spent most of the evening sitting on the throne drinking and talking and only descended when a guest wanted to use the facility. Everyone took a bottle of something so Tania is embarrassed to be left with enough drink to keep a Naval Mess going for a week. Tania is a very nice person. She knows Jack Deverill; her parents' garden in Slough abuts his. She knows the ex-wife quite well – a German Jewess and not quite as nice as one might wish. She used Jack in a most cruel and calculating way.*

I had met Tania Prigorowsky in Paris months earlier, not long after I had arrived in Paris. Each week on Friday evenings, there was a vecherinka (a sort of "at home") given by the Vereschagins, related to the eminent Russian painter, many of whose works grace the art galleries in Russia. All of us officers learning Russian in Paris were invited to turn up at the Vereschagin's vecherinki whenever we could, to chat and socialise. Tania was one of those who sometimes came. Her father had been an engineer who was working in Turkey when the Revolution took place. Unsure about returning to Russia he moved to Berlin, and later to England – to Slough, translating technical publications into and from Russian. He and his wife had two children, Tania and Michael. They both went to good schools and Tania went on to use her knowledge of Russian, German and French as an interpreter, living mainly in Paris, but visiting relatives in Germany and her parents at home. She was also a talented artist and has remained so to this day. Michael (Misha) became an engineer, eventually working in Sweden, he too an artist in photography. Both splendid people of whom there will be more to write.

Letter home, 19 January 1954 cont:

> *Last night I had dinner again with Felix Youssoupoff in his house. This time he was on his own; Princess Irina was out on some social duty. Ostensibly Prince Youssoupoff wished to discuss his book again, but in fact it seems he just felt like a bit of company. We talked solidly from seven until after midnight. He speaks a few words of English, but on*

the whole it is easier to speak Russian. Certainly such conversations have inestimable value from a language learning point of view and it is also valuable for other reasons. Strange to note that Y is a complete fatalist – and from that it follows that he is prepared to excuse any conduct as being an inevitable part of progress towards one's destiny. He also believes completely in God, **blindly** *– i.e. he does not go to church, he thinks the majority of Bible history is bunk, but never-the-less feels that God exists and in some way absolutely controls one's fate. He relies completely in God – rather like floating on the sea. He just lies back, and relaxes, confident that he cannot in any case change his destiny, and that all is for the best.*

His new book is quite interesting, but rather "flat" – the language does not sparkle. It may be that the translator does not know his job, but I fear not. Y thinks a great deal of himself, has always done, and I feel that now he suddenly finds he is getting old, has done nothing really great, and now will not have another opportunity of being great. And he is very lonely – in a land which is not naturally his – with few friends. Most of his friends, Russian and English, have been considerably thinned by time, death, and, most of all I think, by the reputation he made for himself when he was younger – as a rake and dilettante. Now he wants friends – real friends, who will give him the warm feeling that he is still of some use to the world.

Continued the following Saturday. I know, I ought to be shot – but you know, it takes about half an hour to write each page of a typical letter, and I have not had a minute. Every day lessons and translations and reading – every day some sort of social event – every night up to three Russian parties. I am very tired now. Got in at 5 a.m., up again at 8. Worked a bit. Made up the accounts for expenditure so far on our farewell party. Delivered a gramophone. Bought a present for Tania's name's-day party tomorrow. Collected my laundry. It is already 6 o'clock and in an hour there is our weekly meeting at the St. Petersburg Hotel. Yesterday I got up even earlier and took the carburettor of the car to bits as something had gone wrong with it. Then drove to Fontainebleau, about 40 miles away, with Flight Lieutenant Aldwinckle, to have lunch with officers there, and fiddle some drink from the canteen for our party. We are not supposed to use this source of liquor, but we had a successful trip, getting back to Paris at 4 p.m. My wardrobe is now full of bottles.

Squadron Leader Forter came out again yesterday from London and

*I met him at our Embassy. He told me the latest news about our position here. We get back to England on 5 February. Exams start on the 9th and carry on for several days .Then we will have some leave which I will probably spend at the Joint Services Winter Sports centre in Austria. You will be interested to hear **the not to be communicated information** that I have been put forward as the next you-know-what in you-know-where, – **married or not married.** Of course this does not necessarily mean anything, for it is one thing to be put forward and another to be accepted. When I come home on Friday I will only stay over the Saturday. Then I will stay with Russians in London, because I want to continue speaking Russian right up to the oral exams, probably the following Thursday.*

My intention was to stay at the Pushkin Club in Ladbroke Grove, a club started by Maria Mikhaelovna Kullman, the sister of Sofia Mikhaelovna Zernova, whom I had come to know very well in Paris. Maria Mikhaelovna was married to Gustav Gustavovich Kullman, a Swiss, and head of the International Refugee Organisation (IRO) in London. Just as SM was the locus for most Russian charitable organisations in France, so was MM her equivalent in London. At the Pushkin Club at 52 Ladbroke Grove anyone interested in the Russian language, culture and history might meet for lectures and discussions every Friday. She also provided accommodation and food for students, not only of Russian but also in other fields, using several nearby Victorian buildings which she owned, with a central dining room for all in her own house at No. 52. I had an introduction from SM to her sister and had already booked myself in to one of the available rooms.

During my last few days in Paris I had a last dinner with Yekaterina Nikolaevna, the Youssoupoffs, and Grafinia Grabbé, driving the last three to their homes afterwards, and then continued on to a party given by one of my fellow students, Ruth Learner of the Women's Royal Air Force. This was at the apartment of Princess Dadiyanes, with whom Ruth had been lodging. I got back to 1 Rue Claude Matrat at 5 a.m. to meet two girls waiting in the kitchen. They were Russian dancers who, with a friend who accompanied them on his piano accordion, volunteered to play and dance for us at our farewell party several days later. This was a great success.

I drove home to Alton on Friday 29 January 1954, a week earlier than my colleagues going by train and ferry. After a weekend at home I drove to London to take up residence in one of Maria Mikhaelovna's rooms in a house on

Lansdowne Road, close to Holland Park tube station, and a hundred yards from 52 Ladbroke Grove, where I went for breakfast and the evening meal. These were always en famille and gave a good opportunity to meet the two dozen other lodgers in Maria Mikhaelovna's houses. These varied from callow students to, in one case, a Brazilian ballerina, dancing in Madame Rambert's ballet, which was both school and theatre. I got to know her quite well and went with her to a variety of films and plays, for free, because she was employed by a Brazilian paper to attend and write reviews, and she always received two tickets, which we shared. She was a singularly nice person, good-looking but not at all sexy. Most evenings she was sewing the points of her ballet shoes, which need frequent reinforcement.

I attended most meetings of the Pushkin Club on Friday evenings. The lectures and discussions were often in Russian and attended by Russian émigrés of various ages as well as by academics and students interested in the subjects being dealt with, such as "Lev Tolstoy's views on the family" or "Lermontov's prose".

There were also lectures and discussions on aspects of the Soviet Union and attachés from the Soviet and other East European embassies were likely to turn up. All were welcome and MM insisted, usually successfully, that there was no noticeable political bias. MM made a point of involving me quite deeply in the Club and I was sometimes called upon to introduce speakers. One I remember well, because she was outstandingly beautiful – the prima ballerina Violetta Elvin, née Prokhorova, who had managed to get out of the USSR by marrying a Chancery Guard in the British Embassy in Moscow. It took years to arrange her exit. She and her husband divorced soon after; it seems to have been a marriage of convenience, and Violetta went on to teach ballet in Italy, where she married an Italian businessman. At the Pushkin Club she spoke of her experiences training as a ballerina with the Bolshoi Ballet in Moscow.

Also staying under one or other of Maria Mikhaelovna's roofs, was Irina Fröhlich, aged 21, who despite her German surname was of predominantly Russian descent. Her father had been one of the prominent personalities close to the President of Latvia. Her mother was Russian. They had lived comfortably in Riga until the country was occupied by Soviet troops in June 1940 when she was eight. The following year the Germans marched in and remained there until the country was re-occupied by the USSR. By then Irina was 13. She and many other of her Latvian contemporaries had therefore been members of both the Hitler Youth and of the Komsomol (Communist League of Youth). Irina's father had been one of the eight senior Latvian officers to organise the Vlasov Army, Russians, recruited by the Germans to fight Soviet communism under the leadership of General Vlasov. When the USSR forced the Germans back from their frontiers and from the frontiers of other East European countries, steadily occupying all of them in addition to Austria and to Germany herself, the leaders and many of the rank and file of the renegade Vlasov Army were arrested and executed. This process was aided by the Western Allies (Britain, America etc.,) who repatriated any Vlasovites they came across. Irina's father was one of the few who escaped, partly because of his German name and partly because he was useful to the American intelligence agencies.

Irina was very knowledgeable in Russian language and literature, poetry etc., and I gained a lot from her, and, of course she was a lovely companion to take about. I soon introduced her to Valverde and my father. Even Jessie, the housekeeper, liked her, although she frowned on some Russian practices – Irina's predilection for malasalyonniye ogurtsi (pickled cucumbers); horseradish sauce, jars of which were spread on bread and butter; and very strong tea (the Russian way is to add a handful of tea to the teapot, rather than a small spoonful.)

Maria Mikhaelovna introduced me to a former actress of Stanislavsky's Moscow Arts Theatre (MXAT), nominally to improve my Russian pronunciation and diction. Ekaterina Ivanovna Kornakova was a relative of Yul Brynner, the Hollywood actor who made his name in the film of *The King and I*. She was probably in her sixties in 1954 and lived with her teenage adopted daughter Katya (Yul's half sister) in comparative penury in a flat on the second floor of 13 Ladbroke Grove not far from Holland Park and above the ground floor flat occupied by the Kirilovs. They had been in Shanghai immediately after the Revolution, he as part of the international police force. Their daughter, Irina Kirilova, was an academic high flier and became head of the Russian Department in Cambridge. They knew Ekaterina Ivanovna Kornakova well as a fellow Russian and close neighbour.

I paid Ekterina Ivanovna generously for an hour or two each day, when she taught me the shorter poems of various Russian poets, taking me through repetition after repetition. We formed a close friendship and later on, when I was in Moscow, I occasionally telephoned Fortnum and Mason in Piccadilly and asked them to send a hamper to Mrs Brynner, as she called herself, with cheeses, hams, vodka, tinned fish and many other items. I was told that, typically, on receipt of a hamper, she would telephone friends and have a party to consume all the edibles and vodka in one great splurge, after which she was back to her much more modest fare. She was a chain smoker as was Yul. Tragically, she later got work with Imperial Dairies in Hammersmith washing milk bottles. One day she collapsed and was taken to hospital, diagnosed with advanced lung cancer and died. I had tried to contact Yul Brynner to enlist his help in looking after

Ekaterina Ivanovna, but never received a response although I later heard that he paid for her to go into a hospice for her last few weeks and for her funeral so maybe something got through. He too died of lung cancer and at the end of his life campaigned against smoking.

After the exams in early February I stayed on in London at Holland Park making the most of my new Russian friends, keeping in touch with Air Ministry about my next job in Moscow, and arranging to go skiing from the end of February to mid-March with the Joint Services Skiing Association at Ehrwald in Austria, not far from Garmisch Partenkirchen. Driving there on 20 February, I stopped off for the night to see Irina and her mother, Yelena Borisovna Fröhlich, in Munich, where they lived in a partly repaired bombed-out house at 2 Jensenstrasse, not far from the English Gardens (not in the least English). One room was in reasonable condition, nicely decorated and furnished in the Russian manner – tasselled fabric lampshades, loose covered chairs, books everywhere. The loo was extraordinary. It was a large room in the basement and to protect the plumbing from the cold the room was deep in clean straw – very appropriate at Christmas, recalling "Away in a Manger". Apart from Irina and her mother, there was also her brother – Fafa. He was then in his teens, a severe spastic, and very well cared for by Yelena Borisovna. Apart from his disability, which made him difficult to understand, Fafa was a very nice boy. I understood that Irina's father, who was away from home for long periods during the war, had left his wife, partly because of the state of their son.

From Munich I drove on down to Ehrwald to join the Joint Services ski school for the next three weeks. I stayed at the Alpenhof, now rebuilt into a large hotel rather than the pretty building it used to be. I had never skied before but had a very good, quite elderly instructor, who made the learning process easy enough. Within a week I was skiing down the practice slopes without difficulty, and then graduated to off-piste routes among trees where one had to be more careful. I greatly enjoyed the glühwein, served by the tumbler from the bar at the bottom of the one ski-lift, whence I skied home with greater confidence. There were always dances in the evenings in one or other of the hotels. My instruction class was joined by Belgian and Dutch tourists, some of them impossible skiers. One Dutch woman would start at the top of the piste and proceed straight down the mountain on close to all-fours, with the instructor shouting desperately in her wake "Linken ski forwärts!", with no response until she disappeared from sight at high speed, still in the same crouch, and the instructor turned back to us with a shrug of his shoulders. My car and I were high-jacked to help transport bride, groom, guests and even the priest, for the wedding of one of the staff. In compensation I was invited to the wedding on condition I subsequently transported bride and groom to start their "honeymoon" not far away, because they could not be spared during the skiing season. I enjoyed the food – succulent veal, splendid sweets, plenty of good wine.

On 11 March, I drove homewards via Munich, staying the night at Jensenstrasse and collecting a Jewish youth of about 18 who wished to be dropped off near Cologne. Cologne had been badly bombed during the war, and had still scarcely been re-built, apart from the Cathedral, which had survived the war with one of its towers intact. We climbed up inside this and emerged into a maze of narrow pathlets among the roofs, with vertiginous birds-eye views of the ruined city. On Sunday 14 March I arrived back at Boulogne and took the first car-ferry back to Dover. Arriving in Dover I saw the headlines of a paper reading "Constellation Crash in Singapore. 33 Perish". Below was a photograph with the burning Constellation in the background, and in the foreground two firemen, one on either side of Jo Butler, still on her feet, being hurried to an ambulance. Long afterwards I was reminded of this picture by the photograph of a burning child on a road in Vietnam, scorched by Napalm, which moved the world. The newspaper article reported that all the passengers and one steward had been killed in the crash and subsequent fire. Jo and several passengers had been recovered from the aircraft after a hole had been hacked in the fuselage with axes, but they all died on the way to hospital.

The seven crew on the flight-deck escaped with superficial injuries when the nose of the aircraft broke off. The 31 passengers included some very distinguished people, many of them senior academics from Australia and New Zealand. Eye-witnesses said that the aircraft landed short on what was a short runway. The undercarriage was damaged on the runway threshold, a wing came off; the fuselage somersaulted and caught fire. There were deficiencies in the available rescue equipment; the emergency vehicles arrived late; they had no metal cutting equipment, nor sufficient water. The official inquiry later thought that the Captain of the aircraft may have been tired after the long flight from Sydney.

I was devastated. When I got back to London, I telephoned Jo's aunt who lived in west London who was also distraught. She advised me against contacting Jo's parents. I had to handle this thing on my own. There was a sequel years later in 2000 when Herta and I were returning from seeing our youngest son, also Jo, a doctor in Australia. I knew from much earlier correspondence with the Padre of RAF Changi, that Jo had been buried with 15 passengers and her fellow-steward in Bidadari Cemetery, north of Singapore city. Herta and I decided to stopover in Singapore, and visit the graves if possible. On Tuesday 7 November we took the bus north and alighted at Bidadari Cemetery. On the way in we saw a notice on the main gate announcing that work on the exhumation of the 80 thousand graves in this Christian cemetery would be started in November 2001 and that any relatives wishing to claim remains should inform the relevant department of the Singapore Development Board before then. A gardener showed us where to find the graves, in a well-spaced line among trees and shrubs. We were warned about possible snakes in the undergrowth. The graves, in white stone, were in good order and their position was very attractive, a short distance from the nearest path. Apart from the names of those buried there, only Jo's grave had an additional inscription – Nana Buts – her maternal grand-mother, of whom she thought so much.

Leaving the cemetery to catch the bus back to Singapore city, I determined that Jo at least should not be exhumed and disposed of elsewhere. If need be I would recover her remains myself and add them to the Deverill grave in Alton. When we arrived back in England, I identified the *Torquay Herald* as the local paper covering Jo's home town, in the sense that she was born and brought up in Torquay. I provided the editor with material for an article about the forthcoming Bidadari exhumation as well as a photo of Jo in her BOAC uniform. They printed this, and I was contacted within a week by Jo's brother, Jeremy, living in Kingsbridge.

At the London Library, I consulted the Times of Monday 15 March 1954 and copied details of the accident report and the list of casualties. From the Singapore Development Board I obtained details of the passengers and crew buried in Bidadari cemetery – five Australians, five New Zealanders, one from South Africa and the rest from the UK except for two Dutchmen, on contract, with one of the Britons, to Far Eastern oil companies, including Royal Dutch Shell. I wrote to Lord Marshall, Chairman of British Airways, giving the story, and saying that in so much as they were the successors of BOAC, they might wish to be involved in locating and assisting the relatives of those killed in the crash. Lord Marshall put me in touch with Paul Jarvis of his office, whom he had asked to help in the matter. Paul asked me to help track down relatives and keep him informed.

I asked my cousin Grahame Deverill in Perth and another close relative, Rob Aspden in Wellington, to help. They responded splendidly and helped by articles which I managed to place in The Australian, The Daily Telegraph, and through press associations in New Zealand and South Africa, I succeeded in identifying relatives of all those buried in Bidadari, except for the oil company employees. The Singapore Government had agreed to arrange for the exhumation of the remains of the Constellation crash victims on dates which would be notified to the relatives, and British Airways agreed, where they had scheduled air services, to provide return air fares for relatives to fly to Singapore for the cremation ceremonies and to bring the ashes home. Qantas agreed to do similarly for some of the Australian relatives and those in New Zealand made private arrangements assisted in some cases by local airlines. All relatives who wished to recover and repatriate the ashes of their grandfathers, grandmothers, aunts, uncles, etc., were able to do so. The operation took a great deal of coordination and rather more than a year to complete. The relatives were all deeply grateful and wrote me many touching letters. Only in Jo's case was her family's reaction different. Her sister, Lady Anne Wakeford, flew out courtesy of BA and brought Jo's ashes home, but died a month later. Sir Richard wrote to me afterwards and said that he and his late wife would have preferred her sister's memory to remain undisturbed.

Notes:

1. *Lost Splendour.* Prince Felix Youssoupoff. Jonathon Cape. 1953. Prince Youssoupoff inscribed my copy: To John Deverill "Съ волками жить, по волчьи выть" Youssoupoff. Paris 1953. In English: "When you run with wolves, howl like a wolf".

Moscow '54

In early 1954, Air Ministry DDAFL had informed me that it would be some time before I would relieve my predecessor in Moscow, Squadron Leader Peter Knapton. He had recently married one of the Moscow diplomatic community and her tour of duty would not be over for some months. After the Civil Service Interpretership exams, taken several weeks after I returned home from Paris, and my month skiing in Ehrwald, I was posted to take an all-weather flying course on Meteors, this time at RAF Station Western Zoyland in North Dorset. There I joined No 40 All Weather Course of 209 Advanced Flying Training School on 6 April and finished a month later. The course involved a lot of instrument flying with, or as, a Safety Pilot and I accrued about the same amount of flying as at Tarrant Rushton nine months earlier. My mood was different, much more sombre after Jo's death. I often drove to Wells to meditate in the Cathedral, and for good meals at a restaurant opposite the Close. The Cathedral and associated buildings, very reminiscent of Trollope's setting for Barchester Towers, were beautiful (and architecturally interesting). Weekends I usually went home to Alton.

Several days after I had completed the course, Mr John Hogan, a civil servant, Director of DDAFL, arranged for me to be transferred to the Special Duties List, and attached to his office, part of Air Ministry, but located not in Adastral House, but further up Kingsway. I did not need to report to the office each day, but had to follow courses and briefings designed to inform me of a great variety of situations in the USSR where my observations might help colleagues at home get some idea of how the Soviet government and its myriad agencies, armed forces, economy, industry, etc., were developing. Our Embassy's job included monitoring the pulse and other vital functions of the Soviet Union. We attachés were extensions of the Ambassador's senses, his eyes and ears and more, helping him, and through him the specialists in the Foreign Office and other Ministries, enabling the formation of British policy and the Ambassador's representation of it to the Soviet government.

For instance, in my case, I would hope to travel within the USSR, and after the death of Stalin there should be more opportunities to travel, until then restricted by Stalin's paranoia which infected the whole of the Soviet state apparatus. When travelling, I was bound to see factories, private houses, shops and any other of the many manifestations of life. As to factories, even the colour of smoke emitted from chimneys could indicate something of the chemicals being used or the products being made – officially still state secrets. Most ordinary people do not even know what a blast furnace looks like, or a rolling mill or a fertiliser factory. Our Joint Intelligence Bureau (JIB) organised tours of industry for attachés elect to familiarise them with industrial techniques and enable them to diagnose processes, or at least to report significant features of the processes observed, leaving it to the experts at home to make more informed guesses.

Appointments were made for me to visit iron and steel works, foundries, chemical factories, rolling mills and every type of heavy and not so heavy industrial concern. This involved a lot of travel, mostly by train, to the midlands and north – Sheffield and Newcastle, Wales, usually staying overnight, sometimes for several days. Visits were grouped in batches lasting a week or so each, with a great deal of hospitality from the Public Relations people of the companies concerned in whose hostels or favoured hotels I often stayed.

At the ICI fertiliser plant in Billinghurst I climbed to the top of the chalk tower, a hundred or more feet up, and then attempted to emulate a technician who faced outwards while descending the vertiginous vertical metal ladder on the exterior of the tower. My protective overalls caught between rungs behind my back and I had to be disentangled.

Scorched by blast furnaces into which I gazed through smoked glass screens to observe the changes of colour caused by chemical additives or oxygen lances; choked by emanations from retorts in oil refineries; soaked by water coolers – I greatly enjoyed myself. I had never seen industrial processes at such close range, and came to know the most prominent features of all of them, especially as I had plenty of time on my hands to visit so many factories. The knowledge I gained turned out to be very useful, not only for Moscow, but for the rest of my life.

Photography was another aspect of my briefing. From a photograph of an aircraft one can deduce surprising detail about its performance. For instance, in many Soviet aircraft the landing lights were standard. By scaling up the diameter of a landing light one could estimate the dimensions of parts of the engines and airframe to arrive at the approximate thrust of the former and the flying characteristics of the whole. The Air Ministry included a department specialising in this sort of work, estimating performance from minimal impressions, or better, photographs of aircraft in part or in whole. As I was already a fairly experienced photographer, I was more than keen to develop this aspect.

At the same time there were any number of things to find out about my future life in Moscow, and in June 1954 I wrote Peter Knapton a long question and answer letter, where all he had to do was to fill in the answers to my questions and return the letter to me. Some questions related to uniform – might I buy his aiguillettes (the gold braided, tagged, shoulder-straps worn by the attachés of the armed services and aides-de-camp), which were expensive to buy new. No, he wished to keep his, so I had to order new. Would tropical uniform be useful? – Yes, Moscow was hot in summer. Had Peter any furniture, cutlery or glass for sale? No, he and his new wife would need it all when they returned to the UK. How many blankets would be necessary? At least four. Other questions about books, social contacts with Russians, sport. Was there any horse riding for Embassy staff? Not really, except that the daughter of the Swedish Ambassador some years earlier had managed to get hold of a horse on at least one occasion. I decided to take my riding breeches and boots anyway.

Buying everything I would need was a great expense. As a result of Peter's replies, I ordered suits, uniforms, jackets to be made for me by Hogg and Sons of Hanover Square, to whom I had transferred some of my tailoring from Wilkinson. Hoggs were more expensive but provided better quality. Hardware and groceries, including drink, were ordered from Lawn and Alder of 16 Clifford Street, off New Bond Street – suppliers generally to embassies and high commissions. Advice from DDAFL was to take with me to Moscow sufficient provisions and drink to last 12 months, bearing in mind the expected entertainment load – cocktail, lunch and dinner parties, receptions etc. After a year, if I were still *persona grata*, I would have mid-tour leave, and on returning to Moscow, might take another 12 months worth. The normal tour for an attaché was two years. Note the verb "take". All stuff imported with me to the USSR had to be listed on my "*laisser passer*", a permit in my name as a "diplomat", enabling me to import tax-free.

This meant that I had to travel with the goods, or the goods with me. The situation was complicated by the fact that all diplomats taking up or returning to posts in the Moscow Embassy (and others elsewhere where this convention applied) were duty bound to import articles for colleagues in the Embassy and for the Embassy Commissariat. This latter retained a stock of provisions, including pharmaceuticals, to be purchased by entitled members of the Embassy. They were all difficult or impossible to acquire in the Soviet Union – things like

Marmite, breakfast cereal, golden syrup, custard powder, Bisto, etc., necessities in British households, as well as sanitary towels (possibly condoms too), toothbrushes, even toilet soap.

An Embassy committee decided what should be imported in this way. Items were rationed because diplomatic staff entitled to a *laisser passer* did not arrive every week. The convention was of course reciprocal, with Soviet Embassy diplomats in London being similarly entitled to import accompanied freight free of tax. Consequently each diplomat was accompanying a ton or more of goods nominally for his or her use. The shippers, Lawn and Alder in my case, had to pack and list and label everything very carefully. Otherwise who knows who would end up with what. I note that my invoice from Lawn and Alder included 12 jars of patum peperum, numerous rolls of Bronco toilet paper, 200 Gillette Blue razor blades and large amounts of shampoo and Kolynos toothpaste. The impression is that I was setting up a general stores, as in a sense I was.

As I was establishing a "household" for the first time in my life, I ordered crockery, cutlery, glass – sherry, wine and champagne glasses, kitchen utensils and some smaller items of furniture, lamps etc., and it all cost a great deal – the equivalent of a year's salary, (£720 net then: c. 50+ times that amount now). On the other hand I knew that as a Squadron Leader and Assistant Air Attaché I would receive, in addition to my RAF salary, allowances of more than that amount again. So I was not reticent about ordering cases of the best champagne (Mumms), and whisky and gin to cover what I thought might be needed for twelve months hospitality in Moscow. Of course there was always the risk that I might transgress some Soviet law or regulation and be sent *persona non grata*, as sometimes happened. That would mean a considerable financial loss.

When I was not on briefing courses I spent time at home, gardening as often as not, or in London living at 52 Ladbroke Grove, attending Pushkin Club meetings, and seeing as much as I could of Irina Fröhlich and the other Russian friends I had made in London (and in Paris, where I occasionally returned for a few days). A friend of Irina's and a devotee of the Pushkin Club, was Yevgenia Borisnovna Gourvitch, whom Irina and I wickedly called Zhaba (the toad in Russian). Yevgenia and her brother Sasha (Alexander), he may have been a year older, were Baltic Jews whose parents had come to Britain with their children at the time of the communist revolution. In Poland they had been timber merchants, selling softwood to England mainly for the construction industry. Much of it was shipped from Gdansk, and some ended up in my father's timber yard at Phillips. It was splendid stuff – straight, no shakes (splits). When the parents died they left Phoenix Timber, the firm they had started on the Thames estuary near

Rainham, to their children, Sasha and Yevgenia. Yevgenia set up what was initially a subsidiary of Phoenix, Rainham Timber Engineering, specialising in laminated softwood structures including large beams to replace steel girders in some buildings, where timber has important advantages other than aesthetic. In a fire, steel members with their higher coefficient of expansion, can pull a building to pieces, whereas laminated timber, treated with fire retardant, will char but not endanger the structure to the same extent.

Yevgenia had been in England for most of her life but her English remained imperfect, especially her written English. But she was a superb manager, identifying with her employees and capturing their love and devotion to an extraordinary extent. Almost invariably she had an unsmoked cigarette stuck to her upper lip, and fag and lip rose and fell as she talked. She was overweight, slow-moving, pear-shaped, very kind and generous in everything she did and I came to know her very well later. Although genetically Jewish, she was an anthroposophist and devotee of Rudolph Steiner, with elaborate ideas about re-incarnation.

As I was now living, when in London, at Maria Mikhaelovna's house, 52 Ladbroke Grove, rather than at one of her other houses in Lansdowne Road, I saw much more of the family at meal times. They had an only son, Misha, an Oxford graduate in philosophy with a brilliant brain, who liked to exercise it on anyone venturing an opinion with which he disagreed. He sometimes reduced his mother to tears because her thinking in religious matters was decidedly obscure. Occasionally he was downright cruel to his mother and this annoyed her husband, the Swiss-born Gustav Gustavovich Kullman, head of the International Refugee Organisation in London, rousing him from his usual equanimity to outspoken anger.

Another friend of the house was Eric Harley, of Anglo-Russian provenance, a brilliant linguist, who later made a career for himself in instantaneous interpreting – English/Russian and Russian/English – for the United Nations. Irina was particularly friendly with Eric and I was rather jealous of him. Eric's mother had been Russian, a communist, but she loved Britain inordinately and toured the country by bicycle. Her husband had been a trades union official and was more of a communist and less of a British patriot than his Russian wife. Their son was a true internationalist, and at home with everyone whatever their origins and language. It was known in Russian circles in London and Paris that I was taking up the Assistant Air Attaché post in our Moscow Embassy later in September. Irina got in touch with me and invited me to go with her to the Russian Orthodox Church in Knightsbridge for a service to wish me a successful journey to Moscow and a successful sojourn there.

The Russian minister officiating was Father Anthony Bloom, a remarkable man, born in Persia, of a father who was a Russian imperial diplomat, and a mother – the composer Scriabin's half-sister. After the Revolution in 1917 they moved to Paris where the young man grew up a convinced atheist. Later he reverted to the Orthodox Church, studied oncology, led Christian organisations in Paris and taught among the poorer Russian émigrés there. In the Resistance during WW2 he became Monk Anthony in 1943, was ordained priest and moved to London with his mother and grandmother in 1948. He always considered himself a warrior-monk and, had they met, would have seen eye to eye with Father Eugene of the Church of All Nations in Jerusalem.

So Father Bloom had been in London six years by the time he blessed me at a very moving service, well attended by many of the Russians I had met in London at the Pushkin Club and through its founder Maria Mikolaevna Kullman née Zernova. During the service I was presented with a small, engraved, brass, triptych ikon, blessed by Father Bloom and which he used to bless me. This was not the first nor last time I met Anthony Bloom, because I occasionally attended his services with Irina who was very devout. Later he was made Bishop, then Archbishop, then Metropolitan. Born in 1914 he died in 2003, at the age of 89, an influential and much loved man.

On Tuesday 7 September 1954, during the Farnborough Air Show, the week-long show-case for the Society of British Aircraft Constructors, there took place the annual get-together of all British Air Attachés, home in any case both to see the show themselves and to accompany delegations from the countries to which they were accredited. The occasion was written up by the Evening Standard of 8 September under the heading:

GROUP CAPTAIN IN A FALSE MOUSTACHE DOES A TURKISH DANCE

This was the Air Attaché from Ankara who also gave "*comic impersonations*". From Tel Aviv, Wing Commander Micky Martin, a much decorated ex-Dam Buster pilot led a group of attachés in singing a Cypriot chant. And then, the report continued: "*At one table the toast was in Russian. The proposer, Squadron Leader J.J. Deverill takes up an appointment in Moscow on September 24. Missing attaché was Group Captain Peter Townsend from Brussels. He sent his apologies.*"

Herein lies a tale. Peter Townsend was well-known as the officer courting Princess Margaret, and on occasions I was taken for him. In my view it was difficult to mistake us, but we were both tall, with longish faces and similar hair.

He was a Group Captain and I a Squadron Leader, which, in uniform, as we were as often as not, even a journalist might have noticed. Several times when I left DDAFL I was pursued down Kingsway by reporters until they noticed or I pointed out the difference.

On 22 September Dad drove me to London to the East Surrey Docks, used by the Soviet merchant navy partly because it was cheaper than other liner terminals and partly because it was an insalubrious area where Soviet passengers and crew could see that social conditions were inferior in some respects to those in Leningrad. Dad left me at the gang-plank and drove home, leaving me to cart my cabin bags aboard. The ship, the Byeloostrov, was austere. The voyage to Leningrad via Stockholm and Helsinki was scheduled to take five days. I had a cabin to myself and soon met a number of US military people also travelling to Moscow to take up positions in their Embassy. They included Colonel Charles (Chuck) Taylor USAF, the new US Air Attaché, and his Assistant Air Attaché – Lt. Col. Charles (also Chuck) Jones, both pilots. With them they had their wives and families (two daughters in Chuck Taylor's case). We later all became firm friends, especially because our tours in Moscow lasted three years. Also aboard was RAF Warrant Officer Field, coming to Moscow to run the admin. side of the Air Attaché's office, with his wife and four children. We formed quite an English-speaking group and had a good time despite a rough sea as far as Stockholm.

I found Stockholm a really beautiful city, clean and bright. I was met off the ship by the Assistant Air Attaché there, who took me to lunch and helped me buy a pair of skis. Helsinki was not so impressive, much smaller and giving the impression of being frightened of their vast Soviet neighbour. I wrote home that Finland had always been a no-man's-land between Scandinavia, largely western, and the Slavs, traditional enemies.

Back on board the Byeloostrov Chuck Taylor was feeling pain in his lower right abdomen, and he and Chuck Jones suspected appendicitis. The pains increased and, when we docked in Leningrad, Chuck was hauled off by the other Chuck to a Leningrad hospital, where the diagnosis was confirmed. The condition was acute – no time to fly out to Germany for treatment in an American hospital. The operation had to be performed at once. Chuck Taylor was given the option (there were no alternatives) of being operated on by two female Soviet surgeons. A Major Fife of the US Air Attaché's staff was one of those who had travelled up from Moscow to meet their compatriots. He spoke reasonable Russian and before joining the USAF had studied medicine for two years before transferring to theology and thence to the Air Force. It was thought that he would make the ideal companion for Chuck Taylor to take to the theatre. The operation was carried out under local anaesthetic, several hypodermic syringes being pumped into Chuck's guts. This was the conventional Soviet technique – no general anaesthetic for such a minor op. Half way through the appendectomy Chuck announced he was in great pain and demanded a general anaesthetic. Eventually a cylinder of nitrous oxide was produced (as for tooth extractions in the West) and Chuck was finished off. The surgeons packed the wound with Soviet penicillin and after a few days Chuck continued on to Moscow, but only to be flown out immediately with his wife and children to a USAF hospital in Germany. He did not rejoin us in Moscow for several months.

Meanwhile, I had only stayed a few hours in Leningrad before taking the overnight train to Moscow. I had a sleeper, but a sleepless night. The train went extremely slowly, with long stops at intermediate stations and in the open countryside, invisible in the dark night. The stops and the slow travel between them was punctuated by the howling of the train siren, very like the American trains I had seen and heard in Hollywood films, answered by the sirens of other trains near and far, very like packs of wolves communicating.

Letter home from Moscow, Wednesday 6 October 1954:

> *The voyage out was reasonable, maybe a little boring. Once I was on the ship, about half an hour after you left, it was like stepping behind an iron curtain. At once one noticed the Soviet atmosphere – drabness, rudeness, a lack of colour and freedom. I am not by any means alone in noticing this. Yesterday I had lunch with a Daily Mirror reporter here to cover the football match between the Dynamos and Arsenal. He noticed a changed atmosphere in Sweden directly he transferred from the bright lively Scandinavian Air Services aircraft to the drab Soviet LI2 (their copy of the Dakota), with an Air Hostess at the top of the steps dressed in a black military raincoat, suit, black stockings and a green 1932 hat.*
>
> *Back to our arrival in Leningrad on Wednesday afternoon – it took an hour and a half to clear the ship and get established in the Intourist hotel. After a meal I walked around the town. It is very beautiful, especially because the sunset was fine and red, but of the northern, cold, misty, rosy-pastel type, which I remember from Iceland.*
>
> *The great palaces are peeling; the streets and squares are enormous; the people are very depressing. The Soviet people, to my amazement, are not the colourful singing peasants and soldiers, that broadcasts of their*

patriotic songs would have us believe, but grey-black masses who stream along the pavements, for all the world like migrating ants.

Met by several US assistant air attachés, who had been asked to add me to the arriving American group, I travelled with them to Moscow on the 2030 train, arriving next day at 1000. Here in Moscow I am staying at the National Hotel until my flat is ready. From my window I look out towards the Kremlin just across Revolution Square. The Lenin/Stalin mausoleum is just visible. The Kremlin is a beautiful sight on a fine day, but the Mausoleum is an architectural abortion in pink granite.

Walking about in Moscow confirms my first impressions that the Soviets have absolutely no good taste, not one atom. The large new ministerial and university buildings, in a style sometimes called "Wedding Cake", but to my mind more like Gibbs Dentifrice "Ivory Castles", are prominent features but little more. The post-war tenements housing myriads of flats for the Soviet "ants" are devoid of style, drab, even sordid.

Groups of Soviet students sightseeing in Moscow have asked me for directions to this or that street, and when I have replied that I also am new to Moscow they have been amazed to find that I am English. My Embassy chauffer, Vasili Karasyov, is a grand chap who has driven for any number of past British air attachés. His driving is awful but we get on well. A few days ago he drove me to the football match between Arsenal and the Dynamos in the latter's stadium. People could not have been more friendly. But at the official level, most of those I meet are surly, morose, unsmiling boors. I cannot yet make out what these people are. Some are like the Russians I know in Paris and London; sometimes they come straight from the classics of Russian literature – Chekhov, Tolstoy, Dostoevsky. More often they are dull, nitwitted oafs.

On Sunday I wanted to visit the main Russian Orthodox Yelokhovsky Cathedral to attend a service. When I asked the Intourist office in the hotel for directions, they did their best to deter me: the services were over; it was a long way, etc. Eventually I found a taxi to take me. A service was in full swing. The cathedral was packed to the doors. The singing was beautiful and I shall never forget when the whole congregation sang the Our Father – "Oche Nash" – like a great roar of defiance against the exterior atheism. Outside on the cathedral wall a poster advertised a lecture "The Incompatibility of Science and Religion".

AD ULTIMO

I am already in the grip of the social octopus here – daily lunches and dinners, receptions for national days, etc., and often more than one cocktail party every evening.

My second floor rooms in the National Hotel were very extensive and comfortable, even palatial. One entered an anteroom with sofas and armchairs, and a large desk. To call staff, for a meal in one's room, or for laundry service or help of some other sort there was of course the telephone, but also brocaded bell pulls hanging from the ceiling adjacent to the sofas against the embossed papered walls. From the anteroom one entered the bedroom with large double bed and more chairs and tables with bathroom "en suite" as they put it today. The bath was not unlike a Pharaoh's sarcophagus, in the centre of the room, nearly needing a ladder to enter, with faucets for hot and cold water, which would not have disgraced a warship's engine room. Both bedroom and anteroom had windows overlooking Revolution and Manezhnaya squares (the latter taking its name from the Manezh or riding school, which is still there, adapted for exhibitions).

From my bedroom I could see up the paved ramp leading into Red Square. This was all of particular interest to me because in October the Soviet Army was already starting to rehearse for the vast parade on 7 November to commemorate the October Revolution, conventionally dated 24 October 1917, before the post-Revolution adoption of the Gregorian Calendar. The armoured cars, tanks and self-propelled guns and rocket launchers would line up along the sides of Gorki and Pushkin Streets adjacent to the National Hotel. The rehearsal for the massed drive-past through Red Square would start about midnight, when of course the thunder of the diesel engines and the tracked vehicles made sleep difficult. I was deputed to survey the parked military vehicles to detect any new designs of weapons or their carriers. It was a dramatic scene with the hundreds of armoured vehicles manned by uniformed tankisti in their padded helmets tending to their roaring charges.

I took most meals in the restaurant of the National, one floor down from my room. With careful use of the menu one could get decent meals. Breakfast took some getting used to because, as on the Byeloostrov, caviar, salami type sausage, ham and various delikatessenerie were normal fare for Russians, with vodka and wine, whereas I preferred the odd bacon and egg and more often just toast with butter and jam (no marmalade here) and coffee. The waiters had to be trained as to my preferences and after a week or two got the message. However, even my minimal breakfast was difficult to get in under an hour. I therefore read books and got through quite a lot of Russian literature over breakfasts, and more so lunch, which usually took at least two hours. Our working hours were flexible and 1pm to 3pm were normal lunch hours, with up to an hour more for formal lunches at the Embassy or at home, when I got one. There were a great many Chinese visitors living in the National at that time, and it was disconcerting to hear their hawking at meals. There were spittoons on the main hotel stairs but I do not think the Chinese used them. Russian eating habits were different: under the influence of vodka etc., they fell over forwards with their faces in their plates, or backwards onto the floor, to be rescued by colleagues or waiters.

The flat I was to share with the Assistant Assistant Air Attaché, Flight Lieutenant Dennis Spilsbury, clerical rather than aircrew background, was on the third floor of a block in Narodnaya Ulitsa (People Street), in the south of Moscow. In October it was still being refurbished and I went there occasionally to check progress. Usually there were eight or ten young Soviet women in overalls sitting on the floor of the future lounge, with their backs against the walls, smoking, drinking and chatting. They were very good-humoured and utterly lazy. The flat took several weeks to whitewash with a distemper that was, for ever after, coming off on the clothes of anyone who leant against the walls. The electric wiring was not chased into the plaster, but ran over the internal walls between nailed insulators to the switches and light and power fittings. Meanwhile I enjoyed my luxurious rooms at the National.

Within days of starting work in the Air Attaché's office I was offered a ticket to the Bolshoi Ballet. Each embassy in Moscow received four seats for every Bolshoi performance, ballet or opera. These had to be paid for but, at the special British Embassy rouble rate of 40 to the £, were cheap at the price. Applications for tickets had to be made to the Embassy Secretariat, run by Mr Costaki, a Soviet citizen of Greek origin, whose brother had a priceless collection of impressionist paintings, many of which ended up in the Ermitage in Leningrad. Mary Kirk, a junior secretary working in the Embassy, offered me a ticket originally intended for a friend of hers who was now unable to go. The ticket was to Zolushka (Cinderella). The performance amazed me. Hitherto I had thought ballet nice, sometimes beautiful, the philosophy expressed admirable, good always defeated evil by curtain close. But the Bolshoi performance was out of this world. The enormous stage enabled more than a hundred dancers to people the scene.

The scenes were elaborate, often being transformed as one watched, and receiving rapturous applause even before the appearance of any dancers. The quality of the dancing was superb; the corps de ballet faultless. There was never any question of the corps dancers standing idle, gawping at the prima ballerina fouetting centre stage. All were doing their own thing, but not detracting from the principals. The choreography must have been extremely complex. One might be driven to cheers or tears. I was! My views on ballet (and opera later) were changed completely. Thereafter I got hold of every seat at the Bolshoi that I could (and that I had time for, because evening events were always competing.) To ensure a seat for a performance I especially wished to attend, I cultivated the smaller embassies – Icelandic and Afghan and one or two others with a *chargé d'affaires* and minimal staff, but still receiving four tickets daily. Hence, once I got my own flat and started entertaining, the Icelandic and Afghan *chargés* frequently came to lunch or dine.

Within a week I had also attended the opera Boris Godunov, a four hour feast (with two intervals), based on Pushkin's text, music by Mussorgsky. The intervals at the Bolshoi were about 40 minutes long, time to have a vodka or two and a doorstop of rye bread, thickly spread with butter and beluga caviar. No G&T's and salted peanuts here!

Our embassy had originally been the Moscow house of a wealthy Russian sugar merchant. The very fine nineteenth-century Italianate main building faced onto the Moscow river embankment (Sofieskaya Naberezhnaya) and across it to the Kremlin. At right angles to the main building two wings extended back, and parallel with them were two secondary buildings, one on each side, built in the same style. The western of these buildings was the administration and the eastern for adjuncts to Chancery, the heart of the Embassy, the "Operations Room" as it were, which was on the ground floor of the main building, on the right as one entered the main door. On the left were the offices of the Military and Naval Attachés and at the back of the western wing were the Air Attaché's rooms, the RAF being the junior service. To get to the Ambassador's office, one entered by the main door, booked in with the Chancery Guard, who had a desk on the right, and then proceeded straight ahead up the Gothic panelled staircase. That is – assuming you were welcome. Unwelcome visitors were detained by the Chancery Guard(s) and the Soviet militiamen manning the main gate, with their sentry boxes outside the Embassy compound, could be summoned to assist in expelling anyone who would not otherwise depart.

The Ambassador had his accommodation on the first floor, and very fine it was. The square, high-ceilinged dining room, expensively wall-papered, was flanked on each of its four walls by four large full-length paintings, in heavy gilt frames, of erstwhile members of our Royal family, and very few could tell whether they were British, Russian or German royals – two male, two female. The reception rooms resembled those that might be found in stately homes in the UK – Osborne House, Blenheim, etc. In many respects the Embassy was a museum piece, and the Soviet government was only waiting for the expiry of the lease to reclaim the building and force the Foreign Office to find an alternative site for an embassy. This did not come about until comparatively recently, in 2000.

A disadvantage for the Soviets of having the British Embassy smack opposite the Kremlin was that there was no better position than the Embassy roof for observing and photographing Soviet fly-pasts on May Day and 7 November. On each of these occasions the Soviet Air Force mounted a fly-past over Red Square exhibiting its latest fighting aircraft, ostensibly for the predilection of the Politburo lined up on the roof of the Mausoleum, where the Premier and the General Secretary of the Communist Party would take the salute flanked by the Commanders-in-Chief of the three armed services. The fly-past followed the same route as the march/drive-past, and this took the aircraft no more than 50 metres east of the British Embassy at a height of 50 to 100m (Soviet aircraft measured height in metres). On each of these festive days I was obliged to attend the parade with all the other Service attachés in a compound just west of the Mausoleum. But rehearsals for the fly-past were flown on most of the previous ten days, usually at the same time – 11a.m. By that time I had climbed the stairs into the Embassy attic and out of one of the small dormer windows onto the sloping roof, where I was able to take up a more or less concealed vantage point behind the stone parapet wall.

I was often shadowed by the Embassy Head Butler, a Soviet "servant" provided by Burobin, the official Soviet agency for the provision of locally recruited staff. He was also obviously in the employ of, or briefed by, the KGB (Committee for State Security) or MVD (Ministry for Internal Affairs) and it was his job to see what I was up to. However, once I was in the loft space I locked the door from the inside so that interference with my activities would be difficult. Settled against the parapet wall behind the gutters 50 feet up, in rain or shine, cold or hot, I waited for the fly-past with my camera in my arms. My "camera" was a Robot 35mm miniature, with a repeat motor base, so that when I pushed the release button the camera would take a series of photographs at intervals of about one second. The lens was no miniature but a massive telephoto about half a metre long, to which the attached camera was a minute accessory. When I heard or sighted an aircraft approaching and saw it appear over the Kremlin towers I raised the "apparatus", sighted, and pressed the release. After the fly-past I descended from the loft, brushing cobwebs from my clothes and hair and removing any rain-soaked or snow sprinkled clothes, locked everything behind me, and returned to my office looking as innocent as ever, in case any Embassy "servants" were observing. I sometimes achieved splendid results from these operations –

obtaining the first photos of new Soviet fighters and bombers. Some of the photos became classics in their field, and I saw them for years after in histories of aircraft design and development.

My US colleagues, Chuck Taylor, Chuck Jones and their assistants in the American Embassy had much more sophisticated equipment for the photography of Soviet fly-pasts. The US Embassy was much further away from Red Square than were we. They therefore installed a vast telephoto camera in one of the higher floors of their Embassy, with the nose of the lens directed through a window towards Red Square. With this they photographed an aircraft in several sections which could be joined together in the fashion of a line overlap. Every rivet came out clearly. The Americans also had an odd method of keeping conversations secret. Whereas in the British Embassy we had a quiet room, a hardboard room suspended within a larger room, windowless and surrounded with devices to create diversionary noises designed to confuse any microphone, the USAF staff had aircrew helmets which all concerned had to don, with intercommunication by voice tube as in the Tiger Moth. Electronics might be intercepted it was thought, so there we sat talking into our calabashes. The Soviets were supposed to have devices trained on our office windows which could detect and convert into speech the vibrations of the window glass caused by our voices. One could not be too careful.

On 8 October I received a letter from Dad announcing the death of Arthur Deverill. He was the last but one Deverill in the family business of John Deverill in Slough. But he had been poorly for some years and unable to do much in the business. He was succeeded by Jack Deverill, his son, (see Chapter 1 – Men of no Meane Antiquitie) who presided over the last years of what might be called the family firm. A not uncommon fate for businesses. Rags to riches and back in three generations!

Later in October I attended an Ambassadorial lunch for Georgi Malenkov, the Soviet Premier who had succeeded Stalin on his death in March 1953. I sat close to him and was able to engage in conversation when his attention was not taken up with his food or with Sir William and other senior diplomats. He seemed to me to be rather a boring man, full of smiles on his fattish face on which he was soon to fall. Sir William thought there was something creepy about his appearance but that he was quick, clever and subtle, in marked contradistinction to Nikita Krushchev, who was clumsy and impetuous, sly (khitriy in Russian) but intelligent. Immediately after Stalin's death, Malenkov had held both the post of Premier and that of First Secretary of the Communist Party, but very soon Krushchev took over this second post, arguably the more important. Mikoyan, the Soviet Minister for Trade, was also present for this lunch, but sitting too far from me for conversation. I heard Krushchev speak on many subsequent occasions, and he endeared himself to Russian audiences because he so closely resembled the archetypal Russian peasant.[1]

The protocol for Embassy lunches, dinners, receptions etc., was quite complicated for one unused to such occasions. A lot of it was normal politeness, but taken further than in most households. My presence was needed for interpreting, not so much between Russian guests and Embassy staff, but more for the many other guests, from other embassies and organisations, unlikely to speak conversational Russian. One rule was that an Embassy guest should never be left without someone to converse with. Lady Hayter, Iris, like most ambassadors' wives, took great care to seat guests next to or within speaking distance of people with whom they might have common interests. Guests should not be plied with questions or comments which interfered too much with eating and drinking. But nobody should ever feel or look ignored. Nor should guests feel daunted by the glass and silver adorning their place at table. Here it was up to the Ambassador's wife to give a lead by starting to eat and drink using the appropriate knife, fork or spoon and the waiters attending guests would make sure that the right glasses were filled in the correct order so that there was little opportunity for a guest to make a gaffe.

At one ambassadorial lunch we were served with small corn on the cob (not the best food for formal occasions) for which two small forks were provided, one to be inserted in each end of the cob. Lady Hayter gave a lead. However these cobs, being Russian, were wood-hard, and one guest on my right, pressing hard on his forks, had the cob break away and career down the table into his neighbour but one's plate, something which in normal company would have raised a smile. Here the incident was obscured by conversation and discreet mopping up by the nearest waiter. If a guest started to drink soup from the plate, hosts would immediately follow suit. Staff with an interpreting duty, like me, were always on standby to help others having difficulty with conversation. But we were not to intrude on conversations in which more senior staff members were engaged. Who knows, they might be involved in very important diplomatic matters. Sometimes interpreting held up one's own feeding – tough luck!

Sometimes the subject for interpreting might be dull. Charles Thayer, a secretary to the first US Ambassador in Moscow in 1933, in his book *Bears in the Caviar*, writes how he was interpreting for his Ambassador, Mr Bullitt, at a dinner for the top generals of the Red Army. He was sitting awkwardly behind Bullitt and the War Commissar, Marshal Voroshilov, with General Budenny, father of the Red Cavalry, not far away. Mr Bullitt asked Voroshilov about his preferences for ballet and some desultory remarks were exchanged until Charles Thayer started his own conversation with the two military men about polo, which he had played at college. Meanwhile he continued to interpret their responses, as if they were still on the subject of ballet. Eventually the Ambassador realised that the length of the remarks in Russian did not fit Thayer's much shorter interpretations. A climax was reached when Voroshilov and Budenny both directly addressed questions to Bullitt to which they clearly wanted answers.

Thayer was then obliged to come clean and explain that the Russian cavalry would like help in learning how to play polo, with Thayer as Senior Polo Instructor and the Ambassador, who was getting on, as referee at a match to be arranged between the Embassy and the Red Army. When, the question was, could this be arranged? I met Charles Thayer later in Moscow when he visited Chip Bohlen, who had been a Third Secretary in the US Embassy at the same time. When interpreting I never went as far as Charles.[2]

In October the British Embassy in Moscow hosted a Parliamentary delegation from London with which I was called upon to help. It was a mixed lot, including some arrant socialist pro-communists such as Tom Driberg, as well as MP's more sceptical about Soviet achievements. They followed a programme made for them by their Soviet counterparts, including touristic events and a performance at the Bolshoi where Ulanova danced the lead in Romeo and Juliet.

Letter home 20.10.1954:

> *Last Friday, when the Parliamentary Delegation was here, the Embassy applied for, and wonder of wonders, received, 70 seats at the Bolshoi for a performance of the ballet Romeo and Juliet by Prokofiev, Juliet danced by Ulanova. I therefore saw her without having to wait for months for a ticket. People have waited for a year before now. Outside the theatre in Sverdlov Square stand dozens, if not hundreds, of Russians asking if anyone has spare tickets to sell – there is quite a black market in theatre tickets. I notice that this happens outside nearly all theatres, but it is always worse outside the Bolshoi.*
>
> *The production of Romeo and Juliet is magnificent. Our Royal Opera House and the Sadlers Wells Ballet would pack up their tights and pumps and take up farming if they saw how things are done here. The stage at the Bolshoi must be nearly as big as the auditorium. Hundreds are on the stage at the same time and their costumes must*

cost a sizeable part of the national budget. It is of course well known that the theatre makes big losses every year – these are borne by the government.

But in the same letter:

So far I have found Russia to be by far the most depressing place I have ever visited. Everything seems to be miserable – people, houses, clothes, food, weather. There are of course many wonderful, even incredible, sights of great beauty, but all seem to be waiting inwardly to withdraw at any moment into misery and nostalgia.

In respect of my role in the Embassy in escorting delegations such as this Parliamentary Delegation, it should be explained that surprisingly few Embassy staff spoke fluent Russian and felt at home in the language. There were one or two Foreign Office people in the Chancery fluent in Russian, but he or she would usually be preoccupied with the translation of important documents, writing papers on political developments, assisting the Ambassador in his contacts with Soviet dignitaries and counterparts – all of which were more important than interpreting for the many individuals and groups arriving from Britain each week. The Ambassador for my first year and a half in Moscow, Sir William Hayter, spoke enough Russian to understand his Soviet interlocutors, but his French was better than his Russian and his particular interests were on the arts side. On important issues he was usually accompanied by his personal secretary, John Morgan – (studied Russian, polished like mine in a Russian family in Paris but with Prince Dadiani rather than a taxi driver). John's job in Moscow was to monitor discussions, get messages across (in both directions) and be a support for Sir William.

There were usually one or two Russian speakers attached to the Embassy from FORD (the Foreign Office Research Department), but they usually had their own fish to fry. I was called on to help, more than the other Defence Attaché staff, who were less fluent in Russian. As there were very few specifically air matters to be dealt with, my duties were largely diplomatic. My boss as Air Attaché for my first two years, Air Commodore Peter Donkin, was New Zealand born. He had joined the RAF before the war and studied Russian for a short time under their auspices, but was already less than fluent except in swear words. The Military and Naval Attachés hardly spoke Russian at all. I had an Assistant Assistant Air Attaché, Dennis Spilsbury of the RAF Secretarial Branch. He had been taught Russian with me, but was less keen on the diplomatic work, whereas for me it was my lifeblood.

On Thursday 22 October at 0600 I set off with the Assistant Military Attaché, Major John Marshall, and Jill Shepherd, a Second Secretary in the Embassy, tour-expired and returning to the UK by ship from Leningrad. She wanted to take her Volkswagen Beetle back to Britain with her. We drove to Leningrad from Moscow in two cars – the Beetle and John's official Land Rover. The latter was driven by John's Soviet chauffeur, while John drove the Beetle with Jill and me as passengers. The distance from Moscow to Leningrad was (and remains) about 650 km with road and rail running parallel to each other SE to NW. No great task one might have thought.

Letter home from the Astoria Hotel Leningrad 25.10.1954:

> *Everybody said we were mad – that there was no road – that it was impossible to get through after so much rain, and so on. But by persistence, helped considerably by God, we made it! The first couple of hundred kilometres were not too bad – bumpy asphalt, with only one or two diversions – muddy of course, but not seriously. From then on the road is being reconstructed. This means that the soil is scraped and bull-dozed into positions on top of which a concrete road can be laid later. This soil, after several weeks of rain, was mud – **a sea of mud**, about which I will have nightmares for years. Our two vehicles towed each other out of mud, or were manhandled out of mud dozens of times by ourselves and helpers whom we managed to recruit from teams of road-workers, when they could be found. The mud came over the top of my knee boots; in places a man could quite easily have disappeared into the mud upright and drowned. Great boulders were mixed in with the mud, and Jill's Beetle, which is very low, was knocked about a lot, bottoming on rocks with all four wheels spinning helplessly in the air, disappearing in sheets of liquid mud, and battering through great sticky morasses.*
>
> *Both bumpers were nearly torn off by collisions with boulders and by towing ropes attached to vast Soviet tractors heaving us out. The sheet metal bottom of the Beetle suffered a lot. The wings and nave plates were bent, and the engine, when we arrived in Leningrad was found to be attached to the chassis at one point only. Twice the Land Rover, in which I was travelling for a while to help the driver, nearly turned upside down in the mud, with both me and the driver clawing for the door handle on the other side trying to escape. At different points*

we received considerable help from Russians – soldiers, workers and civilian truck drivers, but also considerable abuse. Many times we were up to our knees in mud, bodily lifting or pushing stalled vehicles in front of us. When Jill and I were outside pushing and pulling in mud up to our knees, with John sitting at the wheel inside the Beetle, a burly Soviet peasant banged on his window and shouted in Russian: "What are you doing sitting in there like the Empress!" This was not John's world at all. He was an aesthete, very knowledgeable about wine, a cultured man. Wrestling in mud with intransigent machinery was not his metier.

We finally reached Novgorod at two in the morning, after 20 hours of nightmarish driving. We put up at the Intourist Hotel. Novgorod is a nice place. It was the first capital of Russia and is one of its oldest towns. Small, but there are many small churches. In one small area of about an acre there are seven churches, one against another, all of different design. Jill and I walked to the Kremlin from whose bell tower, up which I climbed, there is a fine view of the town. From Novgorod to Leningrad was not too bad. We were stuck several times, but it was light and the road improved all the time to a reasonable track. John Marshall developed a severe cold, not surprising. Jill and I went to the ballet in the old Marinskiy Theatre – The Nutcracker. Absolutely splendid and I nearly burst into tears. Also attended Chekhov's Cherry Orchard, very good, and Lakme, a quite awful opera. We also visited the Ermitage museum which is very fine, before I delivered Jill to her ship and she sailed away to England. Flew back to Moscow with John on Tuesday morning.

Letter home, 7 November 1954:

Today is the 37th anniversary of the Bolshevik Revolution, Great October Day as it is called. This morning there was the mammoth parade of troops and civilians through Red Square. All of us foreign defence attachés were invited and were in our places by 0930 on a special stand to the right of the Mausoleum. Not far for me to walk, for the National Hotel is just across the road in Revolution Square. About 5000 troops of different forces, the military academies, parachutists etc., and a wide variety of self-propelled guns, rocket carriers and armoured vehicles drove past the Mausoleum. The parade was led by a Marshal of the USSR standing upright in an open ZIM car, accompanied by the Commander of the Parade, a General, in his ZIM. (ZIM stands for Factory in the name of Mikoyan – the cars are of Rolls Royce dimensions). These two officers cursorily inspected the formations halted in Red Square, greeting each unit and were then saluted by each with a roared ovation, not unlike a long cheer followed by a series of short barks.

The Parade Commander then approached the Mausoleum and saluted the General Secretary of the Communist Party, flanked by other members of the Politburo. Marshal Bulganin made a speech lasting some ten minutes about the successes of the Soviet people in the year just past and the plans for the next. Reference was made to the Soviet Union's wish for peace, coupled with the affirmation that Soviet forces would win the arms race which they had never sought. The National Anthem was played by the 1,000-piece band and a 37 gun salute was fired in the Kremlin somewhere behind our backs. The march past then resumed, and after the military came tens of thousands of civilians representing every aspect of Soviet life – factories, sports, culture – with each detachment carrying their banners and flags, rather like a Trades Union demo in the UK but much larger.

I got back to the Hotel National for lunch at 13.00. The afternoon was less noisy but more thousands of civilians continued to march (but now more walk or even amble) through Revolution Square, past the hotel and up into Red Square. By 18.00 the crowds milling about outside my window were waiting to attend events to be presented from a raised temporary open-air stage at one end of Revolution Square. A troupe of ladies in long white dresses (woollen I hope, for it is cold now) are singing patriotic songs and dancing and I am going down to have a look.

Did so. It is now 22.30. The dancing and singing are still going on and I saw a rather silly item by some circus clowns. Dennis Spilsbury and I went off for an hour or so to have supper in our flat but Galya our maid, has the day off so we had to open tins and fry chips to accompany some awful tinned steak. At 22.00 there was a fireworks display over Moscow; nothing special – coloured rockets all of the same type. I am told these parades on May Day and 7 November are standard and take place every year in roughly the same way.

I am reading a book The Thaw *by the well-known Soviet writer*

Ilya Ehrenberg. He has been in hot water over this book, which professes to show a picture of fairly ordinary life in the USSR today. It is a very difficult book to get. I bought the only two copies of the autumn allocation to a small bookshop in Novgorod – grabbing them off the counter as they were unpacked from the just delivered parcel. It is a very readable book. I wish I had time to translate it for you.

Obtaining books for FORD was a job we were asked to do whenever we could. There were bookshops in every largish town, selling for the most part retreads of Lenin's and Stalin's magna opera. These political and ideological works were as tedious as they come and impossible for most people to read. Fortunately not many people read them and as both Lenin and Stalin had pronounced on almost every subject under the sun it was easy, when refuting some communist apologist's argument on a social or economic problem or almost any other sort of problem, to preface one's own preferred dogma by saying *"As Lenin said in 1925 ………"*. As no Soviet apologist had the slightest idea whether Lenin had said such a thing or not, but was unwilling to risk criticising the great leader, as often as not one had won the argument. Chip Bohlen, the American Ambassador when I was in Moscow, used this technique to perfection, with the great advantage that he knew what Lenin had said and written on different occasions, and knew it much better that most other Soviet experts. I never knew whether he was bluffing or not, but adopted the technique with success.

Chip Bohlen was a great friend of Sir William Hayter, and at my junior level, I got on very well with him too. He had had years of experience in Soviet affairs, having been posted to Moscow on a number of occasions in different diplomatic grades, eventually ambassador. My close hand-in-glove relationships with most of the US defence attachés and many of their civilian colleagues meant that we worked almost as one embassy. Collette Schwartzenbach was a very attractive girl of about my age, who had studied Russian and then particularly wanted to get active experience in Moscow. She applied for a job as an au pair for Chip Bohlen's children and went to Moscow in that capacity. When she had finished her term of a year or so, whatever it was, she had become so useful that the US Embassy kept her on until she obtained another job with a press agency reporting Soviet affairs. Later still she returned to the US and soon had her own TV show on the same subject. I enjoyed her company but she was a dyed-in-the-wool blue stocking.

The US and UK embassies organised a joint choir, in which the British held many of the key posts, including that of the conductor. CofE church services were held on Sundays, turn and turn about, in the British and American embassies with the choir performing. The British Air Attaché's staff was considered to be a British Council simularcrum in Moscow (at that time there was no other). In culture we were the bees' knees, from madrigals to Scottish dancing organised by Lady Hayter helped later by Air Commodore Donald MacDonell, when he took over from Peter Donkin as my Air Attaché. Donald was the head of the clan Macdonald, wore the kilt and knew his Scottish dancing backwards.

Another book in intentionally short supply that I obtained for FORD was *Not by Bread Alone* by Vladimir Dudyentzev. Like *The Thaw* this was another seminal book, describing Soviet society and its flaws. Such books paved the way for Krushchev's denunciation of Stalin and all that followed, to Gorbachev's policies and the decline and fall of all communist regimes at the end of the millennium. Not only was I looking for books but also for a variety of other things. Penicillin for example. It was rumoured that penicillin was obtainable over the counter in chemist shops and there was interest in the west as to the strength and purity of Soviet production. I was asked to visit apotekas in Moscow and elsewhere to see if I could get some. I failed. When my accent in Russian was noticed, the penicillin was openly put under the counter and its availability denied, although it might have been different had I had a prescription from a Soviet polyclinik. I was often asked to check market prices of a list of commodities. Prices in the Government shops rarely changed but they fluctuated in the "free" markets of which there were a number, and this probably gave FORD something to work on.

Just before the end of October Dennis and I moved into our own flat in Narodnaya Ulitza. It was furnished with Foreign Office tables and chairs, beds and all the vital pieces of furniture, and by that time we had accumulated some pieces of our own from departing Embassy staff who held sales of effects they did not want to take home. Decent lampshades, light fittings, standard and desk lamps were in great demand because over a tour of two or three years these get scorched and virtually unusable.

On 18 November it froze. There had been cold weather earlier in the month with the occasional snow, but after a wet front of some sort on 17 November, the next day the temperature dropped to -30°C or thereabouts. I donned the overcoat made for me by Hoggs in London, lovat cloth lined with kapok, with a sheepskin collar transferred from my wartime Irwin jacket. Even so I had not yet managed to buy myself a fur hat with earflaps and while out looking for one in GUM (Gosudarstvenniy Universalniy Magazin = Government General Store) in Red

Square opposite the Kremlin, I was stopped several times by old women who mentioned the possibility of my ears freezing off. I bought an earflapped hat and from then on, with the flaps down, resembled a cocker spaniel, or more likely a Russian peasant. GUM was the Russian equivalent of a department store, a cross between M&S, Harrods and Woolworths.

Several days later Dennis and I left on a ten day visit to Kazan, Kuibyshev and Saratov, all on the River Volga, and from there to Astrakhan and Rostov-on-Don, and back to Moscow. We took the train from Moscow to Kazan and thence another as far as Rostov, stopping off at Kuibyshev, Saratov and Astrakhan for a day or two in each. Such journeys took a lot of planning. The Naval Attaché's office kept cabinets of maps of most parts of the Soviet Union and from these, intending travellers traced into self-compiled miniature notebooks the routes and parts of towns they might traverse, annotating them with details to act as aide-mémoires. It was important not to emerge from a railway station looking as if you were unsure where you were going. This was usually a signal for the KGB followers to pounce and insist you proceed immediately to the Intourist hotel, or even that you return to Moscow. On leaving the train you should be able at once to step off in a known direction towards your destination, whatever that might be, or hail a taxi or take a bus with every sign that you knew where you were going. So a well prepared note-book was vital to read up before arriving at the station or airport, and as it might be confiscated by police or KGB, it was better written in some sort of personal code. I used Arabic abbreviations, surmising that even highly trained intelligence officers would be unable to decipher my amateurish hieroglyphs.

One might ask, why not use Soviet maps and guidebooks? They were not available to purchase, for us or for the Soviet people. Such information was secret, issued on a need-to-know basis. One of my most useful guidebooks was a Baedeker Guide to Russia in French published in 1911, bought in a London antique bookshop before I came to the USSR. I also used a Soviet school atlas annotated with dots and dashes and underlinings. This was especially useful for air navigation, i.e. to work out the exact route being followed by the Aeroflot passenger aircraft in which I was flying. I developed this to a fine art and probably knew our position more accurately than the aircrew. On this visit Dennis and I started off from Moscow by train. The scene for most of the first leg to Kazan was snow-covered forests and fields, with the occasional town and village – nobody working outside of course. Traditionally the Russian did very little work in the winter except essential repairs to tools, bringing in logs for the pechka, the enclosed fire kept alight throughout the cold months, and on top of which the peasant and his family often slept.

On this particular journey, about 40km from Moscow, I noticed a great deal of work going on beside the railway line, with high wire fences of the sort often surrounding military installations. Within the fences – considerable earthworks around a large concrete bunker, still incomplete but with, centrally on the sloping southeast side, a protruding metal axle or mast, at some 45° above the horizontal. On the axle was mounted a segmented circular spool or "yo-yo" as I later described it, of about 20' diameter. As the coast was clear I grabbed my Leica camera, always available in my coat pocket, in a specially large zipped "game" pocket sewn by Hoggs into the interior lining, and snapped the structure twice or three times. After our return to Moscow my report to the Air Ministry mentioned this and with the report we had sent them the film and drawings made by Dennis and myself. Much later, when pressed, they said that the installation might be a stone crusher for manufacturing road metal.

We were convinced that the bunker with its yo-yo, wire defences, military guards etc., indicated something much more important than anything connected with roads. As it turned out much later, by which time we had accumulated information on many other sites, the bunkers were radar installations for the Moscow SAM (surface to air missile) defences.

The missiles, whose large covered transport vehicles we sometimes identified and followed traversing Moscow, had been developed from the German Wasserfall rocket, many of which had been captured by the Soviets at the end of WW2, together with many of the German technicians who were carted off to the USSR to help develop the Soviet version. These SAM were sited on a large number of launching platforms in two concentric circles at 40 and 80km from Moscow. These had a concrete herring-bone pattern each covering an area of air strip size, and each with its own acquisition and guidance radar – the yo-yo. The segmented yo-yo was a rotating aerial array capable of broadcasting on a variety of changing frequencies to make jamming more difficult. I always thought that future archaeologists might be puzzled by the hundreds of platforms which they might think associated with a cult as for Stonehenge.

There was a pregnant moment in the train when Dennis leaned across to me and hissed: *"I have dropped my camera lens"*. It had fallen out of his pocket while he was extracting his hankerchief. We were immediately concerned that the lens might be found by a "Soviet citizen" who could denounce us for photography, which was of course forbidden, not only for foreigners, but for everyone. Nor could we easily recover the lens from the floor if it were rolling about among Soviet legs. Fortunately I discovered the lens, a cylinder about 4" long and 2" in diameter, not far from my hand. It had fallen onto a shelf below the window at which I was sitting and had rolled backwards and forwards until my hand touched it. Divine intervention?

Being denounced as spies, or worse, was always a worry, and not uncommon. A Komsomol, or any devout Soviet citizen, sometimes tipsy, sometimes put up to it by the goons, would announce to as many people as could hear that, we, visiting foreigners, had transgressed the norms of Soviet law or behaviour. He, always male, would appeal to listeners to help him detain us until the arrival of the militia. To be surrounded by shouting "citizens" as if one were a thief or paedophile caught in the act, was frightening. And one was always concerned that derogatory articles in the press (Komsomolskaya Pravda usually obliged) followed by expulsion from the Soviet Union might well follow. This sort of thing happened frequently, especially when your country was in the doghouse for some political reason. The Americans usually were and suffered disproportionately. These acts could be turned on and off to embarrass or offend this or that country as the Kremlin might decide.

We stopped in Kazan for a couple of days. Originally a Tartar town, it had a Kremlin at its centre and many churches – all in all a very pleasant place. Taking the train on to Kuibyshev we moved into slightly warmer air and the snow diminished. The train was a slow one, stopping at every station and taking three days. The stops were sometimes quite long because there was only one train each week.

Waiting in the train at halt we were surprised to see a procession winding down the straight road from the village a kilometre away, with several youths playing piano accordions in the lead, playing folk music, and girls in national dress singing and dancing behind them, followed by the procession and at the end a group of young men. Our questions were answered with the explanation that these young men had been called up for national service and might be away from home for three years. The ceremony of seeing them off from their village was a tradition deriving from Czarist days, when each family contributed a son for a life in the army, and he might never be seen again. This pattern was repeated at each village, which was why the train's scheduled stops were lengthy.

On many trains the last carriage or two were Black Marias, with barred but unglazed windows and locked doors, for the transport of prisoners, criminal and political. I frequently sought these out and was sometimes able to talk to the miscreants about their circumstances, destinations (usually unknown) etc. As often as not I could tell them more about the immediate destination of the train. I never saw any warders or escorts; they may have been drinking in the buffet car.

Drunkenness in trains was common. On one occasion a Soviet Army Colonel was initially all over us with slobbering friendliness and toasts from a vodka bottle to us, the Queen, etc. and returned minutes later to accuse us of espionage and threaten us with his revolver. After several repetitions of his mood reversals we stopped the Train Commandant (there always was one if you could find him) and complained. The Colonel was removed by militiamen at the next stop.

Between Kazan and Kuibyshev Dennis and I were sitting in a coach type carriage with a central aisle with two seats on each side. The doors at the end of our carriage opened and a poorly dressed woman appeared. She stood at the end of the carriage and addressed the passengers giving an account of her years in an Arctic prison camp from which she had just been released. After a few harrowing moments she walked down the aisle soliciting money from each passenger. None was given until she came abreast of us when we reached into our pockets for a few rouble notes. She passed on through the door into the next carriage, to have her place taken by another beggar, who again addressed a similar plea to the passengers before walking down the aisle. Our Russian neighbours whispered to us we should never help these beggars because they had been enemies of the people and would be looked after by the state if they had a reasonable case. At least a dozen beggars processed through our carriage and we felt awkward about helping them all. It occurred to us later that these were concentration camp prisoners released from places like Vorkuta following the death of Stalin. Many had been the bezprizorniki (unsupervised) children who ran wild in bands in Russian cities during the war, and were rounded up and sent to the camps.

On the railway station in Kuibyshev we came across more of these Russian bezprizorniki, sitting on the tarmac floor in groups, singing folk songs, or dancing, often accompanied by a balalaika or piano accordion. It was a strange and romantic scene, ineffably sad, beautiful and not without hope. In both Kuibyshev and Saratov we explored the local aerodromes to see what was going on. Both had aircraft factories but it was difficult to get near them because of our KGB followers and the local militiamen who helped them, closing roads and diverting us away, or sending us back to the Intourist hotel. Industry seemed very run down. We walked miles along concrete roads between lines of factories, noting any evidence of production – nothing much.

Astrakhan was interesting because we visited the local caviar factory. Here all three varieties of sturgeon – Beluga, Sevriuga and Ocetrina – were landed and transferred to cool storage. On arrival they were probed with a hollow needle to check caviar content. They were then slit open and the caviar scooped out and put into jars, pasteurised and sealed by a simple machine. This was the only mechanisation. Half a dozen women and a few men did the work. Fish without caviar were passed to another shed for smoking and packing for sale as smoked Ocetrina, which I found in general to be tastier than caviar.

Dennis and I got back to Moscow on 8 December. He had caught a bad cold in Saratov which he passed on to me, but I had already recovered sufficiently to attend a dinner given by the Minister. I discovered that I had been summoned to Berlin later in December, partly because the Air Ministry wished me to have another health check to see if there might still be any sign of amoebic dysentery. The nearest RAF hospital was in Berlin. I did not mind. I had never been to Berlin, which was then divided into different sectors, each under the administration of one of the major allies – Britain, the US and the USSR. Britain and the US worked hand in glove of course. The main crossing point from the Soviet sector was the infamous Check Point Charlie, often featured by Le Carré in his spy stories.

Meanwhile normal life in Moscow continued with the daily cocktail parties, lunches and receptions.

Letter home, 10 December 1954:

> *A few days ago, in fact the day after we arrived back here, it was Iranian Army Day, with a reception at the Iranian Embassy. Major Popov (yes, Russians do have such names) of the Foreign Department of the Ministry of Defence, was there. Up to that evening I had never cared much for Popov – he always stood alone in a corner and smiled superciliously at the diplomatic community holding their dry martinis and gossiping their heads off. Somehow, this time we started to argue. We argued for all the two hours prescribed for receptions. There was one break for food when we were separated by a French General asking cocktail party questions about health and weather, and after a moment to gulp down a few hot sausages, I was overjoyed (my self-esteem rose two points) to see Popov bearing down on me again with a "Where were we?" The argument was of course about communism – the Moscow Metro – skyscraper design – the freedom of artists. Every subject of interest to me was drawn in. Wonderful! Best argument since I last saw Irina.*

I was supposed to fly to Berlin the following day, 11 December, but the flight was delayed for bad weather until 15 December. A decision to fly was made at the last minute and there was quite a panic to get to the airport in time. The previous night there had been a Christmas party given by our Embassy staff, including me and the other defence attachés of course. Dennis and I had two Embassy girls coming in for drinks beforehand and the party did not end until 4 a.m. Dennis drove me as fast as possible the 20km to Vnukovo airport and I caught the flight with minutes to spare – a new passenger aircraft – an IL (Ilyushin) 12, with tricycle undercarriage, rather larger than their Dakota variant. It vibrated so much I thought the rivets would pop. We landed at both Minsk and Warsaw, getting to Berlin (Schönefeldt) in the Soviet zone that afternoon. I was met off the aircraft by an official of the British Consulate in Berlin and driven through Check Point Charlie to Spandau and the hospital there where my blood and guts would be checked over the next couple of days.

Letter home, 21 December 1954:

> *Extraordinary contrast between the lifeless grey of the Soviet sector and the bright bubbling life of our civilisation. No bugs found. Today I am off to tour Berlin. Everybody here is kindness itself. I am treated like a refugee from the east. The weather is warm and sunny. People are so happy here, it is amazing! Children chatter, people talk, church bells ring. Friends have rung up from all over the place. Mike Laing, who studied Russian with me, is here with Brixmis. The Accountant Officer came out yesterday with £50 for me. I am now off to buy stuff for the Moscow flat.*

Brixmis was short for British Exchange Mission. This was one of three small motorised formations set up by each of the three occupying powers to monitor what might be happening in the other zones of occupied Germany, including of course the Berlin sectors. Because the British and Americans worked together they were interested solely in what the Soviets might get up to, and the Soviet equivalent (Soxmis) monitored the British, American and French zones. It was a type of spying, mainly concerned with military formations and movements, their equipment, aircraft, etc. Both sides were at liberty to frustrate the opposition, prevent them from seeing what they wanted to, etc. Each side needed technical linguists to observe and interpret and, as often as not to justify their movements to the other side. Mike Laing was one of these. Brixmis was based in Potsdam.

Letter home 29 December 1954:

> *Over Christmas I fixed up accommodation in the Families' Hostel in Berlin. This is a place to which married families come before moving*

to their houses or flats. Once I was out of hospital I was met with a series of invitations to parties. I spent Christmas Day with Mike Laing and his family – three lovely children. We had a wonderful time. All stomachs were like drums when the children went to bed at 8 p.m. and I made my way back to the hostel, close to the Olympic Stadium, a fine place but with grass growing between the stones. Boxing Day I spent with the boss of the RAF section of Brixmis, a Wing Commander, and his family. This included a cocktail party given by the Brigadier commanding Brixmis. I spent the next day seeking out and visiting an old friend of Irina's mother, Herr Enkelmann, a very interesting character – a professional photographer who has spent his life specialising in photography of ballet, a German Baron (the English photographer). He was born in Russia and spent the first 12 years of his life there. He looks like a very kind edition of Bertrand Russell, with long white hair almost to his shoulders. His flat is exquisitely furnished and everywhere one sees photographs of dancers. Big expensive books of his ballet photographs lie on simple pieces of modern furniture. He recently fell off a step-ladder breaking his wrist and pelvis, so he limps on a stick. His thin body, slack clothes, long white hair and enormous kindly eyes remind me of a character in The Third Man. Initially he was very reticent. Later, on my second visit, he opened up. In Hitler's time he was a pacifist, and suffered for it, but now he says that he would fight communism if it came to a war. He had not spoken Russian for years and was very halting to start with, but we soon found ourselves chatting and arguing reasonably fluently.

I had an interesting experience a few days ago. I had been to a concert of Bach and Brahms in the Hochschule für Musik (this is a new concert hall, rather like a small Festival Hall). I was in the pleasant dream-like mood one gets into after good music and did not wish to have my evening coffee in the rowdier cafés on the Kurfürstendammerstrasse. So I entered a small restaurant not far from the Families' Hostel. I was the only client. I sat down and ordered something. Then I noticed a striking water colour on the wall opposite, 15 feet away – two sailing boats frozen solid in a frozen sea. The treatment was impressionist, colours all shades of blue, with one touch of red. A lanky German youth appeared with my order and I said how much I liked the picture. He leaned over, very pleased, and said in halting English "I did it! I did all the paintings here." He sat down and we talked. Although he looked *no more than 22 years old, he is actually 34. He served in U-Boats during the war, and in 1942 surfaced off the American coast and saw the lights of New York. When the Russians re-captured Riga he was captured and was in a POW camp there for two years. There he met a Jewish girl, a helper in the camp, and they fell in love. Eventually she got away to America where she has a job as a nurse. When released from the camp in 1947 he had contracted TB and spent a long time being treated in a Swiss sanatorium. Then he returned to Berlin to study art, living with his parents and helping them with their café, and painting. A few days before I met him he had received his US visa to rejoin his Jewish girl. They plan to marry and he hopes to do anything to make a living, especially painting. He is a charming chap – tall thin and blonde, with blue eyes, typically German – amazing that he is marrying a Jewish girl – very moving and romantic.*

On Christmas Eve I walked through the Tiergarten, past the Brandenburger Tor, into the Soviet sector and up to the Unter den Linden. The difference between the sectors is striking. At the boundaries life dies, the streets become empty, the ruins are still ruins and there is little evidence of reconstruction – the few people one sees about become drab and grey and do not smile. In restaurants talk, which in the west is open and normal, quietens to whispers. There are only a few cars on the streets, and most of them old. Grass grows in lifeless rail yards, and pokes up between the street cobbles. The shops, which in our sector are like Oxford Street with neon signs and brightly and tastefully dressed windows, a mass of light and colour, especially now at Christmas, in the Soviet sector are dim poorly lit affairs empty of anything to buy. The communist atmosphere blights everything – Dull red banner slogans, as can be seen in any Russian street, flap across the facades of some buildings: Forward to the Victory of Communism! Denounce the instigators of the Paris agreement!

Notes:

1. *A Double Life, The Memoirs of Sir William Hayter*, Hamish Hamilton, 1974
2. *Bears in the Caviar*, Charles Thayer, Michael Joseph, 1952

Moscow '55

I did not get back to Moscow from Berlin until 8 January 1955, carrying with me some lampshades and cushions and other small items for the flat. I found a letter from Dad reporting on Michael's wedding to Pat, which had taken place on Saturday 18 December in the church at Hurworth in Yorkshire. Dad had journeyed there by train with Titus and Mary, with whom he had spent the previous night in London. The journey was long and uncomfortable. They arrived at Darlington at 6 p.m. to be met by Mike and driven to the Croft Spar Hotel for the night. The wedding was very nice, with the bride and groom escorted by Mike's fellow officers in full dress uniform, followed by a real Yorkshire meal, no fork business, and oceans of champagne. Dad, Mary and Titus returned to London, and Dad to Alton the next day. Mike and Pat were hot on his heels, spending Christmas at Alton, with Mary and Titus and their baby son John. Mike was posted to the Glider Pilot Regiment (the Army Air Corps from 1957) and later went to Middle Wallop to seek accommodation, etc. I was pleased that Mike, who had originally wanted to be a pilot, was now to become one, if only on small aircraft.

Additional news from home was that old Mr Daysh had died on Christmas Day, and that the weather was very cold, with two sparrows roosting nightly in the front door porch and a blue tit entering Jessie's bedroom late each afternoon and not leaving until let out in the morning. The Delph pipe works (Wyndham and Phillips), the business at Ruabon in which my father had worked for some time from the age of 11, was going into liquidation, partly, in my view, because Arthur Phillips had not managed it correctly.

Back in Moscow I found that Galya, our housekeeper, was ill, and had not been to the flat for two weeks, to the distress of Dennis, who was no house-keeper. I wondered if she was swinging the lead and to the surprise of my driver, Vassili,

I asked him to drive me to her flat. I was appalled. In a single room, about 15' x 10', lived Galya and her sister and their old mother, the sister's 11-year-old daughter and Galya's nine-year-old son. These five had communal use of a loo and kitchen somewhere else in the block. They had two beds for the whole lot of them. Galya was up, in a ragged house-coat and worn fur boots. She looked at death's door. The little girl was also ill. I left nearly in tears and sent Vassili back with a large box of food. Interesting that when I said to Vassili that Galya seemed to be having a hard time, he thought I was just referring to her health and said that she was on her feet and would soon be at work again. I wrote home: *"It seems that these living conditions are either normal, or else Russians are hard-hearted. My God, what a system! If Marx were alive today he would be interested to find that the first society to adopt his philosophy has created the social conditions he observed in England during the Industrial Revolution, which led him to the theories he formulated"*.

Later when I got to know Galya better, she told me what had happened to her husband, something that had puzzled me. He had been arrested under some earlier purge and sentenced to a long period in a prison camp in Vorkuta in the far north. After some years prisoners were allowed out of the camp but forbidden to leave the area. Their wives might join them and they could live together but in what might be called "durance vile". The KGB was always looking for more presentable girls (men too I expect) whom they could use to collect information about foreign diplomats etc. Galya was given the opportunity of working for the KGB as a housekeeper for diplomats assessed as being susceptible.

The quid pro quo would be that her husband would be allowed back to Moscow (comparative civilisation compared to Vorkuta) earlier providing Galya won her spurs, in our flat as it happened. Galya's story is not unique. Tens of thousands of ordinary Russians were sent to prison camps in Stalin's time (and in Lenin's) for what we would think was no good reason. They were denounced by neighbours or by jealous colleagues who wished to advance themselves, for criticising some aspect of the regime or on thousands of other pretexts. There are numerous accounts of these cases, including the books of Anatoliy Rybakov *Children of the Arbat* and its sequels, published from 1987 on.[1]

Later Galya became quite blasé, and after a lunch arranged by me for other attachés, when they had gone and before she got on with the washing-up, she would come into the living room and slump down in an armchair, light a fag, and try to lead me into a conversation about the departed guests. And we discussed politics and got on quite well, although never could she lead me astray. Although quite pretty, she was always slightly desperate, as was not surprising. In winter she suffered chapped cheeks. Her hair was usually neat and shoulder length, but frizzed and permed in the 30s fashion, probably at KGB expense. Galya's standards lacked in some respects. I once came home to find her washing my laundry in the bath and herself as well, naked among the suds. Her cooking was variable. Chickens were roasted spread-eagled, as on the Austrian flag, possibly because it was easier on the oven – the heat might penetrate more readily. In any case chickens were very small. Her greatest success was baked crab (tinned spider crab meat from Sakhalin) in a rich cheese sauce. This was always very popular with guests, with a good Georgian white wine – a number three. Number one was very thin. Georgian whites had odd numbers, reds even, and the lower the number the drier.

Galya, and the other staff appointed to serve members of the diplomatic corps, were paid wages by Burobin (Bureau for Foreigners) but in addition had to be provided with spetzovka by the diplomat they served. This covered things like uniform, aprons etc. for domestic staff, hat, gloves and shoes for drivers, etc., but the definition was flexible. Some staff preferred hard currency they could use in the foreign currency shops. I gave Galya whatever she asked for – dresses, stockings and especially Morlands zipped fur-lined boots which were made to much higher standards than Soviet footwear. I am sure Galya informed on me to the KGB because she told me she was obliged to, but I was careful not to tell her anything that might be of use to them although they probably ended up with a fair knowledge of my likes and dislikes.

The KGB (State Security Committee) successor to the OGPU (Unified State Political Directorate) and SMERSH (an abbreviation of Smert' Shpionam – Death to Spies), and to other such organisations going back to Ivan the Terrible, had an elaborate system for following us and checking up on our activities. The Embassy, which was of course bugged, as were all our flats, had sentry posts with militiamen on duty at every gate. Same with our flats, in blocks allocated to foreign diplomats, each block having limited access and egress also guarded by militiamen. Their boxes all had telephones connected with their HQ. When a diplomat arrived or left the building, on foot or by car, the militiaman at once phoned HQ who alerted follow-cars, in those days Pobeda saloon cars with five occupants each. In common with all other defence attachés, I had three cars and their 15 occupants allotted to me.

From house bugs HQ may already have had a good idea of where I was going. My three cars would be parked in roads close to my flat, so that at least one of them would be on the scent within seconds. I would then be followed, not by all three cars in a line, but on parallel or intersecting roads. Were I to be on foot or should I leave the car and continue on foot, one or more followers (we called them "goons") would dismount and follow us into shops, houses, churches – anywhere we went. They had walkie-talkies and if they could not be used (during a church service for instance) a system of hand signals. In the Yelokhovskiy Sobor, the main working cathedral in Moscow, I would be followed to a position close to the altar by one goon, who when I turned to leave would give a hand signal to a colleague goon at the cathedral doors, who would signal or radio one or more of the follow cars to prepare for my reappearance. It was almost, but not quite, impossible to evade this surveillance, but one could get one's own back now and then.

So Galya, in telling me her life story and giving me her robust views on the authorities, would, if it were not provocation, have been brave, bearing in mind that all our words were being monitored. Sometimes this could be turned to good account. Peter Donkin and his wife Betty, when they had a plumbing fault, a broken window pane, or something else wrong with their flat, would proclaim this loudly, with more than implied criticism of Soviet maintenance standards, and within a short time the maintenance men would turn up, but much more quickly than had one used the proper channels, via Costaki in the Embassy Admin. Department.

In late January I was in charge of the lighting for a drama evening when the Embassy amateur theatricals group presented three plays in the White Room, the large 'Empire' style ballroom of the Embassy, on the first floor, opening off the Gothic staircase and the Louis Quinze dining-room (the sugar magnate had liked a bit of everything!). The three plays, performed in succession on the Sunday and Monday evening, were *The £12 Look* by J.M. Barrie, *Ivy Cottage* by Ernest Hill, and *The Proposal* by Chekhov. Apart from Soviet bloc diplomats, who declined invitations, the audience included just about every other ambassador in Moscow, who occupied the first two rows of seats. There were many applications for the other seats and some of our own Embassy staff, other than the performers, had to crowd in at the back. As lighting engineer I had a privileged place, manipulating 12 switches and dimmers on a temporary switchboard beside Sir William's party.

The same week, I accompanied our Military Attaché (Colonel Chamier) and Peter Donkin to meet the new Italian Military Attaché, living temporarily in the Metropole Hotel as I had done in the National. He was a charming man who turned out to know Monsignor Trossi very well, having been interned with him in a British POW camp in Kenya. We had to make do speaking in broken French and Italian because our new colleague had no English or Russian.

On 9 February 1955 Malenkov was deposed. Nikita Khrushchev was largely responsible, and Bulganin was made Premier in Malenkov's place. Ostensibly the reason for removing Malenkov was the failure of his agricultural policy, but in fact it was more complicated than that. Sir William diagnosed this somersault in the leadership as the result of a difference of opinion on Soviet policy generally. Malenkov had shown a tendency to change the original Stalinist emphasis on developing heavy industry with the aim of outstripping western production of iron and steel, whereas Khrushchev and Bulganin were still keen to compete with the west in this respect. They had won.

Malenkov was not shot, as might have happened in Stalin's time. Nor did he disappear without trace, a fate often overtaking discarded leaders. He was appointed Minister of Electric Power Stations and was thus still a member of the Presidium. Later he visited Britain in that capacity, with me as it happened. I heard about Malenkov's replacement on the BBC World Service and told Galya. She was amazed, but smilingly said: *"What! Our Malenkov? It can't be! I don't believe it!"* But when I said I had heard it from London, she said *"Oh, I suppose they haven't told us yet!"* I agreed. She then gaily said in so many words *"Goodie! Now I am one of the first to know"* and as I left for the Embassy I heard her saying to a friend, who had dropped in to discuss cooking successes and disasters: *"Of course I don't believe it, but..."*

I had been keen on starting to ride horses again, but so far had seen no easy way forward. One evening, driving home from the Embassy through freezing fog, I spotted five horses ridden by groom-like riders, trudging somewhere along a fairly main road, with steam rising from their nostrils (of both horses and riders; the temperature was well below zero). I trailed them back to a collection of sheds on a rather derelict building site. There I left the car and spoke to the leading rider, who had dismounted, obviously the horses were to be stabled here. He told me that the stables were still being built but that if I were keen to ride I might care to approach the establishment run by the MVD (Ministry of the Interior) or that of the Komsomol (Communist League of Youth), the latter being near Sokolniki Park, a large park of about the size of Regent's Park, in north-east Moscow. As the MVD had sinister connotations, I favoured the latter and drove out there. When I stated my interest the Manager invited me into his office and we discussed arrangements he might be able to make for the diplomatic community to ride again for the first time since the Revolution. I was shown round the stables and could see they had some very good horses and was told that these were the stables where the horses for the next Olympic games were being groomed, and Soviet riders came there to train for the equitation events. It was agreed that he would consult his committee and come up with a price per hour, after which we could talk about formulating programmes for diplomatic riders. He suggested that riding on two days a week might be permissible. This was later extended to three.

As might be expected, Lady Hayter was very keen on this idea and even more so was Betty Donkin, who was a qualified riding instructor back in the UK, and who saw herself becoming the chief instructor to the Moscow diplomatic community, as she did. The upshot of all this was that in February 1955 I was put in charge of negotiating riding facilities for diplomats in Moscow, and later was asked to be Secretary of the club we formed. The Swedes, as doyens of the diplomatic community, agreed to take over the formal side of negotiations, while I was responsible for letting all interested parties know, ensuring with Betty Donkin, that diplomats ignorant of horses would be inducted only after instruction, and for programmes to be submitted to the Soviet riding school preferably a week in advance. The riding school, or stables, established to cater for riders in the Komsomol, formally changed its name from Krasniy Moryak (Red Sailor) to Urozhai (Harvest) this being considered better diplomatically. Fees were set at 25 roubles per hour.

Choice of horses was left to the Manezh management until individual riders established preferences, which they might put in the programme. This was splendid. I rode for a couple of hours each week when I could. Betty Donkin and her girls rode on every possible occasion. The Austrian Ambassador Herr Norbert Bischof turned out to be a high school rider, used to riding the Lippizaners in Vienna. Soon he was teaching Soviet horses to gavotte, walk on their hind legs, etc. Betty started to take jumping classes. The Thai Ambassador complained that his very short legs made riding some of the larger Russian horses uncomfortable. One Russian horse, scheduled for the Olympic Games in 1956, was named Sport and was 17 hands, an unusual size. In fact he was too heavy by half and was quickly relegated from the Olympic show jumping. Riding other than in the covered riding school became a problem, because the KGB obviously thought that they might have difficulty providing horse riding goons. However riding in the Park was approved and then prohibited on the grounds of safety. A horse ridden by the Canadian Military Attaché bolted, and he fell off. He did not injure himself but we were slightly put out because the KGB was given an excuse to confine riding to the Manezh again.

Letter home, 9 February 1955:

Our Thursday lunch parties, which Dennis and I have been giving for the last six weeks, are a great success. We cook up some wonderful mixtures of people (and for people). Today we had Christiane de Vericault, a sweet little French archivist; the Pakistani Chargé d'Affaires Mahmud Hamed; and the Norwegian 2nd Secretary and his wife, Mr and Mrs Nils Dahl. Ages – Christiane 20; Mahmud 34; Nils 32; his wife 28. Last week we had Major and Mrs Fife, US Assistant Air Attaché; Daphne Park, one of the diplomats in our Secretariat; and Major Marinkovic, Yugoslav Assistant Military Attaché. We are excellent friends with the French, Italians, Americans, Canadians, Yugoslavs, Pakistanis, Israelis, Swedes. Finns, Norwegians, Austrians and Belgians. Dennis and I have particular friends among those underlined. I want to get to know some rather nice Abyssinians and South Americans. Most of the guests we invite are young, have brilliant futures ahead of them (I hope) and are full of the latest theories and arguments. Lunches invariably continue (I nearly said drag on, but that is the last expression to use for time that disappears) until half-past four or even later.

The Finns included Colonel Kursaala, the Finnish Military Attaché and his Assistant Major Loikenan, both highly decorated for gallantry in the war between Finns and Soviets in 1939/40.[2] They wore their medals with pride. Both had been seriously wounded and bore the scars, especially Major Loikenan. In his cups, i.e. at every reception, Major Loikenan would come to attention after a few vodkas and rather embarrassingly start singing Finnish national songs at the top of his excellent tenor voice, with, as often as not, tears streaming down his scarred face. His boss, the Colonel, was of sterner stuff. At an early reception he told me always to stand near him if I wanted a drink, because he knew every drinks waiter at these receptions and he only had to click his fingers and a new bottle of champagne would appear even when the party was nominally over or the drink exhausted. This never failed.

At one of our Thursday lunches a piece of plaster fell from the ceiling into the casserole carrying the crab "lasagne". Where the plaster had been we noticed what appeared to be the end of a thin glass rod several mm in diameter, depending vertically down, possibly from the flat above. There was great interest among the diners, including Major Yves Michaut, the French Assistant Military Attaché and we climbed on the table and worked on the glass rod with a nail file and a pair of scissors. It was too firmly plastered in to be removed, but we concluded it was some surveillance device.

Letter home, 18 February 1955:

> *Thanks for the book I asked you to send –* Love and Fear, *which arrived by the Dip. Bag with your letter. I am not surprised you do not like it, an emotionally raw book, although this may not be the reason you do not like it; the story of a girl dying of TB is not to everyone's taste. I am quite puzzled by what you do and do not like. In some respects your taste is like mine. "Like father, like son" they say. You live in me up to a point, for I often, to my annoyance, find myself using your tones of expression, but your part in me is mixed up with a lot of other parts – parts I suppose of others – great grandfathers, people from Mummy's side, ancestors and influences producing the individual, who continues being influenced by others all his life, until he too becomes an influence and an ancestor. Life everlasting, Amen!*

In February in Moscow there was, of course, a lot of snow about and we went skiing into the countryside. A place for skiing favoured by the diplomatic community was Tzaritzino, a village some 15 miles south-east of Moscow, where there was a large park with the ruins of a chateau originally started under Catherine the Great but later abandoned by her when she decided she did not like it. The park, in English style, says Baedeker, with lakes, bridges, grottoes and pavilions (this was the 1902 edition in French!), had the advantage for skiing of not being completely flat, and from its low hills one could get closer to downhill skiing than anywhere else near Moscow, other than the Lenin Hills, which for us amateurs were steep and dangerous. A great plus for air attachés was that with a little effort, one could ski to hills from which one could see Ramenskoye fairly clearly. Ramenskoye was the Soviet equivalent of Farnborough or Wright Pat. Field, an airfield dedicated to aviation research. All sorts of Soviet research aircraft flew from this airfield and we, the staff of air attachés in various embassies in Moscow, were always keen to get a glimpse of what the Soviet Air Force had in mind. Any attaché setting out from Moscow with skis on the roof of his car was always followed by goons with their skis. They were not always very good at the sport and the Canadian Assistant Air Attaché, who was a skier of Olympic standard, was always able to outpace the goons with ease and photograph Ramenskoye with his long focus lenses without hindrance.

I used to go skiing with Dennis, but initially he was much less proficient than I, so I left him struggling in the snow like a stranded beetle, weakly waving the odd arm or ski in attempts to get to his feet, while I consorted with the Russian scallywags on steeper inclines where we fell over continually, recovered, fell over again, and so on. On one occasion I followed a Russian youth down a slope, jumping over a frozen stream at the bottom of a gully. To my surprise the far side was much softer snow, and I came to on my back with the tips of my skis beside my face. As I could still feel my feet and legs I realised that I was still in one piece, plucked my broken ski tips from the snow, and that was the end of that day's sport. These Russian boys were great fun – dirty, dressed in drab, ragged but warm odds and ends of clothing – rather like south Wales mining children. They were strong and self-reliant in a fatalistic way – "Well, I'll do my best, but if things get too bad I'll just die, and who can say if that isn't preferable" type of child. Mongrel Mongols. The better class Russian children playing in the courtyard below our flat, from walking stage to about seven years old, wore the most wonderful "shubas" or fur coats of every imaginable type of animal fur. They looked like small bears and behaved like that. No adults looking after them. Completely self-reliant.

Soviet Army Day, letter home, 24 February 1955

> *Last night there was a long and interesting reception at the "House of the Soviet Army" to mark Soviet Army Day. I had to dress up in all me' splendour, chains of office, medals, boiled shirt, etc. We were received by Marshal Sokolovsky, who later came and sat down at all the tables occupied by foreign attachés, and talked and toasted. He is a charming chap, but depressed me considerably by constantly harping on the "war" theme. "Where would it be best to be if there were a war? Land, sea or in the air?" (Toast – to beautiful ladies present, nodding to wives of American Military Attaché and our Assistant Naval Attaché). "What would happen to ladies should there be a war?" He said all this very sadly and seriously. We argued that nobody wanted war, so therefore there would be no war. He left saying "I endorse that **we** do not want war and **I** am in a position to say that, but are **you**? We drank and danced in moderation until midnight.*

What with my work, in and out of the office, diplomatic and recreational (especially riding), and just occasionally RAF, I came to know the Donkin ménage quite well. Peter Donkin was an interesting man. Born in 1913 in New Zealand, he was taken as a toddler to the UK by his parents largely because of WW1, his father regarding it as his duty to fight. After the war the family moved back to New Zealand, but Peter was sent "home" to a prep. school in Rugby, from where he went on to Sherborne School. He was not much of an academic but was pretty good at sport. After Sherborne he joined the RAF and was sent to Cranwell RAF College from 1931 to 1933. In those days it was the equivalent of a degree course + pilot training. At the end of the course he was commissioned and posted to 16 Squadron (Army Cooperation) at RAF Station Old Sarum, near Salisbury, a short flight from RAF Odiham, where I was welcomed by other Army Cooperation squadrons when I was a boy, at times when Peter may have been there, as he often was. In addition to his RAF flying, Peter also started to race cars, MG's in particular, at Brooklands, which also played an important part in my early life. Soon promoted to the rank of Flight Lieutenant and made a Flight Commander, he had to give up car racing in 1935 to concentrate on his RAF career.

By this time 16 Squadron had converted to Lysander aircraft and in 1939 Peter was promoted to Squadron Leader. There was then an interlude in his flying life when he spent several months studying Russian at London University (as I did a decade later), and then living with a Russian family in Estonia to improve his spoken Russian. After three months he had to beat a hasty retreat when the war broke out with Hitler's invasion of Poland, and Peter was nearly cut off in Warsaw during the Luftwaffe blitz. He got back to Britain via Turkey and was posted to 239 Squadron, initially equipped with Lysanders, but soon re-equipped with American Tomahawks and later with the Mustang, an American aircraft with a Rolls Royce Merlin engine, after the Spitfire probably the most successful allied fighter aircraft of WW2, with great range and hitting power. He was soon Wing Commander commanding 239 Squadron, supporting Canadian ground forces on the Continent. In 1941 he met and married Betty Cox, an archetypal English country girl, horsewoman and huntress and very direct and pushy. Peter and Betty were much of a muchness, very down to earth, feet on the ground, calling spades bloody shovels, kind, decent, but no holds barred. After a fairly heroic war, much decorated, Peter had various staff appointments until his study of Russian led to his selection as Air Attaché to Moscow.

Peter's Russian had by then got very rusty and it may never have been very fluent. He could understand some of what was said to him, but he could not engage in continuous conversation. Of course that was part of my job – to interpret and make sure there were no misunderstandings, rather as John Morgan did for Sir William Hayter. I liked Peter immensely – his direct approach, his inability to suffer fools at all. Physically he was a spare and lanky man with greying hair and piercing light blue eyes. A great friend of his was the Canadian Air Attaché Group Captain Stan Turner.

Like Peter, Stan had also been born in 1913, but in Devon. When he was young, his parents emigrated to Canada and settled in Toronto. While at the University of Toronto reading engineering, Stan learned to fly with the equivalent of a University Air Squadron and in 1938 he joined the RAF as an Acting Pilot Officer and moved back to the UK, and, after various conversion courses, joined 242 Squadron flying Hurricanes from Biggin Hill and then in France where the squadron supported the British Expeditionary Force. Back in England after the fall of France, 242 Squadron operated from Coltishall with several other squadrons including Douglas Bader's. Initially there was some friction between the two, because Bader was punctilious about discipline in dress and behaviour, whereas Stan couldn't care a damn, and reputedly replied to one of Bader's disciplinary injunctions with "Horseshit!". Later they became close friends. In 1941 Stan commanded 145 Squadron (Spitfires) and then 249 Squadron in Malta. Peter and Stan got on very well together. They were men of the same ilk. Stan's Russian was even less than Peter's. Peter Donkin and Stan Turner had a lot in common and I enjoyed working with them. They shared a poor impression of Russians: "straight out of the trees" as Peter used to put it.

On 6 March 1955 I attended a party at the Indian Embassy to meet a new Indian Military Attaché. I wrote to Dad: *"I like Indians – they have good taste and sense, are cultivated and their women dress like flowers. I had a long argument/discussion with five Indians at once about Christianity and the commandment Love thy Neighbour, which is apparently also a Hindu precept"*. Little did I know then that 50 years later a son of mine would have a wife of Indian origin. We got on well with the Indians and played a lot of squash with them. Their Embassy had a squash court, I think the only one in Moscow. We British could only manage tennis on a court behind the Embassy which was flooded in winter for skating.

Two days later I set off on a trip to the Donbas, the basin of the Don river, where there was a lot of Soviet heavy industry which we wanted to have a look at. I went with Humphrey James, the Assistant Naval Attaché, and two diplomats – Roland and David. Our idea was to book a railway compartment (sleeper) from Moscow to Stalino, but we failed and Humphrey and I were allocated two bunk beds of a four-berth compartment with two Russians for company and surveillance, with the two diplomats similarly provided for next door. We tried to get the Russians to share one compartment, with us in the other, but no way! They had almost certainly been briefed to keep an eye on us and make sure we did not take photographs. Our companions were a Russian woman who slept most of the time and a Soviet Army Colonel.

The Colonel was a fairly modest looking chap, rather like Fred Lawrence, the Phillips lorry driver, in a WW1 uniform, except that in trains all Russians, in those days, and possibly even now, doffed their formal clothes at the start of the journey and donned pyjamas of striped flannel. For form, officers of the armed forces kept their tunics ready in case they needed to impress anyone with their rank and status, and put it on loosely over their pyjama top if leaving the train to buy half a chicken or pickled cucumbers. It was unusual then for even a long distance train to have a restaurant car, but, if there were one, a jacket or tunic over pyjama bottoms would be de rigueur. At every station, on the ballast beside the track and five feet down (no platforms) there would be women or children with buckets of pickled gherkins, baskets of scrawny roasted chickens, boxes of smelly dried fish, and other staples of Russian diet, including black bread of course. Tea, the other necessity, could be brewed inside one's compartment using boiled water, piping hot, obtainable from a kiosk at each station labelled prominently "Kipyatok" (boiling water) which led some strangers to think that every Russian railway station had the same name.

Our Colonel was a military historian, in a small way, and was embarking on a lecture tour of five military bases in south Russia at 150 roubles (say £4 then) a lecture. He badly needed the money to eke out his pension, particularly as the book he had just written had not been favourably received by the publishers, who had ordered him to rewrite it, introducing new material under a changed title. He was 53 years old, in the Army Reserve prior to retirement at 55. He gave me his name (unusual for a Russian, but in fact he turned out to be a Ukrainian) and invited me to call on him and his wife in their flat in Kiev if I was ever there.

The train had left Moscow at 23.00 on 8 March – travelled all night and all the next day and night and arrived in Stalino on the morning of 10 March, an average speed of 15mph. But there were many stops for kipyatok and gherkins. If two Russian express trains were to collide head on it would scarcely spill the tea. However there was an advantage in never being late (or early); if early the train stopped outside the station until it was on time.

Stalino was named after steel, not Stalin (although his adopted name came from the same root) and with the whole area had an economy based on iron ore, limestone and coal, all just below the Ukrainian steppe. The three towns we visited were Stalino, Makeyevka and Gorlovka. For the first time the knowledge derived from my tours of the British iron and steel industry paid off. Humphrey and I even found a metal bridge spanning the width of the blast furnaces and Bessemer steel-making retorts of the plant at Makeyevka. Suitably supported at a high level the bridge enabled us to survey most of the activities at the plant. We even saw evidence of continuous casting, a process developed in Britain by Bob Feilden FRS, whom I came to know later when I worked for the Royal Society.

Despite the grime of the heavy industrial plants – rolling mills, foundries, etc., the towns of the Donbas were very impressive. They had been destroyed by the Germans during WW2, when many of the installations had been transported east and re-established in Siberia. In 1955 they were being rebuilt, with a great deal of work going on – cranes erecting blocks of flats, scrapers levelling ground and excavating lakes. Only ten years after the war there were already tree-lined boulevards, imposing public buildings, libraries, theatres, schools, roads being built. This was being repeated in hundreds of Russian towns and villages. They did not want all this to be destroyed again. It was true that they did not want war, despite aggressive policies towards the West.

We stayed in Stalino at the Donbas Hotel, the best in the area, but not as good as the National and Metropole in Moscow. From Stalino we travelled to the other adjacent towns by taxi or tram, usually the latter, a journey of an hour or so. There we walked as much as 15 miles a day, seeing how the economy ticked. What are the main industries? (mostly iron and steel but also chemicals). How do the workers live? Is there a food shortage? Of what specifically? What are the houses like? Are there any ruins left from the Second World War? What are the cinemas like? Is there a theatre? Showing what? What are the audiences like? Well or poorly dressed? Any drunks on the streets? Roads? Churches? Airports? Taxis? Schools? And so on.

If this was spying I did not mind at all. Being interested in Russians and Russia I wanted to know it all. We were of course followed by our goons (a different provincial lot from those who followed us in Moscow), but they did not prevent us from seeing anything. They just wanted to know what we were looking at. All the time the weather was beautiful – blue skies, cool, lovely. The Ukraine in March! We flew home to Moscow via Kharkov, spending a couple of days there. Kharkov was another town largely razed by the Germans. Some older buildings remained, notably the blocks in the town centre designed by the French architect Le Corbusier, one of the few of his avant-garde projects ever constructed.

When I got back to Moscow I found myself involved in an idea the Military and Naval attachés had had to entertain senior Russian officers in any or all of the Services. The RAF had a 16mm film projector "on charge", i.e. supplied as necessary equipment. This was often operated by Warrant Officer Field to show films to the British and American Embassy clubs, attended by many of the less senior staff members fairly regularly and by seniors occasionally. The idea was to get out films from the UK suitable for naval and military audiences. Initially these were: *The Cruel Sea* for Soviet naval officers, and *The Sound Barrier* for the Army and Soviet Air Force. This worked very well and both films were well attended by our Soviet counterparts. This gave me an idea – the female secretaries in the Swedish Embassy, a very beautiful lot on the whole, had made friends with a number of Soviet young people.

The Swedish Embassy was privileged in that Sweden was officially neutral in the Cold War (between East and West) and the Swedish Ambassador had no objection to his staff making friends among the Soviets. The flats occupied by Swedish Embassy staff did not have the same surveillance as we did, and Soviet youths had less objection to visiting them. Some of us younger "diplomats" thought up a scheme whereby the Swedish girls would invite Soviet boys (and girls) to parties in their block nominally to see films, which we could obtain from the UK, France and the US through our diplomatic bags. We would use the RAF projector to show these, with eats and drinks provided by us hosts. This had to be vetted by the various Ambassadors involved – Sweden, the UK, France, the USA and one or two other countries whose diplomats joined the scheme. When we finally got this off the ground it worked very well and we made many new friends among the Russian young, mostly of about university age.

There were always present one or two particularly regular Soviet guests, rather older than the rest, and "writing theses". They were the KGB plants to keep an eye on both hosts and guests. Sometimes when the Russians accepted our offers of lifts home, in the rear mirror we could see cars stopping at each home obviously to question them. Not only did I acquire some more Russian friends, but also I got to know the beautiful Swedes. Apart from western films we also got to see a number of Russian ones. Many were the old communist story of heroic tractor driver meeting heroic nurse and after many adventures driving off (in the tractor) into a Soviet sunset. A few were very good. We also visited the Moscow film and television studios to see programmes and films being made. On 1 April 1955 I wrote home: *"I saw more beautiful females than I imagined existed here. One was a ravishingly beautiful eastern maiden, with a thick rope of glossy black hair and slanty green eyes – broad face – dark skin."*

I also attended a Soviet fashion show with Daphne Park. Letter home, 5 April 1955:

> *On Sunday morning I went to a Soviet fashion show in GUM (Gosudarstveniy Universalniy Magazin), a bit like Harrods or Woolworths, you can buy almost anything there, were it available. I went with Daphne Park. Imagine a small theatre – stage, plush curtains*

— a piano on the audience side of the curtain in one corner of the stage — fat plush woman playing a selection of "hits" from films, both Hollywood and Soviet. From the stage a long platform, 6' wide and 60' long projects into the auditorium — shaded lights. The audience sits in four lines of chairs (plush upholstered like their mainly female occupants) along each side of the piste. A young stout girl of about 23, dressed in a floor length black satin dress, announces each dress through a microphone and crackly loudspeakers in the usual damned silly fashion lingo.

There were five mannequins — one for the fuller figure; one for the not quite so full figure; one for the ordinary figure (which in Russia tends to be fullish); and one ravishingly beautiful girl with a mass of dark hair, a perfect figure and brown eyes as big as saucers. What she was supposed to represent I don't know. In Russia one can count on one hand the number of beautiful women one sees in a year (other than in theatres and film studios). Dresses varied — most were badly cut. The designs were all based on last year's fashions, Daphne tells me. Oh! I forgot the man! There was an appalling male model, who showed atrocious brown suits with stuffed shoulders and vertical red stripes — blue flannel pyjamas and fancy tweed overcoats. The suits were worse than any I have ever seen anywhere. My favourite girl looked wonderful in everything of course.

Soviet fashion was parodied by Ilf and Petrov in their books *The Twelve Chairs* and *The Golden Calf.*[3] In a fundamentalist communist state there should be no room for waste, in women's fashions as in any other area of commerce or industry. And decisions on the design of clothes must be made democratically — by a committee. Assuming a decision at the highest level that 12 or 20 or however many new designs for frocks next year should be put in hand, there was then the need to designate one or more workshops to produce them, to allocate appropriate textiles and haberdashery and to see whether earlier designs might be modified or tarted up to suit or create fashion. So was born Ilf and Petrov's idea of the State Bow, a ribbon tied in a bow to be sewn to a dress to jazz it up for next year. Should it be placed between the breasts, at the waist, or in the small of the back. The (in Russian) Kazyony Bantik, its position decided by committee, would grace one of next year's frocks. Committees rarely produce what the public wants, and the result in Russia of choice limited by economists and other "experts" sitting in committee, was that the dresses went unsold and women made their dresses themselves or turned to friends skilled in dressmaking.

AD ULTIMO

After the Fashion Show I had supper with Daphne Park and then collected Mary Kirk from her flat, in the same block as ours at Narodnaya, and we went to the Bolshoi to see both Ulanova and Plisetskaya dance in "The Fountain of Bakhchiserai", a wonderful fable and the title of a poem by Pushkin. The story is about the Crimean Tartars. Their capital in the Crimea was Bakhchiserai, which I visited later on several occasions. During an incursion into the Ukraine to capture booty and slaves (this could have been at any time after the Mongol invasions up to the defeat of Charles XII of Sweden by Peter the Great at Poltava) the Tartar Khan had captured a beautiful Polish girl, with whom he fell in love. Despite his protestations of love and his willingness to do anything for her other than returning her home, she pined away and died. The Khan commissioned a fountain in her memory, a stone wall-mounted fountain where water emerges at the apex and trickles down to the floor through a succession of sculpted cusps like half saucers, each containing a small amount of water and overflowing into those beneath. This represented the girl's tears. As told by Pushkin and interpreted in the ballet, the story is sadness itself – an emotion esteemed by the Russians.

Although Russians, especially the Cossacks, were always fighting the Muslim tribes and fiefdoms on the Christian-Muslim borders from the Crimea to the Caspian, they thought highly of the independence of these peoples, their fierce loyalties, bravery, fighting spirit, and of course the romantic highlands in which they lived. Russian writers, especially Pushkin, Lermontov and Tolstoy wrote fine poems and novels about them, and Russian composers similarly fine music. Their feelings may have had something in common with the English feelings about the Scots and Welsh. Tolstoy served with the Russian artillery in the Caucasus, mainly against the Chechens, and his novel *Hadji Murad* is about a Chechen leader – a tragic figure, whom Tolstoy actually met, whose heroic character contrasts with those of the Russian invaders from Czar Nicholas I downwards.

Tolstoy had a number of Chechen friends including one, Sado, who paid off heavy gambling debts Tolstoy had incurred. Russian children used to be brought up on these tales and on Lermontov's verse. Then the Chechens and their neighbouring tribes were not stigmatised as they are in 2004, when they are categorised as terrorists and Muslim extremists. In an earlier chapter "Palestine Arab Refugees", I write of the Chechens and Cherkassi in Jordan, exiled after the Russian victories in Daghestan in the 19th century. They suffered exile again under Stalin in 1944 when tens of thousands were sent to Siberia, where the Crimean Tartars had been exiled earlier. Putin's policies in the first decade of the second millennium are in the same dreadful tradition. All these people want is to run their own affairs, as do we all.

Letter home, 12 April 1955:

I cannot express how much I want to be home. Of course it is an interesting life here, but it is very much an "operational" life. One does work of incalculable importance, but one is always hemmed in by the restrictions imposed on us by our host country – the USSR. "Ops" are a very good parallel. Just as in an aircraft, no matter how exciting the mission, there is not much room to stretch – one is shut up in the little world of one's crew, always on the alert, heart in mouth at every unusual manifestation, every change in engine note, bank of cloud or unexpected light in the sky (star? or night-fighter?) – so we live here in a similar circumscribed state, mentally and physically cramped, always on guard, in a limited society of close friends and trusted colleagues – the Embassy our aircraft, its personnel our crew. Even one's taste gets warped here. After a time one comes to accept Soviet standards not maybe as normal, but at any rate as tolerable. Even sentimental dullards returning from trips to "western" countries talk of the extraordinary elation – joy – felt on entering the first western aircraft, ship or port. Even I, after a couple of months here, took the experience of crossing from east to west Berlin like the onset of some strange hysteria. Prisoners of war probably feel the same when liberated – a lightness of spirit as if one's cranium had come off. One gasps in the free air and feels – well, most extraordinary.

The weather over the weekend has been terrible. Winter has come back. It has been snowing for four days without a let up. The temperature is just above 0° C so there is slush everywhere.

I am a bit fed up with Russian plays. They come in two sorts: pre-revolutionary classics – these are all magnificently presented and acted, but they are selected – i.e. only those that depict, shall we say, the terrible lot of the peasants under the Czars; the stupid cruelty and lack of humanity of the upper classes of those times, and so on, are allowed to be played in theatres. All true of course, but after a dozen or so plays like this one feels one knows penniless clerks and ragged peasants well enough. A few more evenings in the stalls and you begin to feel that it is all too repulsive and sordid for an evening out.

*The other class of plays is modern Soviet. These are, without exception, tripe, trash, balderdash. **All** are about victorious revolution, victorious five year planning or something of that sort. Love interest is invariably: husband has to work like a Trojan at his revolution, five* *year plan, building project or lathe – wife feels neglected and goes off with villain – husband has working with him a "girl who understands", but he, with his good Soviet heart, disregards the temptation. Villain meets his deserts (arrested for sabotage or something). Wife sees light and "understands". Husband forgives wife. All return home to children, or into rising sun, or gaze into light of blast furnaces.*

I have lied. There are a few good plays, usually satires, often satirising the sort of play I have described above and the boy-and-girl-meet-tractor type romance. But satirists have a dicey sort of job – insurance premiums would be high.

Interesting that the outward manifestations of Soviet life show very little of what is under the surface. Russians are a passionate, big-hearted, intelligent people, quick-witted, with a sense of humour much like ours. The inside of a volcano is always more interesting than the grey crust. I see no signs of an eruption, but there is plenty of stuff boiling about down there. I just broke off to listen to a few jokes in a radio broadcast from Leningrad. Usual two comedian act – a shopwalker and a prospective customer:

C "What on earth are those?" SW ""Night slippers". C "Why particularly night?" SW "Well in daylight they would look far too awful".

C "What's that?" SW "A dressing-gown". C "Bit big isn't it?" SW (unfolds, saying at the same time) "Of course we stock all sizes, but at present only this size is available". (Roars of laughter from studio audience). C (Affecting astonishment) "That's not a dressing-gown. That is the embodiment of relations between dressing-gowns and humanity".

SW "What about one of these saucepans – see – genuine cast-iron lid". C "But it's too heavy to lift. Leningrad makes the best turbine wheels in the world. Why can't they make decent saucepan lids?" SW "Ah, turbine wheels are all metal: saucepan lids have to have wooden handles!"

There were plenty of jokes about the quality and quantity of Soviet products. A fairly hackneyed one was about shoes for left feet being made by one factory and for right feet by another, without coordination, so that as often as not only shoes for one foot or for the other were available and they in different styles and colours. While we are on about footwear, I had a pair of leather mid-calf RAF flying boots, which stood me in good stead when I had to walk in snow (quite often). However, I wanted to obtain a pair of Soviet Army officers' knee boots, which came right up to the knee, which, I thought, would be handy for walking in deeper snow. I visited Voyentorg, the store selling clothing for the Soviet armed services, and showed them a letter I had from my contacts in the Soviet MOD authorising me to buy a pair of boots. The girl brought me boots in several sizes to try on. They were difficult to get one's foot into because of the stiff leather at the ankle, but I persevered and got them on. They were quite comfortable. The problem arose when I tried to get them off. Pulling hard I was dismayed to see the top of each boot separate at the ankle as the stitching came apart. The girl serving me had disappeared from view, and so too did I, discretion being the better part of valour, placing the boots in several parts back in their box and closing the lid before I made for the exit, thus avoiding a possibly difficult explanation. Do not imagine that all Soviet products were shoddy. I bought a Soviet floor polisher with three rotating brushes on which one could stand while the polisher waltzed about the floor.

May Day 1955 was very much like Great October Day 1954, with much the same massive military parade through Red Square followed by the civilian march pasts, general rejoicing in the evening with street dances and predstavleniye (performances) of popular music, comedy acts, song and dance, folk music etc., on stages erected in the streets and squares with a colourful and noisy fireworks display at midnight, this year preceded by a display by searchlights wheeling their coloured beams through the night sky in a more or less synchronised "dance". In the previous two weeks there had been some new aircraft in the fly-past rehearsals that I had already photographed from the Embassy roof. On one morning two heavy jet bombers appeared and had been given the code names Bison and Bear by the Pentagon and the Air Ministry, who worked together in this regard.

All Soviet bombers were given code names starting with B (fighters – F, such as Flashlight, other types similarly). The reason for this was that initially the aircraft designer and the factory where they were made were unknown. The Bison was a four jet aircraft and Bear had four contra-rotating turboprops. Bear was later discovered to have come from the Tupolev design team – the TU95. Many variants were constructed and it was arguably the best Soviet nuclear bomber, capable of reaching the USA. I came to know Tupolev quite well later. On this Mayday the weather was none too good and although I could see a flight of Bisons or Bears circling in the distance to the north, they did not actually fly-past.

Bears were produced at No.18 aircraft factory at Kuibyshev. Hence our frequent visits there. It is of interest that Irina Fröhlich's future father-in-law, a von Schlippe, was deported with his family from Munich to Kuibyshev at the end of the Second World War to continue his work on airscrews such as those used on the Bear, developments of those used with the German Junkers Jumo range of engines. The propeller tips exceeded the speed of sound, which posed special problems for aerodynamicists. The von Schlippe family remained in Kuibyshev for the best part of ten years before being repatriated. The two sons, Dima and Yura, attended university in Kuibyshev.

From early in April 1955 we in the Embassy had heard the roar of jet engines being tested at an airfield, Fili, just outside Moscow to the west. This led Dennis and me to drive along a still quite rural road on a ridge from which the runway at Fili several km away was visible through binoculars. Fili was an aircraft factory, No. 23, originally a German aircraft factory for Junkers transport aircraft, set up by the Nazis before WW2 to avoid the restrictions imposed by the Geneva Convention. By 1950, with the Germans long since gone, it had been given the responsibility of producing the Myasischev Molot (Hammer), code name Bison, which first flew from Fili in 1953.

From the road where Dennis and I had parked our car we could see a Bison at the end of the east-west runway, testing its engines and possibly preparing for a flight. When, was the problem. We could not camp out indefinitely within sight of the runway. Engine tests continued for a week or more. One day when we had an hour to spare, Dennis and I drove out again. As we watched through our field glasses Dennis suddenly said: *"It's moving!"* And so it was. We were parked exactly on the extended centre-line of the runway, 3km to the west. After slowly gathering speed, the enormous aircraft, like a great bat, with pronounced anhedral (drooping wings), left the ground and, gaining height, passed directly over us at a height of 50'. On this occasion for some reason we had no goons nearby. So Dennis and I obtained the first of many photographs of this latest Soviet bomber. It had a chequered career, being under-powered and with insufficient range to attack the USA, so ten years later after some 80 Bison had been produced the design was dropped. Bear was much more successful and, in numerous variants, was still in service in 2000.

Shortly after May Day I left by train with Peter Donkin to visit Chkalov. Chkalov was a city close to the southern end of the Urals, 1,200km east of Moscow and 350km beyond Kuibyshev. Before the Revolution it had been called Orenburg but on 21 June 1937 an aviator named Chkalov, the Russian equivalent of Charles Lindberg, flew non-stop from Moscow to Vancouver – 5,300 miles across the North Pole. As he had been born in Orenburg the town was renamed after him – local boy makes good! As Chkalov was a "good" revolutionary I expect the town has now reverted to its old name Orenburg again. Why we decided to go there is a mystery. I think we expected to see something there associated with aviation. Originally Dennis and I planned to go there but Peter Donkin decided to come and Dennis dropped out. The journey took a day and a half by train.

The two of us travelled "International Class", which in this case meant a two bed suite in the last carriage of the train, probably placed last because the carriage was antique, and might have split apart had it not been the last carriage. Our compartment was panelled in mahogany, with crystal carafes in wall-mounted carriers for water, a reasonable but antique toilet/bathroom, table and chairs for meals, etc. Very Victorian – the sort of carriage Queen Victoria or the Czars would have used. As it was the last carriage and last compartment in the train there was a rear "veranda" where we could go out into the fresh air and watch the countryside go by.

The trip was memorable but uneventful, memorable because the last 150km was through forests of wild lilac (Cheriomukha) scenting the entire countryside – not much of a flower but a heavenly scent. In Chkalov we stayed in the one hotel still open (according to my Baedeker there had been three in Czarist days). It was all very run down. Orenburg had once been a Cossack fortress town, part of the Orenburg Line. According to Baedeker, camel caravans used to bring in wares from Tashkent, Bukhara, Khiva, Khokand and other central Asian cities – carpets, silks, fleeces and the like to exchange for European manufactured goods. It was also famous for its salt mines, later coal. As far as we could see from the Intourist hotel register, only two Westerners had been there since WW2. We returned to Moscow by air.

In late May we were joined by a third Assistant Assistant Air Attaché, whom we might call Assistant Air Attaché (3), Peter Lewis, an engineering officer and like me a Squadron Leader. His role was to look after the increasingly technical side of our work, but he did not speak much Russian. Later still we were joined by Alan Stephens, Assistant Air Attaché (4), an officer of the RAF Secretarial Branch. We needed all these extra assistants because with Khrushchev in power we were free to travel much more and needed more staff to take advantage of the possibilities. Compared to us the US military attaché departments were much more generously staffed. There was a bonus in that Peter was good at Scottish dancing and Alan was a choirmaster *par excellence*, so our "British Council" cultural work was augmented and enhanced.

I was planning a trip in June with Alan Stephens, to introduce him to our sort of travel, to Kazan and Kuibyshev by rail, on to Ufa by air and back to Moscow via Kuibyshev, Saratov, Rostov-on-Don and Voronezh. I had to be back in

Moscow by 13 June for the Ambassador's Garden Party on the Queen's official birthday and because Dennis and Peter were leaving on the latter's introductory trip shortly afterwards. It did not work out like this. It never did! In fact we only managed Kazan, Saratov, Michurinsk, Voronezh and back to Moscow. Michurinsk was interesting being named after Michurin, the premier Russian breeder of fruit trees – apples, pears, soft fruit and plants as well. He was an ardent supporter of Lenin and Stalin and communism, who was not? His apples, or those I sampled, were very good. But June is not the best month to sample apples.

Shortly before leaving on this trip I thought I had blotted my copybook at a cocktail party at the Indian Embassy. This was attended by many of the attachés from the various embassies as well as by representatives of OTDEL the department of the Soviet MOD responsible nominally for supervising, "helping" and hindering us. That day I had already attended a lunch given by the Yugoslavs, and a party to celebrate American Armed Forces Day at their embassy, and my wits and tongue may have been loosened. I was talking to Colonel Makharov of OTDEL (Отдел Иностранных Дел Министерства Обороны – Department of Foreign Affairs of the Ministry of Defence) about modern art, anathema for conventional communists at a time when realism was the only art worth esteem. I was giving my views on symbolism, knowing nothing about it, but pointing out that we all use symbols in language and mathematics and that without symbols we would have no earthly way of communicating. A symbol should mean roughly the same to you as it means to me if it is to be of much use. I illustrated this by saying that when he thought of John Deverill he probably thought other than what the name brought to my father's mind, but this did not mean there were two of me. It was a question of each person seeing his own truth, and being unable to be very objective.

Colonel Makharov agreed with my views and said that speaking personally and unofficially, in his view I was a sly cunning agent of a doomed regime. I retorted that also speaking unofficially, our western system of government was closer to the ideal than communism could ever be, and that, although liking Russians and Russia, I hated communism and predicted its end within 50 years. The Colonel was annoyed and called over his colleagues from OTDEL and asked them whether I should be thrown out of Moscow, bearing in mind my views. I feared the worst, and told my father that I should have kept my mouth shut. However, on my return from Michurinsk I attended a reception where Col. Makharov was introducing a new assistant of his and both were as sweet as honey. My forecast of another 50 years for the Soviet state and communism was not far out!

Since the fall of Malenkov and the rise of Khrushchev the receptions at the many embassies in Moscow had become much livelier because Khrushchev came to many of them. In this he was doing his diplomatic duty, but also he liked talking and drinking, and that man could hold his liquor better than anyone I have ever met or could meet. He could drink any of the diplomatic community under the table. At the Danish Embassy one day there was a reception in honour of a visit by the Danish Prime Minister. Peter Donkin and I were both there in the general mêlée, but Khrushchev and the Danish Prime Minister disappeared through a door into another room followed by other Danish and Soviet diplomats, possibly because it would be quieter there. After about 40 minutes the door opened and out came the Danish Prime Minister, supported by two aides, making a beeline for the exit, no doubt on his way to bathroom or bed. Khrushchev then appeared, red in the face, wreathed in smiles, his usual pugnacious self. He went up to Peter Donkin, who was leaning languidly against a wall nearby, punched him, but not hard, in the stomach and asked him if he had done much spying lately. Peter was not the sort of person anyone could treat like that, and I saw his face harden and his blue eyes glint. For a moment I thought he was going to hit Krushchev back, but he recovered himself, smiled and made some wisecrack as Krushchev moved on to the next person who caught his attention.

Usually at these receptions Khrushchev would be encircled by a dozen or more correspondents with their notebooks and tape recorders at the ready, hoping for some noteworthy quote to telex back to their papers. I was just as keen and pushed in with them trying to get in my own questions. Khrushchev knew who I was because I was in RAF uniform and he always had one or two aides close by to remind him. I enjoyed these encounters and got a lot out of them.

I decided to improve my Russian further by taking lessons from a young Russian woman, Lyuba, on offer from Burobin for tuition in conversational Russian at moderate cost. She had helped various people in different embassies and there were good reports. She was a nice girl, almost certainly a KGB informer, married three months earlier and needing the money. We started by translating Crankshaw's article "Belgrade Portent" from the centre pages of the *Sunday Times* of 5 June. She was interested that Crankshaw had written that Krushchev had put his foot in it during his visit to Belgrade when he had assumed that Tito would support the Soviet policy in the Balkans. She thought that much of the rest of the paper was tripe, as I believe it was.

Conversations with people like Lyuba improved my knowledge both of the language and of Soviet attitudes, which were by no means always stupid. I wrote my father that he must not think of Russians as cruel incomprehensible Mongols, or intellectuals with adding machine brains. Nor should he swallow the other myth of laughing, dancing Cossacks and soulful dark-eyed beauties smoking cigarettes in long holders. Most were keen, bright and young-minded. But just as the average Briton left politics to a relative few who seemed to like dabbling in them so did the average Soviet (one must not say Russian because Soviet embraces many other nationalities). I spent many an hour with Lyuba discussing our respective national problems – hooliganism in the Soviet Union; Teddy Boys in the UK; drunkenness in both.

On 14 June I took a party round the Kremlin, acting as interpreter for the Soviet guide. The party consisted of Betty Donkin's aunt and uncle, an embassy typist and her mother who was visiting, the First Secretary's mother, the Donkins' children's new governess, and half a dozen others invited out by their relatives in the British Embassy. I invited Dad to come out, and also Mary and Titus. I thought they would find it interesting and inexpensive as they could stay with me. The next day should have been the Queen's birthday and the Embassy's celebratory Garden Party, but it was postponed until 15 July, probably because Sir William was called home for discussions at the Foreign Office.

This led to a trip home for me. We wanted to have detailed photographs of the SAM defences of Moscow but there was no easy way to achieve this in the days before satellite photography. Sir William and Lady Hayter had to fly home at the beginning of July and a Royal Air Force transport aircraft, usually a VIP Hastings, was available to them. It would fly out from Lyneham (a RAF Transport Command base as it still is) and refuel in Berlin. On this occasion the idea was to load the aircraft with two large hand-held RAF cameras and have someone photograph one or more SAM sites on the flight from Berlin to Moscow. The problem was that without an accredited embassy official aboard the aircraft and its contents could be examined by Soviet officials on arrival in Moscow.

The solution was to send me home by Aeroflot to Berlin. In Berlin I needed to see the RAF dentist to have a filling replaced. From Berlin I would fly home by BEA. I planned to spend several days in the UK to allow time to go home and see Dad. I would then fly out with the RAF Hastings, photograph any SAM sites when we overflew the concentric rings of the Moscow defences, and then offload the cameras (and other less confidential stuff) on arrival in Moscow, under the protection of my diplomatic status. The arrangements worked perfectly. In Berlin on the way home on 3 July I was entertained again by Brixmis. At home there were dock and rail strikes and a State of Emergency had been declared because essential services were threatened. This did not affect me.

I was back in Moscow by 12 July. The only mishap that nearly occurred was when Dennis Spilsbury, helping to unload the heavy cameras, each packed in a cricket bag, dropped one of them while leaving the aircraft. It bounced on the Aeroflot steps by which we disembarked making disturbing metal noises. Nobody paid any attention except for our few anxious faces. We entertained the Hastings crew overnight and saw them off in the morning with the Hayters and Dennis who was going on mid-tour leave.

Three days later the postponed garden party to mark the Queen's birthday took place, in lovely weather, hosted by the Minister, Cecil Parrott, in the absence of Sir William. All other ambassadors and chargé d'affaires in Moscow were invited to attend in addition to scores of prominent Soviet officials, officers and others who were neither but who had helped the Embassy in various ways. For instance, the cheery-faced Russian director of the riding stables where many members of the Moscow diplomatic community were now enjoying themselves. Also important foreigners visiting Moscow were invited to come with their hosts. Letter home, 15 July 1955:

> *Nehru came, Bulganin, but not Khrushchev. I looked after the two senior Soviet Air Force officers present – Marshal Rudenko and General Zacharov. Rudenko is a **first-class** type – fiftyish, but still looks in his thirties, fit, medium height, with small features for a Russian and a devilish look in his ever-chuckling eyes. He has a boyish manner that makes me feel he would be game for anything – any sort of adventure or high-spirited lark that would not hurt or put others out. He is the Chief of Staff of the Soviet Air Force.*
>
> *Also at the party were ballerinas, economists, scientists, doctors, all the other ambassadors of course, the Patriarch of the Russian Orthodox Church. Nice people! Against them you have to put the thugs, hooligans, drunks, beggars etc., who form a disproportionate part of the Soviet population. Yesterday was the French national day. Wonderful champagne. Molotov and Khrushchev were there. On Monday I am off by car to Novgorod with Peter and Betty Donkin and Daphne Park.*

Apart from my duties with senior SAF officers, I cultivated the ballerinas present, and made my number with Ulanova, Plisetskaya and a charming girl, Marina Kondratieva, aged 21, a recent graduate from the Bolshoi Ballet School. I had seen her at the Bolshoi dancing Giselle. She was enchanting. However, although I met Ulanova and Plisetskaya later, Marina Kondratieva seems to have retired from dancing because of some illness and I never saw her again.[4]

The Novgorod trip was quite short, a week from 17 July, but eventful. We went in two cars, both driven by our Soviet drivers. On the way we stopped for the night in Kalinin, a large town on the Volga about 100 miles north-west of Moscow on the Leningrad road, by now surfaced and dry and dusty. We had booked accommodation in the Intourist hotel in Kalinin, but when we arrived there the manageress (they were always dressed in double-breasted blue jackets and tight blue skirts round their 44" hips) announced that she had received no reservations for us. Would we wait a short time. In the next ten minutes we saw a procession of disgruntled and bleary-eyed Soviet citizens, some male some female, with their shoes and outer garments in their hands, proceeding who knows where through the foyer. Another few minutes and we were ushered to our rooms, still warm from the dispatched occupants and still reeking of their tobacco smoke.

The Donkins spent the next morning visiting museums or something and Daphne and I were left to our own devices. I had come to know Daphne as the MI 6 representative in our Embassy. She knew the location of the MVD (Internal Affairs Ministry) HQ in Kalinin so we set out on foot to take a look at it. The four-storey block was typically Soviet, with nothing much to distinguish it apart from soldiers in MVD uniform entering and leaving. The door was wide open so we too entered. On the ground floor there was a line of telephones attached to the wall whereby dutiful citizens could inform on back-sliding neighbours, or people they wanted to get into trouble. A stone staircase led to the next floor where we were interested to see that each office opening off the central corridor had the rank and name of the occupant(s) painted on the wooden doors. We produced our notebooks and copied the names down together with the initials indicating the function of the occupants. At first nobody took the slightest notice of us. We were both dressed as for most of our trips in the USSR, informally and sensibly with clothes and shoes unlikely to stand out too obviously unless a sharp-eyed Soviet looked twice, as one eventually did. Still unchallenged, we decided to retreat in good order and left the building satisfied with our exploit.

Later Daphne and I went down to the shore of the Volga to eat our sandwiches. We soon noted that several carloads of goons were taking a lot of interest in us. To divert their attention, leaving Daphne with my clothes, I put on my trunks and set out to swim the Volga, which was not very wide at this point. The water was cold and muddy and there was quite a current, but not too much of a challenge. After a while I gave up and returned to Daphne and we hired a boat for the crossing and were amused to see the goon cars undecided on what to do – drive to a bridge some distance upstream and then down the other side to intercept our landing, or remain where they were in case we returned. Such goon-baiting was always a welcome pastime, but pointless in the sense that one could never get away from the goons for long.

Driving back to Moscow we stopped in a village to get some water to boil up for a cup of tea and were confronted by gipsy women who offered to tell our fortunes if "we crossed their hands with silver" or ten roubles (each). My fortune predicted I would meet a lovely girl, get married and be happy for ever after, which came true in the long run, if not in the short. So there must be something in it! More immediately, back in Moscow I found that Peter Lewis had gone to Murmansk and that our Warrant Officer clerk, Bob Field, was in hospital with suspected appendicitis.

My next trip was again with Daphne. I wrote home to Dad asking him to send me some Quells by the next bag, because Daphne sometimes felt air sick in rough weather, but I doubt if they arrived in time, because we were already off on 1 August. We flew to Leningrad in the morning and had time in the afternoon to visit the Peterhof, Peter the Great's palace on the Gulf of Finland about ten miles west of Leningrad. It was like a small Versailles, with very fine waterworks – or cascades of fountains, which started to work as a result of activation by some sort of mechanical switch, with the object of drenching unenlightened visitors walking nearby. Peter was a great one for practical jokes. The Peterhof had just been repaired after the German wartime occupation. Not so Tzarskoye Selo (the Czar's village) built to house much of Peter's court in originally fine buildings ten miles south-east of Leningrad. Much of this was still ruined, blown up by the retreating Germans and/or laid waste in the battles accompanying the reoccupation by the Soviet forces.

After a night at the Hotel Astoria we took the train to Odessa, a journey of two days. As travelling companions (sputniki in Russian) we had a middle-aged Soviet equivalent of a Company Secretary, chief administrator of a Leningrad factory and her 23 year old niece, a nice girl, studying the history of Leningrad and making a bit of money by acting as a guide for tourists on excursions in Leningrad. Both were cultured people. The aunt was very much a convinced communist without much brain of her own, but her niece was unconvinced and interested in our views, and in life in England which we described. The two of them were going on holiday to Odessa, and it turned out that the aunt was not the practical woman her dogmatism suggested. She had not booked accommodation in Odessa. They were apprehensive that they might not find a room there, so much so that I offered them one of the two rooms we had booked if the worst came to the worst. As it happened the offer was not taken up.

The idea of making this train journey was that the railway passed close to several airfields from which we suspected Badger bombers to be operating, but although I saw several in the air, the activity was minimal, possibly because bad visibility was hampering operations as well as my observations. Daphne and I stayed several days in Odessa, in the best hotel available, which was very good compared with the Astoria in Leningrad. Aeroflot ran a flight to Baku only on certain days each week, so we were obliged to stay there although there was little to do "professionally". We attended an evening concert of gypsy music outdoors in a park, but the "folk" music and singing was so bad as to be a joke. To the northwest of Odessa there was supposed to be an active airfield and we decided to make our way in that direction and see if there was anything going on. We took a bus for 20 minutes, weaving about in the Odessa suburbs, dismounted when we reached open country and set out to walk the remaining 5km to the airfield.

However, the goons had noticed and we were soon overtaken by a motorcycle and sidecar with two militiamen aboard who forbade us from going further on that road. We protested that we had hoped to have a look at the closer of two parallel "limans", narrow, shallow lakes, at least 10km long, running inland from just east of Odessa towards the hills. The word "liman" comes from Greek for a harbour and in Russian, at any rate, has come to mean a shallow, narrow estuary with low banks subject to flooding with consequent deposits of muddy silt. The militiamen said there would be no objection to our striking off east across the scrubland towards the nearest liman, so we did. After half an hour the tongue of water came in sight and we descended down a slope towards it. A number of nude and none too shapely Soviet matrons were lying about covered all over with black mud, for all the world like modern sculpture (Anthony Gormley?) My 1911 French Baedeker said the mud (which stank to high heaven and stuck to my feet like black Bostick) was good for rheumatic and skin problems. The limans were no longer connected to the sea possibly because the authorities wished to preserve them for their therapeutic value and had therefore blocked the exits.

As time was getting on we turned south back towards Odessa. Soon the track on which we were walking became a lane and then a narrow paved road with huts on either side. Uniformed nurses and orderlies moved about between the huts, sometimes pushing wheelchairs and trolleys with people aboard, seated or supine. We attracted surprised looks and increased our pace, anxious to avoid being challenged. Leaving the compound under an iron arch we looked back and saw above it a sign reading in Russian "ISOLATION HOSPITAL".

It was hot and we wanted to swim in the sea where it was cleaner and less salty than the limans. Several miles across the bay from Odessa was a small town rapidly turning into a resort. This could be reached by ferry from Odessa and we used this to go there one afternoon.

There were only ferry passengers and some who had come by tram. The trams came in useful next day. We decided to take the ferry across the bay for a swim again. In the afternoon I noticed a black thundercloud blowing in from the east and for a while it seemed innocuous enough. However, when it came closer and I could see the veils of rain beneath it I told Daphne that we should get dressed and move to the ferry terminal to take a boat back to Odessa. But, at the terminal we were told that all ferries had been cancelled because of the threatening weather. With a crowd of other people we moved to the tram stop and entered the first westbound. From my letter home of 14 August:

> *The storm broke when we were still about three miles from our hotel. The sky had become as black as night (it stayed that way until the next morning). Terrific lightning, thunder and rain. The tram leaked like a sieve – in fact Russian passengers cracked jokes about their wonderful trams doubling as bathrooms. About three miles from the hotel the trams (ours and others ahead of us) stopped with the water up to the floorboards. It was an extraordinary sight. The streets flowed like rivers. Doors, clothing and all sorts of other loose stuff rushed past in the current. We waited some 20 minutes. Other passengers tried to keep their shoes dry by lifting their feet off the floor but the rising water level made this impossible. I was beginning to feel like a contemporary of Noah. Eventually Daphne and I decided that rather than wait in a flooded tram all night it would be better to continue on foot. I rolled my trousers up to the knee. We took off our shoes and socks and wrapped them in my plastic raincoat together with Daphne's handbag and glasses and my wallet. We then stepped out into 2'6" of rushing water and set out for the hotel, about an hour's walk. As we left our fellow-passengers I heard one say 'Who the devil are they?' and a woman reply: 'English!' Walking was difficult, even dangerous because in that depth of water we could not see obstacles under the surface and manhole covers had been pushed off by the flood water. We therefore walked arm in arm so that if one of us fell down a hole or was sucked into it, the other might provide an anchor. At junctions the joining currents of water were almost enough to carry us away. When we reached the hotel we were as wet as if we had*

121

been swimming with our clothes on. Daphne's thin cotton dress was transparent. We walked across the vestibule to the lifts leaving puddles of water on the carpeted floor. Disappointingly, nobody seemed to notice.

Early next morning we flew on to Baku via Simferopol in the Crimea, Krasnodar and the Caucasus town of Mineralniyie Vodi. Here we stayed the night in a very comfortable hotel. As we entered our rooms we passed a carpenter on his way out and on examining the loo (the first thing to do on entering a hotel room in the Soviet Union in case one needs to express disgust and demand something better) I noted that the carpenter had just re-planed and sanded the loo seat. He had not cleared up all his shavings. People in these parts usually defecated from the squat and on finding a western loo seat would normally stand on it, leaving a splintered surface from the nails in their boots. What a thoughtful management I thought and next day before we left I put a congratulatory comment in the Zhalobnaya Kniga – Complaints Book provided for customers to leave their comments – bad or, more seldom, good.

From Min Vodi, as it is called for short, we took a taxi to Pyatigorsk (pron. PTgorsk) where the Russian poet Lermontov lived and wrote some of his finest poetry, and where he was shot dead in a duel at the age of 27, some said with the approval of Tsar Nicholas I, who wished to get Lermontov out of the way because he was an awkward cuss and had accused the Czar of complicity in the death (also in a duel) of Pushkin. We visited the spot where Lermontov died but could not get out of the car because of a violent thunderstorm, the weather conditions at the time of the duel more than 100 years before. The next day we flew on to Baku via Mahach-Kala.

Around Baku there were derricks everywhere, for the most part of wooden construction. Most seemed derelict with large oily patches on the earth around them but there were a few working wells with nodding pump installations. The old part of the town was quite beautiful with a Middle East flavour. Children, brown as nuts, ran naked about the old narrow streets. From our hotel in Baku we took a taxi to the north of the peninsular for a swim clear of the dirty oil field area. There swimming was a delight in the hot summer sun. Daphne was quite badly sunburnt by evening and I turned a darker shade of brown. I had to rescue Daphne when she swam out without her glasses and could not see which way was back. Letter of 14 August 1955 cont:

From Baku we flew to Astrakhan again, less pleasant this time, stinking hot and full of flies. There were so many flies that while eating in the hotel we had to cover everything with paper napkins, removing them for just enough time to eat or drink or pour. The staff were rude and unhelpful. We had hoped to travel to Stalingrad by train, but were told we could not and that we should go by air. As it happened the aircraft we took was supposed to fly to Krasnodar but went instead to Stalingrad, presumably to satisfy our need, rather than the needs of the other passengers with tickets to Krasnodar. Also the Aeroflot IL12 flew most of the way at ground level, where, because of the heat, conditions were very bumpy. Most of the passengers felt airsick and remonstrated with the cabin attendant, but she was boot-faced and unrepentant, confining herself to giving out more sick-bags to those in need. We deduced that the reason for the diverted flight and low height was to prevent me seeing something of air or military interest. Later the technique was used more and more, because from zero feet one cannot observe much and that only fleetingly.

Stalingrad was wonderful. Very hot and very dry — the sort of climate I prefer. We spent a whole day lazing in the sun on an island in the middle of the Volga river, which is the best part of a mile wide here. The rebuilt Stalingrad (it was razed during the siege in 1942) is a very beautiful place, still incomplete, and with signs of having been influenced by Coventry. One would expect Stalin to take a special interest in making his namesake city into a memorial to the Soviet soldiers who saved it after endless days and nights of bitter battle. Wide stone steps led down from the town to the Volga, and on each riser were carved the names of individual soldiers killed in the battle. For the first time in the Soviet Union I had my taxi fare refused by the driver because I was English. Everyone we met was very friendly towards the English. Stalingrad was a Hero City, and so by implication its "twin"- Coventry and by implication we were from Coventry. And so back to Moscow.

In Moscow within a few days I poisoned myself with the remains of a shepherd's pie Daphne had cooked for me. In the hot weather Galya had not put it in the fridge. I had suspected it had gone off but gave it the benefit of the doubt. I was not too ill but had stomach pains as if the sheep was clawing to get out. Sir William Hayter had been involved in a car accident in the UK and I was concerned that he should fly back to Moscow before the end of the month so that I could return home in his aircraft in time to attend the Farnborough Air Display and the Air Attaché's annual get-together. Peter Donkin and Dennis

Spilsbury were still in London and due to return with HE (His Excellency). I could not really go until they got back. Peter Lewis was off travelling in the Donbas, so I was more or less holding the fort in the office on my own. However I planned to get home on 5 September.

Meanwhile I had lunch with Daphne and a US agricultural expert guiding a group of American farmers round communal and government farms. They were amazed at the profligate waste of manpower in the USSR where 120 men and women would run a farm, which in the USA would need three people, probably the owner and his wife and one farmhand, plus machinery of course. The touring Americans were always being asked to convey warm and brotherly greetings to all American peasants. On being told there were none they could not believe their ears. Who then does the work they asked.

The inefficiency of Soviet agriculture was always being attacked in Russia at the highest level, but to little effect. I attended a meeting of collective farm workers in the Dinamo football stadium where they were addressed by Khrushchev, who was promoting a favourite scheme of his – to plant maize in groups of four seeds (presumably so that there was more than a chance that one would germinate). This was called the Four Square system. Khrushchev was standing near me on a dais in the hot sun, which was getting the better of him. He grabbed the floppy cotton hat of a little girl sitting below him and crammed it on his head, raising a loud laugh from the crowd. This sort of spontaneous peasant action made him very popular with ordinary people, less so with the apparatchiki who thought their leader should be more cultured.

My mid-tour leave would be due in December at the latest and I planned to be home for Christmas and while there to buy myself a Sunbeam Talbot III. These cars had won the Monte Carlo Rally for several years in succession and for fast touring seemed to have no rivals. They were also less expensive than the Jaguar XK that Peter Donkin was buying. As diplomats in an Embassy abroad we could buy cars free of Purchase Tax at 30% and benefit as well from a "diplomatic discount". This was given by manufacturers because they reasoned that use of their cars abroad in embassies would be good publicity. Consequently I could buy the Sunbeam I had my eyes on at close to half the UK price. I would not need to pay the Purchase Tax provided I did not re-import the car to the UK for 12 months after I had exported it. However, promoting Sunbeams apart, the last thing I wanted to do was risk the car on the parlous Russian roads. I therefore set out to find someone who could look after the car for me in better conditions.

I had made good friends with the Swedish Air Attaché, Börje Kwarnmark, and was cultivating that association, not only because of the car, but because he was a very nice person. He was agreeable to garaging the car in his house near Stockholm, provided he could occasionally use it when he was home. This we agreed. I reinforced the link by making friends with his very pretty secretary, Inger Adelsohn, with a beautiful figure, thick black hair and blue eyes the size of soup plates. The Swedish Embassy was a treasury of pulchritude, with secretaries Inger and Anna Hamilton (Countess, no less). I liked them a lot.

Thus, apart from work, there was plenty to distract me from my friendship with Irina, who had returned to her mother in Munich and had failed to get work with the Voice of America, because, she was told, of her connections with the Pushkin Club in London, considered very left wing by the US security agencies. She needed the work because her severely handicapped brother Fafa was ill with asthma and needed special treatment. Irina's mother and father were separated but still not divorced and their antagonism caused Irina much pain. In my own home, things were worrying. Dad was back in hospital for a second operation on his hernia and was very depressed. I needed to get home to see him. I did just that, returning to Britain in HE's aircraft on 5 September and returning to Moscow on Tuesday the 13th. I visited home and commiserated with Dad, who was already pretty fit. I phoned Barbara and we went together to a Prom. Concert at the Albert Hall and I took her to visit Maria Mikhaelovna at 54 Ladbroke Grove. She had just been in hospital where a growth in the womb had been diagnosed. Her husband Gustav Gustavovich was worried about the operation that would be necessary. We discussed Irina's situation.

I telephoned Irina in Munich and after some trouble discovered that the telephone had been cut off because of non-payment of bills. The matter was obviously serious so I posted off to Irina all the pound notes and marks I had in my wallet and asked my bank (Lloyds Cox and Kings) to find out how I could send money on a more regular basis, bearing in mind that exchange control was still in force. An arrangement was reached to send Irina's father £10.1.6 per month for a year in the first place, with the understanding that he would make this available to Irina. In fact I never discovered whether he kept his side of the agreement. The sum was small of course, a tithe of my monthly salary, but I reckoned I could not afford any more, especially as I was buying a car.

On boarding the coach from Euston Station RAF Air Movements Centre to Northolt airport to take the RAF Valetta aircraft to Berlin I noticed a small dark girl in glasses talking to a swarthy, well-dressed Levantine character. Before the coach started he asked the half dozen passengers inside if any were going as far as Warsaw. I was the only one so announced myself. He asked if I would keep an eye on the girl, aged about 15. She was the daughter of the Iranian Military

Attaché in Warsaw returning there after a month's holiday in England arranged by his colleague – the British Military Attaché. I readily agreed to act *in loco parentis*. Had her English been better she could have looked after herself, but after only a month she still had some difficulty in making herself understood. In the Transit Hotel I gave my ward 20 marks plus a lot of verbal advice and instructions, while I rushed into town to buy lampshades and a few other domestic items I had failed to get in the UK. The next day the RAF Valetta was unserviceable so rather than wait another night in Berlin I got the British Consul to book me on an Aeroflot flight to Moscow from Schönefeldt. This was the flight used by the Queen's Messenger, so we travelled together, landing at Vilnius and arriving in Moscow at midnight.

Late in September I travelled to White Russia (Belorus') with Patrick O'Regan. He was the Commercial Attaché, living in the Embassy Dacha (country house) at Perlovka. An Irish bachelor, he seemed to enjoy living on his own. We did not get on all that well although his war service had been interesting. He had been in special forces, possibly SOE, operating in Piemonte and organising, or trying to organise, partisan activity. He knew Sestriere well (on the Italian frontier with France) and said he had come across my mother's cousin Nino Grazioli, who had been a German sympathiser, and possibly even the Nazi appointed gauleiter for the area. Patrick was a difficult travelling companion with sharply defined and inflexible habits. He slept as deep as Sodom and you woke him up at your peril. Consequently after 11 p.m. one had to do all the work oneself; by work I mean packing on arrival at stations, dealing with the officials who are always entering the carriage, etc. Also he never walked, but loitered, a dangerous thing to do when the goons were in close attendance.

In Minsk we found an old Catholic church, formerly used by Poles when the town was Polish. To prevent anyone from entering the church, or chapel, because it was very small, the building had been bound with welded steel bars, already rusty with age and corrosion. But in gaps between the bars and the walls were thrust posies of flowers, some quite fresh, showing that there were still ways of defying the Soviet atheist power.

The main objective of the trip was to have another look at the medium bomber airfields beside the railway track between Minsk and Kharkov. From the train we got a good view, despite the obstructive behaviour of goons who stood in the corridor of the carriage with their copies of Pravda spread out at arms-length, one overlapping another. By dint of many "Excuse me"s *(Izvinite)* and pushing I was able to see what I wanted. On the train we had as a travelling companion a Soviet doctor, a forensic pathologist, on his way to Kharkov to listen to a colleague read a paper on some aspect of forensic science. During the war he had fought with Russian partisans in White Russia, was captured by the Germans and sent to work on the construction of the Atlantic Wall. When his profession was discovered he was allowed to practise as a doctor. On D-day all the Russians were moved back into the interior of France but our doctor was liberated by the Americans and for some time lived in Paris with émigré compatriots. I said nothing of my own contacts in case the doctor had been briefed to pump me for information about them. He seemed a nice enough chap but one never knows.

In the Intourist hotel in Kharkov Patrick and I had to share a room. I observed that the large mirror on one wall appeared to have been recently installed and was plastered in rather than being suspended or screwed. We concluded that this might be a two-way mirror enabling those in the next room to survey our activities. We covered it with a spare blanket. After supper when we had returned to our room to prepare for bed there was a tentative knock on the door which I answered. The "dejurnaya" (staff member, usually female, responsible for each floor in a Soviet hotel, not unlike a concierge) handed me a note in Russian to the effect that a person wished me to help in making contact with someone in the west where there had been difficulties in communication. Could we help? The questioner awaited us in a nearby room of which the writer included the number. Intrigued I decided to find out more, and with Patrick standing by in case this was an attempt to compromise me in some way, I went down the corridor and knocked at the half-open door of the room concerned. Next to the bed stood a heavily made up woman in her twenties with permed hair, dressed a la Deanna Durbin in a flared skirt, puff-shouldered blouse, high heels, all very untypical for the Soviet Union. She seemed embarrassed but blurted out that she was a friend of the son of the German General Spiedel, Commander designate of NATO. Could we arrange delivery to him of the letter she held in her hand. I explained that she might use the normal post and took my leave. Undoubtedly this was an attempt at something! What we never discovered.

The KGB tried every imaginable ruse (and some unimaginable) to compromise diplomats. Sex was often the bait. Lesbians and homosexuals beware. Half a dozen or more from the British Embassy were compromised while I was there, including John Vassall, the Naval Attaché's clerk. The Naval Attaché, being of the senior service, was responsible for all the more secret aspects of service security, including the material used in briefing diplomats making visits in the USSR. Vassall's treachery, if it can be so called, was only discovered a year after I left Moscow but a number of others were compromised while I was there.

Some months later our own RAF Warrant Officer, Bob Field's replacement, was blackmailed while Donald MacDonell was home in the UK. Bob owned up to me and was sent home within two days. This meant considerable financial hardship for him because he had borrowed money for the stuff he and his wife had bought for their Moscow tour. In his case he was inveigled into selling his old clothes (jackets, slacks, shoes) to Russian "friends" for roubles. This was illegal under Soviet law. He replaced these clothes with new items from the UK flown out in the diplomatic bag, and then tempted by the roubles, sold these new clothes, setting up what might be called a nice little racket. Quite apart from Soviet law, it was illegal on our side to use the diplomatic bag for the importation of articles for resale. The next step for the KGB would be to ask for information, firstly comparatively innocent stuff: the names of those turning up at the American Embassy Club, and then slightly more sensitive material, and so on, the victim becoming ever more vulnerable to compromise.

KGB attempts were not only made on junior staff. Sir Anthony Meyer, First Secretary in our Embassy in late 1956, was the object of an attempt at compromise not long after he arrived in Moscow. And Maya Plisetskaya, the Bolshoi Prima Ballerina, who had become a close friend of John Morgan, the Ambassador's Private Secretary, was told that if she did not wheedle information out of him and pass it on, she would find her dancing career adversely affected and would not accompany the Bolshoi Ballet to London as was being planned.

Flying back to Moscow from Kharkov we passengers were all freezing at 9,000', so when a member of the crew came back and asked if everyone was happy we told him that it was much too cold. Ten minutes later I saw the mercury in the cabin thermometer moving rapidly upwards. When it passed 30°C a girl two rows behind me started to swoon from the heat. The "stewardess" was locked in the cabin with us; on his way back to the crew compartment the second pilot or whoever he was had locked the door behind him. Encouraged by wisecracks from the passengers the stewardess banged and kicked lustily at the cabin door for at least 15 minutes, by which time the thermometer was reading 40°C. When she finally managed to inform the aircrew that she and the passengers were being broiled there was a roar as cold air poured in from the ventilators over each seat and in a matter of seconds we were freezing again.

Despite a cold contracted after this little adventure and acting as escort for Wedgie Benn MP and his wife just back from a visit to the Crimea where they had both been stricken with gippy tummy, I was asked to go to Leningrad on 8 October to act as interpreter during a visit to the port by British warships. There was an aircraft carrier, a cruiser/minelayer HMS *Apollo* and four destroyers, two

'D' Class – *Diana* and *Decoy*, and two "C" Class – *Chevron* and *Chieftain*. The Assistant Naval Attaché went aboard the aircraft carrier; I took HMS *Apollo*; Dennis looked after *Diana* and *Decoy* and the two assistant military attachés *Chevron* and *Chieftain*. Enormous crowds of Russian citizens queued to board the ships and have a look round. Some no doubt were naval technicians with tape measures, slide rules and cameras. In the case of *Apollo* we allowed on 80 at a time, divided into four groups of 20, each conducted by a Petty Officer assisted by an interpreter – a Russian naval liaison officer, who spoke poor English; a Commander Pearson speaking poor Russian; an official Soviet interpreter who spoke reasonable English and me, speaking reasonable Russian.

The parties were said to be from military and youth organisations but there were only two youths in our lot; the rest being well over 40. We gave them tours of an hour each – in the engine rooms, on the mess decks and on the bridge. The weather was foul all day and all of us were happy to keep out of the rain. We got through eight groups of 20 each and every morning for five days. The afternoons were supposed to be a free-for-all with any Soviet citizen turning up, but we soon twigged that the Soviet authorities had decided not to let anyone come aboard and had issued tickets to their preferred visitors. Those who did come on board were astonishingly friendly and frighteningly inquisitive. Going ashore was quite an ordeal because one had to run the gauntlet of thousands of eyes, peering into one's face, like pygmies in central Amazonia seeing their first white man. Dozens of notes of welcome, letters and postcards, laboriously spelt out by schoolchildren learning English (at least one in each family) were pressed shyly or furtively into sailors' hands, together with books, rouble notes and little gifts, for which the sailors returned pennies as souvenirs.

Every sailor on going ashore was at once surrounded by a crowd of up to 50 people who followed him wherever he went, asking questions in faltering English, smiling approvingly, laughing. In fact wherever one saw a knot of people one knew that somewhere within it there would be a sailor, rather like a queen bee in a swarm of workers. Sailors got off with Russian girls, were even seen necking with them in parks. There were numerous formal lunches and official parties that I attended. But none were as successful as the informal parties ashore, when the sailors mixed with the people whom the officials had kept out of the ships.

There was the strangest incident on the last day of the naval visit, Saturday 15 October 1955. First thing in the morning when I walked from my hotel (the Astoria again) towards the quay where the ships were tied up, I was surprised to see in the distance that the aircraft carrier was very much higher out of the water than on the previous evening. Likewise the other ships. All of them seemed to be

1. View towards the Kremlin across the R. Moskva from the British Embassy roof from where I often surreptitiously photographed flypasts by the latest Soviet military aircraft.

2. The British Embassy wooden dacha at Perlovka, 20 miles NE of Moscow. Looks ramshackle but was in fact very comfortable and large with wings and 20 rooms, all with Russian pechki (log stoves). My home for the summer of 1956. Just me. Quite exclusive!

3. Party at the dacha on 11 September 1956. Note the modified pechka in the wall.

4. Typical Russian house outside Moscow in the 1950s.

5. The Moscow to Leningrad road in 1954.

6. Staff (and horses) of the riding stables Urozhai (Harvest).

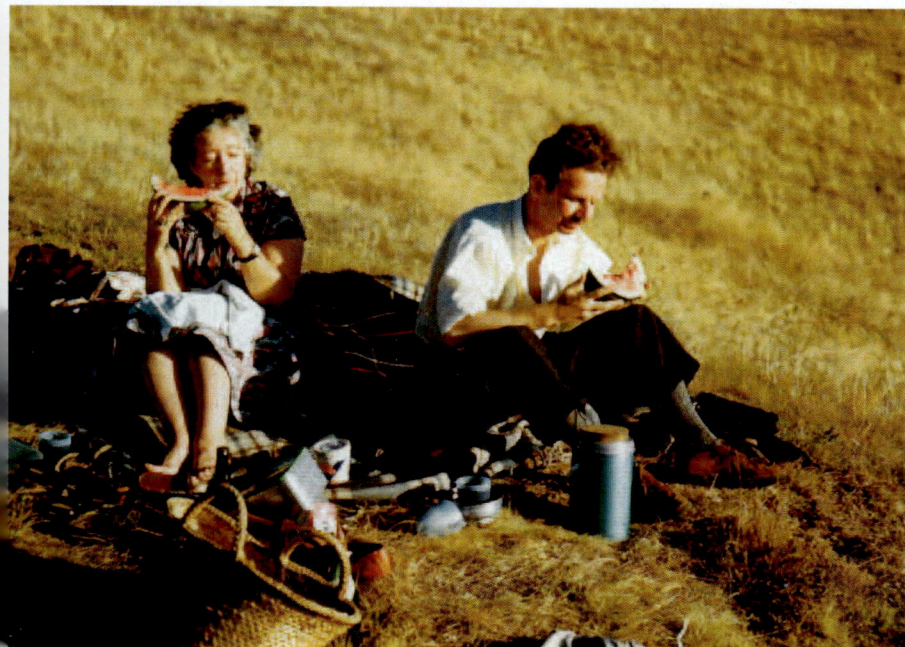

7. Daphne (later Baroness) Park and Donald McDonell (Air Attaché Moscow and thus my immediate boss) having lunch beside the Georgian Military Highway on 15 September 1956.

8. Mt Kazbek, 18 000', which I took at 4.a.m. on 16 September 1956 from a make-shift loo outside the village of Kazbek.

9. View of foothills of Kazbek

10. Ken (later Sir Kenneth) scaling the heights of Chufut Kale in the Crimea

11. The port of Aden in 1960. Its prosperity and population diminished when Britain left in 1967

12. In the 1960s travel from Aden to both east and west was along the shore

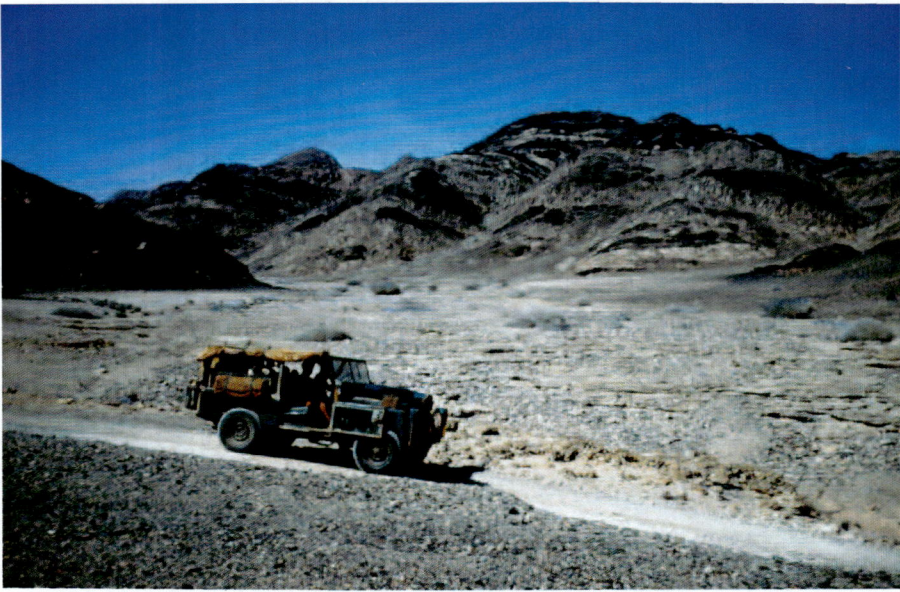

13. Travel inland was much more difficult

14. Bill Shevlin, Field Intelligence Officer, in his room at Beihan.

15. Dinner given by me for some tribal leaders and other locals

16. How to start a war. See text.

afloat in the park where the more than life-size Peter the Great sits astride his enormous horse – the Bronze Horseman. I also noticed squads of men marching purposefully in different directions with shovels, and piles of sandbags on trolleys. Something was obviously afoot. Getting closer I was able to see that the river Neva had risen at least 20' and the ships with it. Water was already lapping over the quay parapets and large expanses of grass were flooded. What had happened was that as in Peter the Great's time, a flood tide and a strong on-shore wind had combined to raise sea level and threaten serious flooding in Leningrad. Hence the squads of workmen. Further tours of the British ships were cancelled and after more parties to say farewell our ships weighed anchor and we attachés returned to Moscow. While the British squadron was visiting Leningrad a Soviet squadron had been visiting Portsmouth, reported Dad in a letter dated the 15th.

Over the weekend I again visited the famous monastery at Novodevichi. It was no longer a "working" monastery like Zagorsk, but the churchyard was full of the tombs of famous Russians, who were not quite famous enough to be interred in Red Square against the Kremlin Wall. Services were still held there and the singing was very good. An old man with a wall-eye tried to sell me a small bible outside the main entrance. He told me in a whisper that he had it wrapped in newspaper in a tattered bag he was carrying, and he had to be careful because it was illegal to sell bibles. I did not buy it because my accompanying goons would have fallen on him after I had moved away. There were always plenty of beggars outside active churches, mostly old and sick people. Daphne kept her small change to give to such people and so did I. On this occasion I gave away a lot before driving fast home to change for a cocktail party in the Canadian Air Attaché's flat to welcome the aircrew who had flown in Lester Pearson, the Canadian diplomat who had played a part in the foundation of NATO. There were 17 crew because Lester Pearson had come to Moscow as part of a world tour – in his own aircraft, carrying with him a maintenance crew as well as a double flight crew. After the drinks some of us were invited to dinner in the Prague restaurant – an excellent dinner, in fact the best I had ever eaten in Moscow.

On 18 October I left with the Donkins and Daphne Park on a visit to Central Asia – Turkestan. Of it Matthew Arnold wrote in his poem "Sohrab and Rustum"

But I have seen
Afrasiab's cities only, Samarkand,
Bokhara, and lone Khiva in the waste,
And the black Toorkmun tents: and only drunk
The desert rivers, Moorghub and Tejend,

Kolik, and where the Kalmuks feed their sheep,
The northern Syr, and the great Oxus stream,
The yellow Oxus.

We first flew to Tashkent and stayed there several days. Tashkent was not a very picturesque city at the time except for some streets of old houses. However these were being demolished to make way for modern four-storey cement blocks of flats, more or less standard throughout the Soviet Union. There was a good market that we visited with carpets galore made in Bukhara but in impossible designs featuring the heads of Marx, Lenin and Stalin together or separately. A new Opera House was being built, with each room incorporating the designs of one or other Soviet Central Asian Republic. One was decorated entirely in small cut pieces of coloured mirror glass, another with complicated arabesques in relief. But this was as yet incomplete. One evening we attended a Schiller play in the Uzbek language which was fairly awful. Another evening we went to a classical ballet performed by the Uzbek national ballet company. This copied Bolshoi choreography but the dancers were less proficient and one "prima", entering left rather fast, traversed most of the stage on her bum.

Peter and Betty Donkin were taken to visit various museums in Tashkent but I had other ideas and Daphne was happy to follow my lead. Tashkent had an aircraft factory which was supposed to be producing Ilyushin Il-12 or Il-14 aircraft, the first being a tricycle replacement of the LI-2 Soviet version of the Dakota DC-3. The Il-12 was a rather unsatisfactory aircraft, unreliable and by no means comfortable for passengers. The Il-14 was a considerable improvement and became an Aeroflot classic in its way. We (by which I mean the RAF) wanted to confirm that Tashkent was still producing the Il-14 or whether it had moved towards producing more modern aircraft – jets even. Daphne and I set off on foot towards the airfield. From maps I had concealed on my person I noticed that there were two large cemeteries between our Intourist hotel and the airfield, as well as several large fields which in summer may have grown cotton or grapes.

I thought that if we were to be stopped by "Soviet citizens" (a sobriquet often used by our KGB followers if they wished to establish their credentials) we could say that we wished to visit the cemeteries to satisfy our cultural interests. A thin story but good enough. However, after negotiating one cemetery and entering the next, shouts from behind us showed that the KGB were calling on all Uzbeks nearby to intercept and detain us infidels for violating a Muslim cemetery. We hastened on across the desiccated cotton fields as fast as we could because no Uzbeks seemed to be paying much attention to the goons and what I wanted to see on the airfield was within sight – nothing there but a few parked IL-14's. I noticed that Daphne was falling behind and, turning to urge her to keep up, I noticed blood seeping from the heels of her shoes which had worn bad blisters on her feet. I suggested she take her shoes off and make do in her stockings until we reached a reasonable track leading back into town.

Daphne was like that – always wanting to keep up, especially with men, unwilling to accept defeat in anything and to put up with any hardship in order to achieve an objective. I found her the ideal travelling companion, much better than most men. Could it have been more? We were almost the same age (33 at that time). No, I was heavily involved with much more glamourous girls, less qualified and experienced than Daphne, but for me very much more beautiful and attractive. I was bewitched by ballerinas but quite apart from physical attributes, I wanted any consort of mine to have a feeling for flight, flying, clouds and the beauty of the third dimension, in some ways like Jo Butler, although other girl friends had been even more interesting, exotic and attractive. Daphne was always a colleague although on one occasion Lady Hayter asked me seriously whether I was not seeing rather too much of Daphne. I thought not.

I had been keen to visit Khiva, an ancient Central Asian city south of the Aral Sea at the head of the delta of the Amu Darya river, formerly the Oxus, originating in the Hindu Kush far to the south. Khiva itself had no airfield so we had to fly to Urgench, not far distant, and take a taxi from there. We stayed in Urgench in a very poor hotel, the only one. Of Khiva, Arminius Vámbéry, the daring Hungarian traveller, who visited Khiva disguised as a dervish in 1864 wrote: *"First you must have seen a Persian city of the lowest rank, and then you will understand my meaning when I say that Khiva is much inferior to it."*[5] We got a strong impression that not much had changed.

Khiva had few modern buildings. It was contained within earth ramparts and a partly demolished high mud-brick wall entered by four gates to the north, south, east and west. Within the wall were a large number of mosques and minarets, many derelict and truncated, possibly for safety, so that they resembled the water cooling towers of a power station, except that the towers were often partly tiled with the turquoise tiles typical of Persian architecture. Khiva had a long history of what would now be called fundamentalist Muslim culture, in the time of Peter the Great being the largest slave market in Central Asia, with a stock of ten thousand. It was said that the cruelty of Khivans displeased even the Tartars. We had the strong impression that the Soviet authorities were allowing the town to decay, the more modern Urgench being promoted in its place.

Returning to Tashkent we next flew to Andizhan in the Fergana Valley, between Kirghistan and Tadzhikistan. This was the valley from which the Moguls rode to conquer India and I say rode advisedly because the valley was always famous for its horses. Not so many horses when we visited. Industry there was mostly based on cotton, and when we were there the cotton had just been picked and was laid out to dry on every road, posing problems for transport, one would have thought. From the air almost all roads seemed to be covered with cotton wool, as they were. Back in Moscow we had asked that we might visit a kolkhoz (collective farm), to see agricultural work in progress and meet the workers. This was more difficult than we thought. We were taken by train to the selected kolkhoz, which was on the route to Osh, where Alexander the Great is said to have looked into China (the border is close), seen the Takla Makan desert, and decided not to go further in that direction.

Collected by car and taken to our kolkhoz, we were met by the director and his colleagues and sat down and lectured for an hour on the organisation and administration of the farm. This was followed by a tour of the buildings occupied by administrators, with introductions to each bureaucrat, each of whom made a presentation. Still no sign of fields or peasants! We were than walked to trestle tables in the open piled high with food. This was for the most part boiled rice imbedded with bits of roasted mutton, called "ploff" (pilaff). Other tables held sweeter confections, still others bottles of vodka and wine. There was enough food to feed a regiment and we soon deduced that after we had finished and left, the "regiment" would arrive to have a splendid meal from our leftovers. After two hours of food and drink with interspersed speechifying we again asked when we could go into the fields and were told that there was no time, our train back to Andizhan would be leaving in ten minutes. After this experience I invented the phrase "Plof v'glazakh" (Pilaff in the eyes) to describe a method of frustrating a visitor's wishes.

Our third expedition from Tashkent was by train to Samarkand, Bukhara and Mari. They were along the railway line towards Ashkhabad on the Caspian Sea, from where we had intended to fly to Tblisi the capital of Georgia and return to Moscow that way. This was disallowed and from Mari we had to return to Tashkent by train the way we had come and fly home from there. However Samarkand, Bukhara and Mari were interesting enough. We stayed a day or two in each.

"For lust of knowing what should not be known we take the Golden road to Samarkand" Flecker "Hassan". Samarkand was Tamerlane's city, with many buildings of his time still there and well cared for by the Soviet authorities. The

Bibi Khanun, the mosque erected by Tamerlane's wife as a present for her lord and master when he returned from a campaign, has to be seen to be appreciated. Partly destroyed by earthquakes not long after it was built, the ruins are still magnificent. Nearby – the Gur Emir, Tamerlane's mausoleum, is equally fine. In 1405 when he died at the age of 70 his embalmed body was placed in an ebony coffin and laid to rest there under a greenish-black jade slab in the floor. This is the largest known slab of that material – 6' long, 17" wide and 14" thick. Like the Bibi Khanun, the Gur Emir was also soon damaged by earthquakes but is well looked after by the Soviet Antiquities Institute associated with the Soviet Academy of Sciences.

Slightly further away is the Shah-I-Zindeh, a complex of small shrines splendidly ornamented in different shades of turquoise blue tiles with geometrical designs in relief. No depiction of live forms of course; that would be contrary to Islam. On the "science side" an immense "sextant" cut in a rock hillside was constructed by an astronomer, Ulu Beg, a contemporary of Tamerlane interred in the Shah-I-Zindeh. He made observations from a chamber at the foot of the cut as different sections of the heavens came in sight with the revolution of the earth. His calculations showed Ptolemy's catalogue of stars to be incorrect. Less scientific was a stone Koran stand of gigantic size beneath which infertile women crawled to better their condition.

The roses I found growing in the side streets of Samarkand were very healthy, floriferous and scented. I was interested because of the importance of the rose in Persian writings – Omar Khayyam. I was also interested to know if the mullahs in Samarkand understood Arabic, and I asked a mullah I met near an "active" mosque. He obviously did not understand my Arabic, so I tried Russian. No, he said, he could read and chant the Koran but he did not understand the words. However he had been taught and remembered the meaning of each surah (verse).

I was interested to meet some Russian teachers working in a Samarkand secondary school. They did not speak Uzbek. At school Uzbek children were taught only in Russian. The teachers lived together with other Russians in a compound exclusive to them. They regarded the Uzbeks as foreign to them and they looked forward to finishing their assignments in Samarkand and returning, in the case of one woman I met, to Leningrad. The tour of pedagogical duty was two years in her case. I was reminded of colonists worldwide.

Determined efforts were being made to Russify the locals, or at least, to prevent children being indoctrinated with Muslim practices considered deleterious. Women were not permitted to enter shops wearing the chador (veil) which in Uzbekistan resembled the Persian black horsehair chador. Uzbek houses were still built without windows on to the street, because wherever you put the windows those on the street could be blacked out.

Bukhara where we next went was one step back from Samarkand – dirtier and less pleasant, as might be thought appropriate for the home of emirs (princes, governors) who were even more cruel than in Khiva. Here again the Russians, who occupied Bukhara in 1868 when they pushed through the trans-Caspian railroad, took care to bypass the city in favour of a railway station ten miles to the south at Kagan, where barracks for the garrison, workshops, storage sheds and amenities for the Russian camp-followers formed the nucleus of a sizeable community.

Bukhara was better built than Khiva. Rather than mud most of the old buildings were of fired brick, and some unglazed shrines, using bricks set in geometric patterns, were very attractive and should be illustrated in any history of brickwork. An example was the shrine of Pasha Ismail, a Samanid king of Bukhara who died there in 907 after a benevolent reign when he brought under his rule immense territories running from the Caspian Sea to the Tien Shan mountains and from the Persian Gulf to the Indian Ocean. In his day the regime was relatively tolerant and Bukhara was home to large Christian and Jewish communities. This changed abruptly when Genghis Khan, a pagan, the Chief of Chiefs of the Mongols, took the city in 1219, seized the Koran from its stand and threw it to the ground, crying out *"Lo, the hay is cut, give the horses fodder!"* and the massacre, looting and burning did not stop until the city was a smoking ruin.

The city was rebuilt by Genghis Khan's sons and regained its reputation as a centre of Islamic learning. Even when we visited there were many buildings, previously madaris (schools) but now just buildings of architectural merit. There was just the one working seminary for mullahs. We asked to visit the Rector and this was arranged. He was a kindly Muslim cleric who told us that we could not meet the students (50 graduated each year) because they were in the fields helping to harvest cotton. He explained that his madresseh was one of two in the Soviet Union, the other being in Alma Ata. He entertained us to tea – greenish brown, without milk or sugar – in small cups without saucers or handles and then showed us the rooms of the students, who lived in pairs in small vaulted cells around the sides of the ancient building.

We stayed in a small and rather grubby tourist hotel. The food was bad, but one could manage on eggs and bread and tea, making sure it was hot to avoid any infection. Not far from the hotel was a pit full of dirty water and we were told of the prevalence of Richter Worm, caught from dirty water in these parts, which, after developing in the liver, migrates to the surface of the skin and can then be seen making its way just beneath the epidermis. To deal with this, one was supposed to make a cut with a knife in the skin ahead of the worm's advance, and when its head and sufficient body emerged, to wind it on a stick until the whole worm was out. This did not help our appetites.

Bukhara is the city of storks and every minaret and relatively high point was crowned with the untidy bushes of stork nests. The high points included the towers of the caravanserai, or complex of bazaars, which Curzon of Indian fame found interesting when he visited, as did we. The complex vaulted buildings from which the bazaars radiated were called "timis". In my experience the souks of Damascus and Jerusalem had a better selection of things to buy, but I bought a splendid Bukharan thick cotton blanket in horizontal stripes which has survived 50 years of children's picnics. There were also plenty of very good Bukharan carpets, but too expensive for me. Most items for sale were utilitarian – primus stoves; coffee pots; samovars, etc. We were in Bukhara on a Friday, when most of the stalls were shut, but even so there was a parking problem, particularly on Fridays when all Muslims must visit the mosque to pray. The donkey park was reasonably full, and there were no parking meters. A Bukharan legend relates: *"The devil says in a donkey's ear 'All mares are dead!' – and the donkey brays sadly. 'Except one' adds the devil. And that is why the donkey always ends his bray with a happier 'Haw'".*

The central structure in Bukhara was the Ark, a brick and mud "Kremlin" in which the emirs once lived. When we visited, it was more or less derelict, but still a good vantage point for photography. As an example of the extremism of the "fundamentalists" before the Russians took over, in 1842 Colonel Charles Stoddart was seconded to the British East India Company and sent to Bukhara to explore the possibility of trade in Turkestan, where it was feared that Russia was stealing the advantage. He was a devout Christian, not prepared to trifle with "heathen". He soon antagonised the Emir, who confined him to a dungeon – a pit 20 feet deep only accessible through a small hole in the roof. The pit was stocked with snakes and scorpions and any other nasties available. Every so often Stoddart was pulled out, threatened with death, offered freedom and then pushed back into the pit. After some months the British in India sent Captain Arthur Connelly to find out why nothing had been heard of his superior. He joined Stoddart in the pit. Later both were brought up and offered freedom if they abjured Christianity and became Muslim. Stoddart agreed but Connelly did not. Both were decapitated.

The British then sent a further envoy to Bukhara – the Rev. Joseph Wolff, a Bavarian Jew converted to Catholicism later ordained an Anglican Minister. He was well off, fluent in Hebrew, Greek and Latin as well as German and English. His nominal objective in visiting Bukhara was to attempt to convert the Jews remaining there to Christianity. After a long and difficult journey he arrived in Bukhara in 1844 and learned of the deaths of Stoddart and Connelly from the Jews he met, who also fed and protected him – from poisoning and worse. He was able to observe the meeting out of justice to those who had offended the Emir. They were laid out on the ground beside the Ark and their eyes were put out by the executioner's thumbs. This was the most lenient penalty. Not much advance since then, judging by the treatment of hostages taken by Muslims in Iraq in 2004. Eventually after great difficulties Wolff was allowed to leave Bukhara and return to England to spend the rest of his life as a country curate.[6]

I had read that in Bukhara the pit in which Stoddart and Connelly had been imprisoned could be seen, and so I inquired as to its whereabouts. We were taken to an Uzbek house, and one of the family living there stripped a carpet from a grill in the floor and invited us to look in. As my eyes accustomed to the light my hair stood on end. Two men seemed to be lying on the floor. The Soviet authorities had rigged up the dungeon as an exhibition of the excesses of the earlier Muslim regime.

From Bukhara we moved on to Mari (Mary on some maps; in Russian Марй) 500km south towards the Iranian frontier. Mari is the modern version of the ancient Merv, or rather Mervs, because there have been at least three earlier cities. Their remains are in semi-desert 18 miles east of the modern Mari. We took a taxi out there. There was little to be seen, other than the mausoleum of Sultan Sanjur, a massive brick building. The Sultan's tomb lies in the centre of the floor. It seems likely that this monument still stands because it was too strongly built to be destroyed by any of the conquerors who regularly sacked these cities. The earliest Merv, known as Giaour Kala is supposed to have existed long before the time of Christ. Alexander built a fort there in 328 BC. In the fourth century the city was the seat of a Christian bishopric. In the seventh century the invading Arabs destroyed it but over the next three centuries the new Merv built nearby became famous for its fruit, cotton and cattle. People came from all over the world to see the unique irrigation systems based on the river Murghab which rises two hundred miles away in the mountains of Afghanistan and Iran, creates an oasis at Merv and then disappears in the desert to the north. Seljuk Turks supplanted the Arab dynasty and developed the oasis and its city to the pinnacle of its fame in the 11th and 12th centuries AD under Alp Arslan and the Sultan Sanjur.

Then from 1153 to 1221 the Mongol hordes under Genghis Khan and his son Tuli Khan descended on Merv massacring the entire population, said to number at that time 700,000.

In the 15th century Shakhrukh, son of Tamerlane, built a new town close to the site of its predecessors, but it lasted only a hundred years. The Russians started to build Mari about 1886 when the trans-Caspian railway reached the Merv oasis on the heels of Kaufmann's Cossacks. By that time the population was Turkomen after the nomadic Tekke Turkomen swept out of the Kara Kum desert in 1856 driving the previous settled population before them. The Tekke were said to be ferocious, dishonest and coarse. It was said that when the Persians found they were fighting Tekke they tied each other up and waited to be taken away as slaves, probably to the slave markets of Bukhara or Khiva. On the credit side they were amiable, frank and hospitable. Many people liked them. The Russians liked them. Donovan, the *Times* correspondent who was fortuitously made Khan of Merv in 1881, was not enamoured of his subjects during his six months of office, but got along with them well enough. They had the endearing anarchic quality not uncommon in nomads of tolerating their leaders *"only"* Vambery wrote *"as long as they do not make their supremacy felt by unusual commands or extravagant pretensions"*.

On our short visit the Tekke seemed to have knuckled down to the new order of things – factories (mainly for cotton, carpets and rugs), some degree of mechanisation in agriculture – tractors and mechanical cotton harvesting machines, etc. The major market-day of the week was Sunday, and we were there over Sunday and thus able to see the fantastically colourful event. Not that the venue was colourful – several dusty courtyards between low concrete outhouses – but because of the people, their colourful dress and proud appearance and behaviour. In this respect I liked the Tekke Turkomen far better than the Uzbeks, whose men-folk wore at most an embroidered skull-cap called a tibiteyka above normal Soviet clothes. The Tekke dressed in more biblical garb – long dark cloaks and loose trousers, soft leather knee-boots and on their heads the best part of a black Karakul fleece. Karakul fleeces with black and curly hair, made into Astrakhan hats, come not so much from Astrakhan, the marketing centre, as from here, the Karakum desert. Kara means black. The fleeces used for hats are taken from as yet unborn Karakul lambs.

The womenfolk favoured red – long embroidered red dresses, with veils on their heads, faces uncovered but often with one corner of the veil held between their teeth. It was said that a city was once taken by the treachery of a woman and thenceforth it became obligatory for women to carry one corner of the veil between their teeth – to stop them talking, unless, of course, they had to talk! Apart from cotton cloth, carpets, sheep and goats, horses , donkeys and mules, and all manner of household articles from samovars and Primus stoves to Chinese tea bowls, there was a section of the market for sales of jewellery and trinkets, not displayed but concealed about their person by the brightly dressed Tekke women. On being approached by another Tekke, after quiet conversation, the woman interested in selling might produce a pectoral worthy of a bishop's ransom or weighty gold and silver bangles.

The whole of this part of Soviet Central Asia has an economy based on cotton, its quality being praised even before the time of Christ. But after the Mongol hordes descended cotton went into decline. When the Russians came with the railway they tried to re-establish cotton culture using American Sea Island seed, which would not flourish in Merv. Too dry maybe. Later they introduced short staple Indian cotton with great success. However they made an environmental mistake on the grand scale by using most of the Amu Darya/Oxus water to irrigate cotton on a vast scale, with the result that the Aral Sea has now largely dried up.

From Mari the Donkins and Daphne and I returned to Tashkent by train – three days and nights, without water. For once a Soviet train could not even provide tea. As we became more and more thirsty I got off the train at a prolonged stop at Chardzhou, where the railway crosses the Amu Darya, and bought as much as I could of the only liquid they had – warm, sweet, pink champagne – six large bottles. We even used it for cleaning our teeth. From Tashkent we flew back to Moscow. We got back with a day or two spare before the 38th anniversary of the October Revolution on 7 November and the parade through Red Square. Both Betty Donkin and Daphne Park were immediately laid up with diarrhoea and the former only left her bed to fly back to Britain to quarantine the second of their two dachshunds (the first had died a month earlier). The Donkins would be time-expired in April 1956 and wanted their dog out of quod then.

I was given the job of looking after Lord Douglas, The Chairman of BEA (British European Airways), Lady Douglas and several officials from the Ministry of Civil Aviation led by Sir George Cribbett. They were coming out from London the following week to negotiate an interline agreement between BEA and Aeroflot. This agreement was to provide for co-ordinated booking arrangements with modified flight schedules so that travellers between London and Moscow for instance could reserve and pay for seats on flights connecting at intermediate airports or on direct flights flown by either airline. These days this is taken for granted but in 1955 it was necessary to reserve and pay for seats separately to each airline, whose flights would not necessarily connect. The agreement was quite complex but the detail was worked out by the officials of the MCA and Aeroflot. My job included interpreting in the discussions between the Head of Aeroflot, Marshal Zhavoronkov and Lord Douglas, with their retinues.

I was a bit concerned because a mistake in terminology might at best delay negotiations and at worst become incorporated in the agreement to be signed by both sides. Fortunately Marshal Zhavoronkov also had an interpreter and I agreed with him beforehand that he would interpret from English to Russian and I from Russian to English, with each of us helping the other over obscure terminology. As far as I know everything was hunky-dory. Other than this official work I also showed Lord and Lady Douglas the sights of Moscow, the Kremlin, accompanied them to the Bolshoi Ballet, and visited the Mausoleum to see the embalmed Lenin and Stalin. On the last day, after the agreement was signed a ceremonial lunch was given by Marshal Zhavoronkov at the Prague Restaurant after which I took Lord and Lady Douglas souvenir hunting before seeing them into their car to the airport. That evening I had supper with the Swedish Air Attaché, Börje Kwarnmark, and discussed bringing my Sunbeam Talbot to Sweden after Christmas for him to garage and look after.

The next morning at 06.00 I drove to the airport and flew Aeroflot to Berlin via Warsaw and Vilnius (too early to use the new interline agreement). A molar that had earlier given me trouble had fallen to pieces, possibly on ploff, leaving an irregular stump. In Berlin the dentist told me that the tooth would have to come out. He extracted it with a certain amount of butchery because there was very little tooth for his forceps to grip. The wound bled copiously and I went to A&E of the Service hospital in Berlin who sewed the wound up. I spent a day or so doing some shopping for friends in Moscow and their children, and a party with my BRIXMIS colleagues ending up at 0100 eating shashlik and frankfurters at a street stall. Later that morning I flew back to Moscow with the Queen's Messenger arriving at 5 p.m. just in time to change and go to a cocktail party at 6.30. Bed, exhausted at 10.

In late November Dennis and I gave a farewell party for the Fields who were returning to the UK tour-expired. Bob had been a splendid Warrant Officer, RAF to the core, knowledgeable about all aspects of RAF life and procedures, a comedian occasionally, a lawyer always, barrack-room sometimes. We were sorry to see him go. Bob had a South African wife, Jean. They had met in Rhodesia during the war when the RAF was thick on the ground and many pilots were trained there. They had four sons aged between ten and two, who behaved very efficiently with their own "service discipline" as befitted a Warrant Officer's brood. The two year old used his next senior brother as interpreter. Despite their operation as a juvenile unit, or possibly because of it, they cleverly avoided or unconditionally rejected any course of action or disciplinary measure they considered unnecessary. In other words, a true RAF family. Neither their parents nor anyone else could impose on them.

In early December I wrote home asking Dad to book me two tickets to "La Plume de ma Tante" at the Garrick Theatre on 23 December, a horse from Joan

Andrews on Boxing Day, when I hoped to hunt, and another two tickets at the Festival Hall on 28 December to see Violetta Elvin dance. I would take Irina, back in London for a visit, to the ballet and we would go back-stage to talk Russian to Violetta afterwards. My plans were to be the first passenger to use the new Aeroflot BEA interline agreement on 17 December, the 30th day from signature when the agreement was supposed to come into force. I would pay Intourist in roubles for the flight, the first occasion when this would be possible. As the two services did not yet connect I would arrive at Heathrow on Sunday 18 December and I asked Dad to drive there to collect me.

The temperature in Moscow was quite cold: −17°C for the previous ten days, snowing hard on 2 December with snow in the streets building up at several inches an hour. The Soviet authorities had an amazingly efficient snow clearing service. Most of the roads in the city were cleared by large vehicles fitted on the front with two large shares or blades pivoting alternately and meshing like two outstretched arms to scoop lying snow on to an integral conveyor belt. This carried the snow over the top of the vehicle and its cabin and deposited it into a tipper truck following behind. As each tipper truck filled, another replaced it. The snow was driven out of town and deposited in the fields to await the spring thaw.

On Friday 15 December Dennis and I arranged an early Christmas dinner for us AAA's (Dennis, Peter, Alan and me) with as guests Peter and Betty Donkin, the Canadian Air Attaché Stan Turner and his wife, the French Assistant Military Attaché Yves Michaut and his wife, Chuck Klench and his wife (both of them Press Correspondents), Daphne of course and sundry other colleagues and friends. The dinner was in our flat at Narodnaya Ulitza. In all about 30 people came, which strained the catering arrangements and we were obliged to borrow an extra cook, imminently expecting a baby, and the use of next door's cooker, because our oven was not large enough for two turkeys.

Notes:

[1.] As far as I know these were only printed in Russian by ИЗВЕСТИЯ (Izvestia – meaning News), a well-known Russian newspaper and publishing house. By now, 2004, Rybakov's works may have been translated and published in English.

2. An intriguing book about aspects of this war is *The Diary of Politruk Oreshin*, found at Loimola, and privately printed in 1941 in Russian, English and Finnish by Lord Carlow as a present for his Finnish friends. The diary was kept by Politruk (Political Supervisor) Oreshin, of a detached ski battalion of the Soviet 37th Infantry Regiment. The last entry is on 18 January 1940 when Oreshin

was probably killed during a Finnish raid. The Finns used to ski in silently, cut half a dozen throats and disappear into the snow undetected as often as not. Their partisan tactics are also described in "Kaputt", Aria d'Italia, 1948, in Italian, by Curzio Malaparte, the Italian war correspondent and author.

3. ДВЕНАДЦАТЬ СТУЛЬЕВ and ЗОЛОТОЙ ТЕЛЕНОК. These were published in 1953 and 1954 in the Russian Language by the Chekhov Publishing House in the USA. But they had been written much earlier. Ilf died in 1937 and Petrov in 1942. The chapters of their books had been published in the USSR as feuilletons. They are very funny and were accurate depictions of some of the absurdities of Soviet (and Russian) life even in the 50s when I was there. For instance there was a massive neon sign on one high building which read "Eat Meat", this at a time when except for diplomats like us the meat was in poor supply and of poor quality. As it was not possible in Soviet society to advertise individual factories, because they did not exist as such, Soviet town planners, convinced that no modern town should be without neon signs, had to "advertise" products more generally. Another read "Fish is good for you".

4. I managed to contact Kondratieva in 2000 but despite acknowledging her existence she was unwilling to engage in correspondence.

5. *Travels in Central Asia*. 1863. Arminius Vámbéry. John Murray. 1864

6. *Narrative of a Mission to Bukhara in the Years 1843-1845*. Rev. Joseph Wolff. Published by John W. Parker 1845. I can also recommend 'The Great Game' by Peter Hopkirk, 1990, John Murray, which gives a very readable history of the goings on in Central Asia throughout the 19th century.

Moscow '56

I arrived home on 18 December 1955 as planned and Christmas turned out as envisaged except that I could not hunt on Boxing Day; Joan Andrews had no horse for me. Early in the New Year I collected my new car from Rootes' Group distribution centre in west London paying £752.19s.9d for it, six months' salary for my rank of Squadron Leader. The car had numerous extras, a special heater for cold climates such as Sweden and the USSR, a car radio with short wave capabilities and an electrically operated overdrive (now called fifth gear). This last caused endless trouble, but at that time I had not yet worked out that it is a waste of money buying a "top of the range" car when all one really needs is a reliable and cost effective motorised chair, comfortable but without frills. A car is one of the fastest depreciating assets one can acquire.

Several days after Christmas I drove off to Munich in the new car to visit Irina arriving there on 7 January. I stayed with them – Irina, her mother and Fafa – for five days in their partly derelict house. They were seeking a school for Fafa and we visited an Anthroposophist school in a small village east of Munich, where about a dozen children boarded. Anthroposophist principles involve treating all people as equal under the Lord, whatever their states of health or disability, genius or dimness – what might be called truly comprehensive. This is all well and good. However some of their other principles seem questionable. For instance teaching a child to read before he is of a certain age is discouraged because one could "spoil childhood". The aim is to let the child play and use imagination without adult interference until the age of seven, and with as little as possible thereafter. There are a multitude of other principles, some admirable, some ridiculous, many – reasonable. Overall, at a higher level, there is general agreement on the Hindu concepts of karma and reincarnation and Mme Blavatsky, who founded Theosophy, is claimed by Anthroposophists as one of their own. She was a very eccentric person and played a part in establishing Benares Hindu University in India.

Rudolf Steiner knew Mme Blavatsky, and in founding Anthroposophy was influenced by her ideas. There are now many Anthroposophist schools throughout the world. Whatever one thinks of their philosophy, the school near Munich was very good for Fafa. We did not leave him there at once but arranged for him to go later. As a gift I had brought Fafa a small German record player and a number of records (discs) of Russian folk song and classical music. There were no CD's or Walkmen in those days. Fafa loved music.

From Munich I drove on south through the Brenner Pass into Italy and along to Turin where I spent several days with Mariapola and Zia Albina at 2 Via Cristalliera, about a mile west along the Corso Francia from their previous flat at Via del Carmine. Being further from the city centre, the new flat was probably cheaper to rent, and it was much more commodious, with four large rooms on the fifth floor. Pola was taking exams to qualify her to teach art at a more advanced level and she was also painting more and more of her own works, some of which were being sold. She particularly liked painting street scenes in the old hill villages behind Bordighera, where she and her mother usually went in the summer. In Turin Pola and I visited cafés and bars patronised by Fiat workers. Turin was largely a Fiat city, producing cars and aircraft. Apart from teaching in state primary and secondary schools, Pola also gave private tuition to would-be artists and architects.

After several days in Turin I drove to Sestriere, nominally to seek out Patrick O'Regan's partisan friend who had known Nino Grazioli, my mother's cousin from Cuneo. The ex-partisan was managing (possibly owned) the Hotel Diana, where he wined and dined me very well. He had very little information to give me about Nino, except that he had come to a "bad end". Just what this meant I was never able to establish with any certitude, although it seemed probable that he had supported the Germans and possibly worked for them, which the partisans would not have liked. Towards the end of the war Piemonte was full of partisans, or those who later claimed to have been partisans. Some certainly were. In Cumiana, a village south of Turin, I sought and found a street named after Nino Toretta, a cousin of Signor Bersezio, a High Court judge. The Bersezios had been great friends of my parents. Nino was shot dead on 26 April 1945 in an action against German troops interfering with a transfer of arms by partisans to the safe-keeping of a monastery.

Skiing at Sestriere was impossible because of thick fog, in which I lost my way and nearly broke my neck. I drove back to Munich and had several more days there with Irina before driving home to arrive in the penultimate week of January with not much more than a week to prepare for my return to Moscow. The plan was to accompany Daphne, whom I would pick up in Paris where she had been staying with ex-SOE friends. On Friday 3 February 1956 I crossed the Channel with the car and drove to Paris where Daphne had reserved me a room at the Hôtel du Ministère. After booking in at 2100 I made my way to Aleksei Burnashov's flat in Rue Claude Matrat and talked to him and his younger daughter until 2 a.m. Then slept late until lunch with our Paris Air Attaché. Daphne turned up and we planned to leave next morning, Sunday 5 February, driving north via Brussels. That Saturday evening I went round to the Yussoupoffs' apartment and knocked on the door. After some delay a voice asked in Russian: *"Who's there?"*. I replied: *"Vanya, from Moscow!"* (Vanya, Russian for Johnnie, was how I was known in Russian émigré circles). There was no further reply and the door remained locked. I later discovered that Felix thought I might have been an axe-man sent by the KGB to dispose of him, as for Trotsky.

Daphne and I set off from Paris towards Brussels in a snowstorm early on Sunday 5 February 1956. The snow soon turned to freezing rain which coated the car in shimmering transparent ice. The door locks and windows froze. Inside we were OK with the heater going flat out. The roads were skating rinks. Fortunately, while at home I had bought chains and these I now fastened on the wheels and with their help reached Brussels after ten hours. We stopped the night there and next day the roads were not quite so bad after we passed Aachen. From there on via Dusseldorf conditions improved still more, largely because the Germans had cleared and gritted and salted the road.

North of Hannover we stayed the night with friends of Daphne, a Major in 4th Hussars and his family. He helped to find a Staff Sergeant tank maintenance engineer who attended to the overdrive on the Sunbeam, which had stuck "engaged", which meant I could not use reverse gear. The following day, Tuesday, we drove to Grossenbrode on the north German coast, where we booked on the first ferry on Wednesday to Gedser in Denmark, staying the previous night in the ferry hotel. The ferry took three hours and 20 minutes but served excellent smorgasbord, which served to fill the time and our stomachs. On the road from Gedser to Copenhagen the weather was grey and dreary. After lunching well in Copenhagen we crossed the straits from Helsinførs to Helsingborg in 20 minutes. The channel was freezing up but kept open by icebreakers. After another night-stop in a magnificent state hotel in Värnamu, a third of the way to Stockholm, we arrived there late on Thursday evening. I contacted Major Gösta Hellstrom, the Swedish Military Attaché in Moscow, but then back in Stockholm. The

Swedish Defence Attachés divided their time between the capitals of the countries to which they were accredited, often more than one, and their Ministry in Stockholm. Gösta took over my Sunbeam, which he would leave in Börje Kwarnmark's garage at Lidingö, for his attention when he came home in his turn. Daphne and I flew on to Moscow by SAS flight on Saturday 11 February arriving at 2100. This gave us Sunday free for unpacking and preparing to start work on Monday.

A week later on Sunday 19 February, after lunch with a new member of the Embassy secretariat, Daphne and I visited the Dostoyevsky Museum, recently redecorated in honour of the 75th anniversary of the author's death. I had been there before and was sorry to find that the refurbishment had been carelessly done, and domestic articles that had previously been positioned as if the dwelling were still occupied by Dostoyevsky and his father (a doctor) had now been placed in sealed glass cabinets. The elderly lady who had previously been the curator had been replaced by an Intourist guide in double-breasted black jacket (as in Intourist hotels). She knew nothing and cared less. communist slogans now decorated the walls. This was all a great pity. Earlier one could imagine the family still living there, as was still the case with Tolstoy's town house, kept as if the family were still in residence. That evening we went, Daphne and I, to a quite dreadful play *Overseas Guests* about a British Parliamentary delegation visiting the Caucasus – boring and an insult to the intelligence of any normal person. We walked out after the second act.

Monday 20 Feb. I took Inger (Börje Kwarnmark's secretary) to the Moscow Conservatoire to listen to graduate composers attending the performance of their graduate compositions – five of them. The first to come on the stage to receive plaudits was about 23 years old and looked like a miner coming off duty, the last sort of person you would suspect of composing symphonies. I was going more and more to the Conservatoire; not so many diplomats went there and I could usually get good seats (or seat because I quite often went on my own) in the centre of the front row within feet of the soloist. Rostropovich was a frequent recitalist on the cello and it was quite embarrassing to sit close in front of him because when playing he was a man possessed, contorting his face and grappling with his cello like a monkey on a stick. During passages where the orchestra was playing without him, he would hum or almost sing the music. But what inspiring music he extorted from his cello! I am sometimes amazed that before I went to Moscow my musical sense was mute and dumb, or quiescent. In Moscow I was often inspired by music, moved to tears and cheers. After the concert Inger came home to my flat and cooked us a passable omelette, which we washed down with champagne. Wednesday I took her to a performance of Faust at the Bolshoi.

Thursday was Red Army Day, which I attended with Betty Donkin, Peter being away again in London. We arrived late at the reception and Betty hurried off to join a table where Stan Turner and other senior attachés and their ladies were sitting, while I joined a table of Russian generals, both Soviet Army and Air Force. They had already been drinking. One roared *"Shtraff! Priyekhal pozdno!"* (Penalty! Arrived late!) and poured 100g of vodka into my glass with the order *"Zalpom!"* (In one!). This was to be expected. But another General then refilled our glasses and beckoned me to my feet with the toast *"Za vashei korolyevoi!"* (To your Queen!) The second 100g went the way of the first and so did more, although I was trying to get away with sips rather than gulps, difficult in company of this sort. After about an hour I exchanged glances with Betty at her table, where she was having similar difficulties. We rose as one, bade farewell to our Russian hosts, and, clutching each other as discreetly as possible, retrieved our coats from the *garderobe* (cloakroom) while Soviet NCO's used a walkie-talkie to summon the Air Attaché's driver and car, a large Humber Super Snipe limousine with a retractable glass screen between the passenger seats and the driver. After dropping Betty at her flat I was driven home and collapsed into bed.

On Friday Daphne gave me a 34th birthday party at her flat. There were no Russians present but we spoke Russian because it was the only common language. The day after, 25 February 1956, was memorable in Russian and Soviet history – in world history one might say. At a plenary session of the 20th Party Congress of the Communist Party of the Soviet Union, Khrushchev denounced, dethroned and unmasked Stalin. In a long speech he demonstrated beyond any doubt that Stalin had been a crude and cruel tyrant, acting against the interests of the Soviet people, against its institutions and organisations, contrary to the doctrines propounded by Lenin and even by Marx and Engels. Khrushchev started right back when Stalin had replaced Lenin on the latter's death; he produced detailed cases of communist leaders and groups who had been liquidated on Stalin's orders to preserve his own position – the cult of personality, Khrushchev called it. The full text of the speech can be read on the Internet. The address was a bombshell. Until then Stalin had been treated as a God. At a Soviet secondary school (No.1, where all tuition was in English), which I visited later, both teachers and students told me of the dismay occasioned by the fall of their God, by the irrefutable evidence that he had been a devil all the time.

We at the Embassy quickly learned about this. Of course nobody other than Soviet delegates and officials could be present at the Congress. However the denunciation of Stalin was soon being debated at meetings of various Soviet organisations, including Moscow University. Here we did have an informant.

Max Hayward, an Oxford graduate in Russian, had been in Moscow in 1946 and 1947 as Third Secretary in the British Embassy. Because of his fluency in Russian he had interpreted in discussions with Stalin and other high ranking officials, Ministers etc., and had come to know the Soviet scene like the back of his hand. After his tour in Moscow he joined the University of Leeds as a lecturer in the Department of Russian. In 1955 he had returned to the Moscow Embassy on a temporary appointment to the Secretariat.

Not only was Max a fluent speaker of Russian. He fell straight into the part (if it were a part and not just his own nature) of a fairly mature Soviet student, dressing and behaving in character (scruffily), even smoking his fags like a Russian, holding his samokrutki (self-rolled shag, in newspaper as often as not) cupped in his hand, drinking like them, speaking like them, indistinguishable from them. In this respect he was a bit of a menace, especially as, like a Stanislavsky trained actor, he could not easily relinquish his role, possibly did not want to, but went on living it for hours or days or weeks, in the company of his Embassy colleagues as well as in the Soviet environment outside. Max had friends in Moscow University and attended meetings where Khruschev's denunciation was debated.

Max went further. Not long after the Congress, he denounced Stalin himself, standing drunk on a table in a restaurant in Tblisi, the capital city of Georgia, Stalin's birthplace in the Caucasus, where even now Stalin is a hero. This coincided with demonstrations against the dethronement of their Wunderkind by thousands of Georgians in the Caucasus generally and especially in Gori, where Stalin was born. Max's drunken outburst, witnessed with acute alarm by an Embassy colleague travelling with him, led to his hurried departure from the Soviet Union. Sir William Hayter was back in London discussing the B&K (Bulganin and Krushchev) visit and Cecil Parrott, the Minister and Chargé d'Affaires, anticipated Max being expelled and sent him home. He returned later as a correspondent for the *Daily Telegraph*, but soon left again, terrorised, he said, by the secret police. I drove him to the airport and he told me that he was constantly followed by the KGB in a car with four goons! I told him that I was always followed by three cars with five goons in each! He was impressed but still thought he was in danger. Maybe he was, because as a correspondent he no longer benefited from diplomatic immunity. Anyway it was from Max that we got the nitty-gritty of the reactions of Soviet citizens to the dethronement of Stalin. I met Max later at St Anthony's College in Oxford where he was lecturing and writing books about Soviet and Russian personalities. What a man! He came to an untimely death in 1979 at the age of 55, of cancer, but his steep decline was aggravated by years of heavy drinking.[1]

On Saturday 3 March I went skiing with Betty Donkin and then to the Conservatoire with her in the evening. Next morning I left with Peter Lewis on a trip that should have taken in Minsk, Vitebsk, Kiev, Simferopol, Zaporozhe and Kharkov. It did not work out like this. We had sent Vasili Karasyov, my driver, with the Standard Vanguard, to Kiev, from where we had intended to drive to Kharkov. Close to the main road there were several Soviet Air Force bases, which we wished to check for activity. The weather was very cold but not so much as to freeze the mud hard. For several hours the road was passable but we were then stopped by militiamen who refused to allow us to continue to Kharkov by the direct road and diverted us onto unpaved roads through open country and the occasional village and communal farm. The dirt roads were deep rutted mud that our Vanguard could not cope with. Fortunately we still had our escort of goons in their GAZ 69, a jeep-like, off-road vehicle. They were also having trouble with the mud. We decided to help them if they would help us and agreed with them that we would keep each other company as far as Kharkov, towing each other as and when necessary. This worked very well, but we never saw the airfields.

A week or so later, our American colleagues made the same journey. The weather was better and they were not forced to use dirt tracks. When they neared the airfields a motorcycle and sidecar passed them and stopped a short distance ahead where the officer in the sidecar could be seen struggling into his uniform preparatory to stopping the US attachés. When they drew abreast, the officer had his tunic on but no time to change into his service trousers. The US Assistant Military Attaché called out: *"Where's your trousers?"* and drove on past. The same thing happened a few miles further on but this time neither side could keep straight faces and the matter was treated as a great joke. A few miles further still and the US vehicle broke down. To the rescue came the Russians on their bike. By radio they summoned a military breakdown vehicle, which towed the Americans right into the air base they wished to survey.

In both cases the goons were provincial and not our Moscow teams, otherwise they would have had to be changed to follow some other foreigner with nefarious intentions. They did not like this because it meant studying the new target to find out as much as possible about his or her aims, habits, likes and dislikes. We were not entirely sure about goons and their ways, but reached conclusions on the basis of experience. When particularly fed up with them we arranged for confrontations which we assumed would lead to their being switched between targets. About this time a whole clutch of US Embassy staff, including some good friends of mine, was declared *persona non grata* and had to leave by the next available flight. I cannot recall why, but probably they were suspected of blatant espionage. Subtle espionage was only to be expected, but blatant espionage was indecent behaviour (sometimes literally).

After seeing off this batch of Americans from Vnukovo Airport, I was driving back to Moscow followed by the usual Pobeda full of goons when I decided to get my own back.

In the suburbs I turned off the main road in the southwest suburbs of Moscow (an area I knew quite well) and then jinked round several crossings, stopping immediately to let the goons get ahead on the previous road, and waiting for them to double back on a parallel road. It was then fairly easy to get on their trail, following them as they tried to get back on mine. I arranged my route to get them to lose themselves in a region of lanes and building sites until they entered one building development with deep mud and mountains of building materials (bricks were never stacked as would be the case at home, but deposited higgledy-piggledy from tipper trucks in heaps which would have stopped a tank). Here the goon car stalled in a building site morass from which no amount of revving up could unstick it. I got out of my Vanguard and approached them, not bent on violence but on embarrassment. On my approach the five occupants spread newspapers in front of their faces as if they had come solely to catch up on their reading, conveniently hiding their faces from my eyes. I drove back to the Embassy satisfied with myself.

Baiting goons sometimes backfired. They could get their own back. There was an area in NW Moscow where the out of bounds area for us attachés was much less than the usual 40km.

The line on our maps delineating the forbidden area came within about 12km of the Moscow inner ring road, forbidding our access to quite a large area of woodland, with no obvious features such as factories, airfields, military installations, or concentration camplets. Of these latter there were quite a few scattered about Moscow, one clearly observable from our flat. Daphne and I determined to see if we could find out why we should be prevented from entering those woods. Driving the Standard Vanguard, with Daphne in the passenger seat, I first concentrated on losing our goons. After about ten minutes driving round side-streets I was fairly confident that I had lost the goons for enough time to get to our target. The road I followed should have crossed the area we wished to examine. However, it narrowed to a track and then to very little more than a footpath through trees and dense undergrowth. Realising I could not take the car any further I stopped and dismounted to walk forward and see if the path possibly widened beyond the tangle of shrubs.

I had gone 50 yards when Daphne called from the car, and looking round I saw I was being approached by a Major of Frontier Troops, recognisable from their green pogonies (shoulder boards). He introduced himself, flashed his identity card and said: *"Major Deverill, you have entered a forbidden area and I shall have to report this to the Ministry of Defence".* Not often at a loss, I replied: *"No, I am not. The forbidden area starts 200 metres along that path"* pointing at the path down which I had just walked. *"Let us compare our maps".* He either had no map or did not wish to produce it, but I showed him precisely where we were on my own map borrowed from the stock of maps held in our Embassy, many out of date, but good enough for my purpose. The Major agreed. He had no other option and I heard no more about the incident. But how, we wondered, did he know we were there at all. We thought that possibly my Vanguard, serviced entirely by Soviet mechanics, might have been bugged with a simple radio responder beacon as had some of the cars of other embassies.

For some of these sorties by car I would drive myself; for others it was better to have Vasili driving. He would do exactly what I asked him to, because he was associated with the KGB and MVD and would report whatever we had done. There were other dangers in driving oneself. We drove on our UK licenses and they were enough for identification. We also always carried our Diplomatic Cards, small booklets with our personal details, appointments etc., issued to us by the Soviet Ministry of Foreign Affairs. However, one wrong step, a road accident or contravention of the Soviet traffic laws, could mean being debarred from driving until one had passed the Soviet driving test – a difficult examination, part written, part practical, including a technical examination to show that you could repair your vehicle in simple breakdowns, adjust a carburettor, change tyres, modify timing etc. The exam could be delayed or marked so as effectively to prevent a candidate from ever driving on his own again in the USSR. So one had to be careful.

Once I very nearly had a road accident that could have been serious. Driving to Tsaritzina to ski, I came over the brow of a hill from which the narrow tarmac road ran downhill in a dead straight line for several miles. About half a mile ahead I could see a blue motorcycle and sidecar stationary in the centre of the road waiting to turn left when a heavy truck had passed in the opposite direction. The truck was travelling slowly and the motorcycle combination could easily have turned in front of it, but the motorcyclist preferred to wait. As I approached I could see that the occupants of the motorcycle combination were uniformed militiamen. I applied my brakes but the road was a sheet of frozen snow packed down by earlier traffic. I started to skid, eased off on the brakes and changed down to a lower gear, lightly stabbing the brakes to the point when skids recurred. At 300m the heavy truck was still approaching and the motorbike and sidecar were still in the centre of the narrow road with no room to pass on the near side where there was deep snow piled up with the trees poking through. By now I was down to 20mph and slowly slowing but a crash seemed inevitable. The militiamen had not seen me coming; they were focussing on the approaching truck. Down to 10mph but still sliding. At the last moment the truck passed and the motorbike and militiamen turned into the side road with me glissading past their rear, metaphorically mopping my brow.

News from home that Pat and Mike had had their first child, Jacqueline (Jackie), born in Salisbury in Odstock Hospital on 5 February 1956, while I was driving out to Stockholm. Not to be outdone (were they ever?) Mary and Titus had their second child, Mary Ann, at St Mary's Hospital Paddington on 9 March. Dad went up to see them on Sunday 11 March. He was disappointed that they had not named her after Angioletta, or used one of her other three names. In southern England there had been three weeks of snow and frost and quite a few plants in the garden had succumbed. I wrote home that I was very sad and angry that Glubb Pasha had been dismissed as Chief of Staff of the Arab Legion. He had been dismissed on 2 March by the 20-year-old King Hussein. He flew home via Cyprus with his wife and Naomi and Godfrey. Several other senior Arab Legion officers were dismissed at the same time and many others followed. The Legion was being Jordanised, but with hindsight this was inevitable and the best thing to do.

In Moscow I was looking forward to my next trip and studying for the RAF Staff College entrance examinations. On Sunday 18 March 1956 I had a telephone call from Peter Donkin to explain that he had just been telephoned by OTDEL (Department of Foreign Affairs of the Ministry of Defence if you have forgotten) to say that they wished to fly a Tupolev (TU) 104 passenger jet aircraft to London the following Thursday with Colonel General Serov, the head of the KGB (Committee of State Security), for discussions with Special Branch and others involved with security during the proposed visit to the UK of Bulganin and Khrushchev (B&K) from 18 to 27 April 1956.

Serov would be staying in London about a week. OTDEL asked for a British screen (safety) pilot to interpret for the Soviet pilot and his crew, none of whom spoke English. Peter told me what I already knew – that it would take the RAF more than a week to identify a pilot who spoke Russian fluently enough to be safe in this role, which would involve a knowledge of transport flying, Air Traffic Control, and experience of flying jet aircraft. I seemed to be ideally qualified.

Would I like to go? Would I! I responded enthusiastically and set about collecting together the equipment I might need – pencil, ruler, note-book, and a navigational computer, developed from the Dalton computer, a hand-held, aluminium, circular slide rule on one side and on the other a rotary plastic window enabling one to use a wax pencil to mark in a triangle of velocities. Using this I could convert kph to mph, feet to metres, etc. and find true airspeeds by marking in drift and wind etc., all aspects of pilot navigation, some of which might be needed on the flight. Lucky we still had that computer in the office!

The TU 104 was a passenger jet aircraft said to have been developed from the TU16 Badger medium bomber of which a number of units were based in White Russia and on bases which I had seen from the train, travelling from Leningrad to Odessa for instance. The passenger variant had not yet been seen close-up by western observers, although one had flown past at Tushino during the 1955 air show. It was obviously going to be a fascinating business to fly in one. For the forthcoming visit of B&K to the UK it had not yet been decided whether they would travel in TU 104s or by Soviet naval vessel. As the group including the two leaders was likely to number the best part of 50, at least two TU104's would be needed, and probably more because high level delegations always have to carry a large amount of supporting equipment and material. Apart from anything else Krushchev had responsibility for the Soviet armed forces, including their nuclear weapons and would need the technical back up in case of a war breaking out, unlikely, but it had to be planned for. Then there would be presents to give to British counterparts and a multitude of other sizeable bits and pieces.

On 19 March Sir William Hayter spoke on Soviet TV about the forthcoming B&K visit to Britain. He spoke in English with John Morgan interpreting. John at once became a TV star. He looked very handsome – dark, broad-shouldered, widely spaced eyes – and spoke clearly in excellent Russian, without any self-consciousness. Sir William looked every inch the British diplomat but John Morgan outshone him as the sort of man Russian women liked.

Meanwhile Malenkov, a Deputy Chairman of the USSR Council of Ministers, and, conveniently, Minister for Electric Power Stations, was sent on a mission to the UK to liaise with the Central Electricity Generating Board and make a variety of visits both in the field of his ministry and more general visits fairly clearly designed to test the water for the B&K visit later. He and his supporting officials flew to London in two IL12 aircraft (rather like a Convair) on 15 March. He had been expected to stay a week but in fact stayed for three, visiting industrial centres all over the UK and finishing with a pilgrimage to Burns' cottage in Alloway where they bade him farewell with an impromptu chorus of Auld Lang Syne.

Earlier at lunch at the British Embassy, Malenkov had admitted to being a fan of Burns, who was approved by the Communist Party as a "social reformer".

In the meantime further details of the B&K visit emerged. The party would number 44 including two doctors, two cooks and two waitresses. They would travel by cruiser to Portsmouth from Kaliningrad. Security would be in the hands of Colonel General Serov, who would also accompany B&K throughout their visit. This is why he was going to fly to London in the TU104 on Thursday 22 March. That morning I was collected from my flat in Ul. Narodnaya at about 8a.m. by a Soviet staff car with Major Chuvilsky, one of my friends from OTDEL, and his superior, a Colonel, who sat beside the Corporal driver. Senior Soviets always liked to drive in front, which sometimes led to awkwardness when a British chauffeur alighted to open the rear door for his Soviet passenger, who had already opened the nearside front door and was getting in next to the chauffeur's Thermos flask and sandwiches.

We set off at a brisk pace down the Kutusovskiy Prospekt in the direction of Mozhaisk, a city 100km west of and close to Borodino, where the battle between Napoleon's French army and Kutusov's Russian army took place in 1812. At 40km from Moscow I was interested to pass quite close to the bunkers of the inner ring of the Soviet Wasserfall defences of Moscow. We were travelling through thick forests of conifers and silver birch. Much of the winter snow had melted but some was left in drifts among the trees. Our driver apparently knew this area and started to talk about the abundance of mushrooms (*griby*) to be found, indicating particularly favoured places.

The Colonel proposed we stop to have a pee and a look round and we all disembarked and made our way over fallen trees and matted undergrowth into the forest. It was very muddy.

We found quite a few mushrooms of the sort categorised as toadstools in England, highly doubtful, but stowed away in the car for taking back to Moscow. There was a shout from the driver who had slipped up to his knees into a ditch, emerging very muddy indeed. We decided to drive on. At about 70km from Moscow (the roads were marked with kilometre posts) we turned off not far from a small town, Kubinka, with an air base close by, easily identified from afar by its characteristic water tower.

As we approached the runways I was able to see a large jet aircraft drawn up, surrounded by some 20 military personnel, some obviously senior, and a similar number of engineers and ground crew. Several generals stood together in a group close to the access ladder to the aircraft. They seemed to have been waiting for us; not surprising because we were over half an hour late for take-off. The OTDEL

Colonel approached a senior general to report our arrival, and explain why we were late. ("*Collecting mushrooms, Comrade General*"). Our driver looked sheepish standing at attention in his bare feet with his muddy boots in one hand. The explanation was accepted. To collect mushrooms is practically a sacred Russian rite, like a Muslim praying to Mecca.

I was introduced to Colonel General Serov, the centre of all attention, and to Lt.Col. Starikov, the Captain of the TU104. Serov had succeeded Beria as the head of the KGB. He had a record almost as bad as Beria's. Apart from various purges and executions in the 30s he had led the persecution and exile of much of the population of the Baltic states during WW2, was held responsible for the massacre of the Polish army officers at Katyn and later the execution of many of the Vlasov army who had sided with the Germans hoping to liberate Russia from the communists. Later Serov was dismissed and liquidated but right now he was flying to London with me. Lt.Col. Starikov was a splendid person, a pilot from the Soviet Farnborough at Ramenskoye, quiet, level-headed and a master of his craft, as I soon discovered. In addition to Starikov, the aircrew comprised a second pilot (First Officer) who also acted as navigator, and a flight engineer and radio officer. General Serov also had an un-uniformed steward with him to do the "house-keeping". I was told to sit in the cabin with General Serov until I was needed after Berlin.

There was a main cabin aft, with room for about 28 passenger seats or freight, and in front of it four smaller "VIP" cabins, the first across the whole width of the aircraft, where Serov and I sat down, with two smaller cabins further forward, both on the starboard side. These were faced on the port side by the galley and a pantry where Serov's steward established himself. In our cabin we sat in two armchairs for take-off. There was also a sofa and circular table within reach. As a concession to safety the furniture was fastened to the floor by chains, as in public rooms in some ocean liners. The three-piece suite was deeply upholstered in red plush. The circular windows were trimmed on the inside with mahogany mouldings and could be shaded by adjusting the cords of brocade curtains. The bulkheads between the smaller cabins were lined with transparent cabinets with similar shelves to which porcelain Dresden shepherdesses and suchlike were stapled. All in all a folksy scene.

Take-off was interesting for me because the jet engines made a great noise, acceleration was exhilarating and initial climb steep. I busied myself with a book (of technical terms I might need to use) while the General rose and went forward to speak to the aircrew and look ahead through the windscreen. The steward shuttled between our cabin and the galley, preparing lunch. At an early stage

General Serov invited me to eat with him. We first had vodka and selyodki (herring filets in brine), very tasty and a Russian speciality. This was followed by a large chunk of cold boiled beef with potato salad and pickled gherkins, also rye bread, butter and hard boiled eggs, boiled in sand, the General explained, far better than water, because the eggs never broke. This was accompanied by red wine from the General's vineyards in Georgia. All very good. We finished with cognac from the General's Armenian estate. Then black tea, very sweet. We spoke of my travels. Serov asked if there was anywhere I particularly wished to visit. I said Vorkuta, the place to which he had exiled more than one Soviet citizen. Certainly, he said. Remind him when we were back in Moscow.

By the end of lunch we were already approaching Berlin so I moved forward to the crew compartment with my computer. I had to stand in the gap between and just behind the two pilots' seats, in a position where I could shout in their ears. The weather was fine. We were flying at 10,000m at a speed of about 800kph. I was given a throat microphone for communicating with air traffic control over western Europe, but at that stage it was just a matter of booking in with the various centres involved, who had already been warned that a Soviet aircraft would be crossing their airspace. The navigation technique was radio beacon crawling – that is, the First Officer tuned in one of the on route beacons and the radio compass needle pointed towards it and when the aircraft was overhead and the needle reversed, the next beacon was tuned in. There was little for me to do other than convert barometric pressures so that Starikov could adjust his altimeter. After Amsterdam and towards the middle of the North Sea I contacted London Radar and from that time on we were under their guidance, altering course to follow the airways on which Starikov had already been briefed.

Let-down started soon after. Landing was going to be on runway 27 (i.e. due west) and the idea was to bring us in from the north-east, losing altitude in steps to maintain separation from other aircraft, reducing speed as we came lower, with a shallow turn on to final approach some eight miles from the runway threshold. I was kept busy passing Captain Starikov instructions from London Radar until London Airport (LAP) Approach Control took over about ten miles out. Then it was a matter of converting speeds from kilometres per hour (kph) to knots, heights from feet to metres and rates of descent from feet a minute to metres a second and vice-versa.

The TU 104 had the disadvantage of having no air brakes and a reduction to circuit speed could only be achieved reasonably quickly by lowering the undercarriage, which Starikov preferred not to do until late in the approach because the increased drag would mean using more fuel. And fuel was a vital concern. London Radar and Approach Control therefore had the job of fitting our TU 104 into a queue of slower piston-engined aircraft (Constellations, Stratocruisers etc.) also on the approach. It all worked out OK. On the ground we were led by a "Follow me Vehicle" to a position on the tarmac well away from the other aircraft parked nearer the terminal buildings. This was to provide space for the reception party, which was allowed out to the aircraft, and to make it easier to guard the aircraft over the days it was staying at Heathrow.

The flight had taken three hours and 36 minutes for the 1564 statute miles from Kubinka. In addition to "interpreting" I had noted down as many details as I could of the operating temperatures, pressures and other salient details registered by the cockpit instruments, as well as operational techniques used by the crew. As we had very few details of this aircraft and its engines, anything I could note would be useful. The RAF Deputy Directorate of Intelligence (DDITech) knew I was coming in on the TU 104, and one of their photographers was able to photograph the TU 104 as it was landing.

The Media met us in force, and after Serov and his party had disembarked a BBC journalist who had entered the aircraft came up to the front where I was packing up my gear in the cockpit. He asked me questions about the flight and I was nothing if not complimentary. *"She flies beautifully"* I said, and I think these were the only words of mine reported. Two years earlier, the flights of the De Havilland Comet, the first passenger jet aircraft in service, had been stopped after two disastrous crashes, later discovered to have been caused by pressure cabin fatigue. This was a great setback for British aviation and the appearance of a Soviet passenger jet of about the same capacity must have been disturbing to say the least. Flight, The Aeroplane and Aeronautics, three British journals specialising in aviation, published comprehensive articles about the TU 104 in late March and early April 1956, mostly complimentary but pointing out possible or probable deficiencies, only to be expected of an aircraft modelled on the Badger bomber.

The view was that the TU 104 was a Badger with a new body, and modified engines of a size much larger than any the UK and USA were considering for a passenger jet at that time. The engines were probably inefficient (they were, as I discovered later). The undercarriage was very high, having been adapted from the Badger when its mid-wing was moved to a low wing format. The nose and crew cabin were pure Badger, even incorporating the transparent nose and flat bomb panel, and the chin radar, used in the Badger for target identification, and in the TU 104 for storm spotting and probably other things. Overall, the journals thought, the TU 104 was not a threat to western passenger jets under construction. I was told later that I was on BBC TV that evening and caused a stir locally in Alton. The Alton Herald gave me a mention. Fame indeed!

As I needed to be within reach of Heathrow for the return flight and had to be available for various meetings at Air Ministry to talk with technical boffins about the TU 104 and its performance, I found a hotel in the Bayswater Road, the Coburn Court Hotel, a nice quiet, comfortable and comparatively inexpensive hotel, where good meals were always obtainable. This became my base, and I used it for subsequent TU 104 flights, of which more anon. Over the weekend I took the train home to see my father and fill him in on all that had occurred and would be occurring.

Serov had his talks with Special Branch and I expect MI5 and people from the Foreign Office. He did not get a good press because his misdeeds were known to large numbers of immigrants to the UK and there was no end to the insults he received from the press, on the radio etc. When I met him again at Heathrow on Tuesday 27 March, he was distant and less friendly than on the way to London. We took off at 0815 and after performing my interpreting duties and getting us to 10,000m and out of our airspace without incident I spent the time after Berlin helping Serov's steward to sideline and cut out from the previous weeks' daily and Sunday papers the press reports relating to his boss. He was keen to ignore some of the more virulent but I was not having that and made sure he served up the lot.

Lunch was not as lively as that on the 22nd, and the food not as good, having been loaded at Heathrow. I thought it unwise to mention Vorkuta again. Getting back, we landed at Moscow Vnukova rather than at the airbase at Kubinka. Serov was met by a panoply of senior military officers who made much of him. I was left to collect my things and trudge back towards the terminal building hoping that Vasili would be there with the car. Halfway, there was a swish of tyres and Serov's large black ZIL limousine came to a halt beside me. Out stepped Serov and a tall elegantly dressed woman. He said: *"Major Deverill, I could not leave without thanking you with all my heart for your work in getting us safely to England and back. May I introduce my wife"*. We shook hands all round and they re-entered the car and went their way. I was quite moved. Could this be a cruel tyrant! Vasili met me and drove me back to Narodnaya. I was not there long. A week later OTDEL were on again. Could Major Deverill accompany another TU 104 flight to London on Friday 6 April. The aircraft was going there to bring back Malenkov from his visit to the UK. I said I could. This time we went from Moscow Vnukovo airport. It was a different crew. Boris Pavlovich Bugaev was Captain. Nominally he was an Aeroflot Captain but also a Soviet Air Force Lieutenant Colonel. There was overlap here. At the met (meteorological) briefing we noted that there would be a strong head wind for the flight, which might stretch our ability to reach Heathrow with enough fuel to cover a diversion or stand-off.

But we took off anyway. On this flight we were not carrying much, other than spare tyres, to be stock-piled in London for possible use on later TU 104 flights. The flight was as before, without obvious complications until we were approaching the mid-point of the North Sea. I noticed a red warning light come on and asked what it meant. Half an hour's fuel left I was told. This was slightly worrying. Landing at London would be on runway 27 as on the previous occasion but with a lower cloud base of about 1000'. There was a lot of traffic (air traffic) at Heathrow and we were led south of the airport and intended to make a clockwise circuit before joining the queue on final approach. However, Bugaev was getting very worried about his fuel state. Looking out of the window to starboard he shouted in Russian: *"I can see the runway and am going to land"*. I said: *"No. You must land from the other direction"*. In vain – we turned over Windsor Castle at about 300 feet (strictly forbidden) with the Air Traffic Controller asking me why I was not obeying his instructions. I replied: *"Pilot refuses to do so. Turning final on 09!"* The Controller stood off all traffic using that runway and allowed us in on 09, partly downwind, but the runway was long enough for us to stop using a lot of brake (and tyre rubber. Hence the spare tyres).

On this occasion we were staying one night only and there was no time for me to do more than phone Dad from the Coburn Court Hotel, where I established myself again. Early next day I took a taxi to Heathrow and waited by the parked TU 104 until Malenkov and his retinue arrived. We took off at 08.30 or thereabouts. Climbing away from Heathrow led to another argument with Bugaev who wanted to climb to height at once, whereas Control kept us at 3,000' until we were clear of other traffic near the North Foreland. Climbed to 10,000m and flew the airway as far as Berlin where my role as "leader" (Russian *lider)* ended. This time I was expected to stay up front in the cockpit, already an accepted member of the crew. Over Poland Bugaev contacted Moscow and received reports of bad conditions there – driving snow (Russian *metel*), low cloud base and bad visibility. Closer to Moscow we were initially diverted to Ramenskoye, the Soviet Farnborough, a place I had never managed to get near to, because of the secret work going on there.

I envisaged a scoop *par excellence* "RAF Pilot lands at Secret Soviet Airfield" the London headlines might read. But it was not to be. The diversion was probably vetoed by the airfield MVD representative. We were told to land at

Moscow Vnukova, from where we had taken off the day before. Bugaev told me that he would land using the Soviet equivalent of GCA (Ground Controlled Approach), when the pilot had to do little but obey the patter of the Ground Controller working from a radar equipped cabin at the approach end of the runway. Standing between the two pilots I was keeping my eyes on the altimeter and at the murk through the windscreen – no sign of anything but snow whipping past and the grey mass of cloud through which we were descending.

The terrain at Vnukovo and for miles around was flat, covered with small conifers and silver birch, better than hills and mountains for landing in these conditions. Several of Malenkov's party pressed up front, obviously apprehensive and trying to get a better view. At about 100m the aircraft broke cloud and I saw that we were approaching the illuminated runway obliquely at an angle of 30° and would intersect it at a point several hundred metres down its length from the threshold. Worse, the runway had been partially cleared of snow, dumped, probably blown by the powerful snow clearance machines, in two ridges ten feet or more high one each side of the runway. Initially Bugaev seemed determined to try to land from this position and foreseeing a crash I slipped behind the bulkhead between the pilot's seat and the navigator's position and braced my back against it, sitting down on the floor. One bounce and Bugaev opened up the engines again and we climbed back to 1,000'.

With an oath Bugaev abandoned the GCA option and turned his attention to the Radio Compasses. These were tuned to the two radio beacons positioned on the runway centre line, one 8km and the other 1km from the threshold. Making a circuit of the airfield using two radio compasses, whose needles pointed in different directions depending on the relative positions of the aircraft and the beacons was more than my mind could encompass, but Bugaev's training made this look easy. On this occasion when we were lined up with the runway I could see the two radio compass needles both pointing straight ahead and the aircraft descended and broke cloud at about 50m, more or less in line with the runway, I say more or less because the strong wind was blowing across the runway and a correction was necessary at the last moment before the wheels touched down. For the previous ten minutes Malenkov, and as many of his entourage as could squeeze up, had filled the entrance from the cabin to the cockpit and they had not hesitated to shout words of encouragement and advice to Bugaev, who had his hands full and could have done without this. He touched down and streamed the emergency braking parachute with which these aircraft were fitted. We stopped in the middle of the runway and the passengers raised a cheer and shook hands all round. Only then could we taxi in and disembark.

We were met by officials from Malenkov's office and by representatives from several foreign embassies because Malenkov was still a member of the Presidium and an important man. Sir William wrote it up in his memoirs:[2]

> *I went to meet him on his return, a rather hair-raising experience. It was a blustery overcast day, and his TU 104, the then very new Soviet jet airliner, appeared out of the clouds at Vnukovo, failed to land and took off again into the overcast. My Air Attaché who was with me told me the aircraft could not have fuel for more than five minutes flying time left, and we were worried for Malenkov's safety as well as that of our Assistant Air Attaché who was on board (the latter told us he was sure a crash was imminent and had taken up an appropriate position in the aircraft). We kept our anxieties from Malenkov's wife and daughter, who were standing with us, and in due course the aircraft came round again and landed safely, its parachute brakes trailing. Malenkov appeared beaming at the top of the steps and invited us on board to look at the new aircraft. Outside its lines were splendidly smooth and modern; inside it was furnished, as Miss Nancy Mitford said of another Soviet plane, like a cottage, with a great deal of red plush and china figurines in glass cases.*

Over the next few days the Russian media reported that some organisations in the UK had shown themselves to be unfriendly towards the Soviet Union. These reports probably derived from Serov's press clippings! On the other hand Malenkov was reported to have been met by friendliness everywhere. On 11 April he and his wife lunched at the Embassy and I was seated nearby and heard his accounts of his visits especially to Scotland and Rabbie Burns. By now it had been decided to rule out the TU 104's as transport for B&K to travel to London, possibly because it was realised that westerly winds made the westward flight too long to be absolutely safe. The party would leave on 15 April in the Soviet cruiser Ordjonikidze from Baltiysk, the naval port of Kaliningrad, once Prussian, but Soviet since the end of WW2. They would arrive in Portsmouth on 18 April. Already on 12 April an RAF Hastings of Transport Command landed at Vnukovo to take Sir William and Lady Hayter back to the UK to meet B&K at Portsmouth with Prime Minister Anthony Eden, and then accompany the party on their programme. Captain Adrian Northey, the British Naval Attaché in the Embassy, left for Kaliningrad to sail with B&K on the Ordjonikidze.

At about the same time Lysenko was removed from his post as President of the All-Union Academy of Agricultural Sciences. He had propounded the doctrine that nurture rather than nature drove evolution, a doctrine that was ridiculed by western scientists, and held back Soviet biological sciences by many years. He had been a protégé of Stalin, who liked to think that Soviet Man was a product of advances in Soviet society, especially politics, rather than genetics.

On 18 April B&K were met at Portsmouth by Anthony Eden and his Foreign Secretary Harold Macmillan. They then took the Royal Train to Victoria Station where the Soviet party was to stay at Claridges, taking over an entire floor. That evening there was a dinner at the hotel hosted by Eden. John Morgan, who had flown back to London with the Hayters, and Tom Brimelow, Head of the Russian Department of the FO were there to help. That same day I was on another flight from Vnukovo to Heathrow in a TU 104, carrying presents for the British hosts, from a brown bear for Princess Anne, through works of art, down to nesting wooden babushkas for the less important people. No one was forgotten. The bear, named Nikki, possibly after Nikita Khrushchev, (a good example of his humour) was a young but surprisingly large cub, transported in a wooden cage, and tended by his keeper. I was warned not to try to touch it. On this occasion there was another pilot flying – Nikolai Alekseyvich Usanov. We had no difficulty with the flight or landing. We returned to Moscow the next day. I had spent the night at the Coburn Court Hotel where I had more or less been allotted a room of my own, because I had been warned that there would be more flights.

While B&K were in Britain, there were two more TU 104 flights, one with Bugaev again and another with Konstantin Ksefondaryovich Kashova. I was able to note down details about practically every obvious characteristic of the aircraft and its operation. One thing that intrigued me was the management of the fuel. An illuminated display on the roof of the cabin between the two pilots showed which tanks were feeding the engines. As far as I recall there were five or seven tanks in the wings and fuselage. The display showed which tanks were in use and their contents and there were switches to allow the flight engineer to override the automatic sequence in which the tanks were used. This was to compensate for movement of the centre of gravity away from the centre of lift. As a transport captain (on Dakotas) I had been instructed in loading techniques, stowing freight in different locations in the cabin to ensure that a balance was achieved where the centre of lift and the centre of gravity did not diverge so much as to affect adversely the handling of the aircraft.

With jet aircraft, using enormous quantities of heavy fuel from tanks in different parts of the aircraft, there was (and still is) a need to preserve the balance of the aircraft. To take an extreme example, if tons of fuel are used from a tank in the tail, it will tend to rise and the nose to dip, eventually leading to a situation where the pilot will have to pull back on the control column and use his trimming tabs to maintain attitude and height. One can get the same effect in a small aircraft like a Dakota (DC3) if too many passengers queue up at the back to visit the loo, or run up and down the aisle in the passenger cabin to look out of a window at some interesting sight. This used to lead to peremptory orders to passengers from the Captain via a stewardess for passengers to return to their seats. The fuel management system in the TU 104 was very sophisticated and I had not come across this before.

On one of these flights I was invited by Bugaev, whom I had come to know better than the other skippers, to sit in the First Officer's seat to sample the aircraft's handling. I had asked about directional stability, and with Bugaev sitting in the Captain's seat and me next to him, he demonstrated by putting both his feet on the starboard rudder pedal and then pushing it with all the strength of both his legs. The aircraft yawed violently to starboard and then, left to its own devices, returned, after a bit of hunting about, to stable flight. He then did the same using the elevators, pushing the control column hard forward to the dashboard. The nose dropped and the negative G (gravity) resulted in pencils, notebooks, coffee mugs (empty fortunately) and dust and grit from the floor, flying up towards the cabin roof. Once again, with hands off the control column, flight quickly returned to stability in the vertical plane. We were carrying two stewardesses on that flight and they rushed in from the passenger cabin to find out what the emergency was and to complain at the spillages that had occurred aft. Fortunately we were not carrying passengers on this flight.

I did not get as far as landing or taking off, but one can understand that the pilots would want to retain responsibility for these most critical events in flying. Landing, and even more take-off, are potentially the most dangerous moments for an aircraft and its crew, when a technical or personal failure can bring disaster and a well-trained pilot at the controls is essential. The TU 104 was a very heavy aircraft to fly at low speeds, as for instance when landing, and on several occasions I witnessed both Captain and First Officer wrestling with the controls, which at that low speed needed all their physical strength.

I got the distinct impression that the TU 104 had been designed to be "peasant proof" and there was lots of room for crew members. This contrasted greatly with the Comet where one had to be careful when getting into the pilot's or co-pilot's seat that one did not switch on or off any one or more of a number of switches, push levers and buttons the effect of which might not be immediately apparent. The crew of a Comet fitted their seats like hands in gloves. In the TU 104 everything seemed to be immensely strong. A booted 20-stone peasant could scarcely damage much. On entering the cockpit before a flight a pilot or the flight engineer ran his forearm up a line of tumbler switches mounted on a neighbouring bulkhead, switching all 30 or so to "ON". To start the engines there was a metal "biscuit tin" between the pilots' seats with a hinged lid. One opened the lid, turned a switch to select the engine and pressed a large 1" diameter button. Various starting noises were then heard from the engine, dials flickered and if they all settled down the engine was OK. If it were not, the pilot switched off and radioed for another aircraft. Take-off and landing were always bumpy, either because of an uneven runway or square tires or both, but although instruments, lights etc. fell off the cabin ceiling and walls, nothing was broken and nobody concerned.

The last TU 104 flight of this series landed back in Moscow on 19 April, the day after B&K had embarked for their return on the Ordjonikidze from Portsmouth. One regrettable incident that had occurred during their stay, which had not been widely reported until after their return, was that the Royal Navy, or an intelligence service acting on its behalf, had attempted an underwater survey of the bottom of the Ordjonikidze or one of its Soviet escorting warships. A Commander Lionel Crabb, as he was later named, had carried out an underwater reconnaissance "training" mission from Gosport while the Soviet naval vessels were at Portsmouth. He failed to return, but a headless corpse in a wet-suit was later washed up. The full story of this episode has never been revealed.

The B&K visit was not unreservedly welcomed by the British public. There were demonstrations by many thousands of Poles, Czechs, Bulgarians, Latvians, Lithuanians, etc., around the UK wherever the visitors went, especially Oxford. Sir William, in *A Double Life* wrote:[3]

> *In point of fact their reception must have been something of a surprise to them. This was their first visit to an industrialised capitalist country, and their stereotypes told them that while the Government would be hostile the people would greet them as the beloved representatives of the Worker's State. But the opposite occurred; the Government was hospitable and welcoming, while the reception was, to put it mildly, mixed. Once we were driving together in our huge hired car Krushchev said to me: "What is the oo, oo noise they make?" "It isn't oo, oo," I said "it's boo, boo."*
>
> *"What does it mean?"*
>
> *"It doesn't mean anything, it's just a noise".*
>
> *"But does it indicate disapproval?" he persisted.*

I thought it was no good trying to conceal this, and admitted that it did. "Well next time they do that to me I shall do it back to them" he said, and for the rest of the drive he was saying "boo, boo" most of the way.

B&K arrived back in Moscow on 30 April and the visit was reported in the Soviet press as having been very successful. Eden had been invited to visit Moscow the following spring. In fact the invitation was not confirmed, because later in 1956 there occurred the Suez *débâcle* and the Soviet armed intervention in Hungary, when Anglo-Soviet relations went into steep decline. Before then the BBC had noted that their Russian language broadcasts to the USSR suffered less from jamming. This jamming was a highly professional and technological achievement. Every Soviet city sprouted a number of jamming installations. These could be identified by their metal pylons, over 100' high, carrying at the top a "flower" of four diverging "petal" antennae at approximately 45° to the vertical, on which were mounted the radiators of the jamming signals. These imposed a warbling noise on a number of frequencies covering the western target broadcast, and making it quite inaudible. Each jammer was effective to a distance of about 40km, and although some overlapped, it was sometimes possible to hear the broadcasts if one drove out into the country and listened from there. We helped the BBC discover the coverage of its broadcasts by driving to various distances from Moscow with a portable radio which we tuned to the BBC frequency being used at that time and noting strength and clarity. Target broadcasts for the jammers were mainly the BBC, the Voice of America, and Radio Free Europe. After Suez jamming increased again. There was seldom a moment in Moscow when we had nothing to do!

On May Day there was another of the May Day Parades in Moscow, which we all attended. Because of the B&K flights I had not been able to give the practice fly-pasts my usual close attention, but on the few mornings when I could get on the Embassy roof I took some very good photos of several new aircraft types particularly some new, probably supersonic, fighters, which gave us an impressive display on 1 May. The parade of about 5000 troops and many rocket transporters and other armour, was commanded by Marshal Zhukov, who had come close to being executed by Stalin, but was now back as a blue-eyed boy.

On or about May Day Peter Donkin and Betty and their children returned home tour-expired and Air Commodore Donald MacDonell arrived to take his place. He attended the May Day parade but because of the visits in which I was involved, the flights backwards and forwards to London and duties elsewhere, I was not present for the Goodbye parties for the Donkins nor for the Hallo parties for Donald. He came to Moscow unaccompanied because his wife suffered from schizophrenia and was often in and out of hospital. She stayed at home with the children, two sons and a daughter, the sons being at school at Bryanston. Donald was born in 1913 in Baku, where his father Ranald MacDonell, 21st Chief of Glengarry, had been British Vice-Consul in southern Russia.

Born in November Donald was a few months younger than Peter Donkin and Stan Turner, but of the same vintage – a good one for Battle of Britain pilots. He came to Britain as a child with his parents, towards the end of the communist revolution and although he cannot have learnt his Russian out there, he probably had a Russian nanny who gave him the basics. He joined the RAF from school (Hurstpierpoint) in 1934 and flew Bristol Bulldog fighters and the first ship-borne fighters, later as an instructor, until the war. He was then given command of 64 Squadron flying Spitfires. During the Battle of Britain he shot down a number of German fighters and was awarded the DFC. Subsequently he led fighter sweeps over the Continent and on one sweep over France was shot down, captured and spent the rest of the war in a POW camp. After the war he filled several staff appointments before becoming Chief Flying Instructor at the RAF College, Cranwell. Then he spent a year studying Russian in Cambridge and another two years as Senior Instructor at the Joint Services Staff College. He then came to Moscow as Air Attaché.[4]

Donald's Russian was much better than Peter Donkin's. He had a much softer character than Peter, more complex, more difficult to relate to, but worth the trouble trying. He could get bees in his bonnet (Glengarry) and was difficult to move, even with rational argument. I believe his experience as a Prisoner of War had deeply affected his character. Also his wife's illness affected him a lot and quite often he seemed unhappy. He was considerate to a fault, easy to feel affection for, and to sympathise with. Less easy to follow, especially when one could see he was leading in the wrong direction. He was very proud of his father, whom he had succeeded as Chief of Glengarry. As Vice-Consul in Baku, Ranald had played a leading role in the arrest and execution of the 18 Communist Commissars in that part of Russia and this was on record and even affected a visit that Donald, Daphne and I made there later.

In May 1956, shortly after Donald's arrival, I was involved in a programme for a delegation from the Royal Society of London, led by their President Lord Adrian, with their Foreign Secretary Dr Mary Cartwright and three other senior Fellows of the Society. They had come at the invitation of the Soviet Academy of Sciences to discuss conclusion of an agreement providing for exchanges of senior scientists and scientific research workers. After visiting various Soviet laboratories they returned to Britain intent on developing this initiative, having invited Academician Sisakyan, the Chairman of International Relations of the Academy, to pay a return visit to London with some colleagues. I mention this because ten years later I would be working for the Royal Society in charge of their department of international relations.

At about the same time I visited south Russia and the Crimea in the company of an American attaché, but this was not a success. Possibly the goodwill I had accumulated in the eyes of the Soviet officers of OTDEL did not apply to the same extent if I were travelling with Americans. I had planned to visit the south coast of the Crimea but we were prevented from doing so by militiamen who intercepted and stopped us. I tried to go instead to Evpatoria, on the west coast, home to many Karaite Jews, some of whom had moved from Chufut Kale, the fortress city later occupied by Crimean Tartars. Once again, no way! When we returned to Moscow thoroughly frustrated I stormed round to OTDEL in uniform and gave them a piece of my mind. They calmly advised me to try again.

In early June six English models with attendant administrators came to Moscow to put on a fashion show of 72 lower priced dresses (c. £10.10s) to which all Soviet personalities, representatives of clothing factories, and anyone else who could establish that they had serious interests, were invited by the responsible Soviet Ministry. The fashion show was mounted in the Metropole Hotel, where a piste was established and music laid on, plus a public address system for the commentaries. I helped our Commercial Attaché, Patrick O'Regan, with interpreting and negotiations with the Soviet officials involved. There was a show every day for five days and the first of these was attended by Galina Ulanova and Maya Plisetskaya, the prima ballerinas. They were amazed at the slim waists of our models, and I heard one call to the other across the piste *"Where do they keep their guts (Russian – kishki)?"* At the end of the visit, before the models went home, Patrick gave a splendid party for the girls at Perlovka, the Embassy dacha (country house) where he lived. Champagne flowed like water and Sir William and Lady Hayter attended.

The party was so lavish I concluded that the Embassy paid. The party was primarily for bachelors, as one might hope, apart from VIP's, and guests of ambassadorial rank. The girls were beautiful but none more so than my girl-friend of that time Countess Anna Hamilton (from the Swedish Embassy). I wrote home to Dad about Anna:

…a Swedish girl of Scottish descent, she is of the Russell-Flint variety. 5'8" in her stockings. She likes dancing with me, not because I samba very well, but because I am three inches taller than she is (most diplomats here are short).

The Hamiltons were an interesting family, descendents of one of Bernadotte's generals fighting with Napoleon. Originally they were from Scotland, devout Catholics, like Mary Queen of Scots. They suffered from discrimination when extreme forms of Protestantism took root there and sought refuge in Sweden of all places. When Sweden became Protestant, the family had to import their own priest. They had a number of grand houses in various parts of Sweden, with a family schloss, Wrangelsberg, at Färlöv a few km north of Kristianstad in Skåne, the southern province of Sweden. At another schloss on a lake north of Stockholm there was a family museum of sorts, housing antiquities, some very large, brought back from Russia, Poland and other countries where Hamiltons had served. In Napoleonic times, war meant loot. Elderly Hamilton spinsters, bachelors, widows and widowers, were welcome to live in the lakeside schloss.

2 June 1956, a Saturday, was the Italian National Day and Molotov attended the evening reception looking more subdued than usual. He had been given the sack that morning to get him out of the way before President Tito arrived in Moscow from Yugoslavia. There had been differences of opinion about what to do about Yugoslavia. Some, like Molotov, were in favour of cracking down and bringing Tito to heel. This might not have been a good idea when noises of rebellion were being heard from Hungary. This may have been one reason why my visit to the Crimea had been obstructed by the authorities. The chances are that aircraft were being moved from the Caspian and Black Sea areas to bases in the Ukraine. Some western military attachés were also having difficulties with travel itineraries. At the Italian reception I talked to the ballerina Struchkova who hoped to travel with the Bolshoi ballet to London in the autumn.

Dad had decamped to Italy for a three-week holiday with Les and Nan Kerridge and friends George Foster and his wife. It was a rather rushed motorised tour, with Les doing the driving. Some visits to cultural centres were more than rushed with Les advising his passengers to look down that road as we pass and you should be able to see the Leaning Tower. Dad took several days off, leaving his fellow travellers in Alassio, and took a coach to Turin, staying in a hotel overnight, but with Albina and Mariapola during the day, two days in fact. He re-invited Mariapola to visit Valverde in September (in fact she did not come until I was home the following year). He rejoined Les and party in Alassio, where

Les had been stationed in the war, and after several more days they drove home across the Simplon Pass.

Dad mentioned Khrushchev's denunciation of Stalin, to which the English media were giving great attention. What did it mean? He asked. In a letter on 15 June I replied:

Briefly, a break with the past – possibly not genuine or permanent, designed to show what was previously known to most but only discussed in whispers: i.e. that Stalin's rule was one of the most bloody and inhuman periods of history that man has known. B&K want to show that everything now has been started afresh, that there will be no more terror. You see, the regime was based on a set of such obvious falsifications that it made unstable the whole monolithic communist structure. And as they intend to go on increasing its size to encompass the whole world some pretty radical work has to be done on the foundations. Of course the whole structure is built on sand – but nobody can see this – only the vast amount of rotten brickwork that has to be replaced by good stone. The system is rotten because there is nothing to prevent any number of other Stalins and Berias turning up in the course of time. Or to stop Krushchev becoming a little Stalin himself. These repairs to obvious structural faults have provided the opportunity (as in house repair) to alter or patch up things the present bosses do not like, including some holes, cracks and unnecessarily ornate decorations for which these same bosses were responsible when they were part of the builder's team. All these faults are blamed on 'poor old Joe' for he is dead and cannot answer back. Thank God for that they think. The plans still provide for building on the same old Marxist sands, swamps and quagmires.

24 June was to be the annual Soviet air display at Tushino, just outside Moscow to the north-west, when they liked to show some of their aircraft to invited delegates from foreign countries including Britain and the USA of course. This was of course partly propaganda spiced with braggadocio, but advances in their development of modern fighting aircraft deserved being demonstrated, if only to show that in some respects they were abreast of the US and UK. In 1956 the Soviets really pushed the boat out. Delegations were invited from the US, UK, France, Sweden, Norway, Egypt, Finland, Yugoslavia, Switzerland, Indonesia, and India. And there were others we were told less about, for instance the Iron curtain

countries and China. In all there were 20 delegations invited and all came.

Britain sent the largest delegation, led on the civil side by the Rt. Hon. Nigel Burch (Secretary of State for Air) and on the RAF side by Air Chief Marshal Sir Ronald Ivelaw-Chapman, the Vice Chief of Air Staff. Two Air Marshals (Broadhurst and Pike) and three Air Vice-Marshals (Cheshire, Silyn Roberts and Cross) were in support, with two Group Captains, a Wing Commander, and three Squadron Leaders, including Michael Forter of DDAFL, as tail-end Charlies. For those unfamiliar with RAF slang, a tail-end Charlie was the last aircraft in a fighter formation responsible for weaving about and watching for attacks from the rear. Broadhurst and Pike were respectively AOCs-in-C (Air Officer Commanders-in-Chief) of Bomber and Fighter Command.

The USAF sent ten delegates led by General Twining, the French ten, and the Scandinavian countries and odds and sods up to half a dozen each. Truly a mighty gathering of brass hats. Our RAF delegation came by Comet, one of the later marks no longer endangered by pressure cabin fatigue. Nigel Burch came by Viscount, the four turbo-prop transport, flown by Vickers Chief Test Pilot Jock Bryce, with George Edwards, Vickers Managing Director, aboard. Jock promised me flights in the Viscount when I came home. The other delegations had no jet transports operating and came in their piston-engined equivalents. I think they were impressed by the Comet and by the TU 104's which the Soviets took care to park close to the visitors' aircraft for comparison. Our Comet arrived at Vnukovo Airport on Saturday 23 June, the Americans in a Globemaster ten minutes earlier and the French ten minutes later. Each aircraft had to be met by attachés from their embassies and by Soviet officials and SAF (Soviet Air Force) officers to welcome them, make sure the aircraft were parked and guarded, and accompany the visitors to their accommodation in hotels and embassies.

June that far had been extremely hot and dry but on Saturday 24 June, the day selected for the display, the heavens opened and there were line after line of thunderstorms, torrential rain and a low cloud base. Many demonstrations had to be cancelled, supersonic fighters could not direct their sonic booms at spectators, the parachutists could not be dropped. This непогода (nyepogoda = non-weather, i.e. very bad) lasted all day, and the next day – Monday. To compensate for the propaganda failure, on the Monday a visit was laid on at short notice to a large Soviet air base in what for us attachés was an out-of-bounds zone. It was out-of-bounds for me, but I thought I might get away with it by jumping into the limo carrying AVM Cross, AOC No. 3 Bomber Group (who took over Bomber Command from Broadhurst in 1959). Cross also had a Group Captain with him. At this air base we were driven slowly past parked bombers and fighters, some of which we had not seen before, and others which I had photographed from the Embassy roof rehearsing for the May Day fly-past. We were not allowed to stop or get out of the cars, which was just as well because it was still pouring with rain.

The cars drew up beside large inter-connected marquees into which we were invited for lunch. In one, the pilots of the aircraft on display, some of whom had flown or should have flown the day before, were marched up to have their hands shaken by Broadhurst and Pike. Lunch was partly sit down and partly stand up, i.e. buffet style with some seats for those who could find them and for the more senior visitors and their Soviet counterparts. The Soviet Air Attaché, Colonel Konstantinov, from their London embassy was present and so were many of the OTDEL officers. On seeing me they held a quick conference and then confronted me, saying that I had not been invited so what was I doing there. I tried to justify my presence as an interpreter, but they seemed pretty miffed. Konstantinov did not seem to mind and we toasted each other and others in vodka, and ate up our caviar, black bread and sausage. Hard drinking Russians often hold a piece of black bread while downing vodkas, not to eat but to sniff between swallows. This obviates catching one's breath. They even have an expression for it *'vnukhat' khleb"*= sniff bread. Marshal Budyonny was present and Michael Forter said to him: *"You were my Regimental Sergeant Major in the Cavalry before the Revolution".* Later Budyonny has been a Cossack commander, a cavalry (later tank) man. Now he was a senior Marshal, a great friend of Zhukov, and Michael Forter, once his superior officer, was now a Squadron Leader in the RAF. This was good for a few vodkas.

That evening our own Embassy laid on a big reception for the UK visitors and their immediate hosts and the next afternoon Khrushchev and Bulganin gave a quite extraordinary party for all the delegations. On this occasion the weather was good. The party was held outside, I believe in the grounds of one of the dachas allocated to members of the Supreme Soviet, on the Moskva River to the west of the city. I did not attend because only the most senior diplomats and their families were invited, apart from the members of the delegations. Donald described the occasion to us juniors next day and Sir William writes in his memoirs:

> *Another (party), which was significant for its curious political overtones, was given in June 1956 to the delegates who had been attending the Tushino air-show. It was held in the open air, in a park, and after some curious antics in the course of which the Secretary of State for Air, Mr*

Nigel Burch, was rowed about by Bulganin in a small dinghy on an ornamental lake, we all settled down to some heavy drinking round a table in the open. Bulganin went hard at it, and it was the only occasion when I myself ever saw Khrushchev the worse for drink. As Bulganin drank more and more he became more and more sentimental. Khrushchev on the other hand became aggressive, and in a series of short speeches managed to insult literally every country in the world. First he said that only the great powers counted, which put all the small countries in their place. Then he said only the United States and the Soviet Union mattered. France was too poor to make an atom bomb. The Royal Air Force (he was just back from his visit to Britain) had only obsolete bombers; I thought some of the numerous Air Marshals present were going to get apoplexy. Then he had his usual go at America and proposed a toast to China, which the American Ambassador could not drink and to East Germany which none of us could.

There were no Chinese present but Molotov produced a little general from somewhere; Khrushchev ignored him. Bulganin stood up during some of Khrushchev's speeches and tried in a maudlin way to soften his asperities. Khrushchev told him to sit down. Molotov, Malenkov and Kaganovich at the other end of the table were pursing their lips and drumming their fingers on the arms of their chairs. Eventually they brought the proceedings to a stop by remaining standing after one of Khrushchev's speeches and going round saying good-night.

Other guests at this party told me that before the speeches and serious drinking, while guests and hosts were talking to one another, girls (devushki) dressed in traditional Russian costumes walked slowly out from among the birch trees with trays of food, while Russian folk music was played and songs sung by an orchestra and choir among the trees. Soviet senior officers rowed guests about in dinghies on the lake, and they included Teresa Hayter, the daughter of Sir William and Iris. She was apprehensive that someone might fall overboard, because her General was manifestly unfamiliar with boats and oars.

The next few days I was kept busy taking parties of Soviet officers and members of the aircraft industry and Aeroflot round the Comet and Viscount. The Comet flew home with most of the RAF delegation but the Viscount stayed on so that George Edwards could meet Tupolev for discussions, no doubt on common problems in the operation of transport aircraft and designs for the future. George Edwards and Tupolev got on very well together, professionally and personally.

The Comet flew in again on 30 June, nominally to take a number of senior Soviet officers on a flight and then to return home with a few of our delegates who had stayed on. This was a bit of a disaster. I briefed the 30 officers, including the Head of Aeroflot, on the flight to come.

They were already sitting in their seats in the Comet, and then the pilot sent a message back to me in the cabin that he could not start the engines; the battery was flat, as a baker's 'at, in RAF parlance. We tried everything, but no good, a Soviet battery would not do – different specifications. Eventually, after I had made profuse apologies in Russian, the officers disembarked and went their way in their respective cars, leaving me to confront the press and TV. That night, Dad let me know, I was on television on the ITA (Independent Television Authority) news. Our papers, especially the *Daily Mail*, were quite cruel, not to me personally, but about the fiasco in general. The Comet could not fly home until Soviet engineers managed to recharge the battery overnight. It was a new type of battery and the Comet Flight Engineer thought that his Soviet opposite numbers had taken the battery apart to learn about any innovations. Egg on our faces all round! Just before the last of our RAF delegation left for home I had visited America House to see a film and there met up with the Ethiopian and Pakistani Chargés d'Affaires and two French defence attachés. We had a hilarious late night supper in the Hotel Moskva, where to get served we posed as the "English Air Delegation" because the cook was said to be going off duty. As Vasile, the Ethiopian, was black with short curly hair and under 5' tall, and Mahmud, the Pakistani, was overall dark brown with long black hair, and the French were very French, the management must have wondered.

I was tired and slightly fed up and decided to take a week off in Sweden. At the Queen's birthday garden party in the Embassy I tuned in to somebody else's conversation, as is necessary at these events, and discovered that the Russian guest he was talking to was Gliere (Reinhold Moritzovich) in his sixties and old enough to be classed as one of the successors to Tchaikovsky and the great Russian composers of that period, late Czarist early Soviet. He was of Belgian ancestry and a devoted communist. As a faculty member of the Moscow Conservatoire he had taught younger composers like Khachaturyan and Prokofiev. They were favourites of mine, especially Prokofiev. Maybe Gliere was the Professor said to have rushed out of the concert hall with his hands over his ears to escape Prokofiev's 1st Piano Concerto. In my frequent visits to concerts at the Conservatoire I had heard some of Gliere's music. This was lyrical rather than Schoenberg and Webern, and more to Stalin's taste, and to mine. I was therefore glad to talk to Gliere and tell him I liked his music. The others drifted away and there were just Gliere and I talking.

A short clerk-like man in a brown suit and cheap spectacles seemed to be trying to push in, so I turned a diplomatic shoulder to exclude him. But Gliere extended an arm and said: *"May I introduce you to Dmitri Shostakovich!"* Did I make room! I asked Shostakovich what he was composing. He said he was in difficulties because a year earlier he had felt moved to compose something and had been given leave to move residence to a House of Creativity *(Dom Tvorchestva)* in the countryside near Zvenigorod, but the spirit had left him and after a year with no newborn compositions he would have to move back to Moscow. The Soviet authorities had this idea of providing nest-boxes for creative artists, authors, composers, poets, etc., to lay eggs, as one would for birds.

Increasingly I had been going to concerts of classical music in Moscow, often to the Moscow Conservatoire, where I could get a seat quite easily. Frequently Cecil Parrott, later Sir Cecil, but known by all as Joe, was also there, usually like me, in the front row of the stalls. Joe was the Minister in our Embassy in Moscow in 1956 and he and his wife were very enthusiastic about culture – music, art, opera, ballet. Occasionally Joe and I crossed swords although in the Embassy hierarchy I was much his junior. He was number two in the Embassy, deputising for the Ambassador, and Chargé d'Affaires in his absence. He sometimes thought I was engaging too much in political rather than Air Force matters, although he was often the first to ask for my assistance as interpreter or guide when his staff or their visitors needed it. We eventually became firm friends and later when I was with the Royal Society I was able on his behalf to present to the Czechoslovak Academy of Sciences his translation into English of The Good Soldier Švejk and his biography of its author Jaroslav Hašek. At that time Joe was *persona non grata* in Czechoslovakia because of an alleged association with MI5 during his time in Prague as our ambassador from 1960 to 1966.

On Thursday 5 July I took the SAS flight to Stockholm. Travelling on the same flight was Max Hayward, on his way home, anxious to get away from persecution, as he saw it, by the KGB. Another travelling companion was a pretty American girl of Armenian parentage who had just visited the Soviet Union to seek out relatives in Yerevan (the capital of Soviet Armenia), normally out-of-bounds to foreigners. She managed to get there only after appealing to Mikoyan, the Armenian-born Minister for Trade. She had stayed there a while, and had been appalled by the unhappiness of her people who implored her to tell Armenians abroad about the plight of their Soviet compatriots. She was now going to a small, impoverished village in northern Syria where others of her family lived, to compare conditions and then write some articles about it for a magazine. A bit cold-blooded I thought.

Many minority peoples in the USSR had a relatively bad time. I have already mentioned the Crimean Tartars, the Karaite Jews, and other Caucasian and Central Asian minorities. If one wished to differ from the standard Soviet Man (includes women) whose characteristics had been planned centrally, there was bound to be trouble. We had an Israeli Embassy in Moscow, manned by a Jewish Chargé d'Affaires whom I knew well and sometimes had for lunch, and two assistants. He was on my list for spare tickets to the Bolshoi. On one occasion he visited the Jewish Autonomous Region in the Soviet Far East, not far from Khabarovsk. This region was half the size of Ireland, with a population of 60,000, including 15,000 Jews. On his return the Chargé quipped that the Jewish Autonomous Region was neither Jewish nor autonomous. The capital city was Birobizhan. The people there complained, much as did the Armenians, Tartars and most of the other minority peoples.

In Stockholm the weather was not very nice – a great deal of rain. Midsommar was just past but Midsommar parties were still going on. I reclaimed my Sunbeam Talbot from Börje Kwarnmark for a week and located and met up with Daphne Park's friend Terry O'Bryan Tear and his wife Sandra. He was half Irish and half French, 38 years old, and a tearaway character in many respects. His wife was a small Scot, tough enough to keep Terry in order for some of the time. They had an elderly Humber Hawk car and with me in my Sunbeam we used to drive about at speeds of up to 100mph, although I later discovered that the Swedish upper speed limit was 80kph. Luckily I was never stopped. With Terry and about ten of his friends we went out on boats to a crayfish party on an island in the Stockholm archipelago. One is supposed to eat each small crayfish (they are fresh water and very small) with a glass of Aquavit.

It poured with rain but this had little effect on our eating and drinking. Afterwards at about 2 a.m. while sailing home, one of the boats foundered about a mile out from the quay, the four occupants climbing out of the water into whichever boat was nearest. We took refuge in the house of the British Assistant Air Attaché, John Ramsden, who had been with us. Those who had been submerged took off their clothes and donned blankets and warmed up in front of a blazing log fire. We drank hot punch for the rest of the night. It being midsummer the sun scarcely set; there was twilight between 23.00 and 01.00 but it was never really dark, even when the sky was overcast.

I had hoped to see more of Inger Adelsohn who was temporarily home in Stockholm, but apart from finding me a room (very small and dark; I immediately changed it for something better) she was busy with her parents and friends and we only managed a meal together and a visit to Uppsala, where she had been to University. Her father was the Head of the Legal Branch of the Swedish Foreign Office. Terry O'Bryan Tear had introduced me to Ulla Berling, the beautiful 20-year-old daughter of a Swedish Admiral. She was very tall, with dark hair and green eyes, secretary to a German firm in Stockholm but she found the job boring, partly because she spoke no German. From the age of ten she had hoped to become a ballet dancer, but as she grew taller she had to give up that ambition. I was greatly taken by Swedish women but puzzled by the Swedish extremes of behaviour. I wrote home:

> Swedish women are quite something and I have had a daily party and even more frequent lunches, coffees etc. with much alcohol and gaiety. Swedes, the men at least, are atrociously formal and conventional if they are of parental age. Consequence is that children go out of their way to be unconventional to the point of eccentricity. It is therefore difficult to generalise about the national character, which varies in direct proportion to age, from Left Bank existentialist in slacks and sandals to extreme Puritanism. One thing they seem to have in common is a love of fish; the young worship the sun and "natural phenomena" and their elders – family pedigree, business relationships and bridge.

After leaving the Sunbeam with Börje I was back in Moscow by 11 July. Patrick O'Regan was going home, and I fancied going to live in his place – the Embassy dacha at Perlovka. This was 24km to the north-east of Moscow on the Yaroslavskiy Shossé. The dacha was a rambling wooden building built for the Metropolitan Vickers engineers who had come to Moscow in the 1920s to install escalators in the Moscow underground. They had been accused of espionage in Stalin's time and after a show trial they were allowed to return to Britain. They bequeathed their dacha to the British Embassy with a 50-year lease (due to expire in the 70s).

The dacha had about 20 rooms on two floors, each heated by one or more pechki (tiled stoves or Kachelofen). These consumed considerable quantities of wood in winter and close to the dacha was a small house and garden belonging to Vanya the dvornik, or yardman, whose job was to cut down trees in the summer and split them into logs to be piled up for use in the winter. The ceramic-tiled brick stoves, extending from floor to ceiling, kept warm day and night and it was usually enough to rake the ashes and insert several logs each morning through the small loading door at the base of the pechka to keep it going. Vanya and his wife and children lived there all the time doing odd jobs in addition to servicing the pechki. No doubt they also told the KGB what the dacha occupants were up to.

From Patrick I bought many of the household effects he did not want to take home to Britain. He was a bachelor and never spoke of any family at home. From him I bought for £20 a mass of domestic items, curtains, bits of furniture, bed linen, a wrought iron standard lamp and what may well be a rare Chinese funerary pot. In the week starting 20 July I moved all my own belongings out to the dacha from Narodnaya Ulitza and set up something close to a home. I was the only person living there except for the occasional week-end when some Embassy staff might come out to stay in one or more of the many rooms. They never got in the way. There were several small kitchens. With my gear I also appropriated Galya to cook and clean for me. She preferred to move with me rather than to accustom herself to a new diplomat.

The dacha was several hundred yards off the Shossé and on three sides the taiga (mixed conifer and birch forest) came right up to the perimeter fence round the house. It went for miles and was wonderful for walks except that it was easy to get lost especially in overcast weather when one could not see the sun and shadows to get one's bearings. On one occasion, walking in the forest in a vaguely southerly direction, I turned back, but there was no sun and the tree trunks had no moss on any side, which Boy Scouts used to be told can indicate direction. I almost panicked, but to my surprise stumbled across a knapsack, just dropped or left on the ground, containing toiletries as well as documents and passes, including a Komsomol membership card, presumably belonging to the owner. There was no doubt that whoever it was had only just left the scene. Had he been following me? Had he left the knapsack expecting me to come across it and pick it up. I did and a few minutes later found the tracks of a forestry vehicle, which I followed back to the Shossé. I handed in the pack and documents to the Embassy MI5 representative and he probably sent them back to London. My own view was that this had been a "plant" intended to deceive and that the planter had retreated or hidden in the undergrowth while I picked it up.

On 19 July I flew off with Daphne to Kharkov, from where we took a train to Minsk, probably doing a recce of airfields beside the railway. Thence back to Moscow by air. I was now studying hard for the RAF Staff College examinations, which I had not yet passed. I needed to because I wanted my next posting to be to the RAF Staff College at Bracknell. To sit these examinations I had to fly to Berlin in mid-August for a week. The studies for the general knowledge paper included communism and Marx. I knew quite a lot about the subject. I stayed in Berlin for several days, taking the examination at Gatow, the RAF base. I reckoned I had passed.

A very interesting young woman, Camilla Gray, came out from London to stay with Daphne in her Moscow flat for a month or so. Her mission was to study Russian ballet and write an article about it for one or more British institutions. In her teens she had been a budding ballerina, with, I believe, the ballet Rambert. But she grew too tall and heavy to continue towards important dancing roles, so she looked elsewhere. Writing and art generally attracted her. Her father was Keeper of the Department of Oriental Antiquities of the British Museum which probably helped. I accompanied Camilla to the ballet several times and enjoyed her company. Either on this visit or a subsequent one she met Oleg Sviatoslav Prokofiev, the composer's son. He was an artist and poet and the two fell in love. In the course of many more visits to the USSR Camilla studied the revolutionary Russian artists – Constructivists and the like, who had been prominent at the time of the Revolution. Her seminal book *The Russian Experiment in Art 1863-1922*, which was and remains one of the best on that period of art in Russia, greatly annoyed the Soviet authorities and for six years they did all they could to prevent Camilla and Oleg from meeting. Only in 1969 did they marry, in Moscow, and the sad thing is that Camilla died after the birth of their only child, Anastasia.

In the last week of August I was asked to escort Isaiah Berlin to meet a Soviet philosopher. Isaiah Berlin needed no interpreter because he spoke better Russian than I. I had not met a professional philosopher before. Isaiah Berlin was an extraordinary man. He was visiting Moscow with his wife Aline. They had married in February. They were staying with the Hayters who were very much involved with Oxford University, as was Isaiah Berlin. Probably I was chosen to accompany him to meet this Soviet philosopher because I knew Moscow fairly well and drove the Standard Vanguard everywhere. As it happened this particular meeting had been set up in the forest dacha-land west of Moscow near the river Moskva. Like Irina, Isaiah Berlin had been born in Latvia, in Riga. He was Jewish, but not observant, indeed very sceptical, an enemy of dogma, but he liked the Jewish religious traditions and religious traditions generally. A benign sceptic. When we found the dacha it was a small and very damp single storey wooden house. It looked as if some Ministry or other, of Culture maybe, had allocated the dacha for this meeting and the Soviet philosopher and his wife had been told to clean it up, start a fire, produce the table and chairs and a bottle of red wine and zakuzkis (nibbles they might be called now). We were ten minutes late because the dacha was hard to find.

We were asked to sit down on the damp chairs and were offered the wine and eats by the rather embarrassed hosts. After the niceties had been fulfilled the Soviet philosopher (SP for short) introduced a Marxist / Leninist apologia for the concepts of Soviet morality and the Soviet man. Then stopped and invited Isaiah's opinions. He erupted in streams of comment, on each element of which he enlarged to lead to further ideas for development. After some minutes he stopped (for breath maybe) and the SP tried to get back to Soviet morality etc. Another space for the thin end of a wedge and Isaiah was off again. With one hand raised in explanation he knocked over the bottle of wine, which soaked the damp doilies on the damp table, with the SP's wife mopping up with a rag. Isaiah did not stop until he needed to blow his nose, which started to bleed profusely, mixing blood with wine! When all this was cleared up the SP was mute with confusion. Not Isaiah, who continued to elaborate on his ideas – the fallacy of a Soviet morality and anything based upon it. Handshakes all round and I drove Isaiah back to the Embassy.

While in Moscow, Isaiah, with other escorts, met Pasternak, who had just given the text of Dr Zhivago to an Italian publisher, and Anna Akhmatova, 20 years older than Isaiah, who is said to have been rather glum because he had just married Aline. I managed to pick up some of Isaiah's ideas from our visit to the SP and from our conversations in the car, because Isaiah was an unstoppable conversationalist. Later he sent me the text of "Two Concepts of Liberty", a lecture he gave in Oxford in October 1958. One conclusion I reached was that to achieve freedom in any sphere of activity one has to subordinate oneself to certain disciplines, which limit other freedoms. For example, to be free to drive a car one has to learn and to abide by rules limiting your freedom to drive on the wrong side of the road, at high speed, to the disadvantage of the freedom of others to walk, cycle or drive in safety. Common sense? Philosophy is codified common sense!

I might well have looked after Isaiah on his other visits but I was needed for flying again. On 2 September I flew back to London with a TU 104 taking some 30 senior Soviet Air Force officers and officials to attend the Farnborough Air Show. The flight from Vnukovo included Konstantinov, Soviet Air Attaché in London, who had flown in earlier so that he could accompany his senior colleagues to the SBAC show, and Donald MacDonell who was also tasked to accompany the guests. After all the passengers had embarked and I was in the cockpit with the crew awaiting clearance to start engine, Colonel Chuvilsky of OTDEL came through the small door from the cabin with outstretched hand to shake mine and wish me godspeed. His words were interrupted as he failed to notice that a hatch in the floor through which the crew usually entered the aircraft on a ladder through the nose-wheel compartment was still open. The drop to the tarmac below was the best part of 20'. As Chuvilsky fell I held on to his hand from which he dangled until he managed to put one foot on the ladder, which was still in place. Needless to say, his breathless thanks were even more generous than he may have originally intended. I particularly liked Chuvilsky, a SAF technical officer in his fifties. He was always helpful if he could be, a decent civilised person, as were most of the Soviets I met, including the KGB, who were sometimes pests, but carrying out their orders.

We stayed a week and I took the opportunity to go home for a couple of days, although my father was away for the week in Bexhill. I promised to come and see him in October if I were able to accompany the Bolshoi Ballet to London. As the exhibitors at Farnborough mostly had large caravans or temporary buildings to give hospitality to prospective customers, I both saw the air show and accompanied the Soviet visitors to get free drinks and lunches. By this time I was getting very familiar with the TU 104, was looked upon as one of the crew, and was presented with the wings of a SAF Pilot First Class. On the return flight to Moscow on 9 September there was a SAF photographer on board who took a photograph of me in the cockpit, festooned with maps and microphones, and, over my shoulder, Marshal Sudetz, Head of the Soviet Strategic Air Force, with an arm around my waist. I had hoped that this would appear in some journal I could lay my hands on, but if it was printed, it must have been in some SAF magazine. The SAF officers were very pleased with their reception at Farnborough.

On 11 September Donald and I gave a very good goodbye party for Dennis Spilsbury, returning home tour-expired. We gave it at the dacha where there was plenty of room. Between 70 and 80 guests came from 11 different embassies. Champagne flowed like water and the food was very good, provided by cooks borrowed from the Embassy and from Donald's household. It cost us at least £100 each, a lot of money then. Living with Dennis at Narodnaya we had been obliged to entertain modestly, because he had a large family at home, and I had to keep in step with him. At this party Donald and I were able to return hospitality on a lavish scale. The best party of the year it was rated. Dancing went on until three next morning.

On Friday 14 September Donald, Daphne and I flew off to Mineralniyi Vodi (Min. Vodi) to be met by Vasili Karasyov, whom we had sent off to drive there the previous week in the Standard Vanguard. He met us off the aircraft and we put him on an Aeroflot service back to Moscow while we drove in the car the following day towards the Georgian Military Highway. This road, much of it unmetalled, runs north-south through the Caucasus mountains from Ordzhonikidse, once Vladikafkaz (meaning key to the Caucasus) through Mtskheta, the old capital of Georgia, to Tbilisi the present capital. The road became known as the Georgian Military Highway during the Russian conquest of the Caucasus in the middle of the 19th century.

The scenery was magnificent. Soon we were among really high mountains, approached by rocky foothills. We stayed the night in the village of Kasbek, under the mountain of that name, 18,000' high, and first climbed by a Scot (and not much since). I had been told that Kazbek's peak was usually covered with a cloud cowl, except very early in the morning. So I was up at 4 a.m. and from the "hotel" (hovel) loo, an outside wooden kiosk with a halved door (as for a stable). I did get a splendid view of the peak when the sun came up and woke up Donald and Daphne to see it. Later in the morning I set out to climb the foothills of Kazbek to a small church or shrine. Daphne tried to follow me but gave up. The views from the church were very fine and I then knew what Lermontov was writing about in his poetry, much of which is about this area. The road, or track, through the village of Kasbek was a wilderness of rock, brought down in a recent landslide and covering both road and river, the Terek, running north, another subject of Lermontov's poetry.

Beyond Kasbek we met another stream, the Aragvi, this time running south to Tblisi. The weather remained fine and clear. We had no time to stop in Mtskheta, other than to photograph the church, of a distinctive Georgian style. The Georgian Church is one of the oldest in Christendom, not in communion with Rome, more Orthodox but with a different liturgy. We arrived in Tblisi ready for bed in the Intourist hotel, where we had booked rooms from Moscow. After a couple of days in Tblisi looking at museums and a collection of Georgian church silver, we flew by Aeroflot to Baku, a flight of about two hours in the IL12 along the broadening valley between the Caucasus and anti-Caucasus mountain ranges. Most of this was over the Azerbaijan People's Republic and where the terrain flattened out along the Kura river, there were several important Soviet air bases. In the fine weather I was able to observe quite large numbers of Ilyushin 28 ground attack bombers and later concluded that these were being readied for action in Hungary, where discontent with Soviet hegemony was building up.

In Baku we had trouble. Although we had booked into the Intourist hotel we were told that they had no accommodation and that we would have to return to Tblisi that evening there being no room on the daylight train. Although we pleaded that Donald was visiting his birthplace, this cut no ice, quite the reverse. The night train had obviously been chosen to ensure that we would be unable to see the airfields I had already reconnoitred from the air. I had hoped to have another look at Baku harbour which we were always asked to check if we were visiting. Although I was unable to do so the task was competently covered by the Assistant Naval Attaché, Humphrey James. Using psychology, he had noticed the comparative prudishness of many people, not only Russians, who do not stare if somebody's flies (zip or button) have accidentally been left undone. One normally looks elsewhere. Humphrey attached a small camera in front of his vital part, with a remote release cable running to one of his trouser pockets. With hands in pockets standing on a hill overlooking the harbour he gaped his flies and pressed the release. The photographs came out well, each print framed by his flies.

We stayed in Tblisi another day, having a swim in the reservoir/recreational lake just north of the city. Then we drove on west through Stalin's home town of Gori, not a very prepossessing place, to Borzhomi. At that time there were two popular bottled mineral waters available in Moscow – Narzan, which came from springs near Min. Vodi, and Borzhomi. Borzhomi had a flavour of sulphuretted hydrogen (bad eggs) and could seriously ruin your Scotch.

We did not go there for the waters but because I had read in a book from the London Library that the writer had eaten *"arshinniyi forel"* (28"-long trout) caught in Lake Tabatskuri, a lake some 25km south-east of Borzhomi and not far from the Turkish frontier. The road leading there was very difficult – lumps of rock and very little surface. It led steeply uphill for most of the way by which time we were driving through thick cloud, and then steeply down hill. We broke cloud to see the lake ahead of us, with a cluster of poor dwellings, apparently deserted, and then a quay and boathouse on the north side of the lake. In the village we spoke to the village idiot, which did not get us far, and then to a peasant woman who waved us towards the boathouse, saying, in Russian, that there was somebody there.

We drove to the boathouse, the lower part of which was on piles sunk in the mud with pieces of boats rotting beneath. An exterior staircase led up to a wooden door. We climbed up and knocked. A growled injunction seemed like an invitation to enter. Inside we met the gaze of a grizzled fisherman, in a thick woollen sweater with a torn blue apron round his waist. In accented Russian he asked our business. I said I had read that big trout could be caught on the lake. We would like to buy some. He sighed: *"I am just an Armenian fisherman. We are not allowed to catch the trout now. It is not the season".* *"However"*, he added, *"I just happen to have a few here, in the corner under those sacks".* He moved them aside and there lay half a dozen enormous trout, not *arshinniyi*, but from 18" to 2'. We considered what we could carry back to the hotel in Borzhomi, where we had booked rooms on the way through, and selected two fish – a 20" one for Donald, who was wearing a belted trenchcoat in which a trout of that size might be concealed, and an 18" one for me to conceal under my Russian coat. The trout were great fat heavy beasts.

There was then the question of the price. *"Ah"*, said our fisherman *"Our splendid government has thought of that, and I must weigh the fish"*. He produced a balance with two plates, suspended from each end, and put the trout, one by one, on one plate, while on the other he piled stones randomly. When they balanced he asked *"OK …what will you give me for them?"* I suggested 10 roubles for the two. At our special rate of exchange that equalled 5/- but of course it would be difficult to work out the value now in 2005 – maybe £5. *"Khorosho!"* (OK) he said and I handed over the money. While doing so, Daphne advised that a car, GAZ 69, Jeep type, was speeding down the mountain road towards the village. Goons we concluded. Realising that the fisherman was going to get into trouble, we stowed the fish under our coats, belted them up fast, and made for the door, saying goodbye. We escaped just before the goons arrived and, looking back, could see them running up the steps to the fisherman's room intent on doing something nasty.

I drove the Vanguard back up the road into the hills and fog, pulling off after a mile or so for us to dismount and have a pee. Daphne went off behind some rocks and undergrowth. A few minutes later we heard a crash and oaths in Russian and when Daphne rejoined us she said that the goons had been watching her from behind some bushes. So she had lobbed a large stone among them. We drove back to Borzhomi and asked the kitchen to grill us our trout for supper. They were very good eating, with kartoshki (potatoes) and carrots, and probably fed most of the staff as well, so big were they. We washed them down with white wine, Tsinandali, very cheap in Georgia.

Next morning we continued our journey to the west driving over roads littered with the debris of rock falls with a narrow, barely negotiable passage bulldozed to enable lorries and military vehicles to pass. Apart from our Standard there were very few other vehicles about, other than our KGB followers and often there was no sign of them. Occasionally we turned off the road to look at a Georgian church or other interesting building. At Kutaisi we came out of the mountains into the Rioni delta, on the Black Sea littoral. Numerous branches of that river ran out to the sea and because of recent rain these watercourses had to be forded. As often as not the road was invisible under the flowing water for up to several hundred yards and, driving the Vanguard, I was concerned that we should not get in so deep that the engine would stall and we would be stuck. Here and there were lorries and even the occasional bus to give me a lead.

We were flagged down by a lone woman who requested a lift as far as Sukhumi and we squeezed her in beside Daphne. She was in her fifties or sixties, poorly dressed, but well-spoken. She told us that she was a recently retired school-teacher. To obtain a pension she had to provide evidence of teaching for the requisite number of years. During the war she had taught at schools in this area, but all records had been lost, and she now had to seek out former colleagues and pupils of hers, and obtain from them affidavits confirming that she had taught at this or that school over this or that period. As many of these people had been killed or dispersed during the war, or exiled in the years since, her task was a difficult one. We dropped her in the outskirts of Sukhumi, the Black Sea port, while we went on to find the Intourist hotel.

This was closed for repairs (in Russian *pod remontom.* At that time practically all buildings in the USSR were pod remontom, especially if the authorities did not want you to go there). We were advised to go to a hostel for "workers". They were able to find us beds in the communal dormitories, one for men another for women. After a bad meal we retired. Next morning Daphne told us that she had found our schoolmistress was also lodging there in the next bed to her but several. Many of the "girls" wanted Daphne to tell them of the latest books popular in Britain. So Daphne spent much of the night relating to her audience the gist of Rebecca by her namesake Daphne du Maurier.

On 22 September we drove on westwards along the northern Black Sea Coast, once home to Greek and Venetian colonists. The idea was that Vasili would fly from Moscow to Krasnodar on 26 September where we would meet him and hand over the Vanguard for him to drive back to Moscow while we flew back there. We drove through Sochi, the premier holiday resort for many Soviet citizens in those years, and the home town of the Zernov family before the revolution. Both Maria Mikhaelovna and Sofia Mikhaelovna (See chapter "Russian") lived there. Outside Sochi we were overtaken by a fleet of black ZIL limousines obviously carrying VIPs. I decided to follow them and see where they were going. They turned downhill towards the sea, through wide gates, stopping in front of a mansion among the trees. Flunkies were opening the doors of the lead cars when I decided to drive out before the gates closed behind us, which could have caused us to be delayed for explanations.

We stopped for the night at Lazarevskoye, a very small village on the hillside above the Black Sea, with beautiful views over the coast. There was a little hotel there, busy in the summer, but not in September, when we were the only guests. On the menu were roast ptarmigan, of all things, probably shipped down from the northern forests for the delectation of some important guests who had never turned up, and kept in the fridge since (no deep freezes in the USSR then). These birds were delicious, their crops full of pine nuts or something, but in any case carrying the scents and flavour of pines. With *grechnevaya kasha* (roast buckwheat cooked like rice, knob of butter on top) to which I had become addicted in Paris, the meal was one of the best I ever had in the Soviet Union. Ptarmigan are *tetereva* in Russian, pronounced *tittirivá* (see chapter "Russian"), and I was glad to have my vocabulary justified.

On 23 September we arrived in Novorossiysk and stayed there two nights to await Vasili's flight to Krasnodar. Novorossiysk was a cement town with a very large cement factory covering everything for miles around with a thick layer of white cement dust. It was also a port of significant size and it is interesting that in 2005, with the Ukraine intent on joining the European Union rather than continuing as a Russian satellite, Novorossiysk was seen as replacing Sevastopol' in the Crimea as the future naval base for the Russian Black Sea fleet. Now in 2014 the problem has been solved, if only temporarily, by Russia annexing the Crimea.

We had a swim in the sea there which was pleasant enough and it was interesting to note the "orders" for swimmers and sunbathers painted on large notice-boards on the beach. These tabulated the prohibitions and orders: sun-bathers to turn every so many minutes; no cars, dogs or laundry to be washed, and so on and so on.

Vasili arrived at Krasnodar on 25 September and we drove there, handed him the car and flew back to Moscow. Our poor old Vanguard was found to be a write-off with a broken chassis, and we later replaced it with a Soviet Pobeda, which could be written off (in the accounting sense) more easily than an imported car. Meanwhile I used a Land Rover.

I was only back in Moscow a day or two before we were asked to provide three screen pilots – one for each of three TU 104's flying the Bolshoi ballet to London for a repertoire lasting a month at the Royal Opera House in Covent Garden. The aircraft were to take off together from Vnukova in the morning of 1 October 1956. There was again no time to line up extra pilots from London so it was agreed that if I guided the lead aircraft, the other two could be accompanied by Peter Lewis and Alan Stephens, who, although not pilots, would be OK for interpreting. As we would be flying in a loose formation the two aircraft behind me in the lead aircraft could just follow us to land safely. Nothing better could be done. All three of us drove early to Vnukova to attend crew briefing.

The weather forecast was bad, with a strong wind, low cloud and bad visibility at Heathrow. Marshal Zhavoronkov, head of Aeroflot, had an open telephone line to Colonel Konstantinov (Soviet Air Attaché in London). They spoke at intervals over the next hour while we all waited for a decision as to whether we should go or not. I was inclined to think that conditions were too dangerous for safety, bearing in mind that we would probably have to land using GCA (Ground Controlled Approach) talkdown, when Peter and Alan might have difficulty in interpreting and relaying to the pilots the dozens of instructions and corrections coming from the GCA Controller. But then Zhavoronkov announced that we would go, and the crews set off towards the three aircraft, already loaded with the dancers, administrators and double air hostess quotas, four for each aircraft – over 150 people in toto. I admired the "Press on Regardless" attitude of the aircrew which I thought was very much in the RAF aircrew wartime tradition. Despite the awful weather forecast, and in full knowledge of the deficiencies of the TU 104 – range especially – there were no gloomy prognostications. Zhavoronkov told us that he would be on an open line to Heathrow, and the Soviet Air Attaché in London was already on his way there, for the whole period of the flight, until we were all on the ground. Zhavoronvov would be watching conditions and give us further instructions if necessary.

As usual I had little to do until we passed Berlin and I used some of the time chatting up the ballerinas. Ulanova was especially nice and I asked her if I might get some tickets for her performances at Covent Garden, which she assured me would be possible. I only had to telephone David Webster, the Chief Administrator of the Royal Ballet, or John Sullivan, the Technical Director, and she would make sure some of the seats allocated to her for friends would be made available. Most of the dancers were anxious about their reception in the UK, which they had been told was an American armed camp, and a base for their nuclear weapons pointed at Moscow.

By mid-North Sea, the weather forecast for Heathrow had if anything become worse and I anticipated difficulties in getting all three aircraft down in safety. Minutes later my Captain (Bugaev again) received a message from Zhavoronkov to divert to Manston. During the war (WW2) RAF Manston had been a Master Diversion Airfield, one of a number equipped with FIDO, a fog dispersal installation. The acronym stood for Fog, Intensive Dispersal of, one of those cack-handed acronyms thought up before the title of the thing to which the acronym referred. The very long runway for those times of 9,000' was five times normal width and flanked by lines of interconnected kerosene burners. When ignited, FIDO could clear a path through overlying fog in about half an hour, enabling Bomber Command aircraft in difficulty to land. I only knew three such aerodromes – Manston, on the Kent coast near Ramsgate, Blackbushe, south of

Reading, and Waddington south of Lincoln. The very long wide runway meant that Manston, the closest aerodrome to the continent, was an ideal diversion for three TU 104s with a precious cargo and short of fuel. Incidentally FIDO was abandoned because it burned 250 000 gallons of aviation kerosene per hour of operation, something to make environmentalists blench.

London Radar confirmed that I should contact Manston on an international emergency frequency for which all three TUs had crystals, and we were instructed by the Approach Controller to use GCA even though weather conditions over Manston were not bad at all, with cloud base at about 1000', some slight rain but good visibility. My aircraft landed first and we were directed to follow a vehicle to a far corner of the airfield where we were instructed to park. I left the aircraft and asked a meeting vehicle to take me to the Control Tower to monitor the landings of the next two aircraft with Peter and Alan aboard. All OK.

On the other side of the airfield I could see a dozen or more USAF (United States Air Force) aircraft parked. These later turned out to be a USAF squadron of fighter-bombers with nuclear capability. Several military trucks drove towards us and from them debouched armed USAF infantrymen, many of them black, who established a cordon round the Soviet aircraft. This greatly upset Bugaev who used his MF radio to contact Moscow and ask for instructions. They told him not to allow any passengers or crew members to disembark. The dancers in our aircraft were also disturbed, metaphorically wringing their hands and saying that this was what they had been told Britain would be like – an armed American camp. The Manston Control Tower asked me to accompany a USAF *lootenant* in his Jeep to the Tower, where they had the Soviet Air Attaché at Heathrow on the phone and wanting to talk to me.

He told me that all was confusion at Heathrow because a Vulcan bomber, carrying the CinC Bomber Command, Air Marshal Sir Harry Broadhurst, had just crashed. Sir Harry and the pilot, Squadron Leader D.R. Howard, side by side in the cockpit, had used their ejector seats and had escaped with minor injuries but the four other crew-members had been killed (they had no ejector seats). Would I please, Konstantinov asked, hire coaches locally, and arrange for the Bolshoi group to be driven to Covent Garden. The crews should be found accommodation for the night locally and the aircraft were to fly back to Moscow the next day. With him at Heathrow was John Sullivan, who then spoke to me and confirmed what Konstantinov had said about the dancers.

There was a difficulty! When I returned to the aircraft and told Bugaev of the arrangements he refused flatly to leave the aircraft, saying that his instructions from Moscow were quite clear. Nobody should leave the aircraft except me. Back

I went to the Control Tower and phoned Konstantinov. He told me to persuade Bugaev to leave the aircraft and to come to the telephone in the Control Tower. He would be given his orders, and Konstantinov would ask Marshal Zhavoronkov in Moscow to confirm them by radio direct to Bugaev. Back to the aircraft. After half an hour, when Bugaev had received amended orders from Moscow, he agreed to come with me to the Control Tower and I put him on to Konstantinov.

There was an amusing misunderstanding when Konstantinov told Bugaev that the Bolshoi ballet should be driven to Covent Garden in coaches Major Deverill would arrange. Bugaev exclaimed: *"V Kopengagen!!??"* (To Copenhagen!!??). Further explanations.

While Bugaev was driven back to the aircraft to explain to crews and passengers what was about to happen, I telephoned a local coach company in Ramsgate and they agreed to send seven coaches to Manston immediately, five to take the ballet to Covent Garden and two to transfer the crews to wherever I could arrange rooms for the night. The first hotel I telephoned in Ramsgate said: *"Yes. Of course we can accommodate the Russians. Who will pay? The Soviet Embassy? Fine. No problems".*

Within half an hour the ballet was off to London, and after bedding down the aircraft and leaving one crew member (probably the KGB man) on board each for security, the rest of us were driven by coach to our hotel on the front at Ramsgate. When we entered there was a surprise. We were met by two motherly figures who addressed us in fluent Russian. They were Russian émigrés from 1919, who had settled in England after the Revolution. I imagined that some of the more KGB inclined Soviet crew-members may have thought that this was a put-up job and that MI6 had installed "plants" in the hotel before we arrived.

Needless to say there were many more telephone calls to and from the Soviet Air Attaché, Covent Garden and the Air Ministry, whom I needed to keep informed. I learnt that the Vulcan had crashed on the runway at Heathrow at 1108 that morning in rain, fog and bad visibility. The pilot had landed short and hit the runway threshold, the same type of accident that killed Jo Butler and 31 passengers in the Constellation at Kallang on 11 March 1954. The Vulcan had crashed at about the time that we should have been landing at Heathrow. Whether the crash brought about our diversion or whether we might have arrived in the vicinity at the time of the crash I do not know. Had the latter been the case all of our three TU 104s might have run out of fuel within the 20 minutes it could have taken to divert elsewhere. Either way we were lucky. I was very sorry for the Vulcan crew killed in the crash. The pilot and co-pilot were in the cockpit forward, seated in Martin Baker ejector seats, and were able to eject from the runway. The rest of the crew were low down in the aircraft, without ejector seats, which could only eject upwards.

In taking down details of the crews to enter into the hotel register I found out that it was the 21st birthday of one of the hostesses. We agreed to have the best possible dinner to celebrate the occasion and I ordered a three course meal with champagne. While making the arrangements I had another message from Konstantinov to say that he was sending an Assistant Air Attaché by car to Ramsgate to keep the aircrew happy (they already were, but possibly the Soviet Embassy was more concerned that some of the aircrew might defect) and to arrange for the payment of hotel and other expenses, including refuelling the aircraft for next day's flight back to Moscow. He arrived during dinner, in time to have his champagne and slice of cake, provided by the management. *"My God"* he said *"What is this going to cost!"* Next day, 2 October 1956, there was time for the aircrew to visit a fishmonger to buy crates of fresh fish to take home to Moscow. We then flew back without incident.

The Bolshoi ballet made its debut at Covent Garden on 3 October with Ulanova and her partner Yuri Zdanov dancing Swan Lake. It was a *tour de force* of course. I was determined to attend one or more performances for which Ulanova had promised me tickets, and ten days later I was back in the UK for a week, during which Irina and I went twice, and sat in some of the best seats in the house to watch Ulanova dance in two ballets – *Swan Lake* and *The Fountain of Bakhchiserai*. The dancing was everything I had come to expect although the sets could not be as splendid as at the Bolshoi in Moscow, the stage there being so much larger. Beforehand I had purchased a box of chocolates, emptied the contents and filled the box with the gherkins preserved in brine beloved of Russians and so much less noisy to eat than chocolates.

Back in Moscow on 19 October I found that the atmosphere had changed. Hungary was in the run-up to its revolution against Soviet power, a revolution led by Imre Nagy. Our travels in the USSR were meeting much more hindrance than in the previous two years; the Soviets were moving troops and aircraft preparatory to the suppression of the insurrection and they did not want us to know too much about it. At the same time, regrettably, Anthony Eden was colluding with the Israeli and French governments to intervene in Egypt and recover the Suez Canal which Nasser had nationalised a year earlier. At the beginning of October it seemed as if Khrushchev was having second thoughts about invading Hungary, but when it became clear that Britain was on the wrong foot in Egypt, opposed by the US and most of the rest of the world, Soviet troops moved on Budapest on 23 October (another landmark birthday date for my sister) and in the ensuing conflict Budapest was bombed by Soviet aircraft and more than 1,000 Soviet tanks invaded the country.

The rest is history: over the next three weeks 30,000 Hungarians were killed in street fighting; 200,000 sought exile, many leaving the country across the Austrian frontier; thousands more were arrested and imprisoned. Nagy and other Hungarian leaders were arrested and later executed. Meanwhile the radio link between the FO in London and our Embassy in Budapest had been cut and our Ambassador there relayed his reports via us in Moscow. He called for Western assistance in combating Soviet aggression. But with Britain in trouble in Egypt there was little to prevent the Soviets having their way in Hungary.

On 1 November the Bolshoi ballet returned to Moscow from London, in several conventional IL 14 aircraft. On 5 November Hungarian street fighters gave up in the face of a Soviet ultimatum. That afternoon an organised mob broke into our Embassy grounds to demonstrate against the British action in Egypt. It was fairly good-natured and I met a pair of elderly Russian ladies who enquired about the garden and some of the plants. That same evening I was attending a party in the Embassy Club when Ken Scott, John Morgan's replacement, was called out to Chancery to translate a note that had just arrived from Krushchev. We translated it together and it turned out to be a not-so-veiled threat to use nuclear weapons against Britain if we continued to oppress Egypt, or words to that effect. We boycotted Revolution Day ceremonies on 7 November and the Soviets withdrew their invitation for the Sadlers' Wells Ballet to visit the USSR. Things became bleak.

Sir William Hayter was outraged by the British action in Egypt, a potent factor in allowing the Kremlin hawks to get away with their invasion of Hungary. He was due for relief in January, and although earlier I had thought of having another Christmas at home, I then thought it might be better to fly home with Sir William and return to Moscow with his successor – Sir Patrick Reilly. Meanwhile I went off with Daphne Park on her last trip before tour expiry. She would finally go home in December. We re-visited Central Asia, including Samarkand and Tashkent, but it was not as much fun as on the previous occasion. We were hounded by goons wherever we went.

In November, walking in the centre of Moscow, I noticed a temporary kiosk with a few people queuing in front. Looking over their shoulders, I saw that a girl behind a desk was issuing invitations to meet a local deputy up for election. Printed invitations were being given to interested citizens, so leaning over their backs, I took one, thinking that this might be an interesting occasion to attend.

The girl reacted immediately and demanded the invitation back. I refused, saying that it was surely an open meeting and in no way confidential. I admitted that I was from the British Embassy and would like to attend with a friend. She promised that if I returned the card and left my name I would receive two invitations the next day, still well before the meeting. I agreed, and the invitations were delivered.

The meeting was in the evening in the conference room of a public building a short walk from the Embassy. I invited Daphne Park to accompany me. We turned up about half an hour before the meeting. The hall was about half full with some people sitting on wooden benches and others standing around gossiping. Several benches at the back were occupied by Red Army soldiers, who had obviously been drinking, some still drinking from bottles. They were making a lot of noise.

About five minutes before the speaker was expected, the audience was called to order, an injunction ignored by almost everyone except Daphne and me, sitting on a bench several rows from the front, facing the podium from which the delegate-elect would speak. He duly arrived, was introduced, and commenced a very boring speech about his past appointments and achievements in his factory and in the Communist Party. Several times the Chairman had to call for order and silence and was ignored. We were far enough forward to hear most of the dissertation.

Two benches behind us and the 20 or more soldiers seated on them went over backwards with a great deal of noise and raucous laughter, and voices calling in vain for order and quiet. The speaker finished after 15 minutes and the Chairman proposed the election of the candidate. All in favour to raise their hands – all did, (except Daphne and I, who imagined that we were ineligible to vote). *"Who is against?"* the chairman asked. No hands raised. The Chairman, looking pointedly at us, asked: *"Who has not voted?"* We did not dare raise our hands, for fear of exile to Siberia. Someone whispered in the Chairmans's ear, and he closed the meeting.

In December the weather became too bad for me to commute daily from Perlovka to the Embassy and I applied for a recently vacated flat in a diplomatic block on Sadovaya-Samotechnaya, a segment of ring road 60-70m wide, the Sadovaya related to Russian *sad* meaning garden, referring to the trees in grass originally lining the road in some places. The circumference of the ring road is almost 15km, centred on the belfry of Ivan Grozniy in the Kremlin. This ring was originally a fortification, a vallium (ditch and wall, *"val"* remains a Russian word) built to protect Ivan the Terrible's Moscow against attackers, the Turks in the person of the Crimean Tartars. After their defeat and as the threat of attack waned, the defences were removed and dwellings erected, initially modest, but later houses for aristocrats and the new bourgeoisie. Initially the ring had to provide for the renewal of defences should these be needed, so the houses had extensive gardens running down to what soon became a ring road. After the Revolution, when battles took place between Reds and Whites at places on the ring road, the gardens were used to construct the present unusually wide Sadovaya Ring (Садовое Кольцо). Sadovaya Samotechnaya was a short section of the ring road on the north side of Moscow and got its second name from the stream Neglinnaya (un-clayed) which passes beneath the road at its eastern end. The Samotechnaya probably means "free-flowing" to distinguish it from a ditch.

My new flat was being re-whitewashed and I lodged with Donald for six weeks in his superior flat on Skatertny Peryulok ((Table-cloth Lane). There was plenty of room there because Donald was unaccompanied and he had a very good cook, Klava. I had sometimes been able to borrow her for important parties when I was living at Perlovka. Her *pièce de résistance* was a large "swan" made of meringue with tinned fruit and ice cream between its partly folded wings swimming in more ice cream. However, Klava called these creations Goosi (geese), more abundant than swans in Russia.

From Skartertny Pereulok to the Embassy was only about 15 minutes, driving carefully on the beaten snow. Following the demise of the Standard Vanguard, I used a car from the other Attachés' stables. Once I moved into my new flat it was quite nice. However, as at Taganka it was for diplomats of approximately my grade (Second Secretary or thereabouts) of all nationalities and as neighbours on one side I had a family of Indonesians who made strong smelling oriental food and a lot of noise. Above I had neighbours who often disposed of evil smelling refuse down the rubbish shute, which led to the basement. These common waste disposal shutes were a constant source of bad smells and noise (cans were thrown down it). I insulated my shute lid (in the kitchen) as far as possible to avoid smells leaking out.

In winter, and this was winter, the large opening double windows, had to be closed and the cracks between caulked with tightly packed cotton wool. Only the "fortochka" a small storm window set in the larger window, was left unsealed for ventilation. Pot plants could be lodged between the outer and inner windows, and frozen food could be hung out of the fortochka if the temperature was -10°C or below. The Russians would hang "pelmeni" (large meat-filled Siberian ravioli) out of the fortochka in a string bag.

I had planned to spend Christmas with Irina in Munich but changed my ideas when I discovered that she was in London and shortly returning to Munich but not necessarily over Christmas. I liked Anna Hamilton and decided that Christmas in Moscow might have its compensations. Anna was a very attractive girl, intelligent but no blue-stocking, a doer, with lots of initiative. There was also the point that I expected to accompany Sir William Hayter back to the UK early in the New Year, and probably escort his replacement, Sir Patrick Reilly, back to Moscow in the RAF aircraft that would undoubtedly be laid on. At that time I was expecting to return home tour-expired in February and hoped to travel home via the Soviet Far East – by the Trans-Siberian railway to Nakhodka and then back to the UK by ship or plane via Japan – a journey of several weeks at least.

I had passed the Staff College Qualifying Examination and there was now no obvious reason why I should not attend the next course at Bracknell starting in January 1958. I had to be selected, but with recommendations from Sir William Hayter and my two Air Attachés, Peter Donkin and Donald MacDonell I envisaged no difficulties. What naivety! Would I never learn? I had discussed my ambitions with Chuck Taylor, the US Air Attaché, before his return to the USA and he had asked *"Why not do the USAF Staff College course? I can fix it."* He arranged with the Pentagon that I should be invited to visit them in Washington shortly after my return to the UK later in 1957. We could then discuss going to the USAF Staff College. I thought that if I failed to be selected for the RAF Staff College I could go to the US equivalent.

Meanwhile my plans to return home via the Soviet Far East had run into trouble. Because of Suez and Hungary, relations between the UK and the USSR had deteriorated and OTDEL had become much more unhelpful over our travel. All Western attachés were affected. My return to the UK was still several months in the future and it was becoming clear that my replacement could not arrive in Moscow until February or even later. He was to be Squadron Leader Dale, who had completed his course in Russian but for whom a visa to enter the USSR was being delayed (another case of the Soviets making life difficult for us).

Christmas worked out as reported in my letter home of 30 December:

> *Happy New Year. You have had no letters from me for the past week because the bags have been running queerly over Christmas.* (More Soviet nastiness!). *There have been no incoming bags since the Sunday before Christmas and there will not be another one until the day after tomorrow – Wednesday. But I have received your Christmas letter. Thank you. I hope you had a good time. We did here.*
>
> *On Christmas Day I went to a joint lunch given by Peter Lewis and*

Peter Rouse-Moore, respectively the Assistant Air Attaché 2 and the Assistant Naval Attaché 1. That evening I dined with the Ambassador who by tradition gives dinner to all the bachelors and unmarried women in the Embassy. This was followed by a ball to which all the staff of other Commonwealth embassies are invited. There were 30 of us at the dinner starting at 7.30 p.m. and at 9.30 the other guests arrived, having dined in their respective embassies. Our ball lasted until about 3 a.m.

On Boxing Day I gave a party in my old flat on Narodnaya, which I used to share with Dennis Spilsbury. I am in and out of there as well as my new flat on Samotechnaya. I had 20 people for dinner followed by a film (an opera) followed by dancing – Rock and Roll (ask Mick what that is). The whole thing was most successful. I had all the most interesting people (in my view) in Moscow and certainly all the most beautiful women. (Two of the beautiful ladies were Anna Hamilton and Mrs Isham, the wife of a Second Secretary in the US Embassy. The latter, green-eyed and black-haired, in her late twenties, professed to be of Red Indian descent). The last guests left at 3 a.m. again. The next night was also a three o'clock affair as have all the nights up to now. Tonight I am having a rest and writing this letter at midnight hoping to be in bed by 1 a.m.

On Boxing Day I sensibly went riding to shake off some of the effects of Christmas pudding and alcohol, and again yesterday. Yesterday was not so pleasant because all the best horses, including my "Bouquet" had been sent off to the New Stadium to take part in a pageant. I was given the best horse available, which was awful. I asked for another and it was even worse.

Today I have been skiing with Anna, in the vicinity of the 40km limit of the forbidden areas west of Moscow. Had a most enjoyable and strenuous afternoon. The temperature has at last gone down to about - 10°C (it had been much higher and slushy earlier) giving good snow conditions.

My trip to Khabarovsk has been forbidden by the Ministry of Defence, quite groundlessly it seems to me. It is very annoying. I had so wanted to visit the Soviet Far East. Tomorrow I will probably try to argue with OTDEL to allow us to go later but I have my doubts because they do not like us at the moment and are trying to make things as difficult as possible for all travellers, especially attachés.

Daphne (Park) visited my father at home on 19 January and stayed the night, meeting Mike and Pat at lunch on the Sunday. The previous evening she had visited Mary and Titus at their London home in Circus Road. This was not the first time she had met the family. Meanwhile Sir William Hayter and Iris had returned home in an RAF Hastings aircraft on 15 January. I had hoped to accompany them but permission came through from OTDEL for me to visit the Crimea with Ken Scott for a short visit from 16 January. This was too good to miss, so I saw off Sir William from the airport and then put my things together for the trip south. Ken was now the Ambassador's personal secretary. We had not travelled together before but he seemed a nice enough chap, a first impression borne out subsequently. We flew Aeroflot to Simferopol, the capital of the Crimea and lodged there in the Intourist hotel. For some reason or other the restaurant in the hotel was closed and to get supper we had to walk across the road to a crowded restaurant which was difficult to enter because of the tumult at the door.

By announcing our diplomatic status we were allowed to the front of the queue and then joined another to await places at a table. After half an hour or so we were ushered to a table with two vacated chairs. The occupants of the other two chairs were Army officers in uniform. One, a Colonel, was already drunk and his companion, a General, kept straightening his colleague out and preventing him from falling backwards on the floor or face down in his plate. Ken and I were a bit fed up with our treatment in Simferopol so far and were openly critical of the arrangements in the hotel and restaurant. We ordered and eventually food came (and drink which we shared with the General who shared his with us). In conversation the General, on learning whom we were, wanted to know what we thought of the Soviet Union and its people. We told him that it was very difficult to meet any ordinary people because they were not allowed to meet us.

The next morning we decided to visit Bakhchiserai,[5] the Crimean Tartar Khan's "palace" once upon a time, now a museum kept, nominally, in the state it had been in during the Khan's residence. We went there by taxi from Simferopol, about half an hour's drive over frozen streets, because the temperature was -11°C, unusually low for the Crimea in January. Bakhchiserai, Bakhchè Serai in transliterated Tartar, meaning Seraglio of Gardens, was very well maintained and worth a visit. We were particularly interested to see the fountain on which Pushkin based his poem and which gave its name to the ballet *The Fountain of Bakhchiserai*, very moving when danced by Galina Ulanova. I had seen it several times. There were no longer any Tartars there, or in the Crimea. Hoping to regain some of their independence the Crimean Tartars had supported the German occupying forces during the Second World War.

Following liberation in 1943 Stalin exiled the entire Tartar population to Siberia and replaced them with Russians and Ukrainians.

The Fountain of Bakhchiserai was surprisingly modest, mounted vertically in a wall. Water trickled from a spout at the top and was split by features of the fountain so that drops ran down the stone slab being further split into further trickles. These represented the tears shed by the Polish princess who pined for home. The reception rooms where the Khan dispensed justice and conferred with other Tartar leaders were very fine, with carpeted floors and low divans and sofas along the walls, very much the style adopted by modern Muslim leaders in any part of the Middle East, in tents or buildings.

The capital of the Crimean Tartars had originally been Chufut Kale, once again probably transliterated Tartar. We had read about this "fortress" in my 1902 French Baedeker and as it was only a few km east of Bakhchiserai, Ken and I walked towards it, over frozen roads and paths along what was known by some as the Valley of Jehoshaphat. Before we got there we noticed steps on the face of a vertical cliff leading to galleries and caves with painted ikons some visible from down below. This was the Uspenskiy Monastery, Uspenskiy meaning "Assumption", dedicated to the Virgin Mary. We climbed the vertiginous steps to the chambers hollowed out of the cliff. The "monastery" was without any guardian or even doors.

It seems that after the arrival of the Mongols, or Turkomen, or Tartars, the Muslims were less than tolerant of the Orthodox Christians, who found it safer to establish a monastery carved rather like Petra, from the cliff face and high enough up to deter any would-be intruder. This would also deter any tourist although according to Oliphant about 20 thousand Christian pilgrims used to visit the church in August on the feast of the Assumption.

Leaving the monastery with aching legs (descending a great number of steps is unusual exercise for most legs) we approached Chufut Kale, looking for a way in. There were steps up to a large portal, but is was locked and barred as if the place were uninhabited, so we decided to scale the city wall and cliff on which it was built, about 50 feet up, not as high as the monastery, but no steps and the more or less vertical climb was made hazardous by frozen snow in the crevices available for toes and fingers. Ken was dressed in a black Crombie greatcoat and shoes suitable for a Third Secretary in Whitehall. My gear was less posh – my covert kapok-lined coat, specially made for me for Moscow by Hoggs in Savile Row, and lace-up boots (flying boots but of the type made for escaping on foot from a Gulag Luft). I led the way and photographed Ken following more warily.

When we got to the top and over the wall, who should meet us but the Russian caretaker whose first question was why we had chosen such a difficult way to enter. We should have knocked on the door. We asked him about inhabitants. He said that the previous month a Tartar, returned from exile, had tried to settle in the ruins but had been caught and thrown out.

The Tartars had inhabited Chufut Kale for hundreds of years, together with Karaïte Jews who had been there very much longer. Muslims tolerated Jews to a greater extent than Christians, and they got on well enough together, but when the Khan moved to Bakhchiserai in the 17th century, many Tartars moved with him to the much more verdant valley, leaving Chufut Kale to the Jews. The Karaïtes were a sect who did not accept the authority of the Talmud or interpretation of scripture by rabbis. They appointed their own rabbis and had their own synagogues. The Soviet authorities had little sympathy for either Jews or Tartars, exiled the latter to Siberia and forbade their return to the Crimea, and "resettled" the Karaïte Jews in Evpatoria, a coastal town about 70km northwest of Simferopol. Chufut Kale was cold and dreary and we did not stay there long but were let out of the gates by the caretaker and walked to Bakhchiserai where there was a taxi to take us back to Simferopol.

That evening we returned to the restaurant across the road, sat down and ordered. Shortly after a young man in his thirties (like us) rose from his table on the other side of the room and approached us, wishing to drink a toast with us Englishmen. To our surprise he drew up a chair and sat down, saying that he was interested in England and asking quite well-informed questions. He then said that his wife was with him, might they both transfer to our table. We agreed. The wife in her late twenties was very nice, slightly awkward, but friendly. Ken and I immediately twigged that this unusual event had been arranged by the General with whom we had dined the night before.

We were game for anything and wondered what was coming. Our unexpected friend said he was a bee-keeper. Times were hard for some reason or other; of course January is not the best time for honey, especially in frozen Crimea. We finished our meal, borsch or something like that and the Soviet couple insisted that we should go home with them for a drink. We agreed and piled into their small car in which they drove us to the eastern outskirts of Simferopol. Their house was single-storey, small and in its own garden where the beehives were kept. This was preferable to the usual pokey Soviet flats in which most of the population lived, more on the lines of the old Russian wooden cottages to be seen on the outskirts of Moscow and rapidly being replaced by concrete blocks.

The bee-keeper explained that he had no ordinary vodka but for his bees he received a great deal of proof spirit which he and his wife used instead. He poured us out a glass each. It was ice-cold as befits vodka, tasteless and with remarkably little noticeable "kick". Conversation ranged over every subject in the sun: politics, history and religion (the Tartars, Jews and Ukrainians). Our opinions of the Soviet Union, the Great Patriotic War (i.e. WW2) were sought and listened to with interest. Some time after midnight the bee vodka was having a strange effect on me at any rate. On turning my head I seemed to be still looking straight ahead, and I felt disassociated from whatever I was saying, with a sort of paralysis creeping over me. Ken too was starting to behave oddly. We decided to make our adieus, politely refused a lift back to the hotel saying we needed the walk, and stepped into the cold night which had a drastic effect on our already slightly comatose brains.

We had no idea how to walk back to the hotel but fortunately there were tram lines leading downhill and we remembered that we had driven uphill to the bee-keeper. By walking (arm in arm) between the tramlines we reckoned that we might at least get back to the centre of Simferopol and our hotel. And so it was. Next morning we were more or less OK again, without the hangover we might have expected. It may be true that pure alcohol is better from this point of view. Generally though this Soviet hospitality was very unusual, indeed unique, the only time such a thing happened to me in more than three years in the Soviet Union. And the bee-keeper and his wife were genuinely friendly, even if they may have had to report on us to the KGB next day. One might well ask: is this the sort of thing Air Attachés and diplomats should be doing – sight-seeing and partying at public expense. Yes! Money well spent! Finding out how the other side lives, sharing their worries and hopes, gaining insights into the influence and operation of the authorities (even the General) contributes to the knowledge necessary for good international relations.

Despite further attempts to travel to parts of the Soviet Union I had not yet reached, diplomatic relations between the UK and USSR had reached such a formal nadir that we could not get permission, and without permission, from OTDEL in our case, tickets could not be bought, so there was nothing for it but to knuckle down to the *status ante quo*, i.e. the Soviet Union as it had been when I arrived in 1954. Not quite. I myself was *persona grata* with my Russian colleagues in the ministries, in Aeroflot and even in the KGB as a result of my flights backwards and forwards with the TU 104s. There was no particular grudge held against me; it was just that the politics had led to a change of policy. Ah well. I only had a few months left to go before returning home.

On Wednesday 13 February I flew home by Aeroflot and BEA, arriving at tea time, staying in London and visiting Air Ministry on Thursday and Friday for orders related to my flying out with Sir Patrick Reilly a week later and discussions about my return home and what I would then do. I found out that no decision had yet been made about my attendance at the RAF Staff College but that the USAF had been in touch about my visit to Washington in May, when I was expected to be home. I should stay in Moscow until May Day and then fly home directly afterwards.

I was home over the weekend 16/17 February and then made my way to Lyneham to join a Hastings carrying Sir Patrick Reilly and his wife to Moscow to take the place of the Hayters, already home. The flight, on 19 February, was not without incident. We night-stopped in Berlin where the Reillys took themselves off to stay with senior diplomats there. I went shopping for cheese and bacon and to attend a contemporary ballet with a German friend.

Next day, 20 February, after taking off from Gatow (Berlin), the aircraft, a Hastings of Transport Command, normally a freighter, but adapted for this flight to carry several reasonably comfortable seats for the Reillys and their escort (me), was instructed to land at Minsk rather then continue to Moscow, where a severe blizzard would have made landing hazardous for the RAF crew.

I would have preferred to divert to Warsaw but the Soviets insisted on Minsk, so we landed there without trouble. The Reillys were driven into Minsk to stay at the Intourist hotel (the only one, which I knew well) while the crew and I stayed at a small hostel on the airfield. We needed to re-fuel the aircraft which involved much telephoning to Moscow over a terrible line (they probably heard my voice through the ether rather than the telephone line) and we then had to take turns guarding the aircraft overnight. There were confidential mail bags aboard. All was done and we were airborne next day 21 February at 0900 arriving Vnukovo at midday. As it was a freighter, conditions on the aircraft were less than luxurious, very noisy. The Air Quartermaster, normally responsible for the security of the load, did his best to keep the Reillys comfortable. When they accepted his offer of a mug of coffee, he broached the large Thermos full of the black stuff, and poured measures into the mugs arranged in a semi-circle on the floor boards. *"Milk?"* *"Yes please"*. With a penknife he made holes on opposite sides of the circumference of a tin of Nestles condensed, applied his lips to one and blew an arching stream of milk from the other into the Reilly's mugs. The look on Lady Reilly's face was something to behold.

For the rest of the week I was kept busy with the aircraft and crew, because the radio compass in the Hastings had packed up on the flight into Moscow, and the Soviet screen pilot refused to accompany the aircraft back to Berlin until it was replaced. The Soviet pilots depended entirely on one or preferably more radio compasses for navigation. A spare compass had to be flown out to Moscow via Copenhagen and Helsinki but by 24 February, my 35th birthday, it had still not arrived. The crew members had to be accommodated and the aircraft guarded (one of the crew slept in it each night) and transport for the crew members had to be provided backwards and forwards between Vnukovo and Moscow, quite a business at that time of year with snow, sleet and slush making driving difficult. Donald MacDonell was away at home and I was doing all his work, including attending the reception for Soviet Army Day on 23 February. We got the Hastings off to Lyneham by the end of the month.

I tried to do more travelling in March and April, but OTDEL would not cooperate and apart from short visits by car as far as the monastery complex at Zagorsk and skiing at Tsaritzina I (and all the other service attachés) were confined to Moscow. There was plenty to do there and I continued to frequent the theatres and the Conservatoire, making the most of the cultural opportunities while I could. I packed up most of my personal belongings, some brought out to Moscow and some acquired there – books, furniture, cutlery, crockery, lights, riding and skiing gear – in wooden cases for dispatch home by ship from Leningrad. Anything for which I could not envisage a use in England I sold to colleagues staying in Moscow. From the US Embassy I acquired a large deep freeze (literally named "Deepfreeze"). This was the property of Chuck Jones, the USAF Assistant Air Attaché, returning home on 8 May. I thought this freezer would be very useful at home, where we had no such thing, but it was very large, so I initially consigned it to sister Mary, at her home in Circus Road, Maida Vale. To get it back to her I had the US Ambassador's Globemaster drop it off at Tempelhof airport in Berlin, whence it was collected by a truck from RAF Movements at Gatow, who loaded it on to the next RAF transport flight to RAF Lyneham. Another RAF truck delivered it to Circus Road. Mary kept the Deepfreeze until years later when I retrieved it once I had a wife and family and a house in the UK.

There was a succession of going away parties given for me by many of the defence attachés of embassies with whom I had been closely associated. Usually Anna Hamilton was invited with me because it was assumed that we would eventually form a closer association (not to be, as it happened!) In late April and May, up to May Day, I played my usual role on the Embassy roof, getting some more very good photographs of new Soviet aircraft. My swansong with communist students was on 17 March, when I showed them Richard III in the Swedish flat, followed by a showing in our own Embassy to staff from the other embassies the following evening. A reception for the Italian Armed Forces Day, another for the departing Finnish Military Attaché , a large American reception for I knew not what – life much as normal in Moscow in those days.

Easter Monday, 22 April 1957:

> *Dear Dad,*
>
> *Beautiful weather here now. Warm sun and clear skies. In a couple of days the Air Attaché arrives back and on Sunday my relief arrives at Leningrad. On Saturday the Air Commodore (Donald MacDonell) is giving me a farewell party. Horrible idea. I hate such affairs. I hand over my duties on 2 May. I may be coming home on the SS Molotov, leaving Leningrad on 6 May arriving London (Surrey Docks) on 13 May. I shall probably start my leave on the 13th, spending a month in Sweden and then a month in Italy.*
>
> *Please tell Mary that the Deepfreeze will be turning up at Circus Road in the near future. She can use it until I need it, which may be a very long time.*
>
> *Not much is happening here. As you may have heard on the news, our travel has been more and more restricted. This applies not only to us but to all non-communist embassies. Of course it makes life very dull here if one cannot travel. I have been winding up my affairs and preparing for the arrival of my successor – Squadron Leader Dale. He is going to have to live in the dacha out at Perlovka. There is no other accommodation available. It was much the same when I arrived here. After two months or more in a hotel I had to go into a flat with only the minimum of furniture, chucked out by others who had been newly furnished.*
>
> *I have been very tired lately. Last night I went to a small cocktail party for some Labour Party MPs going through Moscow to Laos. When I got home to my flat I changed to go to a film at America House (the US Embassy Club), and then somehow or other went to sleep fully clothed on my bed, waking up too late to go out, and only in a state to undress and go to bed properly. I need a change and am looking forward to it. I have had enough of the Soviets for a few years.*

In fact I did not return home by ship but by air, on 13 May via Helsinki. I stayed the night in the Coburg Court Hotel so that I could visit Air Ministry early next day to discuss my visit to the Pentagon in Washington the following week. Then – home on leave.

Notes:

1. See Patricia Blake's introduction to *Writers in Russia 1917-1978* by Max Hayward, Harvill Press 1983.

2. *A Double Life. The Memoirs of Sir William Hayter.* Hamish Hamilton 1974.

3. Ibid

4. Donald MacDonell drafted some sections of his memoirs before he died in June 1999. His widow, his second wife, Lois, edited the memoirs with Anne Mackay and they were published by Pen and Sword Aviation in 2005 as *From Dogfight to Diplomacy. A Spitfire Pilot's Log 1932-1958.* Donald gives an excellent picture of his early life in the RAF and as a prisoner of war in Germany where he spent four years until his release in 1945. The chapters describing his 2½ years in Moscow as Air Attaché, including a year when I was his assistant, add some details to my own story.

5. A good account of this whole once Tartar area may be found in *The Shores of the Black Sea* by Laurence Oliphant, originally published in 1853 and re-issued by Könemann in 1998. Oliphant was a British diplomat and MP, born in South Africa. Jewish in origin he was a pioneer of Zionism. For an excellent review of the history of the whole of this part of the world, especially the Crimea, read *Black Sea. The birthplace of Civilisation and Barbarism* by Neal Ascherson.

Staff College

I flew back to London on Monday 13 May 1957 and immediately visited Air Ministry (DDAFL) who had received my air tickets to fly to Washington the following week by "Blue Plate" service as it was called. That week-end, 18 to 20 May, I had time to visit home to see the family and check the arrival from Moscow of some of my heavy kit from which I needed to extract clothes suitable for wear in Washington. The following Thursday I flew to Paris by RAF flight from Northolt and thence took a USAF car to an air base near Fontainbleau from where a DC4 flew me as a passenger with a load of senior yanks to Andrews Air Force Base outside Washington. There I was collected by Colonel Charles (Chuck) Taylor and driven to his home 20 minutes south of Washington at 2517 N. Kenilworth Street, Arlington 7, Virginia. Chuck's wife, Carol, and his two daughters were at home waiting for us and we immediately got involved in a series of barbecues in their garden or in the gardens of other USAF families. Arlington was a favourite domestic area for officers of all services working in the Pentagon.

Chuck and Carol lent me their second car, a large Chevrolet with automatic gears, the first I had come across, but quite easy to master. In this monster by British standards I was expected to drive myself to the Pentagon for meetings with various officers in various offices in the rabbit warren which the Pentagon then was (and probably still is). I had always assumed the Pentagon would be a five-sided building but had not realised that it is a series of concentric pentagons, joined by radial corridors, very like a spider's web in many respects.

Driving to and from the Pentagon was complicated, on multi-lane highways, with frequent clover-leaf junctions and flyovers and underpasses, dense traffic, and the necessity of being in the correct lane for the direction in which one was aiming. I soon got the hang of it. It was hot and humid in Washington as it always is in summer, so one of the first things Chuck Taylor did with me was to visit a drug store to buy a light-weight suit, good quality and ridiculously cheap. Any size and taste could be suited and the trouser legs, left un-seamed on the peg, were hemmed to your leg length before you left the drug store, wearing the new suit. I chose a blue-grey crease-proof cotton mixture, single-breasted. It lasted me many years back in the UK. At the same drug store, we bought readymade meals on plastic covered foil plates for the evening. Carol heated these in the oven for all of us when we got home. I discovered this was normal fare. For most of the people I met home cooking did not exist, except for barbecues, which might be categorised as cooking. Once we went to a drive-in cinema and ate our plasticated meal there, watching a bad film.

The plan was to spend Monday and Tuesday 27 and 28 May in the Pentagon visiting various air intelligence departments. Officers concerned with Soviet bombers wanted to talk to me about my experiences in the TU 104, because of its similarity to the Badger bomber from which it had been developed. They already knew much of what I had to say because my reports to Air Ministry had been copied to them. One visit intrigued me greatly. I was sitting in an office waiting for the officer, who strode into the room and introduced himself as Major ...... "from Clandestine". He was dressed in brown slacks, loud check jacket, kipper tie, and two-tone shoes. He sat down opposite me and asked whether from my flat in Samotechnaya I had ever noticed pigeons flying about or roosting. I said – ravens yes occasionally, sometimes starlings, but not pigeons in my recollection. I thought pigeons would have trouble surviving the low winter temperatures in Moscow. Why did he wish to know? He would not be drawn on this question, shook my hand and left the room, leaving me wondering whether the CIA or some other intelligence agency might be interested in using carrier pigeons in Moscow (for 007 type agents), or whether they wished to introduce toxic materials or viruses to infect Muscovites.

I was to see General Walsh of the USAF, towards the top of the USAF Intelligence structure, on Tuesday at midday. Before then I decided that I would have time to ride in Rock Creek Park, where one could hire horses and kit. Setting out early I had no difficulties finding the stables, and set off at a trot into the myriad drives and tracks criss-crossing the park, densely wooded with occasional lakes. At about 1030 I thought I should turn for home but then the problems started – I could not find the stables. Eventually I was galloping madly from one drive to another following the instructions of black gardeners and sweepers, each of whom told me exactly how I could get back to base, but all incorrect. Luck eventually took me and my lathering horse to the stables, where I left the animal to the grooms, paid over my dollars and drove at high speed to the Pentagon. I was half an hour late but General Walsh was understanding and rather astonished that I had been riding at all that morning and on my own. He was very friendly, in the American back-slapping way, on Christian name terms from the start. He had been briefed by Chuck Taylor on my wish to attend the USAF Staff College, and immediately telephoned them, after a few minutes conversation informing me that I had been reserved a place in the autumn.

Chuck Taylor and his erstwhile No.2 in Moscow, Colonel Chuck Jones, then told me that some officers at Wright Pattison Field, a two hour flight from Washington, would like to meet me, and that we would take a B25 Mitchell medium bomber over there the next day. We took off early from Andrews Field, close to Washington but on the far side of the Potomac (later used a lot for presidential flights) with Chuck Jones flying, because he had flown the type during the war. We spent a day at Wright Pat. looking at captured Soviet aircraft of which they had quite a number. I was told I could not fly a MiG 15, because not long before a Royal Air Force Group Captain had pranged it – a sore point with the Commanding Officer. I felt all RAF officers might now be tarred with the same brush. Not that I wished to risk my life in a MiG.

Later that day we flew to New Orleans in Mississippi. Neither of the Chucks had been there before so we were all tourists. The fish market was extraordinary with thousands of live crabs in baskets and trays following me with their prehensile eyes. We ate a "basket o' crabs" in a fairly frenchified restaurant. One used hands to pick this or that cooked crab out of your basket and tore it to pieces to eat. Very tasty! We joined a coach tour of the richest houses in town gawping through electronically controlled gates and learning from a guide which famous person lived there. One got the impression that there were a lot of seriously rich people in New Orleans to contrast with the poor blacks of whom there were very many more.

We spent the night in New Orleans and flew back to Washington on 30 May via Maxwell Field, another important USAF base. The next day there were more interviews for me in the Pentagon and then dinner, quite formal, with Chip Bohlen, the US Ambassador in Moscow, who was home on a visit. We (Chuck Taylor and I and a certain Colonel Hamblin) spent the weekend driving in the area south of Washington searching for a house for the latter. We looked at several properties on "estates" – large scale housing developments of not dissimilar design, which had not yet become common in the UK. Although the houses were similar, they were not identical because of a building regulation that the same design might not be repeated at a lesser interval than five. Some houses were split level; others what we would call bungalows, others with two floors, with features such as garages, gables etc., differently placed to achieve variety. Houses were not substantially built but had a multitude of gadgets, especially in kitchens. These developments were for the moderately well-off middle class who had abandoned the centre of Washington to the blacks. We had one lunch hosted by a friend of mine in Moscow, a US Cultural Attaché who had been in Moscow and helped with the entertainment of the Soviet students for whom we had arranged films. He still lived in central Washington with black neighbours but planned to move directly he could find a house outside.

During my second week in Washington we visited Annapolis, the home of the US Naval Academy, and toured nearby Baltimore, very like some parts of the UK. I was then tasked with driving several wives to Jamestown, where the Pilgrim Fathers had landed in 1608. I used the Chev. lent me by Chuck and Carol, and Betsy Essoyan (another ex-Moscow friend) took her car. The journey was about 150 miles. I had not realised that the speed limit in Maryland was 55 mph and initially I drove at 60. This worried my passengers so much that I reduced speed to an acceptable 45. Jamestown had been turned into a theme village with a cluster of thatched cottages surrounded by a wooden palisade. The cottages were occupied by families in 17th century dress and they busied themselves with the sort of things that the settlers might have done – the women baking bread, growing vegetables, tending goats and chickens, making and mending clothes and the men building, making furniture, agriculture, horticulture, etc. Offshore in the little bay was moored a reconstructed version of the Mayflower, which had, I think, been made in Europe and then sailed across the Atlantic to anchor in Jamestown, joined by two other small sailing ships representing those accompanying the Mayflower in 1608.

I was interested in Jamestown because of George Deverill, who had emigrated to Jamestown in 1628 aged 13 (see chapter: "Men of noe meane Antiquitie"). He certainly survived there until he was 18, but there is no record of him thereafter, possibly because these early records were kept in Williamsburg where they were burnt with all the archives in a fire. The "Mothers of America" had an office in Jamestown and were helpful but not hopeful. Apparently lots of people would like to be able to trace a family root to Jamestown.

Back in Washington living with the Taylors I was able to experience at first hand some of the gadgets and gimmicks peculiar to American houses of that time. There were several bathrooms in the house, small, but bathrooms nevertheless. All rooms were wired for communication with each other via an "exchange", in the Taylors' house located in the kitchen. This meant that any room might have access to music (taped or radio) and the occupants of rooms could be summoned for meals, etc., children woken up and told to do things. In the UK we were still years away from multiple bathrooms and house intercom.

None of the gardens of adjacent houses were separated from their neighbours by fences or hedges and this enabled neighbours to visit each other without let or hindrance and the children of the locality were all thoroughly mixed up. Barbecues were communal rather than family because nobody seemed to mind if others joined in. Sometimes hosts did not even know the identity of some of their guests. I was uncertain about the advantages of this aspect of American life.

There were many parties given primarily for me by Chuck and his wife Carol and their friends, frequently Service officers from the Pentagon. One aim was to introduce me to marriageable girls – match making. Many of the girls were pretty enough but came to parties in little girl outfits, with pleated gauzy organza skirts and frilly tops which reminded me of Shirley Temple films. The strong American twang in their voices turned me off and their knowledge of elementary geography was abysmal. The pretty daughter of an Admiral thought England was adjacent to the Soviet Union and as to the Middle East even the parents had no idea. Of course I was pretty hazy about the location of the different American States so maybe they too had doubts about my geography.

On Friday 7 June my hosts must have thought I had been with them long enough and decided I should finish off my American visit in New York, where I would be left to my own devices. I was booked a room on the 34th floor of the Stadtler Hotel and seen off by the Chucks and their families on an inter-city train from Washington. When parting, Chuck Jones repeated an invitation to me to join him in developing a vast area in Oregon which he had inherited from a relative. It was covered in trees which would take some time to fell. We would both need to retire from our respective air forces. It was nice to be invited. In New York a couple of hours later I took a cab to the hotel and settled in. Next day I visited the Empire State building, then the highest in New York if not in the world, was impressed by the high speed lifts (elevators) and by the view from the viewing platform at the top, although New York was fairly murky at the time.

I did not like New York. Even Fifth Avenue seemed dirty and tawdry and the food was awful in the burger bars which were the only reasonably priced eateries I could find other than the hotel restaurant. I was collected by a USAF car on Sunday and driven to Trenton Air Force Base from which I flew to Burtonwood in Lancashire in a DC4 arriving at 0900 on Monday 10 June. Took the train home to Alton via Waterloo and was pleased to be back. America had been somewhat of a disappointment.

Back in England and based at home in Alton my first task was to return to the Air Ministry in London. I was sent round to the Deputy Directorate of Intelligence Technical (DDI(Tech)) to arrange a simulated reconnaissance by Soviet Air Attachés of Boscombe Down aerodrome. After Farnborough, the historic RAF station devoted to developing and testing aircraft, Boscombe Down became just as or more important after WW2. It is larger, well away from densely populated settlements, in the country one might say, and well placed for the trials of modern high speed aircraft. The Empire Test Pilots' School, originally based at Farnborough, soon had a strong presence at Boscombe Down.

It was, as it were, the British equivalent of Ramenskoye which we were always trying to observe when I was in Moscow. DDI(Tech) had had the bright idea of improving the security alertness of some key airfields in the UK by mounting simulated recces by pseudo-Soviet attachés and I was to be the first one. The defence ministries in the countries where the attachés were serving would have had prior notice of their travel to the areas concerned, even if they did not know the actual targets. Therefore all airfields in the area were alerted to the threat. The types of vehicles and their licence numbers would be known and could also be given to prospective airfield targets. I had no car; mine was still in Sweden, so I borrowed Dad's blue Hillman Minx, licence number POT420, and set out with an Assistant Air Attaché u/t (under training) down the A303 to the vicinity of Boscombe Down, not far from Amesbury, arriving early in the morning. We found a place to park the car in the shade of a haystack in a field half a mile from the main runway, on which a Lightning fighter was being readied for some sort of test flight with a number of other at that time secret aircraft parked nearby.

I noted a disused concrete pillbox within 50 yards of the runway and we took a circuitous route along hedges and entered it by a rusty door. A gun aperture opened towards the runway and with my camera I took photographs of the work in hand on the Lightning and adjacent aircraft. Nobody came to confront us for about half an hour when we saw some movement and a Fire Tender and two service cars debouching from the camp in our direction. We returned to our car through a pigsty and only managed to get into it shortly before an officer of the RAF Police arrived and asked us to get out and accompany him to the guardroom. I told him that we were Soviet Air Attaché staff, and that as he was well aware he could not make us leave our car or detain us. These were the rules of the game. We drove back home well satisfied with the success of our mission and next day took the train to London and reported to DDI(Tech) that the security at Boscombe could be improved.

The following week I accompanied two more u/t attachés on their industrial tour of factories in the Midlands. There was an awkward moment when I was summoned to P (Personnel) Staff at the Air Ministry and confronted by an irate Group Captain who berated me for having fixed myself up with a place on the USAF Staff College Course. Confirmation had been received from the Pentagon that I was awaited in the autumn. This was the first that P Staff had heard about it. I was ordered to write a letter of apology to General Walsh regretting my inability to attend USAF Staff College because the Air Ministry had other ideas about my future employment. As it turned out they did not, but I had no other option than to write to General Walsh explaining the predicament. This was not my first contretemps with senior staff and their decisions, and certainly not the last.

The 22nd July was Camilla Gray's 21st birthday to which I was invited. It was celebrated in her parents' house in Greenwich and to get there they had hired a river boat which took the hundred or so guests from Westminster to Greenwich. The weather was good and the voyages, in both directions, back after midnight, were memorable. Early the following week I went north again with the u/t attachés and later Börje Kwarnmark arrived at home in Alton driving my Sunbeam Talbot car. We put him up for a couple of nights and then drove him to London Airport to take a flight home to Stockholm. I was now free to go on leave, of which I had built up an entitlement of about three months. I set off in the car from home on Friday 5 July crossing the Channel by a flight from Lydd to Le Touquet in a Bristol Freighter, which had been adapted to carry four cars. With hindsight this was a waste of money but at that time I had plenty of money in the bank from my allowances in Moscow. Reverting to normal rates for a Squadron Leader did not show up in my account immediately.

I arrived in Stockholm on Sunday 7 July 1957 and stayed with Börje and his wife Syssy in their house in Lidingö partying with his friends and my friends until Thursday, when I met Janeta Hamilton, Anna's sister. Anna was already at the family farm near Kristianstad in the south of Sweden, the province known as Skône. On the Friday I drove with Janeta to the farm, met the father and mother of the sisters and a brother, Klaus, aged 18, said to be doing badly at his studies. Staying at the farm, which was more like a small schloss, gave me a good idea of how the family lived – in some respects above my usual lifestyle; this was a titled family and they behaved in character. Breakfast was prepared by staff and one served oneself from silver dishes arrayed on a sideboard: fish, bacon and eggs, toast. All very well presented. Count Hamilton, the father of Janeta and Anna, breakfasted in a silk dressing-gown and slippers and engaged me in conversation about Russia and England. He was very well-informed and knowledgeable about problems of international relations, interesting and a little formidable. The girls and their brother were more slapdash.

I was invited to go with the family to attend the Swedish equivalent of the Grand National at Falsterbö near Lund on the south coast of Sweden. This was on Saturday 13 July 1957. We drove there to arrive before lunch which was provided in marquees. Members of the Swedish Royal Family were there, the King, the Queen, and their daughters, and I was introduced to them, having been briefed by an aide to spend no more than a minute or so speaking to the princesses. In fact Princess Birgitta was a very nice tomboyish girl and I spent well over my allowance talking to her. In those days, and possibly still, the Swedish Royal Family was renowned for "informal" behaviour, cycling in the streets of Stockholm, shopping and going about their everyday lives without escort or fuss. I was favourably impressed although I had seen at close range Queen Elizabeth and Princess Margaret headscarfed at one or more horse shows in the UK, but not to speak to and I imagine I would have got short shrift had I tried.

We lodged in a very nice hotel close to the beach near Falsterbö. The beach was of pure white sand and lovely to swim from in the hot sunny weather. That evening we all attended a dinner and ball given by another aristocrat in his castle nearby. I had to hire a dinner jacket and all the trimmings because I had omitted to bring my own from England. After pre-prandial drinks I was teamed up with a lady to accompany in to dinner, arm in arm. We sat down to several courses of very good food: entrées, fish, meat, sweet, the last-named especially memorable being trays of alpine strawberries, in heaps a foot or more high, flown in from Italy and served from giant silver dishes, with cream of course. Wines to accompany the spread were very good and I was interested to see that the dinner, which had started so formally, by the coffee and liqueurs had degenerated into a drunken mob, with some young men actually under the table and not in a state to stand up. Lady Hayter would not have approved.

Anna was otherwise engaged with admirers in Skône so on 15 July I drove back to Stockholm with Janeta who had work to do. She had studied psychology at Uppsala University and initially worked in an abortion clinic which, as a devout Catholic, she disliked, moving to become a case supervisor in an institute treating the deaf. Janeta had a more mature character than Anna, as one would expect as at 29 she was eight years older. She was a very pleasant companion. We visited the Royal Theatre at the palace of Drottingsholm, the usual residence of the Swedish Royal Family. The theatre was built in the 18th century and then lost or abandoned until 1930, when the apparently derelict building was opened up again and found to be still furnished with all the original theatre and stage equipment used 200 years before. Performances of period plays were restarted and we booked for one on Saturday 27 July. Meanwhile Janeta and I drove to Värnama where the Hamiltons had another schloss full of loot brought back by the generals from their military campaigns and where maiden aunts, widows and widowers of the family were accommodated – a sort of family care home. We then drove north through the Swedish forests to Leksand for a couple of days to see a folk play performed there annually. Forests all the way, in which it is unwise to walk at this time of year. We made a couple of forays but were driven out by swarms of mosquitoes. Back in Stockholm on Friday 26 July, we attended a British Embassy cocktail party and next day the Swedish play at Drottingsholm, of which I understood no word, sitting on seats which may have been tolerable two hundred years earlier but not in 1957.

In early August I drove from Stockholm to Munich via the Danish ferry, taking two days, having alerted Irina to my impending arrival. Staying in their still war-damaged house at 2 Jensenstrasse, with Lalya (as Irina's mother was called, or more formally Yelena Borisovna) and Fafa, Irina's severely mentally handicapped brother, I was greatly impressed by the differences from the life I had seen in Sweden. I only stayed there for two nights because I had arranged to see Mariapola in Bordighera the following week. She and her mother, Zia Albina to me, went there regularly for the summer every year, always to the same guesthouse, with a view of the sea and good food, a sunny happy place. While I had been in Moscow Pola had written to me that she had come to know an elderly Englishman, Karl Walter, who had for many years (including the war) lived in a flat on the top floor of the walls of the old town of Bordighera, with a rooftop view of the Mediterranean and down the coast towards Nice (Nizza). She had told me that Karl wanted to marry her and she was thinking about it. As Karl Walter was in his seventies I had doubts about his suitability as a bridegroom for Pola in her twenties. I therefore wanted to meet this Karl and Pola took me to his flat for an introduction.

I found Karl to be a splendid chap, bearded and suntanned, very fit, slim and agile and a mine of interesting information. Karl's father had been German and his mother English. His wife had been an American who had died several years earlier, to Karl's infinite distress. Initially they had lived in Texas but they favoured England and then Italy. He was an anarchist of the variety known as Syndicalist, which indicates that they believed in some sort of government, democratic and minimal. He had written several books on the subject,[1] and had hoped to convert Mussolini's fascists to Anarchism Syndicalism. Needless to say he failed. Anarchy is basically the absence of any formal or state imposed law. Syndicalism was a movement to transfer the ownership of enterprises to unions of workers, not necessarily trades' unions but committees managing industries, housing associations etc. One can see how this might have led to complete chaos. Despite being starry-eyed in their politics, Karl and his wife were writers, journalists at times, who loved Italy, wished to live nowhere else, and managed on their comparatively small income.

They had one son, Grey, who was similarly off-beat, but very distinguished in his way. Grey Walter had taken an initial degree in the natural sciences at Cambridge and then further specialised in nerve physiology and electronics, not unrelated subjects. In his thirties during the Second World War Grey worked on radar, more specifically the PPI (Plan Position Indicator) where a rotating scanner in the aircraft maps radar echoes on a circular screen. This became the H2S used by Bomber Command and the PPI is now the standard display method. When I met Karl, Grey was Director of the Burden Neurological Institute in Bristol, part of the Frenchay Hospital. Partly as a result of his early interest in electroencephalography and his work on radar scanning during the war, Grey had developed the electroencephalograph as a potent weapon in the diagnosis of brain functions and disorders. I was to meet him later. Meanwhile I concluded that there was nothing much to worry about in a link between Karl and Pola. He obviously esteemed her highly and would never do anything to harm her. The age difference did seem a bit excessive but I quickly appreciated Karl as "salt of the earth" at a much higher social level than the class to which one usually applies this appellation.

During the following week Pola guided me in my car to see the places she particularly liked to paint – the mountain villages inland from Ventimiglia on the French/Italian border, clinging to the precipitous flanks of escarpments, nestling in deep and shady ravines, with buttressed houses on many levels and lavender growing in every front yard where there was room. We also drove up the Val d'Aosta among mountains where there was still plenty of snow and where we observed the militia trying to locate smugglers moving tobacco and cigarettes across the frontier, using the rocky hills to hide their activities.

On one trip in early August the Sunbeam's electric overdrive packed up and I had to telephone home for spares to be flow out to Nice. The car could still be driven there but I was unhappy about driving home until all was in order. After two days the parts arrived and were fitted in a garage in Nice. From Bordighera I drove Pola back to Turin and on the way she showed me the small town of Racconigi where she taught art in a secondary school. I left her in Turin and drove back to Munich via Innsbruck where I needed to collect a briefcase to be delivered to Irina. Stayed there for a day and then drove back to Sweden via Frankfurt. All this driving at fairly high speed was playing havoc with my tyres, the treads of the rear tyres, the driving tyres, this being the conventional rear wheel drive, being worn down unevenly. Tyres were not made as well in those days as they are now. Sometimes I was driving for hours at over 100mph, this on the various motorways in Europe, on many of which there was no speed limit.

There was a party in Wrangelsburg on Tuesday 20 August at another country house. I took Anna, Janeta being back in Stockholm. When I left Anna at the family home at 3 a.m. she asked me to drive some junior aristocrat back to the hotel where we were staying. He vomited all over the upholstery of my beloved Sunbeam, said he would clean it up later, but never did. Next morning I borrowed a pail and cloths from the hotel and cleaned it up myself, but so disgusted was I that I left for Stockholm without taking leave of Anna, resolved never to see her or Wrangelsburg again. After a couple of days in Stockholm meeting Janeta and inviting her to visit us in Alton when she could get away from her work, I drove to Göteborg and took the ferry back to Felixstowe.

I had to be back for the Farnborough Air Show in early September, to escort Chuck Taylor and some USAF friends. I also had an introduction from Karl to his son Grey Walter in Bristol. In his research on learning processes, monitored using electroencephalography, he needed access to a flight simulator, a synthetic pilot trainer – the simplest form being a Link Trainer, the sort on which I had trained to fly on instruments. His research showed that it usually took seven repetitions of a cause and effect sequence for the mind to learn the association and act to anticipate the effect. He could wire a Link Trainer to enable him to reverse the controls at the turn of a switch so that, for instance, pulling back on the control column would push the nose down rather than raise it. How long would it take a trained pilot to learn the changed effects of the controls? Would the experience of the pilot be a factor?

I drove to Bristol on 6 September and met Grey, who gave me a tour of his laboratory, which was highly practical in the sense that there was any number of patients being investigated, given drugs of different sorts, wired up to various mechanisms, etc. I was very impressed by Grey and decided to introduce him to the Chief Scientific Officer of the RAF, a civilian working in Air Ministry. They met later and the CSO was also impressed. Grey got his Link Trainer, and, later still, demonstrating what he was doing to Sir Harry Broadhurst, CinC Bomber Command, he sat him in the Link Trainer, closed the hood and after some minutes of normal operation reversed elevator and aileron controls and waited to see Sir Harry's reactions. Sir Harry got the Link into a spin and in his disorientation damaged the Link hood so anxious was he to get out. It is possible that someone who has flown a great deal and to whom the effect of the controls has become second nature cannot easily learn to cope with an unusual cause and effect sequence.

While waiting in a nearby room for Grey to get something sorted out in his office, I was drinking a coffee when I met a very attractive girl, also making a coffee prior to returning to her research on some aspect of electroencephalography. She turned out to be an Icelandic postgraduate psychiatrist, Maia Sigurdarsdottir, attached to Grey's lab to pursue a research project on the effect on the brain of lysergic acid (LSD) as seen using electroencephalography. Grey was her supervisor. We struck up a friendship, which became more than that. On learning that she was short of a guinea-pig willing to take LSD and be observed while under the influence, I volunteered and she agreed to get in touch with me and call me down to Bristol when my turn came. The things one does for science! And for girls!

I was back in London later in September for discussions at Air Ministry about my future. I was of course keen to go to Staff College and I had written a formal letter to Personnel Staff to emphasise this but when I visited them at Adastral House on 16 September I was given the impression that they had not seriously considered this option. They were keen that I should get back into flying practice and so was I, and it was agreed that in mid-November I would join No. 3 Flying Training School at RAF Feltwell for a two week course on piston-engined Provosts, largely to brush up my instrument flying. Then in December I would do a course at No.4 Flying Training School at Worksop on Vampires, the Vampire being a somewhat dated single-seat jet fighter.

About that time I was seeing Daphne Park quite often and we decided to mount a joint party in her London flat for many of the diplomats we had known in Moscow. Knowing that a Transport Command aircraft was visiting Moscow to take out or bring back the Ambassador, Sir Patrick Reilly, I contacted the crew at RAF Lyneham and asked them to get me two 500g cans of beluga caviar for our party. These were not the tiny little jars at £20 each available from Fortnum and Mason in Piccadilly but really substantial tins which had to be opened with an old-fashioned tin-opener. I think they cost me about £20, but their value was immense for those who like the stuff. The party was a great success and attended by Sir William Hayter, by then Master of New College Oxford, and Iris, Lady Hayter. We ate the caviar with soup spoons and black bread, accompanied by vodka and/or champagne. Sir William asked me what I was doing and I told him the whole story about my vain attempt to attend the USAF Staff College and Air

Ministry's apparent reluctance to send me to our own. He said he would see if he could do anything about it.

At home Pola arrived for two weeks, the first time she had been to England. She was enchanted by the warm little houses scattered around in the towns and villages, something I had never thought about. Also the green countryside; all Italians are surprised at this. Their own countryside is brown for much of the year and England is in complete contrast. Pola settled down to paint, and as she had not brought her paints and brushes to England we visited Phillips' shop in the High Street and bought a dozen or more tins of enamels and other paints and half a dozen of the smallest brushes available and she set to it. Very soon, her room, facing north, once my sister Mary's room, reeked of gloss paint and was festooned with paintings on paper and card and wallboard. It happened that I was phoned by Air Ministry on 24 September to ask me as an Italian speaker, to drive to Biggin Hill RAF Station on Friday 27 September to help entertain an Italian Air Force football team, arriving to play a representative RAF team on the Saturday. I explained I had my Italian cousin with me and was told to take her down with me.

Pola was a first class person to have at the reception. She was absolutely beautiful in a scarlet Fortuni type pleated dress. She charmed everyone, visitors and hosts, and especially me. I had sometimes thought of the possibility of marriage to Pola but it was a step too far. I was always restrained by feelings that it would be too close a family connection, anathema in Catholic eyes. Apart from genetic objections, marriage would not have been a good idea because Pola was an artist with a great many devoted Italian friends. She could not have left Italy without being miserable. She had had a tragic life and art and her artistic friends were everything to her, everything she had ever known. Even Jessie, our sometimes difficult house-keeper, liked Pola and put up with her foibles, the paint splashes on the bedroom walls, the constant cigarette fumes. I learnt a lot from Pola. She said "Always behave as you think you should. Never mind what others might or might not think of your behaviour. If they like you: fine. If not: move on."

I was sorry to see Pola go back to Turin but a week later, on 21 October, Janeta Hamilton arrived at Harwich. I fetched her in the car and brought her to Alton, where she had to put up with paint fumes and cigarette smoke left from Pola's occupancy of the same room. This was the time of the first Soviet "Sputnik" and one evening walking back from Selborne we saw the satellite pass over in the sky. We went to see *The Chalk Garden* at the Royal Court theatre in London and I accompanied Janeta to the Silver Cellars to search for and buy a butter dish of the sort where the domed silver lid hinges over to display the contents. Very expensive I thought. Janeta wanted to visit Lady Astor, who was a friend of hers, at her home at Sutton Courtenay. I drove her there but was less than happy to be left outside on a chair while Janeta went in to chat to her friend for the best part of an hour. I was offered a cup of tea by one of the staff. But I felt treated as someone below the salt.

I ran Janeta back to Harwich to catch the ship home. As I was returning, driving along the A12 at 60mph plus, with the radio on and the window slightly open (it was October) there was an explosion and I found my face and upper body covered with warm yellow stuff. Initially I thought that something might have happened in the car, but what. I stopped directly it was safe to get off the road and discovered that the yellow stuff was corn on the cob. A driver travelling in the opposite direction must have thrown out of the window the corn cob he had been chewing. By an infinitesimal chance the cob, approaching me at the speed of the other vehicle plus my own, probably 100mph, had entered my car through the three-inch aperture above the glass of my side window and fortunately hit me in the chest, where it disintegrated. Was this an omen? It could have been a nasty accident.

Omen or no, on 8 November I received a letter from Air Ministry to the effect that I was an additional selection for No. 48 Course at the RAF Staff College, Bracknell with whom "...*you will communicate without delay to arrange for joining instructions to be sent*". The 12-month course would start in January 1958. I was very pleased. I stayed at home at Alton with occasional sorties to London until 17 November when I reported to Feltwell to start my flying course on Provosts. The following weekend I drove to London for supper with Daphne, at which we drank a glass or two of wine. Driving back to Feltwell towards midnight on Seven Sisters Road I was crossing a major road at traffic lights when I ran into a small van travelling at right angles to me from west to east. I came to a stop immediately but the van described several pirouettes in the road and seemed to be heading for a large plate glass window on the corner of the crossing furthest from me. Fortunately the kerb of the road slowed him down and the van stopped and a pale and shaken driver emerged from the driving seat. He accused me of driving through a red light, which I did not admit, although I knew I must have done so. We exchanged details of insurance companies etc. and I drove on equally shaken, leaving the other driver to find some way of getting to his destination because his vehicle would go no further. My Sunbeam was damaged in that the bonnet was distorted but appeared to have suffered little else. I carried on to Feltwell and next weekend left the car at Abbots Garage (and Coachworks) in Farnham for repairs.

At Feltwell I flew morning and afternoon, one or two and occasionally three times a day. We flew teamed up with another pilot, taking turns to fly and be safety pilot. My brother Mike, who was still in the Army Air Corps, was also at Feltwell, flying Austers and other small Army communications aircraft but somehow or other we seem not to have met. Between Feltwell and Worksop I had less than a week off before starting to fly Vampires. This was an aircraft I did not like very much. The cockpit was almost too small for me and I was told that were I to have to bale out I should not attempt to use the bang seat (ejector seat) but turn the aircraft upside down, jettison the hood, and drop out with the aid of a bit of negative G. Otherwise I would lose my knees on the cockpit cowling. The Vampire was an aircraft for small pilots, or for pilots with short legs. Landing was rather like sitting down on the runway, because the aircraft was so low that only when one's bottom was a few inches from the tarmac did the wheels touch. Flying was interesting in that my face was so close to the glass windscreen that the experience resembled that of a bird, but without the draught. Unfortunately Worksop suffered from smog from the neighbouring industrial areas and bad visibility, including snow, kept us in the crewroom for much of the time. In a month to 4 January 1958 I completed only eight hours' flying. I then had to prepare for Bracknell Staff College Course, to start on 13 January. In the interim I spent the best part of a week in Munich, seeing Irina.

I had great affection for Irina but she told me of her devotion to Tom Sheasby (See Chap. Russian). She asked me if I could find him for her because she had received no replies to letters and cards written to the only address she had for him. I agreed that I might be able to help through Army channels and over the next few months followed this up, sending a letter for the War Office to forward to him, to which he might reply if he wished, and contacting the couple, two elderly ladies, who had fostered him. Because Tom was a foster child, I do not think he knew who his biological parents may have been. The two ladies, sisters I think, whom I eventually contacted living near St Leonards, had not heard from him for a considerable time but knew that he had been farming in Cornwall since his retirement from the Army not long before. In my letter to Tom via the War Office I had given Irina's address in Munich and eventually she had a reply. Tom was married for the second time and was farming on a small scale in Cornwall. A second separation was looming. There had been several children.

The story was unhappy and I never knew much of it, collecting scraps of information from Irina and other informants. I was not greatly upset by Irina's link with Tom, because I could see there would be difficulties if I reinforced our own relationship. Many of the things predominant in Irina's life were not so attractive to me. The Russian "soul" was all very well but I was more of an unbeliever and realist, regarding doubt as more important than faith. My life in Moscow had shown me faith in various forms, the Soviet faith in their Revolution and in the personalities who had developed it – Marx, Lenin, Stalin etc. And the Russian Orthodox Church and the apparent idolatry of worshippers. Not much different from Catholicism! There might be grains of truth here and there but I would not have been able to base a philosophy on such things. Subsequent experience has not diminished my scepticism.

On 13 January I drove to the RAF Staff College at Bracknell and was allocated a large room next to another housing Major Donald Fletcher, an Army officer on the RAF course. There were always cross-Service appointments at Staff College available to a few officers of each service and of the Civil Service to ensure common knowledge of procedures used by staff officers; in other words we should all know how the other Services did things. Similarly we had a couple of USAF officers and one from the Rhodesian Air Force. Donald was a good friend – a solid character, not given to flights of fancy, thorough, knowledgeable, reliable. This compared with my comparative impetuosity, sometimes too way out lateral thinking, flexibility rather than solidity. We worked together in some exercises. I think Donald got less out of our professional association than I, but he had many other friends. As too did I. Sandy Gordon-Cumming had flown with me at Feltwell and was a typical RAF pilot type. David Martin-Jones was an RAF Engineer Officer of brilliance. Tony Talbot Williams was a businessman. He intended to retire early to pursue a second career in property and did so after a subsequent tour in the Far East. He had built up a portfolio of properties in Cornwall, especially in Rock, which he renovated and hired out to holidaymakers. He arrived at Staff College with a large filing cabinet containing details of his properties which he administered from his room using his telephone a great deal. The students of 48 Course covered the whole spectrum of Service characters, most being fairly "normal", boring even, but with an admixture of eccentrics.

The first week or so of the course was concerned primarily with briefings about what we were going to be doing and elementary exercises in writing Operation and Movement Orders, Signals, etc., and mastering the systematology of Service appreciations, i.e. how to set about defining a problem and planning its solution, and suchlike. The next week I was warned that the Soviet Embassy had asked for my assistance as Screen Pilot on a Soviet TU 104 flying to America taking the new Soviet Ambassador to the USA. This would land in Copenhagen to pick me up on 5 February. This was good for my image at Staff College and I was delighted to go. I flew BEA to Copenhagen very early on Tuesday 4 February from

Heathrow, leaving the Sunbeam there, having stayed for several nights at the Pushkin Club, meeting Marie Rambert and Tamara Karsavina there on the Friday evening, attending a Russian choral concert with Daphne Park on the Saturday and then another Russian concert at the Festival Hall on the Monday evening.

The crew of the TU 104 were mostly already known to me, with Bugaev as Captain. We flew from Copenhagen to Heathrow, refuelled and continued immediately to Keflavik in Iceland to the east of Reykjavik, familiar from my time in Iceland with 221 Squadron in 1941. Landing at Keflavik was tricky because they had only two runways to land on. One was into wind but covered in deep snow, and the other shorter by a third, clear of snow but 45° out of wind. We decided to risk the latter although the crosswind was in excess of 25 knots. Crabbing in towards the runway threshold, I had doubts about how we would manage but Bugaev yawed the aircraft straight just before the wheels touched and then deployed the braking parachute. We stopped after a lot of swerving and bumping but we were down with some tyres scorched from fully applied brakes. But we were carrying four sets of spares.

The Soviet Ambassador to the US was whisked away to the Embassy in Reyjavik, while we were put up in rooms in the airport hotel, where we also had supper, which was very good. The next morning would be a long day flying from Keflavik to Gander in Newfoundland and thence to Baltimore – six and a half hours in the air, and possibly more than an hour at Gander refuelling and possibly changing more tyres. We were driven to the aircraft where the Ambassador was already waiting in the aircraft passenger cabin and after settling in, Bugaev started the engines. Then panic! The KGB member of the crew ran into the cockpit having discovered one of the crew was missing. *"Ubezhal!"* (Done a bunk!) he shouted. Bugaev shut down the engines and the KGB man disappeared accompanied with two of the burlier crew members. Half an hour later they reappeared with the missing crewman, whom they had discovered still asleep in bed.

Off again. The flight to Gander in Newfoundland was fairly uninteresting. Nothing much to see except sea and frozen terrain once we reached it. Refuelling was uneventful and we were soon off again on the last lap to Baltimore. The flight was more interesting being over land and I was able to do some sightseeing as well as communicating with the radar stations controlling our flight. The Ambassador departed to Washington in a convoy of American and Soviet limousines and the Soviet aircrew with their Air Attaché. I was met by Colonel Chuck Taylor and taken off to a party with Chuck Jones and Major Fife, also ex-Moscow, and their wives, with a very similar party the next evening of Saturday

8 February. We were supposed to fly back to Europe the next day but the flight was delayed for bad weather and we did not take off from Baltimore until the morning after, stopping again at Gander and spending one night at Keflavik before reaching London Heathrow early on 11 February.

Driving back to London where I had to visit Air Ministry for debriefing on my latest TU 104 flight, I was overtaken by the Soviet Air Attaché, still Colonel Konstantinov, who had seen off the TU 104 to Moscow. Konstantinov opened his car window and shouted that I should follow him to the Soviet Embassy where we would have a chat and a drink. I did so and we got into Konstantinov's large flat with some difficulty because his wife was out shopping. However one of Konstantinov's assistants found another key and we let ourselves in to a large room with leather covered furniture and little else. Konstantinov marched into the kitchen and reappeared with black bread, a pound of butter in its greaseproof paper and a bottle of vodka. This we dispatched in double quick time reminiscing at length about Moscow and the Soviet Union to which Konstantinov was longing to return.

We were well into a second bottle of vodka when Konstantinov's wife returned with provisions from the shops. She looked at our somewhat flushed condition, and said in Russian something like "I'll go make coffee!" However, before she returned I realised that I might pass out within a short time, and for an RAF officer and Staff College student to be found drunk in the Soviet Air Attaché's flat would be a "black" of the deepest variety if discovered or revealed. I therefore made inadequate excuses and fled from the door to my car which I managed to drive to Daphne's flat. She was entertaining two children but I mumbled something and made straight for her bedroom where I passed out for an hour or two. I cannot have been too bad because in the evening I went to dinner with my sister Mary and Nonie, visiting from Paris. On the Friday, after visiting Air Ministry, I had lunch at the Royal Aeronautical Club with Donald MacDonell, who was on his way back to Moscow the following day. I returned to Bracknell to restart work on Monday 17 February.

A week later I was down in Bristol again visiting Maia. She came to a Guest Night in the College at Bracknell on 20 February, four days before my 36th birthday. On that day we went to a performance by a Ukrainian choir in London after which I moved some blankets, sheets and pillows to Maia's flat in Bristol. It was sometimes easier to sleep down there. She came to London again on 26 February to a play *A Touch of the Sun* at the Saville and on the 28th to *Lysistrata* at the theatre in Oxford. I had persuaded Maia to take an interest in parachuting and twice we visited Fairoaks airfield to make our first jumps. Fortunately on both occasions the weather was too bad.

Staff College work was mostly related to communications in the broadest sense, writing and speaking, and in the narrower sense – communications in the Armed Services: appreciations, orders, and other specialised methods of recording information and passing it and receiving it, all in a form which had to be correct, clear, concise, and in time, i.e. when required. I already knew a lot about this, as did most of my fellow students, but the practise was very useful not only then and in the RAF thereafter, but for ever, even now when I am writing these words.

There were about one hundred students on No. 48 Staff Course, the majority RAF officers of the rank of Squadron Leader, my rank. For our work we were divided into syndicates of six, each looked after by a member of the DS known as a Syndicate Leader, usually of the rank of Wing Commander. The Syndicates were also divided into three groups under DS Group Leaders of Group Captain rank. Above them were an Assistant Commandant and the Commandant, a splendid person, Air Vice Marshal Ellworthy, CBE, DSO, DFC, AFC.

At a lunch given by the Commandant, which I attended, I suggested a lecturer to talk to the course about communism. A feature of the course were lectures on subjects of interest and importance, often international importance, given by experts in the various fields. On communism, of which I had recent experience in Moscow, I was able to help by recommending Wolfgang Leonhardt, who had been trained in the USSR after the war to take an important position in communist East Germany as part of the communist hierarchy. He had defected to the west a year or so before my course at Bracknell and I had come across him when he lectured at the Pushkin Club, which I still patronised whenever I was free to go to their meetings and lectures. He came and spoke extremely well, not only on this occasion but to subsequent courses at Bracknell.

Maria Mikhaelovna Kullman had accepted my offer to reorganise the record of members of the Pushkin Club, which were in typically Russian disorder. While so engaged I came across the name and address of Lonsdale, the Soviet spy, whom I had not met but who had been a member of the club. At the time I did not know that Lonsdale was a spy but was intrigued by the name, famous in the boxing world and the name of a shop in Soho where I bought the occasional bit of sporting equipment. Lonsdale was arrested by Special Branch in 1961. He was the mastermind of the Portland spy group which contained four other spies, all caught at the same time and sentenced to long prison terms. In fact Lonsdale's real name was Konon Trofimovitch Molody, a Colonel in the KGB, for whom Lonsdale was chosen as a nom de guerre. In 1964 he was exchanged for a British spy caught in the USSR, Greville Wynne. It is not surprising that Lonsdale joined the Pushkin Club because at the time he was studying in the School of Oriental and African Studies of London University, and the Pushkin Club had a number of their students as members.

Another spy with connections to Portland, or to the British Navy more generally, was John Vassall. He was not arrested until 1961 but when I was in Moscow he was clerk to the Naval Attaché, then Wiggy Bennett, a delightful Naval Captain who was often the life and soul of parties. Vassall turned out to be a homosexual and was identified as such by the KGB, photographed in compromising situations with Soviet citizens and then blackmailed into revealing some of the secret information with which he was dealing on a daily basis. On several occasions I was called to London to contribute to the case about Vassall, but all I could say was that he had always been very helpful and respectful to me and that there had been other members of the Embassy staff I would have suspected as crypto-homosexuals before Vassall.

Some of the appreciation type exercises we were set at Staff College were soundly based intellectually but others less so. One we liked was a re-run of Operation See Adler (Sea Eagle) the Nazi title for the air attack to precede the planned invasion of Britain in 1940. As this was planning with hindsight, with the outcome known, it was not difficult to see the factors unexamined or given inadequate weighting by the Nazi High Command planning what became known to us as the Battle of Britain. A less popular appreciation was named "China Tea" involving an attack on China using V-Bombers dropping nuclear weapons. This exercise situation excluded allies, no USAF; the UK was in it on our own. Nevertheless the cities of China were destroyed on paper to such an extent that there was no Chinese government with whom to discuss terms. Exercises were usually subject to much subsequent discussion; the solutions we submitted were returned with the comments of the Directing Staff, criticism, praise or condemnation. With China Tea, solutions never came back, there were no subsequent discussions, all exercise papers were withdrawn and China Tea disappeared down the drain. Maybe it was just too controversial!

Over Easter, 27 March to 14 April 1958, I had arranged to go to Bristol to take my LSD as part of Maia's research project and then to fly to Australia on a Comet of the RAF from Lyneham, nominally, I argued, so as to be able to compare the aircraft with the TU 104. First – LSD. I dove to Bristol on 31 March and stayed with Maia the night after she had done an EEG to check my "normal" brain rhythms to compare with readings later when I took lysergic acid. The next day (very appropriately April Fool's Day 1958) I drove to the Burden where Maia had prepared her apparatus. She glued the EEG electrodes to various places on my scalp and I then swung my legs on to the couch beneath the terminals for the electronics and was given a medicine glass of 100mg of lysergic acid diethylamide. My pigtail of wires was connected to the EEG and I put my head back on to the pillow. Here is my report, completed three days later at El Adem in North Africa on the first leg of the Comet flight to Australia:

Fifteen minutes after swallowing the LSD I noticed that colours were becoming abnormally vivid. The muscles of my legs began to shiver in convulsive ripples. These shivers, pleasant to feel, spread to other muscles, first in my limbs and then in my chest, back and stomach. A sensation of slight nausea and lightheadedness such as that experienced in conditions of negative G afflicted me. I felt a growing paralysis in the nape of my neck. It became increasingly difficult to control my movements. I felt able to maintain physical and mental equilibrium only by staring at some small object and fixed my eyes on a two inch square embossed plate in the centre of the nearby central heating radiator.

After some 20 minutes on Maia's instructions I closed my eyes and at once saw before me a cloudscape of grey cumulus limned in silver against a deep blue sky. It was as if I was lying on the ground gazing upwards into an infinity of sky, a scene of great beauty. I wanted to share this with Maia, not difficult because I had been told to give a running commentary on my experiences over the intercom provided. I climbed towards these clouds at great speed while trying to continue my commentary on the rapidly changing scene. The clouds changed with my approach, becoming globular, coppery and leaden. They seethed like boiling metal. The blue sky disappeared. All became dark. I emerged into a strange existence. I was part of a system of rotating whorls with which I moved at awful speeds away from and out of myself. I identified myself with any or all of the filaments of which the whorls were composed. They had no substance other than energy, and pulsed in amplitude and frequency, all the while rotating at varying speeds, faster with increasing frequency, slower with increasing amplitude.

The fibres or filaments of the whorls appeared as moving specks of white light, like bright tracer flak fire or cats' eyes reflecting a car's headlights. The rotating translucent whorls or funnels were suffused with colours from violet to rose and through them I could see neighbouring whorls. These vast skeins of moving pulsating colour expanded with me away from myself and reality. The pulses would

223

lengthen smoothly with a delicious vortiginous acceleration or shorten and broaden into short choppy frequencies which hurt me, as if the tendons of my mind were being stretched, as in the eye-ache of a migraine headache. Centres of particular discomfort were behind my right eye and in my right shoulder. The whorls rotated anticlockwise and my association with them was accompanied by a metallic whine, fluctuating in intensity and frequency with the pulses.

It seemed I was directed by a fatherly influence to continue ever deeper into space and to synchronise myself with the pulsing coloured skeins. At first this was pleasant but the short pulses were too painful and became faster and faster eventually bringing back consciousness with a terrible pang of emotional pain. I called out to Maia and grabbed her hand until I felt sufficiently reassured to close my eyes again. Returning to the same space-world of pulsating skeins, I penetrated even deeper in a strange hope of arriving at something, but not discerning more than the medium in which and with which I moved, and of which I was both part and whole, becoming ever more lonely in the constricted vastness. Many times I was irritated by the intrusion of extraneous noises. They destroyed the continuity of experience and obliged me to relocate and resynchronise myself with my, as it were, "carrier wave". At some of these interruptions I called to Maia for silence.

I became very cold, particularly my stomach. Maia brought blankets and a hot water bottle which I gladly accepted. Every muscle of my body shivered uncontrollably. Imbecile mutterings shocked me into consciousness and I opened my eyes. I thought I might be hearing my own distorted voice. I called for Maia and the sound of my normal voice reassured me. It was explained that the mad voice was of a youth being tested in an adjacent room. Now with open eyes I saw that imperfections of the ceiling and walls had become ghastly ghoulish ranges of Daliesque mountains dripping sepia streams of filth which quivered like dying entrails. A bare electric light bulb hanging from the ceiling on a flex was endowed with surreal significance. The incident of the lunatic voice initiated a fear of madness and death. With the former I associated the distorted view of reality I had seen with open eyes, the latter with the divorce from reality towards which I was urged by something unknown when I closed my eyes. Only Maia appeared normal and the personification of reality. All other objects and beings were distorted and ugly. At some stage I got off the couch for some electrodes to be refixed. The pain caused by Maia's efforts to break down skin resistance and re-cement the contacts to my scalp was exquisite — so real. I told her to pull my hair hard, simply to feel more pain, and so be more aware of my existence. Time ceased to have meaning. An hour might take seconds to pass, or a minute an hour.

As part of the experiment Maia had planned to see what effect flicker stimulus might have on me as seen by the EEG. A powerful strobe light was mounted above my face and this could be switched on and adjusted to strobe at the frequency of one or other of my brain rhythms. Influenced by the rhythmic flashing the brain rhythm would modify its frequency, try to get away as it were. But feedback from EEG to strobe would modify the strobe to match the brain. That was the idea. In my case, when Maia switched the strobe on, after a few seconds the flash was intolerable and I swept the light and nearby fittings out of the way with a sweep of my arm.

Readjusting the equipment, Maia inadvertently played a snatch of symphonic music, Scheherazade, used earlier to test a tape recorder on which my voice was being recorded. The few minutes of music gave me enormous comfort and seemed indescribably beautiful. Returning to the couch I re-entered the same space world immediately I closed my eyes. But by now I was worried that with increasingly deeper penetrations I might never get back to reality. An influence still directed me to let go of reality entirely, but the attraction of life was stronger and made me determined to retain consciousness. The stirring vortices were carrying me away from life but I was now determined to go no further and I would not close my eyes again.

I descended from the couch from under my heap of blankets and resisted all requests for further EEG recordings. I wanted no more disembodied experiences, but warm living beings and hot sweet tea. A doctor was summoned to give me an antidote, probably a tranquillizer. The muscular spasms decreased. Earlier even my heart had seemed to shiver, now only my limbs and stomach muscles quaked. I also felt warmer, and the feelings of paralysis in neck and back diminished. Emotionally I felt ineffably kind. I wanted to talk and describe my experiences to anyone interested to listen, but time and time again forgot the purpose of a train of thought before reaching its conclusion.

I was taken upstairs to the laboratory for tea. In the lab I saw many

17. The Incense Road at the Mablaqa Pass between the Wadi Beihan and the Wadi 'Ain.

18. Grave robbers

19. Funerary plaque dug from the ancient cemetery above Timnah by local grave robbers. The inscription records that a Qatabanian named Zabiy Sabah was buried there at about the time of Christ. Now in the Boston Museum of Fine Arts.

20. Boys weaving camel rugs in Beihan. Used for camels and for sitting down for meals on the floor or sand.

21. Beating indigo into lengths of cloth for futahs

22. A 'purple' herdsman who has been to Mecca, judging by his green shimagh.

23. Driving with Andrew Fuller from Aden to the Bab el Mandeb. NB radio and picnic equipment.

24. Loading salt from Shabwa for distribution in the Yemen and elsewhere

25. Bill Shevlin in front go the Qatabanian temple complex at Timnah

26. On the way to the Wadi Hadhramaut. The flat topped scarps are the remains of the'jol' long since eroded by wind, water and sand.

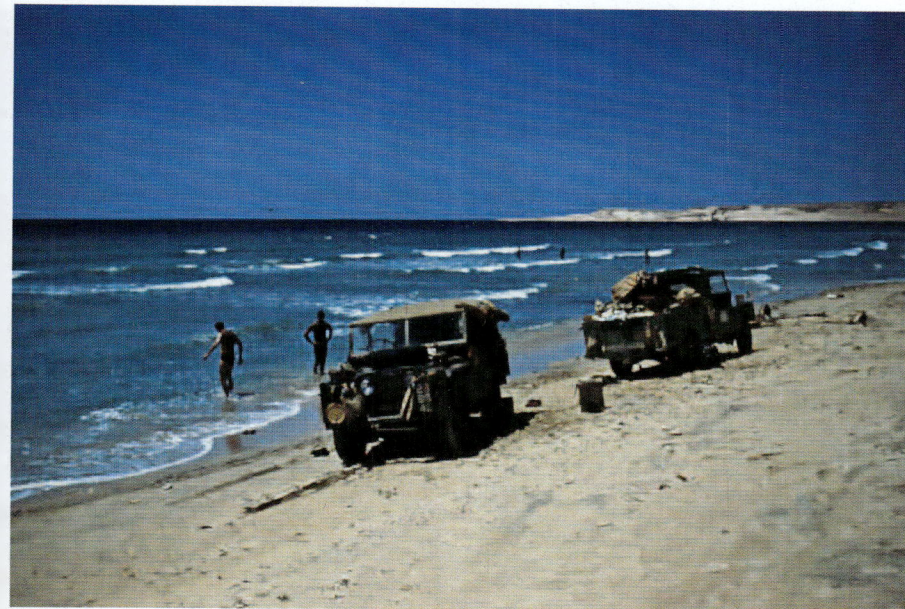

27. Travelling east along the Somali coast in August 1959. This is where Sgt Kaka, to the right of Andrew Fuller, later wrestled with a shark as described in the text.

28. Climbing from the coast towards Erigavo we came across this man picking globules of hardened gum, possibly myrrh, from trees beside the track.

29. A dhow in the port of Aden. Ships like this were the foundation of the Roman Arabia Felix, bringing wealth from Africa and the Far East to send up the Incense Road to Mediterranean civilisations.

30. Four Shihuh women come out to defend their village above the Straits of Hormuz. Speaking Kumzari (related to Farsi) they are thought to be descended from the original Yemenis who came to Oman after the collapse of the Marib dam. See pp 246 & 288.

31. The Yemen mountains rise from the coastal plain.

32. March 1960. Threshing at Al Qatn in the Wadi Hadhramaut. Note the paired camel and ox and the women's tall straw hats.

dead and eviscerated rats lying among the teacups, sugar bowls and plates of biscuits. One rat was in a cage awaiting its fate. For this live animal I felt great love and wanted to fondle it. The corpses of rats did not affect my enjoyment of tea, but I suddenly thought that the party had been arranged to check my reactions to death. A Dr Davies was concerned with some or all of these rats. His research seemed to be to teach tricks to rats and then kill them, centrifuge their brains and compare their characteristics with those of untrained rats. He was about to kill the caged rat.

I felt disgusted and determined to attempt to ridicule Dr Davies and his staff, and attack them, physically if need be. For his part, Dr Davies embarked on lengthy arguments about psychosis and said that my behaviour was typical of some psychotic states. Maia left the room and I followed her, no longer prepared to tolerate the laboratory staff, apparently chiefly interested in death and madness, the two things I had fought against. I walked downstairs and made much of a dachshund wandering among the offices. This partially appeased an intense desire to be kind to something living. I went to my Sunbeam and turned on the radio. It was already 1720 hrs, five hours after taking LSD and an hour after taking the antidote. Viennese waltzes soothed my mind and produced a flood of emotion close to tears. The sky was blue and clear. The contrail of a high flying aircraft was extraordinarily beautiful. Trees and birds and all living things were wonderful. I farted and relished the smell as a gourmet might relish a good cheese. All colours were extremely vivid. My limbs still occasionally shivered convulsively and I had a numbness in the back and sides of my head.

I became aware of my sly suspicions that I was being watched and that people passing the car on the way to the canteen or lab. were spying on me. Realising that this was paranoia I made a point of smiling graciously at such passers-by. I imagined prying eyes behind every curtain and round every corner. I was concerned to hear one of two small boys passing precariously on bicycles say to the other: "Watch out for im! E's one of the nuts!", but reassured to hear the other boy reply: "Nah, e's in luv!" I collected Maia from the Institute and we drove back into Bristol. My driving was OK although my arguments were rambling and I felt free of all inhibitions. In the restaurant where we had supper, Maia had to stop me addressing other diners on the importance of normality and kindness.

Next day, 2 April, I drove home to Alton after getting Yellow Fever and Cholera inoculations in preparation for my Comet flight to Australia. I was depressed. On 3 April I drove to RAF Lyneham to join the Comet which took off at 1000 hrs on 4 April, Good Friday 1958. I finished writing this account at El Adem in the evening after supper in the Transit Mess.

Flicker stimulus, mentioned above, was discovered by Grey Walter to trigger epileptic fits in a significant percentage of the population, many more than suffered fits "naturally". Using flicker stimulus it was possible to diagnose a tendency to epilepsy, and as a result of Grey meeting the RAF Chief Scientific Advisor, a pilot study (of cadet pilots) was started to screen aircrew entrants for this predisposition, which might be dangerous if a pilot were to have a fit while flying. An interesting example came to my notice later. Three small piston-engined aircraft were to be delivered to the Far East, I think to the Sultan of Brunei, and the RAF had allocated three young jet Provost pilots to deliver the aircraft. Because of the limited range of the aircraft, they flew out via Gibraltar and then followed the coast of north Africa as far as Egypt, where they should have turned south down the Red Sea and onwards. However, after turning east at Gibraltar one of the pilots started to feel poorly to the extent that he had to make emergency landings at various north African airfields. Eventually, when the aircraft landed at Nicosia in Cyprus, he said he could not continue and arrangements were made by the RAF to replace him – a considerable inconvenience because the other aircraft had to wait until a replacement arrived.

The "sick" pilot was examined by medicos and consultants at the RAF hospital in Cyprus but they could find absolutely nothing physically wrong with him. It was decided that it was entirely his own decision not to accompany his colleagues in the third aircraft and he was arraigned for court martial in Cyprus. Serving in the Middle East was a Wing Commander Medical Officer who had also qualified as a RAF pilot, a doctor with wings – a rare bird. Earlier he had submitted a thesis which had involved research in electroencephalography and, crucially, flicker stimulus. Acting on an idea, he asked the pilots when and where they had been flying when their colleague had felt poorly and the relative position of the sun at those times. He established that at the time the sun had only just risen in the east and that the three aircraft were heading towards it. The low sun had shone through the propeller discs of the single piston-engined aircraft. From the known revolutions of the propellers, in cruising mode for the long flight, the aviation doc. was able to establish that the flicker of the sun's rays through the propeller blades would be at a frequency to trigger the equivalent of an epileptic fit in one so predisposed. Flying jets would have no effect on him because they lacked propellers. An electrocephalograph and flicker test of the pilot confirmed his predisposition. Case dismissed! I met this doctor pilot and heard the story from his own lips.

It must be said that mind-bending drugs are to be avoided at all costs. All are dangerous. One must differentiate here between these and the drugs which are better called medicines, which may have physical side-effects, but seldom adversely affect brain function. Those who choose for amusement to deform their perception of reality by taking chemicals are downright stupid, criminally irrational. Reality perceived by a healthy mind is extraordinary enough to satisfy the most exacting sensualist, intellectual or those between or outside such categories. In life dangers abound and, whether you are a would-be hero or complete funk, in reality you may confront the whole gamut of experience without risking your wits with drugs.

Something I find surprising about my LSD experience and the eyes-closed hallucinations of expanding space/time or whatever one might choose to call it, was its resemblance to the descriptions of the expanding universe by cosmologists. Spinning, pulsing, filaments are terms I have used in reporting what I saw and felt.[2] If things as apparently different as cauliflowers, snowflakes, trees, our own organs and a thousand and one other things can be shown to share common patterns (named fractals by Benoit Mandelbrot) might not the mind be capable of discerning such patterns within itself? In nature, which is everything, everything is possible. Before participating in this experiment I had mentioned my intentions to the one RAF doctor on my course as a Staff College student – Wg Cdr (Doc) Urquhart and asked him for his views. He thought I was foolhardy and said that were my RAF superiors to know, they would forbid me to take the matter further.

The Comet flight to Edinburgh, near Adelaide, was to ferry equipment and a few personnel to Woomera, the British Nuclear Bomb test site, for which Edinburgh was the main transport airbase. We stopped on the way, first at El Adem, where I finished the report for Maia, later included in Maia's research paper (shortened I expect). After Bahrein we stopped in Katunayake (Ceylon) and Changi (the Singapore airfield I already knew well). We stayed there the second night and then on to Darwin in Northern Territory, Australia, getting to Edinburgh on 7 April. I had nightmares all the way to Australia and did not sleep soundly until we were in Adelaide where we stayed for a couple of nights.

Adelaide was a revelation. I put on my trunks and ventured into the sea for a swim. When I returned to the beach I was confronted by a lady dressed in tweeds and hat who told me I was committing an offence. My trunks should have a chest piece and a skirtlet extending at least 4" down from the crotch. Times have changed. Adelaide may no longer be said to be where every Australian has a maiden aunt.

We started back to the UK by the same route on 10 April, getting home to Lyneham on 12 April – for the round trip about 55 hours in the air. I liked Darwin. There were frogs everywhere, even in the loo cistern. Of course these days in a Jumbo Jet the actual flying takes half the time, with only one stop to refuel, but the Comet did not have the range or speed, although it was an improvement on piston-engined aircraft. The Comet II, in service in the RAF, did not suffer the fate of several Comet I's used by BOAC, which broke up following fatigue failure of the pressurised cabin.

While night-stopping in Singapore I had time to take a bus to Changi cemetery to find the grave of Josephine Butler. It was damp, as it often is in Singapore and initially I had difficulty in following directions I had received from the RAF padre at Changi some time before. However a gardener showed me the line of white stone graves where the deceased passengers in the Constellation had been buried. Jo's grave was particularly moving with an engraved farewell from her beloved grandmother, whom Jo regarded with more profound love than her parents.

After Easter the course at Bracknell started again on 14 April and we embarked on a series of visits to acquaint students with how the various RAF Commands (Bomber, Fighter, Coastal, Transport etc.) and the other Armed Services were organised, with a trip to the Continent to visit NATO Headquarters. I remember how the coach in which we were travelling from Calais to Fontainbleau stopped in France for officers to relieve themselves and how some hared off to buy bottles of wine which was then drunk beside the road, as if some of our number had never been away from England before. They took off their jackets and rolled up their trouser legs like schoolboys on an outing. I was rather shocked.

Back home, I was trying to get Vickers at Brooklands to agree to let me fly a Viscount, using the rather spurious argument that the Soviets might call for me to fly as "leader" in a turboprop transport. As a result I got in touch with Jock Bryce, Test Pilot of the Viscount, who was only too happy to agree to show me the controls. On 13 May I drove to Brooklands and Jock took me up for ten minutes in a Viscount (G.APLX) and then, to my surprise, got out and said I should carry on flying for an hour or so. As apart from the control column and throttles I hardly knew where anything else was, and I had never before flown a four-engined aircraft, I thought that both Jock and I were taking a risk. I flew the aircraft for two hours, landing twice, once, very daring, with one of the four engines feathered. As a result of getting to know Jock I also met Barnes Wallis, always a hero of mine for his work on the Wimpy, the bouncing bomb, and other outstanding inventions and developments.

I discovered that he was having difficulty interesting the Air Council in the swing-wing aircraft he was developing with Group Captain Cheshire VC, the officer who flew as observer with the USAF crew on the nuclear bomb drop on Nagasaki. Group Captain Cheshire was by then also working on his humanitarian project which became the Cheshire Homes, the first of which was at Lee Court between Alton and Petersfield. That is a story in itself.[3]

The swing-wing prototype, or model rather than prototype, was called "The Swallow". I discovered that Barnes Wallis would welcome an invitation to lecture on swing-wing aircraft generally and the Swallow in particular to our course at Bracknell. I told the Commandant about this possibility and he reacted at once, inviting Barnes Wallis down to a truly memorable lecture with subsequent discussions far into the night. In the event, failing to interest the British government, Barnes Wallis took his invention to the United States where it was the basis for the development of the F111 fighter. Of course I never was invited to fly in a Soviet turboprop aircraft, but flying the Viscount was an interesting and enjoyable adventure. All General Duties (Pilot) officers at Bracknell were expected to keep in flying practice during the Staff College course and aircraft were made available at Booker, a small nearby airfield. A number of us flew aged but very safe Ansons from there, often down the coast to Cornwall and back, which was easy to navigate.

In May, in a fit of extravagance, I bought an emerald ring which I thought Maia might like. I had spotted the ring in Longman & Strongitharm, a jeweller's in Berkeley Street, on one of my trips to have my hair cut by Eburne's in Dover Street nearby. The ring cost £248 or two months of my net salary at that time, say £7,000 on today's salary scale. At the time I was also subsidising Maia's meagre research grant by £50 per month. One might say the girl was to some extent being "kept". We had plans to visit Italy in the summer stand-down at Bracknell. I was doubtful whether, with Maia in tow, I could visit Irina in Munich or Mariapola in Turin, but I wrote to them anyway to warn them I might be turning up. Just as well as it happened.

I was very busy with my final thesis on the Russian enigma, the difficulty for those brought up in the west in understanding the Russian philosophy, always a problem but even more so when overlaid with communism.[4] My "research" into this morass involved me (or I involved myself) in frequent visits to St Anthony's College in Oxford and to the Pushkin Club in London. As it happened, later in

1958 Maia obtained a place at Somerville College, Oxford, to pursue her work in psychiatry/sociology and moved into a room there. It was a women's College and there were strict controls on men entering except at certain hours, rather like the visiting hours in a hospital. I was able to gain entry with reasonable freedom provided I left by 22.30 hrs. There was no question of staying the night; Maia might have been expelled.

Later the restrictions on conduct and the entry of "guests" led Maia to find rented accommodation, shared with other students (one of whom committed suicide later, said to be lovelorn with Maia). This was not so unusual; one of her other guinea-pigs in Bristol for LSD EEG experiments had been a self-styled artist, Stan Barber, married with two small children. Some time after taking his dose of LSD he attacked Maia with a knife. But she knew how to look after herself. Stan's paintings were devoid of much talent, incorporating boots and sunsets and other ill-assorted objects without much rhyme or reason. Eventually he left his wife and boys, and years later she blamed me for promoting Stan's relationship with Maia, which was certainly not the case and would have been contrary to my own interests. They were a very ill-assorted couple. I was very sorry for their children, but I expect they survived.

Grey Walter himself came to a premature and tragic death. A brilliant man, he knew it only too well, dressed eccentrically in western cowboy garb (after all he had been born in Texas), and played the eccentric in every way. He was author of many professional papers in his field and *The Living Brain* a Pelican Book[5] for the less professional reader. With his father Karl he was also joint author of *Further Outlook* a science fiction book. He was a splendid communicator, and was quite often on television demonstrating the robots he was developing. Grey was lionised by associates. His behaviour could be and was anything he pleased, but there were raised eyebrows and the scientific equivalent of tut-tuts when he "swapped" wives with one of his major collaborators.

His first wife, Lorraine, was the analyst of much of his EEG recordings and she continued in this role even after their divorce. He and Lorraine had two sons; the elder, Nicholas, followed his grandfather, Karl, becoming an apologist for anarchism. Both wives died prematurely. So did Grey. He used to drive a scooter in Bristol and in 1970 was knocked down in a collision with a car, suffering severe brain damage. He never recovered and died in 1977. For me he was *persona non grata* because, having met Mariapola in Bordighera, he introduced her to drugs, initially methedrine, an addictive amphetamine sometimes called "Speed", which adversely affected her mental and physical condition. However it may be that Grey expected Pola to take the same informed attitude to drugs that he did and as did Maia and many other specialists in that field. How tragic that a man who had made such important contributions to the understanding of the brain should have died as a result of damage to his own.

On 26 July I drove with Maia to Ferryfield (Lydd) and flew with the Sunbeam in the Bristol Freighter to Le Touquet, thence driving via Brussels to Yugoslavia, which we soon decided we did not like and returned to Italy. We drove across to Bordighera and for a few days stayed with Karl but had to find other accommodation when Grey and his wife Lorraine and a pre-teen boy, I think their second son, arrived. A grower of carnations, Pietro, a friend of Karl and admirer of Mariapola, let us use for free a small bungalow in his hillside plantation above San Remo among the flowers and vines. A problem was that the only water came from a standpipe from which the irrigation hosepipe had to be detached for enough time for us to shower and (for me) shave. We spent some time with Karl, Grey and his family, but Maia was keener on the bars in San Remo, where she soon picked up a young (younger than I) man who claimed to be a racing driver and titled, a Conte.

He certainly behaved in character as a well-off minor aristocrat, and before I knew much about it he had driven off with Maia and several other young men and women to Monza, then a Grand Prix racetrack. I was left to my own devices so contacted Pola who was still in Turin, not yet having accompanied her mother to Bordighera. I drove there but both Pola and her mother had bad colds and I took time off to re-visit Cuneo returning to San Remo after a week or so to check with Karl if Maia had returned. She came back a few days later and as I had to get back to Staff College and she to Somerville we decided to continue with an earlier plan to visit Venice and then drive back to the UK via Germany and France. In Venice we were touted by various youths who knew of rooms to let and chose a fairly cheap and scruffy place on a small cross canal. That evening we stupidly jumped into the canal to cool off and got dirty with oil and unmentionables, sewage etc. The environment was not so well cared for then.

Next day we did all the usual things, photographed each other with the pigeons in St Mark's Square, ate expensive ice creams and poor overpriced pasta dishes. Maia wanted to ride in a gondola but they were fiendishly expensive so we instead went out in a motorboat for an hour. After some bitter recriminations about Maia's behaviour in absconding for more than a week with a doubtful Italian Conte, I carefully stood up and removed my suit jacket (mohair from Savile Row) put it down safely on the coaming at the front of the quite large boat, collected Maia in my arms (she did not resist thinking it was an act of affection coming up) and threw her overboard. We were about half way between the Lido and St

Mark's. The driver of the boat was incredulous. He immediately turned the boat back to where Maia was floundering. In case she might risk drowning, I took off my shoes and dived in to help recover her. She was OK but shocked, as I had intended. Back in the boat, soaked to the skin (as was I) she was speechless, but not the boatman, who shouted that he would call the police, that nothing like this had ever happened to him before, that it was a disgrazia, etc.

I felt quite pleased with myself and Maia showed signs of being chastened, if only temporarily. In many respects she was intolerable, using her undoubted attraction to win male attention but then, when won, abusing it, with no concept of loyalty or fidelity. Not a good basis for a permanent relationship! Next day we started the drive home. Thenceforth I no longer regarded Maia in quite the same light, better kept at arms-length, metaphorically if not physically, i.e. reciprocal treatment, involving the hardening of the heart.

I drove Maia back to her digs near Somerville College and returned to Bracknell to restart Staff College on Monday 25 August. 1 December was Daphne's birthday, for which I went to London and the next day I had dinner with Karl Walter in Highgate where he was buying a house. His health was not good and he planned to return to London primarily to utilise the National Health Service. The sort of treatment he now needed was expensive and not so good in Bordighera. He told me that one thing he regretted missing in his life was making love to a black woman. To some extent this was said in jest, but he was the sort of free-thinker who would have taken to qualified promiscuity but for his devotion and loyalty to his wife who had died in 1953 after they had been married 49 years. Most of that time they had lived in the same flat in Bordighera.

Over that and several subsequent weekends I learnt to fly gliders and sailplanes, initially at Booker airfield and later near Alton at Lasham. However I could never raise much enthusiasm for gliding, because one was too dependent on thermals and I preferred powered flight, which I could still engage in; indeed I had to keep in practice, otherwise I would lose my flying pay, a substantial allowance introduced for RAF aircrew. At Bracknell we were turning our attention to the postings we would prefer after completing the course. After years with the Arabs and in Moscow I opted for V-Bombers and a serious flying job and put in an application for such posts. However, after a Staff College course the norm for an officer of my rank and seniority would be a Staff post at Air Ministry or in one of the Headquarters – Bomber, Fighter, Coastal, Transport, Middle, Far East, etc.

I had the disadvantage, emphasised by the DS, of not having a "normal" RAF career. For most of the war I had been abroad and after rejoining in 1946 I had again been abroad, mostly in diplomatic or, at any rate, abnormal appointments.

More than three years studying Arabic and Russian, five years or so in Moscow and Amman, was no alternative to the steady progression of the usual RAF officer to senior rank via junior command positions on squadrons in the UK. Mind you, this is what I had always wanted. I had successfully volunteered, intrigued and conspired to obtain these special courses and quasi-diplomatic appointments.

The course visited Cranwell, Shrivenham (like Cranfield already considered a Service inclined university) and the Army Staff College at Camberley and the Naval at Greenwich. The Camberley visit lasted a week during which we participated in Army Staff College exercises. I was kept busy. On one occasion we had an exercise which should have taken two weeks to complete. I was so busy with other activities that I ignored the task until there were a scant 48 hours before the papers had to be handed in. That evening Maia came to a dance at the Staff College and I told her of my predicament. When I returned her to Oxford after the ball she gave me some Dexedrine tablets and told me to take two before starting work. I finished writing at 8 a.m., handed in the exercise solution and went to bed, sleeping for an entire day and feeling awful when I finally arose. I received a higher mark for this exercise solution than for any other submitted while I was at Bracknell.

As to marks more generally, I had done quite well at Staff College. Most of my exercises and their solutions had been thought well of by my Syndicate and Group Leader, Wing Commander Tyler and Group Captain Mavor respectively, although the former did not like my rather loose (he thought) language. I could not help, or more probably did not wish to help, using words and phrases which may have seemed flippant or chosen to lighten or dramatise or otherwise leaven the dissertation or whatever it was. I have never been able to avoid this tendency because most of my writing is intended to be digested by the reader and digestion is helped by accompanying sauces, gravy and plonk. A more serious criticism at my final interview was that I did not suffer my superiors lightly, or, in their words, I should give greater respect to my superiors in rank. That was a well-deserved criticism except that if it is a plus not to suffer fools lightly, what if they are your nominal superiors?

The course was due to end on 13 December with a final ball, after which we might disperse. Prior to this I learnt that I would be posted to RAF Ballykelly in Northern Ireland, as a Flight Commander on a Shackleton squadron. The Shackleton was an ageing four-engined coastal reconnaissance aircraft. I would retain my rank of Squadron Leader. This was a disappointment; I wanted something much grander and immediately submitted an objection to the posting, requesting a review, bearing in mind that I had asked for an appointment to V-Bombers. My letter disappeared into the maw of Air Ministry and I was told that no immediate decision could be made, but I would be kept informed.

I had not been home in Alton more than a few days when a letter arrived to say that I would now be posted to Aden as Command Intelligence Officer (CIO) with the Acting Rank of Wing Commander. I protested about this too. But the die was cast. Aden it must be. It was a consolation to be promoted and to be going back to the Arabs, whom I knew and liked. This was another way-out appointment which I later discovered had been made because there was nobody else suitable for the post, which required a knowledge of Arabic and of the Middle East. My predecessor as CIO HQBFAP (Headquarters British Forces Arabian Peninsular) was none other than Lionel Folkard, the one-armed fellow student on my MECAS course nearly ten years earlier.

I spent Christmas at home but decided to visit Maia in Iceland over New Year's Day to see if I could find out more about her, meet her parents and see her home and where she had been brought up, in Akureyri on the north side of Iceland (proper name Island, *eesland*, no connection with ice) facing the North Pole. On 27 December I flew British European Airways to Reykjavik and then took a local air service to Akureyri. Maia had made it clear that I could not stay in her parents' home; there was no room and her father suffered from a heart condition, which meant he could not risk excitement or emotional stress. Maia thought that my presence might cause one or other or both. Her father was in fact the retired head teacher of the local school, which she had attended. I was interested to note that he was regarded as a very important figure in the community rather as head teachers and doctors and other professionals used to be respected in England.

As I had not pre-booked accommodation, I tried the YWCA (there was no YMCA) and they gave me a bed, in a room shared with another chap. The YW was crowded with drunken youths when I arrived, and one of them tried to get me to share his schnaps from a Coke bottle. The youths were so rowdy trying to use the office telephone that the manageress in angry desperation pulled the telephone cord out of the wall, thus stopping all communication by that means. I was surprised at this behaviour although I had been told that in temperance Iceland, where government bottle shops were the sole purveyors of alcohol, there was more intemperance than anywhere else in the world apart from other Scandinavian countries who had tried to control drunkenness in the same way.

I visited Maia who was home for Christmas and met her parents, who were very nice I thought. Their apartment was in a concrete block, a material much used in Iceland where there are no trees to speak of for beams, nor clay for bricks or tiles. Roofs were of corrugated iron or asbestos, weighted to prevent them blowing off in the great gales afflicting Iceland. From the YW I had a splendid view of Eyjafiord, the 30-mile-long narrow fjord at the southern end of which Akureyri stands. The morning after I arrived I saw two fishing boats sail from the little port going north as fast as they could steam. I was told the two owner/Captains of the ships were chasing each other to the fishing grounds. In the afternoon I was told that one of the ships had been towed back to Akureyri with extensive damage because the Captain had forgotten to check the water in his boiler. He had of course been drunk, as were many people in this benighted town. Benighted in more than the figurative sense, because at this time of year the daylight lasted very little more than three hours.

However an Icelander I met in the YW said he was going skiing up (and down) the mountain to the west of Akureyri, quite high for Iceland at up to 5000'. He said he would lend me a pair of skis and I was in any case travelling in my ski trousers for warmth, with an anorak and pullovers. I readily agreed and we set off to climb the slope when it was still dark at 10 a.m. There was of course no ski lift; we had to climb in our skis, taking them off for the steeper stretches. By lunch time we were quite high up above Akureyri and ate our sandwiches. Starting back at 2 p.m. it was already nearly dark again.

My companion, who was experienced, disappeared into the gloaming while I was hampered by a low mist obscuring the slopes and dips in the snow, filling me with apprehension because I could not be certain I was not heading for a precipice. I could see the lights of the town reasonably well and reckoned that if I kept them ahead I would arrive there eventually, in one piece with a bit of luck. However lower down the mountain I ran into loose barbed wire strands and my ski trousers were literally ripped to shreds from my bleeding legs.

Limping through the streets to the YW, with the wind chilling my nether parts, I fortunately met nobody and resolved not to be so stupid again. How many times in my life have I made such resolutions!

On 2 January 1959 what should I receive at the YW but a telegram addressed:

SQDLDR DEVERILL. AKUREYRI. REPORT LYNEHAM 1600 JANUARY 15 FOR DEPARTURE 0700 JANUARY 16 STOP REPORT BRACKNELL FIRST – RAF BRACKNELL. How RAF Bracknell and the Postur og Simi at Akureyri tracked me down one can only guess. In Akureyri I was probably the only visiting Brit.

Notes:

1. *The Class Conflict in Italy.* Karl Walter. P.S. King and Son Ltd. 1938 and *Towards Democracy*, same author and publishers, 1939.

2. *Before the Beginning.* Martin Rees. Simon and Shuster. 1997.

3. T*he Biography of Leonard Cheshire VC OM.* Richard Morris. Viking 2000

4. Churchill described this somewhere as "… a riddle wrapped in a mystery inside an enigma" but he may have been mostly concerned with Russian politics.

5. *Further Outlook.* W. Grey Walter. Gerald Duckworth & Co. Ltd. 1956. *The Living Brain.* W. Grey Walter. Same publishers 1953 & Penguin Books 1961.

Aden

I flew into Khormaksar, the international and RAF airport for Aden in the evening of 17 January 1959. The aircraft was a good old RAF Hastings to which I was already accustomed. We stopped on the way in Cyprus and stayed the night of the 16th. I was not displeased to be returning to the Middle East, although Aden had for some years been known as a place where delinquent officers were sent! The climate was hot and damp for most of the year and recreation might be seen by some as difficult – no access to any fleshpots, not the sort of place any tourist in his or her right mind would pay to visit.

From the historical point of view Aden is fascinating. On 19 January 1839, 120 years and 48 hours before my arrival, Captain Stafford Bettesworth Haines of the Royal Marines took possession of the port of Aden in the name of Queen Victoria primarily to deter pirates operating against British shipping sailing to and from India. Until then Aden and the area around it had been controlled by the Sultan of Lahej, residing at Dhala, a small town or large village about 100 miles north in the foothills of the Yemen. The population of Aden was then recorded as 132.

The history of Aden goes back 5000 years or more before then. It was one of the ports serving the Incense Road, along which frankincense and myrrh and much else were transported to the Middle East and especially to Egypt where the gums were used extensively in the funeral and other rites of the civilisation of the pharaohs. Over thousands of years the routes followed by the carriers varied depending on the dangers of the desert and its tribes and the dangers of the sea and its pirates. Sometimes the route followed might be part sea, part desert track, and Aden was one of the ports used. Frankincense grew mainly in Dhofar in the east of south Arabia where the mountains drew moisture from the SE monsoon. Myrrh grew more on the Somali escarpment below Erigavo, but both aromatic gums and many more were harvested and sent to the Middle East in caravans up the Incense Road and rafts and ships along the coasts and up the Red Sea.

The ancient Egyptians named south Arabia "God's Land" because the sun and moon, which they worshipped, rose from that direction. The crescent moon was symbolised by the crescent of a bull's horns, deriving from the bull cult, their roaring, snorting and hoof pounding reminding the ancients of the noises accompanying the volcanic activity and earthquakes in the Mediterranean area. The bull cult was a Middle Eastern creation which spread to south Arabia and India. India's "sacred cow" originated in the myth. Funerary ornaments in south Arabia often incorporated a bull's head. In the Bible south Arabia was often called Ophir or Punt, both names probably covering adjacent areas of Africa. Later the Romans called south Arabia "Arabia Felix" thinking that the incense, gold, slaves, exotic animals, silks and spices arriving in the Mediterranean up the incense road from the southern deserts had originated there. In 25 BC Augustus Caesar sent a military expedition under his commander Gallus to conquer this source of wealth.[1] They mostly perished in the desert after discovering that apart from the gums, the other riches were shipped in from Africa and the Far East by Hadrhamis who had long since discovered how to use the Trade Winds and Monsoons.

As the market for incense declined and other trade found less arduous routes, Aden became less important except as a comparatively safe hideout for pirates and refugees from the much harsher territory inland. The original settlement and port were part of the crater of a long extinct volcano, providing a protected anchorage, with an ample source of fresh water at Sheikh Othman, a few miles to the north.

As a base for British imperial enterprise Aden was very convenient. With the advent of steam a coaling station was established on Perim Island, down by the Bab el Mandab, at the southwest corner of the Arabian peninsular, where shipping from the Red Sea would turn east towards the Persian Gulf and the Indian Ocean or west to Africa. Aden was the best port south of Suez between Africa and the Gulf (sometimes called Persian). When construction of the Suez Canal was finished in 1869, Aden became even more important for shipping.

After the arrival of Haines, Aden was ruled as part of British India until 1937 when it was made a Crown Colony. The Indian connection resulted in Aden becoming in many respects a part of India in more than name. The lives of the initially few British expatriates had much of the flavour of life in India. There were exchanges between the secretariats in India and Aden; civil administration developed on the same pattern and even domestic life was affected – members of the secretariat lived and worked in similar buildings and Anglo-Indian jargon was common – as in India lunch was tiffin and a pukka sahib and his mem-sahib wanting their whisky or tea would shout "boy" for the servant, who might be a teenager or a greybeard but was still known as a boy. In Aden not only was the term used but an Arabic plural for boy (boyat) entered the local dialect.

Anglo-Indian mores were also imported, and Richard Burton notably inveighed against them describing life in Aden as:

> "... comprised in ignoble official squabbles, dislikes, disapprobations, and 'references to superior authority'; where social intercourse is crushed by 'gup', gossip and the scandal of small colonial circles;....... where, briefly, the march of mind is at a dead halt, and the march of matter at double quick time to the hospital or sick quarters".[2]

I was in Aden over 100 years after Burton's visit but much of Burton's criticism still applied. On arrival I was given printed guidelines on those I might expect to entertain and be entertained by. They included Service officers of my rank and one or two ranks above and below, together with civilians assessed to be of equivalent rank. Judges were too illustrious, but their juniors acceptable as long as they were not too junior. Barristers OK, but solicitors not necessarily.

The civilian population had increased more than a thousand-fold since Haines – a polyglot, ethnically diverse community of Arabs, Yemenis, Indians, Somalis, Greeks and Italians and of course the British, some civilian but mostly Service, the latter totalling over 7000 in 1959 with many still living in the buildings of 100 years earlier.

Because there were, when I arrived, no suitable rooms available in the RAF officers' mess at Steamer Point, I took a room in the Crescent Hotel, the best hotel in the commercial centre of Aden, where the many Indian enterprises had their offices and shops. The Crescent was run by Italians, Sig. Volpe being the proprietor, living nearby in a luxurious house of his own. Key members of his staff were also Italian, notably the chef and the restaurant staff. The food was very good at the Crescent especially the lobster (caught locally) thermidor and the fillet steak (flown in from Kenya). My room was on the top floor of the hotel and although the roof above was insulated, the tank for washing water was outside the insulation and by the evening the 'cold' water was hotter than the hot and showers impossible until late, or preferably next morning. The Crescent was about ten minutes drive from Headquarters British Forces Arabian Peninsular disposed on a ridge named Tarshyne above Steamer Point.

The Intelligence Branch to which I was posted was large, larger than any HQ unit I had come across until then. There were 20 officers of the Army and RAF, a dozen civilians, and several dozen Warrant Officers, non-commissioned officers and OR's (other ranks). This was the first integrated tri-Service intelligence HQ set-up in the British armed Services – an idea of the Chief of the Imperial General Staff – Lord Louis Mountbatten. He was set on eliminating counter-productive inter-Service rivalry and started with Aden where he had only recently ordered the Army, the Navy and the RAF to integrate the intelligence and planning aspects of the Command's activities.

In the Intelligence Branch served roughly equal numbers of officers of the Army and RAF, but not the Navy. They had declined to participate in the integrated branch "until later", and maintained their separate intelligence organisation at Bahrein, in the Persian Gulf. This was ironic because the Navy was Lord Louis's Service. In the Intelligence Branch in Aden we had to make do with a Naval Liaison Officer, who was in fact a civilian. The Senior Intelligence Officer (SIO) currently commanding the Branch was Lt.Col. Dennis de M. Carey, an affable and cultured officer many years my senior who had taken over from Lionel Folkard, referred to earlier. The idea was that Dennis would be SIO until his retirement later in 1959, when he had a job lined up working for a London impresario, the sort of work he much preferred. I would then take over as boss, establishing a pattern whereby the Army and the RAF would command the Intelligence Branch turn and turn about, with the Navy joining to make it a threesome should they so wish.

Dennis also lived in the Crescent Hotel so we were able to exchange notes outside the office over the dinner table or in the bar, which was very well frequented, not so much by the soldiery, who could get cheaper booze in their respective messes, but by representatives of all the other Aden government offices, judges, administrators, medical people, visiting potentates, spies. As would-be informers of any nationality could enter the Crescent freely the hotel was a hothouse for the exchange of knowledge, including intelligence, and this was a great advantage because I could act rather as I had done before in Amman when I could pick up titbits of crucial information by talking to all and sundry without them being inhibited by check points, guard rooms, passes, etc.

Our "parish" from the intelligence and planning point of view was very large. In terms of latitude it ran as far north as the Caspian Sea, and south to South Africa. In longitude the meridian central to the Indian Ocean and westwards as far as central Africa might be said to delineate our sphere of interest. Of course, being in Aden we were vitally interested in things going on immediately around us in the East and West Aden Protectorates, and the surrounding countries – The Yemen, Saudi Arabia, the Trucial States, Kuwait of course, always threatened by Iraq, Iran, and on the other side of the Red Sea – Egypt, Somalia and the various British colonies and protectorates. "Protectorate" was a term covering weaker, less developed states (especially tribal areas) protected by stronger ones and it used to be that the stronger states agreed or imposed their protection on the weaker. Sometimes the UN or its predecessor the League of Nations officially provided the protecting state with a mandate, but not in the case of Aden.

The Western Aden Protectorate derived from agreements between British governed Aden, a Crown Colony after 1937, and 16 tribal states or emirates, the rulers styling themselves emirs, sheikhs, sultans or whatever their tradition decreed. Over years they amalgamated into the Federation of Arab Emirates, each with a traditional ruler usually resident in the main settlement of his state. In the more important places he was provided with a resident political officer responsible to the British Agent for the Protectorate, based in Aden, responsible in his turn to the Governor of Aden. The Eastern Aden Protectorate (EAP) was different from the Western because it was further from Aden and had fewer tribes and less population in a much larger territory.

In both WAP and EAP there were two larger British officered or commanded local armed forces – the Federal National Guard (FNG) operating in both Western and Eastern Aden Protectorates and the Aden Protectorate Levies (APL), primarily an Adeni force. Further afield there were the Somaliland Scouts (Somscouts), in British Somaliland; the Trucial Oman Scouts (TOS) in the Trucial States; the Sultan of Oman's Armed Forces (SOAF) in Oman, and others. Additionally the tribal leaders had their own forces of armed tribesmen. As Command Intelligence Officer I would need to know about them all and meet as many as possible.

Dennis and I agreed that first of all I should set out to tour the parish and meet people, starting from Aden and moving progressively further away. In the Protectorates we had three RAF Field Intelligence Officers (FIOs), Flight Lieutenants, speaking fluent Arabic, stationed in areas within a hundred miles of Aden from where we needed reports on events and incidents which might affect the security or stability of the base. They usually lived near the Junior Political advisor and FNG/APL detachments provided some protection from the wild and woolly tribesmen, all of whom carried firearms as City businessmen might carry umbrellas.

My first visit outside Aden on 29 January 1959 was to Tor el Bahr, a hill village some 60 miles north-west of Aden where our FIO Roy Wade lived in a small stone house. I had trouble getting to Roy because although Aden is usually very dry, that year there was torrential rain and the tracks and airstrips were waterlogged for some days. The wadi beside which Tor el Bahr stands was by no means arid. In much of south Arabia thunderstorms form over the escarpment once or twice in a fortunate year. The rain-water rushes down through numerous and normally dry wadi beds to be spread by cleverly placed embankments, once made by hand but later by bulldozers. The land around Tor el Bahr bore good crops of maize, sesame, limes, vegetables and dates. For the occasional meat feast there were goats.

We were entertained to a meal by the local sheikh and a dozen of his lieutenants. We sat on either side of woven goat hair mats on the floor of his large tent and two roasted goats were served on mountains of rice heaped on enormous brass trays, rimmed to prevent spillage of the juices. I was lent a dagger with which to cut off bits of goat to eat. With rice the form was to use the fingers to make mouth-sized balls. Only the right hand may be used, the left being for other purposes. Another convention is never to show the soles of your feet, especially to your host. This is difficult if you are not accustomed to squat cross-legged on the ground. As male south Arabians usually wear futas, sarong-like skirts worn between knee and calf-length, one is sometimes told one's nose is showing, but it is another appendage the speaker has in mind. Wearing pants is a good idea. This is something to bear in mind. My neighbour beside me on the mat, a villainous-looking tribesman in his fifties, cut off a particularly horrible piece of gristle and gave it to me. I managed to get it down and reciprocated. I was surprised when with an oath he threw it over his shoulder into the corner of the tent. Some Muslims have reservations about food handled by infidels.

From Tor el Bahr one could see the neatly terraced slopes of the escarpment climbing up to the not far distant Yemen. These terraced hillsides have probably been cultivated like this for thousands of years and from the air I saw similar terraces reverted to desert but with darker circles between the outlines of old irrigation channels where frankincense trees once grew and had left the imprint of their roots. Roy drove me back to Aden in his Land Rover.

I was only back in Aden for three days before flying to Mukeiras in a Pembroke aircraft. The Secretary of State for the Colonies, Mr Alan Lennox-Boyd, was visiting and after meetings and entertainments in Aden, was flown in his RAF aircraft, a modest Anson, to some of the regional Protectorate capitals to meet local leaders and people. I made a point of reaching Mukeiras earlier. Mukeiras was a small town on the escarpment 80 miles north-east of Aden, the home of the Na'ib Jabil deputising for the Sharif Hussein, the Emir of Beihan, an important local leader whose palace was at Nuqub about ten miles north of Beihan. The Sharif, related to the Hashemites of the Hedjaz and later of Jordan, lived most of the time in Aden where he had the ear of the Governor, Sir William Luce, and many of his senior administrators, including Ken Trevaskis, British Agent, Western Aden Protectorate, who became Governor some years later. The Sharif used to attend many of the High Commission receptions wearing Adeni dress – turban, loose shirt over a futa, held around the waist by a broad leather belt decorated with buttons, pockets for coins, rifle bullets, etc., with a jambia (a "J" shaped dagger) in its sheath thrust behind the belt, and sandals worn with green nylon socks. Adeni sandals were often in two parts with a loose top element on the lines of a spat which flapped as one walked and was said to warn snakes to get out of the way.

The Na'ib (Arabic for deputy) Jabil, exercised power on the Sharif's behalf and controlled his armed retainers. Mukeiras is at about 7,000', high enough for it to be cool and clear compared with Aden. Our FIO Bill Mackintyre drove me in his Land Rover to the top of a hill overlooking the airstrip from where we watched the parade of thousands of tribesmen being reviewed by the Secretary of State. The parade was not so much a parade as an immense crowd surrounding the dirt runway and kept to the perimeter by FNG and APL soldiers. The Secretary of State stood erect in a Land Rover accompanied by Ken Trevaskis and drove around the inside of the perimeter to be saluted by the tribesmen as he passed. The traditional salute was for the tribesmen to fire their guns as close as possible in front of the visiting dignitary without hitting him. That would warrant a black mark.

The guns varied from WW2 rifles back through Boer war carbines to blunderbusses, and the Secretary of State's progress was marked by the explosive ripple of the firearms and a lot of black and white smoke. Afterwards he was given the usual goat and rice lunch before his departure in his Anson to the next outpost to be visited. In the evening we entertained the Emir and Na'ib to films in the FNG officers' mess (built to accommodate six officers), showing an American film about the US army beating up redskins and vice versa, which was appropriate to the audience who were delighted by the battle scenes.

I returned to Aden for a week and then it was Bill Shevlin's turn. Bill was our FIO in Beihan, 40 miles further north from Mukeiras. This adjoins the ancient city of Timnah, the capital of the Qatabanian civilisation which was founded and grew on the commerce along the Incense Road until the fourth century AD. There were many ruins, some showing very fine ashlar stonework with enormous blocks cut so accurately that it would be hard to insert a knife between them. The city had been the subject of infrequent archaeological digs often abandoned because of local hostility. An American named Wendell Phillips had been the last there, fleeing the country before he had achieved all his ambitions there but writing a good book about it.[3]

Letter home, 20 February 1959:

My trip to Beihan was most enjoyable. I toured the south and west of the region partly on foot and partly in a Land Rover with Bill Shevlin and the Junior Political Adviser. The countryside is not like Aden but a mixture of sandy plain and hills rising to mountains. Beihan is situated in a large wadi running in a northerly direction into the sand sea of the Empty Quarter. Immediately to the north it is bounded by the Ramlat Sabatein "Desert of the Two Lions", with enormous egg yolk yellow dunes. To the south, east and west stretch networks of subsidiary wadis into rising hills and then mountains of bare igneous rock. Beihan itself is at 2500' and the hills around up to twice that height. In the wadi beds there is a little cultivation – grain, dates, sesame.

Besides visiting various government guard "forts" and inspecting the two or three men in each, drinking tea with them, etc., we shot at game – birds much like snipe and grouse. They were almost sitting on the barrels of our shotguns but I invariably missed, as did Bill Shevlin. I had a five shot repeater but still missed.

We drove as far as we could up the old Incense Road, built over 2000 years ago, which leads from the Wadi Beihan over a pass into the Wadi Ain and on to the Yemeni frontier. The Works Department is trying to open up this route again to wheeled traffic, but it was made for camels and donkeys and the bends of the ascending originally paved track are of too short radius for even a Land Rover and then of course much of the road, originally stone flags, has been washed away by centuries of rain (infrequent but torrential when it comes) and rock falls. At the top of the pass, the Mablaqa Pass, the road is still beautifully paved and perfectly preserved for stretches of up to 20 yards. Towards the top where the climb is steepest, the Road is stepped, like Clovelly in Cornwall, but with 10" risers which are impossible to negotiate in a vehicle. At the top, on the almost vertical wall of the final cut through the pass are inscriptions in the Qatabanian language celebrating the opening, and naming the "chief engineer" responsible for what still seems to be quite an engineering feat.

In Timnah I took many photos and Bill and I ourselves excavated a tomb in the cemetery, finding nothing more than broken bones and fourth-century pottery. However I purchased for £2 an alabaster funerary plaque from a grave robber (it is a profession here). It has a bull's head protruding from the top with a Himyaritic or Qatabanian inscription lower down, giving the name of the person buried there I imagine. On the temple ruins I was approached by a little girl who held out something in her hand – a small lump of apparently fused stone with what looked like a bronze spike sticking out from it. I gave her two shillings and when I got it back to Aden I chipped at it with a nail file. The fused stone fell off revealing a bronze bull's head on a piece of bronze casing, possibly part of the decoration of an altar. Maybe the altar had been burned down when bedu from the desert invaded the city when it declined in the third century AD or about the time of the collapse of the Great Dam of Marib, the Queen of Sheba's capital, now in the Yemen.[4] This dam provided, in its day, for the irrigation of much of this part of the world, and when it silted up and disintegrated it set in train the migration of many people from these parts to the Jebel Akhdar in the south-east of Arabia.

I also visited a rug-maker's house and took photos of two small boys weaving the long lengths of dyed goat hair cloth on which one sits in most south Arabian houses. (I had one made for me to my design!). And I also photographed the ancient process of beating indigo dye into cotton cloth to make the purple futas many tribesmen wear. The dye is the equivalent of woad. Some locals cover themselves with the stuff and I got covered with it when I borrowed the dyer's mallet and did some beating myself.

Incidentally I was at the S of S's goat eating party which you saw on TV. There were 3,000 people there (30 Europeans). Three hundred goats were eaten. The SofS was very worried when he stained his white dinner jacket with grease. But no doubt he will be able to have it cleaned when he gets home.

Don't imagine these trips I do up-country are at all formal. In Beihan Bill Shevlin and I lived in a room of a mud house. You pee through a hole in the floor and it runs down the outside of the wall into the street. All sewage in the town goes the same way, but for solids Bill has the luxury of an Elsan chemical closet. All sorts of disgrazie happen all the time. The cook tried to make a blancmange with lemonade powder.

Someone shat on the Elsan lid and seat. The aerial of the radio in the Land Rover snapped off when we passed under a low tree. There was a second luxury in Beihan. Every evening two little boys carried in a tin bath and then buckets of hot water so that we were able to have truly British baths, sitting inside with legs and arms out like a Victorian soap advertisement.

The bulls' heads mentioned in my letter home of 20 February 1959 were the subject of some debate at home ten years later, concluding with the decision that for their safety museum pieces should be in museums. In 1969 at Valverde, a cleaner woman, recruited to help Herta once a week, reported that while dusting the bookcase in the living room she had accidently broken our 'door knocker'. We concluded that this must have been the small bronze bull from Timnah. And so it was. In the course of the next year I discovered that the Gimpel Fils art gallery, then in South Molton Street, W1, planned to mount an exhibition of South Arabian sculpture from December 1970 to January 1971. I had been introduced to the Gimpel family by Daphne Park when we were both home from Moscow in the 50s. Some of them had done gallant work in SOE during WW2. Titus Oates, my sister's husband, also knew them. Being interested in all sorts of art I often visited the gallery.

We discussed the exhibition they were arranging and I offered my alabaster plaque and bronze bull as exhibits and introduced Andrew Fuller, who also wished his own collection to be shown. Bearing in mind my interest in South Arabian sculpture, Peter and Kay Gimpel asked me to write an introduction and provide photographs for their catalogue. I needed to find out more about my bulls and consulted the greatest expert of that time – Professor Jacques Ryskmans of the Institut Orientaliste in Louvain, Belgium. He provided me with an excellent potted history of the bull cult in South Arabia and in the area more generally. In Timnah, the capital of the Qatabanian Kingdom, the moon-God was Amm, personified by a bull, whose curved horns evoke the crescent moon. The bull represented the Moon God as well as the idea of fertility. Bulls' heads therefore appeared on coins, altars and funerary monuments. In the case of my alabaster bull the inscription on the base is the name of the man buried there and his clan name, to be read as Zabiy Sabah. The palaeography indicated a date of the tomb of about the time of Christ. The second name, Sabah, derives from Sheba, (the Queen of Sheba had been a Sabaean living on the plains round Marib, now in the Yemen). Pliny described the Sabaeans as *wealthy, owing to the fertility of their scent producing forests, their gold mines, their irrigated agricultural lands and their production of honey and wax'. (Pliny Natural History, Bk VI, xxxii, 159 -162.)* Bearing in mind that Zabiy Sabah lived at the time of Christ, he may have been related to one of the three wise men (sheikhs) said to have presented the infant Jesus with gold, frankincense and myrrh all products of south Arabia and the horn of Africa.

The Gimpel Fils exhibition was a great success. Peter Gimpel indicated that if I were to offer my bulls for sale through the gallery I could expect to receive about $2,000 for the alabaster and $1,000 for the bronze. With such a valuation I wrote to several American museums and after considerable correspondence agreed to sell the alabaster plaque to the Boston Museum of Fine Arts for $2,000. They were considering purchase of the bronze head when Sir Mortimer Wheeler (a Fellow of the Royal Society despite or because of his fame as an archaeologist), with whom I was often in touch, told me that the British Museum would like to buy it. And they did. We have not located it in the BM but on a visit to Maine in 2006 we found our plaque in the Boston Museum of Fine Arts, splendidly displayed in a cabinet and still, I believe, the only exhibit of South Arabian sculpture they have.

Back in Aden: I had invited Dad to visit me, taking a ship out, spending a week with me, the most I thought he could stand, and then sailing home. However I did not disguise the facts.

Letter home, 10 February 1959:

> *I do not think you would like it here though. Polo, tennis, swimming, officers' mess – conjure up pictures of colonial life with Sudanese servants in tarbooshes and white nightgowns, whiskey sodas, etc. Slightly pukkah! In fact this is a seedy desolate spot and most people behave in a rather seedy way with a lot of petty bourgeois snobbery – looking down on the "natives" and on "that haggish woman Mrs ...." And suchlike. Not edifying. For me there is the consolation of associating with wild and woolly officers and wild and woolly Arabs, Somalis, Yemenis and a score of other nationalities bursting at the seams with dynamism, courage, weapons, treachery and every other extremely individualistic characteristic.*

Not surprisingly Dad decided not to come.

I was able to get to know quite a bit about my fellow officers because within a week of my arrival in Aden I was appointed President of the Mess Committee (PMC), that is, of the Officers' Mess at Steamer Point. It was usual in the RAF for the PMC to be the most senior officer living in the Mess, because that being his home he would make sure it was comfortable and efficient and everything that the other living-in, younger and more junior officers would want. The appointment was made by the RAF Station Commander, under a system whereby the HQ, although very large and commanded by an Air Vice Marshal, was a lodger unit of RAF Steamer Point. The Station Commander was Wing Commander Bill Howell DFC, a war-time pilot but afterwards transferred to a ground branch. He was a rather conventional officer in his late forties, married with his wife accompanying him. He thought I would be the ideal man to head the Mess Committee, involving all aspects of Mess life – food, accommodation, services, the bar, events etc.

I moved to a large room in the Mess about six weeks after getting to Aden but immediately saw that I would not like it there. It was customary to dress for the evening meal in a cut down version of tropical Mess Dress. I preferred the informality of life at the Crescent. In the Mess life centred on drink, and I never liked binge drinking, as it is now called, with the necessity of all present standing their round of drinks to those grouped at the bar, even if all concerned had already had enough. There was a stifling lack of life and interest in the Mess and after a few days I returned to my room at the Crescent, making the excuse that I needed to be able to follow up intelligence contacts and it was impossible to talk to be-futa'ed Adenis in the Mess even if clearance could be obtained for them.

However I continued to be nominal PMC for a month or more until some other sucker could be found. Undoubtedly the Officers' Mess was in a superb position, on a promontory several hundred feet above the sea, looking out towards Socotra. The sea was always changing and often rough, with dolphins sometimes to be seen cavorting among the waves. The Officers' Club was down below the Mess on the beach, with excellent swimming behind a shark net which rose and fell on floats in the water. But for my purposes the Crescent Hotel was much superior.

In the Mess we had Ladies' Nights, when wives, older daughters and girl friends might be invited to join in drinking themselves silly. I loathed these occasions. For my part I arranged what I considered to be much more cultured occasions – once a recital of Under Milk Wood on records (78 rpm in those days) and a recital, records again, of Russian and Soviet folk songs I had brought back from Moscow. These were very popular and under a bright moon and stars in the silky Aden night it would have been difficult not to have been moved. The roof of the Crescent Hotel also provided "cultural" evenings with recorded concerts of classical music in the evenings once a week or so, with the audience seated at chairs around tables and drinking for the most part glasses of wine. Listening to Mozart was all the better for the occasional intervention of ship noises, a liner's hooter, the clank of an anchor chain.

The day after my 37th birthday I flew to Mukeiras again. Bill Mackintyre wanted me to join him to witness an action to be started by the Na'ib Jabil's merry men, when, if the Yemenis could be provoked into opening fire, RAF Shackletons from Khormaksar would by prior arrangement beat the hell out of them. I was collected from the airstrip by Bill in his Land Rover and spent the night in his house. Very early next morning, when it was barely light, we drove to the Na'ib Jabil's house on the outskirts of the town of Mukeiras and were welcomed to drink mugs of strong sweet tea flavoured with ginger and cardamom.

Then, in a fleet of small and mostly clapped out vehicles we headed north for about an hour to the place on the Yemen frontier selected for the "provocation". The frontier was along a wadi overlooked by hills (hills on hills because we were already at about 7000') on the ridges of which the Yemenis (regular or irregular troops, we did not know) were ensconced in sangars (stone breastworks). In much the same way we were sheltering behind boulders on our ridge. The distance between us was about 1000 yards. The Na'ib Jabil checked on his walkie-talkie that a Shackleton aircraft was in the air and on "cab-rank" waiting to be called in directly the Yemenis opened fire, if they could be persuaded to do so. On orders from the Na'ib, his retainers fired their rifles towards the "enemy" but nobody fired back. Led by the Na'ib Jabil some of us (including me) strode forward 50 yards or more, waving rifles in the air and occasionally letting them off in the direction of the Yemen. Finally a shot was returned. The Na'ib raised his walkie-talkie and called in the RAF assistance. The Shackleton flew over at about 10000' and dropped its load of 250lb bombs singly and in sticks among the said to be Yemeni occupied rocks, without apparent effect.

Back in Aden, at my next meeting with Ken Trevaskis, to compile the weekly report on happenings in the Western Aden Protectorate, I found that he had drafted a paragraph on the action in which I had been involved explaining that the Yemenis had opened fire and the RAF had been called in to help defeat the violation of the frontier. As I had personally taken part in the provocation, I had to disagree with his statement that the Yemenis had started it. He was quite unable to see my point of view but asserted that I did not know the truth of the matter. Maybe I didn't! But it seemed to me unreasonable to deceive the Governor and HMG. Apart from anything else it would have been dynamite for all concerned if the press had come to know the reality. This was by no means inconceivable.

At the Officers' Mess Steamer Point we received copies of most of the British Sunday papers, including the Sunday Express. One well-written article on the Yemen and its ruler, the Imam Yahya, who had assumed power when the Turks were defeated in 1919, appeared over the signature of Ralph Barker. An Int.3 (grade of intelligence staff officer) in my Intelligence Branch was Flight Lieutenant Ralph Barker. Could it possibly be the same man? I checked with Ralph and it was! Ralph was in charge of a cell in the Intelligence Branch which was indeed a cell – a concrete cubby-hole without windows and one locked door which would be opened following a coded knock. It was of course air-conditioned but a bit of a hell-hole to work in. Ralph was responsible for our most highly classified intelligence, receiving and summarising material from signal intercepts, the sort of things Bletchley Park and Cheltenham collected. Ralph was assisted by a charming WRAF officer – Margaret Stewart-Thompson, who later married Captain David Overton, a Sapper in Aden, and they sailed back to the UK together in their yacht.

I accepted Ralph's assurances that he would never use knowledge gained in his intelligence role to colour his journalism, but thought it inappropriate to have a stringer for the Sunday Express in charge of the most secret intelligence in the HQ. Somebody else may have had the same views because Ralph was detached to Bahrein leaving Margaret in charge of Sigint, something that caused problems later.

David Collet may have had something to do with it. He was the MI6 representative in the HQ, a young (few years older than I) open-faced, cheerful, educated and cultured person whom I liked very much. Additionally he was always on my side in the rows I started having with my superiors. His nominal role was Political Advisor to the Commander (later the Commander-in-Chief). As MI6 means counter-intelligence I was never sure what advice he had to offer or whether this was just a cover. Certainly I later discovered that he was surreptitiously organising air drops of arms to Yemenis thought to oppose the Imam Yahya, ruler of the Yemen, who as a Zaidi, a Shia Muslim minority sect, differed from most of his subjects who were orthodox Shia or Sunni Muslims. The Imam was much influenced by the Italians and more-so by the Russians, who provided him with aircraft for a small air force, including obsolete fighters and helicopters.

It was at a party to which I was invited by David and his wife that I also became involved in an episode where I was formally interviewed by the MI5 representative in the HQ – Mr Arnold. He too was a friend of mine but not so much socially as officially, sitting on some of the committees on which I served. At this dinner party I was sitting opposite an officer of the Army Pay Corps who was denouncing Soviet communist influence in the world and lauding the supremacy of the Western democratic alternative. I said I would act as the devil's advocate and argue the case from the Soviet point of view. I explained dialectic materialism – thesis and antithesis argued over by elected and appointed representatives of "the people", resulting in synthesis which became policy. The process was just as "democratic" as our parliamentary system and had been debated by the prisoners in gulags (concentration camps) in Siberia, who concluded that our system had as much to offer as theirs. I gave some concrete examples of apparently fair policies achieved and implemented in the USSR.

To my amazement the Major went redder in the face (he had drunk a lot), rose to his feet and exploded – "You are a dangerous man Deverill! You have convinced me!" He carried on in much more personal vituperation and as it was quite late a number of diners rose and started to say their goodbyes. I was horrified to find I had broken up the dinner party.   Next day I was summoned to Mr Arnold's office to discuss the matter on which he had received a report from the Major denouncing me as a Soviet sympathiser. Mr Arnold thought that I was unlikely to be a Soviet agent if I had been posted in as SIO, after the very stringent security checks which even included investigating my long dead Italian mother, all my girl-friends, my conduct in Moscow and much else. I explained that I could have argued the Western case just as cogently.

It was agreed that it might be better for me to avoid being drawn into such arguments in future. It might not have helped my case had Mr Arnold known that the previous week I had used the British Council lecture room in Crater to give a gramophone recital of Russian and Soviet folk song, similar to the one I had arranged at the Officers' Mess. My audience numbered about two dozen, including two Lebanese Arabs, two French, three Indians and two British. They had many questions to ask about my time in Moscow. The British Council representative was away on leave and his Indian deputy had raised no objection to my using the premises. But when his boss arrived back he was at pains to explain to me that the British Council's task was to promote British and not Russian culture.

From home Dad reported that Maia had driven down from Oxford with my Sunbeam which I had left with her when I left the UK on the understanding that she would deliver it back to Alton where Dad would arrange its sale. Apparently it was very dirty and Maia was accompanied by Norma, a Jamaican student studying chemistry at Oxford. With Dad in his car and my sister Mary in the Sunbeam as navigator, they took the car back to Abbotts Garage at Wrecclesham and left it there for servicing and cleaning, returning to Alton for lunch after which Maia and Norma went back to Oxford by train. The car eventually fetched £228.18s.7d. compared with the £752.18s.9d. I had paid for it in December 1955, not bad for four years occasional use and a lot of fun. However the expense of maintaining it had been horrendous. The two months net salary equivalent was especially welcome because otherwise I was essentially broke apart from my net pay and allowances of £150 pm.

Maia was in trouble as usual. She was fed up with her work at Somerville College, more probably with the restrictions on her behaviour. As to which on 18 February Dad had spotted an article in the Daily Express that Pierre de Giselle, son of a French refrigerator manufacturer, visiting Oxford to improve his English, had offered a crate of champagne to any college girl willing to be driven through the city on the roof of a car dressed only in a bikini and then immediately swim the Isis. This was made public at an undergraduate party and accepted by Maia who said that the temperature in England in February was mild compared to the temperature in Iceland, her home country. The project was going ahead but the Principal of Somerville forbade her to do it. This must have riled Maia even more. Not long after, I had a letter from Karl Walter in Bordighera saying that Maia had turned up again hoping to renew the acquaintance of the "racing driver" she had met the previous year. Karl said that Maia had soon concluded that the racing driver was "of the species serving best in absentia". She left him and then tried to find free board and lodging by the sea, hoping to stay in Karl's flat. She initially tried to obtain the key from Teresa, Karl's house-keeper, but when that failed she tackled Karl himself. He wrote: *"I let her know, anyhow, that I'm very hard up, having earned not a penny last year. But I admit she is very ingratiating and once again I am grateful for the riches I have not".*

Letter home, 12 March 1959:

> *All the Army members of the staff went away for 18 days conferring in Cyprus. Just routine stuff but for the life of me I cannot understand why they have so many conferences. The Chairman always sounds imposing and dull, and everyone else sits around biting the ends of pencils and holding the inevitable pieces of mill-board with a dozen pages of paper bulldog clipped to the front: very military – like a "going map". It is for doodling on and passing to people with invitations to have drinks afterwards.*
>
> *I have been doing a lot of flying recently – in fact every morning I have taken the first detail in the Meteor here, or rather at Khormaksar.*

As a result I am very tired, for quite apart from the mental and physical strain (if one can call them such) of flying, it means I have to get up at 05.30 each morning in order to have breakfast and then drive the ten miles to the airfield. I get back to the office from Khormaksar at about 10.00 and work until lunch at 13.30. Then more work (mostly reading reports) or a swim. Tea – visit somewhere or other to meet people or see places and take photographs – dinner – then collapse into bed – and sleep badly it being hot. I am looking forward to my next lot of travels to the Persian Gulf.

Flying had become very dear to me. The ability to divorce myself from the petty aggravations and tediousness of Headquarters' life in Aden was life-restoring. While flying I could commune with nature, encounter my old friends the clouds (not so many) and physics.

It was usually very hot when I taxied out to the end of the runway, wearing no more than a pair of Y-fronts under my flying overalls. If I had to wait at the end of the runway the heat built up and I could almost see the sweat rising up my goggles. Then "OK to take-off"! Turn onto the runway and open throttles. Wheels off the ground and retracted and I would stand the aircraft on its tail and rocket up at 7,000' a minute, with the sweat evaporating off me so that I felt as if diving into an ice-cream. I would climb to above 20,000' and then set course for Africa where the Somali coast would already be visible.

Keeping South Arabia on my right I could not easily get lost. After 20 minutes or so I had to think of returning to Khormaksar, sometimes doing a few aerobatics on the way and a maximum rate descent down to circuit height before landing. This aspect of my life could not easily be interfered with by, shall we say "unenlightened" officers on the ground, sometimes called "penguins" by aircrew. On occasions I would accompany Meteor aircraft of 8 Squadron on sorties against dissidents, as an observer, because I was usually flying a two-seat Meteor trainer. This gave me a good idea of the futility of trying to find, let alone attack, individuals and small groups sheltering among the tumbled rocks and caves.

Of course it would be wrong to label all the staff officers as "unenlightened". Most were highly intelligent, kind, and considerate. On the plus side was Flight Officer Liz Avery, born Oldershaw in Alexandria on 14 February 1921, her father being a British Army officer and her mother Maltese. Liz went to schools in Egypt and graduated from St Clare's College Heliopolis in 1939 at the age of 18. She had been brought up speaking English, Arabic, Italian and French. In 1940 she met Sgt. Frederick Edwin Avery, 23 years old, a wartime recruit to the 8th Royal

Hussars. They were married in the Catholic cathedral in Heliopolis on 12 August 1941 but had very little time together before he was killed in action in his Stewart tank on 20 November near Sidi Resegh during Operation Crusader, General Auchinleck's attempt to destroy the Afrika Corps before Rommel started his advance up the desert to El Alamein.

Liz returned to the UK and trained to be a teacher at the Hampton Training College, then taught in various schools in southern England. In August 1953 she joined the Women's Royal Air Force as an Aircraftwoman on the administrative side but after a few months was selected for officer training and was commissioned in February 1954. After more administrative posts she was selected to attend the Middle East School of Arab Studies (MECAS) after an initial three-month course at the School of Oriental and African Studies in London University.

Promoted to Flight Officer, Liz was on the 13th course at Shemlan from January to November 1957. She passed the Civil Service Interpretership examinations with flying colours, her distinction undoubtedly helped by her prior knowledge of Egyptian Arabic. She was then posted to Aden and joined the HQ Intelligence Branch where she was responsible for the analysis of intelligence gleaned from local and other sources. She was outstandingly loyal to me and became a close family friend. Liz returned to the UK in 1961 and retired from the WRAF to restart her earlier career – teaching, in Australia, Papua New Guinea and South Africa until the age of 60 when she finally retired to live on the Isle of Wight and then in Ashford where she had relatives nearby. She died in 1999, still loyal, loving and loved. She always said that her years at MECAS and in Aden were the high points of her life.

A man to whom I did not greatly warm was Major Andrew Klinghart of East European origin. He was an excellent collator and analyser of intelligence and seemed very happy in his work. At lunch time he was always one of the first to arrive at the bar in the Officers' Mess and join colleagues talking loudly and downing drink after drink, with little thought of lunch or much else. Come 3 p.m. and they all went home fairly sozzled to sleep it off until evening suppers and dinners. Nothing much else, or I discovered nothing. Andrew had a charming East European wife and they lived together in a hiring in Crater. I never met them at any of the evening occasions I attended, and wonder how they managed to survive the hot, stifling environment, physical and intellectual.

Our commanders, the Commanders-in-Chief, were a mixed lot. Air Vice Marshal ML Heath (b.1909) was in command when I arrived and had he wanted he would probably have been able to implement Mountbatten's policy to integrate the HQ. He returned home tour-expired just as I succeeded Dennis as SIO. His successor was Air Chief Marshal Hubert M. Patch (b.1904) who should probably never have been sent to Aden. He had just lost his wife of many years and was distraught and confided his distress to me. He was open in his disregard for "young" officers and kept company mostly with officers of his own age, who had known the RAF between the wars. I was 18 years his junior! He was not much bothered about integration and seemed only too ready to put up with the Army becoming the dominant Service in the HQ. He only stayed in Aden ten months and then retired to Africa, marrying a French widow who lived in a house opposite my office window, so I saw quite a lot of her.

Both Heath and Patch had originally been pilots but early in their careers moved to specialise in armaments. Patch was replaced by Air Chief Marshal Sir Charles Elworthy, who would indeed have stood up to the Army but I saw comparatively little of him because by then I was coming to the end of my own tour. Sir Charles had been an active pilot throughout his career and he was the Commandant of the RAF Staff College in 1958 when I had been on the course there and came to know him. My immediate superiors in the HQ, the Commander, Air Forces and the Senior Air Staff Officer, an Air Vice Marshal and an Air Commodore respectively, were of much the same "mind" as their C's-in-C, preferring the traditional single-Service approach to the new-fangled integration favoured by Mountbatten. How then could I run an integrated Intelligence Branch without their support? With difficulty! But until Dennis Carey left in October 1959 I was relatively free of care, travelling a lot, flying, swimming, riding horses and even trying my hand at polo, initially not knowing that one has to hit the ball with the flat of the stick and not the point, as in croquet.

For official duties I had a battered Land Rover but needed a private car. For £40 I bought a 1953 Fiat Giardiniera. The brakes ceased to function a few days after I bought it and it was difficult to find the Fiat agent in Crater (a buxom Italian lady) to have urgent repairs made but in the meantime I drove on the gears. The car was like a very small estate, personalised by a previous owner who had the roof cut off with an oxy-acetylene torch so that, being tall, I could by craning my neck, drive with my head out of the top like a tank commander. The radiator was crumbling like half-eaten honeycomb but surprisingly did not leak. My vehicle caused raised eyebrows among the other Staff Officers, who thought it infra dig.

Despite the absence of my Army colleagues I was able to get away twice in March – to Bahrein, which I had visited before in 1944 when I was flying on 216 Squadron from Egypt.

It was now much larger, being an important international airport. I also accompanied Lord and Lady Hamilton, distantly related to the Swedish Hamiltons and to the Governor of Aden, Sir William Luce, to visit plantations at Abyan 30 miles east of Aden where agriculturalists were trying to grow cotton. Abyan had been an important town on the branch of the Incense Road leading from the coast, and Aden, to Shabwa and thence north and west to what are now the Yemen and Saudi Arabia.

This led to an invitation for me to visit Lord and Lady Hamilton on their ranch near Nakuru in Kenya where they had a 50 square mile estate with thousands of cattle herded by Masai tribesmen. When visiting them later I helped to count and dip the cattle, numbering upwards of 5,000 and witnessed Lady Hamilton give a dressing down, literally, to a Masai drover who had dared to depart from traditional Masai garb and donned an old Army greatcoat for protection against the keen morning air. Lady Hamilton could not abide the Kikuyu, the majority tribe in Kenya, whom she said had become townspeople and whose settlements were always dirty. The Hamiltons lived the lives of very wealthy landowners, in a splendid house with splendid food, clean white sheets on the beds and everything an exile like me hankered after.

I was soon able to indulge my taste, being summoned to a meeting in London to be attended by all senior RAF intelligence officers worldwide. British Overseas Airways Corporation (BOAC) flights to Aden had been temporarily suspended for some reason and my only chance of getting to London in time for the meeting was to join a twice-weekly BOAC flight from the Far East passing through Bahrein. I had to get to Bahrein quickly to catch the flight that evening, 3 April 1959. I could only do it by flying a Meteor to Bahrein which was OK except that the aircraft would be needed in Aden for flying on 4 April. Wing Commander Hutson, the Wg Cdr (Flying) at Khormaksar, agreed to fly with me and then take the Meteor straight back to Aden. On the way we landed to refuel at Salalah, Masira and Sharjah, RAF airstrips on the South Arabian coast, getting to Bahrein with plenty of time for me to catch the BOAC flight and for Wing Commander Hutson to start the long flight back to Khormaksar on his own. Each leg of the flight at 20,000' took only about 40 minutes, but the turn-round on the ground took about the same time – say four and a half hours altogether or nine hours for the flight there and back.

I spent ten days in the UK, visiting Air Ministry but basing myself at home in Alton and going to London by train. Apart from the conference, which went on for several days, I arranged to take the Civil Service Interpretership examinations in Russian in September. I had passed the London University final exams in

Russian with flying colours but wished to have the Civil Service Interpretership qualification in case I could apply to enter the Foreign Office, more interesting than the RAF, when the linguistic qualification would be useful.

I also visited Maia in Oxford and Stan Barber and his wife and children in Bristol. I had had the idea of making colour slides of some of Stan's paintings and showing them to people I might meet (in Aden initially) in case they might like and want to buy one or more. Maia was her usual selfish self, not that I did not enjoy this, but now looking after my own interests to a greater extent. She was wearing my emerald ring and I asked her for a closer look, slipping it off her finger and into my pocket. I had no intention of returning it other than to Johnson and Stongithearm, whom I asked to take it back. They would not agree to that but said they would sell it for me for a small percentage. I eventually received their cheque for £200 which I added to the £228 for the sale of my Sunbeam and invested the sum in British Petroleum shares. These came in very useful later. Maia made no fuss at all over the ring. With her it was a matter of "easy come: easy go". I was determined not to be taken for a ride again.

I was back in Aden on 14 April. Dad wrote about his worry that I might have been on the BOAC aircraft over-flying Iraq and forced to land at Baghdad. I assured him that this incident occurred on 18 April and that in any case the flight I was on flew via Beirut over Syria and Saudi Arabia to Bahrein, from where I had flown back to Aden by Aden Airways. However the Iraqis were already getting even more uppity than before. From intelligence sources we learned that the Soviet Union had agreed to supply a number of Ilyushin 28 medium jet bombers to Iraq, so I was on the lookout for these. Eventually we heard that a Soviet merchant vessel had passed through the Suez Canal carrying a deck cargo in large crates. We guessed where this might be going and I sent Shackleton aircraft from Khormaksar to photograph the ship when it turned east at the Bab el Mandab. A comparison of the crate sizes and the sizes of the wings and fuselage of the IL28 confirmed without doubt that delivery of the bombers was under way, two to each ship, with the wings and fuselages in crates on deck and the engines in the hold presumably.

From 1 to 7 June I was sent to Nairobi as the senior RAF member of a Court Martial. These things are like Jury Service. One is always liable to receive a summons to serve on a Court Martial. I was able to use the visit to meet up with one of my course colleagues from MECAS who was working with the security services in Kenya and I had a nice time exploring some of the country. To my surprise I was then ordered to Cyprus to attend an intelligence meeting of the former MEAF (Middle East Air Force). A year earlier this had been the more important RAF headquarters in the Middle East, but even then primacy was being passed to HQBFAP which then became the lead RAF HQ in the area, with Cyprus taking more of a back seat. The Command Intelligence Officer there was Group Captain Rupert Clarke, one up from my rank. He accommodated me in his house in Episcopi and I hobnobbed with his wife and charming children. We drove over much of Cyprus, including the Turkish north, over Mt Troodos, staying the night in a Greek Orthodox monastery. We visited the Castle of St Hilarion. We also borrowed the station Pembroke to have a look at other parts of the island from the air. At that time there was not the same animosity that later poisoned relations between the Turks and Greeks in Cyprus making it more or less impossible to travel freely between the Greek and Turkish areas. Then we passed from one to the other without let or hindrance.

I took time off to fly to Beirut where I took a taxi up to MECAS to see how they were doing. The place was largely abandoned because the students had departed on language leave although some of the staff were still there. At the request of the War Office I also took ten more days to fly back to the UK "for discussions". Their senior Intelligence officers did their best to persuade me to support their move to take over command of the Intelligence and Planning branches in HQBFAP. After all, they argued, I must agree that the Army, with its vast experience, was far better suited than the RAF to run the intelligence set-up. I did not agree and quoted Mountbatten's orders to integrate.

I was slightly narked to find that flying back to Aden on 6 July I had a Brigadier from the War Office sitting next to me who continued to try to persuade me that I should support the Army case, which would not affect me, he emphasised. I would continue as SIO when Dennis Carey left, but subsequently the post would become an Army one. In fact they had a point. The RAF had been the lead service in the Middle East because between the wars RAF aircraft had been the punitive arm in operations designed to keep the fractious tribes in order and prevent them raiding each other, cutting roads, stealing goods and generally behaving rather as they still do. However the regional threat now posed by Iraq, supported by the Soviet Union, demanded more than the threat of RAF bombing and the forces in Aden and in the theatre more generally were predominantly Army, with heavy tanks, artillery and much of the equipment of modern war, most of it Army.

It was already July, past mid-summer, meaning the sun was now well to the north of Aden, the temperature a degree or two lower, more humidity and a progressively stronger wind – the southwest Monsoon, with any rain falling not on Aden but on the Yemeni mountains to the north. The wind made for a rougher sea which damaged the shark net at the Services' Officers' Club leading some of us to frequent the Goldmohur Club, or for some of us the more exclusive Italian Club where they had a net of their own. There were subscriptions to pay for membership of these clubs but not much. The change over from southeast to southwest winds was marked in the sea with darker patches and swirls, possibly caused by the different temperatures of water currents or by differences in plankton, I never discovered which. But it was pleasant to watch the behaviour of the sea from the terrace of the RAF Officers' Mess.

At about this time, possibly just after I had returned from London with the Army Brigadier (Int), I was invited to an evening party by Hilary Colville-Stewart, the "civilian" senior intelligence officer working to the Governor. He and his Irish wife Chloe lived in a very nice large flat in Maala, not far from Steamer Point, not on the shore, but in a place like Aden nowhere was far from the sea. I asked Hilary if I might project colour slides of Stan Barber's paintings as a sort of sideshow after we had eaten and he readily agreed. It would only occupy ten minutes of guests' time and might be a welcome "cultural" diversion. And so it was. At the party there were about 20 guests, some military, some civilian, some old, some young, a nice mixture. Among the young were two very attractive girls, air hostesses with Aden Airways I was told. Rosanna Rizzi was Italian, in her early twenties, dark and slim. Her companion, Herta, Austrian, a few years younger, was fair and slim, with a very direct way of looking at you – or at me at least. I later discovered that Rosanna thought I might be the painter trying to exhibit some of my work. Herta disagreed. Rosanna bought one of Stan's paintings which I brought back for her when I next visited the UK.

Some days later, on 11 July, I flew to Djibouti, the capital of the small French enclave of French Somaliland on the Africa coast opposite the Bab el Mandab, to meet the Chief of Intelligence of the French forces there. He was a Colonel in the French Armeé, who put at my disposal a car with driver and a whole house to live in, including servant. Apart from an initial meeting with the Colonel I was given no opportunity to discover anything at all about the French presence. My visit was treated very formally and I got the impression that the Colonel had instructions to be polite but give nothing away. Quite right! Djibouti was a charming place. The French were fully integrated with their Somalis and in the many night clubs and bars one might see officers, NCOs and ratings as well as civilians of all nationalities, with equally multifarious women (and men) and dressed in any way they pleased, often an officer in his tunic with a futa below and bare feet, and a black or coloured girl in much less. It seemed that everyone was intent on having a good time. Of course French Somaliland was then treated as an integral part of France, like Marseilles.

In Djibouti I met the Swiss representative of Shell, Pierre Chavannes, and his beautiful wife Andrée. They lived in a Swiss-style chalet, you might call it, in the hills behind Djibouti. Andrée had a tame Cheetah which used to walk beside her on a lead. Pierre and his wife invited me to stay in their house for one night. We got on very well together and remained friends for some years until Andrée died prematurely. Paul retired from Shell after a disastrous tour in Nigeria, married for the second time and from then on lived in Switzerland, initially outside Bern and later close to Lausanne.

Many British 'exiles' in Aden liked to visit Djibouti to get away from the much more hidebound life in Aden. With my swimming flippers in one hand and briefcase in the other I returned to Aden on 17 July by Aden Airways, and who should I see in the hut used for arrivals, departures, customs, migration, passengers, crew, etc., but Herta in Aden Airways uniform departing for a flight to Asmara, the capital of Eritrea, via Kamaran Island, the quarantine station for pilgrims to Mecca. I stopped her and asked for her telephone number which she gave me.

Herta arrived back in Aden next day, but tired from the long flight. However I phoned on 19 July and went round to see her at the Aden Airways house in Maala, Salem Bahakim Flats, where she lived with Rosanna and the other five Aden Airways hostesses. Thereafter I was a frequent visitor. It was only fifteen minutes walk from the Crescent Hotel. Rosanna and Herta were by far the most attractive girls in Aden I had encountered, soon to be joined by Neda Nanut, a Yugoslav girl, also in her twenties. All three were young, intelligent, beautiful and unattached. Of the three I was most impressed by Herta, with her direct gaze, her frankness and her gameness for almost anything reasonable I might propose, reciprocated because I was just as interested in considering anything she might propose. It has always been so. I soon discovered that Herta's family name was Jeuschenak, that she had been born in Klagenfurt, the capital of Carinthia, on 13 January 1940, and had moved with her parents after the war to Addis Ababa.

On 30 July I flew to Hargeisa to accompany Andrew Fuller on a trip round British Somaliland. Andrew was a Major of the Royal Greenjackets responsible for checking out on the ground features shown on the vertical air photographs of south Arabia and the Horn of Africa taken for the Joint Air Reconnaissance Intelligence Committee. These photos were used for making maps and charts, and it was important to know the nature of the very large number of physical features identifiable in the prints. Was an apparent water source, spring or well, seasonal or permanent, and was the water potable? Was an apparently passable track hard or soft sand or jagged rock? Such questions as these could only be answered by inspection on the ground. After my arrival in Aden I very soon found out about Andrew and his work and was very keen to accompany him on at least some of his reconnaissances.

He met me at Hargeisa and we both stayed the night in the Hargeisa Club, primarily for expatriate Brits. Next morning we started off early in the first of two Land Rovers, the second driven by Sergeant Kaka, an Indian from Scotland who had joined a Scottish regiment. With him in his Land Rover Sgt Kaka had three local Somalis, who would look after us from the domestic point of view – cooking, helping to erect our tents, anything we could do ourselves at a pinch, but where it was useful to save time and effort, quite apart from interpreting the Somali language and culture. Andrew was a master at his job including maintaining the vehicles of which he knew every nut and bolt. A lot of maintenance was necessary because savage African thorns frequently punctured the tyres, which had to be repaired using an ingenious vulcanising gadget, in a sense a pyrotechnic, which needed igniting. This vulcanised the patch to the outer tyre, whereas the inner was repaired using the usual adhesive patch. A device screwed into one of the sparking plug ports re-inflated the tyre to a pre-set pressure when the motor was re-started. Andrew frequently diagnosed an engine fault by ear, and dismantled as much as needed dismantling, neatly laying out the components on a ground sheet, repairing or adjusting whatever had been wrong, re-assembling and driving on. This often delayed one's progress. But better than breakdown miles from help!

The former British Somaliland, now part of Somalia more generally, runs from west to east from French Somaliland to within about 150 miles from Cape Gardafui, the eastern Horn of Africa, where the coast drops away to the south more than a thousand miles to the northern frontier of Kenya. Thus, British Somaliland was comparatively small, a strip 100-150 miles wide and 350-400 miles long running along the Gulf of Aden, parallel to the Aden Protectorate coast about 200 miles to the north. The southern border flanked Ethiopia.

In our two Land Rovers we drove east towards Burao on tracks leading through extraordinary desiccated forests interspersed with tracts of desert or desert scrub. We drove until rather late the first day and it was nearly dark when we camped. Thunderstorms were visible to the south-east with great flashes of lightning and frighteningly loud thunder. We got into our sleeping bags on Safari camp beds and dozed off only to be woken at past midnight by the rushing of water under our beds. Surveying the rising flood pouring around us we decided that discretion was the better part of valour and retreated to the greater security and discomfort of the seats in the Land Rovers. The water rose ever higher and swilled about round our feet in the vehicles. It was a scaring situation; vehicles and their occupants have been swept away in wadi floods caused by storm rains. Towards 3 a.m. the storms collapsed and at first light we found we had camped in the middle of a wide wadi and could indeed have been drowned if more rain had fallen.

About 20 miles north-west of Burao we came across a roughly circular lake about 100' in diameter, of warm brackish blue water, blue because of its great depth which we tried unsuccessfully to measure. Most water sources are surrounded by the spoor of wild animals that go there to drink morning and evening, but here there were no traces of game. We decided that the water was not to their taste, possibly toxic. To us it tasted a bit sulphurous but not undrinkable. Not far away was an identifiable volcanic cone of black rock from the interior of which came the noise of rushing water. Water, some of it hot and steaming, possibly from this source, filled rivulets bordered by vegetation on which fed locusts, possibly not yet at the swarming stage. Somaliland was often plagued by locusts and it was in this scenario that I placed "Desert Locust Control" an appreciation style exercise I designed for the RAF Junior Command and Staff School (JC&SS) several years later.

From Burao we altered course north-east obliquely towards the coast on tracks indicated on Andrew's maps where the going and terrain had to be noted. In the early evening we started the routine to be followed for the next two weeks. There were many herds of small antelope to be seen and we would park up close to one of them and then take a rifle and kill the evening meal. These antelopes were so unaccustomed to seeing human beings that one could walk right up to them without their being in the least scared. It would have been easy to put a revolver to the chosen animal's head and pull the trigger, but one had to be careful not to kill it outright because the Somalis would not eat any meat not killed by the halal process whereby the blood is drained by a cut through the throat. The "boys" then quickly skinned the carcase, disposing of any unwanted bits for the jackals and then putting the haunches to roast or cutting them up for stews.

There was no bother about letting the meat hang. It went straight from the herd to the pot. Initially I was rather horrified by this procedure but after a few days I was shooting game and skinning and cutting it up without any squeamishness. I concluded that the ferocity of many tribesmen and their attitude to death is conditioned by their way of life. One can get used to anything, even killing human beings if that is the correct thing to do. After the evening meal round the fire, kept burning for as long as possible to keep away predators, especially hyenas, the boys would use any leftover scraps of meat to make curry and rice for next day's lunch. This would be ladled into outsize Thermos flasks the best part of 9 inches in diameter and 18 inches long, strapped into holders on each Land Rover front wing. By the following midday the curry would be nicely matured and ready for eating.

On rising ground south of Ankhor Peak (1716m) by an abandoned landing ground we turned west through Las Dureh and then north down a wadi to the coast about ten miles west of Karin, a town of possibly a few thousand people, most of them away inland with their herds and flocks apart from fishermen and the elderly. Thence we drove east along the sandy beach where we could, or over the flanking dunes when the coast was too rocky to use. We were often driving parallel to flocks of pelicans going the same way. They fly about 20' up, coasting on the sea breeze where it rises at the shoreline, and rarely flapping their wings. In the evenings and sometimes more often we would have a dip in the waves, not going out too far because of uncharted sea currents and the likelihood of sharks. On one occasion, as the sun was setting, we had ventured out into the sea for 50 yards or so and returning to the beach observed a multitude of splashes in the shallows. These turned out to be small sharks, about 8' long, which seemed to be trying to get at the crabs which were dancing like dervishes on the wet sand. Sgt Kaka got hold of one of these sharks by the tail and for a moment he looked like one of the tritons on the famous Roman fountain 'del Tritone' wrestling with a dolphin. The shark was too strong for him and he had to let it go. After that we were even more careful about swimming.

The coastal villages and occasional small towns like Karin were largely deserted except by the occasional old people looking after small children. This was because storms inland brought by the south-west monsoon had started the vegetation growing on the plateau and the tribes with their women and older children had followed the rain with their flocks of sheep, goats and camels. Arriving at Mait, another such small town, we turned inland and climbed the escarpment on a track which was scarcely made for Land Rovers but just passable. From sea level to 8000' in a few miles is hard on any engine even if there are plenty of hairpin bends. On the ascent we passed through bands of different vegetation, including gum trees towards the top. I asked one Somali what he would do with the gum he was collecting from the trunk of a low sparsely leaved tree and he said it was used locally to burn in household fires to deter snakes. At the top of the climb we came out on to a fairly arid plateau from where it was an easy run to the town of Erigavo. From there we drove inland, roughly southwest for 100 miles or more, passing vast herds of camels drinking from cisterns filled with water by diesel pumps. We continued to stop at each water source, replenishing our Jerricans and chuggles (canvas porous water containers) and pouring a sample of each into small bottles, carefully labelled, for the specialists in Aden to analyse. Sometimes we had to dig to find the water, which might be muddy or sandy, often needing to remove baboon dung and other gunge from the surface before drinking.

Completely isolated in desolate scrubland we came across a store stocking every possible item, from spare spear-heads to tomato sauce. The only customers were trade trucks, usually carrying passengers as well as merchandise, which negotiated the tracks as best they could dropping off people and things and loading replacements. The store was the prototype "corner shop", lacking only a corner. We bought some mango chutney and a few other things to eat. High up on a hook under the corrugated iron roof I spotted two carved wooden "bottles" covered in dust and obviously passed over by customers preferring the lighter and cheaper plastic bottles. I bought the pair, carved out of what seems to be the trunk of a date palm. We have them still.

We continued south-west to the Ethiopian frontier and then followed a track flanking it until just before the Djibouti-Addis Ababa railway where we turned north-east to Djibouti. The track was very wet and muddy from rain for most of the way and also in the hills which were thickly forested and with game abounding. There were antelopes of every variety including the Gerenuk, an antelope which has evolved a longer neck than its fellows (but not as long as a giraffe) to enable it to browse trees more easily. The name gerenuk is Somali for, hold it, long-necked. Sgt Kaka and I shot an eland and only later realised that it was a protected animal. Too late. It cooked up very well. A difficulty was that it had very large hindquarters. We strapped a leg on our Land Rover bonnet, thinking we would eat it later, but very soon we were in the residential suburbs of Djibouti and it was all too obvious that in the hot sun the eland ham had gone off. Disposing of it was a problem because everywhere we tried to dump it turned out to be a children's playground or a bathing beach. Eventually we found a resident's rubbish bin outside his house on the road and left our stinking eland leg there.

I got back to Aden on 13 August and flew to Bahrein the following day to help to sort out some difficulties there connected with a Field Intelligence Officer, Flight Lieutenant Lagnado, we kept in the Gulf, nominally to report on affairs in Muscat and Oman where certain Omani tribes, or parts of them, living generally on the Jebel Akhdar, had for some time been in revolt against their rule by the Sultan of Oman. The rebellion was eventually extinguished by the Special Air Service in operations spread over several years. The revolt had its basis in the antagonism of the mountain tribes, who had originally come from the Yemen, to the tribes from the relatively flatter plain who had arrived in a later migration from the area of southern Iraq. Lagnado was a nice man to deal with and spoke reasonable Arabic, but was always having trouble with his British Army colleagues, who were eventually successful in getting rid of him and using junior Army intelligence officers to do the same job.

By the time I got back to Aden on 18 August I only had ten days before returning to the UK for my "mid-tour" home leave. I had arranged this to coincide with the departure of Dennis Carey, tour-expired and leaving the Army for a second career as an impresario, and the arrival of his replacement Lt Col Peter Castner, scheduled for 8 October, so I had to be back by then. I was seeing a great deal of Herta; our linkage was accepted locally and we were invited together to parties. However there were some raised eyebrows because I was 37 years old and Herta only 19. Many thought I was more likely to marry Herta's friend Rosanna, very attractive but of no vital interest to me, possibly because her interests were limited and she seemed to have her own agenda, whereas Herta's interests were unlimited and she was completely unselfish. I was not yet intent on marriage to anyone but my interest was more than sharpened when Herta talked of possibly moving away from Aden to join another airline.

I flew home on 28 August and immediately went to stay with Russians at the Pushkin Club at 52 Ladbroke Grove, prior to taking the Civil Service Interpretership examinations in early September. These were held at Uxbridge and the written papers were enlivened by an RAF team practising drill on the parade ground outside for the Royal Tournament. The drill was performed entirely without orders, the manoeuvres memorised to perfection and as a result of countless repetitions. At intervals the team members fired volleys from their rifles and this was quite disturbing for 20 of us writing essays in the various languages in which we were being examined. The windows were wide open because the temperature was in the high 80s Fahrenheit. The eventual outcome was that I passed the exam quite well although I would have preferred a First Class Interpretership rather than the Second I achieved.

I then went home for a week, looked up Maia in Oxford and collected Stan Barber's painting bought by Rosanna, and then visited Munich and Italy to see Irina and Mariapola respectively. I told them I had met a girl I liked especially and might well marry. I also briefed Dad on Herta and also Mary and Titus, who treated it as just another of John's infatuations. As presents for Herta I had the bright idea of buying books – a Russian folk tale – Konyok Gorbunok (The Little Hump-backed Pony), a Russian classic, in Russian and beautifully illustrated, and several others. Not only did I wish Herta to appreciate Russian but to buy a girl a classic in a language she does not yet speak can compliment her intelligence better than jewellery and other superficial gifts.

Back to Aden on 6 October and Peter Castner was already there. He reminded me of Conrad Veidt, a film star between the wars who usually played German spy parts, wearing a monocle as did Peter Castner. He was an old hand in intelligence, at least ten years older than I and probably sent out to play his part in retrieving the post for the Army in future. Initially I liked him but I soon came to see that he was not beyond covert scheming over the planned Army takeover, not taking account (or maybe he did) that I had access to his signals home to his superiors reporting on his progress in the takeover. What could I do? The RAF could not care less, the Navy less still. I was on my own in wanting to implement Mountbatten's integration plan. Peter had a wife and two children back in England but they would not accompany him to Aden so he lived in comparative solitude, or maybe not because a year later, by which time I was home, he had left his family and married a Chinese woman with fish and chip shops in Kenya. Or so I was told. I could not forgive his disloyalty to me bearing in mind my own loyalty to Dennis Carey.

Herta went on holiday to Europe on 23 October, visiting Austria and Italy where she had relatives and friends respectively. I felt forlorn but occasionally took Rosanna or Neda, or both, to parties, but my heart was not in it and I resolved to persuade Herta to marry me when she came back as a matter of the highest priority. Of course I was 18 years older, and had got used to doing things on my own. I was somewhat apprehensive about having to take another person's likes and dislikes into account for the rest of my natural life. I wrote in a notebook: *There is the prospect of living with this strange person, who is completely new and profound as well as shallow and frightening, like a forest "дремучий лес". Completely unperturbed by the dangers of an unknown future, oarless canoe in the rapids, she is as composed as a child playing with its teddy.* In retrospect this was a bit of an exaggeration. Poetic licence! The Russian means "dreaming forest" but has other overtones. Herta sent me plenty of cards and letters showing that she was affected in much the same way. On the whole I thought the die was cast and I told Dad in letters. He was none too well, in hospital with various troubles which developed into his final illness – basically cancer of the kidneys probably triggered by smoking.

On 10 November I drove down the coast with Roy Wade to the Bab-el-Mandeb taking four days over the round trip. We followed the coast the whole way, driving on the beach for the most part, the route used by camel caravans. We drove west to Khor Umera, a lagoon connected to the sea by a narrow channel. We camped there for the night and tried to repair the offside rear wheel of the Land Rover, the connecting studs of which constantly loosened for no known reason. Roy Wade was no Andrew Fuller and we failed even to diagnose the fault and therefore had to stop and retighten the bolts every ten miles or so. We had an escort provided by the Sultan of Lahej in a second Land Rover and used their tool kit and spares to keep ours moving. At Khor Umera we were entertained to roast goat by the garrison of the National Guard fort there (ten men and an NCO). We slept in our camp beds on the sand to the lulling sound of the breaking waves, but bearing in mind the hyenas which sometimes bite off the face of a sleeping man. We kept a driftwood fire going to deter such animals.

The camels we met on the coast fed largely on sardines. These were caught by their herdsman in circular nets about 25' in diameter, the edges of which were weighted with small lead weights. Folded over the arm the net weighed a good 15lb and was difficult to throw in such a way as to expand into a circle and drop into the water over the target shoal. That evening an old fisherman who had fed his camels on bushels of sun-dried sardines and was eating supper of the same sardines grilled on the embers of his camp fire, shared some with me as we discussed his problems, one of which was that he needed a new net. Next morning he said, I should come along again and he would show me how to use his net. I sought him out early and he stunned a fish sufficiently for it not to swim too far away and threw it into waist-deep water, demonstrating how to gather and cast the net with a swing of the right arm. He then challenged me to do similarly. I had to have a dozen or more tries before I managed a cast to his satisfaction. When I returned to Aden I got on to the Fisheries Officer and had two new nylon nets made and weighted and sent to the old fishermen who had been my teacher. I later discovered that he had been run down and killed by a car while visiting Aden.

We held a shooting competition with the soldiers of the garrison and I improved my standing by hitting the target five times out of five when the others failed to hit it at all. The second day we were joined by the Junior Assistant Adviser and we continued down the coast to the Yemeni frontier, staying the second night in a border village on the coast. The countryside was more hilly here and covered by much desiccated vegetation, as well as shrubs I recognised as Euphorbia, some as high as 20', when cut exuding similar white sap to that found in garden plants of the species at home. There were plenty of gazelle about and not far inland into the Yemen there were reputed to be wild goats and mountain lion. After a deviation north to the foothills of the Yemeni mountains we were accompanied back along the coast by the representative of the Sultan of Lahej. Back at Khor

Umera I bought two goats and Roy and I entertained to lunch the garrison and the various others who had joined our party. I also arranged a post-prandial air display by two Venoms from Khormaksar, scrambled by Control when I explained that the locals would be impressed.

I had a commitment to visit Muscat and Oman in December. One of my staff, Major George Hutson, had been killed in Oman, when his un-armoured Land Rover had run over a land-mine planted by Omani rebels. We started a programme to armour all Land Rovers operating on the Jebel. The situation there was highly precarious and I had arranged to go and find out more at first hand. Meanwhile I had to go to the hospital in Aden for several days to check if I had been re-infected with amoebic dysentery while sharing food with the local Arabs during my recent visit to the Bab el Mandeb. The pathologists thought not, but the condition of my guts was still teetering on the edge of acute inflammation as a result of earlier infections and cures.

On 30 November 1959 I flew to Bahrein to be collected by Squadron Leader Barry Atkinson, the Commanding Officer of the Sultan of Oman's Air Force (SOAF). He flew me in one of the SOAF Armed Provost aircraft to Muscat, where we landed and I was introduced to Colonel Waterfield, Military Secretary to the Sultan's government. Barry and Waterfield had been great friends for some time which was one reason why Barry had been appointed to his post. However he was fed up with being treated by his army colleagues as a sort of airborne Motor Transport section to be available at a moment's notice to fly any army officer anywhere. I had come across this problem in the Arab Legion. From Muscat we flew to Ibri on the Jebel Akhdar where I met some of the army officers combating the Omanis revolting against the Sultan's rule.

We flew back to Muscat where I had supper with Colonel David Smiley, the Commander of the Sultan's armed forces, and his wife Moy, a bit of a snob and fairly pushy. Colonel Smiley was about 44, small, fair, blue eyes and a brave man who, after commissioning into the Blues in 1936, served the war in the Middle East with the Household Cavalry and later in SOE in Albania and Axis-occupied Greece. Following the war, after two years as Military Attaché in Sweden, he applied for a "golden bowler", a lucrative way of retiring at that time. He was turned down but retired anyway intending to farm in Kenya but accepted an offer from the Secretary of State for War, Julian Amery, to command the Sultan of Oman's armed forces. He did not seem to like the job, spoke no Arabic and seemed to have made little attempt to get to know the Muscati sheikhs.

Over the next few days we flew over the Jebel and I was interested to observe the ancient system for collecting and distributing water both for irrigation and other uses. This is known as the falaj or qanat system and it has other names in the different parts of the Middle East where it originated and continues to this day. "Falaj" is the name used in Oman where the system started to be employed about 2000 BC. Near the source of water, a spring, aquifer or the head of a wadi, often the same thing, a vertical shaft known as the "mother shaft" was dug to a depth depending on the rock formations and other factors, with another shaft and then another from 50m to 100m apart in a line towards the terrain or property envisaged as the end or major user or distributor of the water. The bottoms of the shafts, up to 100m deep, were then connected by sloping shafts, of a size enough for a man to work in, through which the water would flow gently downhill.

The gradient has to be sufficient to keep the water flowing but not at a speed that might lead to erosion of the channel, because maintenance is difficult, with boys often doing the spade work while their seniors supervise the work from above. Water could be used freely by individuals, but for irrigation projects the owners had to negotiate an agreement with those who originally paid for the construction. The system covers distribution controlled by sluice gates and the word falaj derives from a Semitic word for division. 20,000 of these aflaj (Arabic plural of falaj) are still in use in Oman and many more in Iran and other parts of the Middle East and even as far as Morocco and China. From the air the aflaj in Oman look like lines of molehills running from the foothills of the Jebel Akhdar down to the cultivated plains closer to the sea. On the ground we motored up and down these plains and everywhere agriculture was booming with crops of grain and vegetables and groves – trees, dates and other palms.

While in Muscat I was introduced to many of the local leaders and was invited to participate in shooting contests with some of the Sultan's family. Some of them were ace rifle marksmen and I did the best I could, which was not good enough. I felt very much at home with Sayyid Tariq, the Sultan's half brother. He had been educated in Germany and admired everything German. He led a group of other relatives including Sayyid Abbas, the Sultan's uncle and Sayyid Tiwani, the Sultan's nephew, who shot out the bull-eyes of 17 targets with 20 shots. They all spoke excellent English.

I also met the British Residents and Advisors and the British officers seconded to serve in the different local armed forces or recruited as "hired assassins" as we called mercenaries – officers recruited from other than the British Services (often retired British Army officers). The violence in the area was distressing. But in a society without a democratic method for removing unwanted leaders there is every incentive to use assassination. The day after I flew back to Aden insurgents put a bomb under the bunk of the Muscati Minister of the Interior on his way by ship to Bahrein for medical treatment. Fortunately he went to sleep with his feet where his head should have been or he would have needed a coffin rather than surgery to his lower legs.

Herta was back in Aden on 10 December the day after I got back there from Bahrein and we were happy to be together again. Lord Tedder, the Chief of Air Staff, was visiting Aden and was interested in progress in the integration of the HQ. The main purpose of his visit was to see how living conditions for the garrison could be improved. The size of the garrison was always being increased without much consideration as to how they could be decently accommodated, fed, watered, supplied with electricity (there was only one small diesel power station which often broke down) and kept happy. I went to dinner with Lord Tedder and the Commander-in-Chief but I doubt if anything much was done as a result of his visit.

On 22 December I wrote home:

> At this very moment I am talking with Herta and Neda about the "duties" of children to parents. Both have had unhappy childhoods for different reasons. Both agree that unsatisfactory childhoods cause children to forget their parents' efforts.

Herta and I talked a lot about our future life together, which included children. I was still somewhat apprehensive of marriage and wrote to Dad:

> I feel very strange now that I know that I am really getting married. It is rather like chasing rabbits for a long time and then when you finally catch one, you don't really know what to do with it. On the whole I am rather worried because I feel it is such a responsibility. Until now I have been more or less responsible only for myself.

Dad replied that I was right to be concerned about my responsibilities because Herta was so young and he asked what the views of the RAF might be bearing in mind the security aspects of my work. I wrote back:

> Stop worrying about any stupidities that you may have come to expect from me. I emphasise and emphasise and emphasise again that Herta and I are getting married because we do not want to live apart any more and there is no sense in doing so anyway. I have told you a lot

about Herta. She is 20, her hair is tiger colour, eyes the same, she is Austrian, born in Klagenfurt, speaks five languages, plays the piano, cooks, is well read, intelligent and attractive. She loves flying, travel, ideas. She is as Catholic as I am (not very). We want to establish not only a family, but also a "castle" of family security. You will like Herta!

My sister Mary and her husband were less confident about my judgement and Titus wrote asking if I wished to kill my father with worry. Of course I had not written as much to them about Herta and our intentions. After all it was scarcely their business any more than their marriage had been mine. To crystallise my views I wrote for Herta and myself what might be called a "brief" on marital attitudes. It read:

My wife should be a person in her own right, having definite opinions on all matters, and capable of arguing in defence of those opinions whether right or wrong. She should be able to learn easily and be prepared to enter any experience for the sake of learning more and so adapting and developing her personality to greater and greater complexities of greater and greater interest. She and I should stand back to back rather then face to face. In this way we would appreciate two sets of experiences instead of one and, by sharing them, profit doubly.

I realise that just as I have to carry out routine work of a sometimes uninteresting nature in order to ensure a reasonable income, so will she be to a large extent concerned with not overwhelmingly exciting domestic affairs. But I hope that I shall be able to provide for her assistance labour-saving devices, and sitters-in and servants to enable her to get away and enjoy herself. This seems to me fair and right.

In the many exploits I hope to take part in starting from this New Year of 1960 I hope that Herta will follow, accompany and on occasions lead. In any case, neither of us should ever drag our feet or constitute a burden on the other. Stimulating each other, supporting each other, laughing at and with each other, life should become very tolerable indeed.

Considering this more than 50 years later, how have my prognostications worked out? Not bad! Certainly Herta has never been slow with her opinions on anything and we have never stopped enjoying and deploring experiences together. There could have been more labour-saving devices for both of us but in general we have managed as well as most or even better.

Herta and I decided to marry as soon as we could arrange a wedding, either in Aden or to suit Herta's parents, by then in Salisbury, Southern Rhodesia, a part of the short-lived Central African Federation until Zimbabwe, Zambia and Malawi became independent. Herta got in touch with her father and mother and they agreed to do the honours and arrange everything. Both Herta and I could get away from our work for sufficient time, she to go to Salisbury in mid-January for three weeks in advance to help arrange matters, get wedding dress made, etc., with me following on 22 January just before our wedding day, set for 24 January 1960.

We had decided that as both Herta and her family and I were nominally Catholic we should ask Herta's parents to see if we could be married in the Catholic Cathedral in Salisbury, but without a Mass or too much rigmarole. Meanwhile Christmas 1959 was upon us. We celebrated in Salam Bahakim Flats on tinned pheasant and Christmas pudding which I had acquired from the NAAFI. It was not quite the same as turkey with all the trimmings but went down well enough with wine. In Aden one could get all sorts of food from a Cold Store run by Conte da Vico, an Italian expatriate whom we knew quite well. The Officers' Mess did very well for food over and above the Service rations and at Christmas and New Year there were plenty of parties to attend, sometimes as a matter of duty.

Herta and I arranged to fly down to Salisbury courtesy of our respective employers, Herta by Aden Airways and Middle East Airlines, and me by RAF Beverley to Nairobi and on by another Transport Command aircraft to Salisbury. From Salisbury Herta sent me a quick telegram on 20 January saying that before the Catholic Cathedral in Salisbury would agree to marry us they needed a certificate from a recognised Catholic authority to confirm I was indeed a Catholic. This was cutting it fine. I sent a telegram to Dad asking him to telephone my old school, the Mayfield Xaverian College, to request the Principal to cable the Cathedral to the effect that I was a genuine Catholic. I am glad to say that this was done within hours even though I had not revisited the College since 1938.

When I arrived in Salisbury on 23 January the cable confirming my Catholicity was already there. Herta's parents had a small house on the outskirts of the city where they were already accommodating Herta and her brother and they had arranged for me to stay at Meikels Hotel, the best in Salisbury. This was the first time I had met Herta's mother and father, and I liked them at once, and her brother Hermann, aged 19, already working with his father in the transport business they had started, but interested in joining the Royal Rhodesian Air Force (he never did). On the 24th I put on my best RAF tropical uniform and was taken to the Cathedral in advance of Herta to meet my best man, a Wing Commander from an RAF establishment in Salisbury, whom I had never met before nor since. He and a bridesmaid and Father McKinnon (priest and Jesuit monk) who conducted the ceremony, and the many guests who attended our wedding and reception had been organised by Herta's parents. Indeed they had organised everything with what was for me unprecedented kindness and generosity. Fr McKinnon did not dwell much on the religious side of the marriage, but blessed us thoroughly. We exchanged the conventional vows involving loyalty to each other till death do us part. The whole ceremony took about an hour.

I had never thought about the complexity and expense of arrangements necessary for a formal wedding. None I had ever attended had seemed so well arranged with nothing left to chance or improvisation. I had always seen weddings as an agreement between what might be called "consenting adults" probably because during the war most unions had to be arranged on the spur of the moment without frills. Our wedding in Salisbury Cathedral was a solemn plighting of troths before family and friends, admittedly none of ours, but of Hermann and Paula Jeuschenak. They did us proud, sparing no expense and trouble. Our wedding changed my attitude to all weddings thereafter. There is no more important event in the lives of the two people concerned, nor in the lives of their families. New horizons are opened up; new universes created.

The wedding reception was a sit-down late lunch in Meikels Hotel. There were several dozen guests, some of whom brought wedding presents, none of which survived long except a spotted blue and white bowl we still use for grated Parmesan. The food and wine were very good. Speeches were made by Herta's father, by the best man (whom I had briefed on what to say), and by me, in a fairly inspired oration on international relations of which I said we were a very good example. A wedding cake was cut and champagne quaffed before we were let off the hook and could retire in the evening to the room upstairs that I had occupied the previous night. For supper we ate oysters, which we understood were good for these occasions.

Outside the hotel Hermann had left us one of his cars, a large Chevrolet, parked for us to drive away next day on our honeymoon, for which we had a week before needing to return to Aden. Our plans were to drive to Bulawayo and thence to Victoria Falls, and back to Salisbury, visiting game reserves on and off the road.

The first game reserve we came across was on the road to Bulawayo, and stopping at the gate to pay for entrance we were handed a card by the Wardens with various do's and don'ts, prohibitions and warnings. One must not leave the car under any circumstances; lions were dangerous; windows should be kept shut in the presence of monkeys. An odd warning was about Sable (black) antelopes, especially the bull. These might appear innocuous but in fact were dangerous, charging at the slightest provocation. Within a hundred yards of the gate we saw a group of Sable antelopes peacefully chewing mouthfuls of dry grass. Herta encouraged me to get out and take a photo. I had doubts about this but opened the window and pointed my camera. A Sable bull, rather like a black and brown goat the size of a cow and with a bunch of dried grass sticking out of its mouth, lowered its head and charged. I started the car and reversed towards the gate at top speed. The Wardens saw us coming and opened the gate, slamming it shut once we were safe on the other side. We were then given a short lecture and allowed back into the reserve, now more careful.

Another park included a snake garden where all manner of snakes and reptiles could be viewed from fairly close up, but from far enough away to protect observers from bites and spit. A poster advertised for snakes which the reserve would buy from intrepid snake collectors at so much a foot – more for mambas and puff adders and not so much for pythons and the less poisonous snakes. We stayed the night at a guest house outside Bulawayo which at that time resembled a Wild West township where the Sheriff might at any time emerge from a bar, six-shooter in hand.

From Bulawayo we drove north to Livingstone where I had telephoned to book a room at the Victoria Falls Hotel. The distance was not far, about 200 miles through delightful African countryside on a road alternating between tarmac and laterite. We arrived in time for dinner. The room, No 44, was very comfortable and had been occupied the previous few nights by Lady Dorothy MacMillan, visiting the Central African Federation with her husband Harold (next door in No 43), and a retinue of nine other senior colleagues, some with their wives. The whole party had flown home the day before we arrived. Harold MacMillan was Britain's Prime Minister from 1957 to 1963, and a week or so after his stay in the Victoria Falls Hotel he made his famous speech about the "winds of change blowing in Africa" an allusion to the many former colonies seeking and gaining independence, including of course Rhodesia.

We visited the Victoria Falls on 27 January and photographed each other in the falling spray and against the backdrop of these astounding waterfalls. I got Herta to stand, in some trepidation, on the edge of a sheer drop with the main falls behind her. In the hotel I saw an advertisement for observation flights from a DH Dragon Rapide several times a day from the local airfield and booked for early next day. It was a fantastic experience. I was just behind the pilot on the starboard side with Herta on the port side next to me. The pilot, a South African, flew low down the Zambesi to the west and then deviated over the Caprivi Strip, an offshoot of Namibia between Botswana and Angola, flying for the most part at treetop height. We saw countless game, herds of wildebeest, antelope, elephants etc., and I was able to photograph some of them through the pilot's open window just in front of me. Of course I was thoroughly familiar with the Rapide from my many hours flying them in the Arab Legion Air Force. Returning to Victoria Falls we flew low along the Zambesi seeing hippo and one or two signs of local boats. The flight was pretty bumpy and I had doubts about being airsick as did Herta, but we survived.

We stayed in the Victoria Falls Hotel for another night and then wondered what to do with the last couple of days of our honeymoon. A guest at our wedding, invited by Hermann, had been the Chief Engineer of the Italian engineering firm constructing the Kariba Dam. This was south of Lusaka, then the capital of northern Rhodesia, now Zambia. He had invited us to look him up so we decided to take him up on it. We set out early on the morning of 29 January and took the road to Lusaka, a very wide scrapered laterite track running almost due east from Livingstone. Herta was driving. I should explain that I had always thought that Herta was a proficient driver, with a licence, all legal and documented. About 100 miles out of Livingstone we were doing about 80mph on the red dirt road when Herta said something and applied the brakes. A wild dog was running across the road ahead of us and Herta braked hard to avoid it. Our wheels locked and we went into a wild skid, careering towards the right hand side of the road bordered by a deep ditch with scrub and larger trees behind.

I had no time to give any advice and assumed we would have a crash, possibly fatal, when we hit the ditch and trees. As we slowed I thought we might survive and seconds later that although surviving we would be injured and the car probably written off. Come the ditch and the car stopped, with its front wheels apparently missing but when I emerged to survey the damage the wheels were deep in the ditch and apart from superficial damage all major components were still there, if rather bent and scratched. So here we were then, personally in one piece, but with a car immobilised 100 miles from Livingstone and with no means of summoning help.

Within minutes what should appear but a breakdown van. I stopped and negotiated with the driver and he agreed to tow us to his destination in Chirindu more than 100 miles on, at the border between Northern and Southern Rhodesia. Off we went, arriving in the late afternoon. We left the Chev with the breakdown man with instructions to try to get the car into a condition to drive to Salisbury next day. We put up in the Chirundu Hotel where it cost £3.5s for the two of us for the night. Next day sure enough the car was back on the road and we drove on to Kariba, using the name of our wedding guest to be given a tour of the dam site including the vast generator halls as yet incomplete. There was an Italian workers' village there where we had lunch before getting back on the road to Salisbury.

There we stayed the night with Hermann and Mutti, as I soon came to know her, explaining the damage to their car as best we could – not very convincingly I fear. Our borrowed Chev was destined for a customer and some expensive repairs had to be done before it could be sold. I fear we had added greatly to the expense and inconvenience caused to my new in-laws. On 1 February I flew back to Aden via Nairobi. We had hoped that we could return to Aden together but civilian women were prohibited from flying in RAF Beverley aircraft. I was told that because the aircraft had two "floors" and only a ladder connecting them it was thought that women should not be visible from below, even if wearing trousers.

I was back in Aden on 1 February 1960 and Herta several days later. We continued to live as before, with me in the Crescent Hotel and Herta in Salem Bahakim Flats but as we were both travelling the situation was not dire because neither address minded much (if at all) whether we were alone in our rooms or not. In any case Hilary and Chloe Colville-Stewart, at whose home we had first met, were going on leave for three months from March and offered us their very nice flat during their absence.

An incident occurred that took me away from Aden on 6 February. On 5 February I received a telephone call from Ken Trevaskis to explain that during a party attended by the Sharif of Beihan he had told Ken that he now had the first aircraft of his own air force. Intrigued, Ken tried and eventually succeeded in getting more of the story out of the Sharif, who was very excited and pleased with himself. That morning a Yemeni helicopter had landed at Beihan. The pilot had stopped the rotor and disembarked before noticing that a crowd of tribesmen waving rifles was running towards him. He turned back and managed to get into the helicopter but the fastest tribesman stuck the barrel of his rifle into the cockpit and prevented closure of the door. With help from other tribesmen the pilot was winkled out and taken before the Na'ib Jabil, who ordered the captive to be locked in a room in the fort. Although the pilot could speak no Arabic or English, the Na'ib concluded that they had caught a Russian because it was known that the Soviet Union was supplying the Yemen with aircraft and the crews to fly and maintain them. Ken was unwilling to have Aden involved in an international incident, and knowing that I could speak Russian wanted me to rescue the Russian from durance very vile and get him out of the Western Aden Protectorate before the powers concerned started exchanging threatening notes.

It had already happened and a Soviet broadcast had announced to the world that the British had detained a Soviet pilot in Aden. The FCO sent an urgent telegram to the Governor to ask what was going on, and that he should get it sorted out a.s.a.p. Both the Governor and Ken thought that the best thing to do would be to send me, a Russian speaker, to ascertain the situation on the spot and assure the pilot that he was free to fly home to his comrades in the Yemen. This was exactly the sort of situation in which I loved to be involved. Realising that this might be a good opportunity to acquire information about the Soviet helicopter which I believed to be a small machine, NATO-named "Hare", I telephoned the Wing Commander (Flying) at Khormaksar, explained the situation and asked if there was a Pembroke available to fly me, a few knowledgeable helicopter maintenance crew and a photographer to Beihan, where we would examine the aircraft, photograph it and send it back to the Yemen with the pilot. The Pembroke was lined up and I was about to drive to Khormaksar when the Senior Air Staff Officer, my nominal boss in the HQ, phoned to ask what I was up to. He must have heard of my plan from someone else in the HQ because I had informed my staff that I would be away for some hours.

He said No. The Governor and Ken Trevaskis should have approached him in the first place and he would have decided what to do about it. Until he had contacted them I should not fly to Beihan. Needless to say he could not consult either because they were no longer in their offices. Lunch was pending. And so several hours were lost because SASO thought that his authority had been flouted. Eventually later in the afternoon I was given the green light to go but the delay meant that we would have to stay the night in Beihan and put our plans into action next morning.

When I got to Beihan my first concern was for the Soviet pilot. He was a nice enough chap from Smolensk who gave his name as Grisha (Russian diminutive for Gregory). He spoke no Arabic and was obviously fearful of these bearded, dirty tribesmen, bristling with arms, although he must have come across very similar people on the Yemeni side of the frontier. He had been detailed to pick up a patient needing medical treatment from a Yemeni fort (possibly someone shot or bombed from the Aden side) to take him back to a hospital near Ta'iz. He had thought Beihan was the fort and landed there to discover his mistake. He had not had a decent meal since he had landed at Beihan and I arranged that he should get the best that our Field Intelligence Officer, Bill Shevlin, could offer.

I also asked the Na'ib Jabil to move Grisha to a room from where he would not be able to see us examining his helicopter. It was indeed a Hare, of which we probably had plenty of information at home, but there was every advantage in getting more.

Next morning, the RAF ground crew removed cowlings from the aircraft and the photographer did a very good job photographing significant parts. We brought Grisha out to his helicopter but then discovered that before his eviction from it he had attempted to radio his base to tell them what had happened. The services had been left switched on and consequently the battery was flat and the engine could not be started. With mechanics on the spot conversant with helicopters we used one of the batteries from the Pembroke and jump leads to start the engine and Grisha engaged the rotor and ascended at speed, not to be seen again. Not to be seen, but to be heard of. I noted that after take-off he disappeared to the north towards Saudi Arabia rather than west to the Yemen, and after getting back to Aden that afternoon I heard that he had landed 50 miles or more into the desert, probably in Saudi territory. The Soviet radio was still protesting that we were detaining a Soviet pilot and his aircraft. Grisha must have got back to the Yemen later because we heard of him no more. I enjoyed the episode because I was able to talk to Grisha in Russian and about his home and how he longed to get back there. Obviously the Yemen was not a popular posting.

The Russians were giving us quite a bit of work at that time. Iraq had their support; it was all part of their interference in the Middle East and in Asia more generally. Our particular concern was Kuwait, which intelligence indicated was an Iraqi target for incorporation. This could be a threat to our oil supplies. The UK was on good terms with the rulers of Kuwait and we had a treaty obligation to defend them were they to be attacked. The Kuwaiti armed forces were armed partly by Great Britain and to augment their British tanks we also had an arrangement to stockpile our own tanks in Kuwait in case we needed to use them against invading Iraqi forces, largely equipped with Soviet armour.

My Army colleagues in Plans needed to know about the going inland in Kuwait for heavy tanks, and I was asked to furnish a report. The only vaguely relevant information we had in the HQ was in the Joint Intelligence Bureau library – a book by a C of E parson who had travelled that way in the late 19th century, no doubt intent on converting Muslims. This was obviously inadequate. At a meeting I said that I would travel to Kuwait, possibly in civvies, possibly with Andrew Fuller, and we would discover all there was to know about the desert floor that tanks might be required to cross. Cries of horror! I could not possibly be spared from my office (and the Officers' Mess bar it was implied) to engage in such a foolhardy venture. Whether they ever got the information they needed and by what route I do not know, but as we had the friendliest relations with Kuwait at the time and were supplying them with the tanks to operate across their deserts I doubt if it was very difficult.

Over this period Herta and I enjoyed ourselves in Aden, swimming at Goldmohur or at the adjacent Italian Club, going to the open air cinemas in Aden itself or Little Aden, where there was a separate and thriving community mostly connected with the large oil refinery there. Herta was away quite often on Aden Airways flights and I was fulfilling my role in the HQ, becoming more and more disillusioned with the work, or rather with the disorganisation of the work and the workers, including my colleagues. One episode was caused by the Chief Signals Officer, a Wing Commander Joe Beckett. He had noted that Margaret Stewart-Thompson, the WRAF Flying Officer responsible for Signals Intelligence of the highest security category, was nominally on the strength of his Signals Branch, although working in the Intelligence Branch. He was pressed for staff and issued an ultimatum that Margaret should return to his fold the following week. At that time Ralph Barker was away in Bahrein so I told Joe that unfortunately he could not retrieve Margaret because her work was vital to Intelligence, to Planning and to the Commander-in-Chief and his advisors. She could not easily be replaced because her work demanded the highest security clearance and special training unavailable in Aden. Joe persisted and appealed to the SASO, who brought in the bigger gun of the Commander, Air Forces, Air Vice-Marshal Lee.

They ordered me to release Margaret and restore her to Joe's branch. In my turn I appealed to the CinC, Air Chief Marshal Sir Hubert Patch, telling him that his most important operational and political intelligence was in danger of being cut off, there being no officer to handle it, unless Margaret could be kept in her job. He must have spoken to those involved because Margaret was reprieved. However, Air Vice-Marshal Lee took me to task over this, not in the office, his or mine, but at Little Aden where he met me near the beach, me in trunks with my swim fins in one hand. He roundly cursed me for disobeying his orders, shouted, going purple in the face, risking apoplexy. What could I do in my embarrassment but smile – the worst thing in such a situation! AVM Lee went berserk. I was quite upset; after all it was the CinC's decision, not mine.

On 5 March I set off with Andrew Fuller to tour part of the Eastern Aden Protectorate. He was in the Wadi Hadhramaut. The main idea was to visit Shabwa, the earlier Sabota. This town had once been the capital of the Hadhramaut, controlling the trade routes meeting there from Dhofar to the east, where much frankincense was grown, from Qana (now Bir Ali) due south, an anchorage on the Arabian Sea to which incense and other goods were brought by raft and ship from further down the coast, and from Aden, also an entrepot. Taxes on all goods from these sources were levied in Sabota and no caravan was allowed to bypass the city, with walls funnelling caravans towards the city and punishment for any tribesmen trying to circumvent the system. As it had water from numerous wells it was a natural place to develop.

From Sabota the incense caravans passed north through Husn al-Abr to Saba and Ma'in and thence through the desert to Petra the capital of the Nabatean kingdom and to eventual destinations at Gaza and in Sinai and Egypt. In those days most religions used frankincense and myrrh and the caravans carried with them all sorts of other trade goods. With time individual tribes or groups of tribes established exclusive franchises to carry the different products and even when I was there the salt mined at Shabwa was carried exclusively by one tribe and mined exclusively by another.[5]

I flew to Saiyun (height 2,000') where the landing ground was on the floor of the Wadi Hadhramaut between the vertical walls of the jol (plateau) another 1,000' higher to north and south. I met Andrew there and for the night we were accommodated in the ruler's house on the outskirts of the town. This was very comfortable – decent beds and food, and the luxury of a small swimming pool in the basement for ablutions. One soaped oneself on the edge and then stepped in. The depth was about four feet. No plugs but the water came in through one hole and went out through another. Sanitation was also modern in the sense that there were Armitage Shanks flush toilets draining through the walls into the street. The next day we drove west 15 miles to Shibam, sometimes called the Manhatten of the Hadhramaut because of its tall four or five storey buildings with battered walls. The buildings look taller than they are because the rooms on each floor have two windows one above the other. The architecture is typical south Arabian.

The size of rooms, passages etc., depend on the average length of the trunk or branches of the 'ilb tree, about the largest tree growing in these parts. This limits beam lengths to about 10 feet. The walls of the buildings are mud brick, reinforced with straw. The age of a building depends to some extent on the efficient disposal of urine. It erodes the mud bricks and so is usually carried by wood gutters projecting from the walls to fall as far as possible out into the street. Solids fall through another aperture and are already fairly dry on arrival at street level. At Shibam the Wadi is already wider than at Saiyun and the wells serving the town are situated in the centre of the Wadi where one can observe Ruth-like scenes as the women collect water in containers carried back to town on their heads.

From Shibam we drove on to Henin where the Wadi debouches into the Ramlat Sabatein where we needed to take on a guide for the next leg to Husn al Abr. Andrew knew of a guide he had used before and we visited his small tent on the sand outside the town and announced ourselves loudly so that he might prepare to receive us. His wife was pushed out of sight from the back of the tent and we were invited in to squat in front of him. He offered us a drink – goat's milk in an old saucepan. It was crusted with yellow fat with a few floating flies which I tried not to drink, but one must be diplomatic on such occasions. I noticed that at the back of his tent he had the suspended skins of large lizards containing fat or oil of some sort, rather like salami in an Italian grocer's.

He agreed to come with us to al Abr and we left within an hour into a small sand storm where visibility decreased and we were pleased to have a guide. It took the best part of the day to get to Husn al Abr, where we were met at the fort by Sheikh Khurusi whom we had been told would be the best man to facilitate our visit to Shabwa. Sheikh Khurusi had been established at Abr by Harold Ingrams, who from 1939 until 1944 had been the Eastern Aden Protectorate Resident Advisor to the Sultanates comprising the EAP. Until Ingrams took over, the tribes had always been fighting each other but after much negotiation he established between them what became known as "Ingrams Peace". Part of his achievement was thanks to his appointment of personally chosen deputies in key places in EAP. Husn al Abr was one of these, being on routes from the south to Saudi Arabia and the Yemen. Ingrams had met the Khurusi family in Zanzibar, where he had been stationed before. As with many Zanzibaris the Khurusis were of South Arabian origin.[6]

Shabwa had been a very difficult place to visit because the local tribes were very antagonistic to foreign visitors including anyone from tribes other than their own. Very few western visitors had been there because of the danger of being shot. Freya Stark, that inveterate traveller in the Middle East, had failed, and we were told that if we succeeded in getting there we would be the first Western visitors for 22 years, i.e. since 1938. Sheikh Khurusi agreed to help us, gave us a guide and an armed escort of tribesmen known to the Sabians in Shabwa.

From any aspect Shabwa was unprepossessing. The buildings were the usual mud brick without many historic ruins at first sight. However there were ruins of dressed masonry south of the town and we discovered stones such as lintels with Himyaritic inscriptions, incorporated in less ancient dwellings. On being asked about these stones the locals said they had been left by the awali (the first ones) and should not be interfered with. They said they had been told this by Belhaven – Lord Belhaven, the first British Political Officer to serve in the East Aden Protectorate.

The Sabians were mostly black and unfriendly, descended from Ethiopians who had once occupied this part of the world, because from time immemorial the South Arabians had invaded and occupied parts of Ethiopia and in their turn the Ethiopians – parts of South Arabia, with both sides enslaving the others. It would be interesting to know the relationship, if any, between the name Sabian and Saba, or Sheba and the Sabaeans, a civilisation preceding, or rather overlapping, the Himyars and Qatabans, and the Arabic use of the word Sabi (pron. Sobi) for boy, or servant. Now the Sabians mined the salt, salt domes which once capped oil deposits before they drained away east towards the Persian Gulf millennia ago. The salt mines were what might be called open-cast, caverns hundreds of feet deep in the rocky ground, dug out over the course of centuries. A few Sabians could be seen working in the caverns on galleries carved in the salt and connected by rickety wooden ladders. They chipped away at cliffs of salt with sharp mattock-like tools while others loaded the loosened salt into woven goat-hair sacks, which would later be carried by camels throughout south Arabia and possibly further.

Not very nice work by the look of it. At the time of the incense road it may have been better and Pliny the Elder writes a good account in his Natural History, Books III to VII and XII, xxx 53, xxx 56. We were given a meal in Shabwa by some friends of one of our tribal escorts in the family's mud hut. The family was very poor and although it was Ramadan they produced for us Arab bread and sesame oil, the former to be dunked in the latter. To drink – camel's milk with Arab coffee to finish off. They ate nothing themselves, having to wait until nightfall. On the outskirts of Shabwa there were wells, some very deep with plenty of brackish water for stock. I saw one well where a herd of some 50 camels was being watered by husky young bedu women, two of them hauling up buckets of water from a well while others, with much banter and joking, poured it into mud troughs from which the camels and goats drank. I had my Leica at the ready and took a couple of action snaps but had to break off hurriedly when the girls picked up stones preparatory to stoning me.

From Shabwa we retraced our steps back along the southern edge of the Ramlat Sabatein coming across the shells of the once luxurious vehicles, mobile homes etc., abandoned six years earlier by an ARAMCO oil exploration team, which had crossed the un-demarcated border between Saudi Arabia and the Eastern Aden Protectorate. Their activities had been stopped by Federal National Guard and the oil men had been obliged to return to their base in Saudi Arabia leaving their vehicles to the depredations of the weather and bedu. All fittings of any worth had been stripped, together with engines, pumps, furniture, tyres and anything else moveable. Because of the dry air the basic vehicles were in good condition. Although no oil was discovered at that time, it is interesting that modern maps show a network of pipelines connecting wells and storage areas about 40 miles to the southwest. One tall derrick of the ARAMCO "A" rig remained erect – a strange and lonely landmark in the wilderness of dunes.

We drove on as far as Tarim in the Wadi Hadhramaut. At Al Qatn I photographed women threshing the harvest wearing tall wide-brimmed hats against the sun. The cut crop was laid out on a threshing flow and then driven over by mule or donkey pulled sleds to break up the husks which were then winnowed by women who threw the ears up into the air for the wind to blow away the chaff. A truly biblical scene. These settled people are generally much less bellicose than the desert bedu.

We decided to return from Tarim to Mukalla down the western of the two wadis leading that way – the Wadi Idm. This was a less used track than the Wadi Duan but Andrew was keen to reconnoitre it. At one place where the road crossed from one side of the wadi to the other it was flooded by a sudden storm earlier in the mountains behind us and we had to wait until the water level subsided sufficiently for us to drive through. Later we were joined by a second Land Rover with a large escort and various passengers requesting a ride. Andrew took half in his vehicle and I went with the second with six or seven tribesmen for company. They were the typical small, wiry, nearly black south Arabian bedu dressed in short futas, colourful shirts, leather belts with jambiyas, their rifles and an assortment of bandoliers. For much of the drive they sang their very distinctive songs. After a while we were separated from Andrew who stopped to let off some of his passengers. We continued over the jol the surface of which was a nightmare scene of tumbled burnt rocks, often cinders, obviously originally volcanic. There was no water but we had plenty in our chuggles. However I became very hungry and eventually mentioned this to one of the bedu. From a bag he was carrying he produced a handful of rather sandy dates. Never have I enjoyed food so much, and to this day I love dates, preferably stuck together in blocks as sold by Sainsbury in 2006. I flew back from Mukalla to Aden on 14 March 1960.

Herta was pregnant, which was not unexpected and which we welcomed. We decided to tell Aden Airways that she would carry on working until April. She had been doing a great deal of flying and it was tiring because in those days an air hostess was far more than the waitresses in the cabins of modern air liners. The hostess, usually only one per aircraft, was an integral part of the crew, vital in the case of an emergency and a general factotum at all other times, making and serving meals to passengers and crew with wine for the former (and often for the latter) poured from real bottles into real wine glasses. She had to deal with sickness, and there was a lot of it because the Dakotas flew quite low over the deserts and mountains and it was often as bumpy as a rough sea. Passengers had to be ordered, supervised, mothered and shepherded.

The hostess was on her feet for the whole of each flight, sometimes even during takeoff and landing. It was usually hot on the ground and a hostess waiting for passengers in the aircraft on the tarmac at Aden would inevitably be pouring with sweat, with make-up running down her face unless she had been very sparing in its application. On one occasion the cabin emergency exit hatch of the Dakota blew off on take-off from Asmara (capital of Eritrea) and the Aden Airways station officer failing to find it acted on impulse, visited the local market and found it there for sale, bought it and returned it to Aden by the next flight.

Aircraft from Ethiopia frequently flew back to Aden with cargoes of qat, a hallucinatory drug taken by many Adenis to while away their somewhat unexciting lives. Qat was rather like privet clippings and to gain much effect the addict had to chew a kilo or more, spitting out the green fibrous pulp at intervals. The hostess might rest on the sacks of qat if there were not many passengers. Herta had been flying as an air hostess with Aden Airways since 9 April 1957, when she was 17 years and three months old. By the time we met in July 1959 she had flown more than 2000 hours, almost as much flying time as I had flown in the whole of my 20 years in the RAF.

Herta told me how the hostesses used to improvise in performing their duties. All passengers could not be served simultaneously and at breakfast some passengers would have finished their meals before others had started. This was an advantage because if scrambled eggs and baked beans were running low portions might be recycled for later breakfasts. Herta found the pimpled skins of chicken legs aesthetically displeasing and used to remove these before serving. In rough weather when passengers were being sick in the aisle (there was only one in the Dakota) Herta would cover the floor with the tabloid newspapers keeping the more up-market broadsheets for any more serious readers. On one occasion she had an enormous thermos flask of soup to serve as starters for lunch. After opening the screw top she lowered a ladle into the hot fluid but the ladle was very cold at 10000' and the thermos exploded drenching Herta with the contents, in full view of 22 servicemen facing aft in their rearward facing seats.

An immediate decision that Herta and I took was to stop smoking forthwith. This was not difficult because neither of us smoked much more than socially, in my case because I found accepting a cigarette an easier option than explaining countless times that I did not smoke. We had read that smoking tobacco affected a foetus adversely, although there was as yet no firm knowledge linking smoking with cancer. Any risk to the baby was unacceptable and from the date of our decision neither of us ever smoked again.

Hilary and Chloe Colville-Stewart flew off to Italy for their leave and we moved into their splendid flat which although not yet a home of our own seemed very much like one. Herta starting cooking for us, initially with some disasters, but with increasing success, until now when she is an incomparable chef. The fish in Aden was very good and we used to get darak and other fish from the market. For meat we relied on the Cold Store.

On 16 April I flew to Sharjah on the Trucial Coast to meet some of the rulers of the various states, all of them with agreements with the UK for their defence in the event of threats from neighbours or from further afield, Iraq, supplied with arms by the Soviet Union, being the most threatening. The Trucial Oman Scouts was the British officered force best equipped to confront threats, actual or envisaged and I was escorted by a young officer of that force. We first visited the Buraimi Oasis.

Letter home, Sunday 24 April 1960:

Am writing this at 7a.m. in the Officers' Mess of the Trucial Oman Scouts at Sharjah. I am waiting to accompany a string of polo ponies for their weekly bathe in the sea. I have been here for a week and have visited Buraimi (subject of a dispute with Saudi Arabia) and the inland desert (The Empty Quarter or Arabia Deserta) as well as the coastal towns of this erstwhile "Pirate Coast" ending in the mountains of this south-eastern end of Arabia. While I am here Herta has gone across to Asmara in Eritrea, in the other direction, to stay with Rosanna and her parents. She returns to Aden tomorrow and so do I. I therefore thought it would be better to write you a letter from here because there is always so much to do back at Aden. Next Saturday I fly to Cyprus for a big regional intelligence conference with Herta following, I hope, three days later. Trouble is that I go "Priority 2" whereas she can only come on "fill-up" basis if there is a spare seat.

Continued later – before lunch. We took 15 polo ponies down to the sea, pulling them with some difficulty through the little white breakers, of which they are frightened, into deeper water where they swim slightly apprehensively with whoever is looking after each animal hanging on to its mane. I am now quite tired for I also rode last night for an hour, then swam and then ran along the beach to dry off. The Trucial Coast is an odd place. Parts of it are the most awful country in the world – a wilderness of salt-covered sand and mud, dead flat, with shallow dirty lagoons of an inch or two of stagnant water. A vehicle can break through the surface of the sabkha as it is called quite easily and it is best when driving on it to keep going as fast as possible and not stop. The sabkha is blindingly white like a flat snow-covered Russia, but very hot. No fresh water anywhere and it stretches for miles,

Inland from Trucial Oman there is a dune desert, initially scrub covered but becoming sand sea as one runs into the Empty Quarter, with enormous dunes up to 600' high of reddish yellow sand – very difficult to motor over. In the prevailing wind the gentler slope of a dune is more or less to windward and not difficult to take at a rush but with danger of getting stuck in the soft sand. At the crest of the dune an abrupt turn through 90° has to be executed because over the lip there is often a vertical drop of 50' or more. Descending the downwind side requires a careful choice of slopes. Between dunes the desert floor is often hard and smooth. Driving laterally between dunes is often easy enough but as in the sea the waves of adjacent dunes seldom harmonise and crossing over the crests is inevitable. Between ranges of dunes there are sometimes date gardens, coinciding with the few wells. These are owned, in so much as anything can be said to be owned, by families of tribes who live towards the coast but who come back to their date farms at certain times of the year, treating them much as second homes, where they can act the bedu, go hunting with falcons, etc. Buraimi is a cluster of eight greener villages with date gardens with water sources in the oasis. Three villages, quite widely separated, belong nominally to Muscatis, the other five to the sheikhdom of Abu Dhabi. All are claimed by Saudi Arabia. Now Omani rebels plant land mines obtained from Saudi Arabia on the tracks around Buraimi and there are a few incidents each month and some casualties.

Two officers of the Trucial Oman Scouts drove me in their Land Rover the whole length of the coastal road of the Trucial States (now called the United Arab Emirates). In 1960 there were seven independent emirates with individual treaties with the British government and the Scouts were the largely British officered corps charged with their defence and internal security. The coastal road was not much more than a track for much of its course from Dubai to the Straits of Hormuz but the geology and geography were very interesting, with the north-eastern extension of the Jebel Akhdar (the Green Mountain) rising steeply from the coast to more than 6000'. While two of us swam in the Straits, the third was posted with a rifle on a 100' promontory to keep a lookout for sharks. From there one could see scores of very large fish of some sort swimming parallel with the coast several hundred yards out.

Still higher up the mountain slope was a small village and after a while four veiled women appeared and watched our movements. Later when we set up camp for the night some men from the village visited us, their elderly leader holding before him a small elaborately carved axe, which seemed to be a symbol of his authority. It was difficult to understand what he was saying, but it was friendly and he seemed to be speaking in Baluchi, the language of Baluchistan on the Iranian side of the Straits.

Letter home from Herta on 18 April 1960:

> *Asmara*
>
> *Dear Dad*
>
> *Surely you will notice that this is not John's calligraphy but mine. I will try my best to make my handwriting readable. Thank you very much for your last letter. I really hope that you are well and did not have to go back to hospital. How is the climate and do the flowers begin to blossom? In Aden it is beginning to be very hot and sticky, luckily there is the sea, and whenever we have the chance we go for a swim and sit in the sun for hours. Lately this did not happen very often for John had a lot of work. Now he is on a trip in the Muscat and Oman Sultanates, on the Arabian coast near the Persian Gulf and I took this occasion to come here to Asmara to see my friend Rosanna, who has been by 'room-mate' for almost three years while I was working for Aden Airways, and her family.*
>
> *The climate here is wonderful due to the high altitude (8000 ft) and Asmara itself is a very nice town with lots of flowers and green, which we do not have in Aden. After a week I will go back and hope very much to go to Cyprus where John has to attend a conference; it would be very interesting for I have never been there before and it is a very beautiful place.*

I find marriage marvellous; it is like being in seventh heaven. Useless to say that we are very, very happy. Now I have to stop. I hope very much to receive a letter from you shortly, for this way we will come to know each other sooner. With a lot of love and affection, also from John.

Herta

P.S. Hope my English is not too bad. It is improving all the time, but slowly.

In fact Herta's English was improving fast. But it was already good when we met. Her Italian was better than mine. Her French incomparably better. German – well I never claimed to speak it. The fact that she was writing to my father indicates the importance she gave to relating closely to my family, which had become our family. The adjustments made necessary and desirable in marriage were scarcely adjustments – they came naturally to both of us. We went into a "dual" mode as in the Arabic language. All our assets and liabilities were at once shared; we had a joint bank account; everything we owned was owned in our joint names. Initially we owned very little apart from the clapped-out Fiat car, and a bill, dating from Herta's life before marriage, from Bikerjee Cowajee, a local Indian store, for a dozen or more long play records. Thereafter we only bought things we both wanted, paying for them from the joint account. The marriage vows specifically stipulate that we endow each other with what we have. And so it was and has been. Of course we did have my RAF salary as a Wing Commander, £150 p.m. net which in 2014 would amount to about five thousand pounds – not to be sneezed at.

Our visit to Cyprus worked out very well. I had to fly civil airline via Beirut because RAF Transport Command had no convenient flights. Herta followed several days later on an RAF aircraft and we were accommodated in the Officers' Mess on this occasion but I was kept very busy with meetings most of the time. I gave a lecture on the task of British Forces Arabian Peninsula and the specific threats, illustrated by my own colour slides. Herta and other wives attending were given a programme of their own. Herta and I often got away to swim and sunbathe on the magnificent beaches, which on the British base were quite devoid of tourists or local Greek Cypriots. We flew back to Aden together by RAF Comet on 11 May.

Three days later I was away to Nairobi for the East African Regional Intelligence Conference. The conference was one day only but I wanted to visit

Mombasa and Zanzibar, which were in our area of interest. In Mombasa I bought some ebony fruit dishes (or that is how we use them at home now) as well as a topaz and a pearl, which I wanted to have mounted into rings for Herta, who still lacked an engagement ring, although we wore wedding rings bought in Rhodesia. Zanzibar was a lovely island and I greatly admired the very solid carved wood doors in most of the houses on the narrow streets.

Letter home, 20 June 1960:

> On arriving back from Zanzibar I fell ill with dysentery and then with flu' or maybe it was malaria – the doctors do not know, nor do they care much. It is too hot. Our Somali maid also became sick. Her trouble is a tumour that has to be cut out on Wednesday. She will not be coming back to us so Herta is training another Somali girl to do the job. She may not last long because in a week's time British Somaliland will become independent and many Somalis here want to go home.
>
> Committees visit us constantly to review the HQ staff and cut it down and much of my time in the office is spent trying to hold "integration" together. Generally life is a great trial. The weather is at its worst – 100°F, with the highest possible humidity. I go to work at 0700hrs each day and after six hours in our furnace of an office am quite exhausted. Herta and I either sleep air-conditioned until teatime or go swimming. You in your beautiful cool climate will have the energy to write to us daily, but we get the paper saturated with sweat by half-way down the page!!
>
> Herta has started to attend the clinic to do pre-natal exercises. The doctors pronounce her quite extraordinarily fit. She is bulging somewhat now but still manages to get the baby brown above her bikini. Some of the exercises are very odd. I have tried them and find that I too can raise and lower my breasts with my jaw muscles.
>
> We now have no money at all, which is a great relief as I hate having an overdraft. Looking back a year I find that financially I am no better off, but in fact of course I am richer by a wife, a car and fifty Shell shares, apart from all sorts of smaller items like record-players, fruit dishes etc. In Zanzibar I bought two large ebony dishes which weigh some ten pounds each but make magnificent fruit dishes despite the effort needed to pass them about. One has to be careful passing them to old ladies.
>
> With a baby coming I see no immediate improvement in finances but goodness gracious I get £150 a month after tax, so even with high

rents we will not be reduced to starving in mangers. I mean – people have managed on less! Herta now has her driving licence after a series of unfortunate episodes with the traffic police chief, who has been here too long and has lost all sense of humour. Anyway she can now drive to the hospital, go shopping and do all the other necessary things without infringing L-driver regulations or spending fortunes on taxis.

I lie without clothes on in the air-conditioned bedroom of our house (Hilary and Chloe's) while Herta makes up her face in front of a mirror in the corner partly obscured by some three dozen bottles and phials. Smells of unguents and aromas reminiscent of cocktail parties and operating theatres drift about. The air conditioner hums and pours a stream of cool air over our hot bodies, red from today's unusually hot sun. We are going out to eat, fish probably. A gift of corn-on-the-cob is boiling in the kitchen but seems very hard and unlikely to soften. There is no sugar or bread for breakfast so we must call at the small Arab store. We have pseudo-colds from constant changes of temperature from one extreme to another.

Must go and eat fish now, Herta says.

Dad replied that Alton was also unbearably hot, 80°F on 25 June but with thunderstorms in the evening of which the dog, Pat, a Springer Spaniel, was terrified, shivering and shaking in utter panic, as some dogs do. He looked forward to us coming home and added that he had read in the papers that the Commander-in-Chief, Air Marshal Patch, was also due to be replaced in August. God be thanked!

On 28 June I set off on another jaunt with Andrew Fuller. My idea was to visit Sa'id in the Wadi Yeshbum. Sa'id was the seat of the Upper Aulaqi sheikhdom. At the time some of the tribesmen there were particularly rebellious, and one family/clan had openly revolted against their Sultan and looked towards the Yemen instead. Consequently HMG, personified in the Governor of Aden and his agencies, used threats when diplomacy failed and patience ended. Warned of military action the family and supporters took refuge in the maze of rocky cliffs and caves which the RAF was called upon to clobber. The family's house in Sa'id was demolished from the air using rockets. Before the strike they had already decamped to the Yemen which they reached several weeks later with only one casualty, a young man who blew off one of his hands with his own grenade. This despite more than a thousand sorties flown by 8 Squadron and the fighters from a passing aircraft carrier.

I was interested to see the damage done to Sa'id for myself. It was minimal, indeed almost unnoticeable among derelict buildings, ruins, habitations and houses under construction, all of which looked the same. I met Andrew at Beihan and from there we drove along the southern side of the Ramlat Sabatein to Nisab once an important town on a branch of the Incense Road connecting it to the coast. At Nisab we left the main track and turned east across the stony sand for 20 miles to Ataq where there was an RAF landing ground which was occasionally used to supply the Federal National Guard and for casualty evacuation (cas.evac.) There we turned south for another half hour to the Wadi Yeshbum with Sa'id at its mouth.

The Wadi Yeshbum was sometimes called "murder valley" because of the numerous active feuds between families watching each other for the opportunity to assassinate someone important of the offending family. Some people never went out for fear of being killed, others went out specifically to kill. The mud buildings in the town, reminiscent of those in Shibam, had no windows or openings low down for reasons of defence rather than modesty, very like Verona and the castles of the families of Romeo and Juliet. The Federal National Guard had a strong presence and they had erected loudspeakers in the main square to broadcast messages to local residents. There were the shrines of a number of Muslim "saints" outside the walls of the town.

From Sa'id we drove 20 miles east down the Wadi Yeshbum and into the Wadi Habban to the town of Habban, another ancient city on a side spur of the Incense Road connecting Qana (now Bir Ali) on the coast and Shabwa. Bir Ali is situated on a promontory four fifths of the way from Aden to Mukalla, providing some shelter for shipping. There is not much other shelter on the south coast of Arabia. Aden, and Muscat, already in the Persian Gulf, are really the only two properly protected anchorages. Perennial water runs in the wadis Yeshbum and Habban and apart from sparse cultivation we saw small fish in some of the deeper pools. We arrived at Habban in the afternoon just as a sand storm started to clear, and the city looked very romantic. We had been delayed because of noises that Andrew had heard from the engine of our Land Rover, causing him to stop and remove the cylinder head to replace something important – a valve or piston ring I believe. To do this in the teeth of a sand storm seemed risky to me, but Andrew managed to get everything together again in a couple of hours and we had no further trouble.

From Habban we drove back to Aden via Mafidh and Laudar on a track with plenty of evidence of the Himyars and Qatabans who lived here long ago. I found heaps of marble off-cuts and one broken piece which had obviously been the start of a small bull but which the carver may have abandoned when his piece of marble broke. Also a nicely carved piece, possibly from a frieze, showing a very Hellenic vine leaf. Apart from gums, marble was exported from Arabia Felix in the earliest times. We drove the last 20 miles along the beach in the "crab path". I was always sorry for these little crabs, scuttling along in their millions but unfortunately just where we needed to drive in order not to sink in the dry soft sand inland or the wet soft sand towards the sea.

Letter home, 6 July 1960:

I am not a happy man. Three days ago I was admitted to hospital with amoebic dysentery again. Two weeks ago I went away on a trip from Beihan, along the edge of the Empty Quarter to Ataq, and then south and west through the mountains and lava of the southern Protectorate. Immediately after my return I had another attack of "squitters" with a high temperature this time. The medical people checked for malaria and found amoebae. So I have to do the whole nauseous treatment again at such an inconvenient time when our organisation is being "reorganised", we are moving flat, and Herta is "swelling". I took 48 hours off before coming into hospital to move our heavier things to the new flat but now Herta is on her own and of course coping extremely well. But it is unfair. The new flat in Flight House, Maala is squalid compared with the luxury of Hilary and Chloe's flat where we have been living for the last four months. We can make it nice, but at a cost, and all is in doubt because this dysentery might result in our coming home early.

There seems to be some confusion about our coming home date. I am tour-expired on 12 January 1961. I have applied for a course starting 1 January and if selected would have to come back in December. Now dysentery may bring us back earlier still. However, Herta cannot fly for the last two months of her pregnancy nor for the first month after the baby's birth and there are doubts when this will be – could be October. This effectively cuts out a return until November or December. Can we stay at home until we know where we are going, please?

I am very fed up with the Services. We are treated in a very slipshod and bureaucratic way. I notice this much more than when I was single. Although I was always prepared to rough it myself, I am not going to see Herta collect lines on her brow as a result of Service indifference to our living conditions and welfare. And to bring up a baby on "pans, frying 12" C1" and in ugliness! God forbid! Do you know that there is nobody responsible or willing to help Herta move from one flat to another with all the consequent arguments with the Water Authority, the Electricity Department, the landlord and his agent, Lands Officers and God knows whom, and into a flat with no air-conditioning, badly furnished and in an awful area.

She drives around happily saying that stabbing pains in the tum at this stage are quite normal, in heat of 100°F and humid enough to keep rivers of sweat running down your face all the time. If anything untoward happens I cannot even be there to help. Oh well. Maybe I am exaggerating! Herta is indeed amazing. She is strong and fit but with a tendency to overdo things.

She comes to see me twice daily with ice cubes, fresh limes, enormous lumps of cheese, sugar and other food to eat instead of the atrocious hospital diet.

When I am out of hospital (this is not a continuous course of treatment, but a series of phases with time off between them) Herta and I are dashing (Adeni dash is slower than European walking pace) about the backstreets of Crater, among goats browsing rubbish and offal, trying to buy a plastic bath, a carry-cot and all the many things needed for babies. When exhausted we lie in pools of sodden sheets reading Dr Spock's Baby and Child Care, *musing over ruptured umbilicuses and their importance and child psychology. I worry about the RAF and our living conditions and Herta over the colour of curtains and lampshades. We are as fit as can be expected. Sometimes morale drops in the heat of the day, but never too far.*

Certainly the conditions in Flight House were very bad for an officer, or indeed an airman of any rank, let alone a Wing Commander. In the centre of the un-tiled floors of bathroom and kitchen there were central drain holes from which cockroaches emerged at night. There were no cupboards for storage but rough shelves. We were one floor up from the ground, reached by a concrete staircase. Sand and dust blew in through the windows overlooking the street down which passed noisy traffic and herds of goats. The flat was smelly, dirty and drab without any redeeming features. And we had to pay a lot for it. When I was discharged from hospital I was advised that only a stay of at least a couple of years in a temperate climate would placate my bowels and our return from Aden to the UK would be arranged on medical grounds four weeks after Herta had given birth, the earliest she might fly. Meanwhile I was on sick leave but occasionally recalled to hospital for further tests.

While Herta was visiting me there on one of these occasions thieves broke into our flat at Flight House and stole the radio, my Leica camera and lenses, a slide projector, tape recorder and all my colour slides. All of this was insured but the colour slides would have been an irreparable loss because I had taken these photographs all over south Arabia during the previous 18 months with the support of the *National Geographic* Magazine. However, on checking the stairs from our flat to the roof of the block we found all the slides, most of them still in their Kodak boxes, scattered by the thieves as they made their getaway. Every single one was recovered; none was even damaged.

My support from the *National Geographic* Magazine was a result of encouragement from an Italian "stringer" for *Paris Match* – Dante Vacchi. The arrangement was that I sent my captioned films for processing by the *National Geographic* and they returned them with comments and more 35mm Kodachrome films, usually ten at a time. However they never used my photos but in the end sent out their own team of photographers who in my view compiled a very inferior article.

Dante then proposed that I try sending photos with captions to Camera Press in London, a firm started by Tom Blau, a Hungarian. Camera Press accepted photographs from photographers and journalists worldwide, copying them and distributing lists to any periodical or author in the world needing to find an illustration for an article, advertisement or book. There was no fixed price for this service. Camera Press negotiated a price with each applicant, sharing the proceeds 50:50 with the photographer. From this association I made quite a bit of money and over the next ten years my photos appeared in dozens of journals, from Paris Match to the journal of the Jesuits' mother-house in Ireland. This showed me other professions I could have followed – journalist and/or photographer. I was seriously thinking of leaving the RAF and embarking on another career and I was greatly attracted by the Foreign Service, having experienced that sort of life in the Soviet Union and in other countries where I had served. Most entrants to the Foreign Service were recruited as university graduates, but I discovered that there was an "over-age" competition that I would be eligible to enter. Fluency in at least one foreign language was a requirement. I had Russian, Arabic and Italian. I resolved to explore the matter further.

In August we had a visit from Sheikh Khurusi from Husn al Abr, who had helped Andrew Fuller and me to get to Shabwa in March. He was on his way to

AD ULTIMO

Zanzibar for a holiday with his folk and had an overnight stopover in Aden. Herta and I invited him to come with us in the afternoon to an open-air cinema in Maala where they were showing something which we thought he might enjoy, to be followed by a meal at home. We got the cinema tickets and sat down in a row as yet unoccupied by anyone else. As the cinema filled up an Indian sat down beside Herta who was three seats in from the central aisle.

Khurusi looked uncomfortable and then exploded: How dare he (the Indian) sit down beside a woman. The Indian remonstrated that this was a public cinema and he could sit anywhere he wished as long as he had paid for his seat. This led to a loud and angry argument. The film had already started and others in the audience were objecting to the noise. I offered to change places with Herta but Khurusi was having none of it. Eventually to a chorus of shushes from adjacent rows the Indian rose and moved to another seat further away from the irate Sheikh, who himself moved to a seat behind Herta from where he could "protect" her. For the rest of the evening the Sheikh was complaining that these Indians had no knowledge of how to behave.

On 7 September Herta and I bought some rubber sheeting, the rest of the nappies (Paddi Pads and similar did not exist then), and some "little vests". All that day Herta had complained of nagging pains in her tum and we intended to bring this up at the next clinic visit in the afternoon. But by then the pains were severe and with an obvious regularity about them so that, despite Herta's disinclination to sound a false alarm, we telephoned the hospital and were advised we go there for a check. We hastily packed a bag and ironed the necessary things just in case. At the hospital they said Herta should stay. I drove off in a bad state of mind wondering what next. At midnight I was at Reuters' office where I sometimes went to check world affairs as they were reported by telex. Very emotional I wrote a poem on the back of a telex dated 24 August reporting troubles experienced by United Nations troops in Katanga where Mali troops had revolted against their officers.

Years of experience locked within these cells
Forebears with crested fleurs-de-lis ride
Asiatic seas stir
Wars pass.

Far within, far from human eye,
The tumblers click

Franz Josef's world smiles
A saddler stitches in Cuneo
A farmer ploughs
Victorians build and build.
The Great Wars: Tipperary faintly heard.
The tumblers click.

Bombers moan across the skies
Khaki trucks caterpillar the Ukraine
Tyrants tyrannise and draw the net of chance
Summits and sputniks fizz and soar.

The tumblers click
And in a bright flare of passion
Chromosomes lock
Re-starting the time sequence
Where months run down
Through clinic visits
Iron pills
Exercises
Quiet happiness
To the last pain
For the next man.[7]

Next day, 8 September, I phoned the hospital at 7 a.m. and was told that Herta was in labour and doing well. I rang again at intervals and was told that the baby might be born at midday. In fact it was born at 08.40 – a boy, 7lb 3oz with a big head that gave Herta a lot of pain and tears to the womb that needed stitching up. He needed no slap to start breathing but was shouting from the word go, for food no doubt, because when I got there an hour later he was sucking anything to hand, including his thumb. The hospital did quite well but there were a few shortcomings. No doctor was available to stitch up Herta's womb for five hours. The ward was not air-conditioned and even the drinking water was warm and came in coffee cups because there were no glasses. Later I was delayed in seeing Herta because of a Commanding Officer's inspection of the ward when all patients including hot new mothers had to be tucked into their beds with nothing hanging out as per parade ground. John Edwin had a lot of dark hair and china-blue eyes, big feet and hands, and papery skin. His face was red from his efforts to be born. He had a philosophic air and rested his chin on his clenched fist like Rodin's "The Thinker". Herta looked splendid and wanted to leave hospital at once but was not allowed to do so.

Back at Flight House I was trying to get contractors to install air-conditioning in the bedroom and making sure the Somali maid had things as clean as possible, pending Herta's return. She did not come out of hospital until Tuesday 20 September 1960, having spent 13 days there, longer than usual, but it gave me time to get some improvements made to the flat. I wrote home:

> *I enclose the first photos of the family when John was two days old. He has a weepy eye at the moment, having stuck a thumb in it in his frantic search for the appropriate thing to suck. His hunger is fabulous and he sucks for three minutes at start of feed without a decent breath, consequently going red in the face with much panting.*

I was informed that we would fly back to the UK by RAF Comet to Lyneham RAF Station, the main base for Transport Command passenger flights, on 21 October, so it was time to say Goodbye to all our friends and colleagues in Aden and prepare for our arrival in England. Herta had no winter coat so I ordered one (from Vogue magazine) to be flown out by the next Comet. We had bought a carry-cot and blankets for Johnnie as our son was known to differentiate him from me. We had named him John Edwin, incorporating my father's name although we had after much discussion decided against a formal christening because we were doubtful about the advantages of children being inducted into religions without their agreement. We thought that they could decide that for themselves later on. Up to the last day I was of course working at my desk in the Intelligence Branch, but conscious that directly I left command would revert to the Army in the person of the monocled Colonel Castner and stay in their hands indefinitely unless the new CinC took a strong line.

Notes:

1. *The Eagle and the Sun* by Lord Belhaven, John Murray 1951. This is a novel constructed from fairly sparce historical facts. However Lord Belhaven served as a Political Officer in South Arabia, travelled widely and knew his South Arabians.

2. *First Footsteps in East Africa* Richard F. Burton. Longman, Green and Longmans 1856

3. "*Qataban and Sheba*". Wendell Phillips. Victor Gollanz 1955

4. *Southern Arabia.* John Doe. Thames and Hudson 1971. This gives a very fine overview of much of the archaeology and history of the Incense Road and South Arabia.

5. I am not the first to conclude from reading the literature, and learning about South Arabia at first hand, that the three kings "of orient old", said to have visited the infant Jesus in Bethlehem, were not kings but the "wise men" of St Matthew's Gospel. In Arabic a Sheikh is a term for a wise man, often an elder and leader of a family or tribe. I myself was often hailed as "Ya Sheikh", especially when I commanded the Arab Legion Air Force in Jordan. It is only a step from there to imagine that the three Sheikhs in the Christmas story were leaders of tribal caravans with the right to carry the gifts offered to Jesus – gold (from Africa or from the Yemen, where some was mined), frankincense from Dhofar in the east of south Arabia towards Muscat and Oman, where the best frankincense came from, and myrrh, probably from the Horn of Africa. That Balthasar was black would be understandable because the Ethiopians (Habashi in Arabic) had frequently settled in south Arabia and vice versa. To offer as a gift or tribute part of their stock in trade would have come naturally to these people. The dominant ethnic group in Ethiopia, the Amharas, and their language Amharic (deriving from Geez) came from south Arabia. They are Christian rather than Muslim because Islam travelled down the Incense Road long after Christianity and the Judaism that preceded it.

6. *Arabia and the Isles.* Harold Ingrams. John Murray 1952. This is the more comprehensive edition.

7. Poets should have no need to explain themselves, but, as an amateur, I am conscious that the analogies may be obscure. A jet engine is usually started by a time switch, which automatically turns on, successively and proportionately, the feeds of fuel and air at the right times and temperatures to start the engine. Once the pilot has pushed the button to start the engine the cycle cannot easily be modified. It is as inevitable as fate. This is the point I am making. In the Meteor aircraft the engine starting cycle made sufficient different noises for the pilot to know how far the process had gone. One could hear the different stages clicking in, as when opening a combination lock. In a sense this is a pilot's poem.

Last Post

Ibn Saud, the Wahabi leader, who may be said to have founded Saudi Arabia, after recruiting tribes to his banner, and pushing the Hashemite family out of the Hedjaz, said: "In the first part of my life I have created my country; in the second part I will populate it". It is no surprise that the royal family is large by western standards with thousands of great grandchildren. In my case, although Herta and I started small with our first son John, we originally thought of having six children, but after having one and experiencing the disruption of ordinary life and the expense, we modified our ambitions in that direction. Ibn Saud had all the oil money behind him. We had to manage more modestly.

In which connection – while in Aden I had been informed that there was a surfeit of officers of my rank in the RAF and that unless my acting rank of Wing Commander were to be made substantive I should see my retirement date as my 43rd birthday, normal for Squadron Leaders under the earlier career structure. I was not disturbed. For some time I had hankered after life in the diplomatic service. I had become acquainted with this during my time in the Middle East and much more so in Moscow. International relations interested me greatly, far more than flying, which had become more of a recreation and an aesthetic experience. For me flying was beautiful, akin to classical music and poetry, a communion with physics. Fear was a component of that beauty. Such feelings might not be appropriate for a professional pilot, apart possibly from Antoine de Saint-Exupéry, a hero of mine. Of course the RAF had given me opportunities to learn languages and their associated cultures in world famous institutions, and to put all this to good use in the countries concerned. Had I anything to worry about? Here was another opportunity staring me in the face. But it had to wait!

On arriving home by Comet from Aden we had been met by my brother Mike, serving at Wilton, near Salisbury and conveniently located to pick us up from

RAF Lyneham. He dropped us in Alton, where we were able to move in with Dad, and Jessie, who had some misgivings about having to look after not only an ageing widower, but his son and family. However, Herta took life in Alton in her stride, helping in every chore. Johnnie, a baby a month old on arrival, made no trouble other than being as demanding as babies are at that age. On arrival from Aden he had over-loose motions, which Dr Wilson, our family doctor, soon cleared up with antibiotics. I too had a medical problem – inflammation following amoebic dysentery and its cures, and had a week in Wroughton RAF Hospital before further weeks spent at home on disembarkation leave. In this period I visited the Air Ministry where I was briefed on the appointment at JC&SS, which I was to take up early in the New Year. The JC&SS was now at Bircham Newton in Norfolk, which I knew well from my service there during the war after my return from Iceland and immediately before flying out to the Middle East.

Meanwhile there was Christmas coming up. My disembarkation leave lasted until the Christmas break, when JC&SS stood down until January when their next course of officers would arrive. It was decided by Air Ministry, that as I was not completely up to date with flying jets I should spend a month in all-weather flying training on Meteor aircraft at RAF Strubby in Lincolnshire, commencing 8 January 1961. I was in favour, because in addition to my salary as a Wing Commander, I received flying pay, a generous allowance supposed to reward the skills of flying and the dangers. Flying pay would cease if I got out of flying practice. I was accustomed to the Meteor and looked forward to a month spent flying them.

Herta and I booked in at the Market Hotel at Alford about five miles south of Strubby and eight miles inland from Mablethorpe, a seaside resort of caravan sites on the bleak Lincolnshire coast. Of course we had Johnnie with us, and our VW Beetle. Before leaving Aden, Herta and I had bought the light blue Volkswagen Beetle previously owned by Rosanna Rizzi, Herta's close Italian friend, also an Aden Airways' air hostess. This we had re-sprayed in Aden by an Italian garage to brighten the dulling of the Aden air on the coachwork. We shipped the car home in advance of our own departure and received it in Alton just before Christmas, which was a boon because we needed to move about.

After a pleasant Christmas at home in Alton, when Titus and Mary with their children, John aged nine and Mary Ann aged four, drove down from London for lunch, and Michael and Pat visited from Wilton, we drove to Alford after the New Year and settled into a large double bedroom at the Commercial Hotel, later re-named the Windmill Family and Commercial Hotel. Our room was over the bar and there was a lot of noise from carousers, piano accompanying raucous singing, and more row when everybody left towards midnight. Meals in the pub were substantial but not cordon bleu. The staff were very helpful with the baby who was feeding on reconstituted dried milk from bottles every hour or so. In the Beetle Johnnie occupied the removable blue canvas body of the pram/carry cot we had bought for him in Aden from Bikajee Cowajee, the Indian factotums. It was a simple sturdy construction which we later used for our other babies. No nonsense about a car seat or the elaborate aluminium and plastic baby carriers of today. Ours cost the present day equivalent of about £50. We used it a lot for walks in and around Alford, especially Herta, who without the car was somewhat isolated.

This was because although she had obtained a driving licence in Aden, after some difficulties involving me in negotiations with the chief of traffic police, the licence was not valid in the UK and she had to have driving school lessons, a lot of practice with me, and, eventually, a driving test. My own course at Strubby, No. 213 All Weather Jet Refresher Course, flying Meteor 7's and 8's, started with a week of ground instruction. I knew most of the stuff taught but other officers may not have done. For "All Weather" read "Bad Weather" or even "Atrocious Weather". All of January it rained cats and dogs and blew gales. Cloud base was usually zero feet. Flying, which started or should have started in mid-January, was held up because instructing in such weather was ruled out. I flew several times before the end of January but did not get off solo until 3 February, when there was a slight let-up in the intensity of the Atlantic fronts. Every time we (with my instructor), or later I, took off, the aircraft was in cloud within minutes. The constant instrument flying in bad conditions got me down and I was usually tired and fed up by the time I got back to the Commercial Hotel in the evening. I had further thoughts about my future. Could squadron life compare with the sort of life I had got used to in the Middle East, in Moscow, in Aden – intellectual, international, cultural. No way. It was in the Commercial Hotel that Herta and I conceived our second son Paul, who was born the following 6 October.

The course finished on 17 February 1961, and by that time we had driven down to Bircham Newton several times to visit the Junior Command and Staff School and see where we were going to live. The Wing Commander (Admin) told me that all suitable married quarters on the station were occupied at the time and that until a suitable house became available we might live in the Neptune Hotel near Hunstanton, one of several on the RAF books. So on 18 February we loaded the Beetle with Johnnie and some of our belongings and drove down there, about 40 minutes by road. They made us welcome. It was warm and tolerably comfortable. They even had a television set for hotel guests – black and white of course and with a tendency to reduce the picture to a horizontal strip several inches high. These were early days for TV and even Dad at Valverde made do with a hired set with a small screen (they all had small screens in those days).

The objectives of the JC&SS were similar to those of the school I had attended in Malta in March 1945 – to teach junior officers of the RAF the skills needed to fill Staff and Command appointments in ranks senior to Flight Lieutenant. Until then most officers had been on flying duties with little opportunity for administrative duties and the other more varied and amorphous responsibilities associated with handling numbers of officers and men cooperating in achieving the tasks of an air force and its subdivisions. Post-war the length of the JC&SS courses had been doubled to six weeks. In that time each course, for up to about 30 officers at a time, to some extent mimicked the senior Staff College, with instruction in the basics of writing Service papers in their various forms, public speaking, current affairs, with exercises to practise these skills and to measure the effectiveness of the tuition.

The Chief Instructor was Wing Commander Stan Baldwin. He had distinguished himself during the war in Bomber Command at first flying Lancasters and then Mosquitoes in a pathfinder squadron, and, after the war, V-Bombers, before joining JC&SS. On my first day at Bircham he told me of my duties which included many lectures on various subjects of which I knew a little but not much, together with notes on several of the lectures given by my predecessor, who had already gone to his next appointment in Germany. It was assumed that I would lecture on Command and Leadership, Organisation, Work Study and Measurement, to name but three, **starting the following morning**. Overnight I read up the first lecture text, disagreed with some of it, made amendments with a mental note to amend much more once I had studied the subject and selected my own illustrations, prepared my own visual aids and drafted my own lecture texts.

I had arrived at the start of one of the six-week courses due to end just before Easter, when the school closed for two weeks. We usually had a two-week break between courses, timed to fit the longer summer holiday of four weeks in July/August. This gave us quite a lot of time off but it was supposed to be used to introduce modifications to the syllabus, with new or modified lectures and demonstrations. Demonstrations were often on stage, with Directing Staff (DS) playing key parts in the playlets, which were usually larded with plenty of humour. One demonstration illustrated how a Commanding Officer should handle a minor disciplinary infraction by one of his junior officers.

Such sins are usually investigated informally and, if proven, honour is satisfied by a reprimand, or severe reprimand by the Station Commander. At JC&SS at this time it was customary to demonstrate how best a Commanding Officer should show his disapproval and the text called for a harsh admonition with implied threats of a worse outcome in the case of any repetition. Starting from a low voice the CO would deliver his words on a rising note of anger and indignation ending up on his feet and speaking very loudly indeed. An enterprising officer had had his wife modify the CO's stage uniform with wings specially embroidered and attached to cables operated from the CO's trouser pocket. At the climax of the reprimand the audience suddenly noted the CO's wings beginning to flap up and down like a maddened hawk. This always raised a great laugh. I had bought a false "handlebar" moustache for this and other roles.

Courses were divided into four syndicates, each supervised by a Syndicate Leader of Squadron Leader rank. Syndicate Leaders could be of any RAF specialisation – aircrew, secretarial, supply, etc., and this was beneficial because they could lecture in and about their specialisation as well as about more general aspects of Service life: public speaking; Service communications such as operation orders; signals; procedures and etiquette in officers', NCO's and airmen's messes; discipline; courts martial and a host of other matters peculiar to Service and RAF life. My Syndicate Leaders included a secretarial officer, an equipment officer, a navigator and a pilot (Ian Worby) with whom I got on particularly well. Each morning would begin at 8 a.m. with a meeting of the Group Commander (me in this case) and his Syndicate Leaders to discuss the day's work, which usually followed a detailed programme worked out for the whole course before their arrival. There would usually be a few problems to deal with related to individual students, absence, sickness etc.

At 0800 the course work would start with Public Speaking, with three students speaking each day, firstly a five minute reading from the Bible or any book preferred by the student and approved by his Syndicate Leader. The next student would give a five minute news review summarising gleanings from the daily papers, BBC etc. Another student would then follow with a 15 minute short talk on any subject he might choose. Each performance would be followed immediately by DS (Directing Staff) comments on structure, language and projection, eye contact, clarity, impact on the audience etc. This first session would last about half an hour. Lectures and exercises would follow, each of 40 minutes, with intervals of ten. An hour for lunch and then back to work in syndicate rooms or organised sport outside.

Evenings were often used for addresses by visiting personalities and experts. Married students were not permitted to be accompanied to JC&SS by their wives and were obliged to live in the officers' mess because the workload was such as not to permit distraction. After all, the course only lasted six weeks.

I was soon enjoying this new (for me) activity and was determined to improve on the procedures I had inherited. With the Chief Instructor's approval I introduced new lectures on command and leadership, visited Cambridge and other academic centres of excellence to recruit more interesting outside lecturers on themes of relevance to junior (and senior) commanders. A knowledge of current affairs was required by the syllabus and, at a time when the Cold War was waging, there was little more important and interesting than communism, in theory and practice, on which I recruited an economist from Cambridge who started his lecture by drawing a large circle with chalk on a blackboard to represent the size of an economy and then dividing it up into segments to illustrate how one might distribute the national "cake", shares of which might only be significantly increased by increasing the size of the economy. Otherwise one would rob Peter to pay Paul. From here to Marx was not all that far! On sociology of relevance to leadership and management I met Phil Sadler from the Scientific Advisor's office in Air Ministry, who became a good friend and from whom I learned principles that have been useful ever since. Later he was appointed Director of the Ashridge Management College.

Likewise Geoffrey Crump, from Bedales School, who came to lecture courses on elocution, of relevance to public speaking. I remember an example he gave of the importance of pronouncing consonants clearly: Question – "Where is Flight Lieutenant Smith?" Answer: "In the ba….!" In the bar or in the bath?? When Herta and I were allotted an RAF Married Quarter following a couple of months at the Neptune Hotel, Phil and Geoffrey always stayed with us on their visits, about six per year in each case. Phil drove a Sunbeam Talbot car, similar to the one I had owned before my posting to Aden. It was usually overflowing with the stubs of cigarettes. As far as possible he refrained from smoking in our house. Geoffrey also smoked, more frugally, but Gauloises with their pungent smell, and in the house, but we could scarcely object. He always preferred a cooked breakfast in bed, which Herta indulged him. Initially we only had the one child, Johnnie, but plenty of spare rooms in the 1930s married quarter. It was a vintage house built out of excellent materials to a good design, the sort which today would fetch the best part of a million pounds.

At JC&SS entertainment was a "must". To engage fully with students, they needed to be fathered by their Syndicate Leaders and Group Commanders, and apart from at least two "drinks" sessions at home for each course, one at the beginning and one at the end, there were occasional suppers for several students at a time, usually with their Syndicate Leader and his wife. Herta was splendid in arranging these occasions, drink, food etc., despite having very little experience to start with. Courses usually included a few foreign officers, from the air forces of NATO or other countries with whom Britain had cooperative arrangements. Jordan was an example, but we also had students from the Israeli Air Force, as well as Indonesians. One German student, a Deutsches Heer officer, Major Schröder, devoted his 15 minute Short Talk to a detailed apology for German conduct during WW2, ending most embarrassingly in tears. As neither he personally, nor any of his RAF fellow students, were old enough to have played an active role in the war, his talk went down like a lead brick. But he was a nice enough chap, whose parents had been involved, and meant well enough.

Some of the exercises at JC&SS involved simulated operations in which the RAF might be called upon to use force and these were usually set in a context where the opposing baddies were named something like "Capricornia", some fictitious country or other, posing a military threat to Britain or our allies. Students were required, as at Staff College, to write appreciations of the situation following study of the factors, and then develop these into plans of action, operation orders, etc. As our courses often included students who might take offence at our fictional enemies, I decided to see if I could introduce an exercise with an obvious enemy who could not be equated to any country – the Desert Locust. Here was a real threat to the economies of various countries in Africa and the Middle East especially. And aircraft had a role. I had witnessed some aspects of the fight against desert locusts when I had visited East Africa from Aden and I could see that this would be an interesting subject which could not offend anyone's national sensitivities.

In London at the time there was an Anti-Locust Research Centre under the direction of Professor (later Sir) Boris Uvarov FRS, Russian originally, an entomologist and expert in the arid countries where desert locusts breed and congregate. The desert locust is often an individual and fairly harmless big grasshopper. However in certain meteorological conditions winds can sweep these locusts together and when a group has formed, given the right conditions, they can breed and transform themselves into the gigantic swarms that invade and destroy all plant life in fertile land over which their wings aided by favourable winds take them. As with war, knowledge of the enemy, good intelligence as to factors affecting their behaviour, technical knowledge as to how best to confront the threat and all the other military planning, organisational and operational procedures play a part. I visited the Anti-Locust Research Centre, met Sir Boris, and his wife Dame Olga, who worked in the Centre and was the first woman President of the Royal College of Veterinary Surgeons. In the course of several visits I collected background material and compiled a dossier for our students to study before they embarked on the exercise. I introduced it in 1961 and 1962. It was a great success and was still being used many years after I retired from the RAF, until JC&SS was changed from a practical to a correspondence course. Note that Sir Boris was FRS, a Fellow of the Royal Society, my second brush with the Fellowship (the first was when I was in Moscow) for whom I would work for 22 years from 1965.

In thinking of what I might do when I left the RAF I took into account my qualifications. I could fly an aircraft, but was not enamoured of a career as a civil pilot. Flying from A to B and back time and time again did not appeal. I spoke Russian fluently as well as some other languages where fluency might be achieved quite easily. Life in the Foreign Service appealed to me a lot. Inquiries revealed that there was an over-age competition for entry to the Foreign Service and I sent off for particulars. For many years I had been involved in Intelligence in various ways, and MI6, the Secret Intelligence Service (SIS), had great appeal. Daphne Park a close friend in the Embassy in Moscow might help here, and I had other friends in the same Service. Both for the Foreign Service and the SIS, my languages would help. I initiated inquiries which bore fruit later.

However, it appeared that my knowledge of Arabic, Russian etc., was not really a recognised qualification if I wanted to join the Foreign Service or any other organisation involved in international relations. I contacted the School of Slavonic and East European Languages, still in Russell Square, and asked how I might most easily convert my knowledge of Russian language and literature into an Honours Degree. Not so easy I was told. I could enlist for an external degree but this would mean several years' part-time study of a select syllabus. OK, my 43rd birthday would be 24 February 1965, so I still had several years in hand before probable retirement. Registering was not all that easy. Firstly I had to have General Certificate of Education passes at "A" level in Russian, which would be my first language, and in Italian, which I chose as a subsidiary subject. To take the "A" level exams I needed first to pass in three subjects at Ordinary Level. This was not difficult. I took Italian, Russian and French "O" levels in the next year or so, followed by Russian and Italian "A" levels. I was pleased to find my knowledge of colloquial Russian and Italian was better than my examiners, and I positively exulted in my written papers in Russian, expounding on Lermontov and Pushkin. Top grades in all subjects, but so I should. I was then able to register with London

University as an external student to read Russian as a primary subject with Italian as a secondary. My studies were not arduous because I had read many of the classics of Italian and Russian literature before. For me it was more of a classical recreation for the evenings and weekends when I had time off from JC&SS.

There was plenty of time off. Herta and I decided that over the long break in August 1961 we would drive in the Beetle to Italy and stay there for at least a couple of weeks. Johnnie was fit and well and was used to regarding the luggage space behind the rear seat as his personal domain. He occupied it all the way from Alton to Gabicce Mare, an Italian seaside resort on the Adriatic 20km south of Rimini. The small hotel we had booked into was not up to much. On the first evening in the restaurant when we started with spaghetti, none was provided for Johnnie (aged 11 months and already omnivorous). We pointed this out to the waiter, who removed some of my small helping and deposited it on a separate plate for Johnnie. This dietary parsimony was unwelcome and next day we moved to a better place in Cattolica, 8km north towards Rimini. It was better there, more comfortable and no trouble over food. Herta was heavily (very heavily), pregnant, to the extent that she could scarcely fit behind the VW steering wheel, and had no decent swim suit, so she had one run up by a dress maker in Cattolica. One day on the sand Johnnie was running around naked as was his wont, when a cassocked monk, escorting a troop of schoolboys to the beach for their PE., approached me and remonstrated that Johnnie should not be naked, but properly clothed. It might give his charges the wrong idea. I pointed out that a baby under a year old would not be much of an attraction, clothed or not. We visited the old hill city of San Marino as well as Bologna, where Johnnie charmed the diners in an excellent restaurant where we ate spaghetti Bolognese of course.

Paul was born on 6 October 1961 in the RAF Hospital Ely. Those were the days when the Services had their own hospitals, specialists and nurses, in the case of the RAF – Princess Mary's RAF Nursing Service. The hospital dated back to the war and possibly earlier and was distinguished for being mainly single storey and therefore with very long corridors, the lino floors of which were always highly polished, by nurses in those days, not contractors. Herta was back at home quite quickly after Paul's birth. We had decided that Herta needed some help with the two babies and through the Austrian connection the daughter of a friend in Villach was identified. We had met her briefly on our visit to Italy via Austria the previous August and she seemed a very nice girl, interested in culture and in England and with quite good spoken English. Her name was Judith and I met her in at the port of Harwich later in October. She quickly settled down with the two boys and stayed for the best part of a year. Later she married an Austrian timber merchant in Villach, Erik Walker, and later still started her own picture gallery, becoming well known in Austria and Italy. She was very interested in Shakespeare and attended many performances of his plays at Stratford-on-Avon. Judith's presence freed Herta from some of her chores as mother and Judith became and remains a firm friend.

We named our second son Paul Alexander because we had given Johnnie the family names of John and Edwin and felt free to name his brother after a traveller with a mission, and who better than St Paul and Alexander of Macedon, both travellers with missions! Herta's mother's name was Paula, so there was a family connection. Paul was a bolshie child from birth and still is, but considerate now that he is married with his own sons. Life continued apace with JC&SS and my extramural studies.

In 1962 I was pressing ahead with various options for a second career. On 15 July I wrote to my father:

> *I have discovered that I am eligible and quite favourably placed for a special competition for entry to the senior branch of the Foreign Office. As far as I can see, if I retire from the RAF next July, I will receive about £7,000 terminal grant and £310 p.a. pension. Were I to stay in the RAF until the retiring date for my rank on my 43rd birthday I would receive 5% more RAF pension but of course less Foreign Office or other pension at the age of 65. I am therefore moving cautiously in the direction of retiring from the RAF next year if I succeed in the FO competition, which takes place next April. My starting salary in the FO would be less than I get now, but it would be augmented by my RAF pension and the £7,000 terminal grant would provide the down payment on a mortgage on any house we would need to buy in London. Could we stay at home over the transfer period? If all this works out I would probably be leaving the RAF one week and starting in the FO the next. It might take a month or so to find a house. Anyway this plan is still only a plan and we will see what develops in the next month or so. Maybe the RAF will not release me. Maybe the FO competition will be too severe. Please do not tell anyone about this idea of ours – not even Mary and Titus. I prefer to keep it quiet until something comes about. We will talk about it when we come to Alton in October.*

My father was none too enamoured of my intention to retire and he never really believed that my 43rd birthday was the statutory retirement age for an officer of my substantive rank, which was Squadron Leader, although I had been an Acting Wing Commander for over four years. There was in those days of apparently permanent jobs, a reluctance to, as it were, "changing horses in midstream", although in these days of short contracts, employees and employers have to accept changes and plan for them. This was my attitude and I was getting on with studies to secure a formal degree and approaches to the Foreign Office, the security services, airlines, and a large selection of public and private enterprises where I thought I might enjoy working.

In August 1962 we drove to Sweden in the Beetle to stay for several weeks in the house of Börje Kwarnmark, who had looked after my Sunbeam while I was in Moscow as Assistant Air Attaché. Börje and his wife had themselves gone away for the summer and were happy that we should stay in their house in Lidingö north of Stockholm. To cross the North Sea we took a ship from Harwich to the Hook and thence to Gouda, the cheese town, staying there the night in a hotel in the medieval town square, not very peaceful because there was a folk music festival going on, which made a lot of noise until about 3 a.m. Next day we drove as far as Ljungby before stopping for rest. After hundreds of miles on the road we were exhausted and although it was early morning we cleared the hotel cleaners out of our room and collapsed on the bed, continuing to Stockholm the next day. Sweden was a nice clean place to take children for a holiday, but somehow it did not have the slightly disreputable charm of Italy, and we did not speak Swedish.

Over Christmas 1962 the Junior Command and Staff School moved from RAF Bircham Newton to RAF Tern Hill. The idea was that we broke off before Christmas for the holiday, and then re-convened at Tern Hill in early January driving via Bircham to collect as much of our stuff as we could get in the car (not much because it was still a Beetle). This was a particularly cold winter and driving from Norfolk to Shropshire the roads were icy and covered with snow in some of the higher places. I knew the address of the married quarter we had been allotted at Tern Hill and on drawing up outside read a notice pinned to the door saying that on no account should we attempt to start the back boiler in the living room because it was frozen up. The dining and living rooms each had a single bar 1000 watt electric stove where a fireplace had once been and we had to manage with these. Upstairs there was no heating at all. Conditions were grim. However we had a serviceable domestic hot water boiler in the small kitchen and an electric cooker, so that apart from being cold, we could wash the children (in clouds of steam in the small bathroom) and cook food. We were not the only officers to be inconvenienced by the freeze. Many others were also transferring from Bircham Newton to Tern Hill over those few days.

At Tern Hill, near Market Drayton, in the heart of Shropshire, work at JC&SS was much as it had been at Bircham Newton. Arrangements had to be made for different civilian lecturers to visit us from the local universities rather than from Cambridge, but Phil Sadler and Geoffrey Crump continued to come, staying with us in our rather smaller house. Recreationally we missed the walks among the dunes on the Norfolk coast but there were compensations in the beautiful countryside around Tern Hill. The airfield was the training base for most RAF helicopter pilots and I got to know a number of them. I had always wanted to learn to fly helicopters, but one could not easily achieve such an ambition while a senior member of staff at the Junior Command and Staff School. I was a member of the Officers' Mess of course, and was duty bound to attend Mess functions, with Herta as often as not. Our entertainment load remained the same. Market Drayton had some very good shops and we especially patronised the fishmonger who was very enterprising, on one occasion displaying the head of a large shark in his window to entice customers.

Inquiring about horses I might hire I met Joan Goddard, a woman of about my age, daughter of a retired city man who had bought a farmhouse near Hodnet Hill. Joan, much indulged by her parents, was an enthusiastic horsewoman, with a horse, Tich, a big grey getting on for ten years old, which Joan used to hunt. However as often as not she preferred to ride another smaller horse of hers and she was only too happy to have me to exercise and hunt Tich. She charged very little for a day out and nothing at all for a hack. So for the first (and last) time in my life I could afford to hunt, with little to pay but the "cap" which for me as a serving officer cost 10/- (50p). I hunted about once a month on Saturdays for the best part of two years with the North Shropshires. The hunt was not a posh affair but mostly farmers in Wellies, with a good admixture of teenage girls and a sprinkling of society ladies, the odd businessman, and, once or twice, Americans wanting to experience Jorrocks Jaunts and Jollities. They were always well turned out in pink by their holiday agencies.

In such rural and beautiful countryside it was a joy to be able to get views of stately homes, half-timbered houses, and ancient farms from a privileged viewpoint, high above the hedgerows and on bridle paths normally closed to the public. On one occasion we met at High Ercall and I entered in my diary:

> *A beautiful crisp day with hot sun – an anticyclone day. We first drew*
> *"The Marl" and a fox went away south at once (wind was north-west).*
> *Unfortunately it led us into very wiry country – a lot of road work* (to
> avoid the barbed wire in the fields). *Over the Tern he went and the*

hounds and the first five riders followed over a plank bridge. The sixth horse went straight through the planks into the river. We had to make a long detour before catching up again. Later we found four or five more foxes which travelled fast, but always south into wire and water. Covered about 40 miles I would say and finished tired out, horse and man, at 16.30.

I then had to ride Tich back to his stable, often miles away. Sometimes Herta followed the hunt in the car, with the children in the back, so she had some idea of when I might get home. Following a hunt used to be quite easy because one could usually hear the hounds and the huntsman's horn. Tich was an extremely sagacious horse. He loved hunting and would be on his tiptoes at the sound of the horn. He knew when to draw the line and when the light became too dim for his eyes he would gently but resolutely refuse to jump any more, and I would then know that it was time to break off. I often found myself in the company of a 70-year-old lady riding side-saddle on an equally sensible horse. This lady was always beautifully dressed in a black riding habit and jacket and a bowler hat suitably veiled in what looked like black chicken wire.

Joan Goddard's father died in 1963 and his wife and Joan decided to sell up in Shropshire and move to the Cotswolds, where Joan wanted to be able to ride with the Heythrop, an important hunt in horsy circles much superior to the North Shropshires. Tich would go with them and I would need to find an alternative mount if I was going to continue to hunt. From introductions I met the Adams family at Lilleshall, who had several horses needing exercising, and Linda Adams agreed to let me ride "Piper", a very good-looking animal, when hunting started in the autumn. Piper was younger and less experienced than Tich, more skittish and with endless energy, rather more of a handful to hunt. As I was to discover.

For our holiday in 1963 I had the idea of writing to Karl Walter and asking about the availability of his flat on top of the town wall of Bordighera. He said it would be vacant because he was to visit his son in Bristol over that period. We could use it rent free for as long as we liked. We drove down in the car and settled in, immediately repairing to what sand there was between the rocks on the shore so that the children could scrabble about. They scrabbled only too well, possibly turning up infected material which invaded their small bodies when fingers were put in mouths. The following morning Johnnie already had loose motions turning soon to streaming diarrhoea. While we were attending to him there was a shaking of the building and the ground, and all the citizens of Bordighera ran into the streets in fright. It was an earthquake. We cowered under the staircase until the tremors ceased. Half an hour later Paul got the runs and then both children started being sick.

We saw a doctor's brass plate on one of the houses in Bordighera, knocked on his door and asked his advice. After examining the boys he threw up his hands and told us to drive at once to a children's hospital in San Remo, a larger town a few miles to the east and put the children into their hands. This we did, but at the door I was shocked to be asked to put down £100 equivalent in lire as a deposit before the children could be admitted. Fortunately I had the money in travellers' cheques. Johnnie and Paul were then put to bed in a ward. They were given antibiotics but Paul was already looking at death's door, paper pale with owl-like rings round his eyes when they were open, not at all his usual boisterous self. Water drips were prescribed but because there was a shortage of staff, we, the parents, were instructed in where and how to arrange the drips. We were worried stiff about their health, and deeply regretted risking their lives on this escapade. After two days, during which we lived in a nearby pensione, but spending most of our time in the ward with our boys, they were assessed as OK for discharge and we loaded them up and drove as fast as we could homewards. We stayed the night in Bolzano, and then beat it for Calais and the car ferry to Dover and home. Paul was only one and a half years old, Johnnie two and a half. At such ages one has to be cautious, more cautious than we had been on this occasion.

Bringing up children is an enormous responsibility, insufficiently recognised by many people. These days, many women hanker after a career, qualify at university, strive for first and higher degrees in their chosen fields. There is a tendency to regard life at home looking after children and husbands as secondary, unworthy of a talented or experienced graduate. This is so wrong. A mother's care is essential for a baby until it is a child, and the close care of both parents is important almost indefinitely. How the parents divide up their responsibilities to each other and to their children is to some extent personal, but cannot be unimportant to the society to which they belong, especially to the wider family who are best placed to help. It is disregard for these responsibilities which has brought society to its present (in 2008) dysfunction, families to disintegration and individuals of whatever age to unhappiness, sometimes despair. At a lecture in Alton by Lord Selborne on biodiversity when questions turned to the deleterious effects of uncontrolled human population growth I suggested that adults wanting children should apply for licences, and be examined as to their suitability as parents. Population growth should be controlled and there might be state allowances for the first child, none for the second, with subsequent children discouraged by taxation. I would not go as far as China but it is clear that they have limited population growth and children have benefited, and have even been spoilt, another problem.

I was gradually getting to know more of Herta's family background, which had not been a bed of roses. Her mother and father, Mutti and Papa, Paula and Hermann, had often been at loggerheads and close to estrangement, separation and divorce. Part of the problem was that Hermann was an incorrigible entrepreneur, prepared to risk all he had on any enterprise he considered likely to lead to advantages to himself and his family. Mutti was much more conservative and unhappy about risking anything they had achieved on options which to her seemed impracticable and likely to lead to impoverishment rather than enrichment.

Their temperaments may well have derived from their backgrounds. Hermann had been born on 4 August 1907 in Knin, now in Croatia, but at the beginning of the 20th century a small town of the Austro-Hungarian Empire on the recently constructed railway joining Zagreb with Šibenic on the coast and various other Dalmatian towns. His parents were Michael and Amalia Jeuschenak (neé Kraus). Michael had been born on 4 September 1865 in Celje, now a medium sized Slovenian town 50 miles south-east of Klagenfurt. Jeuschenak or sometimes Jošenak is the Germanic spelling of Jevšenak, a common name in Slovenia where in 2011 there were dozens of subscribers of that name in the telephone directory.

Amalia Kraus was born on 3 July 1881 in Leoben, now the second largest town in Austrian Styria after the regional capital Graz. The registration of her birth in Leoben says she was born at 9 Judendorf, now a street close to the river Mur, but then part of a small Jewish enclave. The Kraus family was Roman Catholic and Amalia was baptised the day after her birth in the main church in the town, dedicated to St Xaver (Francis Xavier). Amalia's father, Alexander Kraus, was a pithead foreman of the Fridau-Steinkohlenbergwerk coal mine at Seegraben near Leoben. This was the first coal mine opened in Austria and later managed on very enlightened terms for those days with strictly limited shifts for the workers and exemplary to the extent that it was associated with the first mining academy in Europe, the predecessor of Leoben University which to this day is mainly concerned with the mining industry. The mine closed in 1963.

Alexander Kraus married Amalia's mother, Maria Rinnbacher on 3 February 1880 also in St Xaver. That was about 18 months before Amalia's birth. Whether she later had brothers and sisters we do not yet know. Nor do we know how Michael Jeuschenak and Amalia Kraus met. In 1900 Michael had become an official responsible for accounts at Knin railway junction. Initially he was described as a clerk but later as an Assistant Conductor. We have a photograph of him in his railway uniform. One must remember that the railway then was quite a young mode of transport, the equivalent of an airline in the 1950s. Working on a train was like being a member of the cabin crew and quite prestigious.

Michael and Amalia had been married in Derrniš, a small town half way between Knin and Šibenik on 10 May 1900, when Amalia was 18 and Michael was 35. They had three daughters: Amalia Maria born on 6 July 1901 in Sebenico, then in Italy; Olga born on 23 December 1903 in Knin; Stefania born on 24 September 1905 in Knin and then their only son, Hermann also born there on 4 August 1907. The parochial birth registers for Amalia Maria, Olga, Stefania and Hermann give their mother Amalia's 'domicile' as Leschberg, now called Loška Gora, the Slovenian translation of Leschberg, a small village a few miles north of Celje, where Michael was born. The name means col in mountain-speak (depression in a mountain-chain). How Amalia from Leoben got to Leschberg is a matter of conjecture. She was only 18. She might have been in service. Maybe some member of her own family lived there. Church records are the best source of reliable records because they often include details of parents.

Registration of births (and christenings and some other matters) deaths and marriages was originally the responsibility of the church, with entries in books kept in the parish concerned. The state also needed these data and now in most European countries local councils keep registers which often duplicate church records. Hence, when national boundaries change significantly and records need to be shared, many fall by the wayside. All the Jeuschenak children born to Michael and Amalia have their births and other personal details stored in the countries where these events took place, now, in their cases: Slovenia, Austria, Croatia and Italy. Thus the registration of their births can be found in Klagenfurt, Leoben and Zagreb, to name but three. The Croatian certificates record Amalia, who married Michael, was from Leoben, but domiciled in Leschberg when the births were registered. With two major churches, Catholic and Orthodox, and several languages, Slovenian, Croatian, German and Italian, one can see problems for genealogists.

Michael and Amalia were Catholics, as are most Slovenians, whereas much of the population of Knin was and remains Serbian Orthodox. As yet (2012) we do not know what happened to Michael who may have died some time after 1910, possibly during the First World War, when the Balkans were in turmoil after the assassination of the Grand Duke Ferdinand in Sarajevo. Nor do we have any idea what happened to Stefania. Amalia Maria and Olga are buried with their mother in the St Ruprechter cemetery in Klagenfurt where Amalia once took Herta to see the grave plot she had chosen. And of course we know much more about Hermann, Herta's father. After the end of the first world war and after the Rapallo and other agreements setting up Yugoslavia as an independent country, Amalia and her three young children, Amalia Maria, Olga and Hermann moved to Austria, where as a born Austrian Amalia would have felt at home and probably had rights of residence as a result of her birth in Leoben.

In 1918 with the break up of the Austro-Hungarian Empire, what became Yugoslavia was formed from the northern Balkan provinces and some people took the option of remaining there, or moving to an adjacent country if they had relatives there or other links. Agreements were concluded between countries and portions of countries surviving WW1 without much reference to the people living there. Šibenik, which had been Austrian, became Italian Sebenico. Many Italians lived there already because of its earlier history. It was of course Catholic and there are indications that Amalia and her family moved there first and then to Klagenfurt where Amalia took over a "Tabak Traffik", a small shop selling tobacco, a government monopoly, as well as various other products as in "corner shops" in the UK – newspapers, matches, sweets, etc. Amalia managed the shop in St Ruprechter Strasse, close to the main railway station, and lived in the flat above. I visited Amalia there with Herta.

Hermann did well at school in Austria, attending gymnasium, the equivalent of a grammar school in the UK, but may have left early. Of course he had been a month short of seven years old when the Archduke was assassinated in Sarajevo by Gavrilo Princip, the event that precipitated the outbreak of the First World War. Hermann and his mother and sisters may have been in Sebenico until about October 1918 when the Kingdom of Serbs, Croats and Slovenes (later named Yugoslavia) was set up. Hermann was just entering his teens, the right age for entering gymnasium, but he had been in Klagenfurt earlier because there is a photograph of him aged about five taken in a photo studio there named Atelier für Fotografie, Hans Wanderer, Klagenfurt, Domgasse 10.

Any time he spent in an Austrian gymnasium must have helped to perfect his German, maths and other grammar school subjects, including Latin. With a mother named Kraus from Leoben he probably spoke German from childhood. There were many German speakers in what are now Slovenia and Croatia. Hermann was keen above all else to better himself and started work with a firm in Klagenfurt making parts for motor vehicles. In 1938, when he was 31, he already had a firm under his own name which was painted on the lorry he drove, transporting rock, probably for the building industry or for roads, from a site near Sankt Andrä, on the Austrian side of the border on the road from Celje, Slovenia, where his father, Michael had been born. The lorry bears the name Hermann Jeuschenak Autounternehmung, indicating that he hired out the lorry (and himself) for transporting loads, a constant feature in his business life thereafter. A caption inked in below the photo reads 'Erste Tätigkeit' (first work) and the date and place Framrach (on the Celje road) and 20 December 1938, not long before the second world war. Another place mentioned several times in captioned photographs is Legerbuch, a village about 4km south of Sankt Paul.

Hermann's business involved visiting clients, and on one visit in the late 1930s he is said to have met a girl, possibly in an office, and said he would marry her. This was his future wife Paula Seebacher born on 21 April 1915 in Villach, but, when they met, living with her mother and her second husband Grass in St Veit. Paula was a very attractive brunette, as one can see from a photograph of her standing in the snow on a visit to relatives or friends in Obermühlbach, a village in the hills a few miles west of St Veit. Paula and Hermann seemed very well matched, or thought so, because shortly before their marriage they conceived a child, to be Gerti, their first daughter, born on 16 September 1938.

Earlier, Paula and her sister Hilde, several years older, and brother Peter had had a rather unhappy family life. Their natural father, Seebacher, left their mother when the children were small, and she had been obliged to put the two girls into the care of a convent engaging in this sort of welfare. The food was poor and the children treated badly by modern standards. After Paula's mother remarried a Herr Grass, they retrieved the girls from the convent and the family lived together in St Veit in a house close to the old town centre. Paula had wished to study to be a teacher but her mother prescribed home economy, as it might be called now. There was more trouble to come. After Paula met Hermann the two of them sometimes stayed out late and obviously Paula's mother disapproved, until one night, when Paula was very late home, her mother said that she should henceforth look after herself. She and Hermann were married in 1939. They lived in a house, probably rented, in Sankt Paul im Lavanttal. The house was still there in good condition in 2011.

Shortly before Gerti's birth, Hitler's forces had marched into Austria and "merged" it with Germany in the so-called Anschluss, to be followed by the occupation of the Sudetenland and the invasion of Poland, leading to the Second World War. Most Austrians were in favour of the Anschluss. However, Paula's brother Peter had always been a bit of a free-thinker and he soon ran into trouble with the Nazis for criticism of the regime. He twice served terms in the Dachau concentration camp (near Munich) where people heard voicing critical comments were often confined. In those days you had to be careful about what you said in public. Possibly as a result of his experiences in Dachau he developed tuberculosis at the end of the war and died prematurely.

Hermann had always been interested in motorcycles and rode them in regionally organised races on Alpine roads. We have photographs of him riding on one of these occasions, rounding a corner at speed. He was involved in accidents and in his later life made a point of advising young people not to engage in such a dangerous activity. He used to relate how on one occasion he played poker or a similar game of hazard for high stakes. When he had lost all his cash he wagered in lieu his beloved motorbike, and lost it. He was bereft and never again gambled (other than in business). Motorcycles were all very well for what might be called sport, but Hermann preferred good fast cars for personal transport and directly he could he drove an Auto Union which later merged with other German car manufacturers to become Audi, with the merger still celebrated in their badge of four linked circles.

With WW2, in the unified Germany all males over a certain age were conscripted and so was Hermann. However, as he had his own transport firm it seems to have been considered reasonable that he should do similar work for the Wermacht. He spent much of the war trucking supplies to the German armed forces in various parts of Europe – Poland, Czechoslovakia, the Ukraine, France, Italy. He seems to have been an ordinary soldier or possibly an unteroffizier (non-commissioned officer). He certainly succeeded in avoiding close contacts with the SS, the Gestapo and concentration camps although he knew quite a bit about what was going on there. He was away from home a great deal. Home at the time was still Sankt Paul. Paula was there with the children, Gerti, born 1938, Herta born 1940, Hermann (junior) born 1942.

Some time in 1943, judging by photographs, the family moved from Sankt Paul to Krumpendorf, next to friends – the Nageles. The two families were on good terms and in 1944, when Hermann discovered that Arnulf Nagele, about ten years his junior, had been badly injured in a battle with the allies in Italy, he drove down there, no doubt with a Wermacht truck, and brought him back to Krumpendorf for treatment in an Austrian hospital. Paula told me of an occasion when allied aircraft were attacking installations nearby, probably a train on the railway line running through Krumpendorf, and using a cloth she gestured at it from the balcony until it flew away. Herta attended the Volksschule in Krumpendorf and her school reports for several years from when she was six always placed her in the top category or one below. She walked to school and back home every day whatever the weather, a distance of over a mile.

At the end of WW2, with Germany defeated, Hermann was quickly "de-Nazified" by the Allied authorities, and started again in the transport business. He was successful enough to have a large house designed and built for him in Krumpendorf, quite close to the Wörthersee. The architect and builder was Anton Koschat, who had a building firm based close to Amalia Jeuschenak's Tabak Traffik. Anton and Hermann had often kicked a football about when in their teens. Later Anton's son Heinz took over the firm and Herta and I are good friends of Heinz and his wife Sieglinde, The house was large by today's standards, and very well built in the classic Austrian town house style. One disadvantage, according to Paula, were the many kachelofen, the tiled stoves beloved of Austrians, one to each room, for heating in winter. It was heavy work feeding them with logs each day. But Mutti loved the house and was more than distressed when Hermann, needing capital for his business or for the family's livelihood, decided to sell it. For tax reasons the house was in Mutti's name and she at first resisted Hermann's attempts to get her to agree to the sale. This led to substantial disagreement between the spouses, with Mutti demanding a divorce, the papers for which were drawn up and signed but never actioned.

Why not one might ask. Probably because, in the turbulence at the end of the war, separation would not have been to the advantage of either spouse nor of course to their children. With the sale of the Krumpendorf house the family moved to Vienna, still occupied by the Soviet Union on the one hand and the French, British and Americans on the other. Austria was treated as a defeated enemy nation and both the country and Vienna were divided into zones, each administered by one or other of the victorious powers. The city of Vienna, like Berlin, was deep inside the Soviet zone, which included all of Niederösterreich bordering on the Soviet dominated countries of Czechoslovakia and Hungary.

The rented Jeuschenak house in Vienna was in Küniglberggasse, Hietzing, a fashionable part of the city, but then close to a large Allied military camp. This was in the British sector, but near the border of the French sector and not far from the Russian, although the sectors were like pieces of a jigsaw puzzle, with the Americans closest to southern Germany, the French to the south of them, the British closest to Italy and the Russians to the East European countries they had occupied. Herta, then aged nearly 10, attended school in the nearby Volksschule at 5-7 Steinlechnergasse, a short walk from their house. But she was only there until the following July when there were further developments to change family life.

The occupation of Austria including Vienna was to last until 1955. No part of Austria was then ideally suited to an entrepreneurial spirit like Hermann. But it seems that he had already decided to move away from Austria. Vienna may just have been a temporary staging post. A friend in Klagenfurt, a doctor of medicine, had moved to Addis Ababa, and reported back that the streets, if not paved with gold, were free for business. The western-minded Haile Selassie was head of government there and development could be expected to take off. Hermann disposed of most of his remaining assets in Austria, and bought a large American Mack truck and trailer, in whose successor vehicles much of America's freight is still transported. On the advice of another friend he filled the truck with crates of Austrian Gösser beer and shipped the whole caboodle to Assab in 1950, driving it himself up the torturous roads through the arid mountains to Addis Ababa. There he discovered that the cargo of beer had gone off during the long, hot voyage. But the truck was sold and the money spent in establishing a motor business in Addis.

Paula and the children aged 13 (Gerti), 11 (Herta) and 9 (Hermann) followed by air in early January 1951, taking the train from Klagenfurt to Rome. Hermann had arranged flights from Rome to Athens and from there to Cairo, where he met Paula and the children and flew with them to Djibouti and thence to Addis Ababa. Herta was entranced by the change of climate from the winter cold of Austria in January to the warmth of Cairo and the heat of Djibouti. They had arrived in Djibouti at breakfast time and looked forward to a nice meal in the airport restaurant. However Hermann strode off into the restaurant kitchen and soon appeared shaking his hands in a sign of dismissal. He had found flies everywhere and food was out of the question. The children were very disappointed.

In Addis Ababa Herta was initially put to school in the French Lyceé, where the teaching was all in French of which she initially had no inkling. But she soon picked up some of the language. The following year, 1952, Hermann and Paula decided to send Gerti and Herta to a convent school in Switzerland in Chatel St Denis (a state school now that there are too few nuns to provide teachers). Herta did not mind leaving home in Addis because her father and mother were often getting at each other and the convent provided a comparatively calm and ordered environment. She returned to Addis each summer for the long vacation, but not otherwise. As Hermann established his business as garage proprietor and agent for German firms in the automotive industry, Herta was moved to another convent school at St Maurice, close to the skiing resort of Verbier, which the girls sometimes visited in winter to ski, supervised by Algerian nuns. Both convent schools were very international, Switzerland being famous for "finishing schools", with well-off parents from all over the world vying to send their daughters there, just as my mother had attended the Theresianum in Schwyz. Herta met a number of girls at the school from good families in different countries and wished to

33. I meet my match.

34. Force-landed at Mukeiras in February 1960 - a Russian helicopter code-named Hare which might have been the foundation of the Sharif of Beihan's air force.

35. Andrew Fuller driving through the Wadi Idm between the Hadhramaut and the coast after a wadi flow. Half an hour earlier the water was higher than our roof.

36. Moving north from the Jebel Akhdar towards the Empty Quarter.

37. Approaching Habban through a sand storm at the end of June 1969. Habban was an important city on the Incense Road two thousand years ago.

38. The Royal Society at 6 Carlton House Terrace. My office window is behind the tree on the left, on the second floor (above that with balconies) overlooking the Athenaeum.

39. The Royal Society. Me in my assistants' office opening off mine.

40. Tania Prigorowsky. My deputy in the Department of International Affairs at the Royal Society for the best part of 20 years.

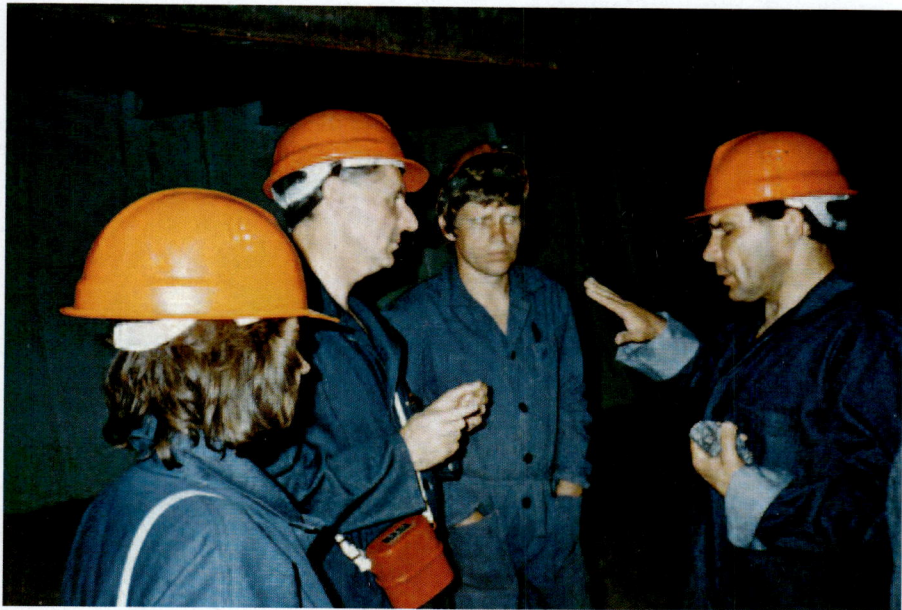

41. Herta in foreground with on her left Professor (later Sir) Arnold Wolfendale FRS (physics Durham), 300m below Mt Elbrus in the Caucasus, being briefed on the Baksan Neutrino Observatory

42. On Elbrus, rising to 5,636m, which is behind me

43. Academician Aleksandr (Sasha) Chudakov (cosmic rays), who developed the Baksan Observatory, talking to us after our visit. Professor Wolfendale is second to his right and the second to his left is his wife Marina Chudakova, Hero of Soviet Sport for earlier victories in yachting at the Olympic Games.

44. Feet of Clay Daniel 2:41-43. Seen behind a Soviet block of flats at the time of Yasnost'. Lenin's feet must have sunk in the wet cement of his plinth!

45. Max Perutz FRS and Sir John Kendrew FRS, of the MRC Laboratory of Molecular Biology in Cambridge, use a model of the haemoglobin molecule to explain their work on it that led to Nobel Prizes for both. I took this photograph when visiting them with a delegation from the Chinese Academy of Sciences.

46. Sir Martin Ryle FRS and Professor Anthony Hewish FRS at the Mullard Radio Astronomy Laboratory, Cambridge, under one of the large aerials there, explaining their work to improve knowledge of galactic and extra galactic radio sources.

47. John Deverill at work initialling a joint project. These were the preferred formal links between scientific institutions here and abroad.

48. Me with some of my staff in the early '80s. They were a splendid lot. Intelligent, carers, linguists!

emulate them in some respects. By now she was fluent in French, the language of tuition and was picking up English from stays in Addis.

This was just as well because several years later the business in Addis Ababa was not doing well and the girls were brought home from Switzerland at the end of 1955 and Herta, nearly 16, went for a short time to the Sandford English School in Addis Ababa, started by Mrs Christine Sandford during WW2 when her husband, Colonel Sandford, was head of the British Military Mission there. They were on good terms with the Emperor Haile Selassie, who later gave them land on which to build a larger school. It still exists as the Sandford International School, with 700 students, many of them Ethiopians. In the early days, and that includes 1956, Mrs Sandford took some of the classes Herta attended.

Even this did not last long because Herta soon found work as a copy typist with the American Embassy. Attracted by the work of an air hostess, she applied to join Aden Airways in that capacity. It was a small airline, a subsidiary of British Overseas Airways Corporation (BOAC) operating Dakota (DC3) aircraft on routes in East Africa and the Arabian Peninsular. An interview was arranged with Mr Bennett, the Aden Airways Commercial Officer, and Rosanna Rizzi, the head air hostess. The interview was in a bare room of the Ghion Hotel in Addis. Mr Bennett asked Herta what she would like to drink, probably expecting her to opt for a coffee or soft drink. Herta asked for a Dry Martini, which sounded sophisticated although she had never had one. Being only 17, to join Aden Airways she needed the written consent of her father, who gave it readily. Aden Airways was of course based in Aden so Herta flew over on an Aden Airways flight to be accommodated in a small block of flats reserved for the half dozen air hostesses in Maala on the road running northeast from Aden to Khormaksar, the airport. She was flying within days; her first flight being from Aden to Nairobi via Hargeisa and Mogadishu on 10 April 1957.

There was no formal training course but a new hostess flew with a more experienced one and learned on the job, with additional training in aircraft evacuation, safety procedures, etc. In the two years before I met her, Herta had flown well over 2,500 hours, more than I had flown, albeit in a different capacity, in 20 years in the Royal Air Force. Poetic that according to the late Sir Cecil Parrott, Slav linguist and translator of Hašek's *Good Soldier Švejk*, the name Jeuschenak probably derives from the Slavonic word for ash tree "jesen" with the diminutive suffix "ik", or "little ash tree". That a little ash tree should stand beside a "stream in fertile uplands" seems especially appropriate.

On 14 April 1964 I was summoned to the FO in London to have my Russian and Arabic tested. I managed very well with Russian after an interesting conversation with a female interpreter. The Arabic interviewer was a fat bespectacled Palestinian who fortunately spoke very slowly and deliberately. By straining my memory I was able to make reasonably fluent conversation. In fact I surprised myself and decided that I had been underrating my Arabic. On the Friday back at Tern Hill there was a formal dining-in night in honour of four members of the Board of Management of Westland helicopter factory at Yeovil. They had flown up from Yeovil in a Widgeon. After a reasonable dinner I had a very interesting conversation with the Works Manager of Westland, when I probed him about possible appointments with them when I retired.

Our son Paul, aged two, used to ride his bicycle like a maniac aiming for any large puddles he could find in the road and regularly getting soaked, bruised and dirty. On 22 April he ran the front wheel of his trike over a steel grating near our back door and shouted with pain. He ran towards me weeping. Not thinking he was badly hurt I went to pick him up and was horrified to find blood streaming from a deep cut in the back of his head. Calling Herta we put a cotton wool pad on the wound, tied it tightly with a nappy and after a quick call to Station Sick Quarters I drove him there. The Medical Officer and assistant orderlies were waiting in the Emergency Ward and soon Paul was sewn up with three neat stitches.

We needed a larger car for ourselves and the two children. The old Beetle got smaller and smaller as the boys got larger and their impedimenta increased. We decided to stick with the Volkswagen marque but get the larger Variant, which had just come on to the market. We collected it in early June hoping to use it for a run to Alton on 9 June. About 4 miles short of Faringdon, south of Oxford, the oil pressure warning light lit up. I checked with the dipstick and the sump was almost empty. We drove on gingerly to a garage in Faringdon and tried refilling with oil, but this was at once pumped out onto the garage floor. There was no alternative other than to abandon the car and continue to Alton as best we could, chartering a taxi from a very considerate young man who got us home at 10.30 p.m., charging £4. The next day the VW Swindon agents collected the car and reported that the factory had not installed the sump drain correctly. They would put it right and I would be able to collect the car from Swindon once I had paid £30 for its recovery and repair, which I did on 12 June. I thought this was unreasonable especially as I was taking examinations in Russian in London in that same period. To add to our woes Herta had lost her purse and a pullover of Paul's on the roof of a friend's car in which they were travelling to Hayling Island. She kept this from me at first but told me about it later. I suggested phoning the police, and lo and behold, the lost items had been found by an Army Major and could be collected from Alton Police Station.

In our quarter at Tern Hill we had a coke central heating boiler named an Ideal Neo Classic. It was none of these things, being an antique which caused quite a lot of dirt and damage. We closed down the dampers each evening before going to bed leaving several inches of coke combusting slowly at the top. The boiler fed one very small radiator in the hall as well as the cylinder in the airing cupboard on the landing. One of the first things to do in the morning was to re-activate the boiler, which would have been smouldering sullenly for most of the night. Getting the boiler going again involved opening a front grill and breaking up the coke with a poker. This sometimes worked well with the coke re-igniting ready for replenishment. However, as often as not there was a dull explosion inside the boiler which blew open any flaps still closed, ejecting clouds of ash and soot across the kitchen and into the face of whoever was performing this duty. All of us got caught at different times, especially our batwoman, who used to come in early to help Herta during the mornings. Another fault was that the domestic hot water, used for washing and baths as well as washing up, sometimes boiled. This could be at any time of the day or night. The steam and scalding water escaping through a vent pipe in the roof made a lot of noise and was definitely frightening.

Diary Tuesday 30 June 1964:

> Today went down to London on the 7.40 a.m. to see the FO co-ordinating people re a possible job. Arrived London 11. Carlton Gardens at 12. Met by Peel who introduced me to a colleague John Quire and another elderly dispirited sort of chap in charge of Department. Started by asking me what I knew about them. We then talked for an hour and a half. Terms offered were favourable – £2,000 p.a. etc. But proposed appointment was most unattractive. We continued over lunch at Quire's club – Royal Naval Volunteer Reserve. I said I would await a letter from them re my suitability for the post and would let them know before 1 September whether I accepted. In fact, after discussion later with Herta we decided that it would be impossible to accept and I informed the co-ordinating office accordingly.

The co-ordinating office and people were the Secret Intelligence Service, MI5 and 6, etc. The things I objected to related to loyalty to friends. It was made clear that in such posts one must be prepared to betray friends, or at least be disloyal to them, if this were in the interests of the Service. For me this was inconceivable. Loyalty is a most important character trait, probably the most important: first – unquestioning loyalty to one's immediate family, then to one's more distant relatives, then to one's friends, then to one's country and then to the wider community and the world. This relates to the proximity of relationships: one's family is closest and best known and then there are widening concentric circles of loyalty and responsibility. On one occasion I even designed a tie to illustrate this, to be available for anyone subscribing to the ideal. Ripples of loyalty and responsibility, represented by dotted silver lines, spread out in concentric and increasingly more widely spaced circles from a central i, in lower case to differentiate it from the more egotistical higher case I. The further from the centre: the more widely spaced the dots. I even had a quote for the tie from Gieves: £7 in polyester. But I would need to order 1000. I decided not to risk it. Anyway, the SIS was one second career I would not embark on.

My application to join the Foreign Office proper under the over-age competition was going ahead and after a number of quite taxing Civil Service examinations where I was doing very well there came the final interview in July. I was informed shortly afterwards that I had come 11th out of about 500 in the competition, but that there had been only nine posts to fill. Another blank drawn.

However there was another dining-in night in the officers' mess at Tern Hill in September, when I sat next to the sales director of Westland, a Mr Gordon. We had an interesting conversation although I did not like the man much. However, on 18 November, out of the blue I took a telephone call from Westlands and was asked to visit Yeovil on 30 November to meet the managing director. I drove there on 30 November. Diary entry:

Set off from Tern Hill at 08.15 in cold freezing fog. Visibility about 50 yards. In Kidderminster the weather cleared becoming sunny near Bath. Arrived Yeovil 14.15. Met by Penrose for short discussion and went together to see Gordon. After an hour we all adjourned to the Managing Director's office. He is a charming Yorkshireman. Starting salary mentioned as £1,200 pa + 15% annual bonus. I disagreed with this because Gordon had earlier told me I would start at £1,800. All seemed very keen that I should accept but it seemed that Gordon could go no further without authority from Finance. We parted gloomily. Penrose is a good type, ex-test pilot. Gordon puts on polished airs. Drove home starting at 16.15. Dark, torrential rain, gales! After Cheltenham the rain cleared then fog descended. Visibility from Kidderminster to Bridgenorth was down to 10 yards. Home at 22.00, very tired.

Penrose was Harald Penrose, born in1904, who had joined Westland as a Test Pilot in 1926 (when I was four) and was promoted to Chief Test Pilot in 1931. He had flown more than 5,000 hours on hundreds of aircraft and did most of the test flying of the Lysander which I also flew. He was a man who greatly appealed to me, a jack of all trades who wrote books and designed his own house in which he and his wife lived for many years. The following day Penrose phoned to let me know that progress was being made and asked me to phone Gordon on Friday 4 December. I did and he told me that he could raise their offer to £1,500 + 10% bonus = £1,650. I accepted provisionally because it seemed a reasonable opening and might lead to helicopter flying. In any case I was fed up with hawking myself around. A possible snag was that Gordon said he wanted me at work in Yeovil as early as possible in January. I asked the Ministry of Defence if they would have any objection to my starting at Westland before my RAF retirement date, which remained 24 February 1965, my 43rd birthday. This would not be possible I was told, but my terminal leave could be used as I pleased and I could have six weeks "training" for my retirement job. Added together I could start work on 1 January if I wished. This meant I would get two salaries for a couple of months, which suited us.

I went out with a bang – on the head. Diary Saturday 12 December:

Oh, what a day this was, to be sure. It was to be my last day with the North Shropshires. Met at High Ercall. None too promising a day, wet drizzle and low cloud. Drew several useless covers before trying the Long. Found here at about 1 p.m. and hounds went away fast towards Ercall Park. Piper went very well taking all manner of jumps. But the field was very trying, all sorts of undisciplined horses – kickers – getting in the way all the time. Approaching the park I was baulked at a low hedge, circled right and came in again about two lengths behind a pony and a larger horse, jumping together about eight feet apart. Set Piper to go between them but they converged on the far side and even drawing up my legs I got a hefty crack on my right thigh and was nearly unseated. Stirrups lost I decided to press on. But while searching for them a couple of hundred yards further on two things happened at once: my hat flew off and Piper shied to the left. Realising I was bound to come off I cleared my feet and went into a roll over Piper's off shoulder. That was the last I remember until asked to see if I could step into a Mini which had been driven into the field. Two kind people then drove me to the Master's house nearby and made me hot tea while phoning Herta to collect the remains. Felt very sick and with a splitting headache. Doc. Pallister visited me on arrival at home and diagnosed concussion – fed me with sedatives. Slept well overnight but still felt frightful all Sunday and was unable to attend Mess Party that night to mark our departure. I also slept most of Monday and Tuesday and only went back to work on Wednesday.

Later I was told that I had been unconscious on the ground for half an hour. The hunt had gone on and Piper had been boxed home to his owner. I did not hunt again, not because I did not want to but because when we moved south, hunting was too expensive. And move south we did in quick order. After getting back to work on Wednesday 16 December I had several days to complete reports on my last batch of students; on Saturday we packed as much as possible of our possessions in the car, and on Sunday drove to Alton for Christmas. Herta and the boys had colds. I was still aching from my fall from Piper. The following Tuesday we spent in London where we bought a fine handbag from Woolands for Herta and a trampoline and various toys from Hamleys for the children.

The next day, while Herta was shopping for Christmas in Farnham, I spent an hour with our solicitor, Mr Arthur, in his Alton office discussing purchase or rental of a house in Yeovil. His advice was not to rent but to buy, using a Halifax mortgage with a bank loan as down payment until my terminal grant was paid. I knew very little about buying houses and even less about mortgages after a life thus far in the RAF, cushioned from such problems, as we were in those days. Christmas Eve was spent trying to find presents for Mary and Titus (individual enamelled frying pans for them, records for Johnny and Moppy). After Christmas lunch in Alton we were to drive to Bourne End for tea with Titus's parents.

Christmas Day went off very well. It was icy cold but no snow fell. On 28 December my father went into hospital with another bout of bleeding from his bladder. His surgeon, Mr Haysom, arranged everything. Herta stayed at Alton with the boys, while I drove back to Tern Hill to meet Pickfords, whose pantechnicon collected our belongings on 30 December to store until we needed them next. I was back in Alton on the last day of December 1964, having visited the Goddards in their new house in the Cotswolds and lunched in Moreton-in-Marsh at the Manor House Hotel.

We were not in Alton long. Asking about possible houses when I visited Westland in November I had discovered that an engineer of theirs wished to move from a house he and his wife occupied at 9 East Coker Road, Yeovil. During the Christmas break Herta and I drove down there (via Salisbury and Wilton, where Mike lived) and had a look at the place. The engineer had already moved out, and the house, though small, stood in a quiet road on the edge of the town, five minutes drive from Westland factory complex, with views over open country, and a small garden. It seemed an obvious choice for a quick buy for slightly over £7,000. The deal was soon done and we moved from Alton in early January.

I had visited Heals in London and had been attracted by a large 7' square bed composed of two linked lower sections with a single sprung mattress over, the fillings of which were natural fibres, including horsehair, Peruvian lama wool and other expensive adjuncts. I was told by Mr Narramore, Head of Bedding, a formidable character, that the bed had been of interest to a film star only the previous day. They had gone away to think about it, but might decide to buy any day. As the bed's price had been reduced to £400 for the end of year sale I would do well to clinch the deal. Thinking of our rather uncomfortable RAF beds and of the luxury of spreading my long legs, it did not take me long to decide. While visiting Heals so that Herta could view our purchase, we also ordered other furniture to add to anything we could borrow from Valverde to provide a basis for our forthcoming civilian life.

By mid-January I was working with Westland. I was discontented to find that I had to share an office with another "Sales Engineer", a poorly spoken young man whom I would not have chosen as a subordinate officer, let alone welcomed as a colleague. The office, like most of the other offices at Westland, was made of adjustable metal walls, rather like a filing cabinet, and the walls could be moved to accommodate more or less employees. Senior employees, like Harald Penrose, had a slightly more luxurious office for himself in a corner of the building. The Directors, Sales, Managing, Production, etc., had more comfortable offices in other buildings. I got a strong impression that Sales were considered rather down-market, possibly because the turnover of personnel was considerable. My predecessor in Sales had moved to East Cowes in the Isle of Wight to work in sales there. Some years earlier Westland had taken over the Saunders-Roe interests in helicopters and hovercraft and the SRN 4 hovercraft were being developed. Later we often crossed the Channel in the SRN 4s.

Small helicopters were also being produced at Hayes close to London Airport – the Scout and the Wasp, the Scouts mostly for the Army Air Corps. Sales staff were treated as being capable of selling anything and were moved around among the subsidiary companies if there were good reasons to do so. As Westlands also manufactured up-and-over garage doors I imagined that sales staff might end up there.

One of the first things I did at Westland was to get to know the helicopter pilots and about the helicopter with which we were all most concerned, the

Whirlwind. It was a revelation to me to see that each blade on the rotor was a work of art with small components fixed together just as one might a balsa model wing. There is no doubt that a helicopter is very, very complicated and a product of extremely sophisticated design. Computers were used in the design process and the engineer from whom we had bought our house was an aeronautical engineer specialising in what we now call CAD (computer aided design). However he complained that he was only rarely called in to deal with problems, but only when things went wrong, and they rarely did. So in his spare time he had designed and was manufacturing at home a harpoon gun for underwater hunting of large fish. It used powerful springs and compressed air. I think this work had been done in the garage and that in moving to another house it had been an objective to get more room for the assembly of his harpoons. He and his wife had no children and he spent a lot of time on his hobby.

I was given a very dusty answer to my requests for tuition on the Whirlwind. I was referred back to the Sales Director, Mr Gordon. I deployed the argument that if I was to recommend and sell Whirlwinds I would need personal knowledge about their performance. I would not buy a car if those selling it to me had not driven it. And similarly with any other product. Mr Gordon dismissed this argument on the grounds that selling helicopters was no different to selling detergent. Any necessary demonstrations could be given by the trained helicopter pilots Westland employed. I felt I was already on the way to the garage door production unit.

A current problem for Westland in connection with the Whirlwind was that King Hussein of Jordan had bought three Whirlwinds to start with, but his wife of that time had nearly been killed in an accident brought about by engine failure. Consequently, the King ruled out any further purchase of Whirlwinds and was considering buying French. I thought that I, having commanded the Arab Legion Air Force in 1949, and knowing Arabic and Arab customs, might be able to influence the King to reconsider buying from Westland. On no account, said Mr Gordon. Any visit to Jordan would be by him and in any case the matter had gone too far and was irretrievable. Nominally I was "in charge of" helicopter sales to the Middle East and western Europe.

Agitating for something to do I was asked to accompany someone from the engineering staff to attend a helicopter "fair" in Hamburg. We flew over by BEA and were accommodated in a two star hotel. The "fair" was extremely uninteresting but I managed to meet some people who might be useful as future contacts. One was a senior Greek Army officer. I knew that they were looking for a helicopter with a specification such as the Whirlwind. The Greek officer invited me to visit Greece and have further discussions. I went there several weeks later and met a number of senior officers and government figures. A problem was that the Greeks were clear that they could not pay in cash but only in Greek currants and wine to an equivalent value. When this was reported back to Mr Gordon he made the point strongly that Westland could not go into the wine and dried fruit business. I understood later that the French and Italians could.

I was rapidly becoming disillusioned with Westland. Meeting the representatives of prospective purchasers in London was interesting but any major hospitality was arranged by Westland's London representative. I was called upon to attend and report back. The policy was to accommodate Westland's staff in a very grotty hotel in Earls Court, but drinks, lunches etc., on the firm's behalf would be in the Savoy Hotel. This is where I met a businessman from Lichtenstein, Manfred Harrer, a middleman who had set up the sale of Westland helicopters to the Austrians in a deal involving various women, one of whom acted as the Westland representative in Vienna. The intrigue seemed complex.

Our Heals' bed was delivered but when the Heals' men tried to get the bed, even in two parts, through the door and up the stairs of No.9, it would not and could not go. Not to be outdone I called in builders, who removed the bedroom window, used ropes to slide the bed up two obliquely placed ladders through the brickwork and into the bedroom, and then refixed the window. As this was for a comparatively short period one might say that the bed, though supremely comfortable, had a downside. There were also other problems. The dining room was very small and the walls stippled with brownish plaster. However, we had excellent neighbours who were a great help. Mrs Sartin in the white house next door was very sympathetic. She was an heiress to the News of the World fortune and had a lot of money which she was using for the education of her only son at Marlborough. Her husband worked for Dents, a firm famous for gloves and fine leather, with a factory in Yeovil. The Sartins became good friends and helped with the children who often went next door to play.

We found a small school for Johnnie in Yeovil – The Park School. He was not there long, the spring and summer terms of 1965. The Head Mistress in her report in June 1965, when Johnnie was four and a half years old, said that he was a quiet, helpful and rather reserved child, who sometimes had difficulties in expressing himself, but enjoyed engaging with other children in group play. His reading and number work were going well.

The Royal Society

The reason Johnnie and Paul did not continue long at the Park School in Yeovil was that I had decided that selling helicopters, garage doors, detergents or baked beans (even Greek currants) did not suit me. I was not enamoured of my colleagues, my superiors or the workers, who lined up every day close to the factory gates, like sprinters on their starting blocks, waiting for the factory siren to signal the end of the working day, and then racing out, endangering the lives of incautious pedestrians going about their business. I told Herta about this and we agreed I would need to seek other employment. A day or two later, on 28 April 1965, reading my Times, I saw the following advertisement:

> *The Royal Society intends to make an appointment to its senior staff. Applicants should preferably be between 35 and 50 years of age, have a university degree, facility in at least one European language, preferably Russian; a wide knowledge of scientific affairs would be an advantage. Duties will primarily be concerned with exchange visits of scientists between the United Kingdom, Eastern Europe (including the Soviet Union), and China, and with the Royal Society's relations with government departments and other bodies in this country and with academies of science abroad.*

The advertisement continued with salary details (scales related to university salaries), start date – 23 June 1965, need for referees (mine would be my ambassadors in Moscow Sir William Hayter and Sir Paul Reilly) and how to apply.

I knew a bit about the Royal Society (RS) because in 1954 I had helped to escort a visit by Lord Adrian, then their President (PRS), visiting the Soviet Academy of Sciences in Moscow with a delegation of senior Fellows (FfRS) to negotiate an exchange agreement. But I looked out details of their history and activities in the London Library and wrote to my predecessor at the RS. He turned out to be John Coates, Daphne Park's successor as MI6 representative in our Moscow Embassy and my friend and former colleague there. John had only been at the RS for a year. Before the Second World War he had read foreign languages at Cambridge, graduating just before the war.

As a conscientious objector John was posted to the Army Intelligence Corps to interrogate German prisoners of war, but soon renounced his conscientious scruples and joined the Commandos, troops of whom were drawn from various allied nations fighting with the Allies. To enlarge his experience he applied to join the Special Operations Executive (SOE). With two companions he was parachuted into Hungary on 13 September 1944 with the aim of negotiating a Hungarian surrender before the arrival of Soviet troops. However he and his colleagues were captured and tortured but successfully maintained that they were captured British prisoners-of-war who had escaped from their camp. Helped by Hungarians, John escaped from captivity in December 1944, and hid near Budapest during the Russian attack, surrendering to a Red Army patrol when it seemed safe. For his conduct he was awarded the DSO.

Back in the UK he joined the FCO and served in the British embassies at The Hague, and later in Vienna, Helsinki and Moscow, where we met. He left the FCO to pursue his academic ambitions, and being fluent in Hungarian and Finnish sought to specialise in the Finno-Ugric language and literature of the Komi people, who had remained in Russia when others had settled in what are now Hungary and Finland. John had come across the Komi while serving in the USSR. By then they inhabited the Komi Autonomous People's Republic, capital Sytykvar. Very few westerners spoke their language, and their literature occupied a single shelf in John's bookcase. In 1964, while seeking support for studies of Komi, John joined the Royal Society's staff, but early in 1965 was informed by Clare Hall, Cambridge, that he had been awarded a Fellowship to enable him to complete a PhD in his Komi studies. Hence, his resignation from the RS and an opportunity for me.

At a lunch at the RAF Club John briefed me on the work and environment at the Royal Society in Burlington House, on my future colleagues, and, most importantly, on the members of the board likely to interview candidates for the post. These would include the Foreign Secretary, Professor (later Sir Harold) Thompson, an Oxford physical chemist and Chairman of the Football Association (I brushed up on my football); the Biological Secretary, Professor Ashley (later Sir Ashley) Miles, who was involved in Royal Society research projects in Latin America; the Deputy Executive Secretary Dr Ronald Keay (a forester with a previous career in Nigeria, the Treasurer and several others.

I turned up for interview at Burlington House in Piccadilly together with half a dozen or more rather academic characters – dark suits, briefcases, spectacles. At interview I stressed my fluency in Russian and other languages and my embassy experience and excused my comparative ignorance in any one scientific field by pointing out that as a pilot I was an engineer, a meteorologist, astronomer, etc. etc., with a smattering of much of science but without any specific loyalties or preferences for one field or another, which would be an advantage in a post involving the award of bursaries and fellowships.

Although it was not specifically mentioned at interview, I was given to understand that my associations with the intelligence world were an important factor, because both Tommy Thompson and Ronald Keay knew that the Soviet Union and other communist countries were trying to obtain scientific information (some classified, some commercially confidential) by covert means.

On 29 May 1965 I received a letter from the RS offering me the appointment and I accepted by return of post. I phoned Dad that evening to explain what I was doing. I would have my own little Foreign Office at Burlington House without having to specialise in a few foreign countries as in the FCO, but in all and every one of them, developed and developing. We now had to dispose of 9 East Coker Road and find somewhere to live in or close to London. I had the pleasure of seeing the Westland Sales Director, Mr Gordon, and giving him my letter of resignation.

The letter offering me the post came with an invitation for me and Herta to attend the June Soirée or Conversazione of the Royal Society. These events were arranged annually in the Society's rooms in Burlington House with the object of demonstrating recent interesting and important advances in science. Key scientists responsible for these advances were invited many months beforehand to mount demonstrations and provide equipment for stands in the main meeting rooms of the Society and to attend personally to explain to invited guests what they had achieved. Guests included the Fellowship, such Royal patrons as might wish to come, the Ambassadors in London (or their representatives) of the major scientific powers, Government Ministers and representatives of non-governmental organisations involved in science and many other people whose presence would be welcomed by the Society. The invitation to the Conversazione arrived by post at our house in Yeovil on the day it was due to take place, so we could not go, but in thanking John Coates I asked him to write to me explaining the social activities in which I might be involved while working for the Society.

He replied:

You will be invited to attend two or three Soirées a year. You are not obliged to attend, though I have found it a good thing to do so, because it is one of the very few occasions when it is possible to meet British scientists and various distinguished strangers en masse. You will find yourself in correspondence with many Fellows and it is always refreshing and occasionally a little alarming to be able to put a face to a name.

Apart from Soirées, you will attend various formal lunches (of which you are usually the organiser) given for visiting senior scientists from East Bloc countries. These are formal in the sense that a sprinkling of Fellows and those connected with the visit are invited; the host is usually one of the Officers of the Society and we all sit around a table in the so-called Tea Room, which is in the Society's so-called apartments – i.e., Burlington House. We are served by waiters in formal dress, some of whom will remind you of Firs or Feramont, and there are sometimes comparatively informal toasts and speeches at the end. We do not dress for these occasions however; any old office suit suffices. Other functions are teas on Committee days. You can drift into these upon those occasions when there is some pretext for your presence.

A Soirée is a sort of buffet supper cum cocktail party (indifferent food, indifferent drinks) in full evening dress. A feature of these affairs is a series of very skilfully arranged scientific demonstrations mounted under the auspices of Fellows or other close associates of the Society. These demonstrations occasionally hit the press; at the last Conversazione, for instance, two live chimpanzees were produced and demonstrated their learning skills to the assembled company. Russians, Chinese, Americans, etc., do attend Soirées, and you will be able to exert some influence over the invitation list so that, as a general rule, those people you need to liaise with most will be invited. Full evening dress, then, is de rigueur as far as Soirées are concerned. This means white tie and tails and miniature decorations. Black ties are only worn at one of the normal soirées in preference to white ties.

You can, of course, hire evening dress of all sorts and miniatures from Moss Bros, but if you are going to be with the Society for more than a year it will obviously pay you to buy rather then hire. Herta could wear either a long or a short evening dress, though there is a preference for long dresses on the white tie occasions.

You will find yourself lunching with your opposite numbers in Government Departments and Embassies, also visiting foreign scientists for whom you are responsible, fairly frequently, and they will, of course return your invitations. This they will do in many interesting ways. Thus, apart from lunches, you will find yourself invited to national days and other similar functions, and you will be sent tickets for things like the Bolshoi Ballet, Chinese ping-pong, dramatic Polish films and the like. For all these occasions, of course, a lounge suit, with or without concealed dagger, is the thing to wear.

The programme for our three-day hand-over is shaping well. So far I have fixed the following:

For the Monday: a call on the Romanians; lunch with the Chinese

Tuesday: call on the Russians; lunch with the principal scientific contact

Wednesday: call on the East Germans; lunch with our principal Foreign Office contact (Richard Speaight)

I had to give one calendar month's notice and therefore left Westland's service on Wednesday 30 June but started at the Royal Society the previous Monday 28 June so that I could follow John's hand-over programme. Over the weekend Herta and I had driven to Alton with Johnnie and Paul. I had remained there but Herta and the children had driven back to Yeovil where she would remain in the house until it was sold. I would commute to London from Alton or stay in London at the RAF Club.

For much of the summer I stayed in the Club but on Friday evenings took the train either to Yeovil, or to Alton where Herta drove with the children to stay with me and Dad. He was not always there because he was having increasing trouble with bleeding from his kidneys and spent a lot of time in hospital having treatment supervised by Mr Haysom, his surgeon. This was usually at Dad's expense because he preferred to have Mr Haysom as surgeon rather then rely on the NHS. Having nominally retired from Phillips and Son, he received a pension of £2000 p.a. but this soon became insufficient to cover the medical bills and he had to draw increasingly on capital. This distressed him a lot.

Herta and I spent some time in the London suburbs looking for a house that suited our pocket and taste but drew a blank and were eventually attracted to Guildford, where we found a very nice house for sale in Eastgate Gardens. This was a quiet road more or less in the centre of the town, opposite the King Edward VII School playing grounds and a short walk from the main station. The price was about £11K which we could manage with a slightly increased mortgage and money from my RAF terminal grant and commuted pension. The house had four bedrooms, two quite large, a very nice lounge and dining room, but the latter with signs of a damp floor, and a long kitchen also with signs of damp. Over the garage a previous owner had built a very large extension, a single room, which we thought of using as a play room. While negotiations to buy this house were going on a retired British High Commissioner of a Commonwealth country made an offer of £9000 for 9 East Coker Road, which we accepted, but he could not complete until later and it was not until 15 November that we could finalise purchase of 4 Eastgate Gardens and move in. We moved with our bed of course and had to ask the builders to revisit, remove the bedroom window and let the bed down into the garden on ladders to be taken to Guildford by our movers. The window was put back and we never let the purchaser of our house know about the problem and its solution.

In Guildford we needed a school for the boys, now five and four years old respectively. Both had attended the Park School in Yeovil, which had made delivery and collection easy. In Guildford we decided to try a Catholic school in the state sector. Both boys could already read. We had taught them using the Janet and John books. The school reported that they could not read, which was obviously incorrect. After one term we moved them to Drayton House School, a private primary in Austen Road, Guildford, about a mile from Eastgate Gardens, where they fared much better.

For Herta shopping was easy because the house was within easy walking distance of Guildford High Street and North Street with shops of every sort. For me commuting to Waterloo Station was also easy, taking 35 minutes, with several non-stopping trains an hour. A snag was that I could rarely get a seat; they had filled further down the line. From Waterloo I could either walk 15 minutes across Westminster Bridge and across Horse Guards Parade to Burlington House in Piccadilly or go by underground to Piccadilly Circus and walk from there. Either way I could complete the whole journey in an hour which was convenient because working hours were nominally from 09.30 to 17.30 with an hour for lunch. Times were flexible for us in the "international relations" office because we often needed to attend Embassy, FCO and Ministry receptions until late evening as well as meeting visiting scientists whenever they might arrive at Heathrow, escorting them to their hotels and getting them settled.

In those days looking after scientists arriving under formal arrangements was very much a "hands on" job, far more than now. As often as not the visitors did not speak much or even any English. We knew about their linguistic capabilities before they arrived from proposal forms arriving by post or telex from the country concerned. Also most of their other personal details, from which we made programmes for their visits, approved in advance by both visitors and hosts. This took a lot of time and effort, liaison with laboratories up and down the country, with travel agents, British Rail, ministries, the Foreign Office, the British Council, etc. Each visit was preceded by scores of telephone calls and endless filling in and amendment of draft programmes for each visitor until the final version was ready to be duplicated and sent to all concerned. To help in this I had two staff: Nadia Slow, who had been No.2 to John Coates, and Veronica Kendle, nominally his Secretary. Veronica was a really charming girl with artistic talent, who wrote very good poetry and included actors, musicians, conductors, sculptors etc., among her friends. Our offices were in the old servants' quarters of Burlington House, reached by a converted food lift, with enough space for two face to face, with a few inches between noses.

In 1965 there were not all that many visiting scientists under formal agreements. Before WW2 scientists came and went under arrangements they made among themselves, between their universities or laboratories or as individuals. The war had diminished international visits by scientists (and indeed by anyone else) unless there were important reasons to go or to come, usually related to the war effort. After the war things started to return to normal, except that there was the Cold War and the Iron Curtain cutting off the Soviet Union and its satellites from the West. However, knowledge is not easily confined by frontiers, and scientists and their countries needed to exchange knowledge just in order to aid their development. There were spies who succeeded in getting access to knowledge and passing it on, but this was no substitute for scientific interchange. There remained the problem for the communist governments of retaining a high degree of control of their scientists and their knowledge, and the problem of foreign exchange when non-convertible roubles and zlotys could not purchase board and lodging, etc., in the Cambridge Arms and equivalent hotels and hostelries.

The answer was to have a nominal equivalence of visits in terms of value expressed in time and currency on a reciprocal basis, with sending sides paying international air fares and host sides paying local costs. On the British side the British Council, acting for the FCO and the government, negotiated and concluded agreements with their counterparts in the east – ministries of culture and academies of science. It was soon discovered that most scientific interchange at postdoctoral level could be delegated to the Royal Society to agree with their scientific counterparts, with the resulting agreements incorporated in the intergovernmental cultural agreements. British Council and FCO sponsorship made it easier to obtain visas and to comply with other official formalities. The British Council and the Royal Society jointly funded scientific visits under the agreements, which called for very close liaison between our offices, fortunately fairly close-by, and with the British Council representatives in the capitals of most countries worldwide.

The first countries with whom we had reciprocal agreements on scientific exchanges were the USSR (Soviet Academy of Sciences), Poland (Polish Academy of Sciences) and China (Chinese Academy of Sciences). Other scientific visits to and from the UK took place without the Society's direct participation, but as UK hosts usually needed money to fund the visits, fares for outgoers and local costs for incomers, help with visas etc., the Society became more and more involved in that it had access to government funds and close ties with the British Council and its parent the FCO, both with overseas representation in the capitals of the countries involved.

Of course none of this overarching bureaucratic structure should have been necessary. Science has always been international. "Science" means knowledge, from the Latin *"scientia"*. The Greeks had a word for it *"philosophos"* – love of wisdom. But science seems more explicit and so it came about. The first scientists called themselves natural philosophers to distinguish themselves from those who were less concerned with nature than with logic, including mathematics, architecture and a number of other disciplines, which were sometimes more speculative than factual. There was a lot of overlap until a logical method of scientific research had been worked out, the method being divided for convenience into stages – observation, measurement, hypothesis and experiment. The experiment had to be repeatable by others and thus verified. Without any of these stages the science was invalid. As it still is on the whole. Science had come to mean verifiable knowledge.

The early Greek philosophers such as Pythagoras in the sixth century BC and Plato and Aristotle in the fourth laid the foundations of much of science (not all because the Chinese had followed a different route). Other Greeks had laid the foundations of other aspects of our culture. Why? Well some say that it was because the physical and intellectual climate in Greece then was particularly conducive to thought. Socrates taught outside in the garden of his friend Akademos, giving us our name for Academy, used for any number of learned societies. Greek influence, especially in respect of inquiry and scholarship, spread explosively with Alexander's conquests, but declined when he died and his empire started to come to pieces.

One piece survived for many years in Alexandria where a great library was established for the conservation of Greek knowledge and scholarship, a Yale or Harvard, Oxford or Cambridge of the ancient world. Euclid and Archimedes taught there and, in the Library, Eratosthenes, who measured the circumference of the earth to within a few % of what we now know it to be, and who first devised a system of latitude and longitude, was a Librarian. There were few restrictions on inquiring minds. One result of this open atmosphere, a prerequisite for the pursuit of knowledge, was a flourishing medical school where many anatomical discoveries were made, including that the role of the heart is to pump blood, which had to be re-discovered in Europe more than 1000 years later. In Alexandria, Ptolemy, the greatest of all Greek astronomers, wrote his astronomical text Almagest, a word deriving from the Arabic al-mujisti, in its turn derived from the Greek for the Greatest or "The Great Treatise". This was to be a standard astronomical reference for 1000 years and epitomises the relationship between the Greek savants and their Arab counterparts who preserved the Greek inheritance throughout the years of the Christian/Muslim "Iron Curtain" which lasted centuries rather than the 50 years of our own more recent Soviet/Western split.

Alexandria as a centre of learning was destroyed largely by religion. Apart from the possibly accidental burning of the Library by forces under Julius Caesar in 48BC, when they were attacking adjacent buildings, the Patriarch Theophilus, with the approval of the Emperor Theodosius, did much more damage in AD 389, and what was left of the job was finished off in the seventh century when Muslims overran the country. Their attitude was that writings in accordance with the Koran were unnecessary and any conflicting with the Koran should be destroyed. Much probably remained but the scholars, preferring peace for the pursuance of their work, moved with many of the records of earlier research to places less affected by strife, some back to Byzantium, others to India, Ceylon and Iran, and later to Damascus, Baghdad and the cities of north Africa and Spain, especially Seville, Granada and Toledo. In these sanctuaries they established new nuclei of learning, where original Greek writings were translated into Arabic, and where the store of knowledge was augmented from Arab and oriental sources – Hindi numerals including the concept of zero (we call them Arabic numerals); Arabic astronomical names for the stars and terms such as "zenith", "nadir", algebra (Arabic el jibr = the symbol), are some of the things from these sources with which we are now familiar.

Western Europe at that time was in the dark ages, cut off from its cultural roots not only by the Christian/Muslim barrier, but also by barbarian invasions from

Asia – Huns and Vandals, Goths and Visigoths. But in 1085, after Bivar the Cid recovered central Spain for the Christian Alfonzo VI, a vast store of knowledge became available to western Christendom setting the scene for the Renaissance. Toledo became a scholastic Mecca where Hispano-Arabs and Jews worked together with visitors from France, Germany, Italy and Britain especially. Michael Scot, Robert of Chester and Adelard of Bath, to name but three famous British translators, established themselves in Toledo, working with others to translate into Latin and the vernacular the writings from all over the known world for which Arabic had been the vehicle. These included the original works of Aristotle and it was now only a matter of time before their theories would be re-examined.

Quite some time because the dissemination of knowledge at first involved the circulation of original documents and manuscript (hand writing) had long been a speciality of the church. Arabic numerals did not come into general use for another 400 years. The invention that was to give the Renaissance a tremendous boost was the printing press, more specifically moveable type, which arrived in Europe in the 1420s, having been used in China for six centuries before then. It was first used in Europe for printing playing cards and holy pictures, but especially in France and Italy it was soon used for printing books and by the end of the century eight million printed books were in circulation, more than had been produced by scribes in the previous thousand years. In Britain, the first book was printed on Caxton's press in 1477. It was a translation of an Arabic original from Toledo.

Nicholas Copernicus (1473-1543) probably read some of these newly printed books, acknowledging his debt to Greek and Arab scholars who had studied the solar system earlier and propounded a heliocentric structure. His great work *On the Revolutions of the Celestial Orbs*, published on his death, raised quite a few eyebrows and Martin Luther commented *"The fool will turn the whole of astronomy upside down, Holy writ declares it was the sun and not the earth which Joshua commanded to stand still"*. Had he not died when he did, Copernicus might well have been burned at the stake as a heretic, as was Giordano Bruno, for such views.

Galileo, born 21 years after the death of Copernicus, courted the same fate by supporting the Copernican theory, taking it further by using the telescope, newly invented in the Netherlands, but quickly taken up and improved by Galileo using lenses made by Venetian glass makers. Galileo invited sceptics, including the Jesuits, set up to counter the Reformation, and masters of the Inquisition, to see with their own eyes that Saturn's moons circled that planet and not the Earth; that the moon was not flat, nor the sun a pure disc as Aristotle had written, but suffered from observable spots and that the three comets visible at that time could be seen to be circling the sun, not the Earth. This was all too much for the church. When he was 70 Galileo was brought before the Inquisition, forced to recant and put under house arrest for the remainder of his life. His writings were placed in the newly devised Index, forbidden reading for Catholics. He later wrote *"And who can doubt that it will lead to the worst disorders when minds free by God are compelled to submit slavishly to an outside will. When we are told to deny our senses and subject them to the will of others. When people of whatever competence are made judges over experts and are granted authority to treat them as they please. This will bring about the ruin of commonwealths and the subversion of the state."* This sentiment is embodied in the ethos and motto of the Royal Society – Nullius in Verba.

Because religions are for the most part based on faith dictated by a self-elected elite, or priesthood purporting to be inspired by the founder, there is little room for curiosity, doubt and inquiry to establish facts and probabilities. Hence, rather than the church, literate but bound by the scriptures, it was lay free thinkers who led scientific inquiry, and being relatively few in number, and needing time and money to pursue inquiries, they tended to band together in "clubs" as do many with common interests. The first two scientific clubs were formed in Rome and Florence, the Academia dei Lincei and the Academia del Cimento respectively, but both were soon closed by the Inquisition.

Fortunately the Inquisition held no sway in England and, since Henry VIII's split with Rome, free thinking had been easier than on the Continent. Already in Elizabeth I's time her physician, William Gilbert (1554-1603), in his book De Magnete had described how he had shown by experiment that the earth was a magnet, as well as giving us our word for electricity, deriving from the Greek *electron* or amber, which he had used to generate a static charge. William Harvey (1578-1657) influenced by works from Toledo, had confirmed, again by experiment, the circulation of the blood in the body. Francis Bacon (1561-1626) laid down a scientific methodology for the study of nature, expressed in his book The New Atlantis. In it he proposed the formation of a society of natural philosophers, who would seek out knowledge by the experimental method, so that it might be used for the betterment of mankind. This was published in 1627, a year after his death, but ran through many editions in the next 25 years. In 1636 and 1638 respectively Thomas Hobbes and John Milton visited Galileo under house arrest in Arcetri, in the hills overlooking Florence, and there is a painting of them looking through his telescope. Shortly afterwards the philosopher Comenius, from Charles University in Prague, spent nine months in Britain at the invitation of Parliamentarians to discuss his ideas for the setting up of an international scientific academy. However he had to return home because of the outbreak of the Civil War and the regime of Cromwell.

In England sundry natural philosophers, including Robert Boyle and Christopher Wren who are now well-known, and a dozen or more others including some probable Royalists had met together much as Francis Bacon had expected. Their first meetings were in London in Gresham College, earlier the house of Sir Thomas Gresham a wealthy merchant and agent for Elizabeth I. He had left his house to be endowed as a College for public lectures and as a centre for natural philosophy more generally. Professors were appointed and the College seems to have become a sort of University College, well adapted to host meetings of natural philosophers. With the Civil War the scientific meetings were moved to Oxford where they were held in the lodgings of one or other of the scientists who participated, notably in Wadham College. When the Roundheads occupied Oxford the meetings were transferred back to London often in Gresham College, but sometimes elsewhere. These were difficult days, in which it was impossible to set up a scientific entity because of the generally religious flavour of government and administration.

With Cromwell's death and the restoration of the monarchy in the person of Charles II, the entire scene changed. The King knew something of the new philosophy as a result of his stay in France, and he had men around him who were much interested in it. One was Sir Robert Moray who returned to England in May 1660 two months after the King. On 28 November 1660 it is recorded:

> These persons following, according to the usuall custom of most of them, mett together at Gresham College to heare Mr Wren's lecture, viz. The Lord Brouncker, Mr Boyle, Sir Robert Moray, Sir Paule Neile. Dr Wilkins, Dr Goddard, Dr Petty, Mr Ball, Mr Rooke, Mr Wren, Mr Hill. And after the lecture was ended they did, according to the usuall manner, withdrawe for mutuall converse. Where amongst other matters that were discoursed of, something was offered about a designe of founding a Colledge for the promoting of Physico-Mathematicall Experimental Learning. And because they had these frequent occasions of meeting with one another, it was proposed that some course might be thought of, to improve this meeting to a more regular way of debating things, and according to the manner in other countries, where there were voluntary associations of men in academies, for the advancement of various parts of learning, so they might do something here for the

promoting of experimentall philosophy.

In order to which, it was agreed that this Company would continue their weekly meeting on Wednesday, at 3 of the clock in term time, at Mr Rooke's chamber at Gresham Colledge; in the vacation, at Mr Ball's chamber in the Temple. And towards the defraying of occasionall expenses, every one should, at his first admission, pay downe ten shillings, and besides engage to pay one shilling weekly, whether present or absent, whilest he shall please to keep relation to this Company. At this meeting Dr Wilkins was appointed to the chaire, Mr Ball to be Treasurer, and Mr Croone, though absent, was named for Register.

Thus was the Society born. A week later it was further recorded that:

Sir Robert Moray brought in word from the Court, that the King had been acquainted with the designe of the Meeting. And he did well approve it, and would be ready to give encouragement to it.

On 15 July 1662 the Society received its first Charter, in which the King stated:

...we look with favour on all forms of learning but with particular grace we encourage philosophical studies, especially those which by actual experiments attempt either to shape out a new philosophy or to perfect the old.

And in respect of the Fellows:

...whose studies are to be applied to the further promoting by the authority of experiments the science of natural things and of useful arts to the glory of God, the creator, and the advantage of the human race.

In 1663, in a second Charter granting arms, the Society is given an extended title: The Royal Society of London for Improving Natural Knowledge. At the same time the Society adopted the motto "Nullius in Verba" from a work by Horace in which the full text implies that Fellows should not revere the words of any master. I myself interpret this as "Never believe anything you read or are told until it has been verified to your satisfaction". This is more satisfying than the

RAF's "*Per Ardua ad Astra*". In signing the Charter, the King declared himself Founder and Patron of the Society and presented the Society with a mace, a symbol since that time of the monarch and Founder.

Robert Hooke was appointed the first Curator of the Royal Society responsible for setting up the experiments, which were the centre pieces of the Society's meetings. Apart from these meetings the Society was anxious to disseminate scientific knowledge through the printed word and Henry Oldenburg was appointed Secretary in 1663 to correspond with scientists at home and abroad and arrange for the publication of the correspondence in the Philosophical Transactions, a series parallel to the Proceedings of the Royal Society, both of which continue today. Oldenburg was born in Bremen, and might be called a German, but he spoke several languages and epitomised the international nature of science and scientists. It got him into trouble and confinement in the Tower of London for two months in 1667 as a result of including in letters exchanged with scientists on the continent injudicious remarks about the conduct of the Anglo-Dutch war. Sir Robert Moray probably interceded with King Charles to get him released.

Other European scientists submitted their work to the Royal Society, Huygens, Malpighi, Leibnitz, Leeuwenhoek and many others. In 1698 Peter the Great of Russia came to Britain at the age of 25 to study ship building in the East India Company's shipyards at Deptford, lodging nearby at Sayes Court, a large house belonging to John Evelyn, then Secretary of the Royal Society. During his ten weeks stay the Czar asked to be introduced to a scientist interested in naval problems, and met Edmond Halley, who had done more than give his name to the comet, being interested in navigating and naval architecture, diving (in diving bells) and compasses, besides having close links with the East India Company. Peter and Halley got on very well together by all accounts, indulging in wild games at Sayes Court, reminiscent of the behaviour of RAF officers during dining-in nights. One game was to load each other in wheelbarrows and push them through Evelyn's prized holly hedges, doing great damage, as did dancing on polished tables in hob-nailed boots. The contact made may have influenced Peter to plan for an Imperial Academy of Science in St Petersburg, implemented in 1725 by his widow, Katherine I, originally a servant girl picked up during the Russo-Swedish war by Peter's friend Prince Menshikov, FRS and, as it were, passed on.

One could go on about these early Fellows at great length but they have been written up extensively by others.[1] There were 41 proposals for Fellowship at the first meeting of the Society on 28 November 1660 and of these 31 accepted invitations to join. They were not all what we would now describe as scientists. For instance John Evelyn who became Secretary of the Royal Society later, is better known as a diarist, as was Samuel Pepys, to be President in 1684. The important thing was to support the Society's aims expressed in the Charter. Some Fellows could help the Society financially, others politically. Most were polymaths with interests spilling over from one field to another. Robert Hooke was such a one, who invented many devices, developments of some of which (the Hooke universal joint) we still use today. Newton, admitted to the Fellowship in 1671 and elected President from 1703 to 1727, was, as it were, the booster rocket of the Society, taking it into orbit as the premier scientific organisation of its day, and today, many would argue.

In 1847 the criterion for election to the Fellowship became work of an original scientific nature and enthusiastic amateurs were largely excluded. Of course no science can be entirely original; one can only build on foundations laid beforehand by others often long since dead. But contributions to knowledge considered by existing Fellows to be of noteworthy originality became the measure. Thus the Fellowship became for the most part an exclusively professional scientific body. And so it has remained. Fellows may not apply to join; they must be proposed by at least seven existing FfRS and these proposals, accompanied by evidence of the candidate's work justifying the proposal, is considered by committees of FfRS in the candidate's and related fields. The number of FfRS elected each year has varied with the growth of science and the growth of the responsibilities of the Society, which is now called upon to advise Government on scientific matters, especially when these are in an international context, and to administer schemes for the encouragement of scientific endeavour where the Government prefers purely scientific criteria to be applied. Some schemes are funded by Government, some by the Royal Society from its own money, some jointly.

So here was I responsible under the Foreign Secretary of the Royal Society, and the Executive Secretary, Dr David Martin more directly, for many aspects of the Society's international affairs. On arrival at Burlington House I met David and agreed that initially I would be concerned with the Soviet Union and East European countries and their academies of science and delegations between them, usually FfRS on our side and Academicians on theirs. I would liaise with the science attachés in their embassies, with officials of the Cultural Relations Department of the FCO and with the British Council departments who would share responsibilities for visits in both directions. This led to a plethora of visits around London and lunches hosted by me or by my counterparts. All very enjoyable.

In conversations with Dr Martin he told me of some of his wartime experiences fire-watching on the roof of Burlington House, of incendiary bombs extinguished and stirrup pumps and buckets of water used to put out any small fires started. He told me of his confrontations with cranks, which had led to his having a button on his desk so that he might summon the doorman if he needed help. One such episode was when a visitor wishing to discuss a scientific problem had explained how he had learned how to fly and was about to launch himself through the open window into the courtyard until restrained by David and the doorman who had arrived in the nick of time.

David, later Sir David, had been a physical chemist, but when the opportunity arose between the wars, applied for the Secretaryship of the RS, a plum job for a young researcher interested in more than his own field. He and his wife were Scots, and associated with the Royal Society of Edinburgh, set up in 1783, later than the Royal Society of London, but in some senses a parallel body and with some Fellows in common. A condition for being Secretary of the Royal Society was that he, or she, although there had not been a female Secretary until March 2011, had to be a scientist. The Secretary also had to be in attendance at all Royal Society meetings, not only of the Governing Council but also of the innumerable meetings of committees set up by Council to consider special issues in each and every field of science. The Sectional Committees were particularly important because they were responsible for the vetting of candidates for Fellowship.

When I joined there were round about 100 different committees. I was responsible for servicing only three – on international relations. The number soon grew as other members of staff, until my arrival servicing committees concerned with less foreign aspects of international relations, asked me to take them over. Royal Society and Nuffield Foundation Commonwealth Bursaries for instance. These were bursaries awarded to promising young scientists whose research for periods of about a year in the laboratory of another Commonwealth country might benefit both visitor and host. I welcomed taking on more and more of these schemes involved with science abroad because they brought me into ever increasing contact with scientists and many others from every country in the world. This was work that some of my staff colleagues found distracting, whereas I loved it.

It was never a matter of sending cheques out to cover the expense of visitors. Outgoers had to be briefed on aspects of life abroad and they were always in and out of our offices. Incomers needed scientific programmes made in advance, possibly with several visits every day to different laboratories in different universities or other organisations, including firms and factories. This meant a lot of telephoning and telexing to negotiate aspects of the programme. When the visitor arrived he was usually met at the airport, escorted to his first hotel, accompanied to the Royal Society to be introduced to the Executive Secretary, and given his per diems, railway tickets and detailed programme. Throughout the visit we had to be on hand to deal with emergencies, modify the programme, arrange for interpreters where needed, fix medical care for visitors who needed it, and carry out a host of different tasks for which I and my staff were soon too few.

Needing someone else to help, my attention was somehow drawn to Tania Prigorowsky, whom I had first met while studying Russian in Paris. I discovered that her parents had died quite quickly one after the other, and that Tania had returned to London from Paris with a guilty feeling that she should have really returned home earlier to look after them in their later years. She was now working with Ladybird on the sale of children's clothes. This I thought was a waste of Tania's talent for languages (fluency in Russian, French, German, Polish and later Swedish) and for her ability to empathise with others whatever their origins. I got in touch with her and invited her to join me in my office at the the Royal Society. In those days it was unnecessary to advertise a competition for employment, as it became later. I could recruit whomsoever I wanted, providing the recruit met with the approval of the Executive Secretary. Dr Martin immediately took to Tania, who started work at once and took a lot of the weight off my shoulders.

Apart from the countries with whom we had agreements and arrangements for visits (including exchange visits) there were many others with whom Tommy Thompson wished to develop relations and still others where various individuals and organisations here and abroad thought we might help in their work or aspirations, even by a word here or a word there. The name of the Royal Society was sufficiently prestigious to transfer some prestige even to a completely unscientific fête. Once it was known that I was, as it were, in the Chair of the Royal Society department responsible for international relations, I was increasingly approached by those needing to strengthen a case for something – for photographs, for recommendations for Fellows who might be persuaded to give their names to some cause or objective, for written contributions to papers and journals, an infinity of aims and methods.

When I joined the RS staff, Tommy Thompson was interested to find out whether many British scientists visited continental west European colleagues and counterparts about research matters. He asked me to carry out a survey, entrusted largely to Nadia Slow, and we soon discovered that although there was some interchange, it was not nearly as extensive as one might expect between near neighbours. At Tommy's initiative we therefore developed the Royal Society European Programme to provide monies and encouragement (largely the same thing) to promote European scientific exchanges. This involved concluding agreements with the senior scientific bodies in all those west European countries. (Exchanges with east European communist countries had more in common with the USSR and were dealt with similarly).

The European Programme grew very quickly and it was agreed that Nadia would take charge of it and recruit her own staff for a separate (but closely related) office. She continued to service certain Russian visits until I was able to recruit more Russian speaking staff for my own office. This was often quite difficult. Some applicants, although with first class Honours degrees from reputable universities, knew a lot about Russian literature but were quite unable to carry on a conversation in Russian beyond conventional greetings. One applicant whose Russian was good enough turned out to be the wife of a Russian priest seeking to augment his meagre income. She had duties which would have conflicted with work at the RS and was turned down like so many others. My favourite way of recruiting was to ask an applicant to sit down in the office with the rest of my staff and just get on with the work on a temporary basis, answering the telephone, typing and duplicating programmes like their office mates. If this worked out to general satisfaction she (and they were usually shes), was asked to sign up for a permanent appointment. They often left after months or years to get better jobs at better pay, or to get married.

Linguistic ability was always important. For most visitors from the Soviet Union and eastern Europe we had to provide an interpreter and to get one from an outside agency cost a lot of money. So it was usually Tania, or I, or Beata Grabowski (a Polish girl I had recruited) who acted in this role, sometimes using Russian as a common language for eastern Europeans who had mostly learned Russian as a second language at school. An early visitor whom I helped in this way was Professor Petrusievitch, a Polish small rodent ecologist. He spoke no English but fluent Russian so I accompanied him for the best part of two weeks on visits to laboratories all over England, mostly in deep countryside, on moors, mountains (such as we have in the UK), wetlands and, of course, at various universities. I liked this sort of activity and the people involved.

The Society had long since outgrown the accommodation at Burlington House, in the East wing constructed specifically for its use between 1867 and 1873 after the Royal Academy of Arts had moved into Burlington House itself and while a West wing was being built for various other learned societies. The

Society moved in on 12 September 1873 with a staff of two (the Secretary and his secretary). After the Second World War, with the many tasks assumed by the Society or given it by the government, the staff soon grew to over 50, and from 1958 to considerably more, some of whom were moved to offices in Cornwall Terrace, Regents Park and elsewhere. This dispersion of staff was inconvenient and inefficient and, when it became clear that the Nash Terraces on the north side of the Mall would be renovated, the Society entered into discussion with the Treasury and the Ministry of Public Building and Works to see if 6, 7, 8 and 9 Carlton House Terrace could be rebuilt internally to provide a new home for the Society with enough room to house all the staff and provide for the many scientific meetings that were part of the Society's modus operandi. Answers were affirmative, the die cast, the architects briefed and work started, aiming for a completion date in 1967 with Her Majesty Queen Elizabeth II, the Society's Patron, formally to declare the premises open on 21 November.

*****

Quite a few books have been written about the Royal Society's rooms at 6-9 Carlton House Terrace (the postal address) and probably none better than the Society's own publications such as *The Royal Society at Carlton House Terrace* published by the Society in 1967, with an introduction by the then President (PRS), Professor (later Lord) P.M.S. Blackett.[2] He acknowledged that his predecessor, Lord Florey, played a much more prominent part in the organisation of the new home. Lord Florey was my first PRS, whom I had met at Burlington House. It was he and Professor Ernst Chain who developed penicillin from Fleming's original discovery. Lord Florey was an Australian, very casual and informal, as one would expect of Australians, friendly and modest, approachable by the likes of me, and easily identified in the street by his grubby cotton raincoat. A feature of most scientists that appealed to me was this lack of "side", a complete absence of assumed airs.

The Chairman of the Commonwealth Bursaries Committee, Sir Frank Engledow, was another such. He was a plant geneticist working on wheat and cereal crops initially, Director of the Agricultural Research Council Plant Breeding Institute in Cambridge (PBI). He was the nicest possible person to work with, and had enormous experience of developing countries, especially of the Commonwealth. He was another of the grubby mackintosh cohort, in his later years entering the RS Committee Room with his briefcase hanging from his neck by a length of binder twine. After his retirement from the PBI he was replaced as Chairman of the Commonwealth Bursaries Committee by another director of the same institute, Professor G.D.H. Bell, and later still by Sir Frank Reilly. All of these eminent scientists played an important part in providing India and other Commonwealth countries with more food for their growing populations, training and working with scientists from the countries concerned. They also advised me on problems in the garden – plants, weeds, trees, how to promote or kill them. The Director of the Nuffield Foundation was a member of my committee and I quickly got to know of the funds donated to science by such industry based Non-Governmental Organisations (NGOs).

The Leverhulme Trust and the Commonwealth Foundation were another two NGOs supporting some of the Society's schemes, in particular Overseas Visiting Professorships, where senior academics after retirement but still young enough to do useful work, could be supported financially in visits to developing countries for periods of four months or more to initiate and help with scientific research. There had to be an invitation from the university department to be visited, which had to pledge its own support of appropriate personal and work accommodation together with such equipment as might be needed for the research. The Royal Society paid the Professor a generous honorarium and first class international air fares for him and his wife, if accompanied. We arranged about half a dozen such Professorships each year and as they often took more than a year to arrange and more than another year to get reports completed and final accounts passed, we usually had the best part of two dozen Professorships on the go at any one time.

At Carlton House Terrace I was allotted an office on the first floor overlooking the Athenaeum (to which many FfRS belonged) and obliquely to Waterloo Place. The view through the large casement window behind my desk was delightfully rural thanks to the London plane trees. The locality suited me down to the ground because the London Library of which I was a member was close by in St James's Square. My office had a door into a large adjacent office (originally two rooms) where there was enough space for two (later three and then four) of my staff and their related paraphernalia, official and personal.

At home in Guildford, 4 Eastgate Gardens, we were now well established. However, the kitchen floor was in a state, with damp barely confined by cheap plastic sheeting. There were no decent carpets in the house, nor curtains and if we were to use the "playroom" over the garage something would have to be done about the unsightly wallpaper and the pine floor with splinters and protruding nails. One evening I decided to see how easily the wallpaper would come off. I prized up one corner and pulled and the paper and attached plaster weighing several hundred pounds came off the longest wall in a frightening crash amid clouds of dust. This needed immediate attention and the plasterer we engaged did a good job. At the same time I hired a sander, knocked in all the floor nails with a punch and hammer and then created a lot more dust sanding off the entire floor which we then covered partially with a Belgian made carpet square. The playroom was then used a great deal by Johnnie and Paul both for playing and for reading because the dining room and the lounge made less provision for children.

Curtains were bought from Heals and made up by them (I was still using my RAF terminal grant monies without much regard for frugality). For the kitchen floor we engaged builders who excavated the earth floor to an amazing depth of several feet, poured concrete into the cavity (it was a big long kitchen) and then finished the floor with large hexagonal heather brown tiles about 1" thick. When Mutti (Herta's mother) examined the tiles on a visit later, she thought the floor was the sort one might see in a castle. It was certainly very strong, physically and in appearance.

Most weekends we visited my father in Alton, either at home or in hospital. He was increasingly ill with kidney trouble. He knew both Johnnie and Paul as small children but I am sorry he did not know how well they developed and their later achievements. He would have been proud of them, and of Jo who as yet had not been born. Later in 1967 Dad's health went downhill quickly and he was taken to the Treloar General Hospital in Alton, where after a few days in increasing pain, he died on 12 October 1967. Earlier he had told me that he would be asking his doctor, Mr Haysom, to stop treatment in early October to allow him to die as close as possible to my mother's birthday – 10 October. In this one could say he succeeded. This was a very sad period for us all. In his will Dad left all his estate to be divided equally among his three children, my sister Mary, my brother Michael and myself. We were also named as executors of his will and in it he said specifically that if any one of us wanted to carry on living at Valverde, he, or she in the case of Mary, might buy it at probate value if the other siblings agreed.

Apart from my love for the home in which I had been brought up and the garden in which I had worked since childhood, there were other reasons favouring a move to Alton or further into the countryside. One factor was the restricted size of the garden in Eastgate Gardens, Guildford. Our two growing boys were for ever kicking and throwing footballs and suchlike into our neighbours' gardens and the Civic Centre car park at the back. We would have had to move somewhere with a larger garden quite soon and it seemed as if the longer commuting from Alton to my office in London would be worthwhile putting up with.

At the time my sister Mary and Titus and their children were living in their house at Rowledge, near Frensham Heights School which their children were attending. Michael and Pat and their children were in an Army married quarter in Cyprus. Herta and I had only just moved to our newly bought house in Guildford. None of us immediately thought of moving to Valverde and we put it on the market for £11,000, at the time a reasonable price for a property of that size in Kings Road. Meanwhile my father's remains had been cremated and interred next to Angio in the family grave in Alton cemetery. Jessie the housekeeper retired to live in a council house in Alton. Her nephew, the gardener, was still needed to maintain the large garden until Valverde was sold. In fact he said he could not help us; he had found alternative employment with a neighbour. Herta and I decided to do whatever we could to keep the garden and house in order pending sale. However it was sad for us to see the place deteriorating.

But no buyers came forward even when we reduced the price to £10,500. After a year we received an offer of £10,000. I let my brother and sister know of this and said that if they agreed, we ourselves would buy Valverde from the executors (us) for £11,000 and divide this between the three of us once creditors had been paid off. They agreed. There were quite a few debts, including a hefty one to Phillips, my father's old firm, the Alton builders' merchants. In the event we paid Mike and Mary £3,000 each, using money from the Halifax mortgage which I had transferred from our Guildford house recently sold very speedily to a Professor Laurence Martin returning from a post in the US to head the Department of War Studies in Kings College, London. He initially agreed to our asking price of £14,200. This was £3,200 more than we had paid for it in November 1965, but we had done a lot of work there, especially to the kitchen. The Professor's surveyors, after inspecting the house, especially the loft, where they scratched holes in the roofing felt beneath the tiles, reported that the house would need re-tiling and that the work should be done by us or the asking price greatly reduced. Within hours I told our agents to put the house back on the market at the original price. Within days the Professor's agents responded, agreeing to the original price, roof or no roof. Completion a.s.a.p. because the Professor had to take up his post in the autumn.

In June 1968 Herta was eight months pregnant with our third child. During my father's final illness I had thought a good cure for a soul departing would be another child, to be named Joseph (my confirmation name or Josephine, my mother's second name). On 3 July 1968 our third son, Jo, was born in Guildford, a month before we moved to Alton. We moved, with Johnnie and Paul, and Jo aged one month in the carry cot in the back of the VW Variant, to Alton through torrential rain and summer floods in August 1968.

Commuting to London turned out to be very tolerable. For one thing I always got a seat because Alton was the terminal and only about a dozen others commuted that far to London. I always had time to read the Times and much else and after a month or so I was able to write papers and edit books with such concentration that had Alton not been the terminus I would have been carried on further. I was very busy editing the proceedings of one of my first important tasks at the Royal Society. Following my arrival at the Royal Society in 1965 I had been asked to organise in 1967 the second Royal Society Conference of Commonwealth Scientists. The first had been in 1948. The aim was to acquire information as to the state of science in the Commonwealth countries to assist the framing of the international policies of the Society. All Commonwealth countries agreed to participate and to provide in advance background statements to be used for discussion. The Conference would last a week and Merton College Oxford agreed to provide the venue including accommodation for delegates and conference facilities. This was a big project and took up a lot of my time. To a large extent it was the brain child of Lord Blackett, then Professor PMS Blackett, who had taken over the Presidency of the Society when Lord Florey retired in November 1965. Professor Blackett was the eminent physicist and Nobel Prize Winner who had been Scientific Advisor to Coastal Command during the war and played an important part in the operations in which I was involved over the Atlantic and Mediterranean. Patrick Blackett had a great deal of experience of India and love for it.

Over the period of the Conference 7 to 11 April 1967 my staff and I moved into accommodation in Merton College to supervise all aspects of the Conference. There were 80 delegates from 19 Commonwealth countries including the UK, plus journalists and various other useful people. I hired a minivan to drive the staff, including Veronica, to Merton College with typewriters, a duplicator, copies of background statements and all the clobber associated with conferences including two tape recorders. In case our notes of dissertations missed out anything important I was determined to record everything everybody said. I had a small room at Merton to use as an office. The accommodation was fairly bleak. April 1967 was cold, rather like April 2008, and many of the College rooms were inadequately heated and without what they now call en suites. Some elderly scientists from warmer countries, including the venerable Indian Professor P.C. Mahalanobis FRS, had to cross the quadrangle early each morning to wash and shave, shivering in their dhotis.

Meals were all in Hall and very good and the other academic facilities splendid. The Merton College Library was admired by all. There was of course no nastiness but a great deal of common sense (a synonym for science). Many friendships were renewed and many more made. Tape recording what was said, especially the questions and answers, was very difficult because many delegates had accents making their English indecipherable and unintelligible. I spent much of the next year writing the Report on the Conference while commuting to Waterloo. The Report was printed and bound for the Royal Society by Staples of Rochester, whom I visited on several occasions to check progress. It was and remains a very fine volume, in blue cloth with the Society's shield in gold. The scientific contributors mostly achieved even greater distinction in their fields after 1967, some ennobled or decorated in other ways, some becoming household names at least in their home countries.

An interesting thing happened on New Year's Day 1968 while we were still at Guildford. We were at home and it was snowing. There was a telephone call from the assistant to Professor Harold Thompson in Oxford to say that he was away but a telephone call had been received from Academician M.M.Shemyakin in Moscow asking for help for his wife, who was dangerously ill in hospital in Moscow. The doctors looking after her urgently needed some equipment for her treatment. It had been ordered several weeks earlier from a firm in Lancing, Eschmann and Walsh Limited, then part of Glaxo. Would I be able to take the matter up on behalf of Professor Thompson. I tracked down the firm but assumed the staff would be away on New Year's Day. When I telephoned I was answered by a technician who was, by chance, stock-taking. He agreed to find the order and check if it could be fulfilled immediately. He phoned back after ten minutes to say that he had the equipment in front of him. It was ready to fly out if I could collect it and get it to an aircraft to Moscow. I asked the technician if he could drive it from the factory to a pub in Midhurst which we both knew and there await Herta who would drive there and bring it back to our house in Guildford.

I then telephoned the Soviet Scientific Attaché, Vladimir Ivanovich Kiryushin, at their Embassy and asked if he could drive to Guildford to collect the package and take it to Heathrow. When he arrived at home I would tell him to whom he should deliver the package at the airport. I telephoned British European Airways and spoke to an Operations Officer, impressing him with the urgency of the matter and reading to him the details of the equipment. He agreed to do the documentation there and then to save time. Both Vladimir Ivanovich and Herta with the packet arrived at Eastgate Gardens at the same time. I gave him the packet and instructions where to take it at Heathrow. After a coffee off he went. The packet was on the first flight to Moscow the following morning and was collected from the airport by a representative of Academician Shemyakin whom I had briefed. A week later we received the heartfelt thanks of Academician Shemyakin for "saving his wife's life". This cemented my friendship with Vladimir Ivanovich, but he returned to Moscow not long after and I never heard from him again. It should be noted that Tommy had studied chemistry in Germany and this had brought him into contact with Soviet chemists, amongst whom Professor (later Academician) Shemyakin, later Director of the Institute for the Chemistry of Natural Products was a leading light.

Lord Blackett, as he soon became, played a leading part in the Conference of Commonwealth Scientists. Subsequently he decided to encourage an Indian scientific institution to become the Indian counterpart of the Royal Society, out of a number choosing the Indian National Science Academy (INSA), which soon adopted many RS methods and produced a Year Book the format, binding and even colour of which was copied from the Year Book of the Royal Society. Not long afterwards the Society concluded an agreement with INSA providing for visits by senior scientists and research workers much on the lines of our agreements with the Soviet, Chinese and Polish academies of science. I used these early models to draft others, refining the texts and changing content to suit the individual countries. By 1970 countries' scientific academies were practically queuing up to conclude agreements on scientific collaboration with the Royal Society.

Dr Martin, the Executive Secretary, was not at all keen to let staff travel abroad even if it could be argued that this would benefit the Society. Either he, or the Deputy Executive Secretary, Dr Keay, might travel singly or with delegations to discuss agreements with scientific counterparts abroad, but not other members of staff. The trouble was that neither Dr Martin nor Dr Keay kept detailed accounts of what they had done or discussed which made it difficult for us to follow up. In 1968, following the ousting of Dr Nkrumah from Ghana, and its adoption of a version of democracy, the Royal Society was asked to send a group of FfRS to Accra to advise on the restructuring of the Ghanaian Academy of Sciences, which had previously been organised on Soviet lines. A group led by Sir John Cockcroft, first went out to advise on the organisation of the Academy, and he and other scientists also examined the Ghanaian nuclear facility, partly constructed under Soviet auspices. Sir John was asked if another group could later be sent to advise on Academy institutes, and how their research might best be directed.

After discussion as to the aim of the second group, Professor (later Sir) James

Beament (Cambridge, applied biology) was invited to lead a group to visit Ghana in February 1969. Accompanying him would be Dr Ray Millard (Deputy Director of the Road Research Laboratory) and a Forest Products expert would join the group from Nigeria. To look after the delegation and keep a record of their advice and the Ghanaian responses I was sent with them. Jimmie Beament told me that were he to fall ill I should prevent him from being given penicillin to which he was allergic. He had numerous other ailments on which he briefed me.

We spent a week in Accra and Kumasi visiting the Ghanaian institutes of Standards, Building and Roads Research, Cocoa Research, Forest Products Research and Aquatic Biology. Because some research was conducted by the universities of Accra and Kumasi, we also made visits there and to their controlling ministries. I kept comprehensive notes and wrote the report later. I made a very good friend in Letitia Obeng, director of the Institute of Aquatic Biology, and together we made a boat trip on Lake Volta, still building up behind the great dam built on the river. One object was to catch tsetse flies, which I did in a jam jar, while Letty sheltered in the cabin. River blindness was spreading to new areas close to the lake as the fly carrying the disease, *Simulium damnosum* adapted to the new habitat.

For looking at the cocoa plantations I borrowed a horse. There were troubles with various cocoa diseases and with the consumption of chocolate in the world, with on-going research into these aspects. Generally the group of specialists found little wrong with the direction of research, except that, as in the USSR, leading researchers were in the institutes with insufficient contact with university students. Professor Beament had as a hobby in Cambridge the making of stringed instruments and research into their principles. From the Forest Products Research Institute he was able to obtain some pieces of wood similar to ebony to try out as bridges. Later Letty Obeng was recruited by the UN Development Programme to work from Nairobi and her daughter, also Letitia, whom I helped with part of her education in the UK, later became Secretary to the Director of the World Bank. I also helped Letty senior with many other problems, such as spare parts for her car. I liked to keep up with most of the scientists I met because they were such nice people. My usefulness in managing the delegation to Ghana played a part in changing David Martin's reluctance to let me go on further travels where it was clear I could help.

My visit to Ghana led me to meet Ghanaians interested in developing contacts they had made with various British concerns in a variety of fields on the applied side of science. These included Edward Bals, originally Hungarian I believe, but then living in Herefordshire, who had invented and developed an ultra low dosage sprayer for use mostly in developing countries where sophisticated machinery was a liability. The handheld sprayer consisted of a plastic tube about 4' long, containing a number of torch batteries. These drove a rotating plastic toothed disc mounted at an angle on one end of the tube. The herbicide or pesticide, suspended in thin oil, was held in a reservoir in or on the tube, and fed through a small diameter pipe to the eye of the disc and thence spread by centrifugal force to the circumference of the rotating disc and to the teeth cut into it. The size, shape and number of the teeth, and the speed of the disc's rotation controlled the droplet size of the spray produced. The viscosity of the oil and the toxicity of the active agent were also factors. Edward had worked all these out and related them to the droplet size necessary to deposit drops of the active agent close enough together to kill an insect of a specific size (another factor) landing on any leaf of a plant being sprayed.

We tried this out by using spray droplets visible under ultraviolet light. I was convinced and visited Edward at his home near Hereford. Edward was a large man, about 6'7" in height and broad in proportion and he had two children who seemed likely to be on the same scale. I sent a sample sprayer to Letty Obeng in Ghana to investigate its potential usefulness there, and, as far as I could, I publicised Edward and his sprayers wherever I could see a use for them. In fact he sold many of the sprayers, and later tractor mounted versions for use in cotton plantations in Africa. His firm, Micron Sprayers, still operates from Bromyard, Herefordshire and in 2014 was run by his son Tom Bals.

I was also interested in sintered bauxite. Bauxite is defined in the dictionary as an earthy mineral containing alumina, the chief commercial source of aluminium. To use some of the electricity generated by the dam at Lake Volta large aluminium smelters had been constructed and aluminium was already being exported. Much of the bauxite came from Canada. I had learnt from Dr Ray Millard, Deputy Director of the Transport and Road Research Laboratory at Crowthorne, and a fellow member of the RS delegation to Ghana, where he was advising on laterite roads, that sintered bauxite was an inexpensive and superior anti-skid road surface for use at traffic lights and road junctions, much superior to granite chips. Later I corresponded with Ghanaians about this potential export of surplus bauxite. Ray Millard and his wife lived in Odiham, five miles from Alton, and Herta and I visited them there and they visited us and we became good friends.

Furthermore a Ghanaian plant had been discovered that might provide a superior stabiliser for salad cream, cosmetics, etc., to prevent the aqueous and greasy components separating. I was able to put people in touch with each other and hopefully generate something useful.

Notes:

1. A good book to start with is *The Royal Society, Its Origins and Founders* edited by Sir Harold Hartley, GCVO, CBE, MC, FRS. The Royal Society 1960. All the scientists mentioned and many FfRS since have biographies on the internet. As a matter of course, deceased Fellows have Biographical Memoirs written about them by other Fellows at the invitation of the Council of the Royal Society.

2. *The Royal Society at Carlton House Terrace* 1967

Extramural

The Royal Society salary scales were as far as possible based on university salaries, with the Executive Secretary paid as a University Professor and Head of Department, and other senior staff such as I, and most of my colleagues, as Readers, with the addition of a London Allowance. This added up to what was quite a lot in those days and I met many a Fellow of the Royal Society who would have liked my salary.

However, living so far from London, commuting was expensive even in those days and we had our boys in Mayfield School, a private primary school in Alton, with at that time a good headmaster, Mr Bickerstaffe. Johnnie and Paul were doing well and we did not wish to transfer them to a state primary school. We also liked to go to Cornwall or abroad to Italy or Austria, or if possible to all of those places for some weeks every year, usually over the school summer holidays. Also, after moving from Guildford we were extending Valverde, our house in Alton so as to give us more room, with an extra bedroom and modifications to the kitchen and bathroom. Halifax gave us an increased mortgage but we did not want to increase our indebtedness to them too much. Some adjustments to our lifestyle seemed necessary

I, and some other senior staff at the RS were often getting at the Executive Secretary asking for the link between our salary scales and that of the universities to be changed. The work was completely different. For instance I had a colleague, one of whose major tasks was concerned with the administration of the coral atoll of Aldabra, part of the Seychelles group in the Indian Ocean. The atoll was primarily for research into the unique habitat, flora and fauna, and from 1976 the RS had a 14 year lease and was responsible for organising the research staff on the island, their transport and provisioning. My colleague's post at the RS bore little resemblance to any university post. He was not alone. In fact, later the RS salary scale was slowly amended as it became more difficult to recruit personnel at university rates. Miserliness was reflected throughout all staff levels at the RS. Sir David, being Scottish, looked after the pennies. However, I loved the work and that made up for paucity of pay, although I used to say that we had to be able to afford to work at the Royal Society.

In 1968 I was still studying Russian externally with London University, intending to get a degree. However, when it came to a decision whether to attend lectures on Old Church Slavonic and Old Russian texts, I decided that as I was now occupying a position in a premier academic institution, and there could be no institution more academic than the Royal Society, there was little point in pursuing a university degree especially as a knowledge of Church Slavonic would be fairly useless. That was the end of that. However, in a different area I enlarged my horizons. The new Royal Society rooms in Carlton House Terrace were quite close to the Royal Automobile Club in Pall Mall, which I discovered had a magnificent swimming pool, Greek in its architectural style. Mr Norman, my colleague who looked after the Council of the Royal Society, was a member and I got him to propose me for membership. As a seconder I signed up a member of the FCO. Thenceforth I was able to be swimming in the pool within a few minutes of leaving my office. I could take guests and sometimes took all my office staff for a swim, telling the telephone exchange to say, if anyone were to ask, that we were at a meeting with the British Council, also close by in Spring Gardens. The Hall Porter may have noticed that my girls' hair was damp when we trooped back into the Society after an hour, but no questions were ever asked.

Apart from my membership of the RAC and the RAF Club, both of which Herta and I used for various functions when either or both of us had to be in London, I benefited from the clubs of others. Fellows of the Royal Society often belonged, with bishops and other high academics, to the Athenaeum, which was opposite the Royal Society in Carlton House Terrace. I could see into its rooms from my office window to an extent that I could have exchanged hand signals with Fellows (or bishops) having lunch. It was an expensive club and I had no intention of joining, but the Executive Secretary and Fellows who were members sometimes entertained me there, although the food was not very good. It was far better at the Travellers' Club round the corner in Pall Mall, patronised by many British ambassadors and senior FCO staff. The Director of the Great Britain-East Europe Centre, Sir William Harpham, was a member and often gave me lunch there. He had made me a member of the Governing Body of the GB-EE Centre and so we usually had a lot to talk about.

AD ULTIMO

The aim of the GB-EE Centre was to promote and sponsor visits to and from the east European countries, mainly in the humanities, economics, history, law, literature and art, the list was extensive and extendable. As often as not visitors came (and went) in groups, often to discuss a particular problem in their common fields. The other members of the Governing Body were very interesting people, including George Robertson, MP and later Minister in one or other labour government, and University Professors in various relevant fields. We met about once a month at the Centre's offices near Harrods in Knightsbridge, but I most enjoyed lunches with Sir William at the Travellers'. The grilled whole Dover Sole were unequalled. Sir William had served in Czechoslovakia and the Soviet Union, speaking Czech and Russian, later becoming Ambassador in Prague, these appointments being interspersed with diplomatic appointments in the FCO and the USA. He was immeasurably kind and modest as well as very well-informed about international affairs, and art and music.

*****

Sir William did me a valuable service related to beds. At RAF Tern Hill, when Johnnie and Paul graduated from cots, they had slept on metal beds, with rounded ends and comparatively cheap mattresses, purchased from Harrods at the same time as we had bought our own super king-sized double from Heals. We wanted to replace the children's beds because the chain metal mattress supports were tearing the mattresses and bedding. I had the idea of buying proper wooden beds from Heals but was surprised to find how much good beds would cost. So I designed my own and had a prototype made by Mr Chandler, the carpenter/joiner working for Mylwards, Alton builders, who were about to extend our kitchen and add an extra bedroom above. Mr Chandler later made us quite a few kitchen cabinets and built-in wardrobes for the bedrooms. He was a wonderful craftsman. The bed frame was of solid beech with finger joints at the four corners. I had wanted dovetail joints but Mr Chandler had no access to a machine that could cut them, whereas the finger joints were more straightforward.

The legs were a different matter. I had it in mind to have the bed height adjustable to cater for children, lower down in case they might fall out, or higher for housewives not wishing to bend down so far while making the bed. This could be achieved by having easily mountable and demountable legs cut to give the required mattress height. I deduced that a "w" shaped laminated leg with flat instead of pointed lower corners to the "w", and of the width of a ski might do the trick, with the upper arms of the "w" cut to give the height required. How these might be made involved some inquiries. I managed to identify and locate one of the craftsmen who had worked on the laminated structure of the De Havilland Mosquito during the war. Mr A.E.H. Reeves now ran his own firm, Laminated Shapes Ltd. in Horsham. He was very busy with his own products, many exported, and at the time was making some laminated counter furniture for a bank. Although uninterested in producing bed legs, he did let me have a surplus shape, or shell, which could be cut into a "u" rather than a "w" shape. I took this home and cut it to form the first set of legs for the Nature bed, as we decided to call it.

Mr Reeves was useful in that he recommended another firm, Wood Engineering Limited of Billericay. They were interested but referred me in the first place to the owner of their firm, John de Savary, a rich entrepreneur living in the West Country with, among other enterprises, a factory in Dorset manufacturing whitewood furniture as it was then called: down-market cheapo furniture and fittings that appealed to the many penurious Brits of those days. Now they would be IKEA rejects. I needed to speak to Mr de Savary because to make the "w-form" bed legs, Wood Engineering Limited would need to make a mould to heat-press the beech laminates. They would be produced in a "shell", each to be cut longitudinally into half a dozen ski legs. The mould would cost £250 but would last for many pressings. I aimed to get the mould made for nothing. This involved talking to Mr de Savary for the best part of two hours. His office was in the upper half of a corrugated iron outhouse. Two of his Rolls Royces were parked nearby under a corrugated iron awning.

We got on very well. He was interested in my sons and I in his, especially his son Peter, who in his early twenties already owned a fuel tanker shipping Indonesian oil to South Africa, at that time blockaded because of its apartheid policies. Later on Peter de Savary bought up part of Land's End in Cornwall and competed in the America Cup with his own yacht, becoming a media if not a household name. His father told me how he had started off on his first fortune during WW2 when, because he suffered from asthma, he was excused from serving in the Armed Forces. Instead he worked for Lord Beaverbrook in aircraft production, and more particularly for the Ministry in charge of airfield construction. It was his job to survey suitable sites and prepare them for the construction of runways, etc. This often involved the removal of large trees, which, being mostly in hedgerows, belonged to County Councils who had no idea of their worth, nor had even any thought of it. The trees were profitably disposed of by Mr de Savary, and were his foundation in business, as it were. Whitewood furniture was in a way an extension of this early work. Anyway he agreed that the mould might be made, with me to repay the cost when I had made some money out of the Nature bed.

The first sets of legs were not entirely satisfactory. Some of them came out of the hot press twisted and warped to an extent that they would not remain in the frame slots. I contacted numerous organisations whom one might have thought would have researched the resilience of thin laminated wood structures: ski manufacturers for instance. But nobody knew whether such structures under stress would take on a set, or would return to normal after flexion over time. So I had to guess whether my Skilam legs, made of 15 x 1mm or 10 x 1.5mm thick beech plies, would retain or lose their springiness. 10% of the latter plies lost it in some degree and the former were even worse. I consulted the makers of the adhesive used to cement the plies together, Ciba-Geigy, and they agreed with the advice of another FRS friend of mine, Professor J.S. Harley of the Commonwealth Forestry Institute in Oxford. Both thought that the fibres of thicker plies might stiffen up the resistance of the legs to warp and set, and this turned out to be so. Thereafter the legs were pressed from eight 2mm plies. Even in the beds we have been using at home for more than 30 years the legs are still retained in their slots without glueing, screwing or any other inconvenience. I had the idea for the legs while I was having a bath at home, got out and sketched it before I forgot. I later patented it, being helped by an Inspector at the Patents Office in making my application in the appropriate gobbledygook. To obtain the provisional patent was inexpensive, but the full patent awarded after about a year was more expensive and the cost of renewals increased each year.

There was less trouble over the frames. These were initially made by a firm in Downham – Essex Specialised Joinery – recommended by the manager of Wood Engineering. The two firms' workshops were close together and I could visit them consecutively, which was convenient because I could not spare many days from my work at the Royal Society. Two prototypes were made for me by these two firms and I collected them on the roof rack of our VW Variant. These were originally supposed to be the two beds for Johnnie and Paul but I had decided that there was such a paucity of well-made beds that they might be welcomed elsewhere. My father was still alive at that time and in a private ward in Treloar's Hospital in Alton and while visiting him one afternoon I was asked by his Consultant to leave them alone together for ten minutes while he carried out an examination. The door of the neighbouring ward was open and I saw an old friend of mine in bed there. She invited me in and disclosed she had a slipped disc which was being treated. I told her of the advantages of a firm bed and of the one I had designed. She had another visitor at the time, who was introduced as Terence Conran's mother. She said she would mention my design to her son. Not long afterwards I was contacted by Terence who asked me for details of the bed, and then to take a prototype to the Conran base in Wallingford, to be examined for possible manufacture and sale by Habitat, the Conran store. This initiative came to nothing because Habitat took up a much cheaper design, a mattress on the floor, which they thought would appeal to their less discriminating customers.

*****

This is where Sir William Harpham helped. One day at lunch at the Travellers Club he confided that Lady Harpham was confined to bed with a bad back. I told him about the Nature bed and its suitability for those suffering from back pain. I gave him a copy of a leaflet I had drafted. A day or two later he telephoned to say that he had shown the leaflet to Sir Paul Reilly the Director of the Design Centre in the Haymarket. I then had a call from Sir Paul asking if I could bring a Nature bed to the Centre for consideration by his committee choosing products for promotion and display. We stuck one of the two prototypes on the Variant roof rack and dropped it off at the Design Centre tradesmen's entrance. On 21 September 1976 the bed was on display in the Design Centre window, having been accepted for the Design Index the previous week. Within days we were receiving orders! Conscious that selection for the Design Index had a condition that the product must be in production, I hastily ordered a batch of 20 beds and the legs for them.

Selection by the Design Centre and the option of using its logo meant that for the next ten or more years we had a great many inquiries and quite a few orders; we sold about 800 until I retired from the Society on my 65th birthday and got out of beds as one might say. I had learnt a lot, certainly that anyone can do anything if one tries hard enough. Also, that success may not be worth the aggravation, because to have an enterprise succeed means undivided dedication to the project. Spreading oneself between several projects must be to the detriment of one or other. I did as much as I could afford with Nature beds, but there were so many complications. The beds needed mattresses; eventually Dunlopillo agreed that I might sell their Firmrest mattresses to purchasers of Nature beds. They delivered direct and we received 30% of the price charged which increased our profits considerably.

There were often production difficulties and although the frames and legs were delivered to us in Alton in batches, Herta and I had to cut and finish the legs to give the required bed heights and pack and deliver them safely. When purchasers could be reached by road from Alton in up to four hours, we usually delivered them ourselves at weekends using our car. Further afield we had to use rail or carrier, which brought even more problems of damaged beds needing replacement, or of beds ending up at the wrong destinations. The people we met along the way were quite extraordinary. It was very rewarding and sometimes had a funny side. On one occasion a couple walked up the drive at home when we were working in the garden and asked with some puzzlement where the factory was. A gay headmaster and his partner came to investigate the bed for themselves. We left them in a bedroom for a while to bounce about. Delivering two beds stacked one above the other on the Variant roof-rack to a vicarage in Dorset, we thought it too much trouble to sheet them up because no rain was forecast. However it was a cold winter day and hoarfrost coated the bed frames with glistening crystals which had to be cleaned off a few minutes before offloading at the parson's. We sold and delivered two beds for the use of a hotel proprietor in St James's Street, quite close to my office at the Royal Society. Herta and I always went together on deliveries.

Publicity was no problem. I used to invite journalists concerned with consumer goods to visit me at the Royal Society for lunch and a tour of the building, after which they could examine the bed in my office, where I had a bed disguised as a couch/table on which I could leave Royal Society committee papers when I did not have bed visitors. Journalists were very receptive to this treatment, being dazzled by the Society's image, and finding the bed pleasing and efficient. And if they needed confirmation, it was available at the Design Centre only 200m away. Helen Lawson of The Lady published a highly favourable two page critique of the bed. Ideal Home and numerous other publications followed, including the Back Pain Association in whose journal the bed was featured. As a result of one or other of these write-ups I was invited to let the BBC TV Tomorrow's World team have a bed, which they collected and demonstrated for about ten minutes one evening, showing its convenience, light weight and efficiency, and culminating when the presenter easily carried it off-stage on one arm.

But overall the bed business caused us a lot of aggravation and we did not make much money out of it. I established a 30% mark-up over cost price added to by a similar percentage on the mattresses. But it was not worth having the house always cluttered with beds. However, more than 20 years after we ceased 'production', we continued to get inquiries from satisfied customers who wanted to order beds for their children and grandchildren. When we gave up we offered the design to other firms who might have wished to benefit from such a proven design, but nobody wanted it. It is more profitable to mass produce and market short-lived rubbish than quality products.

Half way through the 'production run' of Nature beds, we happened to visit Dartington Hall in Devon and discovered that when the original Hall was reconstructed from its medieval state in the 1920s, the Elmhirsts had set up a joinery to do all the woodwork. This workshop was still in existence as Staverton Joinery, fitting out yachts and making a small range of furniture in English hardwoods, usually oak. The workmanship was very good and I proposed to the Manager that he take on the manufacture of the Nature bed frames. They produced these to a much better quality than Wood Engineering Limited, for whom the writing was already on the wall. Staverton made the frames (with dovetail joints) for us until we stopped production in 1987.

*****

A good source of extra income turned out to be Evgenia Borisovna Gourvitch of Rainham Timber Engineering (see Chapter Moscow 1954). RTE produced laminated timber beams on an industrial scale. I invited Evgenia to lunch at the Society and we agreed that the RTE laminates had little relevance to Skilam legs. RTE made laminated beams a foot thick or more, for modern buildings, where, in fact, laminated wood posed less of a fire threat than steel. The wood might char, but steel would expand and bring down the structure in which they were incorporated. However, Evgenia revealed that she was writing a book on Vladimir Soloviev (1853-1900), the Russian poet and philosopher, and his relationship to Rudolf Steiner and Anthroposophism. This had always been one of Evgenia's obsessions. And now she wanted to put down her thoughts before her death, which she thought was approaching, as it was. She was writing in Russian because despite most of a life spent in England, her written English was not good. Soloviev was said by Evgenia to be the first true Russian philosopher. He wrote a great deal of poetry, some very good, and he is said to have inspired the style of Andrei Bely (1880-1934) and Alexander Blok (1880-1921). Both of them could be said to be Russian Symbolists, the former being the leader of the Russian Symbolist Movement and a follower of Rudolf Steiner and Anthroposophism. Blok was similarly inclined and a very fine poet. They both wrote in Russian of course, as did Soloviev (and Evgenia).

Evgenia's book was highly abstruse with references to all sorts of other savants and their theories. Soloviev too was a good poet but his philosophical ideas were full of nebulous impressions with nothing definite. Had Isaiah Berlin had enough hair he would have torn it out. Translating Soloviev's poetry was a challenge because poetry is never translatable from the language in which it is originally written. In translation one necessarily loses all the connotations and nuances of the original. In translating poetry one has to study the original meaning in depth and then compose a new poem which is the closest possible parallel. One of his poems I particularly liked was entitled "Three Meetings", the meetings being visions he had had, the first as a child; the second in the British Museum (shades of Marx!); the third in the Egyptian desert not far from the Great Pyramid (where he got lost). His visions were of Sophia, goddess of wisdom, or rather revelations of the unity of all things, animate and inanimate, and the elegance of that concept. This is what I have always thought (but with no visions so far!). His poems speaking of nature in Russia are very evocative, especially of snow and cold. Russian poetry is almost as rich a field as Russian music. I love it.

I enjoyed my work for Evgenia, carried out usually in the commuter trains between Alton and Waterloo. I had to visit her in her home in Highgate quite often to collect texts and deliver translations. As often as not she had completely re-written earlier texts, which I had to re-translate. The job took years, because I had other work to do, but Evgenia was always in a hurry because of her assumed impending death. She was looked after at home by a housekeeper cum companion, Mary Trueman, who to some extent shared Evgenia's philosophy. In a sense she was Evgenia's literary executor and as a beneficiary of her will knew that it specified that money should be spent on the publication of her book in Russian, English and German. This eventually came about. A German version was published possibly because of Evgenia's support for a German, a Dr Ernst, who had set up a splinter group of Anthroposophy with a few students at a school in Switzerland supported by Evgenia. Funnily enough the English version was published in 1992 without my knowledge. Our son Jo in Australia found it was available from Amazon and I ordered a copy at much reduced price, probably remaindered.[1] I have not been able to get hold of the version in Russian.

Evgenia's brother, Alexander, gave me her last Russian texts a matter of days before her death in the late 70s. After that I kept in touch with him, Managing Director of Phoenix Timber, the large timber importing business started by his father. It was named Phoenix because it was regarded as a rebirth of their business in Latvia, from where the Gourvitchs had taken refuge in England after the Russian Revolution. It was only a few years before Sasha, as Evgenia called him, also died. He had invited me to take whatever books I might like from his very fine library, but I thought this inappropriate while he was still alive. Shortly after his death I asked his wife if I could collect some of the books earmarked for me, but she explained that Gourvitch relatives had turned up from Russia with a van and removed all the books together with some of Sasha's splendid paintings including original impressionists. Jackals she called these relatives. Evgenia had paid me handsomely for translating her book into English. I considered the work worthwhile, because I learned a lot, improved my Russian and met quite a few interesting people I might not otherwise have met.

*****

In about 1980 I was walking from the London Library in St James's Square back to my office and passed Fischer Fine Art, a gallery in King Street. They always had one or two articles of good antique furniture on show among the paintings and something provoked me to enter and go downstairs. Against the wall stood an ingenious drop leaf desk in solid oak by a Canadian or American craftsman of the 1900s. It was labelled to show a very substantial cost, over £1000, several months' salary for me. The drop leaf hinges were rusted through and I thought that with some design changes we could produce a similar desk for a tenth of the price. I invited the Manager of Staverton Joinery to lunch at the Society and afterwards we walked to Fischer Fine Art and examined the desk more closely. He agreed to see what he could do if I would get the exact measurements and if possible a photo. I managed this surreptitiously the following week and then redesigned the way in which the drop leaf hinged so that it would be removable, and sent drawings to Staverton.

They made me a splendid prototype in a fortnight, to be priced at £125 ea. And to be named the Chalet drop leaf desk. We still have it. We did not produce it in quantity because Staverton would only produce in batches of 25, for which I would have to pay in advance, and what with beds we already had enough on our plate. I also designed some ingenious wall-mounted headboards, based on the metal adjustable headboards on the King's Fund Hospital beds. These too we have for ourselves but did not produce. I had made my point that anyone could do anything, or at least, I could. These were not the limits of my forays into furniture design. Much earlier, when we moved to Guildford from Yeovil, I had designed our dining room table, a dresser and bookcases out of solid oak, but these I had made for us by David Rutherford and Alan Peters who had worked for Edward Barnsley and Gordon Russell, both Arts and Craft furniture designers and makers.

*****

AD ULTIMO

Among our assets we had several South Arabian artefacts I had picked up in Timnah (see Chapter "Aden"). On some of my visits to London, my sister Mary's husband, Titus, had introduced me to the proprietors of the various art galleries in Cork Street and thereabouts from whom he had bought paintings in earlier days, when he had money to spare, and when the paintings of many emerging artists adopted by the galleries could still be purchased for comparatively little. One of these was the Gimpel Fils Gallery where I met some of the Gimpel family, Peter, Charles and Kay, who owned the enterprise and worked there. Peter Gimpel had been very interested for some time in South Arabian sculpture dating from the Qatabanian and Himyaritic civilisations of about the time of Christ, several hundred years before and after. He was planning an exhibition of South Arabian sculpture and needed someone to help with the catalogue. Titus had told him of my experience and Peter asked me to write a sort of keynote historical introduction to the catalogue. This I was delighted to do. We had nearly had a catastrophe with a bronze bull's head, when a daily do, who came once a week to help clean our house in Alton -Valverde, reported one day to Herta that she had accidentally knocked our "old door knocker" off the bookcase in the living room and it was broken. The old door knocker was the bull's head, a piece of bronze cladding of an altar at Timnah. A corner of the cladding had indeed broken off, but fortunately leaving the head intact. This episode made us think whether we should treat home as a museum, where other valuables might be damaged by children or careless adults, or whether it might not be better to find them homes in places of academic study and appreciation where they would be safe.

I decided to put two South Arabian artefacts into Peter Gimpel's exhibition. Apart from the bronze bull's head there was the much larger bull's head funerary plaque, with the deceased man's name Zabiy Sabah in Qatabanian on the plinth, the first word being his given name and the second his clan name, with the bull's head carved above it out of the same piece of alabaster. Professor Jacques Ryskmans of Louvain University, an expert in South Arabian archaeology, had sent me his views about the plaque on 7 January 1969 suggesting that Zabiy had died on a date around the beginning of the Christian era. After translating the name he commented:

> *Bull heads appear frequently in South Arabian art on stelae with inscription, altars, coin and – as in your plaque – on funerary monuments. They have a double symbolism: the bull personifies of course the idea of fertility (in the soil, the animals and humans). But the form of the horns evokes a crescent moon. In Timna, which was the*

capital of the Qatabanian Kingdom, the Moon God (and the national God) was Amm. But in the other kingdoms also, where the Moon God had other names, he was personified by a bull. The bull head is thus a symbol of the Moon God as a fertility divinity. To my knowledge the cult of the bull was not known in the Higaz before Muhammad. But traces of an older cult of the cow are found in much older rock engravings from the south of Higaz which were revealed by our expedition with Philby in 1951.

My introduction to the exhibition catalogue was entitled "God's Land" and in it I wrote that Kaspar, Melchior and Balthazar may well have been the sheikhs of tribes with the right to carry goods along the Incense Road, and their gifts to the infant Christ taken from their stock in trade – gold, frankincense and myrrh.

The exhibition at the Gimpel Fils Gallery ran throughout December 1970 and January 1971 and some artefacts were sold, although Peter Gimpel did not particularly wish to sell any. And neither did the many people who had contributed exhibits, including Andrew Fuller, my colleague and friend from Aden. However, as a result I received several "offers" and deduced that the larger piece might fetch £500 or more and the smaller slightly less. I approached several American museums including the Boston Museum of Fine Arts, which after exchanges of correspondence, sent one of their staff who was visiting Europe to have a look at Zabiy. They agreed to pay me $2000, say £800, which I thought good enough. They wanted the smaller bronze as well but in the meantime Sir Mortimer Wheeler had asked for it for the British Museum so I sold it to them for £300. Sir Mortimer was unique in being a Fellow of the British Academy and a Fellow of the Royal Society and highly decorated for his services to the nation and to archaeology, especially his excavations of Maiden Castle near Dorchester. He was elected FRS in 1968 and toured the offices including mine where I met him. Our two South Arabian artefacts found good homes and we visited Boston and its splendid museum in June 2007 to see our piece prominently on display.

*****

In the late 60s the motorway network in the UK was powering ahead. Much attention was given by the media to the junction of the M5 and M6 and other major roads north of Birmingham, popularly known as Spaghetti Junction because of the complexity of the underpasses and overpasses which cover some

80 acres. I saw an article in the Times mentioning that A. Monk and Co. Ltd., one of the contractors for the section of the junction between Perry Bar and Gravelly Hill, was desperately short of steel reinforcing bar for concrete sections. 50000 tons were required.

At the time I was on good terms with all the east European scientific attachés in their various embassies. It occurred to me that Yugoslavia might be able to provide steel reinforcing bar. The Yugoslavian science attaché doubled up for trade and soon confirmed that Yugoslav industry would certainly be interested in selling reinforcing bar to A. Monk.

I contacted Monks who expressed interest, provided the bar was up to the British Standard (BS). One of our FfRS, Mr Feilden (an iron and steel specialist) was director of the British Standards Institute and arranged for me to have a copy of the BS. I passed a copy to the Yugoslav Embassy but then discovered from other sources that the Yugoslavs would be purchasing the bar from Romania. I therefore transferred my attention to the Romanian science attaché who put me in touch with his commercial colleague. From him I obtained copies of the Romanian standards for reinforcing bar which turned out to be a combination of the Soviet and West German standards, written in Romanian. I purchased a technical Romanian-English dictionary and translated the standard into English – about ten A4 pages. Difficult, but Romanian is a bit like Italian and Latin. A. Monk approved the standards but asked that I obtain 20 samples of bar from Romania so that they could be physically examined and given a bending test at Manchester University, where the engineering department had the necessary equipment. After several weeks the bars arrived, 20 one metre lengths of bar of different thicknesses, which weighed a great deal. I got them to A. Monk's representative in London and waited. They failed the test, fracturing when bent to a certain radius. Oh well.

*****

Some time in 1968 I was cutting through the side streets between Lower Regent Street and Leicester Square, when I noticed a brightly painted craft of some sort behind the plate glass window of a building. I discovered this was Ontario House, at that time concerned I suppose with British trade with Ontario. Usually their window was not particularly interesting but this small beetle-shaped vehicle attracted my attention. All the lights were on in the room behind and I stepped in to find out what was going on. Placards and staff explained that the vehicle was a small hovercraft capable of carrying the "pilot" and one or two passengers or their weight in equipment or freight. As far as I recall it had three engines driving fans, one under the floor for lift and two mounted in housings side by side at the rear for propulsion. An attendant told me that if I was interested, a Canadian, Dick Price, was about to address the small audience about this new hovercraft: the Canahover Hoverover. I grabbed myself a glass of wine and some finger eats, sat down, and in a few minutes a dark-suited man picked up the microphone and described the craft and its capabilities, for sport, rescue and short deliveries. I was impressed and after Dick had finished in 20 minutes I told him of my interest. He let me know that a Canadian colleague, Reg Good, would be coming over from Newfoundland to handle publicity and sales throughout the world.

Not long after, there was one of the tragic but fairly frequent flood disasters in the Bay of Bengal, with the usual problems of a shortage of helicopters for rescue and supply. The Times printed a letter I wrote to them about the suitability of hovercraft (invented by Sir Christopher Cockerill FRS whom I had already met) for this sort of disaster, they being cheaper to purchase and operate than helicopters, and easily transportable to the flooded area. I thought it might be a good idea to inform the Canadian government of the possibilities and did so via the representative of their Science Research Council serving in the High Commission. He was already a good friend of mine through my Royal Society work. He let me know that if it was a question of transporting Hoverovers to East Pakistan, as it still was then, the Canadian Air Force might be able to help with a Hercules transport aircraft. Dick Price could have enough Hoverovers available to fill a Hercules, but before the enterprise could get off the ground the Pakistani government would have to request it. (East Pakistan did not gain independence as Bangladesh until 1971). However the Pakistani government would have nothing to do with it. Possibly just as well, because the Hoverover ran into insuperable problems related to its design. Reg Good came across with his wife Faith, having sunk much of their wealth into the project. They lived for some years near Belgrave Square, in an extremely expensive hired apartment. He must have sold a few Hoverovers but not enough to keep the factory going and it closed down some years later. Reg and Faith returned to St Johns. Faith died and Reg eventually married again. But the Canahover disaster must have wrecked their lives. Peter Ottoway, an engineer living near Farnham, looked after the technical side of the demonstration Hoverover on a stretch of water near Heathrow. He and his wife moved away after Canahover folded. We took over Mopsie, the Goods' small Cairn terrier, run over by a car a year or so later when she escaped from the garden and tried to cross the dangerous Whitedown Lane.

As a result of coming to know about these small hovercraft I also met Mike Pinder, who had developed a small inflatable hovercraft of about the same size as the Hoverover. This was selling quite well for sport. Mike was based in Lee-on-Solent. He had previously worked for an oil company, BP I think, and designed and developed a "strap-on" inflatable skirt for moving large oil tanks. The skirts, on the hovercraft principle, were simply strapped round the base of the empty oil tank, and inflated by compressors for towing to a new site. Mike was fascinated by hovercraft and formed a company, Pindair, which produced a small family of hovercraft, the smallest for sport and small transport jobs, and larger craft up to the 12-seater Skima, which could also transport a ton of freight. Mike kept a four-seater Skima near his London house close to the Thames, and this craft was used for demonstrations, to the police for instance. Eventually I was allowed to take this craft out on the Thames on my own and literally had a whale of a time, learning to pirouette the Skima by applying full rudder and differential thrust when well clear of other craft and preferably in the middle of the Thames somewhere on the boat race course between Mortlake and Putney. It was a very wet business especially in a wind. On one occasion I demonstrated this to two police officers, and despite all of us being dressed in nominally waterproof clothing we were soaked to the skin. I did these trips in the Royal Society's lunch hour, slightly extended, but the Foreign Office lunches I frequently attended often finished at 4 p.m., so I was not missed. The hovercraft principle was excellent in some respects. Hovercraft were ideal for transport over mixed shallow water and mud, sand or ice. They are still used as rescue craft in some places where it can be necessary to skate over mud quickly, and for some short ferry routes it can be economical. But it is wasteful of energy and in this day and age, energy conservation is important.

*****

At home our sons Johnnie and Paul were now coming up to the 11+ examinations. Johnnie sailed through, but Paul failed at the first attempt and might have been disqualified from going on to Eggar's Grammar School in Alton. This would have been unfair to Paul and difficult for us with two children in different schools. I took the matter up with our County Councillor, Tony Barron, a Lib.Dem. but none the worse for it. He was in fact more proactive than most of his Conservative colleagues, of a rational turn of mind and not afraid to stick his neck out. He was also on the Hampshire County Council Education Committee, possibly the Chairman. It was agreed that Paul could have a second try at the exam in 1973 and that if he passed he could enter Eggar's under an "over age" procedure. This worked out as planned. Meanwhile Jo, our youngest son, was still at Mayfield Primary School but Mr Bickerstaffe was retiring and was replaced by a less dynamic Head. Jo always did extremely well. He had been reading from the age of about three, taught by Herta using the Ladybird Janet and John series of books tried and tested on his brothers. He was also writing unusually good poetry, possibly inspired by some of the books on our shelves.

Jo loved words. One evening we heard sobbing coming from his room. We went in and found him in tears. In bed he had been reading one of my books *Great Russian Short Stories* including many of the finest Russian authors. I think it was Leo Tolstoy's "Where Love is, God is" that Jo had been reading – the story of a Russian cobbler trying to find God, translated by Aylmer Maude and his wife, premier translators of Tolstoy. This is what had reduced Jo to tears, as it does me. Jo was still a child. Eventually he followed his brothers to Eggar's.

The Eggar's Headmaster initially was George Grey, who had been an industrial chemist, specialising in explosives during the war. As a chemist he was very science orientated and I had the idea, which he welcomed, of inviting FfRS to speak at the annual prize giving ceremony at Eggar's. I lined them up and Mr Grey then contacted them, in the knowledge that I had already prepared the way and that they would be willing to come. I enlisted Sir Joseph Hutchinson FRS, Sir George Edwards FRS and Dorothy Hodgkin FRS in consecutive years, and had the satisfaction of seeing Dorothy Hodgkin present the science prize that year to our son Johnnie. As to the prizes, these were usually books and I arranged that when our sons were prize winners, especially Johnnie, who was always up at the front, I would purchase the book, always more expensive than anything the school would have bought, to be presented as a "school" prize. There was a fairly definite encouragement by us as parents, for our sons, and others generally, to seek excellence, in any and every field of endeavour. In their addresses the visiting FfRS promoted science and were a great improvement on officials of the Hampshire County Council, local businessmen, etc.

It must not be thought that our sons were swots, although later they all toiled long into the night over homework and preparation for exams. They also toiled physically in the garden, wheel-barrowing tons of soil and chalk from the very large rockeries my parents had constructed. Where these had been I turned into lawn or beds, with the new raised areas turfed over. All of this took several years and even one of my Italian cugini (cousins, the Italian term is often applied to relatives of relatives) Paolo Dulio, found it hard going when he was roped into helping with the landscaping. After he returned home to Arenzano, west of

Genoa, he landscaped and planted out his little garden and was pleased to say that this was a result of his experience with us in Alton.

We continued with our pattern of spending at least four weeks of each year on holiday with the children abroad, often in Italy on the island of Elba, where we had come to know the O'Carrols who owned houses near Capoliveri. Michael O'Carrol was unfortunately murdered in his London flat with his mistress – a much publicised event. The murderer, a hairdresser I think, had broken into the flat and had threatened and tied the two of them up but in gagging them had asphyxiated both. We went to Elba afterwards, Michael's brother having lent us his house free.

In some years we visited Austria, where later Herta's father bought a piece of land in Pörtschach on the Wörtersee and built a house with a magnificent view of the Maria Wörth (the church on the south side of the lake). One year we drove to Sweden to stay in the house of an erstwhile friend of mine in Moscow where he had been the Swedish Defence Attaché – Börje Kwarnmark. That was before Jo was born so we only had Johnnie and Paul in the back of the Beetle.

Visiting Sweden on various occasions both I and later Herta had found the colouring of wooden houses there to be particularly attractive and we thought that it would be nice, in renovating our garden chalet (installed by my father when Valverde was built) to use the Swedish red finish on the lower parts, instead of the dull green Cuprinol of the original. From visits to the Royal Swedish Academy of Sciences in Stockholm, in connection with the International Council of Scientific Unions and Nobel Prize matters, I had met Dr Olof Tandberg, the Foreign Secretary, my counterpart there. He identified the finish as a derivative of iron ore, an iron oxide, called falu rödfärg, obtainable from the firm A.B. Wilh. Becker in Stockholm. I accordingly wrote to them outlining our requirements and was highly gratified when a fortnight later out of the blue arrived a parcel of 10kg of falu rödfärg sent as a gift. Instructions for use were printed on the package, but in Swedish. I sent them to Olof for translation and when this arrived discovered that one needed to mix the brick-red powder with linseed oil, water and soft soap in precise proportions. The result was a sort of red mud, but when brushed on the rough boards of our chalet the colour was splendid and did not fade or wash off in even the wettest weather. As the powder when mixed would have been enough to cover 240 square metres, we still have plenty left.

Of course one might expect that Sweden especially should be interested not only in the Nobel Prizes but in the ability of the prizewinners to travel there to receive their awards. Some countries, especially the USSR, prevented their scientists (and most others) from attending meetings abroad. There was a very good structure for the international coordination of scientific endeavour set up under the aegis of the International Council of Scientific Unions (ICSU) with offices in Paris. This has the aim of promoting international scientific activity in the different branches of science and their application for the benefit of humanity. What a noble aim! At a national level there are scientific unions in most of the scientific fields – physics, chemistry, biology, mathematics, etc. These national unions correspond with international unions in the same fields based in various countries. These unions may set up international scientific bodies to consider and deal with specific problems. The whole ICSU family is non-governmental. Its scope is vast and its structure of committees equally so. In the UK the Royal Society is the national adhering body to ICSU and hosts many of the meetings of the committees of the national unions. One committee of great importance deals with the free circulation of scientists. Science is international and can only proceed satisfactorily if individual scientists can travel freely for discussions and collaboration with counterparts in other countries. I was in charge of corresponding with the ICSU Free Circulation of Scientists Committee (later with a slightly different title) meeting usually in Paris.

The Executive Secretary of the Royal Society was a member of the Free Circulation Committee and directed me in what needed to be done, which was a lot. The Soviet Union and its satellites were the greatest offenders for political and security reasons. They would often not allow their scientists to visit the West and sometimes even exiled them to distant parts of their own countries so that they could not easily meet with scientific colleagues and certainly not be visited by scientists from abroad. Their attendance at conferences was strictly controlled and their communications by letter, telephone etc., were monitored. There were usually several dozen Soviet scientists on behalf of whom we were taking up cudgels. Academician Andrei Sakharov, who played a leading part in the development of the Soviet hydrogen bomb, and his wife Elena Bonner were always prominent among those we tried to help, writing letters and having scientific visitors to the USSR visit them or try to. Later when he was exiled to Gorki, several hundred miles east of Moscow, this became virtually impossible. He was the most important but there were many others.

Many Soviet scientists were Jews and wished to emigrate to Israel and/or the USA (often they initially tried to get to Israel, but if successful, staged through and ended up in the USA anyway). Some were physicists but there were many in other fields. We were also called upon to help make it easier for scientists to move between South Africa and Rhodesia and between India and Pakistan, the Arab countries and Israel, when what might be called intellectual blockades were imposed by wellmeaning but mistaken governments. This was a very worthwhile activity. It is as well to remember that not long after the birth of the Royal Society when Britain was at war with continental countries, natural philosophers moved between them without much trouble. There was a hiccup when the Secretary of the Royal Society wrote to scientists in Holland with criticisms of the Anglo-Dutch war. For a while he was incarcerated in the Tower of London, until released after the intervention of Charles II, the founder of the RS.

Parallel with scientific movement there were similar constraints in the humanities. Pasternak and Solzhenitzin were two well-known cases, but there were many more. Anyone speaking out against the Soviet regime was going to be persecuted to a greater or lesser extent, losing their employment and not permitted to leave the USSR in case they added to the criticism from the outside world. Interestingly enough it was easier to promote the freedom of scientific movement than movement in the humanities. This was because historians and philosophers will argue at the drop of a hat, but scientists amicably discuss their work and conclusions in the realisation that they may be mistaken and that further research may bring them closer to the truth. Inter alia they also speak about politics with much more in common than their colleagues in the humanities.

Another interesting committee which I looked after, in the sense of attending to requests from Fellows involved, was the Pugwash Committee. This was named after the town of Pugwash in Nova Scotia where in 1957 a conference was held to set up an organisation to promote the 1955 Russell-Einstein Manifesto. A leading part in establishing this committee was played by Joseph (later Sir Joseph) Rotblat, a nuclear physicist, Polish in origin, who came to England in 1939, when Hitler threatened, and engaged in research in nuclear fission in Liverpool University. This, with other inputs resulted in the atomic bomb. He was not elected to the Fellowship until 1995, when he also received the Nobel Prize and was knighted. By then he was in his eighties, but many other FfRS were involved in the Pugwash organisation and they were very influential in damping down nuclear aggressiveness throughout the world. They feared nuclear proliferation which might have brought, and still might bring, an end to civilisation as we know it. From 1957 Joseph Rotblat worked with Pugwash until the end of his life, having been made President in 1988. Forty independent national groups were set up worldwide and conferences, symposia and other meetings have been held to consider how best to combat the threat.

Among our FfRS, Sir Rudolf Peierls, the Oxford nuclear physicist; Fred Hoyle, astronomer; Kathleen Lonsdale and Dorothy Hodgkin, X-ray crystallographers; and Norman Pirie, biochemist, all played important parts. I met them all and there were many others, not necessarily scientists but in all fields of endeavour such as Bertrand Russell, Sir Peter Scott and Robert Maxwell. Norman Pirie had developed a system of obtaining leaf protein from trees, which he thought would be useful in combating malnutrition in India especially. On one occasion he offered it to me at lunch! Curried! It was as good as tofu and Quorn. Norman was interesting because although a Fellow of the Royal Society he had no PhD, and did not use a doctorate or professorship as a title. He was however very down to earth and left wing, as were most of his colleagues in Pugwash. I met Robert Maxwell frequently at receptions at the Soviet Embassy, in the same group as Tom Driberg, Arthur Scargill and other fellow travellers as they used to be called. Lord Blackett warned me to keep away from Robert Maxwell whom he thought to be a bit of a crook with a beguiling tongue. Later, when I was the Chairman of the International Disaster Institute, Pergamon Press, one of the Maxwell group, published our journal 'Disasters', putting a lot of money into it.

As head of the international relations office of the RS I needed to work particularly closely with the Foreign Secretaries of the Society, initially Tommy Thompson who had recruited me. He could be a bit crusty but we had a very good rapport. Sir Kingsley Dunham (structural geology) was elected when Tommy's stint was up. He was very pleasant to work with, but had a disturbing way of closing his eyes and going to sleep during committee meetings, even when he was in the chair. Foreign Secretaries did a five year stint unless they had to retire for personal reasons. Sir Michael Stoker (Director Imperial Cancer Research Fund Laboratories) followed Sir Kingsley, followed by Sir Arnold Burgen, (pharmacology, Director of the Medical Research Council in London). Professor Anthony Epstein (pathology, virology) saw me out.

I sometimes travelled abroad to visit other academies, often with the Foreign Secretary of that period (Sir Kingsley, Sir Michael or Sir Arnold) to negotiate or conclude agreements. This gave me plenty of opportunities to talk to these prominent scientists who were always more than happy to talk to less scientifically qualified people like me about their subject, or indeed anything under the sun. As a quid pro quo, on one occasion flying back from Islamabad with Arnold Burgen, I had sent my card up to the cockpit to let the pilot know that I was one of his ilk, and was invited to visit him up front. The First Officer was flying the aircraft, a three-engined Tristar, which had arrived six hours late from the Far East. I was able to hear the Captain, an elderly pilot with thick glasses, inform London that the aircraft would have to remain on the ground at Heathrow because the engine pylon on the starboard wing appeared to be insecure. I was happy to explain the situation to Arnold when I returned to my seat.

Sometimes we were accompanied by other Officers, including the President of the time, and other FfRS who could contribute to the aims of the visit, lecture about their work and get a good idea of the state of the field of their research in the country concerned. Sir Arnold Wolfendale (cosmic rays, Durham) became a particular friend, as did Nicholas Kurti (low temperature physics, Oxford), Professor Guido Pontecorvo, a colleague of Michael Stoker at the ICRFL, and Professor R.L. Wain (plant growth substances, Wye College).

Nicholas Kurti had developed a system of cooking meat by pre-digesting it with injected fruit juices containing enzymes and then roasting it at a very low temperature for hours on end. Also inverted baked Alaskas which were very hot inside and very cold outside. For this he used microwaves before the advent of microwave ovens. His gas stove at home had to be modified to give Regulo ½. He demonstrated his cooking skills at the Royal Society one evening and very good it turned out to be. Helpings were distributed by his daughters. At a later stage he collated and edited a very good anthology on food and drink *But the Crackling is Superb*[2] incorporating the comments and recipes contributed by FfRS and foreign members of the RS. Calling it a recipe book was specifically excluded in the Foreword because it is a book with some recipes but rather more scientific remarks about cooking (or not cooking) food. Nicholas made a very good chairman of the Society's domestic committee concerned with our dining room and its fare. The trouble was the cooks. One, of Polish origin, ran up large bills for the purchase of kitchen equipment and it went unnoticed for the best part of two years, until investigations started by committee and concluded by the police revealed that the Polish chef had used the Society's money to equip his own restaurant.

A Fellow who was very dear to me was Professor William (Bill) McCrea, an astronomer/mathematician/physicist who entered Trinity College, Cambridge the year before I was born. He was Irish, born in Dublin, who worked initially in Edinburgh and Dublin. In WW2 he worked with P.M.S. Blackett in Operational Research and then at the University of London. In 1965 he created the astronomy centre of the University of Sussex when the Royal Greenwich Observatory was at Herstmonceux Castle. He lived in Lewes, near where I had been born. Bill was one of "nature's gentlemen" as put in his obituary. He was a very popular visitor wherever he went and I arranged several visits for him as Overseas Visiting Professor under the scheme I ran. This resulted in us being very friendly. He was the sort of person I would have liked as a grandfather or uncle. He invited me to come to the annual Royal Astronomical Society dinner at the Athenaeum Club as an honoured guest, where I had to give a short speech. I said that I was the only member of the Royal Society's staff to have been intimately involved over a long period with Fellows' applications of science, starting with the Wellington, Barnes Wallis and Sir George Edwards; its engines, Dr Hooker; Sir Alan Hodgkin (the Society's President at that time) who invented the oxygen economiser, etc.,etc. I said that the averaging sextant used to navigate the Wimpy at night was probably invented by a Fellow. A small elderly man put up his hand and said "I did!".

Professor Louis Wain (Agricultural Research Council Plant Growth Substance and Systemic Fungicide Unit, Wye College) helped over weed killers for coltsfoot, from which our garden in Alton suffered when we took over. Louis was a splendid chap always in great demand as an Overseas Visiting Professor. He often brought me gifts of fruit and plants from Wye College. Herta and I visited him several times, once at his home. Showing us the garden he explained that his neighbour had planted quick growing hedging plants which Louis wanted to prevent shading his garden. Surreptitiously he watered them with a non-toxic dwarfing compound from his laboratory. This kept them within bounds and must have perplexed his neighbour.

When Professor Wain visited the University of Hong Kong as Overseas Visiting Professor he was concerned to find post-doctoral students doing some very uninteresting projects quite unrelated to local problems. He asked about medical problems in Hong Kong with a bearing on fungicides, in which he was interested. On discovering that vaginal thrush was prevalent, possibly related to the wearing of tights, Louis had the idea of exploring if any of the anti-fungal preparations which he had developed at Wye College for agricultural use would be useful in its treatment. The first task for his students in Hong Kong was to produce tampons for mice. These were then treated with one or other of Louis's fungicides and tried out for toxicity. Many mice died until the fungicide potency was much diluted. It then emerged that a weak dose of fungicide was tolerated by mice. Whether the experiment was continued later I am unsure because after four months Louis came home and left the students to get on with the research themselves.

FCO lunches in first class West End restaurants were often arranged for delegations from Soviet and east European countries, China and some others, invited to London to negotiate or re-negotiate cultural agreements with the UK. The incoming delegations usually included eminent academics in fields where both sides wished to promote the 'cross fertilisation of minds' as we used to put it. The FCO arranged for the UK 'home team' to be as distinguished in the arts and sciences as the visitors. I was invited because of my position in the Royal

Society and often because my knowledge of Russian and other languages meant I could be seated close to visitors needing an interpreter with at least an inkling of any subject that might crop up over lunch. As a result I met and enjoyed the company of any number of foreign leaders in their fields as well as their British counterparts. Apart from scientists these included people like Felix Topolski, Grahame Greene and a host of other writers, artists, historians and economists. Apart from the company, the food was also very good indeed. The FCO must have spent a fortune in those days on meals in the very best London restaurants.

The security services with whom I worked also liked taking me out to expensive Soho restaurants, I expect partly because they could then justify having a fantastic lunch instead of sandwiches at their desks or in their equivalent of a canteen. The Gay Hussar in Soho was one favoured restaurant, also favoured by east European science attachés taking me out for lunch, and not only me but also other contacts of theirs. Sometimes there was the slightly embarrassing circumstance of my MI6 colleague and me being seated at a table next to a Hungarian attaché with some informant, with one or even two other attachés and their informants at tables nearby. This was a Monty Python situation of which we could see the funny side.

In the Cold War context, my contacts with the SIS and scientific attachés in the Soviet and east European embassies, who were usually part of or linked to Iron Curtain intelligence services, KGB etc., were of some use to our own side. For instance, one of the Soviet research workers we had placed in a northern university gave indications that he would not want to return to the USSR on completion of his 12 month visit. As his supervisor had given glowing reports of his work and was happy to have him for longer, we proposed a six month extension and sought agreement from the Soviet Academy of Sciences. They were adamant that he return to the USSR on the original date planned. He took the train to London to discuss the situation with us and with the Scientific Attaché in the Soviet Embassy. The next thing I heard was from my SIS contact. A trio of English students in a hired minibus driving down the Bayswater Road in the early morning had observed a young man being pursued and waylaid by some dark-suited men who had bundled him, protesting vigorously, into a large dark car, which then drove off at speed. The students drove to Bow Street police station and reported the incident. How this came to the notice of the SIS I do not know, but the subsequent sequence of events was more than interesting. The security services acted with speed. By the time I got to my Royal Society office the police at Heathrow had been alerted and when a Soviet Embassy car swept up to an Aeroflot aircraft being prepared for the daily flight to Moscow, police officers boarded the aircraft and asked all passengers to identify themselves. The flight crew and some of the passengers objected and tried to evict the police using force. By this time the aircraft was cordoned off and permission to taxi out refused. Our research worker was identified, removed from the aircraft and taken to a "safe" house where it took him five days to recover from the sedative drugs with which he had been injected, which, the pathologist later disclosed, was close to a fatal dose. Interestingly, after his recovery, he opted to return to Moscow.

One who did not was Dr Aleksandr Ivanovich Karaulov, a physicist also visiting under our agreement with the USSR Academy of Sciences, working in the University of York for a year initially, extended later to 18 months, with Professor Michael Woolfson FRS on an aspect of crystallography. He too was doing excellent work, but was recalled to Moscow and refused to go. He discussed this with us. His reasons for not wishing to go back were largely because he preferred the Western set-up to the communist, professionally and socially. I advised him how to apply for political asylum – quite simple, the form could be obtained from any police station – and informed the Academy of Sciences of Karaulov's decision. This created quite a row. Karaulov would not visit the Soviet Embassy for fear of being detained. We were surprised when Academician Georgiy Konstantinovich Skryabin, a member of the Presidium of the Academy, announced that he would fly to London to interview Karaulov, whom he alleged we were preventing from returning home. We were asked to set up a meeting between all concerned and this took place at the Royal Society in a committee room. It was attended by Karaulov and his Professor (Woolfson), without whom the former would not come; Skryabin; Oleg Belaventsev, the Scientific Attaché from the Soviet Embassy; me and Tania Prigorowsky as interpreter for Skryabin.

Skryabin, a member of the family of which Molotov was a well known member, but no relation to the musician, had commanded one of the first Soviet Army formations to enter Berlin in 1945, he told me with pride. He first satisfied himself that Karaulov genuinely wished to claim political asylum. He then tried to change his mind saying that although he might receive a reprimand if he agreed to return to Moscow, his scientific career would be safeguarded. When this failed to impress (the Soviets had a bad record for fulfilling this sort of promise) he made the point repeatedly that Karaulov's ailing mother would not give him permission to leave her (mothers in the USSR had this right). Also Karaulov had written to the Director of his former Soviet scientific institute, Professor Weinstein, and had wrecked the collaborative projects between his institute and the University of York. Did he really want to do all this damage in order to gratify his selfish liking for his immoral English colleagues? Karaulov said he had found them all to be decent people, but Skryabin advised him not to be an idealist in this matter. Some might be decent but others not. He then produced a letter from Karaulov's mother for him to read and raised the matter of his wife and ten year-old daughter. I said they could probably join him in England if they wished. Much was made of the immorality of leaving family and colleagues in the lurch. If he defected he would be regarded as a traitor even by his family. I contrasted this with the attitude of the English if one of their number chose to go to the USSR to live and work. Colleagues would think him a little odd but wish him well. Belaventsev said that English and Soviet morality were different (with which we all agreed!)

Skryabin's visit had been in vain. He returned to Moscow having done his best but to little effect. Karaulov continued to work at York and then moved elsewhere. Whether he was joined here by his wife and daughter I do not know. But for all of us it had been a lesson. Soviet morality lives on it seems. The poisoning of Alexander Litvinenko by Russian agents is surely part of it.

Soviet visitors were not the only ones to cause us occasional concern. A Polish scientific visitor (let us call him Dr S) was visiting London as part of a joint project with Imperial College. He was accommodated by us at a nearby hotel, because his visit was for a fairly short period. Late one evening the hotel staff heard shouts from his room and the sound of breaking glass. Entering the room with a pass key they found Dr S standing by a broken window with blood streaming from a deep wound in his right arm. The police and an ambulance were called and the latter took him to University College Hospital to be sewn up. His story, related to me later, was that he had met two friendly compatriots whom he had invited into his room for a drink. The conversation turned to Solidarnost, at that time leading the movement to rid Poland of communism. The visitors turned violent, and, feeling threatened and unable to get to the door, Dr S smashed a window with his fist and got out on to the parapet 40 feet above street level and only returned to the room when his Polish friends had left. I did not entirely believe his story. He spoke Russian fluently but very little English. He may have been anti-Solidarnost.

Even the Chinese were sometimes a worry. A Chinese research worker visiting the Transport and Road Research Laboratory at Crowthorne was summoned one day to the Chinese Embassy in London. At the railway station he failed to realise that one should cross the tracks by the footbridge to get to the right platform. Instead he tried to walk across the line and, being hard of hearing, was knocked down and killed by a train. Looking through the bags he was taking with him to London it was discovered that he had sets of highly confidential papers photocopied from originals he had obtained in the RRL, papers which he had not been authorised to consult. These sorts of incidents were not rare but cropped up every few months and made my links with the SIS and the various foreign embassies useful. The Soviet cultural and scientific attachés were always changing. One, Ivanov, had only been in London a few weeks when he was involved in a fracas with the security services and turned up at an Embassy reception with a black eye and contused face. The following week he came to say goodbye before returning to Moscow.

I was asked to provide profiles on any Soviet Block embassy officials I met. This might help the "authorities" to know more about the "opposition". I got over any moral scruples about informing on people by providing positive reports on the personalities I liked and negative reports on those I found a pain in the neck. Once I was asked if I could help provide an English agent going to Argentina with papers and price lists for the Nature bed. The agent would be acting the part of representative for various English firms. I handed over a selection of well printed leaflets and wondered what would become of them. I like to think that they helped the intelligence effort which largely saved our bacon in the Falklands War.

In 1975 we heard that a Romanian scientific delegation would be visiting the UK primarily for discussions about certain aspects of trade. The leader of the delegation was an aviation engineer and member of the Romanian Academy of Sciences. We were asked to provide a welcoming party at Heathrow, and, to match the aviation engineer, Sir George Edwards, FRS, at that time Chairman of the British Aircraft Corporation, agreed to meet the delegates on behalf of the Royal Society. I was asked to go with him, and, while waiting for the Romanian flight, which was very late arriving, we talked about our first meeting in Moscow, the Wellington aircraft, Barnes Wallis, swing wing aircraft and Concorde, which was then engaged in proving flights. I asked Sir George if he could arrange for me to go on a proving flight. He agreed to fix it and said I would be contacted by BAC staff closer to the time of the flight.

In September 1975 I received a call from Weybridge asking me to present myself at Heathrow several days later for a Concorde flight to Newfoundland and back. Before I went home the previous day I left a note on my desk to say that I had gone to Canada and would be back in the office after lunch. The aircraft took off in daylight and we quickly climbed to about 60,000 feet passing through Mach 1 after we crossed the Irish coast. A large Machmeter on the front cockpit bulkhead showed the speed. The aircraft was full of media representatives and we were given a very good flight meal with champagne and caviar by the cabin crew wearing saris. The British Airways Concorde cabin crews were striking for more money to fly supersonically and their places had been taken by Emirates or Gulf Air. Just past mid-Atlantic the sun set but in the east, as we exceeded the speed of the earth's rotation. On the ground in Newfoundland the sun rose again in the east while we were having further refreshments in the airfield restaurant. We took off again after an hour and arrived at Heathrow at about 2 p.m. I was back in my office an hour or so later. It had been a fantastic experience. At 60'K the sky is almost black and stars visible. The curvature of the earth is noticeable and the view not unlike that from a space craft. This was a never to be repeated experience, especially after the Concorde crash in Paris and the cessation of flights.

On a number of occasions during my years at the Royal Society I speculated whether, despite my interest in the satisfying work, I might not do as well or better with some other similarly public spirited organisation. At one stage I was asked by Frances (Baroness since 2004) D'Souza, at that time the Secretary of Disaster Relief, a London based organisation of researchers concerned with natural disasters, if they might hire a room at the Society for their committee meetings. At that time any such organisation with a broadly scientific purpose could apply to hire a committee room and I informed Frances about this arrangement and attended the first meetings because of my own interests in disasters, such as that in the Bay of Bengal in the late 60s when I tried to get hovercraft to use for rescues. My interest (and possibly my presence at the RS) led to my being elected Chairman of the committee, work which I enjoyed. Other committee members included researchers in disaster housing, earthquakes and eruptions and their alleviation, floods and many of the other natural events leading to disasters. The social effects of disasters were also studied; guide books were compiled and printed. The organisation published a journal "Disasters" very well produced for us by Pergamon Press, a Maxwell publishing house. I knew Mr Maxwell from meeting him at Soviet and east European receptions.

At that time I discovered that the United Nations was establishing an organisation – The United Nations Disaster Relief Organisation (UNDRO) – with offices in Geneva. They required a Director with qualifications and experience such as I possessed. So I obtained an application form, which I completed and submitted. Lord Blackett, my second President of the Royal Society and Sir William Hayter, my first Ambassador in our Moscow embassy, now Master of New College, Oxford, agreed to be my referees. I was informed by the Cultural Relations Department of the Foreign and Commonwealth Office that they had nominated me as their preferred candidate. Game and set! But what in fact happened was that an in-house appointment was made. A senior UN official in New York had an ailing wife of French origin who wished to return to

Europe as close to France as possible. Geneva filled the bill. I was not much upset. I enjoyed my work at the Royal Society where I was able to help individual scientists as much or more than I might have done from a UN desk.

Two such were Professor Abu el Azm and Professor Shams ed Din from Egypt. They were both members of the Egyptian Academy of Sciences, with which the Royal Society concluded an agreement in 1977, when Michael Stoker was our Foreign Secretary. Michael, later Sir Michael, was Director of the Imperial Cancer Research Fund Laboratories in Lincoln's Inn Fields, the premier cancer research laboratory in the UK, and associated with other mainline London hospitals. The agreement with the Egyptian Academy was part of the Royal Society's policy to establish links for research collaboration and exchange visits with most senior scientific bodies in the world.

Following the conclusion of the agreement one early UK visitor under our agreement was Professor Kurt Mendelssohn FRS, a German-born physicist whose interests embraced low temperature, medical and structural physics, as well as the scientific and sociological aspects of the Egyptian pyramids. In 1974 he wrote a book *The Riddle of the Pyramids*, which is worth reading. On his first visit to Egypt under our agreement he was accommodated in the Hotel Horus at the Academy's expense, but on his return he had very little good to say about it. Indeed he complained about the room, the food, the clientele (Dr Mendelssohn suggested to me that the hotel should be named '*The Whores*' rather than '*The Horus*') and the loos. I took this matter up with the Academy because Dr Mendelssohn had owned up to crowning the hotel manager with the broken plastic loo seat about which he had been complaining and which the Manager had dismissed as 'normal'. It was agreed that I should fly out to check any deficiencies and propose improvements. The hotel was indeed a grot shop. While having an evening meal at a table with two Lebanese businessmen, they advised me not to choose the curry option because they had found cockroaches in theirs the previous evening. I examined the food on my plate with a small torch because the table lighting was kept so low.

I was pleased to meet the President of the Academy, Professor Abu el Azm who agreed to change the hotel for our visitors to somewhere more salubrious. One advantage of the hotel was their large garden where local marriages were celebrated. On the night I stayed there I was able to witness a marriage reception below my window where a belly dancer played a leading part in exciting the emotions of the bridegroom.

Later visits to the UK under our agreement by Professor Abu el Azm, and one of his fellow officers Professor Shams ed Din, were enlivened by the medical problems of both. Professor Abu el Azm turned out to have a dangerously enlarged prostate and Dr Stoker arranged for a prostatectomy at Guys. Professor Shams ed Din had a much more serious affliction. He telephoned me from Germany to say that he was on his way to attend a conference in the USA but was having trouble breathing. His Cairo doctor had diagnosed flu', but the matter seemed to be more serious. As his flight to the US stopped in London, could we arrange for him to be examined by an English specialist? I at once contacted Michael and he alerted Guys, where we took Shams ed Din directly he arrived at Heathrow. He had a cancerous lung, which was removed the same evening. Obviously the meeting in the US was ruled out and Professor Shams ed Din would be several weeks in hospital and would then need several months convalescence before he would be able to fly home. The cavity left by the removed lung had to fill. With the approval of the officers, we dreamt up a 'Visiting Professorship' to provide him with funds until he could go home. We also arranged a bursary for his wife, a dentist, to come over from Cairo and look after him. The whole operation was completely successful and rewarding for all of us, especially for Francesca Marcantonio who looked after the programme for scientific visitors to and from Egypt as well as those for most other developing countries.

There was also need to intercede with the police when Professor Abu el Azm's wife and daughter were arrested in Manchester for allegedly trying to sell fake gold coins to an antique dealer. The two of them had come over from Cairo without our knowledge, but Mrs Abu el Azm had given the Royal Society as a reference for the police to consult to establish her credentials. The police agreed not to take the matter further provided she did not return to the UK. Odd business! Francesca coped very well with such problems as did all my staff, who were an absolutely grand bunch.

Francesca was the great granddaughter of Italian immigrants to London (possibly Scotland initially) who brought Italian ice-cream here and made a very successful business of it. Even in the 1970s one might see on British motorways pantechnicons blazoned with MARCANTONIO WAFERS, an ice-cream sideline. Despite Francesca's responsibilities for exchanges with developing countries, she could not abide curries or anything other than what might be called English cooking, which caused her difficulties when she visited countries where garlic and chillies are normal culinary additives. As was my wont, when we needed a new member of staff, having received approval from Mr Le Grand, our Finance Officer, to recruit someone, I either advertised the post in the press or contacted an agency. When applications arrived, I asked the better applicants to come and see me, and either rejected them out of hand, or, if one applicant appealed to me, asked her (or sometimes him) to sit down at a desk with a typewriter and telephone and get on with the work, for an hour, for a day or more or less. If she coped well enough and got on with the other staff, we took her on as a 'temp' or permanently, or more likely as the former, to be made permanent later.

Francesca, who earlier had worked for the British Aircraft Corporation, and many more of my staff, were recruited this way. We usually looked for fluency in at least one foreign language – Russian or an east European language being favoured. Chinese was sometimes a prerequisite. West European languages could be useful because visitors from many countries might be able to manage in French or German. Spanish was useful for visitors from Latin America. Francesca's only other language was Cockney, but her personality was more important.

Most of my staff were female, because they were invariably better than males at caring for visitors who were often at sea in our environment. As often as not visiting scientists had no more than a smattering of English and, if they were from the Soviet block, had little inkling of how the 'free' world worked (and played). Since Gorbachev and Yeltsin and the disintegration of Soviet communism it has become hard to remember the enormous cultural gap between 'West' and 'East' before then, which lasted from the Revolution in 1917 until about 1992. My staff were splendid in mediating between cultures and usually stayed for years, only leaving on marriage if that involved moving away from London. I enjoyed looking after them and even if they made mistakes protected them from my colleagues at the RS, who on the whole were careful not to voice any criticism other than through me. Sometimes they tried, which led to rows. There was sometimes criticism that 'my girls' turned up late for work (9 to 5 were the hours for most) but in the case of my office we all had to be prepared to work at any time of the day or night (7/24) when visitors' arrangements required their presence. In any other organisation, the Foreign and Commonwealth Office for instance, they would have been paid at least twice their salaries at the Royal Society with allowances for their languages. I spent a lot of time taking up their cases with the Executive Secretary and the Chief Financial Officer. I think there were never any problems in recruiting and retaining staff because those who had acquired fluency in foreign languages wanted above all else to use them in contacts with their native speakers, opening new worlds. There was usually a queue of applicants to work in my office; applications arrived every week if not every day from linguists who had heard about our work. We all also got immense satisfaction from visits and conversations with the Fellows and other scientists who were always visiting the office. Candidate Overseas Visiting Professors wished to discuss where they might go and what they might do.

In the mid 80s I was contacted by Dr Richard Fisher, an American by birth, who wanted to travel down the so-called Silk Road from Turkey to Xian, largely by road, or off-road, following the most direct land route. The aim was to record the life and culture of the areas they would travel through, as well as the barriers, physical, social, and geographical, affecting the route now, comparing it with what it used to be when silk and other artefacts were transported from China to the West and between intermediate points. Dr Fisher had assembled a group of three like-minded enthusiasts – Tom Ang a brilliant photographer; Don Baker, a specialist in Arabic and Islamic art and architecture; and Paul Crook, a historian and Chinese linguist. Dr Fisher realised that to traverse parts of the Soviet Union and China he would need to have the cooperation of the senior academic organisations in those countries: that is, with the Soviet and Chinese academies of sciences. This might best be done with the expressed support of the Royal Society, which is why he wrote to me.

I had to tell him that without scientific content, the Society could not even consider his proposals. However I had met a Dr Geoff Clarke working at the Imperial Cancer Research Laboratories who had a theory that the reported unusually high levels of oesophageal cancer in people of the countries traversed by the Silk Road had common factors, possibly in diet. I suggested that Dr Fisher should invite Dr Clarke to join what soon became known as the Marco Polo expedition. Now with a scientific content the expedition was accepted by both the USSR Academy of Sciences and the Chinese Academy of Medical Sciences on condition that their own scientists might participate in their respective countries. The expedition was a great success and a magnificent book was produced as well as more than one scientific paper.[3]

Initially one of the few formal agreements between the Royal Society and other academies of science was with China, more specifically with the Chinese Academy of Sciences. Our agreement, concluded in 1963 during a delegation visit to China including the then Professor Harold Thompson (later Sir Harold, Foreign Secretary Royal Society), provided for two Chinese senior scientists to visit the UK each year and two British scientists visiting China as the quid pro quo, with the scientists exchanging views and giving lectures. About a year after I joined the Society Chairman Mao Zedong started the Cultural Revolution in China in the belief that a new bourgeoisie threatened the socialist framework that he had worked to establish. 'Intellectuals', including scientists of course, were exiled to the country to get their hands dirty working on collective farms and the like. Our agreement with the Academy of Sciences was put on ice. Famous Chinese scientists were ridiculed, some killed. In London there were repercussions when doormen attacked reporters with axes. I remained in touch with the scientific attaché; we had the occasional lunch together and I was invited to receptions at the Chinese Embassy several times a year. Sir Harold Thompson, my boss as Foreign Secretary at the time, was keen to re-open scientific exchanges, but only Dorothy Hodgkin was welcome because of her cooperative venture with a Chinese laboratory on the synthesis of insulin.

During a reception in the Embassy in late 1971 I was quizzing Mr He Guowei, the Scientific Attaché, about re-starting exchange visits and he let out that following the forthcoming visit to China of the American President Nixon in 1972, a visit by a Royal Society delegation might be welcome. I immediately dragged over Sir Harold Thompson to discuss this possibility. It was agreed we might choose delegates who would be most interested in visits to and from China. After the Nixon visit our delegation went out and came back with a draft agreement which would replace the earlier one, making provision for more visitors in each direction for lecturing and research.

The following year there was a return delegation from the Chinese Academy of Sciences including an elderly physicist and his one-time English wife. She had met her Chinese husband while he was visiting the Cavendish Laboratory years earlier. They had fallen in love, and she managed to join a British expedition to the Himalayas in an administrative capacity and left them to find her man and marry him. Returning to the UK for the first time in 20 years she spoke Chinese fluently, and English with a Welsh accent (she had been born in Wales) but had difficulty in separating English and Chinese and frequently jumped from one to the other making comprehension difficult for both sides.

By this time I had recruited Catherine Donovan, an Irish graduate in Chinese from the School of Oriental and African Languages of London University. She was thrown in at the deep end, and managed very well despite being expert in Chinese poetry rather than everyday interpreting. Shortly afterwards we decided we needed another staff member skilled in Chinese to help compile a register of Chinese scientific institutions and laboratories and the scientists within them conducting research – a database of Chinese science which would help us decide how, on our side, we would best be able to promote Sino-British scientific interchange to the advantage of both sides. While accompanying a group of Japanese scientists to the University of Bristol at lunch I was seated next to a Professor of Physics, another Professor Thompson. Talking about our Chinese agreement I mentioned I was interested in recruiting a fluent Chinese speaker and he mentioned that his son, while at Cambridge, had married a highly qualified Chinese girl, Miao Ling Thompson. They now lived in London. I took her telephone number and to cut the story short, we recruited Ling to construct the Chinese database, working three days a week initially. Very soon she was a vital member of our office and much in demand for interpreting, especially after Catherine Donovan left to get married.

With China our exchanges increased exponentially. Our first agreement was with the Chinese Academy of Sciences (CAS), the second with the Chinese Academy of Science and Technology (CAST), the third with the Chinese Academy of Medical Sciences (CAMS). I accompanied a Royal Society delegation to China (via Hong Kong going out and the USSR on the way back) from 5 April to 3 May 1982. I had been there a few years earlier before on my own when I had discussed various admin matters affecting visitors in both directions. As 'recreation' I had been taken to the Great Wall and also to Xian to see the terracotta warriors unearthed near the Qin Emperor's burial site. On this later visit our group was led by Sir Arnold Burgen, the Foreign Secretary, supported by Sir (later Lord) Frederick Dainton FRS (physical chemistry, including radiation chemistry). Both were accompanied by their wives, Judith and Barbara.

We flew via Hong Kong where we were wined and dined and discussed joint projects and funding, especially for Leeds University, of which Sir Fred was Vice-Chancellor. The leaders in Hong Kong industry were equally involved in the three Hong Kong universities, and were generous towards British universities wishing to help their Hong Kong counterparts. We stayed in Hong Kong on 6 and 7 April and flew to Beijing on the 8th. We spent the next two weeks mostly in Beijing with secondary visits to Shanghai and Xian. At weekends there were the expected touristic visits from Beijing to the Great Wall and the Ming tombs, and from Qian to the Qin terracotta warriors and the Huaqing hot springs. Scientifically a great deal of business was done, mostly by me and my opposite numbers in the CAS, CAST, and CAMS with inputs from the British Embassy and British Council. It has to be kept in mind that scientists are interested in science and the arrangements for visits by scientists in both directions are best left to those familiar with the administration of such visits – visas, work permits, finance, etc. These arrangements had to be more or less balanced in terms of benefit and expense and expressed in unambiguous agreements between the organisations concerned, drawn up by the "experts" and signed by the scientists representing those organisation.

Our trip to the Great Wall was very pleasant, good weather, wonderful views not only from the Wall but also of the villages we drove through to get there, about two hours drive through countryside and villages. Part of the wall, maybe a kilometre, had been renovated to allow tourists to walk on it, but much of it is steep hills and the stepped flags make it hard work. Arnold and Judith and I walked east (more hilly) and Fred and Barbara in the other direction, not so steep. Fred was as blind as a bat (having suffered from poor sight since childhood) and we were aghast to see that he had walked to the end of the paved wall and several hundred yards beyond it on to broken boulders and paving stones a good 20 feet above the ground. Barbara was calling for him to return but I had to go as fast as I could to take his arm and get him back to safety.

Judith Burgen had been very keen to visit Moscow on the way home because she was very devoted to Russian literature and culture. While fixing up this trip I took this into account and suggested to Sir Arnold Burgen that we go by train from Beijing to Irkutsk, through Mongolia and across the Amur River to Chita in the Soviet Union and thence to Irkutsk where we could visit Lake Baikal and the scientific institutes associated with it. The train journey started in a Soviet coach but with wheels fitted to the Chinese gauge, narrower than in the USSR. In April Beijing was quite warm, but by the time we passed through Harbin early the following morning (Sunday 25 April) it was much colder with sleet and some snow. In those days it was difficult if not impossible to travel via Ulan Bator possibly for political reasons, and we needed to skirt Mongolia altogether. The train was under Chinese control all the way to the frontier. We tried the food in the restaurant car and it was pretty poor. On the second morning in the train I awoke as we were travelling through Inner Mongolia, which looked pretty appalling, colourless bare steppe with no people or animals to be seen, hour after hour, frozen and cold, no trees. Average speed – maybe as much as 20 mph.

At the Sino-Soviet frontier, Manzhouli, we stopped for hours while the wheels of the train were changed to the wider Russian gauge and then rolled on apparently square wheels into the USSR. The scenery suddenly changed from bare steppe to typical Russian "taiga" – silver birch forest, enough to make one weep after so much colourless desolation. From the train we could see many Soviet defences, guns all pointing towards China, tanks and military vehicles by the hundred. The speed of our train decreased still more, with long stops while other trains passed, many carrying timber logs bound for China which was short of wood. We now had a Russian manned train including the restaurant car and the "devushki" (girls, but fat and certainly not young) who soon set to work to start the stoves to heat hot water (kipyatok) for making tea installed at the end of each carriage of our international class (a class above first). Sacks of coal dust were broken open on the floor of the corridor to feed the insatiable boilers. There was a snag. Fred Dainton and Barbara soon appeared to ask me to help try to stop the black coal smoke entering their two-berth compartment from the roof mounted ventilator. On investigation I found that the chimney from the carriage boiler was next to the Dainton's ventilator intake. We had to cut off one or the other and in the event 'caulked' Fred and Barbara's intake with toilet paper, of which we still had a good stock of rolls.

By the morning of 27 April we were in sight of Lake Baikal which was still largely frozen. The Trans-Siberian railway runs along the shore of the southern tip of the lake for several hours before turning north and slightly west towards Irkutsk, which is not on the actual lake but on the river Angara, about 60 miles from where it empties into the lake. We were met at the station by representatives of the Siberian Department of the USSR Academy of Sciences and lodged and dined in the Hotel Irkutsk, which was very good. Wednesday was spent visiting various scientific institutes in and around Irkutsk. The Institute of Limnology on Lake Baikal was especially interesting. Baikal has its own unique flora and fauna, for example the fresh water seals but there are hundreds of other animals and thousands of plants unique to Baikal. Up to 5,387 feet deep, Baikal is the deepest lake in the world and contains about a fifth of the world's surface fresh water. The area abounds with rare minerals and precious stones of which we were shown examples in the museum.

On Thursday, 29 April we flew Aeroflot to Novosibirsk to Akademgorodok (academic village) where many of the Academy's scientific institutes were, and probably still are, situated. Here, Arnold and Fred were kept busy visiting institutes on the Thursday afternoon and throughout Friday, with a visit to the opera after dinner that evening. Friday was May Day, always an important festival in Soviet Russia. We witnessed the May Day Parade, led by the mass go-carts of Siberia, in the absence of the armoured vehicles leading the parade in Moscow. For that evening there was a special invitation to observe the May Day bonfire where effigies of Margaret Thatcher and Ronald Reagan were to be burnt in protest against the British action in the Falklands War which was happening at the time. For diplomatic reasons we declined this invitation, but although the others went to bed early I could not resist making my own private excursion to the bonfire by which time Maggie Thatcher was smouldering and Reagan still on fire to the strains of various Soviet songs coming from the loud-speakers and sung by groups of slightly blotto 'students'. On 2 May we flew to Moscow and thence to London after discussions with the Presidium of the Soviet Academy of Sciences. Back to work in Carlton House Terrace on Tuesday 4 May.

What about my poor wife one might ask? While I was gadding about she was at home looking after the children, house and garden, and of course me when I got home from London, usually at 7.30 p.m. but quite often later when there was late work to be done for visitors. I had to be fetched from Alton Station in the car, and in the mornings, when I needed to be at my office at 9 a.m. (to be there before my staff arriving at 9.30) I had to catch a train from Alton leaving at about 8. Herta drove me there, dropped me off and then drove the children to their schools. A lot of admin!! Herta came up to London to join me for some of the evening functions at the Royal Society, at embassies or at the FCO. In the last ten years of my RS work the policy on wives accompanying husbands on overseas visits was gradually relaxed. Earlier, eyebrows were raised at spouses accompanying even FfRS on visits abroad.

Under Lord Todd's presidency this changed and he may have had a hand in this, because he usually travelled with his wife. Of course often it would have been difficult for Herta to break off from home and come with me on visits but when the children were older this was less of a handicap. She came with me to Hungary, Poland and Czechoslovakia and there was a notable visit to the USSR in 1986, just after the Chernobyl disaster.

The original plan had been for Professor (later Sir) Arnold Wolfendale to visit Academician Aleksandr Evgen'evich Chudakov (Sasha), who had devoted much of his life to research into cosmic rays using an institute in the Caucasus, deep under Mount Elbrus. Arnold invited me to accompany him as interpreter and administrator. The idea was to visit this laboratory, linked in a joint project with Arnold's department in the University of Durham. Durham had been of great help to this Soviet research because the Soviet institute headed by Sasha had inadequate computing resources to analyse the findings of the Elbrus laboratory. On learning of Arnold's invitation to visit Sasha, taking his wife Audrey with him, the other Arnold (Burgen, our Foreign Secretary) decided to accompany them with his wife Judith. The President of the Royal Society, at that time Lord Porter, and his wife Stella decided to tack themselves on to the delegation (as it was becoming), because George Porter (we all used Christian names because knighthoods and baronetcies meant little to the Russians) had business to discuss with the Presidium of the Soviet Academy. At an early stage it was agreed that with all these wives accompanying their husbands Herta should not be left out. So we had George Porter (fast chemical reactions), Arnold Burgen (pharmacology), Arnold Wolfendale (physics, cosmic rays), as well as me (Poo Bah) all with our wives.

Another of Arnold Wolfendale's aims was to present the gold medal of the Royal Astronomical Society to Academician Yakov Zeldovich, a famous Soviet cosmologist who had not been permitted to travel to London to collect the medal in person.

The Chernobyl nuclear power plant accident occurred on 26 April 1986. It occurred to us that our visit only a month later, in early June, might not be welcome. However, the Academy had no reservations; we should come. Because we had booked our flights earlier, the other delegates were restricted to later flights. On arrival Herta and I were met by the Academy and taken to the Hotel Ukraina, where we were pleased to find that we had luxurious rooms on the third floor, with a large bedroom and an anteroom bathroom and all mod cons. Later when the other delegates arrived and we visited them in the same hotel we found their rooms less well appointed. First come: first serve. At first meetings with members of the Presidium, it became clear that some Academicians had recently been at Chernobyl playing leading parts in attempting to ameliorate the catastrophe. There were arguments over some aspects of the programme Lord Porter wished to follow. Lady Porter, who, if not a ballerina, had worked in ballet for some years, wanted to visit the Kirov ballet (which later reverted to its pre-revolutionary title 'Mariinsky') in Leningrad. The Soviet side stated that there were no institutes in Leningrad concerned with Lord Porter's interests. The Porters got their way and were accompanied by the Burgens, while the Wolfendales and Herta and I left by air with Sasha Chudakov and his wife Marina for Mineralnye Vody in the Causasus, from where a minibus picked us up for the drive to Sasha's Elbrus laboratory. In Min Vody we all wanted to visit the loo and made our way there guided by the stink pervading the airport. The ladies reported that they encountered indescribable filth. The 'gents' may have been no better but we managed.

We drove via Pyatigorsk (pron. *PTgorsk*), where Lermontov died and we then turned south into the mountains of the Kabardino-Balkarskaya Republic. We stopped beside a pleasant stream for a picnic and Sasha recommended we drink the fresh water. However I had spotted a sewage tanker washing out its tank just upstream, so we preferred to drink tea from a nearby café. For the night we were lodged in a brand new hotel not far from our destination. The evening meal was delayed and the hotel manager invited me to play him at snooker at the newly installed billiard table in the basement. I discovered that the table surface was convex so that all balls gravitated to the cushions. That night the Wolfendales were in the room next to ours and we suddenly heard a loud crash followed by laughter. Next morning when we visited Arnold and Audrey in their room before going for breakfast we discovered that while Arnold had been washing his teeth the previous evening he had accidentally knocked his elbow on the tiling round the washbasin. A great many tiles had fallen off the wall and disintegrated. Other signs of hasty construction were apparent in the doors and windows, the frames of which had warped so that none could be opened if closed or closed if open.

The visit to the laboratory was interesting. Workers from the Moscow Metro had been working on tunnels deep beneath Mt Elbrus for many years and had excavated tunnels leading to large caverns. In these galleries had been installed hundreds of tanks containing a special fluid from which passing neutrinos split off atomic particles, enabling the detection and measurement of the neutrinos as they enter and leave the fluid. This gives a direction to their origin in space. These detectors have often been located in deep mines as in South Africa or under mountains such as the Elbrus installation because the rock overburden filters out less energetic particles that might confuse the issue. Cosmic rays (neutrinos) are so energetic that they pass right through the earth without let or hindrance. To visit the laboratories we all had to don protective clothing (against water and stone, not radioactivity of which there was none) and pile into industrial train wagons to be pulled into the tunnels for half an hour or so. At one stage we emerged within spitting distance of the peak of Mount Elbrus, but it was extremely cold there. When we had seen all there was to see, we adjourned for a party down below with the laboratory workers, with speeches, wine, vodka etc. in the Russian fashion.

We made a great friend of Sasha's wife, Marina Chudakova, who had been a Hero of Sport of the USSR for her sailing enterprises in yachts, participating in international events including the Olympic Games. She gave us the address of their Academy flat in Moscow and said we would always be welcome there. Taking this invitation at face value we decided to look her up on our return to Moscow, and to her surprise did just that. In those days visits by foreigners to Soviet citizens were still frowned upon by the authorities. But, after some difficulty locating the entrance to the block of flats reserved for academicians we were helped by another resident and knocked at the door. Marina was surprised to see us but invited us in for a cup of tea, introduced us to their dog Timofei, a dachshund, and told us that Sasha was in bed with a headache. We did not stay long but this contact led to many others when Marina came to Britain on visits.

Back in Moscow we learned that our delegation would attend a performance at the Bolshoi Theatre given by graduating ballet students. We would be collected by Academy cars from the Hotel Ukraina at 7.30 p.m. for the performance starting at 8. Waiting outside the hotel I was disturbed when no transport turned up. The Bolshoi had a rule that at 8 the entrance doors would be closed and from then on nobody might enter until the interval an hour or so later. While I was telephoning the Academy unsuccessfully and then searched for non-existing taxis,

Herta summoned her knowledge of Russian and after some difficulty persuaded a mini-bus driver awaiting another delegation to drive us all at high speed to the theatre, arriving in the nick of time. The presentation of the RAS gold medal to Academician Zeldovich was made at an Embassy lunch arranged by the British Ambassador of that time, Rodric Braithwaite.

An incomer was Dr Darshi Chawla from the Indian Veterinarian Research Institute at Mukteswar in the Himalayas. He was awarded a Royal Society Commonwealth Bursary (Francesca Marcantonio's responsibility) to visit the Animal Virus Research Institute at Pirbright to promote his research on Rinderpest. Although told that the stipend of a Royal Society Commonwealth Fellow would not be enough to support a wife and children, he insisted he would manage and we very soon discovered why. His son Vivek, then a little boy, had suffered from cataract of both eyes from birth. When the staff at Pirbright found out about this they helped Vivek to have an operation under the NHS, and Vivek saw fairly clearly for the first time in his life. At the time there were no implantable plastic lens replacements so Vivek had to manage with thick glasses. This visit led to an on-going friendship between our families with our youngest son Jo later visiting Darshi for six months to work on a medical problem, MRSA, in India. This was associated with Jo's medical studies at UMDS (Guy's and St Thomas's). The visits I have mentioned are but two of many others I could quote. Small wonder that my staff and I loved our work. Apart from visitors from abroad, the office (three interconnected rooms) often welcomed the President(s) and Officers of the Society who came for a mug of Nescafe and a chat. Lord Todd and his wife, Andrew Huxley and his, Lord Porter, the various Foreign Secretaries, who were in effect our bosses, were frequent guests, always happy to discuss our current problems and achievements as well as their own, often related to our field of expertise: how to get a UK visa for a dissident Soviet Jewish scientist for instance and how best to get the USSR Academy to allow him to visit Britain.

The number of scientists visiting the UK each year under our agreements increased greatly over the years, from a dozen or so when I joined the Society to well over a thousand when I retired, with a corresponding number of UK outgoers. Malcolm Longair, later Professor at the Cavendish Laboratory in Cambridge and Fellow of the Royal Society, and Llewellyn Smith, later Sir Christopher, FRS (Theoretical Physics, Oxford) were two of our early post-doctoral research visitors to research institutes in the USSR under our exchange agreement. And there were many others, all bright sparks on the way up. They required programmes negotiated and agreed in advance, not only by the individuals concerned but by their institutions and laboratories and the many other national and non-governmental organisations involved – the Home Office, the British Council, FCO, and embassies and their overseas equivalents. My International Relations Office had a life of its own in many respects.

I enjoyed excellent relations with Jack Mallett, then chief of Passport Control, a department of the FCO with responsibility for the final say on visas for incoming visitors. We had many a lunch together and he was of great help in the problems which were always arising about scientific visitors, considered to be of importance to British science but not especially politically welcome.

As I have written earlier, for me especially and for my staff there was no question of 9 to 5 working hours or sacrosanct weekends. We were always on duty, but I made up for work in 'unsocial' hours by giving extra time off when this was possible and not insisting on formal office hours when my girls had spent late nights or early mornings working. However, most of us thought ourselves well compensated by the satisfaction of our work, not the money, which was close to pitiful for the responsibilities we carried and the skills we brought to the job. After I retired from the RS a clock-in, clock-out system was introduced for all staff, with machines and cards to be swiped. This would have been anathema to me and was abandoned after a year or so.

There were quite a few humorous incidents, as for instance when two very senior, elderly Soviet professors were carefully dispatched by train to the Royal Observatory, then at Herstmonceux, and failed to arrive at Eastbourne station where a car from the Observatory awaited them. They were AWOL for two days and when they surfaced we discovered that they had seen the film *Brighton Rock* on other travels to the West and when they saw that the train was stopping at Brighton they alighted to tour the town and were then uncertain how to get to Herstmonceux. They also had £600 each, received from the Soviet Academy of Sciences on account of their seniority, that they wished to spend in Brighton without supervision.

A less humorous incident was when we sent a zoologist as Overseas Visiting Professor to the University of Khartoum to develop their department of zoology and pursue his own research on jerboas (name derived from the arabic) or desert rats. His three month visit was extended to six at his request but during that time I received letters from his wife who had not accompanied him, accusing me personally of breaking up her marriage and making her four children fatherless. We later heard that he had moved to Canada with his research assistant.

AD ULTIMO

Notes:

1. Vladimir Soloviev. The man and the Prophet. Evgenia Gourvitch. Translated by J Deverill Rudolf Steiner Press. 1992.

2. *But the Crackling is Superb*. IOP Publishing Ltd 1988.

3. *The Marco Polo Expedition*. Richard B. Fisher. Hodder and Stoughton.

Why one should not go ex-Directory

On 15 December 1976 I received the following letter from 4 White Knights, Barton-on-Sea, Hants:

14th Dec. '76

Wing Commander J. Deverill,

Dear Sir,

I am Cicely Deverill, daughter of Ernest William Deverill, grand-daughter of William Baxter Deverill, and great-grand-daughter of John Deverill of Slough, and partly out of my own interest, and partly because of the great interest of Canadian cousins, I am trying to make a 'family tree' and eventually to try to trace my family back to its Norman origins (rather an ambitious project).

I have learned a few details from grave-stones in the churchyard of Upton Church Slough, but there are details I cannot fill in, although I shall seek help from the Parish Registers next year (1977).

I found your name in the telephone directory, and have taken the liberty of writing to ask you if you have any knowledge of the family from John Deverill, my great-grandfather, to the present day that would help me make this family tree for my Canadian cousins who are visiting England this Spring to try to do some more research. They are from the Kember branch of the family and will be staying with me for part of the time.

The letter continued to explain that these Canadian cousins, Joan and Robert Gregg, from Ontario, had visited Cicely the previous year and that they had explored the Deverill villages south of Warminster without finding any trace of the family, though discovering later that Deverills had lived in Wiltshire in the 16th and 17th centuries. Cicely added that she had also written to John Deverill Ltd of Slough, which she thought her great-grandfather had started.

I replied on 26 December 1976:

> *Dear Miss Deverill*
> *I feel I might equally say "Dear Aunt" or "Dear Cousin" for that is what you must be, though several times removed.*

I went on to explain some of the detail of the relationship and history of the Deverill family, correcting her view that the name might have Norman origins; that it was in fact the Celtic name of the stream south of Warminster, where some of the family first established themselves, and that being only eight miles long there was a probability that it was only one family that took that name, whether spelt with an "ill" an "ell" or "all" or with only one "l". I mentioned our association with the family firm in Slough and said that I was interested that there were Deverill progeny in Canada, whom I would love to help elaborate their family tree.

From my father I knew of Fanny Deverill, born in 1840 in Upton, then a part of Slough, where her father was John Deverill (1810-1891) who helped establish the building firm, later given his name. Fanny married John Thomas Deakin in 1860 and with him emigrated to South Africa where he was drowned out shooting duck it is said. Fanny married one of his friends, Charlie Kember, and they had five children, a boy Harry and four girls: Edith, Lilian (1874-1957), Rose (18??-1932), and Florence (1878-195?). Kember may have been a gold prospector because this was a time when the British were being encouraged to move to South Africa to help exploit the gold finds.

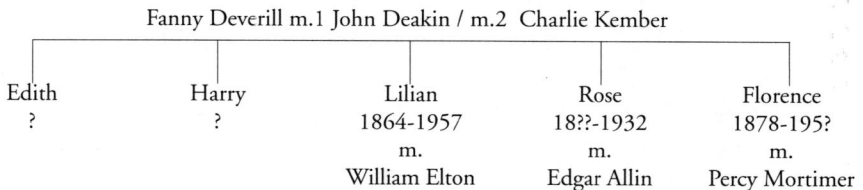

Fanny Deverill m.1 John Deakin / m.2 Charlie Kember				
Edith	Harry	Lilian	Rose	Florence
?	?	1864-1957	18??-1932	1878-195?
		m.	m.	m.
		William Elton	Edgar Allin	Percy Mortimer

More than 30 Canadian families have so far derived from the offspring of Rose and Flo.

The Kember family seems to have established itself in Wakkerstroom, a mainly Boer settlement on the Transvaal border of what is now KwaZulu-Natal and not far from the Zulu heartland where Shaka held sway. The Zulus were inimical to whites generally and the Boers were not at all friendly to the British, one reason for the Great Trek (immigration north away from British adminstration), although the Boer War did not break out until the end of the century. However, the Kembers had trouble with both. Charlie was preparing to move his family elsewhere but suffered a stroke it is said, but I have come across some documents in South Africa indicating that he was sought by the authorities for involvement in some sort of embezzlement. So he might have left his family to escape detention, however unlikely in the South Africa of those times. In any event, Fanny found herself up against it, with a large family and little or no income. She nursed British casualties in the war and had her children go to work on Boer farms around Wakkerstroom. There they were not well treated and Lilian's shoulder was dislocated in an accident for which there was no sympathy.

Flo's version, which she wrote in December 1958 (when she was 80) for an article in the Edmonton (Canada) Journal introducing an exhibition of her paintings, was rather different from what I have written:

> *I was born in Wakkerstroom, South Africa, on December 1st, 1878. I entered this world on a note of tragedy. The Zulu war had just ended and my father had gone to Kimberley where he had an interest in a gold mine when news came through that a fierce band of vanquished Zulus was spreading death and destruction through the country around Wakkerstroom where we were living. The townspeople got together and did their best to make the church into a kind of fortress which they called a laager. All the women and children were moved into it. Just then I happened to be born. Neighbours took the other four children to the laager and my mother waited for my father to arrive. He did so on horseback in the nick of time and managed to get mother and me into the laager. He then collapsed having suffered from sunstroke on his hasty journey back from Kimberley in the tropical sun. The Zulu attack was repulsed when the British Army came to help. My father died shortly afterwards and my mother returned home to England with her five children.*

There seem to be some inaccuracies in her account. At the time she writes about she was a young child so obviously in her article of 1958 she must have been relying on what she had been told later by her mother and siblings. They might have built up a romanticised version of their return home. Kimberley had diamonds rather than gold and is a great distance from Wakkerstroom and if Charlie had interests in gold he would more likely have gone to the Rand, still several days away by horse. Life was hard enough anyway and some time in the early 1880s it seems that Fanny had had enough. On her own she took the family to Durban probably by the recently constructed railway and thence somehow arranged passage on a sailing ship to Britain. This is said to have taken 14 weeks from leaving Wakkerstroom. On arrival they went to Ivy Cottage in Slough, the home of their grandfather, John Deverill, then in his seventies, where Fanny's unmarried sister Polly (Mary Ann Deverill 1849-1928) and brother George (James George Deverill 1850-????) also lived and looked after their father.

After a life in South Africa Fanny's children felt very confined in the strict Victorian atmosphere. The gardener at Ivy Cottage (now demolished) grumbled about "…what them children from Afriki" had done and my great-aunt Polly must have felt the strain. Polly's and Fanny's sister, Lotty (Charlotte Nixey neé Deverill), another of my great-aunts, may have helped, but according to Florence's own account it was John Deverill who paid most of the bills until he died in 1891, the best part of ten years later. He thought highly of Florence's artistic talent and later she painted his portrait in miniature. When John died in 1891 Flo was 13 and went to a boarding school until she was 16, possibly still funded by Polly from her father's estate.

This was a very good example of family unity as is further demonstrated by Hester Harriet Deverill, sister-in-law of Polly, Lottie and Fanny. Hester, the wife of William Baxter Deverill, owned and managed a dame school in Stoke Poges (Gray's poem "Elegy in a Country Churchyard" refers) where not only Hester taught but also two of her daughters, Eva and Jessie. Eva was a pianist and Jessie a painter of considerable talent. On returning from South Africa all of Fanny's children initially attended Hester's school until John Deverill died in 1891 when Florence at least seems to have been put into a boarding school in Bath. Jessie had seen that Florence showed signs of developing into a painter of talent and brought this to the notice of William Harbutt, Headmaster of the Bath School of Art who invented Plasticine, used for modelling at the school. The Bath School of Art was associated with the Kensington School of Art in London, a precursor of the Slade School of Art. Flo was accepted as a boarding student at the Bath school and studied there for several years until she graduated, and spent more years teaching art in a private girls' finishing school in Newport Monmouthshire. She was very well paid there and bought a Bechstein piano with her savings. At the age of 30 in 1908 she met and married Percy Mortimer, a musician. At about the same time Flo's sister Rose had met a Canadian, Dr Edgar Allin, studying for his FRCS in the UK. Edgar and Percy became great friends and Percy was so impressed with Edgar's descriptions of life in Canada that they decided to emigrate there as well (with the Bechstein and little else). These two sisters carried the Deverill genes to the New World.

Edith, Harry and Lilian stayed in England. The Greggs, who were coming to England to look for traces of family were descended from Flo and Percy Mortimer. Joan Gregg was Flo's daughter, and she too was a talented painter, specialising in painting horses, winners of the Kentucky Derby and other prestigious horse-races. Flo herself, despite comparative poverty, went on to become a highly esteemed Canadian artist whose work is in many museums and art galleries in Canada and worldwide. Apart from art, Percy and Flo opened and ran general stores in Toronto and Nova Scotia before moving to Castor, Alberta and then Peace River. Their fortunes were badly affected by the great Depression when they had to leave Peace River for Edmonton. Percy became ill and Flo had to rely more and more on her painting. Notably she was chosen to paint George VI and Queen Elizabeth in 1939, and the painting hangs in the City Hall in Edmonton.

Rose's progeny married into families mainly engaged in medicine and now in 2008 one may say that many Deverill genes are active in professional medical people in various parts of Canada, mostly in the west, where there must be several dozen growing points, all worth cultivating. Most of this information on the South African/Canadian connection came from Barbara Elton, cousin of Cicely Deverill and one of her greatest friends. This is how Cicely came to get in touch with me, thinking from her delvings in the telephone book that I might be able to help. So keep your name in the telephone book is my advice. Barbara is the daughter of Lilian Elton neé Kember who returned from South Africa with her mother and siblings and stayed in England to marry William Elton 1875-1955. Barbara had two brothers Eric and Christopher with children and grandchildren of their own. Do they know of all this historical background? We hope so, because we are all products of our history and can know ourselves and our children, families, friends, relatives and others only by knowing the contexts of their lives.

One of the first things Cicely did was to introduce Herta and me to Barbara, and the two of them visited us in Alton early in 1976. They had been friends since the 1930s when Jessie, the "cousin" of both but their senior by many years, more of an aunt one might say, realised that Cicely was an only child and unmarried and that she would benefit by having as a friend a relative also unmarried and with much in common. Jessie died in 1939, much to the distress of them both, but the link forged lasted until Cicely's death in 1988. The Greggs,

Robert and Joan, turned up in May 1976, and after arrival came to lunch with me at the Royal Society, later visiting us at home with Cicely and Barbara.

After that we received visits by other Canadian relatives. The Spooners, Gord and Marj, he an ophthalmic surgeon, she a nurse, had met in Bath when both were serving with the Canadian navy in WW2. They came from Regina with Rod their youngest son, a surveyor/prospector, from La Ronge in the Canadian arctic and his wife Betty (a GP) on an extensive visit when they toured southern England from a base at our home in Alton. The Canadian extension is most welcome, especially because many of them are so young (or younger than we are anyway). Marj was a daughter of Rose who had returned with her mother from South Africa as explained above.

Cicely became a particular friend and speedily became a proxy grandmother for our three sons, taking a very close interest in them. She soon confided in me that apart from her house in Barton-on-Sea, she had £6,000 invested on her behalf by the Deputy Bank Manager of her bank – the Midland. However, although she had received a small income for some years she had noticed that the capital was diminishing quite rapidly. She wondered why this should be. I did not know much about the relative worth of different investments – savings accounts, bonds, stocks and shares. However, I remembered that my father had sometimes lunched with a certain Mr Leischmann, a London stockbroker who had done work for Phillips and Son (Alton) Ltd., my father's firm, and from whom Dad had also taken advice when acting as executor for relatives who had died. His housekeeper, Jessie Holly, had received a small legacy which she had invested as advised by Mr Leischmann, and had been gratified to find her investment increasing in capital value and providing her with income to add to her wages and later her pension. I found a letter from Leischmann in Dad's files (he always kept correspondence he considered might be useful) and was able to contact Leischmann on the telephone number printed on the paper. He was only too happy to help and by changing her investments on his advice Cicely was able to reverse the previous loss on her investments and receive useful annual dividends. From then Cicely always contacted me about changes to her investments and national budgets likely to affect them. Later Mr Leischmann became a partner in Grenfell and Colegrave, where a Mr Naylor took over Cicely's account. In 1988 another firm took over and proposed charging over the odds for advice to Cicely, and we closed that relationship.

Who was Cicely Deverill? We have to go back again to William Baxter Deverill (1836-1918), son of John Deverill (1810-1891) a founder of the Deverill firm of builders in Slough and his wife Hester Harriet. William had been given the second name Baxter to commemorate the Baxter who had helped John create the firm. William Baxter Deverill married Hester Harriet and they had three children, two girls, Eva and Jessie, whom we have met earlier, and a boy, Ernest William (1878-1961). The girls taught in Hester's dame school in Stoke Poges not far from their home in Burnham High Street. We have a group photo of many of the family in 1892, with Ernest, aged 14 sitting in the background on the branch of a tree, probably in Burnham, maybe one of the famous Burnham Beeches.

In his early twenties Ernest married Esther Emma Wolfsohn (1868-1952) his elder by ten years, whose Jewish grandfather, a walking stick maker, had emigrated to Britain from Poland during the pogroms there. We have two of his walking sticks inherited from Cicely. Esther Emma had dropped her first name and was known as Emma. She was a deeply religious Christian if one is to judge from a Bible given her as a present on 21 April 1894, which is inscribed with philosophical texts and poems, possibly her own, in her beautiful handwriting. She was 37 years old when she bore their first and only child, Cicely, on 11 June 1905 in Lewisham, although she was baptised at St Peter's church in Burnham on 6 August 1905. Ernest may have moved from Burnham to Lewisham because it was convenient for his work with Van den Berghs, the manufacturers of margarine. He seems to have worked with them from 1895, when he was 17, as an accountant or book-keeper as it might have been called then.

Margarine had been invented in July 1869 by a Frenchman Hippolyte Mege Mouries, who aimed to produce a reasonably priced spreading alternative to butter. He used beef tallow and added milk and called the product margarine after the Greek word for pearl because the butter substitute glistened like a pearl. Initially two Dutch family firms started to produce margarine: the Van den Berghs and the Jurgens. The firms then opened other factories throughout Europe but not in Britain until 1917, by which time Ernest was working in Van den Berghs' quite grandiose offices in Mark Lane, London EC3. If he started with the firm before the end of the century as staff manager he would probably have known Alfred Pritchard, who had worked for Mr Jacob Van den Bergh from 1901 in the firm's Despatch Department in Goodmans Yard also in EC3. This was probably a despatch department for distribution of margarine and other food products imported from the Dutch factories. Later, in 1916, Alfred Pritchard's daughter Ivy, worked as an assistant credit clerk for Ernest Deverill in the Mark Lane offices. Lewisham is only about four miles from Mark Lane and Ernest may have gone to and from work by train or bicycle.

A very elderly Ivy gave me an account of some of the Van den Berghs' work at the outbreak of WW1. They imported and sold in Britain things like condensed milk, cheese, smoked bacon and even the original Blue Band margarine, much of it made in their Dutch factories and transported from Rotterdam to London in the firm's own ship *The Sunniside*. In 1917 the ship was torpedoed by a German submarine in the North Sea and the Van den Berghs decided to open their own factory in Fulham, which commenced production of margarine in 1919. It is worth mentioning that my father, Edwin Deverill, would never eat margarine, saying that in his youth it had been made from grease recovered from grease traps, filters installed to filter grease from domestic drains.

Ernest rose through the ranks eventually to occupy a senior management position in Van den Berghs. He was concerned primarily with finance, personnel and their welfare. In 1927, at a dinner for Van den Bergs' sales representatives at the Trocadero restaurant in London, Ernest, then aged 49, proposed the toast to the Company, while Henry Van den Bergh, then Company Chairman, proposed the toast to the King. That same year the two firms of Van den Bergh and Jurgens combined to form the Margarine Union, the head office of which was moved to St Martins-Le-Grand in London EC1. Two years later, in 1929 they merged with Lever Brothers to become Unilever.

It is uncertain when Ernest and Emma Deverill moved with Cicely from Lewisham to Southampton. It seems to have been before 1919 because Cicely started at the Southampton Grammar School for Girls in that year when she was 14. Earlier Ernest seems to have changed the nature of his work while still being employed by Van den Berghs, possibly acting as their sales representative in the south. Cicely said that he had suffered a nervous breakdown, although hinting that he had experienced difficulties at work. And indeed her cousin Barbara wrote that there had been trouble over the treatment of the women working for Van den Berghs in London during the war. It must be remembered that people retired much earlier in those days. Alfred Pritchard retired when he was 54 and lived to the age of 98, hopefully with a pension from his employers, who, being Jewish, were often more concerned than others about their employees.

Ernest and Emma were often at loggerheads and in trying to reconcile them Cicely herself was very emotionally disturbed and spent long periods away from home in Lewisham with Emma's relatives whom she disliked. She was always being shunted between different schools and she resented this. Only in 1919, when she was 14 years old, did she settle down at Southampton Grammar School for Girls where she did well. In July 1924 aged 19 she matriculated and her final school report for that year rated her near the top of the form in all subjects, especially English (literature, composition, grammar), French and history.

Cicely had an especial love for drama. Her parents had opposed her ambition to go on the stage or to be associated with the theatre in any way professionally, so she opted to train as a school teacher. In 1925 in the autumn of the year she left Southampton Grammar School for Girls, she commenced a residential teacher training course with the Diocesan Training College at the King's House in the Close of Salisbury Cathedral. Two years later she graduated with a prize given by Canon Fletcher for distinction in divinity but she had qualifications to teach a number of other subjects including French, history, biology and of course drama.

Despite her parents' dislike of the stage as a career, Cicely continued to excel in many aspects of drama which were welcomed by the schools in which she later taught. She attended a number of specialist courses in vocal music and elocution and was awarded the Silver and Gold Medals of the London Academy of Music for elocution and honours in the examinations of the Royal Academy of Music. She taught drama, French, English and other subjects in four Southampton schools, as Deputy Head Teacher in two of them, ending as Head of the Foundry Lane Junior School in Southampton.

She had a very good rapport with her pupils. On one occasion during a class she noticed that some boys especially were gazing at a rather uninteresting picture on the classroom wall. During a break she examined the picture more closely and discovered that from some of the desks one could see, through a window and reflected in the picture glass, football matches on a nearby sports field. She then told pupils they might watch the football directly from the window for five minutes, provided they concentrated on their lessons for the rest of the period.

Cicely was a staunch adherent of the Church of England and in Southampton to the Church of St Mary. She agreed to produce a passion play 'Christ Crucified' in the church just before Easter 1939. This was a most ambitious venture with a large cast, and requiring three stages and accordingly complex lighting. In this Cicely was offered help by another member of the congregation, a young man of 19, Gordon Pritchard (Note the name. Could he have been related to Ivy?) The lighting plan and other measures he proposed greatly appealed to Cicely and she gave him the go-ahead.

Assisted by an ex-professional stage electrician working in a Southampton garage, Gordon's proposals for lighting and sets worked out very well and the production was a great success, with press acclaim and queues forming for entrance every evening. Cicely and Gordon planned to continue to cooperate on further dramatic productions and it seems that despite, or maybe because of, the disparity in their ages (ten years, as with Cicely's parents) the couple had deep affection for each other.

Not long after the war started in September 1939, Gordon went off to train as an Army officer and later Cicely was devastated to learn that he had been killed in action in Tunisia at Teboura south of Tunis, where the Hampshire Regiment was part of the allied force fighting the Germans in French North Africa as part of Operation Torch. Cicely was continuing to help arrange dramatic productions in Southampton especially for members of the armed forces serving in the vicinity. Later she thought that she owed it to Gordon's memory to start on the work they had proposed to do together – to set up a dramatic company to bring plays to the people, either in churches or other venues, whatever could be found in times of war, to some extent a travelling company, moving with sets and lights to communities which might not be able to visit theatres in larger towns. Cicely approached others interested in her idea and willing collaborators came forward in large numbers, choosing as their name 'The Wayfarers', dedicated to the memory of Gordon Pritchard and others who were giving their lives for their country.

The first productions of the Wayfarers in 1943, were *Motherhood* and the second *The Shepherds' Play*, given in churches, salvation army halls, drill halls, school halls, anywhere willing to host the Wayfarers' visits. Over the following 40 or 50 years the Wayfarers put on many dramatic productions throughout the county of Hampshire and sometimes in more distant towns to the acclamations of their audiences. On average they produced one play each year (39 between 1943 and 1966) including plays by J.B. Priestley, Shaw, Christopher Fry, Shakespeare, O'Neill, Arthur Miller, Dylan Thomas and other well-known playwrights. The plays were sometimes toured round venues in more distant parts of England. The actors were all members of the Wayfarers Dramatic Society, amateurs, but with professional standards. These were attested to by drama critics from many parts of England, many of whom considered the Wayfarers' standards of acting, direction, sets and production superior to those of many professional companies. Cicely gave up active direction of plays in the 1960s when her teaching duties became more onerous, but the concept was hers and it was the love of her life.

During the war Cicely was appointed a Fire Warden responsible for reporting fires caused by incendiary bombs, and if possible extinguishing them using a stirrup pump and bucket of water, sand etc., working with other fire wardens from adjacent streets. Southampton was very heavily bombed at times and St Mary's Church, the venue for Cicely's first dramatic production in 1939, was destroyed in a raid on 30 November 1940. Part of the shell of the building remained and re-building started in 1954 and was completed in 1956 when Cicely produced *Murder in the Cathedral* by T.S. Elliot as part of the re-opening celebrations. Cicely's own account of how the Wayfarers coped with air raids is illuminating:

> *It would be difficult to describe the enthusiasm, the determination and sense of adventure of those early days. Certainly none of those first*

members will forget those early rehearsals. All had war-time duties when there were air raids. Bicycles were ranged outside the hall, and tin hats placed on chairs at the ready. When the sirens sounded, in a matter of seconds tin hats were donned and cast, stage staff and producer cycled at speed to man their various duty stations, first aid posts, fire stations or to fire watch over important buildings in the area. Fortunately this never happened during a performance.

Some of this information comes from Cicely's cousin, Barbara Elton, daughter of Lilian Kember who had returned from South Africa with her mother Fanny and siblings Edith, Harry, Rose and Florence. Jessie Deverill, a favourite aunt of Cicely, had come to know of her unhappiness at having no brothers or sisters or other close family members of her age. Jessie thought her aunt 'Lilian' and her daughter Barbara would be good for Cicely to know, and engineered the introduction as a result of which Cicely and Barbara became great friends, visiting each other's homes and going on holidays together in England and abroad. The bond between them was all the stronger because Barbara was a speech therapist by profession which fitted in with Cicely's predilection for the stage, elocution, voice and drama generally.

Both Jessie and her elder sister Eva had rather tragic lives. Eva went out of her mind after WW1 and ended her life in an institution. Cicely once feared that she might also have a genetic predisposition to mental instability. Jessie went unmarried for many years but met and married a childhood beau, Charlie Harper, in 1938 only to die herself in 1939 with Charlie following in 1941.

On the death of her mother in 1952 Cicely, in addition to her work as a Deputy Head and then Head Teacher, devoted herself to caring for her father until he died nine years later. After his death in 1961 Cicely sold the house in Shirley and bought a bungalow at Rownhams Corner. Only later did she discover that this was to be ruined by the M27. With great reluctance she sold again and moved to Barton-on-Sea, next door to a great friend of hers Ross Scoble. Meanwhile Barbara had introduced her to the Canadian offshoots and so we come back to that first phone call to me.

After a few years Cicely announced her intention of bequeathing to us, her newly adopted family, the residue of her estate and several Deverill "heirlooms" (long case clock, Georgian sofa table, etc.) inherited through her father from her grandfather, William Baxter Deverill. We frequently visited her in her home in Barton-on-Sea, where she showed her talent for artistic taste in the furnishings and the garden and in her hospitality (although often burning things in the oven or boiling over saucepans). Equally she often drove in her Morris Minor to stay with us in Alton, sometimes stopping for a nap in a convenient lay-by. She took enormous interest in our children and in our other relatives and in the history of the family she had never thought she had. She was in all an absolute paragon, a great friend and family member, a proxy grandparent of enormous value, everything that she had ever wanted to be.

I think that Cicely always harboured a longing to 'belong' to something bigger than herself. Without siblings in her youth and adversely affected by parental squabbles she found refuge in friends and in the schools in which she served. Her foundation of the Wayfarers reflects this need for something wider and more important than 'self'. But she always hankered after something even closer in which she might play a 'parental' role. She found this in our family and in the wider Deverill clan.

As it happened we were with Cicely for her last hours. She had gone into the hospital at Brockenhurst after a nasty spell of ill-health. She was diagnosed with an inoperable aortic aneurysm on the point of bursting, a Damocles Sword if there ever was one. Since the time we had met her Cicely had never enjoyed complete health. She suffered from trigeminal neuralgia and the condition of her circulation and heart were always troubling. Later on she could only walk with considerable hesitation and breathlessness. When she visited us by train because her driving was becoming erratic she would take the train from New Milton to Winchester where we would collect her in our car. But even getting off the train was an effort and she usually arranged for train staff to help her out. When we visited her in hospital at Brockenhurst the day before she died she said to me quite rationally "I suppose this is the end, John". I tried to reassure her but it was indeed the end. The following day, 26 July 1988, a nurse asked us to delay entering her ward because Cicely was having lunch but a few minutes later came and told us that Cicely had died when the aortic aneurysm burst.

When Cicely died she left trunks of papers about the formation and development, or maybe it should be called evolution, of the Wayfarers. Eventually I decided that they might be given a safe home in the Museum of Southampton Archives Department, where it would be available to anyone interested in drama in southern Hampshire and in the Wayfarers specifically. The papers included the early Minute Books of the Society, stage directions, press cuttings and reviews of productions and many beautiful photographs.

Thus Cicely left us with many inputs to Canadians of our extended family, some of them being 'growing points' with whom we remained in touch. For much of the time we knew her I was still working at the Royal Society, where she often visited me at my office until ill-health made this too difficult for her.

Vale

On leaving a community, firm, family or other social group one always likes to think that one will have a continuing influence on its philosophy and conduct, preferably in the hands of people one has known or of whom one would approve. Retirement is one such occasion. Approaching retirement from the Royal Society on my 65th birthday in 1987 I was fairly sure that international relations would be in the good hands of Terry Garrett and Stephen Cox and Ling Thompson to name but three. As to leaving more than just influence I pulled off a coup of a sort in late 1985 in respect of our Chinese exchanges, late developers partly because of their Cultural Revolution. The Royal Society's Foreign Secretary and Executive Secretary had been invited to attend a meeting of the Parliamentary Science and Technology Committee at Westminster. They were both occupied and deputed me to attend. I walked down Whitehall to the Committee Room off St Stephen's Hall and sat down. We were addressed by a BP executive who had just returned from North West China where BP were drilling for oil, until then unsuccessfully. One of the questions an elderly gentleman put to him at the end of his talk was whether he thought Chinese postdoctoral research workers would wish to come to the UK to work. The speaker did not know, but thought not, because there were many more opportunities in the US with more fellowships, more generously funded.

Later there was a reception in an adjacent room, where I noticed the elderly questioner sitting on a crate of beer, there being no chairs. I joined him and asked about his question, mentioning that I worked at the Royal Society, and was responsible for Chinese exchanges. He agreed that there was a problem with funding visits by Chinese research workers to the UK. He spoke of the Queen's forthcoming visit to China in 1986 and asked for my view about what she might give to the Chinese to mark the occasion. A leading question! I replied that a

411

suitable gift would be scholarships or bursaries to support research worker visits. He said this was a good idea and he would talk about it to the Queen at tea the following week. I was surprised by his familiarity with the Queen and tactfully asked for his name – Lord Rhodes of Saddleworth, a Yorkshireman who had served in the Royal Flying Corps in WW1, decorated with the DFC and Bar. Between the wars he made a fortune in textiles, with mills in and around Manchester. Later he was elected as a Labour MP and later still ennobled as a Labour peer.

Next day I mentioned my conversation with Lord Rhodes to the Executive Secretary and the Treasurer. They thought the idea was unlikely to go much further, because they doubted if the Palace worked like that. I suggested contacting the Queen's Private Secretary, Sir Kenneth Scott, and ask him. He was an old colleague of mine from the Moscow Embassy in1956/7 and I had already phoned him earlier to check on the plausibility of such a scheme being discussed over tea. Ken gave the Officers of the Royal Society the confirmation they sought.

I was asked to draw up a scheme and did so and the next thing I had was Lord Rhodes telephoning me at the office and saying 'John, I'm going to try and raise money for this scheme from various businessmen, but I'm old and I've still got an open wound on my leg from the Somme, and so can you come around with me'? I agreed and said what about transport, taxi? and he said 'No, I'll borrow a Rolls Royce from the managing director of British Home Stores, whom I know'. And so the Rolls Royce drew up at the Royal Society a day or so later, and I got in it with Lord Rhodes, who proudly showed me his open wound from the Battle of the Somme on his shin; one could see the bone through it still. It must have given him a lot of pain. And we drove off and visited British Aerospace, to see the Chairman. Lord Rhodes asked 'Can we put you down for £100,000?' To my amazement the Chairman said yes, okay. And we went round to about two dozen key managing directors, chairmen, presidents of large firms and they each stumped up £100,000 here, £50,000 there, large sums of money. In total over £1 million. Back at the RS I said 'Well we've got the money now, what next?' Ken Scott told me that they would want to have a vellum scroll suitably inscribed for Her Majesty to hand to the President of the PRC. So we had to find craftsmen with experience in this field. I think it was Catherine Donovan who knew an artist who did inscriptions on vellum. A draft was available within several weeks, approved by the Palace and produced within a couple of months. It was a beautiful thing, costly, but served its purpose. The Queen's China Fellowships remained for many years thereafter as an important stepping stone in the development of Sino-British collaboration in science.

The Chinese scientific attaché in London, Mr He Guowei, (see previous chapter) had become a good friend of mine, but returned to Beijing tour-expired in 1985. He knew I was scheduled to retire from the Royal Society on 24th February 1987, my 65th birthday, and that I was keen to continue to work in the field of international relations thereafter. I was pleased to receive a letter from him well before my retirement asking whether I would be able to work with a new Chinese organisation named the China Association for the International Exchange of Personnel (CAIEP) to which he had been moved in a senior position. Already in 1983 I had set up another firm which I had named Academic and Business Guides. Its purpose was to promote international interchange between individuals and organisations by providing advice on the formalities and practicalities involved (visas, travel, work permits, language/interpreters, health, etc.).

As director of CAIEP Mr He Guowei sent me a telex on 23 March 1987, a month after my retirement from the Royal Society. He named me as one of their main cooperators in the UK and invited me to visit China in April or May to discuss an agreement on collaboration and to interview six candidates for visits to the UK. These would be graduate professionals in various fields including finance seeking placements in UK firms for a year in each case.

CAIEP would pay for my local costs in China, covering hotel accommodation, transport, and a flight back to London after two weeks. I arranged to take up their invitation and fly to Beijing on 3 May, with my flight out paid for by the Royal Bank of Scotland, the Bank of Scotland, Trusthouse Forte and British Aerospace, all of them prospective hosts of future Chinese visitors. From my experience in drawing up international agreements for scientific cooperation, I drafted an agreement between CAIEP and AB Guides for discussion in Beijing.

I was put up at the Beijing Hotel and spent several days there at the CAIEP offices. I was accompanied by them on visits to the Beijing Traffic Management Bureau (keen to get a placement in the Transport and Road Research Laboratory), the Beijing Subway Corporation, and the Institute of Aeronautical Materials. Six candidates for visits came to the CAIEP offices for interviews. I was not impressed. The candidates were deficient in both personal qualities and English. CAIEP had also arranged for me to make a short visit to an aircraft factory in Qian, and I asked them to propose more candidates for me to interview on my return.

Over the weekend 9/10 May I was free, so contacted Mark Kitto, the son of Norman Kitto, a distant relative by marriage of a cousin of mine. Mark had been a Captain in the Welsh Guards before studying Chinese at the School of Oriental and African Studies (SOAS). For the second year of his studies he had opted to visit China for 12 months to practise the language. He was in Beijing in May 1987 so we had supper together on the Saturday. On the Sunday we visited Fragrant Mountain, together climbing the 800 or so steps to get there – fairly exhausting even when I was only 65! We could have used the funicular. The park was built in AD 1186 and covers 395 acres. It is most popular in the autumn when the thousands of *Cotinus coggygria* trees colour the hillside with flame. They do well here at home in Alton too. Later I visited Mark's accommodation provided by the University of Beijing, and was appalled by the conditions the British students were living in.

My visit to the Qian factory was unproductive. They were already making components for Boeing and had arrangements in place for exchanges with the US. I spent several days visiting the burial site of the Qin Emperor and viewing the terracotta soldiers, which had been uncovered nearby.

On my return to Beijing I was introduced to another set of candidates for visits to the UK, several of whom were very suitable, including Li Lian and Zhao Ming, with several others in finance and banking and two aspiring hotel managers (aspiring rather then inspiring!). I immediately earmarked Li Lian for the Royal Bank of Scotland and Zhao Ming for the Bank of Scotland.

On 16 May He Guowei and I signed the CAIEP/AB Guides agreement which established that CAIEP would select candidates for placements in UK firms. Their details would be sent to me for consideration and I would then endeavour to find suitable hosts, and act as an intermediary with CAIEP. The financial aspects were covered in an annex to the agreement. AB Guides would be paid £250 for each placement, plus 10% of the value of any salary or other emoluments paid to the Chinese guests by their hosts. Visits would normally be for a maximum of 12 months, with provision for extension if both CAIEP and hosts agreed. I then flew home to London.

Placements in finance, banking and insurance were very successful, except that some of them decided to stay in the West indefinitely. After 18 months in Edinburgh Li Lian moved on to a MPhil course at Brunel University and after a further year returned to her husband, by now in Hong Kong occupying a senior appointment in a finance house still associated with mainland China. The two of them then surfaced in Vancouver, where Lian made a very successful career for herself, with a young daughter when last I heard. She was not the only one to prefer the West and opt to stay here.

Hotel management was less successful. Trusthouse Forte had one Chinese visitor who could not abide western food and eventually had to be given his own cooking facilities in which to cook his own.

For us the agreement was quite rewarding because most Chinese visitors were paid £500 pm by their hosts, as well as allowances for any travel necessitated by their programmes.

The following year Herta and I were invited to visit China again in May, in this case on the usual basis of sending side paying fares and receiving side paying local costs. For economy we flew Aeroflot via Moscow. We stayed there for six days, some with the science attaché, Terry Garrett and Grace his wife, and some with Marina Chudakova in her dacha east of Moscow. We spent two weeks in China and returned direct from Hong Kong. In Beijing we interviewed candidates for visits under the CAIEP/AB Guides agreement in various ministries and organisations, and were then put on the train to Shanghai and Hangzhou before flying to Hainan island to do much the same. It was explained to us that China wanted foreign capital to develop Hainan as a tourist resort, and that if Trusthouse Forte wanted to invest they would be welcome. Hainan was in fact a delightful place but as yet almost completely undeveloped, with no infrastructure on the part of the coast the Chinese had in mind. I was very doubtful if it would attract Lord Forte – and it did not.

However, it would have obvious attractions for tourists in the long run. Our visit to China had repercussions: some auspicious, some less so. In Hangzhou our CAIEP host was Ye Bo, a charming woman who spoke English well, and who was always available to escort and introduce us on our visits, including one to appear on Chinese TV. We told Ye Bo that we would like to visit a silk factory, Hangzhou being famous for its silk. She arranged a trip to a large factory equipped with rather archaic machinery, and we noted that the manufactured silk was being dyed in garish colours, unlikely to appeal to Western customers. Herta and I agreed that we might help by finding a talented young English designer to feed in new ideas – a counterpart to the Chinese CAIEP visitors. Later we asked Ye Bo for CAIEP support for such a visit and she agreed, subject to her finding a suitable host.

Back in the UK, as a member of the executive committee of the Sino-British Fellowship Trust, I knew of applicants for support for visits to and from China. One was Penelope Tyler, in the final year of her degree studies at Liverpool University in textile design. Penny wanted to further her interests in Eastern textiles, and her referees thought she would be very suitable for an attachment to a Chinese silk factory.

Penny flew out on 29 March 1989 and eventually stayed in China for about three years, far longer than originally planned. Her main host turned out to be the Zhejiang Institute of Technology rather than the silk factory itself, but she considered she had learnt a great deal from the attachment, especially as she was there over the period of the Tiananmen Square protests. These had been reflected in similar protests in Shanghai and Hangzhou, and indeed throughout China. Penny experienced the unrest at first hand, and reported back to us and to her very artistic family in Canterbury.

The quid pro quo for Penny's visit was one we arranged for an architect, Huang Song, from Hangzhou, who spent a year or more working for an architectural practice in Chelsea. I say 'or more' because he too was in favour of staying in the West, and in many of these cases they just disappeared into the undergrowth, and kept their heads down, believing me to be associated with migration and visa, as in a sense I was. Another plus for this country was when Ye Bo, the CAIEP representative in Hangzhou, turned up in London with her husband Ning Yi, who found a place in research at Imperial College, and their daughter, possibly even born here.

While Herta and I were visiting China in 1988 we were taken to an afternoon 'debate' with students of the Qing Hua University in Beijing, by the China Association of Science and Technology, some of whose principals I knew. They must have thought we would be impressed by the students 'free' attitudes and of their ability to speak out. If so, the authorities must have been alarmed because the students were indeed outspoken, calling for much greater freedom in China, particularly for students. They instanced any number of occasions where they had been prevented from voicing their opinions. Having heard them and the veiled threats of some of their supervisors, we were not much surprised at the explosion of dissent in Tiananmen Square the following year.

A less than satisfactory visit that we helped to arrange in 1989 was by a pianist we encountered in our hotel. He was blind and provided occasional piano music for guests. We heard his story about how he had been accidentally blinded at birth by spilt boiling water and was now confined to playing the piano during bar hours at the hotel. We thought that he would benefit from a stay at a RNIB institution in the UK and arranged for his fare money from the Sino-British Fellowhip Trust, and free board and lodging at the host institution involved, in Cheltenham I seem to remember. The visit was a disaster. Medical checks showed that although visually impaired, he was not blind. He used physical violence against his carers, demanded facilities they could not provide and made himself such a nuisance that the police were called and he was deported back to China.

The Tiananmen Square confrontations resulted in some sort of a clamp-down on the sort of exchanges we were trying to arrange. It was gradual and not immediate. We had quite a few visitors here at the time and probably the Chinese authorities did not wish to scare them off and put up with their loss to the West. I doubt if scientific exchanges were affected to the same extent, but our contacts with CAIEP slowly diminished to nil. Their office seemed to have been changed or even closed and the personnel were different. No matter! The experience had been to our advantage and to the advantage of those whose visits we had arranged.

In the USSR, soon to be Russia again, our liaison with Marina Chudakova remained fruitful. She had a particularly soft spot for the Dmitrov School for physically handicapped children not far from Moscow. We agreed to try and create a link between this school and the Treloar College, a counterpart in Alton. The principals of the two schools agreed and Treloars invited a group of up to ten children between the ages of 15 and 18 to visit Alton for two weeks from 25 September 1990. While here, they and their accompanying teachers would live in the College, whose representatives would meet them at the airport and look after them in respect of accommodation, food and transport. Six Soviet boys and one girl came, accompanied by three teachers. The visit was highly successful. Apart from the experience the visitors and their teachers had of Treloars' techniques, there was a social dimension: the kindness and generosity of the Treloars' hosts and of Altonians generally.

On learning that the song and dance group of the Red Army was to visit cities throughout the UK, under arrangements made by Victor Hochhauser, I contacted him by telephone. I explained that a group of Soviet handicapped children was visiting Treloar College in Alton and asked if the Red Army singers and dancers might stop at Alton, on their way to a booking at the Mayflower Theatre in Southampton. He agreed and asked about dates, and whether there was a hall available for a concert at Treloars. There was and never had it had such a large audience, of all the children, their teachers, friends and relatives.

Treloars gave a Ford Transit vehicle to the Dmitrov School. It was driven out by Treloars' staff and later they arranged for the purchase and dispatch of spare parts. A year later, a group from Treloar College visited Dmitrov and liaison continued for some years. A spin-off from the visit concerned Sasha Postnov, one of the students from Dmitrov. He had lost both arms as a child, but the Soviet Union even in 1990 had no artificial limbs such as were available here. We decided to se if we might raise the money to have prosthetic arms constructed and had Sasha measured up while he was here. We raised £5,000 to pay for the limbs and also for his air tickets because he had to return twice for further measurements and fitting at the Roehampton limb fitting centre, over which period he stayed with us at home in Alton. A disappointment was that he discarded the limbs a year or so later, preferring to use his stumps.

Another Russian exchange was brought about by our friend Irina Von Schlippe in Munich. Irina always involved herself in Russian cultural events exportable to Germany in particular, and Europe more generally. In 1991 she let us know that a fine Russian choir established in 1988, the 1000th anniversary of the foundation of the Russian Orthodox Church in Kiev, would be visiting Europe in 1993. The choir, named after its founder Valery M. Rybin, would be singing at a Russian Easter Festival in Blackheath from 30 April to 2 May. Irina asked if further recitals might be arranged in Britain while the choir was here. I thought yes indeed and contacted some of those involved with the choir's visit to Blackheath. Approaching various cathedrals and churches and other less religious venues I was surprised at the lukewarm responses. Even the Soviet Embassy was singularly unsure about welcoming the choir. I then had the idea of approaching St Catherine's College Cambridge, our son Jo's college, because of its historical associations with music. I wrote to the Master, Barry Supple and he referred me to his Chaplain who expressed interest. The long and the short of it was that the choir was booked to sing in St Catherine's College Chapel at 7.30 p.m. in the evening of Sunday 2 May being looked after overnight by willing families and then sent on their way back to Germany on Monday 3 May.

The 16 members of the choir and an organiser of their programme in Germany, Mrs Nadia Hoffman, would travel to Blackheath from Germany in two minibuses, in which they would continue to Cambridge and then back to Germany. All this seemed excellent and we drove to Cambridge to confirm that all their arrangements were in hand.

We arrived early and awaited the choir. We then heard that on their first evening in Blackheath all their formal clothes, dark suits etc., had been stolen from the Youth Hostel in Earls Court where they had been lodged. Alternative clothing had been purchased in charity shops and had served them well enough for their singing in Blackheath. After taking our seats in St Catherine's College chapel the first minibus arrived with half the choir to report that the other minibus had run out of fuel on the M11. This was already half an hour before the concert was due to begin and most places in the chapel were already full. It was agreed that one of the helpers would take a full can of fuel in his car to the stalled minibus, and to the joy of those waiting the rest of the choir arrived no more than half an hour late.

We were then treated to a magnificent concert of some 24 items, some liturgical but mostly less serious, and some downright popular. No music of course – unaccompanied voices, some in the deep bass that typifies Russian song.

As far as we knew the return to Germany and eventually to Russia went well, but the potential cock-up was essentially Russian as was its very successful outcome – all a product of the never-say-die attitude of Russians, which makes them the best people to be with in any dire situation.

Afterword

Other enterprises were legion and continue to this day, or would if we were stronger. However, there come times when one has to leave some things to younger limbs and intellects. Our three sons, all educated in Alton schools, obtained good degrees from world-famous universities and later worked and continue to work in satisfying professions to the benefit of others and themselves. Eight grandchildren seem likely to keep the flag flying.

I can truthfully say that I have never encountered anyone from any part of the world who is in any significant way different from me and those around me. I like the adage which paraphrased reads 'Had I had your parents, your upbringing and environment, I would behave like you'.

Nor would I exclude animals and the inanimate. It is easy to empathise with dogs and cats, horses, cows, sheep and goats. Camels too if you have been brought up with them. Furry animals yes, snakes and spiders less, although I once knew a herpetologist in Ghana who loved snakes. I count trees and plants (including weeds) and clouds among my friends especially when in the war I sought safety by flying in clouds. And the moon and stars to brighten dark nights and give a sense of direction. As we are stardust in the material sense and have achieved consciousness and intelligence only through the ordering of our constituents, it should not be difficult to appreciate them.